Uncle John's FULLY LOADED 25th ANNIVERSARY BATHROOM READER®

By the
Bathroom Readers'
Institute

Bathroom Readers' Press
Ashland, Oregon

OUR "REGULAR" READERS RAVE!

"Your books are the greatest written works since Homer's *Iliad* and *Odyssey*. Uncle John and all his staff at the BRI must be the smartest rubber duckies in the pool!"

—Steven J.

"I've been a fan of your series for years, and I have two shelves devoted to them. I'm now equipped with an arsenal of fun facts for any occasion."

—Alex D.

"I LOVE your books! It is so nice to be able to impress my family and friends with an arsenal of wacky, fun facts!"

—Shayla G.

"My whole family loves your books. We wait anxiously for each new one to come out. The most recent one we are reading has definitely brought conversation out of the bathroom and to the dinner table!"

—Trena N.

"Absolutely brilliant! Your mix of wit and knowledge make these the perfect can't-put-down books for this 11-year-old boy!"

—Grady P.

"I have been an avid reader of *Uncle John's Bathroom Readers* for years. Everyone knows what to buy me for presents. Just wanted to let you folks know that you keep me mesmerized (and seated) for long periods of time!"

—Mitch M.

"I have about 30 of your books, and I want the whole collection! Do you know how much fun it is to start a conversation with a weird little tidbit from Uncle John?"

—Rose P.

UNCLE JOHN'S FULLY LOADED BATHROOM READER®

Dedicated to Allan MacDougall,
friend to bathroom readers everywhere

For information, write:
The Bathroom Readers' Institute,
P.O. Box 1117,
Ashland, OR 97520
www.bathroomreader.com

Cover design by Michael Brunsfeld, San Rafael, CA
(*Brunsfeldo@comcast.net*)
BRI "technician" on the back cover: Larry Kelp

ISBN-13: 978-1-60710-320-2 / ISBN-10: 1-60710-320-6

Library of Congress Cataloging-in-Publication Data
Uncle John's fully loaded bathroom reader.
p. cm.
Includes indexes.
ISBN 978-1-60710-562-6 (pbk.)
1. American wit and humor. 2. Curiosities and wonders.
I. Bathroom Readers' Institute (Ashland, Or.)
PN6165.U535 2012
081.02'07—dc23

2012012548

Printed in the United States of America
First Printing
1 2 3 4 5 6 7 8 16 15 14 13 12

Hiya, Sophie! Hiya, Jesse!

THANK YOU!

The Bathroom Readers' Institute sincerely thanks the people whose advice and assistance made this book possible.

Gordon Javna
John Dollison
Jay Newman
Brian Boone
Kim Griswell
Trina Janssen
Thom Little
Michael Brunsfeld
Sharilyn Carroll
Angela Kern
Jack Mingo
Megan Todd
Brandon Hartley
Jill Bellrose
Michael Conover
Claudia Bauer
Jahnna and Malcolm
Rich Wallace
Joan M. Kyzer
Adam Bolivar
Mary Colgan
JoAnn Padgett
Melinda Allman
Monica and Annie
Aaron Guzman
Ginger, Jennifer, Mana, and Shirley
Lilian the Calm
True Sims
Maggie Javna
John Javna
Sydney Stanley
David Calder
Sandy D'Amato
Matt the Foil Guy
Jeff and Jennifer
Laurel and Hardy
Media Masters
Publishers Group West
Bloomsbury Books
Raincoast Books
Thomas Crapper

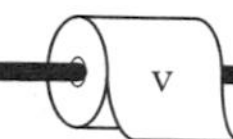

CONTENTS

Because the BRI understands your reading needs, we've divided the contents by length as well as subject.

Short—a quick read

Medium—2 to 3 pages

Long—for those extended visits, when something a little more involved is required

* **Extended**—for those leg-numbing experiences

PLAY TIME

APOCALYPSE, NAH

POP SCIENCE

INTERNATIONAL AFFAIRS

HOW TO DO STUFF

* * *

IT'S OXYMORONIC!

Phrases made up of two words that appear to be contradictory.

New classic
Seriously funny
Crash landing
Deafening silence
Larger half
Soft rock
Living dead
Almost exactly
Working vacation
Center around
Original copies
Clearly misunderstood
Peacekeeper missile
Decreased growth
Found missing
Rolling stop
Same difference
Definite maybe
Specialize in everything
Sweet tart
Virtual reality
Butt head

FROM UNCLE JOHN #1

Late in 1987, when I first took the idea for a bathroom reader to New York publishers, it seemed the series might never even get started. Times were different: The idea of a book designed for the bathroom made editors squeamish. I got a unanimous "No thanks," complete with disgusted grimaces. But when I got back home to California a few weeks later, a message was waiting: St. Martin's Press had decided to give it a try.

The good news for BR fans is that St. Martin's had really just bought the *concept*; they didn't care about the *contents*. So we were free to include anything we wanted. Whatever subjects fascinated us found their way onto the pages—stories about old TV shows and pop music, doo-wop syllables, oddities of American history, quotes from Einstein. A friend showed me a page of church newsletter bloopers her mother had sent her. Voila! It became part of the book. We read a story about some crazed fan sneaking into Elvis' hotel room and using his toothbrush. In it went. And so on.

Putting the first *Bathroom Reader* together was so much fun that I could hardly believe someone was actually paying me—which may be why it was an instant success. It also helped that I found Michael Brunsfeld, the talented illustrator who's created almost all the BR covers, and Andy Sohn, who designed the now-familiar page format. And it helped that St. Martin's Press provided bookstores with cardboard displays shaped like toilets. (Wish I still had one of those.) Who could resist that?

Now, 25 years later, my silly idea is an institution. That's a weird enough story to include in a book like...well, this one.

Go with the Flow!

—John Javna

FROM UNCLE JOHN #2

PASSING A MILESTONE

When my brother John called me in 1987 to tell me he had an idea for a book called *The Bathroom Reader*, I did what you probably did the first time you heard about this book series: I laughed.

But it made perfect sense: John and I both read in the bathroom and so did most people. John recognized that "the reading room" really is the reading room, and if you don't mind my bragging about my brother, it was genius.

"But call it *Uncle John's Bathroom Reader*," I said. And he did.

Over the next 12 years I wrote and edited a ton of articles for the BR—from the Beach Boys to the Buick, GI Joe to Godzilla, Mustangs to Mini-skirts. It was a nutty combination, but amazingly, it worked. Then, in 1999, John decided it was time for him to move on and he asked me to take over the reins. I suggested he find someone else. "There *is* no one else," he said. Still I refused. No, I said. No. No. No. Yes. It was the best decision I've ever made.

Now, here I am, 13 years later, and 25 years after that first phone call, putting the finishing touches on the silver anniversary edition of *Uncle John's Bathroom Reader*. Nobody—not me, not John, nobody—ever dreamed we'd still be doing this after so many years.

But there's a very simple reason that we are: You.

Over the years, we've received thousands of letters from people of all ages and all walks of life telling us how important the *Bathroom Reader* has been to them—kids and adults, teachers and students, people who've been reading our books for 25 years and people who've just discovered us. They tell us they love the short facts, the long stories, the history, the science, the wordplay, the humor. They love that they can learn something new and be entertained at the same time, and it only takes a few minutes.

So here's the question: How can a book with a toilet on the cover be that important to anyone? That's pretty simple, too.

It's because "they" is actually "us." We write *Uncle John's Bathroom Readers* because we love reading about the same things you do—and we love sharing it.

A final note: We couldn't have put together a book like this without a fantastic team. So a sterling silver Thank You to the writers, editors, researchers, and designers who helped make this book shine: John D. (23 years), Jay (14 years), Brian (9 years), Kim (2 years), Thom (10 years), Sharilyn (22 years), Trina (half a year), Jahnna and Malcolm (10 years), Brandon (1 year), Michael C. (2 years), Jill (2 years), Jack Mingo (22 years), Angie (9 years), Michael B. (25 years!), Claudia (4 years), Joan (1 year), Jolly Jeff Cheek (12 years), and Mary (newbie).

And a 25-flush salute to the dozens of people who have contributed to *Uncle John's Bathroom Reader* over the years. We wouldn't be here without them…or you.

Happy reading. And as always…

Go with the Flow!

(What? John already said that? Okay.)

Keep on Flushin'

**—Gordon "Uncle John" Javna,
Felix the Dog,
and the BRI Staff**

YOU'RE MY INSPIRATION

It's always interesting to see where the architects of pop culture get their ideas. Some of these may surprise you.

EDWARD SCISSORHANDS. Screenwriter Caroline Thompson based the character's mannerisms on her dog: "She was the most soulful, yearning creature I ever met. She didn't need language—she communicated with her eyes."

THE BIG LEBOWSKI. The Coen brothers' cult classic was an update of Raymond Chandler's 1939 noir novel *The Big Sleep.* They used the L.A. setting and many of the characters, but changed Philip Marlowe, P.I., to Jeffrey "The Dude" Lebowski.

THE HUNGER GAMES. Suzanne Collins's inspiration for her 2008 novel about teenagers forced to fight each other in a dystopian future came to her while she was watching TV. She was flipping back and forth between *Survivor* and coverage of the Iraq war when the two "began to blur in this very unsettling way."

PHILIP J. FRY. The lead character on the cartoon *Futurama* wears the same clothes—blue jeans, red jacket, and white T-shirt—and has the same blond hair as Jim Stark. Who's that? James Dean's character in the 1955 film *Rebel Without a Cause.*

THE BIG BANG THEORY. Show creator Chuck Lorre named the two leads—Sheldon and Leonard—after legendary producer Sheldon Leonard (*The Andy Griffith Show* and *The Dick Van Dyke Show*).

"CALIFORNIA GURLS." Katy Perry's 2010 hit single was going to be called "California Girls" until Perry's manager asked her to change the spelling to honor Alex Chilton, lead singer of the band Big Star, who'd recently died. The title is a nod to the band's 1974 song "September Gurls."

SEVERUS SNAPE. J. K. Rowling based the character on her short-tempered high school chemistry teacher, John Nettleship, who had long dark hair and a "malodorous laboratory." Said Nettleship, "I knew I was strict but I didn't think I was *that* bad."

Count 'em: On average, an adult human has about five million body hairs.

THE BRI ANTHEM

To mark our 25th anniversary, here's the very first article from the very first Bathroom Reader*: the story of a classic song, a classic controversy...and Uncle John's favorite room.*

SOUL MEN

In the 1960s, Memphis's Stax Records had the most talented lineup of studio musicians and singers in the South: There was Otis Redding, Rufus Thomas, Booker T. and the M.G.'s, Carla Thomas, Eddie Floyd, and Sam and Dave.

Sam Moore and Dave Prater joined the Stax family in 1965. They were assigned to the writing/production team of Dave Porter and Isaac Hayes, and the partnership clicked big, producing a string of Soul masterpieces, including "You Don't Know Like I Know" and "Soul Man." In between was a song that almost made the top 20—a record that would have been a much bigger hit if it hadn't been for radio censorship.

White Top 40 stations were just getting used to playing black soul records in 1966 when "Hold On, I'm Comin'" was released. Because of the suggestive title, many radio stations refused to air it at all. And those that did often made the situation worse as DJs drooled over the sexual implications of the song. In reality, the lyrics were simply about one lover giving the other support "when times are bad." "Coming" just meant "coming to the rescue." Sam and Dave's macho, boastful delivery and sly laughs throughout the song didn't help their case, although it did help to make it a great record. Stax changed the title to "Hold On, I'm A-Comin'" to placate the FCC, but the damage was already done.

WHEN YOU GOTTA GO

If only the radio jocks had known the true story of the song's conception: Hayes and Porter were in the studio, writing some songs. Porter left for a minute, and when he didn't come back, an impatient Hayes went looking for him. His room-to-room search finally ended at—you guessed it—the bathroom door. Porter was taking his time in there, and Hayes yelled at him to hurry. Porter's irritated reply: "Hey man, hold on. I'm comin'!" And a song was born.

The New Jersey coast was once part of Africa.

ADVERTISING FIRSTS

"You've come a long way, baby."

First print ad in the United States: Tobacco company Lorillard placed one in the *New York Weekly Journal* in 1789. It showed the company's logo: a Native American standing over a barrel and smoking a large pipe.

First "spam" message: As early as 1864, telegraph offices and private citizens who owned a telegraph were receiving letters offering dubious investments and other scams. The first "spam" was sent in May 1864 by a London dentist named Gabriel, announcing that his office would be open shorter summer hours.

First "I'm not a doctor, but I play one on TV" ad: The line was first used in a 1984 Vicks Formula 44 cough syrup commercial. It's notable in the advertising world for blurring the line between celebrity endorsement and professional opinion...but clearing the advertiser of any legal claims. First actor to say the line: Chris Robinson, who played Dr. Rick Webber on TV's *General Hospital.*

First movie product placement: In the 1927 silent movie *Wings,* which won the first Academy Award for Best Picture, the characters eat a Hershey's chocolate bar and mention it by name.

First product placement in a video game: In the 1982 car-racing game *Pole Position,* the driver speeds past billboards that advertise other games made by *Pole Position*'s maker, Atari. In 1983 *Pole Position II*'s billboards were for Tang, 7-Eleven, and Dentyne.

First movie inspired by a TV commercial: *Space Jam* (1996), in which Michael Jordan plays basketball against Bugs Bunny, Daffy Duck, and other cartoon characters. The idea came from a 1993 Nike ad in which Jordan plays one-on-one against himself.

First sitcom based on a TV commercial: *Baby Bob* (2002). It was based on a popular series of television ads in 2001 for the Internet service provider FreeInternet.com, featuring a talking baby named Bob (a baby with superimposed moving lips, voiced by actor Ken Hudson Campbell). *Baby Bob* ran for 14 episodes.

Space-suit underwear is water-cooled.

THE TALENTED MISS AMERICA

The Miss America Pageant added the talent portion to the contest in 1935. Most contestants sing or dance, but some display more unusual skills.

1957: Amanda Whitman (Miss Tennessee) did a gymnastic tumbling and trampoline routine to the theme from *The Third Man*.

1959: Elizabeth Holmes (Miss New York) did an impression of French singer and actor Maurice Chevalier. Miss New Jersey, Beverly Ann Domareki, did an impression of a beatnik.

1960: Ann Susan Barber (Miss New Jersey) did a comic routine about a hillbilly attending her first baseball game.

1961: LaVerda Garrison (Miss Idaho) gave a dramatic reading of Charlotte Perkins Gilman's feminist short story "The Yellow Wallpaper."

1967: Jane Jayroe (Miss Oklahoma) conducted the orchestra in a rendition of the #2 hit "1-2-3" (and she won the pageant!).

1973: Ellen Meade (Miss Florida) did a ballet sequence from *Swan Lake*...on roller skates.

1977: Julie Houston (Miss Alabama) played the banjo. The song: the theme from *The Beverly Hillbillies*.

1981: Angelina Johnson (Miss Tennessee) did impressions of the lead characters from TV's *Laverne and Shirley* ...with ventriloquist dummies.

1982: Laura Matthys (Miss Oregon) twirled a rifle to the tune of a traditional folk march from Herzegovina.

1987: Aurelie McCarthy (Miss Massachusetts) played "Hava Nagila" on the marimba.

1989: Tammy Kettunen (Miss Arizona) performed a "freestyle roller-skating" routine to "Amazing Grace."

1992: Shannon Boy (Miss Arkansas) played the theme from *Star Wars* on the flute.

2011: Lauren Cheape (Miss Hawaii) performed acrobatic jump roping to the *Hawaii Five-O* theme.

The expression "in a pickle" was coined by Shakespeare.

OOPS!

Over the past 25 years, we've shared hundreds of outrageous blunders. We'd like to take this opportunity to say a big THANK YOU to all the people who made them. Embarrassing as it may have been for you, you've given a smug sense of superiority to millions of bathroom readers.

NOK IT OFF!

In 2011 a photographer and his assistants arrived at the Manhattan home of antiquities collector Corice Arman to take pictures of her most prized pieces for *Art+Auction* magazine. Arman had one rule: "Don't move any of the pieces." But for some reason, while Arman was out of the room, one of the assistants picked up a large terra cotta figurine and moved it across the room...where it fell to the floor and "smashed to smithereens." When Arman returned, she was horrified. The statue, made in Nigeria by the ancient Nok people, was more than 2,600 years old and was valued at $300,000. She is suing the magazine for the full amount. "I raised two kids around all this artwork," exclaimed Arman, "and they never broke anything!"

IS GLORIOUS KAZAKHSTAN ANTHEM...NOT!

Kazakhstan's champion sharpshooter, Maria Dmitrienko, was standing on the award platform at the Arab Shooting Championships in Kuwait in 2012. She'd just won a gold medal: Kazakhstan's national anthem began to play over the P.A. system. Only it wasn't the *real* anthem—it was a fake one written for the 2006 mockumentary *Borat: Cultural Learnings of America for Make Benefit Glorious Nation of Kazakhstan*. Sample lyrics: "Kazakhstan's prostitutes are the cleanest in the region, except, of course, for Turkmenistan's." (And dirtier lyrics that we can't print here.) The Kazakhstan government—which had banned *Borat*—demanded an apology. Kuwait apologized and blamed the goof on a staffer who downloaded the wrong anthem off the Internet.

NEVER THERE WHEN YOU NEED ONE

Here's a fun prank you can try: Dial a random phone number and send a text that says, "I hid the body...now what?" That's what a

15-year-old girl from Rogers, Arkansas, did. Only problem: The random number she dialed happened to belong to a police detective. She got the scare of a lifetime when the police showed up at her house asking about the dead body. Officers let her off with a warning—and issued this warning to the general public: "While the text was intended as a prank, the Rogers Police Department has no sense of humor when it comes to public safety."

IMPRESSIVE IMPRESSIONIST

Steve Comrie, 20, was invited to a field party in Manlius, New York. He showed up at 11:30 p.m. and saw a sign at the property entrance instructing people to walk through the woods to the field because the driveway was muddy. As Comrie approached the edge of the woods, he thought it would be fun to scare some partiers, who were gathered around a bonfire, so he started making animal noises. Apparently, they were very realistic. One of the partiers, Jeremy Messina, 21, responded by pulling out his shotgun and firing into the forest, hitting Comrie in the face, arm, chest, and thigh. Thankfully, the injuries weren't life-threatening. Police charged Messina with reckless endangerment.

SWINGIN'

One night in October 2011, a group of friends was hanging out at a playground in Vallejo, California. Around 9:00 p.m., a 21-year-old man (name not released) bet his buddies $100 that he could fit into a toddler's swing. So he greased his legs with liquid laundry detergent and then started shimmying into the tiny leg holes. Good news: He won the bet! Bad news: He couldn't get out. Unable to free him, his friends left, and he ended up spending the entire night stuck in the swing. Shortly after sunrise, a groundskeeper heard the young man yelling for help. He couldn't pry the man out, either, so he called firefighters, who used bolt cutters to cut the chains. The man was transported to a hospital where a doctor used a cast saw to remove the swing from the embarrassed man's seat.

* * *

"Looking foolish does the spirit good." —**John Updike**

LET ME WRITE SIGN— I GOOD SPEAK ENGLISH

When signs in foreign countries are written in English, any combination of words is possible. Here are some real-life examples.

A sign in China (instructing people to keep off the grass): "I like your smile but unlike you put your shoes on my face"

Outside a restaurant in Istanbul: "Sorry We're Open"

Outside a Thai building: "Welcome to visit elephant dung factory & souvenir shop"

On the border between Paraguay and Argentina: "The paths to our resort are only passable by asses. Therefore, you will certainly feel at home here"

At a Hong Kong train station: "The toilets will be partially suspended for use"

Next to a staircase in Japan: "Please be careful about a step in a head"

Outside a restaurant in the Philippines: "Try Our Fresh Deli Sandwiches Made with Imported Europeans Meat and Cheese"

Outside a Singapore restroom: "A nearby toilet should be used for the direction of hurry"

On a path in Hiroshima: "10 Min. Walk (7 if run a little) to Ropeway Stn."

Inside Afghanistan's Kabul Museum: "Please Do Not Use the Flashy Cameras During the Photography"

On a winding road in India: "Be Soft on My Curves"

At a French ski resort: "Skiers Entrance Through the Bottom is Compulsory"

At a zoo in China: "Please do not feel or scare the animals"

Outside a church in Costa Rica: "Please no explanations inside the church"

On a vending machine in Tokyo: "Because I Do Not Have A Tissue Always Ready in This Restroom, Please Buy Used One"

Cookie Monster has five fingers; all other *Sesame Street* Muppets have only four.

CANDY HOLIDAYS

Hallmark swears there's no such thing as "Hallmark holidays": holidays created solely for the purpose of selling more greeting cards. But what about "candy holidays"?

SWEETEST DAY (third Sunday in October) Billed as a "Second Valentine's Day" in the early 1920s, Sweetest Day was invented by 12 Cleveland candy companies that wanted to create a holiday around the giving of candy to orphans, shut-ins, the homeless, and other people unlikely (or unable) to buy it for themselves. Their Sweetest Day of the Year committee distributed nearly 20,000 boxes of free candy, hoping to jump-start the holiday and spread it nationwide. No dice: It's still observed in the Great Lakes region, but never caught on anywhere else.

JAPANESE VALENTINE'S DAY (February 14)
It was introduced to Japan in the 1950s by a chocolate-company executive who was trying to increase February sales. Because he didn't understand how Valentine's Day worked in the West, he set it up so that *women* gave candy to *men*, a practice that continues to this day.

WHITE DAY (March 14)
A few years after Valentine's Day was brought to Japan, a marshmallow company created White Day to increase sales of *their* product. It worked: Today, chocolate given by women to male acquaintances on Valentine's Day is called *giri-choco* ("obligation chocolate"), and the recipient is expected to reciprocate with marshmallows or other gifts one month later on White Day.

CANDY DAY (second Saturday in October)
Invented in 1916 when Halloween trick-or-treating was still a local—not a national—phenomenon, Candy Day was an attempt by the National Confectioners Association to spur sales during the slow months leading up to Christmas. We might still be celebrating Candy Day today, had the United States' entry into World War I not forced the cancellation of the 1917 festivities. Attempts to revive it after the war were unsuccessful.

The gym on the *Titanic* included a mechanical camel.

COMRADE SUPERMAN

Superheroes are a huge part of modern folklore. They help us see both the best and worst parts of ourselves. But sometimes their writers get bored and make them do weird things.

***RED SON* (2003)**

Concept: Superman is a Communist.

Details: In the late 1980s, DC Comics created the "Elseworlds" imprint to try a few "What if?" scenarios. Various installments explored such oddball themes as "What if the Joker had been born a woman?" and "What if Batman was a vampire?" This issue, "Red Son," posed the question: "What if Superman's spaceship had landed in the Soviet Union instead of Kansas?" Answer: The Man of Steel would have become the ultimate Soviet weapon in the Cold War. After crash-landing on a farm in the Ukraine, Superman grows up to fight for "truth, justice, and the Communist way" with a hammer and sickle logo on his costume instead of his iconic "S." Lex Luthor vows to stop him but fails; Superman takes over the USSR. Under his leadership, socialism spreads across the globe and America collapses, along with most of the world's civil liberties. But under the influence of Soviet propaganda, Superman becomes a paranoid, Big Brother-like figure and lobotomizes anyone who dares oppose him. Years later, Lex Luthor, now the president of what remains of the United States, convinces Superman of the error of his ways. The hero fakes his own death and goes into hiding, vowing never again to meddle in the affairs of humanity.

***UNDER MY SKIN* (2004)**

Concept: Spider-Man becomes a spider.

Details: In the world of Marvel Comics, Spider-Man (Peter Parker) has always been able to do anything a spider can, with the exception of making his own webbing. Since his comic book debut in 1962, the superhero has relied on a mechanical invention to produce his sticky webs. But for the 2002 *Spider-Man* movie, filmmakers gave Peter the ability to make the stuff organically, as part of the effect of the radioactive spider bite that makes him Spider-Man. This inspired the writers at Marvel to make the switch in the comics, too, but the explanation they came up with was a little weird. In this comic book's storyline, Spider-Man encounters a villainess called The Queen. She defeats him, and then runs off—but not before stealing a kiss, which turns Parker into a gigantic spider…that's pregnant with her spider babies. Sometime later, human-form Peter bursts out of what was really only a spider casing and returns to his normal life, with two big changes: He can shoot spider webbing from his wrists, and he can talk to bugs.

KILL YOU (2009)

Concept: The Punisher meets Eminem.

Details: Real-world celebrities have been making cameos in comic books for years. In 1978 Muhammad Ali took on Superman, and both Jay Leno and Barack Obama have shown up in the pages of Spider-Man. But none was stranger (or more violent) than rapper Eminem's appearance in an issue of *The Punisher.* To promote his 2009 album *Relapse*, Eminem joined the vigilante hero to fight an assassin named Barracuda, who had been hired by the Parents Music Council to murder Eminem for his explicit lyrics. Pun guns down Em's posse, then Em shoots Pun, then Em and Pun kill Barracuda. Finally, the Punisher goes off in search of the Council.

BATMAN: *THE RETURN OF BRUCE WAYNE* (2010)

Concept: Batman travels back to the future.

Details: DC Comics sent the Dark Knight all the way back to the dawn of humanity for this series. After an evil alien called Darkseid blasts him into the past, Batman takes on a group of vicious Neanderthals, then catapults forward in time (through a waterfall) to the 17th-century colony of Gotham. There he meets his ancestor Nathaniel Wayne and helps solve a series of crimes blamed on witchcraft. Another time-jump pits him against the pirate Blackbeard. Then he lands in 1930s Gotham, where he investigates a murder. (The murder victim: his mother.) A final bounce sends him to the end of time and the impending doom of the universe, and that's when things get *really* weird. It's revealed that all this time-traveling was part of Darkseid's elaborate plot to turn Bruce Wayne into an invincible killer android! Fortunately, Superman intervenes and prevents Robo-Batman from jumping back to the 21st century to take over the world. (Whew!)

The designation *Air Force One* applies to any aircraft carrying the U.S. president.

BEHIND BARS: THE MOST TIME SERVED

The stories behind some of the longest-recorded prison sentences ever served in modern history. (Note: All of these people...except one...spent more years in prison than Uncle John has spent alive. Yowza.)

PAUL GEIDEL

The Crime: On July 26, 1911, Geidel, 17, broke into the New York City hotel room of 73-year-old William H. Jackson. Geidel, who had been living on his own since the age of 14, had worked in the hotel as a bellhop, but had recently been fired. Rumor had it that Jackson, a retired Wall Street broker, kept a lot of cash in his room. Geidel jumped the older man while he slept, and suffocated him—possibly unintentionally—with a chloroform-soaked rag. It turned out the rumor was wrong: Geidel fled with just $7. He was arrested 15 hours later.

The Time: Geidel received a prison sentence of 20 years to life, but for reasons that remain a mystery, when he became eligible for parole in 1931, and then every ten years after that, his parole was denied, even though he was a model prisoner. Finally, in 1974, the press got word of the man who'd been in prison for more than 60 years—and Geidel was finally granted parole. Only problem: He didn't want to go. He was finally convinced to leave in 1980, at age 86. He'd spent 68 years, 8 months, and 2 days behind bars. It remains the longest time served in U.S. prison history. (Geidel died in a nursing home in 1987.)

JOHNSON VAN DYKE GRIGSBY

The Crime: In 1907, Grigsby, born in 1885 to former slaves, stabbed a man to death during a fight over a poker game in an Indiana saloon. He pleaded guilty to second-degree murder, supposedly in exchange for not going to the electric chair.

The Time: Grigsby went to prison in 1908 at the age of 23. He was released in 1974—66 years later—at age 89. Johnny Cash heard about Grigsby's release that year, and wrote the song

"Michigan City Howdy Do" in his honor.

> Well, Johnson Van Dyke Grigsby was paroled at 89.
> He never walked on a carpet; never tasted dinner wine.
> His old eyes were slowly fadin' as he walked out of the gate,
> And he breathed the first free air he'd breathed since 19-0-8.
> Howdy do, Michigan City, you're sure a pretty sight....

But that "pretty sight" was pretty disturbing to Grigsby: The world had changed so drastically during his six decades in prison that just two weeks after his release he went back...and stayed in prison until 1976, when he was 91. He served a total of 68 years (although for two of them he was technically a free man). Grigsby died in a Michigan City, Indiana, nursing home at the age of 102.

WILLIAM HEIRENS

The Crime: In 1945 two women were murdered in Chicago. At the scene of the second crime, the killer wrote a message on a wall in lipstick: "For heaven's sake, catch me before I kill more. I cannot control myself," leading the press to dub him the "Lipstick Killer." Then, in 1946, a six-year-old Chicago girl was killed and dismembered. Heirens, just 17 and a student at the University of Chicago, was arrested, and eventually confessed to the crimes.

The Time: Heirens was sentenced to three consecutive life terms. He died on March 5, 2012, at the age of 83, in the 65th year of his sentence. (During his time in prison, Heirens became the first Illinois prison inmate to earn a four-year college degree.)

RICHARD HONECK

The Crime: Honeck and another man, Herman Hundhausen, broke into the Chicago hotel room of Walter Koeller, a former friend who had testified against them in an arson case. They had come armed, according to an 1899 *New York Times* article, with "an eight-inch bowie knife, a sixteen-inch bowie knife, a silver-plated case knife, a .44 caliber revolver, a .38 caliber revolver, a .22 caliber revolver, a club, and two belts of cartridges." Koeller was found dead the next day from a knife wound in his back.

The Time: Hundhausen confessed and testified against Honeck in exchange for a lighter sentence. He told prosecutors that Honeck had killed Koeller with the eight-inch bowie knife. Honeck was sentenced to life in prison in 1899 and released in 1963.

Flu viruses can live up to 48 hours on stainless steel.

Newspaper reports said that during his 64 years in prison, he had received only one letter—a four-line note from his brother in 1904—and had received just two visitors: a friend in 1904, and a newspaper reporter in 1963. Honeck lived with a niece in Oregon after his release, dying in 1976 at the age of 97.

JOHN STRAFFEN

The Crime: Over the course of three weeks in July and August, 1951, 21-year-old Straffen strangled two girls, aged six and nine, in Bath, England. He had been in and out of trouble (and in and out of institutions for the "mentally defective") since he was ten, but was nonetheless allowed to move about on his own at the time he killed the girls. Straffen was deemed unfit for trial and sent to a high-security asylum for a term to be determined by psychiatrists. In 1952 Straffen escaped the asylum by climbing a fence. His escape was noted almost immediately, and he was recaptured within four hours—but in those four hours he managed to strangle a third girl to death, this one just five years old.

The Time: Straffen was tried, convicted, and sentenced to death. A British official recommended to Queen Elizabeth II—just six months on the throne at the time—that she give Straffen, who was clearly mentally ill, a reprieve from the death penalty. The queen agreed, and Straffen's sentence became life with no chance of parole. He died on November 19, 2007, at the age of 77. He had served 55 years in prison, the longest known sentence in British history.

* * *

THINGS THAT (DON'T) GO BUMP

"British resort chain Butlins has banned bumper car drivers from bumping into each other over fears of health and safety. Now holiday merrymakers are supposed to drive calmly round the track in one direction, following each other and overtaking only when there is enough room to do so. Visitors who flout the rules will receive a driving ban."

—***The Sun* (UK), 2011**

It cost $7 million to build the room in the Louvre where the *Mona Lisa* is displayed.

MR. BLACK & MS. WHITE

Thoughts from the gray matter of people named Black and White.

"I never had much of a vocabulary. My friend would still be alive today if I'd known the difference between *antidote* and *anecdote*."

—Ron White, comedian

"MTV is to music as KFC is to chicken."

—Lewis Black, comedian

"I would never purposely sing a song about someone I love, I wouldn't want to embarrass them. But for someone I don't like, I'd definitely do that."

—Jack White, the White Stripes

"The moment you start analyzing your own rock is the moment your rock is dead. That's why rock is now pretty much dead. Too much analyzation. Not enough rockalyzation!"

—Jack Black, Tenacious D

"The most difficult thing in the world is to know how to do a thing and to watch someone else do it wrong without comment."

—T. H. White, author

"The easiest lies to tell are the ones you want to be true."

—Holly Black, author

"All creatures must learn to coexist. That's why the brown bear and the field mouse can share their lives in harmony. Of course, they can't mate or the mice would explode."

—Betty White, actor

"The layman's constitutional view: What he likes is constitutional, and that which he doesn't is unconstitutional."

—Hugo Black, Supreme Court Justice

"Analyzing humor is like dissecting a frog. Few people are interested and the frog dies of it."

—E. B. White, author

"The only easy day was yesterday."

—Clint Black, country star

"Cement doesn't give as much as snow."

—Shaun White, champion snowboarder, on why he doesn't skateboard

What is the white powder on chewing gum? Powdered sugar or talc, usually.

WORD ORIGINS

Ever wonder where words come from? So do we.

LOITER

Meaning: To stand around idly with no obvious purpose

Origin: "The Dutch brought their word *loteren* to English in the 1500s when many Hollanders moved to Britain. The earliest meaning was 'to totter or shake,' like an old-timer. In England, it was more often used to mean 'to be in the way,' and finally, 'to dawdle.'" (From *Where in the Word?*, by David Muschell)

SOFA

Meaning: A long, upholstered seat with a back and arms

Origin: "The word dates from about 1625 and comes from the Arabic *suffa*—a raised part of the floor covered with carpets and cushions. By the early 1700s, the long, stuffed seats designed for reclining were commonplace." (From *Mothballs and Elbow Grease*, published by the National Trust)

TAWDRY

Meaning: Gaudy; showy and cheap

Origin: "The convent, later cathedral, of Ely was founded in the seventh century in England by St. Audrey, who died of a growth in her throat, which she believed was punishment for wearing sumptuous necklaces. In time, a fair came to be held at Ely on St. Audrey's Day, October 17, at which one of the most popular wares was a necklace called 'St. Audrey's lace.' As the centuries passed, the necklaces got cheaper and cheaper, while the name St. Audrey morphed into *tawdry*." (From *Bedlam, Boudoir & Brouhaha—or Remarkable Words with Astonishing Origins*, by John Train)

ODD

Meaning: Any number not divisible by two; strange

Origin: "From Old Norse *oddi*, it originally meant 'point'—the apex of an arrowhead, or any triangle with one odd angle. Although it applied to a group of three in which one was an unpaired unit, eventually *odd* was extended to any number

When Castro took control of Cuba, he ordered all Monopoly game boards destroyed.

between even ones, or anything out of the ordinary." (From *The Story Behind the Word*, by Morton S. Freeman)

CRY

Meaning: To sob or shed tears because of grief, pain, or joy

Origin: "In Ancient Rome, the word for the citizens was *Quirites*. From this arose a verb, *quiritare*, which meant literally 'to call on the Quirites for help,' or just raise a public outcry. The Gauls got hold of *quiritare* and dropped a few consonants until it ended up as *crier* in French." (From *Six Words You Never Knew Had Something to Do with Pigs*, by Katherine Barber)

SAFARI

Meaning: An expedition for hunting or exploring

Origin: "In Swahili, a *safari* is any journey, even just going to the store, but in English it is reserved for adventures in Africa. It was most likely brought into English by British explorer Sir Richard Burton in the ninteenth century." (From *A Certain "Je Ne Sais Quoi"—The Origin of Foreign Words Used in English*, by Chloe Rhodes)

ALOOF

Meanings: Distant physically or emotionally

Origin: "The Hollanders gave us many words that have to do with the sea. *Aloof* is made up of *a-*, 'toward,' and the Dutch word *loef*, the equivalent of our nautical term *luff*, which is used in ordering the steersman to turn the ship into the wind and thus 'steer clear of' the shore toward which the boat is moving. So, when you are acting aloof, you are 'steering clear of' your fellow men." (From *Word Origins and Their Romantic Stories*, by Wilfred Funk)

TRUE

Meaning: Consistent with fact or reality; not false

Origin: "The words *true* and *tree* are joined at the root, etymologically speaking. In Old English, *tree* was *treow* and *true* was *treowe*. Both words ultimately go back to an Indo-European root *deru-* or *dreu-*, referring to wood and, by extension, firmness. Like a tree, *truth* is thought of as something firm; so too can certain bonds between people, like *trust*, another derivative of the same root." (From *The American Heritage Dictionary of the English Language*)

Game Over! Atari turned down the chance to buy the rights to *Pac-Man*.

TREASURE IN THE ATTIC

Maybe somewhere in your junk-filled attic or basement, a long-forgotten treasure is hiding, just waiting for you to find it. It may sound far-fetched, but that's exactly what happened to these folks.

HAPPY HOUR

Find: 13 bottles of 95-year-old whiskey

Story: In 2012 do-it-yourselfer Bryan Fite, 40, began installing his own central air-conditioning in his home in St. Joseph, Missouri. When he pried up the attic floor boards to replace some old wiring, he noticed a group of odd cylindrical objects wrapped in paper. At first he thought they were old steam pipes…until he noticed words like "Old Crow" and "distillery" printed on the paper. He realized he was looking at old whiskey bottles, still in their original paper wrappers.

Fite knew that the house's first owner was an alcoholic who lost the home after he was sent to a sanitarium to sober up. Fite figures the bottles, which date to 1917, were the man's secret liquor stash. It's estimated that the bottles would be worth several hundred dollars apiece, possibly more, if they were sold at auction. Fite says that's not going to happen: He plans to keep the bottles until 2017 when they'll be 100 years old, and then drink them with his friends.

CARD COUNTING

Find: Baseball cards

Story: When Jean Hench passed away in October 2011, she left her Defiance, Ohio, home and all its contents to her 20 nieces and nephews. Her nephew Karl Kissner administered the estate. When one of his cousins found a box of around 700 baseball cards in the attic, he set it aside until they could determine whether the cards had any value. A little research was all it took: The cards were multiple copies of a rare 30-card set known as the E98 series, which included 15 Hall of Famers, such as Ty Cobb, Cy Young, and Honus Wagner. Though the cards were more than 100 years old, most were in pristine condition. They'd apparently been in the attic since about 1910, when Jean's father, Carl Hench, who

Street musicians must audition for permission to play in New York City's subway stations.

ran a meat market, received them as promotional items from a candy company. Because the cards are so rare and in such good condition, they're considered one of the most valuable collections ever found. The 37 most valuable cards together are worth at least $500,000, and the remaining 600-plus are worth another $1.5 to $2.5 million. As Hench directed in her will, the cards are being divided among her nieces and nephews, most of whom planned to sell them at auction.

MADE IN CHINA

Find: A Chinese vase

Story: When 73-year-old Patricia Newman died in early 2010, her sister, Gene Johnson, and Gene's son, Anthony, cleaned out her house in Pinner, a suburb of London, England. They arranged for a local auction house called Bainbridge's to sell Newman's belongings, which included a 16-inch yellow and blue Chinese vase with a fish motif that the Johnsons found on a bookcase in the attic. According to family lore, Newman's husband, William, had brought the vase back from China many years before. It had never been professionally appraised, and the Johnsons thought the bookcase the vase sat on—which sold for £200 ($319)—might be worth more than the vase.

Not quite: A consultant for Bainbridge's recognized it as having been specially made for Emperor Qianlong (1735–96), and valued the Chinese vase at between £800,000 and £1.2 million ($1.3-1.9 million). So what did the Emperor's vase sell for at the Bainbridge's auction? £53.1 million (about $86 million), making it the most expensive piece of Chinese porcelain ever sold at auction.

Update: Well, it *would* have been the most expensive ever sold at auction, had the winning bidder, said to be a Chinese billionaire, ever paid up. As of July 2012, he still hadn't, apparently because he objected to paying the auctioneer's fee of £10.1 million fee ($16 million). At last report, the vase was in storage, waiting for the winning bidder to make good…or for the Johnsons to cancel the sale and risk the vase fetching a lower price at a second auction.

* * *

"He who knows that enough is enough will always have enough."

—**Lao Tzu**

Coldest month at the North Pole: February. At the South Pole: July.

UNCLE JOHN'S WEIRD TRAVEL GUIDE

You might want to see if you can fit some of these locations into your vacation plans. Because sometimes you want to go…somewhere where it's weird outside.

THAMES TOWN

Location: Shanghai, China

Description: A quaint little English village…in China

Details: In 2001, Shanghai's city planners came up with a plan to draw people out of the center of the packed city: Build nine new towns outside the perimeter. To make the towns attractive, the planners gave each of them a theme—and so Thames Town was born. Built to resemble a traditional English village, it has a main square, cobblestone streets, a large church modeled after the Anglican church in Bristol, statues of famous Brits—including Winston Churchill and Lady Di—and even fish-and-chips shops and corner pubs. The plan didn't work. The homes were snapped up by wealthy Shanghaiians as investment properties, so Thames Town is basically a ghost town. (Although it has become a popular place for people to have wedding photos taken.)

BATTLESHIP ISLAND

Location: Hashima Island, Japan, 20 miles from Nagasaki

Description: A "ghost island"

Details: The island is tiny—just 15 acres in area—and rocky, and was uninhabited until a coal-mining operation started there in the 1880s. Over the decades, massive concrete apartment buildings, so large they almost dwarf the island itself, were built for the mine workers, and an imposing seawall was built around the island's perimeter. The wall and the apartment blocks made Hashima look like a battleship, which led to its more common name—*Gunkanjima*, or "Battleship Island." In the 1950s, more than 5,000 workers lived there; in 1974 the mine was closed, and the island has been abandoned ever since—which is why it's also known as "Ghost Island" today. The Japanese government banned anyone from visiting Gunkanjima for decades, but that policy changed in 2009. You can now visit Battleship Island, but only on an official tour. Authorities still don't allow anyone into the crumbling apartment buildings. (A few people have snuck in, and then posted photographs of the haunted buildings online.)

ALPHAVILLE

Location: Sao Paulo, Brazil

Description: A heavily guarded luxury enclave within a large, dirty, densely packed city

Details: Sao Paulo is the world's seventh-largest city (population: 19 million), and, like all large cities, it has a lot of crime. It also has, like most large cities, a relatively small number of wealthy people living among hordes of poor and middle-class people. That led to Alphaville. Built in the 1970s on the city's western edge, it's basically a gated luxury city within the city. More than 30,000 of Sao Paulo's wealthiest citizens live there in plush, upper-class neighborhoods. They have everything they need: malls, restaurants, stores, golf courses, and even their own hospitals and universities. The Alphaville compound is surrounded by high-security fencing, and the entire area is patrolled by Alphaville's private police force, 1,000 officers strong. And there are a lot of helipads, because many Alphaville residents travel to and from their homes via helicopter.

DHARAVI

Location: Mumbai, India

Description: An unusual slum

Details: Mumbai is bigger than Sao Paulo—it's the world's *fourth* largest city (population: 20 million). Dharavi is located right in the middle of it, and it's almost impossibly jam-packed: Just 0.67 square miles in area, Dharavi is home to between 600,000 and one million residents. (For comparison: Union City, New Jersey, one of the most densely populated cities in the United States, has almost twice the area of Dharavi—and its population is only 67,000.) And although Dharavi is without question a slum, it's also a tight-knit community—and, in its way, prosperous and dignified: Thousands of small businesses have combined sales of approximately $655 million annually. You can go on guided tours of Dharavi (most don't allow cameras, out of respect for the people who live there), but you can also rent a bicycle and ride around yourself. Recommended: Try to get to the roof of one of the factories to get an unforgettable view of the seemingly endless huts piled upon huts piled upon huts that are the homes of Dharavi's residents.

Bonus: If the description of Dharavi seems familiar, it probably is. Dharavi is the slum featured in the Oscar-winning 2008 film, *Slumdog Millionaire*.

AUROVILLE

Location: Southern India

Description: A real-life hippie city

Details: In 1966 the Sri Aurobindo Society (a spiritual society named for Indian mystic and independence leader Sri Aurobindo) went to the Indian government with a proposal for the founding of a new city to be named "Auroville" ("City of Dawn") in the South Indian state of Tamil Nadu. According to the proposal:

> Auroville wants to be a universal town where men and women of all countries are able to live in peace and progressive harmony above all creeds, all politics and all nationalities. The purpose of Auroville is to realise human unity.

The Indian government actually liked the idea and helped buy some land—and in 1968, Auroville was founded. The city is circular, with the outer rim a wide, undeveloped greenbelt. Inside that are four zones: residential, industrial, international, and cultural. In the middle of the circle is the Peace Center, with a large pavilion, an amphitheater, and gardens. It's still not completed, but about 2,200 people representing 45 different nationalities call Auroville home today, and they run several farms and other small businesses there. Want to visit? Or live there? Check out their website. Maybe Auroville is the perfect (hippie) home for you!

* * *

AMERICAN HAIRSTORY

In 1860 a Democrat named Valentine Tapley of Missouri vowed never to shave again if Republican Abraham Lincoln were elected president. When Tapley died in 1910, his beard was 12' 6" long.

FLUBBED HEADLINES

Whether silly, naughty, or just plain bizarre, they're all real.

Climber Who Cut Off Arm to Escape Speaking at MSU

PICTURES FROM UNDERCOVER HOOTERS BUST RELEASED

Farm Bureau Estimates Crap Damage at $207 Million

Garbage truck lands on Saturn

Pedestrian deaths largely flat in U.S., Maryland

New President at Kansas City Fed

UNMARRIED COUPLES FIND DIVORCE DIFFICULT

Padres pitcher Latos writes 'I hate SF' on balls

Four More Newspapers Switch to Offset; Conversions Not Always Soomth

6-year-old girl just found after 26 years

1 in 5 U.S. moms have babies with multiple dads, study says

Marijuana Supporters at Record High

A-Rod Gets Hit, Colon hurt

Bugs Flying Around with Wings Are Flying Bugs

For Towns Hold Elections

Northfield Plans to Plan Strategic Plan

Troutt named to Salmon Board

BISHOPS AGREE SEX ABUSE RULES

Former Jets reflect on impact of 9/11 attacks

Every Students Counts

Woman accused of mugging a man using a walker

150th Year for Dead and Blind Institute

Obama to Recruit Clinton's Top Fun Raisers

Church member donates organ to St. Aloysius

Texans Support Death Penalty, but Only for the Guilty

REEL TIME BOMBS

Ever notice something in a movie that looks wrong—like it's from the wrong time period? When filmmakers accidentally include things that didn't exist at the time when their movie is set, we call it a "time bomb."

MOVIE: *The Last Temptation of Christ* (1988)

Time Bomb #1: The historical Jesus was said to have lived sometime between 7 B.C. and A.D. 36. In Martin Scorcese's film, Jesus is a little more modern. In one scene, when he turns around you can clearly see that his robe has a manufacturer's label sewn into it.

Time Bomb #2: Although Mary Magdalene was historically considered a loose woman, the red nail polish she's wearing in her first few scenes is out of place, even for her. Reason: The first glossy red nail polish wasn't created until 1932.

MOVIE: *The Talented Mr. Ripley* (1999)

Time Bomb #1: Tom Ripley puts his blue passport down on a desk. But in the 1950s (when the film is set), American passports had green covers.

Time Bomb #2: Millionaire playboy Dickie Greenleaf has Miles Davis's LP *Tutu* in his record collection. The album was released in 1986.

MOVIE: *Apollo 13* (1995)

Time Bomb #1: The *Apollo 13* mission was launched in April 1970. Astronaut Jim Lovell's daughter must have received an early copy of the Beatles' *Let It Be*, because she's seen holding the album, which wasn't released until May.

Time Bomb #2: When the astronauts climb into their space suits pre-launch, the bright red letters of the NASA logo (nicknamed "worm") appears on a window. That logo was developed in 1975.

Time Bomb #3: Then there's the Lockheed Martin coffee mug that sits on flight director Gene Kranz's desk. Lockheed Martin was formed with the merger of Lockheed Corp. and Martin Marietta...which took place in 1995.

Do you believe it? Scientists say the harder you concentrate, the less you blink.

MOVIE: *The Ten Commandments* (1956)

Time Bomb #1: The biblical Moses is known for performing miracles. He's also known for living around the year 1600 B.C. That makes several of the "miracles" in this film goofs. Example: As baby Moses floats in a basket on the Nile river, a safety pin (invented in 1849) holds his diaper together.

Time Bomb #2: When Moses listens to God speaking to him from a burning bush, tire tracks can be seen in the sand. (Rubber tires were invented in 1888.)

Time Bomb #3: And when Moses stands atop a weathered rock in the desert, he's wearing…a wristwatch. The first one was made by Swiss watch manufacturer Patek Phillippe in 1868.

MOVIE: *Letters from Iwo Jima* (2006)

Time Bomb: The GAZ-69 off-road vehicle is used as a military vehicle on the Japanese island of Iwo Jima. But the battles on Iwo Jima took place in 1945, and the GAZ-69 is a post-WWII Soviet army vehicle, first made in 1953.

MOVIE: *Almost Famous* (2000)

Time Bomb #1: It's the 1970s. Fifteen-year-old William Miller has a gig writing for *Rolling Stone* magazine. His assignment: follow a rock band across the country and write about the experience. In one scene, Miller's jeans come off and he's seen sporting undies with "Fruit of the Loom" written around the waistband, a style not sold till the 1990s.

Time Bomb #2: Miller attends a Black Sabbath concert, and someone backstage is wearing a Black Sabbath Reunion T-shirt, circa 1997.

MOVIE: *Marie Antoinette* (2006)

Time Bomb #1: When Marie Antoinette first meets members of the French royal family, the year is 1768. King Louis XV's daughter, Madame Victoire, is holding a Pekingese. Until 1860—when British troops looted China's Forbidden City and took five Pekingese pups back to Britain—Pekingese dogs could be owned only by members of China's imperial family.

Time Bomb #2: Jack Russell Terriers also appear. They were first bred in the mid-1800s.

In 2010 a traffic jam in Beijing, China, stretched 60 miles and lasted more than a week.

MY DOG HAS Ph.Ds

These true stories of accredited canines show that you really can get anything online—even a college degree for your dog.

Applicant: Sonny, a Golden Labrador Retriever

Story: On a 2007 episode of the hit Australian TV show *The Chaser's War on Everything*, co-host Chas Licciardello announced that he'd submitted an application for a medical degree to the online Ashwood University, which offers degrees for "what you already know," meaning you can graduate without actually taking classes. The application wasn't for Licciardello—it was for Sonny, his Golden Labrador Retriever. (No last name—just "Sonny.") Under "work experience," he wrote that Sonny "has eaten out of hospital rubbish bins for five years" and "has significant proctology experience sniffing other dogs' bums." Licciardello submitted the application—with the $450 fee—and waited.

Result: A week later, Sonny received a framed certificate proclaiming him the recipient of a medical degree. Not only that, according to his transcript he'd earned As in *Immunology* and *Oral Communication and Presentation Skills*. So where is Ashwood University? An investigation failed to determine its exact location, but noted that Sonny's degree was mailed from Pakistan.

Applicant: Chester Ludlow, a Pug

Story: GetEducated.com is an organization that monitors online universities. In 2009 the company decided to test one of its subjects, and had "Chester Ludlow"—a Pug belonging to one of its employees—apply to Rochville University.

Result: Just days later, Chester received his MBA. It came from Dubai with a letter stating that he'd graduated with a 3.19 grade-point average and passed "with distinction" in Finance. It also congratulated Chester for having been a member of the Rochville University student council. (GetEducated.com made a video about it, featuring Chester and a dog named Bixby, who sniffs Chester's diploma and says, "Something smells funny to me." Google "Chester Ludlow" to see it.)

Camels chew in a figure-8 pattern.

Applicant: Wally

Story: In 2004 Peter Brancato, a reporter with Schenectady, New York, television station WRGB, filled out an application for a degree from Almeda University for his dog, Wally. Brancato wrote that Wally "plays with the kids every day" and "teaches them responsibilities, like feeding the dog."

Result: Wally received an associate's degree in Childhood Development...and a transcript certifying that he'd completed courses in European culture, algebra, and public speaking. (Ruff!) After WRGB aired the story, Almeda University issued a press release accusing the station of waging a "smear campaign" against them. The "university," which is still in operation, gives its location as Boise, Idaho—but its headquarters are actually on the Caribbean island of Nevis.

Update: In 2008 Wally was featured in a political cartoon showing him with a thought bubble that read, "I graduated with Bill Chesen." Chesen—a candidate for mayor of Lake Geneva, Wisconsin—had listed a degree from Almeda University on his resume. Chesen accused his opponent of defamation, but the district attorney took no action. (And Chesen won the election.)

Applicant: Molly, a Basset Hound

Story: In 2012 KHOU-TV in Houston, Texas, began investigating companies that use a state law meant to prevent discrimination against homeschooled kids to hand out high school diplomas to just about anyone who pays the hefty fee. KHOU sent one such company, Lincoln Academy, an application in the name of Molly—a dog belonging to one of their cameramen—and found that in addition to the fee, Lincoln required all applicants to pass a test. Sample questions: *A triangle has how many sides?* and *The president lives in the White House—true or false?*

Result: Molly got an e-mail that read: "Dear Molly, You have truly reached a new milestone in your educational career. Sit back and enjoy your new life of being a high school graduate from Lincoln Academy." KHOU aired their report, along with the story of a young lady who got a similar diploma—for $600—believing it would allow her to fulfill her dream of joining the U.S. Navy, only to have a Navy recruiter tell her the diploma was no good. (Lincoln Academy is still in business; Texas legislators still haven't fixed the law that allows such companies to operate.)

MR. BASEBALL

After a lackluster baseball career, Bob Uecker became an actor, sports broadcaster, and TV personality. And he's funny about it all, too.

"I helped the Cardinals win the pennant. I came down with hepatitis."

"I signed with the Milwaukee Braves for $3,000. That bothered my dad because he didn't have that kind of dough, but he eventually scraped it up."

"When I came up to bat with three men on and two outs in the ninth, I looked in the other team's dugout, and they were already in street clothes."

"I go to a lot of Old Timers games, and I haven't lost a thing. I sit in the bullpen and let people throw things at me. Just like old times."

"I led the league in 'Go get 'em next time.'"

"If a guy hits .300 every year, what does he have to look forward to? I always tried to stay around .190, with three or four RBI. And I tried to get them all in September. That way I always had something to talk about during the winter."

"I knew when my career was over. In 1965 my baseball card came out with no picture."

"The biggest thrill a ballplayer can have is when your son takes after you. That happened when my Bobby was in his championship Little League game. Struck out three times. Gosh, I was proud."

"When I looked to the third-base coach for a sign, he turned his back on me."

"I had slumps that lasted into the winter."

"The highlight of my career? In '67 with St. Louis, I walked with the bases loaded to drive in the winning run in an intersquad game in spring training."

"I won the Comeback of the Year Award five years in a row."

"I set records that will never be equaled. In fact, I hope 90 percent of them don't even get printed."

THE DEATH OF GERALD BULL

Who killed the Canadian "Boy Rocket Scientist" who grew up to design a gun for Saddam Hussein?

BACKGROUND

Gerald Bull (1928-1990) was born in North Bay, Ontario. He graduated from the University of Toronto at the age of 20, got a master's degree at age 21, and a Ph.D. in aeronautical engineering (and a job heading the aerospace division at the Canadian Armament Research Development Establishment) at age 22. While at McGill University in 1962 he designed an artillery shell that hit a predetermined altitude and then fired a second rocket. Magazines called him "Boy Rocket Scientist." His dream was to use artillery to launch satellites into space.

Bull tried to sell his ideas to Western governments, but the United States wasn't interested. (NASA wanted to focus on rockets, not weapons.) So, feeling abandoned and insulted, Bull started the Space Research Corporation in 1967 and sold his gun-making expertise to anyone in the world market. This included a 1980 sale of 30,000 artillery shells to South Africa, which violated an American arms embargo and led to a six-month prison term. Not long after his release, he was asked to lead Iraq's "Project Babylon." Saddam Hussein is reported to have personally invited Bull to design a Supergun, a howitzer with a 32-inch diameter barrel capable of sending 1,200-pound packages 600 miles into space. This meant that Hussein would be able to bomb targets thousands of miles away from Iraq.

MYSTERIOUS DEATH

On March 22, 1990, in Uccle, a suburb of Brussels, Bull opened his apartment door to find a gunman hiding in the shadows. The killer fired five bullets into the inventor's head. Gerald Bull was 62.

There were many suspicious facts. For one, Bull had $20,000 in cash in his pocket when he was shot. The killer didn't take it. For

Let's move there! In Italy, you can buy fresh-baked pizza from vending machines.

another, in the weeks following his murder, British Customs impounded eight steel "petroleum pipes" bound for Iraq. The pipes matched Bull's early designs for an enormous gun. Over the next two weeks, five other components were found across Europe. And finally—Project Babylon's chemical-warfare expert, an American named Steven Adams, had discovered Bull's body. Later that day, Adams vanished.

CONSPIRACY THEORIES

So who assassinated Gerald Bull? No one wanted to see Hussein with a Supergun, so every country is a suspect.

• ***Theory #1: The British did it.*** Did Margaret Thatcher dispatch MI-5 operatives to assassinate Bull to eliminate competition with British interests in the black-market weapons trade? A week after Bull's murder, British journalist Jonathan Moyle was found dead in Santiago, Chile, with a pillowcase over his head. He'd been researching a story on British ties to Iraqi weapons buyers.

• ***Theory #2: The Iraqis did it.*** Saddam Hussein wanted to keep the Supergun a secret. A week before Bull was killed in Brussels, the Iraqis executed an Iranian-born British journalist named Farzad Bazoft, who was asking questions about Bull and Adams. Sources say the Iraqis sent a jet to get Adams out of Brussels, but the Belgian defenses intercepted it. It's also possible the Iraqis thought the two were spying for the United States.

• ***Theory #3: The CIA did it.*** The U.S. was no friend to Saddam Hussein, and no friend to weapons consultants who helped him. Remember, the United States put Bull in prison in 1980 for violating an arms embargo. Bull's son Michael initially blamed the CIA, but later changed his opinion to...

• ***Theory #4: The Israelis did it.*** And he's not the only one. Two years after Bull's murder, a British engineer named Christopher Crowley testified before the House of Commons that he and Bull regularly supplied Western intelligence agents with information about the Supergun. In the 1980s, Israel was quick to respond to any threats from Iraq, so Crowley believes Israeli intelligence (the Mossad) had the gun's inventor eliminated.

So who murdered Gerald Bull? The case remains officially unsolved.

Four out of 10 workplace dating relationships result in marriage.

ODD VODKAS

Vodka is practically tasteless, which means that distilleries can add whatever bizarre flavors they want to it. For example...

• **GRASS:** Polish company Bak makes Bison Grass vodka. It's not bison-flavored—it's grass-flavored (and bison eat grass). The grass infusion leaves a small amount of coumarin, which is a main ingredient in rat poison and leads to liver damage (but then, so does vodka).

• **HORSERADISH:** Sputnik, a Russian distillery, makes a vodka flavored with "pure organic horseradish." Wasabi, another kind of horseradish, gives Green Geisha from Oregon's Hard Times Distillery its distinctive flavor (and burn).

• **PORK:** Bakon vodka is infused with the flavor of pork fat. The bottle is bacon-shaped, too.

• **PICKLE:** Another Russian distillery, Vodka Garant, makes a pickle-and-garlic vodka. If that's not to your taste, American distillery Naked Jay makes a pickle-flavored vodka. No garlic.

• **PEANUT BUTTER:** Van Goh produces a PB&J vodka, while NutLiquor makes one free of jelly, just peanut butter. Both are, surprisingly, free of peanut products.

• **BUBBLE GUM:** A company called Three Olives makes this vodka.

• **SYRUP:** Birch syrup is a sweetened tree sap, similar to maple syrup and widely used in Alaska. Alaska Distillery makes a birch syrup vodka. (They also make rhubarb vodka and their most challenging flavor: smoked salmon vodka.)

• **DESSERT:** Pinnacle manufactures a line of dessert-inspired vodkas, including cotton candy, cupcake, cake batter, and whipped cream.

• **ARACHNID:** Skorppio-brand vodka doesn't have any particular extra flavor, but it does come with a real, de-poisoned scorpion, much like a worm comes in a bottle of mescal.

In Japan the number 4 is unlucky (it sounds like the Japanese word for death).

MICHIN SAEKKI!

Translated into English, these international insults may sound silly, but trust us: do not say *them in their native lands!*

GOSPOD ODIN DA TA PRATI! (Bulgarian)
Meaning: "Go to h*ll!"
Literally: "God sends you to the fire!"

FANTONG!
(Mandarin)
Meaning: "Useless!"
Literally: "Rice bucket!"

BACHE SHEYTOON!
(Farsi)
Meaning: "Grow up!"
Literally: "You Satan child!"

CON COMME LA BALA!
(French)
Meaning: "Very stupid!"
Literally: "Stupid like a broom!"

GROZNI SI KATO SALATA!
(Bulgarian)
Meaning: "You're ugly!"
Literally: "You look like a salad!"

NAMEH TEN-NO!
(Japanese)
Meaning: "You want to fight!"
Literally: "What are you licking?"

DRECKSCLEUDER!
(German)
Meaning: "Potty mouth!"
Literally: "Dirt slingshot!"

YA NA'AL!
(Hebrew)
Meaning: "You idiot!"
Literally: "You shoe!"

MICHIN SAEKKI!
(Korean)
Meaning: "Nutcase!"
Literally: "Crazy animal baby!"

GEWADEE MASTAWCHI!
(Kurdish)
Meaning: "Sleazebag!"
Literally: "Yogurt pimp!"

NI SHI SHENME DONGXI!
(Mandarin)
Meaning: "You're inhuman!"
Literally: "What kind of object are you!"

SUTKI PALA! (Polish)
Meaning: "Chill out!"
Literally: "Your nipples are burning!"

AIZVER ZAUNAS!
(Latvian)
Meaning: "Shut up!"
Literally: "Close your gills!"

ARMAGEDDON OUTTA HERE!

One of the nice things about the world not coming to an end when the doomsayers predict it will (aside from not dying) is that the rest of us get to have a few laughs at their expense.

Doomsday: September 11–13, 1988

Predicted by: Edgar Whisenant, a retired NASA engineer and author of *88 Reasons Why the Rapture Will Be in 1988*

End Times: Whisenant used biblical passages to calculate the day of "Rapture," on which some Christians believe they'll be taken bodily up to heaven. His calculation: It would occur during the Jewish New Year, which fell on September 11–13. An estimated 4.5 million copies of *88 Reasons* were sold or distributed by Whisenant's publisher; the company closed its offices on the 11th so that employees could be with their families.

Moment of Truth: September 11 came and went. So did September 12 and September 13. No Rapture.

Aftermath: Whisenant announced that his calculations were a year off. (The Gregorian calendar doesn't have a year zero.) His new date: September 1, 1989. This time he was *sure*. "Everything points to it. All the evidence has piled up," he said.

After-aftermath: September 1, 1989, also passed without incident. "I guess God doesn't always do things the way man thinks He will," Whisenant said afterward. He apparently calculated a *third* date, but kept that one to himself. "There's evidence all around, but ol' Ed Whisenant just can't name it," he told reporters. "My job is done." He died in 2001.

Doomsday: April 1990 (OK, it's a dooms*month*)

Predicted by: Elizabeth Clare Prophet, spiritual head of the Church Universal and Triumphant, a New Age religion that's a blend of Christianity, Hinduism, Taoism, Buddhism, Gnosticism, Kabbalah, metaphysics, and anti-communism

End Times: In the mid-1980s, Prophet claimed to receive

messages from spirits called "Ascended Masters" who told her the world was moving from the old Age of Pisces into the new Age of Aquarius, a difficult period of transition that would culminate in a Soviet nuclear attack against the United States in April 1990. At Prophet's urging, some 2,000 of her followers quit their jobs and moved to the church's 28,000-acre Montana compound. There they built giant underground bomb shelters, each large enough to hold 750 people, and packed them with food, vehicles, fuel, guns, ammunition, clothing, medical supplies, and other items they'd need in the post-apocalyptic world. How did they pay for all that stuff? With their life savings, and additional money they raised by taking loans out against their homes. Prophet assured her followers that the money would never have to be repaid, since the banks were going to be destroyed in the nuclear war.

Moment of Truth: As Prophet's followers huddled in the bomb shelters, April 1990 came…and went. No nuclear attack.

Aftermath: When the world didn't end, many church members left Montana and returned to their homes, either because they'd become disillusioned or because they had to find jobs and start repaying all those bank loans. Prophet's reputation never recovered: Her fourth marriage collapsed, her church went into decline, and her children abandoned her ministry. In 1998 she was diagnosed with Alzheimer's disease. She died in 2009.

The Church Universal and Triumphant is still around, though it's smaller than it used to be, and it's still headquartered at the Montana compound (what's left of it—most of the land was sold). And the church still owns the bomb shelters, which, at last report, were still filled with supplies, along with 20,000 hours of Prophet's teachings on video and audiotape…just in case. "Our church has everything in place if we ever need it. At some level, that puts us all at ease," a church member told the *Salt Lake Tribune* in 1998.

Doomsday: September 10, 2008

Predicted by: Opponents of the $8 billion Large Hadron Collider, located on the French-Swiss border near Geneva

End Times: Built by the European Organization for Nuclear Research (CERN), the Large Hadron Collider is used to accelerate subatomic particles called protons to 99.99 percent the speed of light so that they can be smashed into each other during high-energy physics experiments. The giant machine is housed in a 17-mile circular tunnel, more than 300 feet underground. As construction neared completion in the spring of 2008, opponents of the collider filed suit in a U.S. federal court to block it from being started up, out of fear that doing so might create planet-wrecking subatomic particles called "strangelets," or a black hole that would swallow the Earth in as little as four minutes (or as long as four years).

Moment of Truth: Case dismissed—the judge ruled that U.S. courts have no jurisdiction over European research facilities. (Apparently the opponents' understanding of the law is as shaky as their grasp of high-energy physics.) The Large Hadron Collider was fired up on September 10, 2008. No strangelets—at least none that did any damage—and the Earth wasn't devoured by a black hole, either.

Aftermath: Though the collider was *turned on* in September 2008, it wasn't cranked up to *full power* or anything close to it. That isn't scheduled to happen until 2014 at the earliest. CERN says not to worry: "There is no basis for concerns about the consequences of new particles or forms of matter that could be produced by the collider," the agency said in a 2008 safety report. (But they *would* say that, wouldn't they?)

* * *

DUEL THE RIGHT THING

In Kentucky, whenever a politician takes office, he or she must recite an oath that was written in 1847, which reads, in part:

> I, being a citizen of this state, have not fought a duel with deadly weapons within this State nor out of it, nor have a sent or accepted a challenge to fight a duel with deadly weapons, nor have I acted as second in carrying a challenge, nor aided or assisted any person, thus offending, so help me God.

In 2012 State Rep. Darryl Owens proposed a law that would delete the outdated dueling provision from the oath. His reason: "Every time we get to that part of the ceremony, laughter erupts." The bill failed.

Members of Led Zeppelin had a standing invitation for front row seats at any Elvis concert.

GREEN GIANTS

Think the "natural" products you buy are made by crystal-clad hippies living on a goat commune? Think again.

WESTBRAE NATURAL

Grass Roots: In 1970 Bob Gerner and Kristin Brun opened a retail grocery store in the Westbrae neighborhood of Berkeley, California. According to the company website, they offered their customers "homemade granola, organic vegetables from Bob's garden, organic fruits from local farmers and whole-grain baked goods using Kristin's recipes."

Green Giant: Ten years later, they sold the Westbrae Natural brand to a group of investors, who closed the store and moved the company to Southern California, then sold the Westbrae line to international conglomerate Hain Food Group in 1997. Hain owns several other natural-food brands, including Celestial Seasonings and Rice Dream, and is worth nearly $1 billion. Westbrae remains one of their biggest earners.

HORIZON ORGANIC DAIRY

Grass Roots: Horizon was founded in 1991 by organic food pioneers Mark Retzloff, co-founder of Alfalfa's natural food store in Boulder, Colorado, and Paul Repetto, who had once worked for Westbrae Natural. Each invested $100,000 of their own money, and both worked the first year without taking a salary. First product: six different flavors of organic yogurt.

Green Giant: Just seven years later, Horizon—by this time the country's largest supplier of organic dairy products—went public. The stock offering brought in $46 million. In 2004 Dean Foods, the United States' largest milk supplier, bought the 87% of Horizon Organic stock it didn't already own—for $216 million in cash.

NAKED JUICE

Grass Roots: The Naked Juice Company was founded in Santa Monica, California, in 1983 by Jimmy Rosenberg—who made juices in his home and sold them on the beach. He called them "naked" because they were 100% pure juice—not dressed up with additives. Rosenburg's juices were a huge hit, and before long they were in stores all over California.

Green Giant: In 2000 Rosenburg sold Naked Juice to North Castle Partners, a private-equity firm based in Greenwich, Connecticut, for an undisclosed amount. In 2006 they sold it to Pepsi. Sale price: $450 million.

EMERGEN-C

Grass Roots: In 1978 chemist Jay Patrick created Emergen-C—packaged powdered drink mixes that contained large amounts of vitamin C. When he started the company (at the age of 60), he made the mixes on his kitchen table.

Green Giant: Patrick died in 2003...at which point his company imploded. Jay Patrick's widow became embroiled in a battle over control of the company with Ronald Patrick, Jay's son from a previous marriage. The legal smoke didn't clear for eight years. The results were complex—suffice it to say that Ronald Patrick won. Soon after it was over, in February 2012, Ronald Patrick sold his dad's little company to Pfizer—the largest pharmaceutical company in the world. The terms of the deal were not disclosed, but it's estimated that Pfizer paid in excess of $100 million.

NEW CHAPTER

Grass Roots: New Chapter, which specializes in organic vitamins and herbal supplements, was founded by herbalist Paul Schulick and his wife, Barbi, in Massachusetts in the early 1980s. In 1986 the Schulicks moved the company to Brattleboro, Vermont, in 1986, where, according to the company website, they "prepared their herbal remedies in the back room of a redwood saltbox nestled high in the Black Mountains."

Green Giant: In 2012 the Schulicks sold their company to Proctor & Gamble. The terms were not released, but by this time New Chapter was doing more than $100 million a year in business. "For us," said Schulick, "this has been a dream come true."

BURT'S BEES

Grass Roots: In 1984, 33-year-old Roxanne Quimby, struggling single mother of two living in a cabin in northern Maine, met

The United Nations has banned the use of lasers that are designed to blind enemies.

Burt Schavitz, a reclusive beekeeper who lived in a converted turkey coop and sold honey out of his pickup truck. They soon became friends, then partners. Roxanne started making candles from the leftover beeswax, selling them wherever she could. In 1991 she discovered an old recipe for beeswax lip balm and started selling it under the name "Burt's Bees." It sold like crazy, and in 1993 Quimby and Schavitz moved the company to North Carolina. Not long after that, the two had a falling-out, and Quimby ended up buying out Schavitz's stake in the company for about $130,000. Schavitz went back to his turkey coop.

Green Giant: In 2003 Quimby sold 80 percent of Burt's Bees to a New York City–based investment company for $141 million. (The stake Burt Schavitz sold for $130,000 would've been worth about $60 million in that deal. Quimby gave him an additional $4 million after it went through.) Four years later, Quimby sold the remaining 20 percent—to Clorox Company, for another $183 million.

Bonus: While Roxanne Quimby may have sold her little hippie company for millions of dollars, she's at least lived by her hippie principles: She s spent more than $50 million buying forest land—over 100,000 acres, primarily in Maine—to protect it from logging and other development. "I feel the fact that I was able to sell the company accelerated the process of land conservation in terms of what I could do," Quimby told the *New York Times* in 2008. "So if there is any negative karma, I'm neutral."

*   *   *

REVENGE!

In 2005 British DJ Tim Shaw was interviewing British model Josie Marsh and joked that he'd leave his wife and children for her. At least he said he was joking. His wife, Hayley, was listening and didn't think it was funny. Rather than call him out on the air, she went to eBay and listed his $40,000 Lotus Esprit Turbo sportscar for sale. The description read, "I need to get rid of this car immediately—ideally in the next two to three hours, before my husband getrs home to find it gone." The car sold in five minutes.

Seventy-five percent of all U.S. territory above 10,000 ft. in elevation is in Colorado.

IT COULD ONLY HAPPEN IN...

Ever hear about some odd thing that occurs and find yourself saying, "That could only happen in ____"? That's how we felt about these stories.

...DUBAI

In 2008 the luxury hotel chain Palazzo Versace announced that they were building a plush resort in the Middle Eastern jet-setting hot spot Dubai. Besides all of the usual luxurious amenities stuff you'd expect to find at such a $2.3 billion resort—five-star hotel, gourmet restaurants, luxury spas, etc.—the resort will feature a...refrigerated beach. The plans provide for refrigeration lines to be laid under the sand so that visitors won't burn their feet.

...TEXAS

In July 2012, restaurateur Doug Guller purchased the central Texas "ghost town" of Bankersmith on eBay and promptly announced he'd be changing the name to "Bikinis," which is the name of his sports-bar chain (staffed, of course, by women wearing bikinis). "Bikinis, Texas," Guller said in a press release, "will be a world-class destination, and I am thrilled to expand the Bikinis brand to include town ownership."

...IRELAND

The Mullingar Equestrian Centre, located about an hour from Dublin, had to cancel its 2006 Christmas party after a resident camel entered the party area and drank several cans of Guinness. (It bit through the cans to get to the beer.) The intoxicated beast then ate the 200 meat pies that had been laid out for guests. The camel, named Gus, had somehow escaped from his pen when staff left to change for the event. "You couldn't blame him," said owner Robert Fagan. "He's really a very gentle, docile sort of camel."

It takes the silk of 2,000 silkworm cocoons to make one kimono.

Q&A: ASK THE EXPERTS

Everyone's got a question or two they'd like answered—basic stuff, like "Why is the sky blue?" Here are a few of those questions, with answers from some of the world's top trivia experts.

WHAT A WASTE

Q: *Do insects pee? Do they poo, too?*

A: "Land insects cannot afford to lose much water when they eliminate wastes and thus do not urinate at all. Insects produce waste with kidney-like organs called *Malphighian tubules*. Uric acid and ammonia are dumped into the insect's hindgut and mixed with other waste products instead of traveling out of the body through a separate tube, as urine does. As for defecation, all insects must get rid of solid wastes, called *frass*. (Exception: insects on a strict liquid diet, like blood and nectar.) Frass is usually very dry and looks like tiny pellets. Caterpillars, which can consume huge amounts of plant material, leave larger, moister pellets. If there are flies in your house, you may find fly 'specks,' which look like little grease spots on the countertops." (From *Do Bees Sneeze?* by James K. Wangberg)

ALL WET

Q: *What's the difference between an ocean and a sea?*

A: "Oceans are described as continuous bodies of saltwater surrounding the continents. If all of the water in the oceans were to disappear, the continents would be surrounded by great depressions. Each of the individual oceans contains shallower areas that differ physically, chemically, or biologically from one another; these are called seas. Geographers define a sea as a division of the ocean that is enclosed or partially enclosed by land. Based on this definition, there are more than 50 seas on Earth." (From *The Handy Ocean Answer Book* by Thomas Svarney and Patricia Barnes-Svarney)

BAG MAN

Q: *Why are plastic potato-chip bags so hard to open?*

A: Blame chemist John Spevacek. In a 2012 article called "I'm That Guy," Spevacek wrote that while working for a chemical company that made "multilayer polypropylene films for food packaging," he was given the job of creating a seal strong enough to withstand pressure changes without breaking open—which often happened when cargo trucks carrying bags of chips traveled over the Rocky Mountains. "Other options were technically possible," Spevacek writes, "but not economically feasible. While options exist to prevent premature opening of the bag, such as reducing the initial air pressure in the bag, attempting to add this to the existing processing equipment would have been a nightmare. So it was necessary to increase the seal strength." Good news: Potato-chip bags don't pop open at high elevations. Bad news: They're very difficult to open at any elevation.

TIME FOR A PITS STOP

Q: *What's the difference between an underarm deodorant and an antiperspirant?*

A: "According to John Seifert, a consumer researcher for Procter and Gamble, 'Odor is caused by the bacteria that feed on chemical components in underarm sweat. A deodorant works by controlling the populations of bacteria and doesn't help control wetness.' An antiperspirant, on the other hand, helps control both odor and wetness. The active ingredient in an antiperspirant is aluminum—a mineral that does a lot more than just control bacteria. In fact, aluminum travels to sweat glands, where it reacts to obstruct the flow of perspiration. It's not necessary to use a *lot* of antiperspirant. If you're using a solid or roll-on, just a thin layer will give maximum protection. The best time to apply for maximum protection is when your underarms are a little warm and moist. This enables the active ingredients to enter the sweat glands more readily." (From *The Experts Book of Hints, Tips & Everyday Wisdom*, edited by Edward Claflin)

* * *

"If there is anything the nonconformist hates more than a conformist, it's another nonconformist who doesn't conform to the prevailing standard of nonconformity."

—Bill Vaughan

NORA'S NOTIONS

Writer and film director Nora Ephron (1949–2012) was the acerbic wit behind When Harry Met Sally, Julie and Julia, Heartburn, *and many other books and movies.*

"It's true that men who cry are sensitive to and in touch with feelings, but the only feelings they tend to be in touch with are their own."

"When your children are teenagers, it's important to have a dog so that someone in the house is happy to see you."

"I don't think any day is worth living without thinking about what you're going to eat next at all times."

"I look as young as a person can look given how old I am."

"A successful parent is one who raises a child who grows up and is able to pay for his or her own psychoanalysis."

"In my sex fantasy, nobody ever loves me for my mind."

"The desire to get married is a basic and primal instinct. It's followed by another basic and primal instinct: the desire to be single again."

"Never marry a man you wouldn't want to be divorced from."

"Insane people are always sure that they're fine. It is only the sane people who are willing to admit that they're crazy."

"My mother was a good cook, but what she believed about cooking is that if you worked hard and prospered, someone else would do it for you."

"Oh, how I regret not having worn a bikini the entire time I was 26. If anyone young is reading this, go put on a bikini, and don't take it off until you're 34."

"There's a reason why 40, 50, and 60 don't look the way they used to, and it's not because of feminism, or better living through exercise. It's because of hair dye."

"If pregnancy were a book they would cut out the last two chapters."

"You can't retrieve your life (unless you're on Wikipedia, in which case you can retrieve an inaccurate version of it)."

DYING LANGUAGES

Of the 7,000 languages in use around the world, half may be extinct by 2050. Learn about them before they're gone.

LANGUAGE: Aka-Jeru
REGION: Andaman Islands, Indian Ocean
DETAILS: Aka-Jeru is probably the oldest continuously used language on the planet. It dates to the Neolithic Era—about 8,000 years ago. The Aka-Jeru people live on an isolated island almost 200 miles from the Asian mainland, and linguists say their language has no relation to any other currently in use around the world. The Aka-Jeru have words for six seasons, which are all related to the relative availability of honey. The once-large cultural group is now a small tribe. Only about 20 to 40 people still speak Aka-Jeru.

LANGUAGE: Kallawaya
REGION: Bolivia
DETAILS: High in the Andes Mountains live the Kallawaya people, who have been there more than 500 years. The Kallawaya use modern languages (particularly Spanish) to stay in contact with society, but in private they use their own language, which is only passed down—in secret—by men. The Kallawaya are known as accomplished herbalists, and their remedies are used throughout the Andes. The group has dwindled to fewer than 100 people.

LANGUAGE : Yuchi
REGION: Oklahoma
DETAILS: Yuchi, or Euchee, is a language spoken by Yuchi people, who originally lived in Tennessee, but were relocated to Oklahoma in the late-1800s. ("Tennessee" was thought to be a Cherokee word, but some linguists believe it comes from Yuchi.) The Yuchi children were forced to attend government schools, where they were forbidden to use the native language. They were actually beaten for speaking Yuchi. Only five speakers remain, elderly people who learned the language as children and kept it alive.

Marilyn Monroe refused to allow other blonde actresses on film sets with her.

The language has ten genders, including three for inanimate objects, which are separated into "horizontal, vertical, and round."

LANGUAGE: Guugu Yimidhirr
REGION: Queensland, Australia
DETAILS: When Captain James Cook explored Australia in 1770, he jotted down a few words he learned from the Guugu Yimidhirr, the northern Aboriginal people. Cook's writing inspired a missionary named Johann Flierl to visit the tribe in the 1880s, and eventually the Bible was translated into the native language. The language, now known by only 200 speakers, may become extinct if younger people continue to reject it in favor of English, but at least one word will remain—one of the words Captain Cook recorded: *kangooroo*.

LANGUAGE: Tofa
REGION: Siberia
DETAILS: Tofa is a Turkic language spoken in Central Siberia, not far from the Arctic Circle. Reindeer herders developed it into a very efficient way to communicate. To say, for example, "a male domesticated reindeer in its third year and first mating season, but not ready for mating," speakers need only one word: *döngür*. Tofa qualifies as a "moribund" language, which means that new generations are no longer actively learning it—they learn Russian instead. Just 30 people are fluent in Tofa.

LANGUAGE: Nuumte Oote
REGION: Mexico
DETAILS: Manuel Segovia and Isidro Velazquez, a married couple in the southern Mexican state of Tabasco, are the only two people on Earth who are fluent in Ayapaneco, which they call Nuumte Oote, meaning "True Voice." Their children can partially understand them, and they're both helping linguists create a *Nummte Oote* dictionary, but amazingly, the last two speakers of this language aren't speaking to each other. An American anthropologist who studied them said they are "prickly and stoic" toward each other. Also, "they don't have a lot in common."

Top-selling item for the 1975 holiday season: the Atari Pong video game console.

MOO

Moo.

MOO: One morning in 2012, commuters in Rayburn, Pennsylvania, got stuck in a traffic jam when a cow and a bull decided to have "relations" in the middle of a busy intersection. Police tried shooing them away, but, according to reports, "That just got the bull mad and it started to escalate." Game officials arrived and steered the couple into a private trailer.

MOO: In 2012 a cow named Sadhana and her "bullfriend" got married in a lavish wedding ceremony in Guradia, India. More than 1,500 guests attended. Reason for the wedding: Sadhana's owners were unable to have children, so without a daughter to marry off, the well-to-do couple married off their cow.

MOO: An 18-year-old thief wearing a full-body cow costume stole 26 gallons of milk from a Walmart in Garrisonville, Virginia, in 2011. Witnesses recalled seeing him exit the store "on all fours." Hours later police apprehended the human cow "skipping down the sidewalk" in front of a nearby McDonald's.

MOO: In 2012 a cow named Darcy walked up to a McDonald's drive-through window and just stood there. Her owner—Sandy Winn of Brush, Colorado—told police that Darcy had walked the half-mile to the McDonald's because she "just likes attention."

MOO: Why did a cow climb five sets of stairs in an apartment building in Lesogorsk, Russia, in 2012? She was running away from an excited bull that was chasing her through a field. According to reports, the frightened cow "had to be lassoed and virtually dragged to the lobby while mooing in protest."

MOO: In 2011 a two-year-old boy named Tha Sophat got sick while staying at his grandfather's farm in Thailand. He wouldn't eat or drink, and his condition worsened…until he began suckling milk straight from the cow's udder. The cow didn't seem to mind, and after a month of nursing, Tha was better. "The neighbors say he will be ashamed when he grows up," the grandpa told Reuters. "But his health is fine. He is strong and he doesn't have diarrhea."

The leaping lion logo on the Detroit Lions' helmets has a nickname: Bubbles.

ONE-MAN BANS

When most people are offended by a book, they simply don't read it. But that's not enough for the vigilantes—they don't want anyone else to read it, either.

Book: *The Catcher in the Rye*, by J.D. Salinger (1951)

Vigilante: Howard Bagwell, a member of South Carolina's Dorchester District 2 School Board for 20 years

Story: J.D. Salinger's coming-of-age story is widely considered one of the best novels of the 20th century, but because it contains adult themes and profanity, some people find it offensive. It's been in the American Library Association's top-20 Most Challenged Books for decades.

And Bagwell is certainly no fan of the book: In 1993 he tried to get fellow school board members to ban it from the district's two high schools. He lost, 6–1. (His was the only "yes" vote.) In 2001 he tried again, this time checking out all the copies from both high schools as he filed complaints to force another vote. "It's a filthy, filthy book," he told a reporter. "It has two hundred sixty-nine pages or so, and if you took out all the profanity, the sarcasm, the mockery of old people, the mockery of women and decent people, you would get to read about ten minutes' worth."

Outcome: Bagwell lost the second vote, 5–2. He never did return the books—both schools had to buy new copies.

Book: *It's Perfectly Normal: Changing Bodies, Growing Up, Sex and Sexual Health*, by Robie Harris (1994)

Vigilante: JoAn Karkos, a 64-year-old grandmother living in Lewiston, Maine, in 2007

Story: This bestselling sex-education book for adolescents has won numerous awards over the years and has been translated into 30 languages. Because it is illustrated and deals frankly with its subject matter, it is a popular target for book bans. When Karkos checked out a copy from the Lewiston Public Library, she was so shocked by its contents that she borrowed a second copy from a neighboring branch and refused to return either one, hoping to prevent them from falling into the hands of adolescents. "Since I have been sufficiently horrified of the illustrations and the

President Andrew Johnson was buried with his head lying on a copy of the Constitution.

sexually graphic, amoral, abnormal contents, I will not be returning the books," she wrote in letters to the libraries. (She included checks for the cost of the books.)

Outcome: The libraries returned the checks and demanded that Karkos return the books. She refused. The fight dragged on for more than a year, as Karkos attempted to have the book declared obscene by the local police, and the libraries tried to get their books back. The city eventually filed charges against Karkos, only to drop them on the eve of trial to avoid court costs. Karkos's "victory" was bittersweet: The publicity she generated for the book caused a spike in demand, which was easily met by interlibrary loans and multiple replacement copies donated by opponents of censorship from all over the country. "I've actually begun turning donors down," said library director Richard Speer. "I'm thanking them and suggesting they give the book to libraries nearer to them." Karkos is barred from the libraries until she gives her copies back.

Book: *America (The Book): A Citizen's Guide to Democracy Inaction*, by Jon Stewart, and the writers of *The Daily Show*

Vigilante: Robert Willits, director of the Jackson–George Regional Library System in Mississippi

Story: As we told you in *Uncle John's Fast-Acting Long-Lasting Bathroom Reader,* when Willits got hold of a copy of *America (The Book)* in 2004, he was so offended by the "pornographic" (and fake) nude images of the nine U.S. Supreme Court justices that he banned the book from all eight public libraries he oversaw. It was the first time in 40 years that he had refused to allow a book to circulate. "We're not an adult bookstore," he said.

Outcome: The library system was deluged with so many angry e-mails and phone calls that the Board of Trustees scheduled a public meeting to reconsider the issue. A majority of citizens defended the book, so the trustees voted to end the ban. Willits didn't object. He figured a ban was pointless if the public wasn't offended. "What we probably did," he said, "was stimulate sales."

* * *

"Be obscure clearly." —**E. B. White**

THE LAST LIVING...

What's it like to be the last of a (literally) dying breed?

...*TITANIC* SURVIVOR. Millvina Dean was a two-month-old baby and the youngest person on the manifest of the *Titanic* when it crashed into an iceberg April 14, 1912. Her family was planning to resettle in Kansas City. Millvina, her mother, and her brother survived the disaster. (Her father did not.) In the years before her death, Dean ran out of money and was forced to sell her *Titanic* memorabilia. She died in May 2009, at the age of 97, a month after becoming so destitute that *Titanic* (the movie) stars Leonardo DiCaprio and Kate Winslet stepped in to help pay her nursing home bills.

...GIBB BROTHER. The Gibbs, three of them forming the Bee Gees and the fourth, solo artist and youngest brother Andy, dominated the pop music charts in the late 1970s. Andy Gibb died of a drug-related heart attack a few days after his 30th birthday in 1988, Maurice Gibb died of cardiac arrest during intestinal surgery at age 53 in 2003, and Robin Gibb died after a long battle with cancer in May 2012, leaving only Bee Gees frontman Barry Gibb.

...*GOLDEN GIRL*. The hit '80s sitcom was the first TV show to feature a cast made up entirely of older people. Estelle Getty passed away at the age of 84 in 2008, followed by Bea Arthur who died at 86 in 2009, and Rue McClanahan who died at 76 in 2010. Betty White, who turned 90 in 2012, survived the other three and has enjoyed a late-career resurgence in popularity, hosting *Saturday Night Live*, co-starring on the sitcom *Hot in Cleveland*, and hosting the prank show *Off Their Rockers*.

...WORLD WAR I VETERAN. As a teenager, Florence Green joined Britain's Royal Air Force, where she served as a waitress in an officers' mess hall. (She was afraid of flying.) She died in February 2012, at the age of 110. The last surviving combat veteran was British Royal Navy sailor Claude Choules, known to his buddies as "Chuckles," who died in May 2011 at the age of 110.

Closing the book: The last known Egyptian hieroglyphic inscription was made in A.D. 394.

...LITTLE RASCAL. Twenty-nine child actors were regulars in the *Our Gang* film shorts that ran theatrically in the 1920s and '30s. (They were rerun as *The Little Rascals* on TV in the 1950s). As of 2012, only one of the original group survives: Jean Darling, now 90 years old, who was with the group when the films were silent. From 1926 to 1929 she starred in 46 silent shorts and six talkies.

...DIRECT DESCENDENT OF ABRAHAM LINCOLN. Lincoln had only one son who survived to adulthood—Robert Todd Lincoln. Of his three children, only his daughter Jessie had children (with athlete Warren Beckwith): a daughter, Mary Lincoln Beckwith, who died in 1975 at age 77, and a son, Robert Lincoln Beckwith, an attorney in the Midwest, who died at age 81 in 1985. Neither ever had children, making Robert Beckwith the last living descendant of the 16th president.

...STOOGE. While best known with the line-up of Moe Howard, Larry Fine, and Curly Howard, The Three Stooges actually started with Larry, Curly, and Shemp Howard. Shemp quit in 1930 (after one film) and was replaced by his brother Moe. After Curly had a stroke in 1946, Shemp rejoined the group, but died of a heart attack in 1955. Joe Besser came on after that, until he was replaced by Joe "Curly Joe" DeRita in 1958. The group's popularity diminished in the '60s, and they split for good in 1970. Larry Fine and Moe Howard both passed away in 1975. Besser (perhaps better known for his recurring role on *The Abbott and Costello Show*) died in 1988. The last living Stooge, Curly Joe, died in July 1993.

* * *

JUST IN TIME

Harriet Richardson Ames spent her adult life as a school teacher, having earned her two-year teaching certificate in 1931 at the Keene State College in New Hampshire. But she'd always wanted to complete her education, and in 2010 she finally achieved her goal, earning a Bachelor's degree in education...at age 100. She died the next day.

NO, *YOU* STICK 'EM UP!

Being robbed is a pretty common fear, and turning the tables on a would-be robber is a pretty enticing fantasy. So it's not surprising that over the years a lot of inventors have come up with sneaky weapons that could be used to foil an assault. For example…

Weapon: The Chicago Protector Palm Pistol

What It Was: A gun that was disk-shaped, like a ladies' compact, so that it could be easily hidden in the hand

Details: This seven-shot .32-caliber revolver had a small gun barrel sticking out of one end of the disk and a squeeze trigger at the other end. (The bullets and the hammer were inside the disk.) When trouble threatened, it was easy to palm the gun, with the barrel poking out between the index and middle fingers. To fire the weapon, all the user had to do was squeeze his fist. Nearly 13,000 of the guns were made in the 1890s. Today they're worth $2,000—double that if owner still has the original box it came in.

Weapon: The Watch Pistol

What It Was: A gun disguised to look like a pocket watch

Details: The gun was invented by a Missouri man named Leonard Woods in 1913, when pocket watches were popular and usually worn on a chain, making it easy for robbers to see them. The winding knob on this "watch" was really a gun barrel; a tiny lever next to it was the trigger. "The object of the invention," Woods wrote in his patent application, "is to provide a pistol that can be worn in the vest pocket like a watch, whereby it may be presented and fired at a highwayman while apparently merely obeying his command to 'hand over your watch and be quick about it!'"

Weapon: The "Automatic Concealed Firearm for Self-Defense"

What It Was: A gun worn on the arm

Details: Patented in 1929, this gun was secured to the inside of the wrist with leather straps, and was concealed from view beneath the sleeve of a shirt or coat. A pull chain extended from the trigger to a ring worn on the ring finger, enabling the wearer to fire the gun with a backward snap of the wrist. "Such a hidden

1980s quiz: Who hosted Rubik's Cube's American launch party? Actress Zsa Zsa Gabor.

firearm will be especially valuable in case of a holdup where the intended victim, when commanded to hold up his hands, or even before such a command, may shoot at the criminal without any further preparation, automatically when lifting his arms," inventor Elek B. Juhasz wrote in his patent application. And if the robber has an accomplice? Juhasz designed a second version with *two* guns strapped to the arm, activated by a single chain. One pull on the chain fired the first gun; a second pull fired number two.

Weapon: The Frankenau "Combined Pocketbook and Revolver"

What It Was: A combination pocketbook and revolver

Details: In 1877 one Oskar Frankenau of Nuremberg, Germany, received an American patent for a four-shot revolver concealed in a special compartment of a 4" x 2½" metal (leather-clad) pocketbook. All the user had to do was release a hidden trigger on the bottom of the purse and fire away. According to Frankenau, "The advantage of such a combination for travelers and others will readily be perceived, as it forms a convenient mode of carrying a revolver for protection, especially when attacked, as the revolver may be fired at the robber when handing over the pocket-book." Today they're prized by gun collectors. In good condition they can fetch $12,500 or more.

Weapon: The Camera Gun

What It Was: A gun that took a picture when fired, so that the shooter could prove in court that the shooting was justified

Details: Invented in the 1920s by New Yorker Adalbert Szalardi, the gun had a tiny camera mounted in front of the trigger. When the trigger was pulled, the gun and camera fired together. "Policemen, military persons, and private people are obliged to use guns for self defense. After such an occurrence the courts usually have to determine the legality or necessity of the use of guns and have to depend on witnesses, if any, who are very often absolutely unreliable," Szalardi wrote in his patent application.

Bonus: "Fleeing automobiles with the criminals therein," Szalardi wrote, "may also be photographed while being shot at."

Ouch! The blindness and burning effects of pepper spray can last for more than 4 hours.

BEHIND THE HITS: SOUNDTRACK CUTS

Movie soundtracks have long generated popular songs, from "Stayin' Alive" to "Whistle While You Work," to "Goldfinger" and hundreds more. Here are the origins of a few more soundtrack hits.

Movie: *Titanic*

Song: "My Heart Will Go On"

Story: While making his $200-million movie in the mid-1990s, director James Cameron planned for all of the music to be performed by ethereal Irish vocalist Enya. One problem: Enya wasn't interested. So Cameron asked composer James Horner, with whom he'd worked on the 1986 movie *Aliens*, to score the film. Cameron didn't want any contemporary pop music in the film, but Horner disagreed. He secretly wrote the epic ballad "My Heart Will Go On" with songwriter Will Jennings and got singer Celine Dion to record it. Then Horner asked Cameron to watch a rough cut of the movie with "My Heart Will Go On" playing over the end credits…and Cameron relented. The song was almost as big a hit as *Titanic* itself—it sold 15 million copies, went to #1 in 18 countries, and won the Oscar for Best Song.

Movie: *The Bodyguard*

Song: "I Will Always Love You"

Story: The soaring love ballad was written by country pop singer Dolly Parton in 1972, before she was a superstar. At the time, she was best known as the co-star of Porter Wagoner's syndicated country music TV series. She was ready to go solo, but wanted Wagoner to know she appreciated all he'd done for her, so she wrote the song. "It's saying, 'Just because I'm going don't mean I don't love you. I appreciate you and I hope you do great, and I appreciate everything you've done, but I'm out of here,'" she told CMT in 2012. The morning after she wrote it, she played it for Wagoner in his office. He cried and said, "That's the prettiest song I ever heard." He agreed to release Parton from her contract, provided he could produce a recording of "I Will Always Love You."

Surf's up! On average, Hawaii experiences one tsunami a year.

He did, and the song went to #1 on the country chart in 1974, then again in 1982 when Parton remade the song for the film adaptation of *The Best Little Whorehouse in Texas*.

All of that was completely overshadowed by Whitney Houston's 1992 cover version, which was not originally part of *The Bodyguard* soundtrack. Houston's character was slated to sing a version of Jimmy Ruffin's "What Becomes of the Brokenhearted"—until the movie *Fried Green Tomatoes* featured Paul Young singing it. *Bodyguard* co-star Kevin Costner came to producers with a song he thought would work better: "I Will Always Love You." He was right. The single sold four million copies and propelled the soundtrack to sales of 45 million copies, spending a record 14 weeks at #1.

Extra Cut: Among the other songs on *The Bodyguard* soundtrack was soft-rock singer Curtis Stigers's version of "(What's So Funny 'Bout) Peace, Love, and Understanding," written by British rocker Nick Lowe but made famous by Elvis Costello. Royalties for soundtrack sales are distributed among the many different performers on the albums, with an especially high cut for songwriters. Lowe, who has a large cult following, only ever had one hit: "Cruel to Be Kind," which went to #12 in America, Canada, and Britain in 1979. But royalties from Stigers's cover of his song on *The Bodyguard* earned him an estimated $4 million.

Movie: *Con Air*

Song: "How Do I Live"

Story: In 1997 Diane Warren was well entrenched as Hollywood's go-to writer of movie ballads—including Celine Dion's "Because You Loved Me" for *Up Close and Personal*, Starship's "Nothing's Gonna Stop Us Now" for *Mannequin*, and many more. Touchstone Pictures agreed to use her song "How Do I Live" as an end-credits ballad for its action movie *Con Air*. Warren promised LeAnn Rimes, a 15-year-old country music phenom, that she could sing the song. But Touchstone executives thought Rimes's voice was too poppy and young to sell a song about heartbreak. So they hired country star Trisha Yearwood to re-record it, and her version was included in the movie and released as a single. When Rimes and her label, Curb, found out, they were furious, and rushed her version to stores and radio. Both versions of "How Do I Live" were

In 1849 a 20-foot chunk of ice fell out of the sky over Scotland. No one knows why.

released on the same day—May 27, 1997. Yearwood's went to #2 on the country chart and #23 on the pop chart before her label, MCA, refused to make any more copies of the single for fear it would eat into her album sales. The song disappeared by August. Rimes's version, however, was a monster hit. It spent a record 69 weeks on the pop chart, where it peaked at #2. It sold 3.7 million copies, making it the most successful country song and soundtrack song to date. More impressively, Rimes's take stayed on the country charts until February 2003—nearly six years.

Movie: *Armageddon*

Song: "I Don't Want to Miss a Thing"

Story: Aerosmith was huge in the 1970s, had a massive comeback in the late 1980s, and was bigger than ever in the mid-1990s thanks to hits like "Cryin'" and "Crazy," whose videos starred Liv Tyler, daughter of Aerosmith's lead singer, Steven Tyler. When producers of the 1998 asteroid movie *Armageddon* approached Aerosmith with an opportunity to record the movie's love ballad, written by soundtrack song queen Diane Warren, Tyler said no. He feared the band would lose its hard-won rock cred if they recorded a sappy ballad. However, *Armageddon* co-starred Liv Tyler, *really* wanted her father's band to be involved. So she set up a screening of a rough-cut of the movie for him. He later reported that one scene in the movie changed his mind—when Bruce Willis's character gets lost in space, and his image disappears from a monitor as its being hugged by his daughter (played by Liv). The daughter-daddy stuff got to him—he admits he cried, and agreed to have Aerosmith perform the song. Good move: The song became the first and only #1 hit of the group's career.

* * *

THE LONG-TERM PLAN

Hermann Dörnemann was the oldest man in the world until he died in March 2005, just two months before his 112th birthday. He said he lived so long for two reasons: He drank the water left over after cooking potatoes and his only form of exercise was "walking to the corner shop to buy beer and cigars."

UNCLE JOHN'S STALL OF FAME

Uncle John is amazed—and pleased—by the unusual ways people get involved with bathrooms, toilets, and so on. That's why he created the "Stall of Fame."

Honoree: British Prime Minister David Cameron

Notable Achievement: Conducting important negotiations using the "full-bladder technique"

True Story: Not long after Cameron walked out of a summit on the future of the euro in December 2011, word leaked out that he had engaged in the marathon nine-hour negotiating session without once taking a bathroom break. The Prime Minister reportedly did it on purpose, in the belief that the urgent need to pee would sharpen his focus. He got the idea a decade earlier while watching a documentary about a Conservative Party politician, Enoch Powell. In the film, Powell explains to an interviewer that he gave all his important speeches with a full bladder. "You should do nothing to decrease the tension before a big speech," he says. "If anything, you should seek to increase it." So does the technique really work? Not according to a study published in the journal *Neurourology and Urodynamics* in 2011 which states "an extreme urge to void (urinate) is associated with impaired cognition" that's worse than having a blood alcohol level of 0.05 or going without sleep for 24 hours.

Honoree: Mee Yan Leong, a woman living in Singapore

Notable Achievement: Taking history's longest pit stop

True Story: On March 25, 2009, Leong, 55, had to use the bathroom. When she finished her business and tried to get up to leave, she felt, as she put it, "a force" holding her down and was powerless to leave. There she sat…for the next *two-and-a-half years.* On rare occasions, she got off the pot long enough use the shower, but she spent nearly all of her time seated on the toilet as if she was glued to it. She even slept and ate there, dining on bread, porridge, and biscuits that her long-suffering husband passed in to her. Leong might still be sitting there today, had he not finally decided in January 2012 that enough was enough. He called paramedics; they were able to coax Leong out of the bathroom and take her to the hospital for psychiatric evaluation. At last report, she was doing better, but she still has no idea why she couldn't leave the bathroom. In addition to the unseen force that held her down, she says she was terrified that she would be sprayed with water or pelted with rocks if she tried to leave.

Honoree: Li Maizi, 22, a college student in Beijing, China
Notable Achievement: Taking a stand for "potty parity"
True Story: Because women—who can't use urinals—may take a little longer to use the facilities, it's common in many parts of the world for women's restrooms to have more toilets than men's rooms do. The ratio can be 2:1 (two women's toilets for every one for men) or even higher. Not so in China, where the ratio is typically 1:1. Result: There are often long lines outside of women's restrooms.

Inspired by the Occupy Wall Street movement, in February 2012, Li founded Occupy Men's Toilets. One Sunday, she and six other activists took over a men's room at a busy park in the city of Guangzhou. For three minutes at a time, they'd let women use the facilities, then they'd let the men in for ten minutes, then repeat. Similar occupations took place in Zhengzhou and Beijing. The protests lasted only an hour, but they provoked a huge response from the Chinese public in support of the issue. By Wednesday, officials in Guangzhou were calling for legislation increasing the number of toilets for women. "I do think the right to go to the bathroom is a basic right," Li says.

* * *

ALLEY OOPS

"Naked ten-pin bowling fans have been ordered to cover up. Bowling in the nude will be one of the top attractions for 200 members of British Naturism when they gather in Blackpool at the weekend. But bosses at the ten-pin alley have told them they'll have to wear bowling shoes like everyone else."

—*The Daily Record* (UK), February 2012

FUNNY PAPERS

In past Bathroom Readers *we've told you the stories of some of our favorite humor magazines—*Cracked!, National Lampoon, *and* Mad. *Here are the origins of some more of the best satire rags, including a few you may not have heard of…but really should look for.*

THE ONION

Founded in Madison, Wisconsin, in 1988 as a free, notebook-sized weekly newspaper, *The Onion* was the brainchild of University of Wisconsin juniors Tim Keck and Christopher Johnson. They published articles parodying sensational news stories, satirizing college life, and mocking the city of Madison. After 18 months, Keck and Johnson sold the paper (the exact price isn't known—but it was under $20,000) to staff members Scott Dikkers and Peter Haise. Over the next few years Dikkers and Haise expanded distribution to cities around the United States, and *The Onion* grew to the single-fold tabloid format it still uses today. Then, in 1996, they launched a Web edition, and by 2000 *The Onion* had a worldwide audience.

In 2007 the Onion News Network, a daily web-based parody of television news, debuted—and in 2009 it won the prestigious Peabody Award. The judges said, "The satirical tabloid's online send-up of twenty-four-hour cable-TV news was hilarious, trenchant and not infrequently hard to distinguish from the real thing." *The Onion* is still published as a paper—and it's still given away free in major cities around the U.S. and Canada…including Madison, Wisconsin.

Sample Headlines: "Expert on Anteaters Wasted Entire Life Studying Anteaters"; "'I Am Under 18' Button Clicked for First Time in History of Internet"; "Rest of U2 Perfectly Fine with Africans Starving"

FUNNY TIMES

In 1984 husband and wife Raymond Lesser and Susan Wolpert were living in a trailer on a farm in Athens, Ohio, when their first child was stillborn. "After Rose died we didn't know what we were going to do," Wolpert says in a self-interview on the paper's website. "We were so brokenhearted. We decided to take a trip across the country to try to figure out what to do next." They headed back to their old stomping grounds in Santa Cruz, California, where they stumbled upon a new weekly paper—filled mostly with political cartoons—called *The Santa Cruz Comic News*. "I said, 'This is such a great idea.'" recalled Lesser. "This would probably be a fun thing to do." So they moved back to Cleveland and started the *Funny Times*. The paper became a national success, and nearly 30 years later Wolpert and Lesser are still at the helm. Every issue offers around 100 cartoons, as well as syndicated features by some of the world's best comedy writers. Regular cartoons include *This Modern World* (Tom Tomorrow), *Zippy the Pinhead* (Bill Griffith), and *Slowpoke* (Jen Sorensen); regular contributors include Rita Rudner, Dave Barry, and Garrison Keillor.

THE JOURNAL OF IRREPRODUCIBLE RESULTS

On April 1, 1955, Alexander Kohn, a biophysicist at the Biological Institute in Ness Ziona, Israel, published a fake newsletter he called *The Journal of Irreproducible Results, Volume II* to amuse his friends. It contained one article: "The Inactivation Kinetics of Glassware"—about a phenomenon in which glass objects in a scientist's laboratory have a tendency to break—with numerous references to "Volume I"...which did not exist. A year later Kohn was introduced to Harry J. Lipkin, an American physicist who had recently moved to Israel. Lipkin had a reputation as a top-notch scientist and would go on to become one of the world's leading nuclear theorists, and he was a funny guy. In July 1956, he and Kohn decided to make *The Journal of Irreproducible Results* (*JIR*) a bimonthly parody of science journals. The first public issue was dedicated to the zipper. (In true geek fashion, it paid special attention to the behavior of a zipper as it moves over "the paraboloid curves of the substance under the modern female bathing suit.") By 1957 the *JIR* was known to scientists around the world, and has become known to the wider public in the decades since. And while it has changed hands several times (present headquarters are in San Mateo, California), the *JIR* still runs six issues a year.

Sample headlines: "Impure Mathematics: The Adventures of Polly Nomial"; "The Triple Blind Test"; "Global Average Temperature vs. Number of Pirates"

Extra: In 1990 Marc Abrahams, a mathematician at MIT as well as a writer, took over as editor. In 1994 the *JIR* was sold—and Abrahams and his entire editorial staff left to start *The Annals of Improbable Research*, where Abrahams began the annual awarding of the Ig Nobel Prizes for discoveries "that cannot, or should not, be reproduced."

EXTRA HUMOROUS

There aren't a lot of new comedy magazines appearing in print these days…but there are a lot coming online. Here are a few you may want to check out.

• ***The Toque.*** A Canadian-based parody website. Sample headline: "Conspiracy Theory: Vancouver Riot Funded by Big Glass"

• ***Bongo News.*** A parody news site. Sample headline: "Whitney Houston's Songs Will Live On…in Torture Chambers"

• ***Bean Soup Times.*** Parody site geared toward African Americans. Sample headline: "Father of Six Girls Suffers from 'Player's Curse'"

• ***All Day Coffee.*** Website of writer G. Xavier Robillard. Sample: "Arizona to Cover Up Grand Canyon's Unseemly Lady Parts"

• **The Borowitz Report.** In the late 1970s, Andy Borowitz was president of *National Lampoon* magazine at Harvard. He went on to write for TV, and in 1990 created the hit show *The Fresh Prince of Bel-Air*, starring rapper Will Smith. In 2001 he created *The Borowitz Report*, a website featuring satirical news stories. Sample headlines: "Greece Buys Mega Millions Ticket," "Bush Publishes 'I Can Has Prezidensy," "Decision to Stop Making Hummers Saddens A**holes," and "BREAKING: CNN Viewers Severely Burned by Fire from Nancy Grace's Nostrils"

* * *

WHAT, NO FARTY?

Who are Awful, Tubby, Burpy, Baldy, Chesty, Deafy, Hickey, and Gabby? Considered and rejected names for the dwarfs in Walt Disney's 1937 filmed adaptation of *Snow White and the Seven Dwarfs*.

THEY WENT THATAWAY

Think an impressive invention leads to riches and fame? Think again.

PHILO T. FARNSWORTH (1906–1971)

Claim to Fame: Inventor of television

How He Died: The stress of being spurned by the industry he helped create

Background: As we told you in *Uncle John's Bathroom Reader Tunes Into TV*, Farnsworth battled the RCA corporation for more than a decade to stop it from infringing his television patents. He won the legal battle in 1939, but RCA, which owned the NBC television network, used its media and public relations power to steal the credit for inventing TV, effectively erasing Farnsworth from the industry's history even as it paid him royalties on his patents. (His one appearance on national television was in 1957, as a mystery guest on the game show *I've Got A Secret*. The contestants were asked to guess his "secret," which was that he'd invented TV. None of them could; they'd never heard of him.)

Farnsworth owned his own TV company for a time, but he couldn't compete against RCA and was forced to exit the industry. He continued inventing for the rest of his life and did have some successes, but nothing as big as television.

Details: The years of fighting RCA broke him physically and psychologically. He suffered from stomach ulcers and depression, and spent time in a sanatorium following a nervous breakdown. He was hospitalized repeatedly for alcoholism and also battled an addiction to the drugs that doctors prescribed to calm his nerves. Farnsworth never regained his health, and he died a forgotten man in 1971 at the age of 64.

"CRAZY" EDWIN DRAKE (1819–1880)

Claim to Fame: Father of the petroleum industry

How He Died: Broke

Background: Before Drake came along in the late 1850s, "rock oil" (so called to distinguish it from vegetable oil) was collected where it seeped to the surface of the Earth naturally, in small quantities. Since the oil oozed to the surface in such tiny amounts,

The gases that make up Earth's atmosphere are slowly leaking away into space.

people assumed that there couldn't be much oil underground, either. Drake believed otherwise; that's why everyone thought he was crazy. In 1859 he started drilling for oil in the sleepy lumber town of Titusville, Pennsylvania, where the Seneca Oil Company owned a valuable oil seep—valuable because it produced four gallons of crude oil a day. Others had tried drilling for oil before Drake, but had failed because water from the surrounding soil invariably leaked into the drill hole and caused cave-ins. That happened to Drake too, after he'd drilled just 16 feet down. Rather than give up as the others had, he had the idea of shoving a length of cast-iron pipe, soon to be called a "drive pipe," down into the drill hole to keep the water out and prevent cave-ins. Drake expected to have to drill down 1,000 feet before he struck oil, but he hit it at 70 feet. Production at the site soared from four gallons a day to 35 *barrels*—or nearly 1,500 gallons. At that moment, the modern petroleum industry was born.

Details: Drake never patented his drilling technique; anyone could drill for oil using his method without paying him. That was his first mistake. His second was speculating in oil-industry stocks with the little money he did have. His drilling process increased oil production so dramatically that the price of petroleum crashed, wiping out the oil companies he'd invested in. Just seven years after he changed the world, Drake was flat broke and his health was failing. "If you have any of the milk of human kindness left in your bosom for me or my family, send me some money," he begged in a letter to a friend, "I am in want of it sadly and am sick." When associates in the booming oil town of Titusville learned of Drake's plight they raised $4,000 (around $60,000 today) in assistance, and in 1873 the Pennsylvania legislature voted to pay him a pension of $1,500 a year ($29,000), which his widow continued to receive after he died in 1880 at the age of 61.

* * *

YOU'RE MY INSPIRATION

In 1967 John Lennon received a letter from a young fan who said his teacher was having the class analyze Beatles songs. That inspired Lennon to write "I Am The Walrus"—a nonsensical song with bizarre imagery—"just to mess with their heads."

LIVING LIGHTBULBS

Random facts about living things that glow in the dark.

SIMPLY LUMINOUS

From insects and fish to fungi and worms, scientists have catalogued thousands of species of creatures with a unique trait in common: They're all *bioluminescent*, or fluorescent, meaning they emanate a visible glow. The trait is used for a variety of purposes—to communicate, to help in reproduction, to keep away predators, and to lure prey, to name a few. Here we shine a light on these glowing misfits of nature.

• **FIREFLIES.** In the summer, kids like to catch lightning bugs and keep them in jars. That light is vital to the insects' survival. Courting male and female fireflies flash signals back and forth, and when their flickering code is in sync, they mate. Their glow also alerts bats and other predators to stay away, (which is good because fireflies taste awful). This bright warning signal, also used by some colorful, toxic amphibians, is called *aposematism*. When daring frogs do eat lightning bugs, they temporarily take on the golden glow of their dinner.

• **EARTHWORMS.** A species of glowing earthworm found in sandy soil in parts of the Southern U.S., *Diplocardia longa* can grow to a length of 18 inches. Its blue glow is caused by slime secretions.

• **GLOWWORMS.** A type of glowworm native to Australia, *Arachnocampa* begins life as a glowing, carnivorous larva. It drops sticky mucous-coated lines from cave ceilings, then more or less poops out bioluminescent stuff to attract insects. When the prey gets stuck, the larva pulls up the line and feasts.

• **DRAGONFISH.** The majority of the world's bioluminescent organisms live in the oceans and glow blue or green. One exception: the dragonfish, which uses its red glow as "night vision" to locate prey in the dark ocean depths.

• **SHARKS.** A cookie cutter shark's belly glows, except in one spot at its neck. From below, that spot looks like a fish. When predators come up for a bite, the cookie cutter takes a bite out of them!

• **PLANKTON.** Certain plankton produce bioluminescence, and huge concentrations of them—primarily dinoflagellates, single-celled organisms that are considered algae—can make the seashore glow a vivid blue at night.

• **SEA WORMS.** Several species shoot out liquid-filled, green bioluminescent capsules to distract predators, and *Acanthephyra* shrimp can squirt glowing blue vomit into the eyes of predators.

• **MUSHROOMS.** There are more than 70 varieties of bioluminescent mushrooms. Scientists aren't sure why they shine, but the glow may attract bugs, which help spread the mushrooms' spores.

• **FUNGUS.** Foxfire, blue-green light created by a fungus that lives on rotting wood in the forest, can be very bright—so bright that in 1775 it was used to illuminate the inside of world's first submarine, the *Turtle*.

• **TREE BARK.** Quinine, which beams brightly under ultraviolet light and even strong sunlight, was discovered in the bark of the South American cinchona tree. Small quantities of synthetic quinine are present in tonic water, which glows under ultraviolet light. Quinine is used to treat malaria.

• **MAMMALS.** It was long believed that no mammals produced their own glow...until the discovery of iridescent golden moles in the early 20th century. Another mammal that emits a glow? Humans. People emit a faint shimmering aura, particularly from the face. The glow, a very weak biophoton discharge, is brightest in the late afternoon.

* * *

WORDS UNCHAINED

Some of the words from West-African languages that came to America aboard slave ships: *yam*, *banana*, *banjo*, *elephant*, *gorilla*, *cola*, *okra*, *sorcery*, *tater*, *turnip*, and *goober*.

Oklahoma's official state vegetable: the watermelon (even though it's a fruit).

CIVIL WAR BLOODLINES

Two out of every three living Americans have at least one ancestor who lived through the Civil War. A select few have very famous ancestors.

FOREBEAR: Ulysses S. Grant

DESCENDANT: Ulysses G. Dietz, his great-great-grandson

STORY: Grant, Civil War general and president of the United States, was a Republican. But Dietz is a Democrat and, according to *USA Today*, when the military draft was abolished in 1973, he "jumped for joy." (His call-up number was 4.) In 1994 Dietz decided that his famous ancestor deserved better than the years of neglect and vandalism the National Parks Service had allowed at Grant's Tomb in New York City and threatened to have his great-great-grandfather's body moved to Illinois. The Park Service invested $1.8 million to restore the damage, so Grant's remains remained in New York.

FOREBEAR: Harriet Tubman

DESCENDANT: Pauline Johnson, her great-grandniece

STORY: After her parents' passed away, Johnson found a black dress with white lace sleeves and collar in a closet in their house in Auburn, New York, which had a label with a name written on it: Harriet Tubman. Johnson was 25-years-old at the time, and her parents had never told her of any family connection to the legendary conductor of the Underground Railroad who helped many slaves escape to freedom. But Johnson's aunt knew all about it and gave a stunned Pauline the news that she is related to Tubman.

FOREBEAR: Julia Ward Howe

DESCENDANT: John Shaw, Jr., her great-great-grandson

STORY: In 1861 Howe watched as Union soldiers prepared for war. The sight stirred her so much that she started wrtiting a poem: "Mine eyes have seen the glory of the coming of the Lord." When "The Battle Hymn of the Republic" was published in 1861, Howe became an instant celebrity. In 1878 her daughter, Laura E. Richards, moved to a yellow house in Gardiner, Maine, where she wrote 90 books, including the Pulitzer Prize-winning *The Yellow House Papers*, a collection related to her family's history. After his great aunt died in 1989, Shaw bought the original Yellow House from the estate and moved there with his wife and two children. Less than a year later, a thief invaded the home and abducted his wife and children. The children were recovered safely, but Shaw's wife was murdered. Despite the tragedy, Shaw decided to stay on in the Yellow House. "Peg and I were in awe of the people who lived here before. Our goal was to honor these people and be worthy of staying in that house. I still plan to do that," said Shaw.

FOREBEAR: Frederick Douglass
DESCENDANT: Kenneth Morris, his great-great-great-grandson
STORY: As a kid, Morris was terrified of the old man with "the wild white hair" glaring down from a painting on the wall of his home. "He looked mean," Morris remembers. Today that old man—Frederick Douglass—is the model by which Morris lives his life. Douglass escaped slavery and became the leader of the movement to abolish slavery. After learning that slavery (including forced labor and sex slavery) affects more people today than it did in 1861, Morris started the Fredrick Douglass Family Foundation, an abolitionist organization for the 21st century. Human trafficking rakes in more than $32 billion per year. "It's the world's second most profitable illegal industry," said Morris. The average price of a human slave today: $90. Since 2007 the FDFF has educated more than 50,000 students about modern slavery. "Knowledge," Frederick Douglass said, "makes a man unfit to be a slave."

FOREBEAR: Jefferson Davis
DESCENDANT: Bertram Hayes-Davis, his great-great-grandson
STORY: The Dallas geologist owes his hyphenated surname to an act of the Mississippi Legislature. Jefferson Davis, president of the Confederate States of America, had six children, but only his daughter Margaret gave him grandchildren, and all had the last name Hayes. So in 1890, to preserve Davis's historic last name, the state legislature gave them a new last name: Hayes-Davis. Now, every June, the 600-member Davis family gets together at the home of the Confederate leader, Rosemont Plantation outside Woodville, Mississippi. The oldest member gets to cut the birthday cake...with Jefferson Davis's sword.

All NFL game balls are made by hand in Ada, Ohio.

A BRIEF HISTORY OF THE NEGRO LEAGUE

All about baseball's other big league.

BACKGROUND

Baseball's first governing body—the National Association of Base Ball Players—was formed in 1857. The group immediately wrote a rule barring black players. When the National League formed in 1871, it didn't have an official rule banning black players—but it did have a "gentlemen's agreement" to keep non-white players out. So blacks formed their own baseball associations.

• The first official league for black players, the Negro National League, formed in 1920. The rival Eastern Colored League was established three years later. In 1924 the champions of each league played each other in a "Colored World Series." In the best-of-nine series, the NNL's Kansas City Monarchs defeated the ECL's Hilldale Athletic Club (based in Darby, PA) five games to four.

• A season in the Negro Leagues consisted of about 60 to 80 games played against other league teams. Beyond that, players played in 100 or so other games—against black teams, white teams, semi-pro teams, traveling teams, minor-league teams, small-town teams, college teams, and even Major League teams or ad hoc teams with pro or ex-pro players on the roster. Of the 436 games they played against Major League teams or teams with Major Leaguers between 1920 and 1950, Negro League squads won the majority, 268 to 168.

• Despite the wins, the leagues were poorly funded and poorly managed. Teams dropped in and out of leagues every year, particularly during the Depression. More popular teams, like the Kansas City Monarchs or the Homestead Grays, went some seasons without playing *any* officially sanctioned league games. Reason: It was more financially attractive to go "barnstorming," playing exhibition games on the road.

• There were seven primary black baseball leagues. The Negro National League started in 1920, shuttered in 1931, returned in 1933, then closed up again in 1948. The Negro Southern League existed in between incarnations of the NNL. The Eastern Colored League lasted from 1923 to 1928. The American Negro League, made of some former ECL teams, formed in 1929 and lasted for only one season. The East-West League made it halfway through the 1932 season. The Negro American League was the last existing league, playing from 1937 to 1960.

• The Negro Leagues played night games before the big leagues did. In 1930 the Kansas City Monarchs took portable floodlights with them to road games. Five years later, MLB ballparks started installing lights.

• The Negro Leagues began using shin guards and batting helmets before their Major League counterparts. And they originated the screwball pitch.

• Because the league had very little money, records and statistics from that era are wildly inaccurate. It's been widely reported, for example, that Negro League star Josh Gibson hit more than 800 home runs over his career, more than anyone has ever hit in the Majors. But historians estimate that because of the shorter season, Gibson probably hit somewhere between 200 and 300. (He is, however, the only player—in any league—ever to have hit a ball entirely out of Yankee Stadium.)

• Country-music star Charley Pride played for the Negro America League's Memphis Red Sox in 1952. Today, he's a part owner of the Texas Rangers.

• Baseball historians have begun to piece together statistics from old newspaper box scores and first-person accounts. That's led to the increased status of Joe Williams as possibly the best pitcher in Negro League history, ahead of his more famous counterpart Satchel Paige. Some of Williams's stats: In 1914 he went 41–3 in all games (and 12–2 in league play...with 100 strikeouts). In 1917 he struck out 20 batters in a no-hitter. And in 1930, at age 45, he struck out 27 batters in a 12-inning game, allowing just one hit. Williams retired in 1932 and died in 1946, a year before Jackie Robinson would suit up for the Brooklyn Dodgers.

A British study found that eating different cheeses before bed influenced...

• When Major League Baseball began drafting black players in 1947, that didn't immediately kill off the Negro Leagues or the all-black travelling baseball teams. The Negro National League folded in 1948 partly because they lost too many players to MLB, also because the Homestead Greys (who folded a year later anyway) withdrew from the league to solely barnstorm. The last independent Negro League team was the Indianapolis Clowns, which ceased operations in 1966.

• In 1971 the Baseball Hall of Fame's directors voted to admit Negro Leaguers into the Hall of Fame, ignoring a proposal to have a separate wing for those players. A special committee was formed to induct the first round of players. Enshrined that year were Josh Gibson, Satchel Paige, James "Cool Papa" Bell, Oscar Charleston, Martin Dihigo, John Henry Lloyd, Buck Leonard, Monte Irvin, and Judy Johnson. (Only Irvin and Paige played in the Major Leagues.)

• Hall of Famer Dave Winfield has been especially vocal about recognition for the Negro Leagues. In 2008 Major League Baseball accepted his idea of holding a special honorary draft, in which each of the 30 MLB teams would "select" one player from the Negro League era. The New York Yankees picked Emilio Navarro, who was still alive at 102 years old. Technically, that makes him the oldest pro baseball player in history.

• Because of the on-the-road nature of the league and the poor record-keeping that resulted, the Negro Leagues have spawned a lot of baseball lore. One example: Cool Papa Bell was said to be such a fast base-runner that he once hit a line drive down the middle of the field and was hit by his own ball as he rounded second base. Another one: Josh Gibson was said to hit the ball farther and harder than any other baseball player ever. One time, he hit a home run out of the park in Pittsburgh. A day later, during a game in Philadelphia, a ball dropped out of the sky and an outfielder caught it. The umpire yelled to Gibson, "You're out! Yesterday! In Pittsburgh!"

* * *

"I failed to make the chess team because of my height."

—**Woody Allen**

POP-PANTS

The rise and fall of the star-spangled girdle.

HOT PANTS

In August 1965, a girdle maker called the Treo Company cashed in on the Pop Art craze with a line of women's undergarments called "Pop-Pants." Available in panty-girdles ($7) and panty-briefs ($6), Pop-Pants came in four designs:

- "Big Zip," with a large zipper down the front
- "Crying Eye," with giant teary eyes on the front and winking eyes on the back
- "Hamburger 'n Soda Pop" (self-explanatory)
- "Stars 'n Stripes," with red and white stripes on the legs and a few big blue stars on the hips

They all sold well, but not everyone was keen on the American-flag-inspired underwear.

THE D.A.R GETS M-A-D

Within days of the "Stars 'n Stripes" Pop-Pants going on sale, a women's patriotic organization called the Daughters of the American Revolution declared the panty girdle a "mockery" and a "shocking desecration of the American flag." "Patriotism should be encouraged by a proper respect to the stars and stripes," said a spokesperson.

The D.A.R. is still around today, but it isn't nearly as influential, or as able to raise a stink, as it was in the 1960s. After the group complained, the Treo Company moved quickly to diffuse the controversy, cancelling production of the Stars 'n Stripes and recalling the 3,000 pairs it had already shipped. It also asked the D.A.R. to accept its "sincere apology," though a spokesman admitted to a reporter that he thought the controversy was "to a degree, ridiculous," since the girdles were "obviously not made for public wear."

Newspapers, commentators, and humorists had fun with the story, with headlines like "D.A.R. Squeezes 'Old Glory' Girdles Off the Market," "D.A.R. Protects the Foundations of Liberty,"

Flies have two wings—all other flying insects have four.

and “D.A.R. Pressure Pops ‘Stars ’n Stripes’ Girdle.” Some in the press had suggested the idea for the star-spangled girdle had come from an ad man on Madison Avenue, who’d undoubtedly said, “Let’s run them up the flagpole and see who salutes.”

FOREIGN AID

When asked what the Treo Company would do with all those recalled girdles, a spokesperson told the *Herald-Tribune News Service*, “We may have to give them away for charity, or maybe we should take them out and burn the damned things, or ship them to some foreign country.” Then he caught himself and said, “Oh, no, that is the last thing we should do, send them to a foreign country. The D.A.R. wouldn’t like that at all.”

A *Woman’s World* columnist noted that burning was the well-deserved fate of any girdle, new or old, but burning the Stars 'n Stripes girdles would dignify them since it was the honorable end for a worn-out American flag. Humorist Art Buchwald suggested that if they were given away as foreign aid it would, for once, be clear to all where the gift originated. He went on to say that the Old Glory girdles could be sent to Vietnam so the American troops fighting there could tell loyal Vietnamese women from the Viet Cong, although noting that if they fell into the wrong hands it might be confusing.

GOLDEN GIRDLES

When the Treo Company recalled the Stars ’n Stripes Pop-Pants they were only able to take back the unsold stock; an unknown number of the panties had already been purchased by the public. Of these, a handful survive to this day and are highly prized by underwear collectors. (Yes, such people do exist; Uncle John knows a woman who has a complete set of Pop-Pants, including a rare pair of Stars ’n Stripes. She gave him the idea for this story.)

Who knows? If you’ve got a vintage panty-girdle or panty-briefs lying around with blue stars on the hips and red and white stripes on the legs, it might be worth a lot more than you think.

* * *

Every man has a fool up his sleeve. —**English Proverb**

First product on the cover of *Time* magazine: Coca-Cola (1950).

PARENTHOOD

Some thoughts on the hardest job in the world.

"To me, life is tough enough without having somebody kick you from the inside."

—Rita Rudner

"People who say they sleep like a baby seldom have one."

—Leo Burke

"When kids hit one year old, it's like hanging with a miniature drunk. They bump into things. They laugh and cry. They urinate. They vomit."

—Johnny Depp

"Raising kids is part joy and part guerrilla warfare."

—Ed Asner

"When my kids become wild and unruly, I use a nice, safe playpen. Then, when they're finished, I climb out."

—Erma Bombeck

"The thing that impresses me most about America is the way parents obey their children."

—Duke of Windsor

"Like all parents, my husband and I just do the best we can, hold our breath, and hope we've set aside enough money to pay for our kids' therapy."

—Michelle Pfeiffer

"The way we know our kids our growing up: the bite marks are higher."

—Phyllis Diller

"You learn many things from children. How much patience you have, for instance."

—Franklin P. Jones

"If a growing object is both fresh and spoiled at the same time, chances are it's a child."

—Morris Goldfischer

"Before I got married, I had six theories about bringing up children; now I've got six children and no theories."

—Lord Rochester

"You don't know how much you don't know until your children grow up and tell you."

—S. J. Perelman

"You know children are growing up when they start asking questions that have answers."

—John J. Plomp

"Few things are more satisfying than seeing your children have teenagers of their own."

—Doug Larson

TERRIBLE TYPOS

These stories illustrate the old adage that the devil's in the detules...er, details.

TYPER: A group called Citizens Opposed to the Library Project was fighting a tax referendum to build a new library in Franklin, Indiana. In submitting their financial disclosure documents in 2012, they made one little mistake.
TYPO: They listed their name as "Citizens Apposed to the Library Project." Said a pro-library spokesman, "That proves our point right there."

TYPER: *Reader's Digest* ran an article about women's rights.
TYPO: In the headline, the "R" in "Rights" was replaced by a "T," so readers saw "Movers & Shakers in Women's Tights."

TYPER: A clerk working at the Chicago Board of Elections in 2010 entered the name of Illinois Green Party gubernatorial candidate Rich Whitney into electronic voting machines.
TYPO: The clerk left the "n" out of Whitney, so it appeared as "Whitey." Although the mistake was caught before the election, nearly 5,000 machines had to be reprogrammed. But by that point, the press had caught wind of it—and headlines across the country read "Rich Whitey Running for Illinois Governor!"

TYPER: In 2010 a communications firm called Blue Waters Group made an all-too-common typo. What set theirs apart is that it appeared on a billboard in very large letters. It urged residents of South Bend, Indiana, to visit the city's website and learn the "15 Best Things About Our Public Schools."
TYPO: Despite four proofreaders looking at it, "Public" was misspelled as "Pubic." The sign remained on display for several days before a citizen alerted city officials, who quietly took it down.

TYPER: In 2011 Derby, Connecticut, Democratic Town Chair Sheila Parizo meant to add the name of the incumbent candidate to sit on the local tax board. She typed in "James J. Butler."
TYPO: The candidate's name was James *R.* Butler. James *J.* Butler

is his son, and he isn't a politician...but he did receive the most votes. "My son wants nothing to do with this," said the elder Butler. Nevertheless, he had to stand by as his son was sworn into office. (After a few days of legal wrangling, James J. resigned and Dad took his rightful seat.)

TYPER: A graphic designer at the *Pittsburgh Tribune-Review* attempted to create a reflection effect on the words "Suit Yourself" to accompany an article about summer swimsuits.
TYPO: Because of the reflection, the "u" in *suit* ended up looking more like an "h." Before the mistake was caught, more than 40,000 copies were printed that featured a bikini-clad supermodel standing next to a headline that appeared to say "[Bleep] Yourself."

TYPER: In 2012 Mitt Romney's presidential campaign released an iPhone app called "With Mitt."
TYPO: At the top of every page it said "A Better Amercia."

TYPER: On November 11, 2011, the *Utah Valley Daily Herald* ran a front-page article called "11•11•11: Date of the Decade." (The article was about how neat it is for the babies born on 11-11-11.)
TYPO: There were no goofs in the headline or in the article. But for some reason, when setting up the page masthead, the typesetter accidentally typed in the day's date as "November 11, 2010."

TYPER: Realtor Shirley Hunsperger ran an ad for a new home in Mount Shasta, California, with a "huge deck for entertaining."
TYPO: The "e" in *deck* was mistakenly replaced with an "i."

TYPER: In 2003 Sunrise Elementary School in Fort Worth, Texas, changed its name to Sunrise-McMillian Elementary. Reason: To honor its first-ever teacher, Mary McMillan.
TYPO: In 2012 one of McMillan's relatives alerted the school that an extra "i" had been added to her name. (It's Mc*Millan*, not Mc*Millian*.) Embarrassed school officials fixed the sign out front, but admitted that it would take a few years to replace the rest of the signage—along with all the stationery, business cards, library cards, visitor's passes, spelling bee award certificates...

THE NEW YEAR'S EVE OPOSSUM DROP

Think New York's Times Square Ball is the only thing that falls at midnight on December 31st? Here's a list of a few other things that get dropped to bring in the new year.

MAPLE LEAF AND SARDINE DROP

Residents of the town of Eastport, Maine, drop a four-foot plywood maple leaf from the third story of the Tides Institute & Museum of Art building in the downtown Bank Square at 11:00 p.m. on December 31. That's because midnight comes an hour earlier for their friends across the border in New Brunswick, Canada. (That's also why it's a maple leaf.) Then, at midnight, they drop an eight-foot plywood sardine—a tribute to Eastport's history in the Atlantic fishing industry.

RUBY SLIPPER DROP

Every New Year's Eve since the late 1990s, female impersonator Gary "Sushi" Marion climbs from the second-floor balcony of the Bourbon Street Pub in Key West, Florida, into an eight-foot, bright-red high-heeled shoe. Then, as thousands of onlookers shout the countdown, Sushi (in full drag) and the shoe are lowered to the street. "When I was a little kid, I never really dreamed about being in drag," he told reporters in 2011, "let alone being in a giant glittery red shoe at the stroke of midnight. It's fabulous!"

OPOSSUM DROP

In 1996 Clay Logan, owner of Clay's Corner Store in Brasstown, North Carolina, came up with an idea to get Brasstown some well-deserved recognition as the "Opossum Capital of the World" (which Brasstown and about 100 other towns claim to be). So he caught an opossum, put it in a pyramid-shaped Plexiglas box, and, as midnight on New Year's Eve approached, slowly dropped it from the roof of his store. It worked! The Brasstown Opossum Drop regularly makes headlines in newspapers all over the world and

The Times Square Ball is 12 feet in diameter and weighs 11,875 pounds.

attracts thousands of people every year. (And every January 1, one confused opossum is released into the wild near Brasstown.)

DEUCE OF CLUBS DROP

According to local legend, Show Low, Arizona, got its name from a poker game. A few years after settling there in the early 1870s, town founding fathers Corydon Cooley and Marion Clark decided that there was only room for one of them in the area. They agreed to play a game of poker to decide who would move out. When it came time for the very last draw, Clark said to Cooley, "If you show low, you win," meaning that if he drew the two of clubs—the lowest value card in the deck—he'd win. Cooley drew the two of clubs—and the town's been called "Show Low" ever since. In honor of that story, an illuminated "deuce of clubs" playing card (roughly four feet wide by seven feet high) is dropped from the top of a crane in the town square every New Year's Eve.

BOLOGNA DROP

Lebanon, Pennsylvania, is known for "Lebanon bologna," a type of cured and smoked sausage similar to salami. To honor the town's reputation, every New Year's Eve a 12-foot, 200-pound loaf of Lebanon bologna is lowered to the ground by a crane. (And the next day, it's donated to a local food bank.)

MOON PIE DROP

Mobile, Alabama, is the home of America's first Mardi Gras celebration (in 1703). Since the 1950s, moon pies have been a favorite "throw"—things people toss at passing Mardi Gras floats—in Mobile. That's why the city celebrates New Year's Eve with a Moon Pie Drop, in which a 12-foot-diameter, 600-pound electronic moon pie is lowered from the top of the 34-story RSA BankTrust Building. More than 80,000 people watched the Moon Pie Drop in 2012.

OLIVE DROP

At midnight, the good people of Bartlesville, Oklahoma, lower a giant styrofoam olive 221 feet from a skyscraper into a 15-foot-high illuminated sheet-metal martini glass. Happy New Year!

Nearly 40% of childhood dreams are nightmares.

ALIEN, STARRING MERYL STREEP

Some films are so closely associated with a specific actor or director that it's hard to believe they weren't the first choices. But it happens all the time. Can you imagine, for example...

RICHARD PRYOR AS SHERIFF BART (*Blazing Saddles*, 1974)

Pryor was the hottest comedian of the 1970s...and one of the most controversial. His sharp standup routines brutally skewered American racial politics and sentiments. And that's exactly who director Mel Brooks wanted for his comic western *Blazing Saddles*, about a small Old West town that hires a black sheriff. Brooks insisted on Pryor to play Sheriff Bart, even as he was pitching the script to studios. Hollywood studios wanted *Blazing Saddles*, but wouldn't agree to hiring Pryor (because he was a controversial figure and was rumored to be unreliable due to drug problems). Cleavon Little was eventually cast, and the movie became the top-grossing movie of 1974. Seven years later, Brooks tried again to cast Pryor in a movie, this time in the role of Josephus, the slave who tries to smooth talk and bargain his way out of being thrown to the lions in *The History of the World Part 1*. Pryor was set to take the role...until, just before filming began, he was free-basing cocaine and lit himself on fire, burning most of his body and nearly dying. (Gregory Hines was cast as Josephus.)

MERYL STREEP AS RIPLEY (*Alien*, 1979)

The makers of *Alien* weren't out to make a "blockbuster" sci-fi movie like *Star Wars*—they wanted something dark, disturbing, and well-acted. To cast the role of Ellen Ripley, the tough officer on a spaceship confronted with a terrible alien monster, the film's producers and director Ridley Scott went to Broadway in early 1978 to look for a new actress who hadn't done a lot of screen work. Their casting director, Mary Goldberg, narrowed down the search to two women. The first was Meryl Streep, coming off a Tony-nominated performance in *A Memory of Two Mondays / 27*

Wagons Full of Cotton. At the last minute, producer Gordon Carroll cancelled his meeting with Streep, because her fiancé, actor John Cazale (Fredo in *The Godfather* films), had died of lung cancer a day before, and he didn't want to subject her to a tough audition. Carroll did meet with the other actress that Goldberg found for him—Sigourney Weaver, who got the role.

BILL COSBY AS THE DOCTOR (*Doctor Who*, 1996)

Doctor Who had been running consistently on British television since 1963, but by the late 1980s, the show was running out of steam, and viewership had slipped to half of what it was at its peak in the late 1970s. In 1989 the BBC cancelled the series, but sold the film rights to Warner Bros., who wanted to reboot *Doctor Who* as a movie and market it to American audiences. Warner Bros. asked one of the biggest names in entertainment at the time—Bill Cosby, a doctor of education in real life and an obstetrician on the sitcom *The Cosby Show*—to play the main character, the mysterious alien time-traveler known only as "the Doctor." Cosby turned them down. Warner Bros. finally made a *Who* movie in 1996, starring British actor Paul McGann, which aired on Fox.

OWEN WILSON AS TED STROEHMANN (*There's Something About Mary*, 1998)

Bobby and Peter Farrelly were coming off two huge hit comedies, *Dumb and Dumber* and *Kingpin*, when they started their third movie, *There's Something About Mary*. They wanted Ben Stiller for the lead role of Ted Stroehmann, an uptight, put-upon former nerd who reconnects with his dream girl, played by Cameron Diaz. The studio was fine with Diaz, but were reluctant to hire Stiller, who was best known for *The Ben Stiller Show*, a critically-acclaimed but unsuccessful sketch comedy show. So the Farrellys suggested Owen Wilson for the part. It was a trick—the Farrellys knew that if they presented an actor more obscure than Stiller, as Wilson was at the time, the studio would relent and let them cast Stiller. And that's exactly what happened.

* * *

Don't reason with a hungry belly; it has no ears. —**Greek proverb**

First reference to a "red carpet": the Greek tragedy *Agamemnon* (458 B.C.), by Aeschylus.

THE GRUNGE CODE

The slang or vernacular of any subculture develops slowly and naturally over time. Not so with the words and phrases associated with the 1990s "grunge" music scene.

BACKGROUND

In the early 1990s, the biggest thing in rock music was grunge, a mixture of punk rock and dreary guitar riffs that shot bands like Nirvana and Pearl Jam into superstardom. It influenced other parts of culture, too—the leather boots and flannel shirts worn by the bands (because they were from cold and rainy Seattle) became a fashion movement. In November 1992, journalist Rick Marin was writing an article about the grunge scene for the *New York Times*. Wanting to cover every aspect of the movement, Marin figured there must be a lexicon, so he called Caroline Records, a Seattle-based music label. Receptionist Megan Jasper answered and humored Martin with a list of "grunge terms" and their definitions…all of which she made up on the spot. "I thought we would have a hearty laugh, and he would have to write it off as 15 minutes wasted, but it never happened," she says. Ironically, some of Jasper's terms *did* become widely used slang terms, even appearing on T-shirts and bumper stickers. Here's her list:

- **Wack slacks:** Torn-up jeans
- **Fuzz:** Thick wool sweaters
- **Plats:** Platform shoes
- **Kickers:** Heavy boots. "Kicks" became a common term for *all* shoes in the 1990s and 2000s.
- **Bound-and-hagged:** Staying home on Saturday night with your significant other instead of going out to a concert or club
- **Dish:** An attractive man
- **Big bag of blotation:** Drunk
- **Swingin' on the flippety-flop:** Hanging out with friends
- **Score:** Great
- **Harsh realm:** Bad
- **Tom-Tom Club:** Inspired by the name of a dance-pop side project by the mainstream Talking Heads, Jasper claimed this meant "uncool outsiders."
- **Cob nobbler:** A loser
- **Lamestain:** A cob nobbler
- **Rock on!:** See you later!

The *Muppet Movie* (1979) was banned in New Zealand. Reason: "gratuitous violence."

POLI-TALKS

American politicians say the darnedest things.

"We'd like to avoid problems, because when we have problems, we have troubles."

—Wesley Bolin, former governor of Arizona

"What right does Congress have to go around making laws just because they deem it necessary?"

—Marion Barry, former mayor of Washington, D.C.

"American scientific companies are cross-breeding humans and animals and coming up with mice with fully functioning human brains."

—Christine O'Donnell, U.S. Senate candidate

"Stand up, Chuck, and let 'em see ya."

—Joe Biden, to Sen. Chuck Graham, who is confined to a wheelchair

"We want the press to ask the questions we want to answer so that they report the news the way we want it to be reported."

—Sharron Angle, U.S. Senate candidate

"I find it interesting that in the 1970s the swine flu broke out under a Democrat, Jimmy Carter. I'm not blaming this on Obama—I just think it's an interesting coincidence."

—Rep. Michele Bachmann, on the 2009 swine flu outbreak

"Gingrich—primary mission: Advocate of civilization, Definer of civilization, Teacher of the rules of civilization, Leader of the civilizing forces."

—Newt Gingrich

"They don't call me 'Tyrannosaurus Sex' for nothing."

—Sen. Ted Kennedy

"Today's a big day in America. Only 36,000 people lost their jobs, which is really good!"

—Sen. Harry Reid

"This deal is a sugar-coated Satan sandwich."

—Rep. Emanuel Cleaver, on raising the debt ceiling

"Lemon. Wet. Good."

—Mitt Romney, when asked how a glass of lemonade tasted

City with the lowest marriage rate in the United States: Washington, D.C.

FERAL CHILDREN OF THE MODERN WORLD

Stories of children who end up on their own in the wild and survive by their wits—or with the help of wild animals—have been around for as long as recorded history. Most of the stories are hard to believe, and a lot harder to confirm, but there are a few that have occurred in relatively modern times that are actually true.

JOHN SSEBUNYA OF UGANDA

In 1991 Millie Sseba was gathering firewood in the jungle near her village, when she came across a group of monkeys. One, in a tree, looked particularly odd. She looked closer... and saw that it was a boy. She ran back to her village and returned with a group of men who, after battling the monkeys, were able to capture the boy. They took him to their village and cared for him. He was badly malnourished, covered with sores, and had tapeworms. A few weeks later, he was taken to Paul and Molly Wasswa, a Ugandan couple who run an orphange for destitute children. The boy was soon identified as John Ssebunya, the son of a man and woman who used to live in a nearby village.

The story of what had happened to him began to be pieced together. John himself was able to add to it when he eventually learned to speak. About a year before he was found with the monkeys, at the age of three or four (nobody knows his exact age), John saw his father shoot and kill his mother. He fled, fearing he would be killed, too, and ended up in the jungle. A few days into the ordeal, a group of vervet monkeys approached the boy and, according to John, gave him food. Monkey experts say this part of the story is doubtful, and that it's more likely the boy was simply allowed to take the monkeys' extras. In any case, what is accepted as fact is that after some time the monkeys took the boy in. He learned to eat roots, fruits, and other monkey food, and spent most of his time in trees—and his monkey friends are credited with his survival in the jungle. John's story became an international sensation and was the subject of a 1999 BBC documentary called *Living Proof*.

IVAN MISHUKOV OF RUSSIA

In 1996 Ivan, also just four years old, ran away from the home of his mother and her abusive alcoholic boyfriend, and took to a life on the streets of Moscow. He begged for food, and by sharing it with a pack of street dogs, found companionship and protection. For the next two years, Ivan lived with the dogs, making it through Moscow's brutal winters by curling up with them. He survived the city's shadier characters with the dogs' savage protection. In 1998 Ivan was captured by police—it took several attempts, police said, as the boy and his dog pack were adept at evading them—and was taken to a children's shelter. He was filthy, infested with lice, violent and snarling, and extremely wary of humans, but Ivan was eventually "recivilized." (It helped that he had been raised in a home until he was four and that he could speak.) Ivan went on to attend school and live a relatively normal life with a family in Moscow. (His story was adapted into the award-winning play *Ivan and the Dogs* by British playwright Hattie Naylor in 2010.)

TRAIAN CALDARAR OF TRANSYLVANIA

In February 2002, Manolescu Ioan, a shepherd in central Romania, had to walk through a forest when his car broke down. On the way he came across a large cardboard box—and found a small boy huddled inside. The boy was naked, malnourished, and looked to be about three or four. Ioan called police, and the boy was taken to a hospital. News of the wild boy—who couldn't speak, growled like a dog, and walked on all fours—was broadcast around the country. A short time later, a 23-year-old woman named Lina Caldarar burst into the hospital: The boy she had seen on TV was her son. They allowed her into the room—at which point the boy spoke his first words since being found: "Lina mom."

Lina said the boy's name was Traian and that he was actually seven years old. Lina had run away from her abusive husband three years earlier, she explained, leaving Traian behind because her husband wouldn't allow her to take him. The boy, she later learned, ran away not long after, and hadn't been seen since. Doctors and psychologists said Traian could not have survived alone in the woods for three years. His chimpanzee-like manner of walking, the way he sniffed his food before eating it, and the way he growled if someone approached him while he was eating were all indications that he was probably taken in by stray dogs known to roam the Transylvanian forests. Traian was treated for malnourishment and rickets, and has since attended school and is by all reports a "normal" kid today.

* * *

BRITISH COMEDIAN JOKES

Each year the funniest comedian one-liners are voted on by the 30,000 attendees of Edinburgh Fringe Festival in Scotland. Here are some of 2012's winners. (Remember, these are all from the UK.)

"My mum's so pessimistic, that if there was an Olympics for pessimism, she wouldn't fancy her chances."

—Nish Kumar

"I watched a documentary on how ships are kept together. Riveting!"

—Stewart Francis

"I took part in the sun-tanning Olympics. I just got Bronze."

—Tim Vine

"I'm good friends with 25 letters of the alphabet. I don't know why."

—Chris Turner

"You know you're working class when your TV is bigger than your book case."

—Rob Beckett

"I was raised as an only child, which really annoyed my sister."

—Will Marsh

"Last night me and my girlfriend watched three DVDs back to back. Luckily I was the one facing the telly."

—Tim Vine

Hogwarts motto: *Draco dormiens nunquam titillandus* ("Never tickle a sleeping dragon").

MOON TREES

"Scattered around our planet are hundreds of creatures that have been to the Moon and back again. None of them are human."—NASA

ORBITAL ORCHARD

On January 31, 1971, *Apollo 14* lifted off from Cape Canaveral, Florida, launching astronauts Edgar Mitchell, Alan Shepard, and Stuart Roosa to the moon. Roosa, an Air Force test pilot, had also served as a "smokejumper" for the U.S. Forest Service, parachuting out of planes to help put out forest fires. He and a colleague named Stan Krugman wanted to find out whether tree seeds would still grow after a trip to space.

With the approval of NASA, Krugman chose five varieties: sycamores, sweetgums, Douglas firs, redwoods, and loblolly pines. He chose most of them because they grow well all over the country, and chose redwoods because they are so well-known. He kept an identical group on Earth as a control. "The scientists wanted to find out what would happen to these seeds if they took a ride to the Moon," said Krugman. "Would the trees look normal?"

APOLLO FORE-TEEN

Apollo 14 is famous for a different experiment: moon golf. While Roosa (and his 500 seeds) orbited in the *Kitty Hawk* command module 118 miles above the surface, Alan Shepard used a modified lunar collection device to send a few chip shots into the Fra Mauro crater. On the mission's return to Earth, the seeds were accidentally exposed to a vacuum during decontamination procedures. They were "traumatized," said Krugman, but after careful attention, they all started growing.

NASA gave away most of the Moon Trees—which is what they're called—as part of America's Bicentennial Celebration in 1976. One was planted in Philadelphia's Independence Square by Roosa and the Forest Services mascot, Woodsy Owl. Each state got one to plant at their capitol building; others went to Valley Forge, the Kennedy Space Center, and the White House. A few ended up in New Orleans at the request of then-Mayor Maurice "Moon" Landrieu. The locations of the rest were forgotten until

The X on the Confederate flag is called a St. Andrew's Cross.

NASA scientist Dave Williams started looking for them. So far he's located 83 of the Moon Trees, which he catalogues on a NASA website. One was right under his nose—a 35-foot Moon Sycamore growing right outside his building at the Goddard Space Flight Center in Greenbelt, Maryland.

THE TREES TODAY

Moon Trees look and grow like normal trees. Genetic testing shows that they were unaffected by weightlessness or solar radiation, and even exposure to a vacuum doesn't seem to hurt them. Like any other tree, Moon Trees are susceptible to the weather…and to humans. In 2005 Hurricane Katrina damaged one of Mayor Moon's trees so badly that it was later taken down. In 2008 the sycamore at the Cannelton Girl Scout Camp in Indiana lost its top half in a storm. One at the Wyoming, Michigan, Police Station was accidentally cut down during a building renovation.

WHERE THEY WENT

In case you're nowhere near Washington, D.C., or a state capital, here's where you can find some of the other trees from space:

- International Forest of Friendship, Atchison, Kansas
- Veteran's Hospital, Tuskegee, Alabama
- Helen Keller's birthplace, Tuscumbia, Alabama
- Tilden Nature Area, Berkeley, California
- Palustris Experimental Forest, Elmer, Louisiana
- Holliston Police Station, Holliston, Massachusetts
- Forestry Commission Nursery, Waynesboro, Michigan
- Friendship Park, Jefferson County, Ohio
- Siskiyou Smoke Jumpers Base, Illinois Valley, Oregon
- There are two in Brazil—a sweetgum at the Institute for Environment and Natural Renewable Resources in Brasilia, and a redwood growing in the southern city of Santa Rosa.

Termites don't eat ebony. (But what about ivory?)

NBA DRAFT BUSTS

Being at the top of the draft doesn't always lead to a stellar pro-basketball career, as these players found out.

SAM BOWIE (1984)

A top high-school player, a star at the University of Kentucky, and member of the 1980 Olympic team, Bowie looked to be a lock for NBA stardom. In 1984 the Portland Trail Blazers took him as the #2 pick—passing over Michael Jordan and Charles Barkley. But the 7'1" center never lived up to his potential, and had a lackluster NBA career. Over 11 years in the NBA, the injury-prone Bowie averaged only 10 points per game. Ten years after he retired, both ESPN and *Sports Illustrated* called him the worst draft pick in sports history.

BENOIT BENJAMIN (1985)

A year after Bowie was drafted over future superstars Jordan and Barkley, another soon-to-be middling player was picked ahead of two future legends, in this case, Karl Malone and Chris Mullin. During a 14-year career, Benjamin played for nine NBA teams, none of them in their glory years. While he was one of the best shot-blockers in league history (1,581 total), he averaged only 11.4 points per game and was more notable for committing flagrant fouls and getting ejected from games due to his temper.

GREG ODEN (2007)

As a freshman at Ohio State in 2006–07, the 7-foot-tall Oden led the Buckeyes to the NCAA title game. After Oden's one year of college play, the Portland Trail Blazers selected him with the #1 pick in the 2007 draft. So how did he do in his rookie season? He didn't even play. Stricken with chronic knee problems, Oden underwent surgery after training camp and sat out the entire year. In his first game of the 2008–09 season, Oden left the game after 13 minutes with an injured foot, the first of several injuries that would sideline him for more than 75 percent of the time—he hasn't played in a game since early 2010.

That "thump-thump" your heart makes when it beats is the sound of the valves closing.

DARKO MILICIC (2003)

The 2003 NBA Draft class was one of the best in history, including future all-stars LeBron James, Carmelo Anthony, Chris Bosh, and Dwayne Wade—each of whom went in the top 5. Rounding out the top was #2 pick Darko Milicic, a Serbian pro selected by the Detroit Pistons. But he wasn't suited to the fast play style of the NBA and after three seasons as a benchwarmer in Detroit, he was traded to Orlando. Then Memphis. Then New York. Then Minnesota. Career average: Six points a game.

PERVIS ELLISON (1989)

The Sacramento Kings had the #1 pick in 1989 and selected "Never Nervous" Pervis Ellison out of Louisville. In college, he'd led his team to the NCAA title, was named best player of the 1986 playoffs, and was an All-American in 1989. But when he turned pro, "Never Nervous" Pervis quickly became "Out of Service" Pervis, benched for the better part of his 11 seasons. He ultimately averaged 9.5 points a game and retired in 2000.

ROBERT TRAYLOR (1998)

After missing the playoffs for nearly a decade, it looked like the Milwaukee Bucks would finally turn things around in 1998—they had the #9 pick in the draft that year and selected little-known German power forward Dirk Nowitzki. Nowitzki became a superstar, eventually winning the MVP award and leading his team to a title. Unfortunately, that team was the Dallas Mavericks, because the Bucks traded him away on draft night. In return, the Bucks got Robert "Tractor" Traylor, a hulking, 300-pound, 6'8" center out of Michigan. Traylor played two seasons in Milwaukee before being traded around the league until 2005, when he failed his physical and went to play in Europe. Sadly, in 2011, at only 34 years old, Traylor died of a heart attack.

* * *

First celebrity food endorsement: The first celebrity to plug a food item is also the first pro athlete to appear on a Wheaties box: New York Yankees first baseman Lou Gehrig, in 1934.

THE LAST LAUGH: EPITAPHS

Some grave humor collected by our wandering tombstone-oligists.

In New Jersey:
Rebecca Freeland
She drank good ale, good punch and wine
And lived to the age of 99.

In New York:
Lawrence Cook, Jr.
Ma loves Pa
Pa loves women
Ma caught Pa,
With 2 in swimmin
Here lies Pa.

In Massachusetts:
Lady Coningsby
I plant these shrubs upon your grave, dear wife,
That something on this spot may boast of life.
Shrubs must wither and all earth must rot;
Shrubs may revive: but you, thank heaven, will not.

In Colorado:
I'd rather be here
Than in Texas.

In Massachusetts:
Here lies as silent clay
Miss Arabella Young
Who on the 21st of May 1771
Began to hold her tongue

In Connecticut:
Molly tho' pleasant in her day
Was suddenly seized and went away
How soon she's ripe, how soon she's rotten
Laid in her grave and soon forgotten.

In Colorado:
Bill Blake
Was hanged by mistake.

In Arizona:
Here lays Butch.
We planted him raw.
He was quick on the trigger,
But slow on the draw.

In Vermont:
O fatal gun, why was it he
That you should kill so dead?
Why didn't you go just a little high
And fire above his head?

In England:
Here lies the father of 29.
There would have been more
But he didn't have the time.

In Illinois:
John E. Goembel
Attorney
The defense rests.

In Massachusetts:
Mary Lefavour
Reader pass on and ne'er waste your time,
On bad biography and bitter rhyme.
For what I am this cumb'rous clay insures,
And what I was, is no affair of yours.

Half of all the 6 million parts on a Boeing 747 are fasteners.

FLYING FLOP: THE LIFETIME AAIRPASS

Has an airline ever lost your luggage? Thrown you off an overbooked flight? Left you stranded at the airport in a strange city? If so, you might want to save this story until you're on a plane and can enjoy it to the fullest.

GROWING PAINS

American Airlines now flies all over the world, but in the early 1980s, the airline was much smaller, serving the United States, Canada, Mexico, and the Caribbean. They wanted to expand but didn't have enough money to buy planes for new routes. With interest rates peaking near 20 percent, an all-time high, borrowing the money was out. But what if American could get its *passengers* to buy the planes?

BUY NOW, FLY LATER

At the time, ticket prices were increasing about 12 percent a year, and travelers were sick of the endless fare hikes. American thought it might be possible to solve both problems at once, by letting customers lock in the price of future travel by paying for it years in advance. The airline came up with something called an "AAirpass." By purchasing a 5-year pass ($19,900), 10-year pass ($39,500), or 15-year pass ($58,000), a person could fly 25,000 miles a year (in coach) for the life of the pass, without spending another penny. It wouldn't, no matter how much ticket prices went up.

AAirpasses made sense for frequent fliers, but the real winner was American Airlines. They got the money up front, interest free. To repay it, all they had to do was free up a seat whenever a pass holder wanted to fly. Sales of the AAirpasses helped American fund its growth in the years that followed. The program might have continued, were it not for one thing: The airline also sold a pass good for *unlimited* air travel, in *first* class, *for life*. Lifetime AAirpasses cost $250,000, plus an extra $150,000 if the traveler wanted a second ticket for a companion.

FLIGHTS OF FANCY

Lifetime AAirpass holders received the kind of treatment the rest of us can only dream of. They had access to a special 24-hour reservation hotline for the airline's best customers, which made planning trips and booking flights a snap. American also gave the pass holders books of blank tickets that they could fill in themselves—they literally wrote their own tickets.

At the airport, Lifetime AAirpass holders breezed past the long lines and checked in at the first-class ticket counter. Then, boarding pass in hand, they made their way to the airline's plush Admirals Club lounge, where they waited for their flights in secluded comfort (complimentary drinks and snacks included), far from the hoi polloi. When it was time to board, they were ushered on the aircraft ahead of everyone else. On the plane, they received the best that first class had to offer, free. Every flight earned frequent-flier miles good for hotel rooms, rental cars, or additional plane tickets. For years, the airline permitted pass holders with the $150,000 companion seat to sell the extra seat whenever they flew alone. There was no penalty for cancelling a flight, ever.

66 PASSES

Wonderful treatment to be sure (even better after the flight crews memorized your name and food and drink preferences) but the passes cost a fortune. Though American sold them for 13 years, in all that time they only managed to sell 66. Most were purchased by celebrities and business tycoons (baseball legend Willy Mays and Dell Computer founder Michael Dell bought them), but a handful were purchased by people of lesser means looking for a bargain.

Most of the lifetime-pass holders flew as they always had, except that they flew a little more often now that flying was easy and prepaid. Unfortunately for American Airlines, a handful of pass holders enjoyed life in first class so much that they began using their passes far more than the airline had bargained for—some flew as often as 20 times a month, often to no particular destination, for no particular purpose. Pass holders flew across country just to have a sandwich in a favorite restaurant—not once, not a few times, but *hundreds* of times, each time taking up a seat (or two with the companion pass) that American could have sold for many hundreds of dollars to another traveler. One man

Ronald McDonaldov? At its opening in 1990, the Moscow McDonald's served 30,000 people.

flew his daughter from Dallas to London, England, to buy soap. They were in London for less than an hour.

TAKING ADVANTAGE

Why pay for meals and lodging when eating and sleeping on a plane was essentially free? If passengers wanted to spend five nights in Paris, they could book five round-trip flights in a row. If they were getting fat off all that steak and lobster in first class, they could book the companion seat and leave it empty to create extra space.

If the family of a pass holder was planning to visit Mexico over the holidays, the pass holder could book as many flights as needed to rack up enough frequent flier miles to fly everyone to Mexico for free. One such holder who lost his job created a new career for himself: selling his companion seat and escorting buyers anywhere in the world they wanted to go. Had he or any other lifetime pass holder become homeless, there was nothing to stop them from *living* on American Airlines planes almost full-time.

CRASH LANDING

For years, American Airlines management had known that a handful of lifetime pass holders were getting the better of them, but just how much better only become apparent when a 2007 audit revealed that the worst offenders were costing the airline over $1 million in lost revenue a year, every year, for tickets purchased for $400,000, twenty-six years earlier. One man had logged more than 40 million miles, the equivalent of flying all the way to Mars on the airline's dime.

He might have flown *back* from Mars, too, had American not changed the terms of the deal without notifying pass holders. Suddenly selling the companion seat was against the rules. So was the common practice of booking it under a false name, such as "Empty Seat Smith," and leaving it empty for extra room.

In 2008 American used these and other technicalities to confiscate several AAirpasses on grounds of "fraud," then sued their owners to recover millions in "stolen" revenue. Some of the jilted pass holders have filed countersuits to get their passes back, but as of August 2012, the lawsuits are all on hold. Reason: On November 29, 2011, American Airlines filed for bankruptcy.

CROAKERS & SOAKERS

Who says you can't talk like a pro bowler, even if you don't bowl like one? Learn these expressions and you'll sound like a champ on your next trip to the lanes. Steeee–rike!

Clean Game: A game with a strike (10 pins knocked down with one ball) or spare (two balls) in each frame.

Reading the Lane: Studying how your ball performs in an unfamiliar lane, in order to adjust your play and improve your score.

Benchmark Ball: A "starter" ball used to read the lane.

In the Zone: Able to read the lane, and bowl accordingly. Someone who can't read the lane is said to be "lost."

Yahtzee: Five strikes in a row.

7-Up: Seven strikes in a row.

Clothesline: Four pins in a single line, either the 1–2–4–7 pins or the 1–3–6–10 pins.

Late 10: When the 10-pin is last to fall (and slow to do it).

Help: A pin that bounces off the side wall of the lane and knocks down more pins on the return.

Gripper/Pincher/Squeezer: Someone who holds the ball too tight.

Cranker: A bowler who throws a lot of hooks and relies on speed and power to knock down the pins.

Stroker: A bowler who throws straight, non-hooked balls, emphasizing accuracy over speed and power.

Croaker: A bowler whose throws fall somewhere in between crankers and strokers. (Also called a "tweener.")

Soaker: A ball soaked in chemical solvents to give it a softer surface and better hooking ability. (Illegal for league and tournament play.)

Boomer: A powerful cranker.

Brickyard/Graveyard: A lane or bowling alley with a reputation for low-scoring games.

Dutch 200: A score of 200 points exactly, resulting from throwing alternating strikes and spares in each frame.

CANADIAN FIRSTS

Here's a look at some influential folks from the Great White North.

First Canadian in Space: Commander Marc Garneau was selected for the Canadian Astronaut Program in 1983, and served on the Space Shuttle *Challenger* in October 1984 as a payload specialist. After a promotion to captain, then to deputy director of the Canadian Astronaut Program, he went to space two more times—in May 1996 and November 2000. He retired from the space program in 2006 and successfully ran for Parliament. (If he ever becomes prime minister, he'll be the first astronaut ever to serve as a head of state.)

First Canadian in the NBA: Ernie Vandeweghe was born in Montreal but moved to Long Island, New York, as a teenager. He played college basketball at Colgate and was drafted by the New York Knicks in 1949, where, three years into the NBA's existence, he became the first Canadian-born player to join the league. After he retired in 1956, Vandeweghe also finished a medical degree and became a U.S. Air Force surgeon. He's also the father of 1980s NBA star Kiki Vandeweghe.

First Canadian to win a Nobel Prize: In 1923 Canadian scientists Frederick Banting and John Macleod were recognized by the Nobel Committee for their discovery and identification of the hormone insulin. That led to a proper diagnosis and better treatments of diabetes—patients would no longer slowly die from the condition, but could take insulin injections and lead normal lives.

First Canadian to win an Academy Award for Best Director: Filmmaker James Cameron was born in Kapsuskasing, Ontario. He's made some of the world's most successful and popular movies, including *The Terminator*, *Aliens*, *The Abyss*, *Terminator 2*, *Avatar*, and *Titanic*, for which he won the 1998 Academy Award for Best Director.

First Canadian to win an Olympic gold medal in Canada: Montreal hosted the 1976 Summer Games, and Calgary hosted the 1988 Winter Games. Both times, Canadian athletes were shut out

More earthquakes occur in the Northern Hemisphere than in the Southern Hemisphere.

of gold medals. At the third Canadian-hosted Olympics, the 2010 Winter Games in Vancouver, Montreal-born skier Alexandre Bilodeau won the gold medal in men's moguls. By the time the Olympic games were over, Canadians had won a total of 14 gold medals, the most of any country that year.

First Canadian billionaire: K.C. Irving, born in New Brunswick in 1899, began selling cars at age 25, early in the auto industry. He parlayed his earnings into starting Irving Oil, which he grew into the biggest gas station chain in eastern and maritime Canada. Irving is the first native Canadian to reach a net worth of $1 billion. He died in 1992 at age 93.

First Canadian winner of the Pulitzer Prize for Literature: The Pulitzer goes to an author who writes an exceptional book on American themes, but they don't necessarily have to *be* American. In 1995 Carol Shields won for her novel *The Stone Diaries*. Shields was born in Illinois, but married a Canadian man in 1957 and became a Canadian citizen shortly thereafter.

First Canadian Booker Prize winner: This award, handed out since 1969, goes to the author of a book who lives in the British Commonwealth, which includes England, Scotland, Australia, Canada, and former British territories Zimbabwe and Ireland. First Canadian citizen to win it: Michael Ondaatje for his 1992 novel *The English Patient*. (Two other Canadians have won since: Margaret Atwood for *The Blind Assassin* in 2000, and Yann Martel for *Life of Pi* in 2002.)

First Canadian to reach the top of Mount Everest: In 1982 the Canadian Mount Everest Expedition set out to summit the world's highest peak. It was a tragic disaster—a cameraman died in an ice collapse, three Sherpa guides were killed in an avalanche, and six Canadian climbers decided to turn back. On October 5, 1982, one of two remaining Canadians, Laurie Skreslet, and two Sherpas reached the peak of Everest. (Two days later, the other Canadian, Pat Morrow, successfully summited the mountain.)

* * *

A wise man reflects before he speakes. A fool speaks then reflects on what he has uttered. —**French Proverb**

WHAT PRICE BEAUTY?

People will do almost anything to themselves in the pursuit of looking younger and more attractive.

LIPS: In 2010 more than a million American women underwent lip augmentation surgery. In addition to older treatments to plump up lips, such as silicone, paraffin wax, and cow-collagen injections, some women have opted to enhance their lips with purified tissue taken from research cadavers or compounds made from their own skin. Cost: $1,500–$3,000

EYES: A new fad emerged in 2002 in the Netherlands. Ocular surgeons there developed a technique for implanting tiny bits of jewelry into a patient's eyeballs. (It's legal in the Netherlands, but not elsewhere.) Most popular styles of the platinum mini-jewel: a heart, star, or half moon, which is then dropped into a small incision in the eye's clear outer membrane. Cost: €700 ($860)

FEET: The problem with expensive designer shoes—they're often too narrow to fit the average foot. Solution: Some surgeons in Los Angeles and New York are reportedly offering "pinky toe tucks," in which the bones of a woman's pinky toes are surgically shaved to make their toes straighter and their feet narrower. Cost: $1,000 per toe

ABS: The fastest-spreading trend in male cosmetic surgery is "abdominal etching," also known as precision liposuction. Men can have a plastic surgeon suck out only the fat between their stomach muscles. Result: instant "six-pack." Cost: $5,000–$10,000

TONGUE: Body-modification enthusiasts use their bodies like a canvas—they favor tattoos, piercings...and, since it first appeared in 1996, tongue splitting. Surgeons use lasers, a scalpel, or even fishing line to split the tongue from tip to center. Cost: $750

BUTT: Responding to fears of leaking silicone butt implants, some plastic surgeons now offer "Brazilian butt lift" surgery. They liposuction fat from chubby parts of the patient's body, then inject it into their flat buttocks. Cost: $7,000

Odds of making a hole in one in golf: 1 in 12,500. Two holes in one: 1 in 67 million.

I'LL HAVE A FATSO BURGER

Try to match the fast-food restaurant to the movie or TV show in which it appeared. We hope this quiz doesn't make you hungry, because it's not like you can go out and eat at any of these places. *(Answers on page 596.)*

1. Mooby's

2. Mr. Smiley's

3. Krusty Burger

4. Doublemeat Palace

5. The Lanford Lunchbox

6. Los Pollos Hermanos

7. McDowell's

8. Honker Burger

9. Bronto Burger

10. Taco Town

11. The Chum Bucket

12. Burger World

13. Captain Hook's Fish and Chips

14. Fishy Joe's

15. Big Kahuna Burgers

16. Fatso Burger

17. City Wok

a) *Pulp Fiction*

b) *Fast Times at Ridgemont High*

c) *American Beauty*

d) *Roseanne*

e) *Buffy the Vampire Slayer*

f) *Saturday Night Live*

g) *Dogma*

h) *SpongeBob SquarePants*

i) *The Flintstones*

j) *Beavis and Butt-Head*

k) *That '70s Show*

l) *Futurama*

m) *Breaking Bad*

n) *Coming to America*

o) *The Simpsons*

p) *Doug*

q) *South Park*

Stimulus? Hallmark sells a line of "encouragement" cards for people who've lost their jobs.

4 WAYS TO LIGHT A FIRE WITHOUT MATCHES

This might not save you in the even of an apocalypse, but you never know when little tricks like these will come in handy. Not all of these fire techniques are easy, but they do work with practice.

WITH A BATTERY AND STEEL WOOL

Use the batteries from a flashlight, cell phone, or whatever else is handy. Roll a piece of steel wool between your hands and form it into a "wire" long enough to touch both the positive and negative contacts, shorting the battery. (A 9-volt battery is ideal, since the contacts are right next to each other.) When the wool shorts the battery, it will ignite, and you can use it to light a fire.

WITH A FLASHLIGHT

Unscrew the front of a flashlight. Remove the silver reflector, then remove the bulb from the reflector. Place some tinder (lint, dried twigs, moss, or a cigarette work well) through the hole in the reflector, and point it at the sun so that the sunlight is focused on the tinder. When the tinder catches, use it to light a larger fire.

WITH A SODA CAN

The bottom of a soda can has a shape similar to the reflector of a flashlight. Polish the bottom of the can with a chocolate bar until it shines like a mirror (this can take a while), then use it like the flashlight reflector to focus sunlight on some tinder.

WITH A WATER BALLOON

Fill a translucent balloon with water and tie it shut. (Round balloons work best.) Use the balloon like the lens of a magnifying glass. If you hold it one to two inches from the ground, the light passing through it will be focused to a small, bright point. Squeeze the balloon to make the point of light as small and bright as possible, and use it to light some tinder.

Not so sweet: Illinois taxes candy at a higher rate than other food.

DUMB CROOKS

U.S. Supreme Court Justice Antonin Scalia once said, "Law enforcement has many constraints...but the one thing that it has going for it is that criminals are stupid."

ROBBED AT BULLET-POINT

Verlin Alsept, 59, tried to hold up a Family Dollar store in Dayton, Ohio, in 2012. When the clerk refused to open the register, Alsept held up a .38 caliber bullet and threatened her with it. She wasn't threatened. He left and was arrested near the store.

HOUSE OF CARDS

In 2011 Benjamin North, 26, of Eureka, California, tried to make a purchase from his local Safeway using a stolen credit card. He might have gotten away with it, too—had he not assisted local sheriff's deputies in finding him by using his *own* Safeway Club Card in order to get a discount.

THE SCARLET CHICKEN

When employees of the Chicken Shack in Lakeland, Florida, arrived at work one morning, they discovered that the restaurant had been burgled. It didn't take police too long to track down the crooks: Chad Berrien, 35, and Rickey Wright, 31, were found a few blocks away, drinking the beer they stole...and wearing brand-new Chicken Shack T-shirts.

VAN-ITY

As two young New Jersey men, Ryan Letchford and Jeffrey Olson, were leaving a party in a Radnor, Pennsylvania, condo complex one night in 2012 they happened upon a Pennsylvania State prisoner-transport van parked in the condo parking lot. The van's driver, Constable Mike Connor, lived at the complex, and hadn't closed the door all the way when he parked there earlier that evening. So Letchford and Olson, both inebriated, decided to climb into the back of the van and take photos of each other pretending to get arrested. But when they closed the door all the way, it automatically locked. Their friends eventually found them, only to discover that the door was locked on *both* sides. Letchford and

Olson tried kicking out the metal screen that separated them from the front of the van. No luck. Their only way out: Dial 911. Constable Connor got the call at 5:00 a.m. "I came down and unlocked the doors," he said, "and 'Dumb and Dumber' pranced out of the van." Then they were both arrested...for real.

THE COPS MUST HAVE "LIKED" THIS GUY

Suggestion: If you're a fugitive, don't post a message on your Facebook page saying, "Catch me if you can. I'm in Brooklyn!" That's what 29-year-old Victor Burgos did. He was wanted in Utica, New York, on domestic violence charges, and after finding out that his mug shot was on the "Ten Most Wanted" list at the Utica Police Department, he decided to taunt the cops online. That was the break they needed. They tracked Burgos to a Brooklyn apartment...where they found him surfing Facebook.

NOT-SO-CLEAN GETAWAY

Three 19-year-olds—Nicholas Kalscheuer, Nicholas Fiumetto, and Andy Huynh—hatched a plan to steal a case of beer from the Baja Ranch Market in Covina, California, in 2011. While Huynh waited out front in the getaway car, Kalscheuer and Fiumetto snatched the beer and then ran out. Employees gave chase and captured Kalscheuer immediately. Fiumetto jumped into the car as Huynh hit the accelerator. But instead of getting away, they swerved to avoid hitting a store clerk, slammed into a curb, and stopped. By this time, the police had arrived, so the two men ditched the car. Fiumetto ran into a nearby car-wash tunnel and became stuck among the brushes and water jets. By the time he escaped—all wet—the cops were waiting for him. Huynh got away, but had left his ID in the car and was captured soon after.

CARRY-OFF BAGGAGE

In 2011 a woman went to a prison in Chetumal, Mexico, to visit her husband, Juan Ramirez Tijerina, in a private room. When the woman left, guards noticed that she "looked nervous" as she was wheeling out a very fat suitcase. They stopped her, opened the luggage, and found Tijerina, who had curled himself up into a little ball inside. He was sent back to his cell; she was arrested.

In the 1890s, the Univ. of Nebraska Cornhuskers football team was called the Bugeaters.

EDIFICE WRECKS

*Some government buildings, like the White House, the Pentagon, and the U.S. Capitol, are famous. Others are more…*infamous.

THE "TWEED COURTHOUSE" (a.k.a. The New York County Courthouse)

Background: In 1858 the County of New York made plans to build a new courthouse. The legislation authorizing the project stipulated that the total cost, including furnishings, was not to exceed $250,000 (about $4.4 million today).

Controversy: In those days, New York politics were dominated by Tammany Hall, a Democratic Party political machine run by William "Boss" Tweed. Tweed was as crooked as they came. He saw the construction project as an opportunity to siphon millions from public coffers, and soon Tammany-affiliated officials were awarding contracts to "friendly" contractors with instructions to inflate their bills by as much as 100 times the actual cost. Most of the money was then kicked back to Tweed.

A boyhood friend of Tweed's named James Ingersoll submitted a $350,000 invoice for $13,000 worth of carpets; a furniture maker charged $179,000 for three tables and 40 chairs. A man named Andrew Garvey, dubbed the "Prince of Plasterers" by the newspapers, billed the city more than $500,000 for plastering (including $133,000 for two days' work), then charged another $1 million to repair the work. Of the more than $15 million appropriated to build the courthouse between 1858 and 1871, it's estimated that Tweed and his cronies pocketed more than $13 million ($230 million in 2011 dollars). The purchase of Alaska from Russia, in 1868, cost just $7.2 million.

Aftermath: When the law finally caught up with Tweed in 1871, he was put on trial in an unfinished courtroom in the basement of "his" courthouse. Convicted on 204 of 220 criminal counts, Tweed spent only a year in prison before being released for time served. He was then convicted on civil charges and sent to debtors' prison. In 1875, during a home visit, Tweed escaped and fled to Spain, where a sharp-eyed official recognized him as the corrupt politician he'd seen in a political cartoon. Tweed was arrested and returned to New York; he died in jail in 1878.

Update: The Tweed Courthouse wasn't completed until 1881—more than 20 years after work began. The building still stands: Today this National Historic Landmark serves as the headquarters of the city's Department of Education. (In 1999 the building began two years of renovations to restore its original glory. Budgeted at $37 million, the work cost nearly $90 million.)

THE J. EDGAR HOOVER BUILDING

Background: In December 1967, ground was broken in Washington, D.C., for the FBI's first headquarters building. (Before that, the Bureau had offices in the Justice Department.) It was still under construction when Director J. Edgar Hoover died in May 1972; two days later, President Richard Nixon signed legislation naming it in his honor.

Controversy: The Hoover Building certainly has its flaws. It cost $126 million to build, more than double the original estimate, and though it's one of the most prominent buildings along Pennsylvania Avenue, it has been criticized as one of the city's ugliest. But it isn't the building so much as the fact that it's named in Hoover's honor that has generated so much controversy. During his 48-year tenure as the Director of the FBI, Hoover compiled files on the private lives of public officials, allowed U.S. presidents to use the Bureau for partisan political purposes, and trampled the civil rights of ordinary citizens who opposed the federal government. Almost as soon as the FBI building was named in his honor, there were calls for the name to be removed.

Hoover's abuses of power are well known, but if his critics ever do succeed in having his name stripped from the building, it may be due to a scandal that is much less known, involving the murder of a New England mobster named Edward Deegan in 1965. Two days before Deegan's murder, the FBI learned from an illegal wiretap that two gangsters named Vincent Flemmi and Joseph Barboza were about to murder him. The Bureau, with Hoover's knowledge and consent, didn't warn Deegan or try to stop the killing. Then, after Deegan was murdered, Hoover sat by silently while four men he knew to be innocent were convicted of the murder and sentenced to long prison terms. Why did he do it? To protect Flemmi and Barboza, who were FBI informants.

...a dog's mood by measuring the wags of its tail.

Aftermath: Two of the four innocent men died in prison; the other two, Peter Limone and Joseph Salvati, served 33 years and 29 years, respectively, before their innocence was proven and they were set free. (Limone was originally sentenced to death, but his life was spared when Massachusetts outlawed the death penalty in 1974.) Limone, Salvati, and the estates of the two dead men sued the federal government for wrongful conviction and won. In 2007 they were awarded $101.8 million…or just $24 million shy of what it cost to build the J. Edgar Hoover Building.

THE RONALD REAGAN BUILDING

Background: In 1990 the federal government began construction on a massive new office building on Pennsylvania Avenue between the White House and the U.S. Capitol. Only the Pentagon is larger. In 1995 the (Republican-dominated) U.S. Congress voted unanimously to name the building after former President Ronald Reagan, who left office in 1989. Projected cost: $362 million.

Controversy: Reagan was an outspoken opponent of big government, so the idea of naming the largest nonmilitary federal office building ever built after him—and stuffing it with more than 7,000 government bureaucrats—was controversial from the start. It grew even more controversial when the project fell way behind schedule: Two years into the four-year timetable, the contractors hadn't even finished digging the foundation. Any hope of keeping the building within budget was abandoned. Political and bureaucratic meddling made things worse and added expensive new flourishes. (An IMAX theater and a members-only dining club were later removed from the plans in a failed attempt to keep costs at least partially under control.)

Aftermath: By the time the building opened for business in 1997—three years behind schedule and still unfinished—the total cost had climbed to $818 million, including $149 million for "professional advice on keeping project costs contained." Citizens Against Government Waste said naming it after Reagan was "like naming a military base after Mahatma Gandhi, or a battered woman's shelter after O.J. Simpson." Reagan's son Michael said his father would be better honored if "Mt. Wastemore," as Ron called it, were demolished and the resulting hole in the ground named for him instead.

Though they make you feel warmer, hot drinks do not actually raise your body temperature.

WHAT A CARD!

Over the decades, trading card companies like Topps and Fleer expanded from baseball to other sports, then to movies, TV shows...and a lot of subjects that wouldn't seem to be very interesting to kids.

Got Milk? (1999). A take on the "Got Milk" ads that featured celebrities with milk mustaches. The cards in this set from Marvel Comics showed superheroes and villains like Spider-Man, Daredevil, Doctor Doom, and the Incredible Hulk with milk mustaches. Captions on the back told kids that milk makes them superhero-strong. (Sponsored by the Milk Promotion Board.)

John F. Kennedy (1963). There was a boom in John F. Kennedy merchandise exploiting his youth, good looks, and popularity in the Camelot era. Topps produced this 77-card set a few weeks before his assassination. The pictures are all official portraits or news photos, all in black and white. And the captions are pretty dry—the text on the back of a picture of Kennedy and his wife in a car reads, "President Kennedy and the First Lady leave a formal dinner hosted by French President De Gaulle." Topps released a similar set (some cards even featuring the same photos) in a 1968 set about Robert Kennedy.

Johnson vs. Goldwater (1964). The '64 presidential election was one of the least contested in American history. Vice-president Lyndon Johnson, who became president after the Kennedy assassination, cruised to victory over Republican candidate Barry Goldwater, 61 to 38 percent. This 64-card set, made by the same people at Topps who made the Kennedy cards and released before the election, didn't feature images of the election cycle. Instead, they used nonpartisan stock images, such as Goldwater standing in front of a microphone delivering a speech.

***Six Feet Under* (2004).** The 2001–05 HBO series was strictly for adults, depicting the goings on at a Los Angeles funeral home, such as embalming and funeral services, as well as the personal lives of the family who ran it, which included divorce, affairs, domestic violence, and tragic deaths. Shortly after the first two seasons were released on DVD, Rittenhouse Archives produced an

In the 1960s, astronauts trained for moon voyages by walking on Hawaiian lava fields.

81-card series depicting the characters and pivotal moments from all 26 episodes of the show. If you bought a whole set when it came out, you could get autographed cards from the show's regular cast and bit players.

Hollywood Zombies (2007). Have you ever wondered what today's stars would look like if they died and came back to life as rotting zombies? This 81-card set from Topps could answer your question in gory detail, but with silly pun-based names. Stars include: Martha Skewered (Martha Stewart), Melt Gibson (Mel Gibson), Johnny Death (Johnny Depp), Rachael Rot (Rachael Ray), Oprah Winfreak (Oprah Winfrey), Killiam Fatner (William Shatner), and Mike Die-son (Mike Tyson).

Famous Celebrity Tombstones (1993). If you like your celebrity death memorabilia a little less bloody, this 42-card series from Mother Productions just showed photographs of movie stars' gravesites, with information about the celebrity on the other side. Tombstones included James Dean's, Marilyn Monroe's, Liberace's, Sharon Tate's, and Bruce Lee's. A complete set came inside a red felt-lined cardboard coffin.

Flags of All Nations (1910s). Each card depicted the flag of a different country, as well as facts about the country's population and history. These are notable for two reasons: Many of the countries in Flags of All Nations no longer exist (such as Rhodesia), and the flags are all rendered in black-and-white, which doesn't really lend itself to flag art.

A few more unusual card sets:

- **Creature Feature (1973).** Stills from classic monster movies with "funny" captions and cheesy jokes on the back.
- **Napoleon (1915).** Great moments in the French emperor's life. Example: #14, "The Surrender of Vienna."
- ***Sgt. Pepper's Lonely Hearts Club Band* (1978).** A 66-card set featuring scenes from the Bee Gees' bomb movie of the same name.
- ***The Osbournes* (2002).** The first trading cards based on a reality TV show.

Horses can remember people who have treated them well. (They remember the jerks, too.)

UNCLE JOHN'S PAGE OF LISTS

Some random bits from the BRI's bottomless trivia files.

8 TOP BOX-OFFICE STARS OF ALL TIME

1. John Wayne
2. Clint Eastwood
3. Tom Cruise
4. Gary Cooper
5. Bing Crosby
6. Tom Hanks
7. Clark Gable
8. Burt Reynolds

4 ODD OLYMPIC EVENTS

1. Town Planning (1928)
2. Live Pigeon Shooting (1900)
3. Solo Synchronized Swimming (1984)
4. Firefighting (1900)

6 POLITICIANS WHO HOSTED *SATURDAY NIGHT LIVE*

1. Ralph Nader
2. George McGovern
3. Jesse Jackson
4. John McCain
5. Al Gore
6. Al Sharpton

5 WORDS COINED BY *SUPERMAN* COMICS

1. Bizarro
2. Brainiac
3. Kryptonite
4. Superpowers
5. Smallville

6 CELEBRITIES WITH SPECIES NAMED AFTER THEM

1. Barack Obama (Lichen)
2. Roy Orbison (Beetle)
3. Greta Garbo (Wasp)
4. Frank Zappa (Jellyfish)
5. John Cleese (Lemur)
6. Hugh Hefner (Rabbit)

4 FOODS THAT ARE TOXIC TO DOGS

1. Avocados
2. Grapes
3. Macadamia nuts
4. Persimmons

3 JAPANESE SOFT DRINKS

1. Pepsi Ice Cucumber
2. Water Salad
3. Deeppresso Coffee

5 BEST-SELLING BOOK SERIES

1. Harry Potter
2. Goosebumps
3. Perry Mason
4. Berenstain Bears
5. Choose Your Own Adventure

6 THINGS INVENTED IN CANADA

1. Instant mashed potatoes
2. Paint roller
3. Egg cartons
4. Caulking gun
5. IMAX movies
6. Plexiglas

3 VANITY PLATES BANNED IN UTAH

1. BGBOOTY
2. CARGASM
3. UTSUX

STALL OF FAME: THE *U-1206*

This submarine may never be as famous as the Titanic, *but the uncanny story of how—and why—it sank has earned it a place in Uncle John's Stall of Fame.*

GOING TO SEA

On April 6, 1945, a German navy submarine named the *U-1206* departed from the port city of Kristiansand, in Nazi-occupied Norway, and began its first combat patrol. Assigned to the waters of the North Atlantic, its mission was to seek out and destroy British and American ships on the high seas.

For the 50-man crews aboard submarines like the *U-1206*, life wasn't just extremely dangerous, it was also very unpleasant: Quarters were cramped, and the bathrooms were no exception. There were only two *heads* (toilets), and because one of the heads was right next to the galley, the space was often used to store food. When it was, the toilet was unavailable, meaning that the entire crew had to share the remaining toilet.

UNDER PRESSURE

The plumbing on German subs of that era differed from American and British subs in one important respect: The German toilets discharged their contents directly into the sea, instead of into a holding tank. Not having such a tank saved precious space, but it came at a price. The toilets could only be used when the submarine was traveling on or near the ocean surface. When the submarine was submerged, the pressure outside the hull was too great for the toilets to be able to flush.

If nature called under such circumstances, crew members had to use buckets, tin cans, and whatever other containers they could get their hands on. They had to carefully store the contents of all those containers—don't spill!—until the submarine surfaced, when they could be poured into the toilets and flushed, or taken topside and emptied into the sea.

The ventilation systems on World War II German subs were notoriously inadequate, which meant that even in the best of circumstances, the air was foul with diesel fumes, human body odor, and other smells. When the toilets were unavailable and all those buckets and cans were filled to overflowing with you-know-what, the stench was even worse.

HEADS UP!

The *U-1206* had a new-and-improved plumbing system. Unlike many subs in the fleet, it had high-pressure toilets that could be used at greater depths than the standard heads could. But the new system was very difficult to operate. The toilets came with complicated instruction manuals, and a few members of the crew had to be trained so that they could serve as toilet-flushing "specialists."

Barely a week into the *U-1206*'s first patrol, Captain Karl-Adolf Schlitt (who was commanding a sub for the first time) had to use the head while the sub was cruising at a depth of 200 feet, some eight miles off the coast of Scotland. Rather than request the assistance of the toilet specialist, Schlitt tried to follow the instructions in the manual to flush the toilet himself. Something went wrong—and when Schlitt asked the toilet specialist for help, something went wrong again. The specialist opened the outside valve—the one that opened to the sea—while the inside valve was open, causing a torrent of water to flood into the sub.

WHAT A GAS

It was then that another flaw in the *U-1206*'s design became apparent. When a submarine is submerged, it runs on electric motors powered by giant banks of batteries. And the *U-1206*'s batteries were in a compartment directly below the malfunctioning toilet. The seawater quickly combined with battery acid and created deadly chlorine gas, which began to spread throughout the sub.

As the gas filled the submarine, Schlitt had no choice but to order the submarine to surface so that the gas could be vented and replaced with breathable air. Because they surfaced within sight of the Scottish coastline, they were quickly spotted by Allied aircraft and attacked. One crew member died in the melee that followed; three others fell overboard and drowned.

The *U-1206* was badly damaged in the attack and could not

Christopher Columbus wrote the first known report of a hurricane in 1495.

dive. Seeing no way to save his submarine, Captain Schlitt ordered the crew into the lifeboats; then he scuttled the ship, making it the only warship in naval history to be doomed by its own malfunctioning toilet. Thirty-six members of the crew were rescued by small boats in the area; 10 others made it to shore in their lifeboats and were captured.

POT LUCK

In its eight days on patrol, the *U-1206* never did manage to attack any Allied ships. Not that it would have made any difference to the Nazi war effort, which had just three more weeks to go. On April 30, Adolf Hitler committed suicide in his *Führerbunker* in Berlin; seven days later, Germany surrendered and the war in Europe was over.

It's possible that the toilet that sent the *U-1206* to the bottom of the Atlantic may have saved the surviving 46 members of the crew. Though Winston Churchill later admitted that "the only thing that ever frightened me during the war was the U-boat peril," by the summer of 1943 the Battle of the Atlantic had turned decisively in favor of the Allies, who were now able to sink the U-boats faster than the Germans could replace them. The odds of a German submariner surviving the war were slim: 75 percent of the entire U-boat fleet was sunk during the war, and 30,000 of the submarine service's 40,000 crew members went to a watery grave with them.

Thanks, perhaps, to a malfunctioning toilet, the *U-1206*'s 46 surviving crew members were not among them.

* * *

AN UNAPPEALING TALE

Even after World War II and the end of food rationing, exotic and imported foods were hard to come by in England. Shortly after the end of the war, Laura Herbert managed to find three bananas at a London market, one for each of the children she had with famed writer Evelyn Waugh (*Brideshead Revisited*). When he found the bananas, Waugh sat the children down and showed them the bananas. Then, he carefully covered the bananas in whipped cream and sugar…and ate them all in one sitting, all by himself.

LOCAL HEROES

Right place + right time + cool head = life saved.

MILKING IT

Truck driver Michael Coyle's boss describes him as "easy-going and never in a hurry." But he didn't waste a second when his 18-wheel milk tanker came upon a serious accident in Fermanagh, Ireland, in April 2011. Coyle saw a wrecked car that was on fire…with two men trapped inside. Coyle pulled his truck up next to the accident, ran to the back of his tanker, unscrewed the valve, and then sprayed the flaming car with milk until the fire went out. Victims of a hit-and-run collision, the two men were rushed to the hospital with serious injuries, but were reported to be in stable condition.

LOVE, HERTZ

Firefighters were already planning to honor Gus Hertz as a hero for his save on Wednesday when they found out he did it again on Thursday. The two incidents occurred in June 2012 while Hertz—a 37-year-old bank employee from Roanoke, Virginia—was vacationing with his wife and kids in St. Petersburg, Florida. In the first save, Hertz saw a car careen off the road and land in the Gulf of Mexico. He swam out to the car and pulled the driver to safety. A day later Hertz was fishing in his boat when he saw a small plane crash in the water. He sped over and rescued the two occupants before the plane went under. Both times, Hertz left the scene before the press could interview him, but firefighters found out who he was and gave him a commendation. "I was just in the right place at the right time," said Hertz humbly. "Dumb luck."

LITTLE RUNAROUND

Ivan Teece was riding on the upper level of a double-decker bus in London when he noticed a crowd on the side of the road gathered around a distraught woman. She was yelling, "My baby's not breathing!" Then Teece saw the baby. It was blue. And no one was doing anything to help. On a whim, the 24-year-old airport worker yelled for the bus to stop, jumped down the stairs, and ran over to the mother. "It's going to be okay," he told her. Then he gently took the infant in his arms and started running toward a nearby medical center. The baby was still blue. "There was a moment when I thought she was going to die in my arms," said Teece. "But then I heard a gasp of air and then she was groaning." Doctors discovered that the baby, 10-month-old Summer Hodgson, had tonsillitis, which had blocked her airways.

PHYSICS TO THE RESCUE

A Boeing engineer named Duane Innes was driving in Seattle, Washington, in 2010 when he was nearly sideswiped by another car. Innes sped up and looked into his rearview mirror and saw that the other driver was unconscious. And they were approaching a busy intersection at high speed. Innes knew there was only one way to prevent a catastrophe. "Basic physics," he later told the *Seattle Times*. "If I could get in front of him and let him hit me, the difference in speed would just be a few miles an hour, and we could slow down together." So Innes let the other car rear-end his minivan. Then he decelerated slowly and brought both vehicles to a stop on the shoulder. The other driver, 80-year-old Bill Pace, had lost circulation and passed out. It turned out that Pace is somewhat of a hero himself: He's a retiree who volunteers for the Special Olympics. Said Innes: "For all the good that Bill has done, he's probably deserving of a few extra lives."

CATCH ME IF YOU CAN

Kristen Beach, 21, of Medford, Oregon, was standing outside her apartment building in July 2012 when she saw a two-year-old boy hanging from the ledge of a three-story building. Beach (who has a two-year-old of her own) ran over and positioned herself underneath the crying child, whom the press identified as Freddy. "I said, 'It's okay, baby. If you fall, I will catch you!'" Then, after a few tense moments, little Freddy let go and fell 30 feet into Beach's outstretched arms. Her knees buckled from the impact, and she fell to the ground but was able to hang on to the child. (Freddy's mom was charged with child neglect.) Beach was in a daze when questioned by reporters. "I still can't believe that happened."

*   *   *

"Soldiers fight and the kings are heroes." —**The Talmud**

A real train crossing a bridge was blown up for the '57 film *The Bridge on the River Kwai.*

"I'LL HAVE THE HUSBAND AND WIFE LUNG SLICE"

In China, menus in restaurants frequented by Western tourists are carefully translated into English and easy to understand. But if you eat where the locals eat, you may experience a phenomenon known as "Chinglish"—translations that are incomprehensible and often hilarious.

BONE APPÉTIT

Translating Chinese into English is made difficult because 1) many Chinese symbols are *pictographs*, or graphic depictions of the words they denote, and 2) pictographs are combined to create symbols for new words. The word "calf," for example, combines the symbols for "cow" and "boy." That's how "cowboy leg" finds its way onto some menus where leg of veal is served.

Chinese symbols can also mean more than one thing. The character for "dry" (one of the two symbols used in the name for the *dry pot* style of cooking) can also mean "do." In English "do" can be a slang term for...well, this book is G-rated, so we can't really spell it out. But that's why, when a dish called "dry-pot rabbit" is on the menu, the English translation sometimes describes the rabbit performing an intimate act on the cooking pot that, had it involved another bunny instead of the cook pot, would have increased the population of rabbits in the vicinity.

GOOD EATIN'

How would you translate buffalo wings into Mandarin? How about corn dogs, ladyfingers, tater tots, toad-in-the-hole, or spotted dick (two English pub favorites)? It's easy to see where misunderstandings can arise. The Chinese, it turns out, also love colorful idiomatic names. According to legend, a popular tofu dish called Bean Curd Made by a Pockmarked Woman really was created by such a woman. And because a Sichuan dish of minced pork on bean-thread noodles looks like ants climbing a tree, that's what it's called. So sometimes even when a dish is correctly translated, it can seem pretty odd to the uninitiated.

Sad fact: A single cup of ice cream has more cholesterol than 10 glazed donuts.

Here are some real examples of items found on menus in China:

Salty Egg King Steams the Vegetable Sponge

Beauty Vegetables

Blow up a Flatfish with No Result

Bacteria Dictyophore Wu Chicken

Ginger Burping Milk (hot)

Sydney and White Tree Fungus Braise Pig Heart

Elder Brother the Ground Is Second

The Palace Quick-Fries Dices Chicken Powered

Hand Pills to Fight Pork (hand-made pork balls)

Wood Mustache Meat

Steamed Red Crap with Ginger

Pot Zhai Double Dong Belly

Government Abuse Chicken

Fishing Fans to Burn Dry Sausages

Plaster w/Coconut Juice

Strange Flavor Noodles

Spiced Salt Blows Up Pig Hand

The Black Fryings the Breeze Ball

Health Demolition Tofu Recipe

Husband and Wife Lung Slice

West the Flower Fries the Rib a Meat

Open Space Pfiddlehead Stewed Meat

Chicken Rude and Unreasonable

Dishes with Human Pickles

Decayed Thick Gravy Fillet

Peasant Family Stir-Fries Flesh for a Short Time

Carbon Burns Fresh Particularly Most

Good to Eat Mountain

Strange Flavor of Inside Freasuse

A Previous Small

Fragrant Bone in Garlic in Strange Flavor

The Incense Burns Screw

The Farmer Is Small to Fry King

Man Fruit Braise the North Almond

Slippery Meat in King's Vegetables in Pillar

Big Bowl Four Treasure Frog

A West Bean Pays the Fish a Soup

MUSIC ON TV

Music-based shows have been a part of television almost from the beginning. Here's a look at a few of the biggest musical shows of all time.

TOAST OF THE TOWN (June 20, 1948). The program that would later become *The Ed Sullivan Show*—a cultural institution watched by millions of Americans from all walks of life in the 1950s and '60s every Sunday at 8:00 p.m.—began humbly. One of TV's first variety shows, *Toast of the Town* was hosted by Sullivan, a New York entertainment columnist. Fewer than a million people even had television sets at the time, most of them in New York City, Los Angeles, and Pittsburgh. The show's first act was comedy duo Dean Martin and Jerry Lewis, then Richard Rodgers and Oscar Hammerstein II took the stage and talked about their new Broadway musical *South Pacific*, followed by the first singer to perform on the show—nightclub singer Monica Lewis (sister of the show's producer, Marlo Lewis). She sang a song called "I Could Kiss You For That."

AMERICAN BANDSTAND (September 22, 1952). The show's precursor, *Bandstand*, debuted on Philadelphia TV station WFIL on September 22, 1952. Airing 2:30–4:30 p.m. weekdays, it was a showcase for promotional films of pop and big-band music acts and sometimes an in-studio guest, hosted by local disc jockey Bob Horn. That format didn't bring in viewers, so after two weeks Horn revamped the show to make it more like his radio show—he played hit records and showed teenagers dancing to them. It was a smash. The on-air DJ who cued up the records was another local, 33-year-old Dick Clark.

In 1956 Horn got arrested for DUI (ironic, considering he was the face of WFIL's anti-drunk-driving campaign) and was fired. That was Clark's big break. He became the host of *Bandstand* and immediately made changes. First thing he did: put more rock 'n' roll music on the show. Then he integrated the dancers—marking the first time blacks and whites appeared on a dance floor together on TV. Clark also wanted to take the show national, so he personally drove film of the show to ABC executives in New York. In 1957, when the network asked its affiliates for pitches for new afternoon programs, Clark successfully lobbied for *Bandstand*, which became *American Bandstand*. It debuted on August 5, 1957, as a 90-minute daily show. First in-studio guest: R&B singer Billy Williams, who sang his #3 hit cover of Fats Waller's "I'm Gonna Sit Right Down and Write Myself a Letter." (It had a good beat, and you could dance to it.)

Over its 30-year life, *American Bandstand* played tens of thousands of records and hosted hundreds of singers and groups, spreading and helping popularize rock 'n' roll. With the arrival of cable and music video networks MTV and VH1 in the 1980s, *American Bandstand* started to become passé. When ABC wanted to cut the show to a half hour in 1987, Clark refused, and took the show into syndication, then to the USA Network. It went off the air for good in 1989, by which time Clark was a media mogul and one of the most famous people in the world. Through Dick Clark Productions, he created and hosted a number of game shows, radio shows, TV shows, and an annual New Year's Eve special for ABC. Clark and fellow DJ-turned-media-mogul Ryan Seacrest worked on reviving *American Bandstand* in 2005. It failed to come together, but one element, a national dance contest, became the Fox summer series *So You Think You Can Dance?*

***THE LAWRENCE WELK SHOW* (July 2, 1955).** After four years of broadcasting only in Los Angeles, the showcase for "Champagne music" (mostly polka) went national. The first song was an accordion duet featuring Welk and the show's staff accordionist, Myron Floren, performing "The 12th Street Rag."

Each episode had a theme, such as "Songs From World War II" or "Down Mexico Way," and Welk and his "Musical Family" of singers and musicians would wear appropriate costumes. The show was never a hit with younger audiences, but it was a Top 10 show among Americans over 50, because it featured older music—never the rock or R&B that dominated American pop charts in the '60s and '70s. When ABC cancelled the show in 1971, Welk took it into syndication, where it ran until 1982. In 1986 an Oklahoma public TV station picked up the rights to the show and made it available to public stations nationwide. Many still air reruns of *The Lawrence Show* in its old time slot, Saturday at 7:00 p.m.

For music from TV in the '60s and '70s, turn to page 280.

THE DOPE ON ROPE

This article has a real good twist.

According to *Merriam-Webster*, rope is "a large stout cord of strands of fibers or wire twisted or braided together." If it isn't made from strands twisted or braided together, then it isn't properly "rope."

Rope is also referred to as *cordage*. Cordage below 3⁄16" in diameter—twine and clothesline being examples—isn't considered true rope. Cordage above 3⁄16" in diameter is.

Before the invention of plastic, materials used to make rope ranged from plant sources, (palm trees, hemp, flax, grasses, cotton) to silk, animal hides, hair, and intestines.

Twisted rope, also known as "laid rope," is made in three steps: 1) fibers are twisted into *yarn*; 2) lengths of yarn are twisted together in the opposite direction into *strands*; and 3) the strands are twisted in the opposite direction into rope. These opposite-direction twists create tension, which holds rope together and adds to its strength. Twisted rope generally uses a few strands—three is very common—and the strands can be quite thick.

Braided rope is made by braiding (rather than twisting) thin strands together. There are many different patterns, each having distinct advantages of strength, durability, and flexibility. It's common to use from 8 to 32 strands in a single rope.

The oldest evidence of rope-making dates to roughly 17,000 years ago. The decayed remains of a rope about 1⁄4" in diameter, made from two twisted strands of an unknown plant fiber, were found in one of the famous cave paintings in Lascaux, France.

By about 10,000 years ago, rope was being used by people in most parts of the world. Like the wheel, it became one of the vital tools in the advancement of civilization.

Some examples of rope tools that drastically changed the lives of ancient people: lassoes and snares for hunting, nets for fishing, cattle-harness lines for pulling plows, rope-and-pulley systems that allowed for the hoisting of heavy objects, and the many rope tools used in shipping, such as sail rigging and mooring lines.

Ancient Egyptian drawings show people using simple tools to make twisted rope. Further drawings show that ropes were used extensively in the building of the pyramids.

In 2005 archeologists digging in caves on Egypt's Red Sea coast discovered dozens of neat coils of well-preserved grass-fiber rope, each about an inch in diameter and 100 feet long. They had been stored in the caves by sailors more than 4,000 years ago.

At least 500 years ago, the Incas made rope bridges as part of their road system through the Andes.

By the 12th century, European ropemakers used *rope-walks*—long narrow buildings, some several hundred feet long—where strands could be fully laid out. This allowed the ropemakers to avoid unwanted twisting and knotting as the ropes were being made. The first American ropewalk was built in 1635 in Salem, Massachusetts.

Rope is also made from metal. You've probably seen "wire rope," or "cable," on suspension bridges.

More than half of all rope manufactured today is used in shipping-related industries. On boats and ships, ropes are called "lines."

According to the Tug of War International Federation—official tug of war competitions use only rope made from Manila hemp. (It's actually made from the leaves of the abacá, a type of banana plant native to the Philippines). Primary reason: Manila rope is resistant to both stretching and snapping.

Largest rope ever: the rice-straw ropes (against TWIF rules!) made for the annual "Great Tug of War" in Okinawa. The rope for the 2012 event was 4.5 feet thick, 656 feet long, and weighed more than 80,000 pounds. It took several thousand people to move it.

* * *

From the police blotter: "Report of rabid woodchuck on Devonshire Lane. It was actually a porcupine that was not sick."

FAN CLUB FUNNIES

It used to be just Trekkies, Dead Heads, and Hulkamaniacs. But if you're a huge fan of something today, the Internet makes it possible for you to connect with other fans and share clever nicknames like these.

NBC's *Community* has a cult following, members of which call themselves **Human Beings**. Reason: The show takes place at a community college that tries desperately to be politically correct, down to its extremely neutral team name, the Human Beings.

• **Peabodies** sounds like a fancy intellectual kind of name, as in the prestigious Peabody Award or the super-intelligent cartoon dog Mr. Peabody. It's also what Black Eyed Peas fans call themselves. (Get it?)

• The Killers is a rock band. The group's fans are **Victims**.

• The satirical ultra-patriotic *The Colbert Report* has fans called, alternately, **Heroes**, **Colbert Nation**, and **It-Getters** (because, according to host Stephen Colbert, "they get it").

• "Bro" (short for "brother") is a slang term that means "guy" or "dude." For some reason, there's a following among these bros for the latest My Little Pony cartoon show, *Friendship is Magic*. These fans call themselves **Bronies**.

• Hardcore fans of the band They Might Be Giants call themselves **Giantheads**, and derisively call casual fans **Floodies**, because *those* fans only started following the group after its third and only platinum album, *Flood*.

• Fans of Barry Manilow are "loony" for the soft-rock singer. Thus: **Maniloonies**.

• Pop singer Bruno Mars has had two #1 hits: "Just the Way You Are" and "Grenade." Both are on his 2010 album *Doo-Wops & Hooligans*, which also provides his fanbase nickname, **Hooligans**.

• People who never miss an episode of *Wheel of Fortune* are called "elderly." Just kidding. They call themselves **Wheel Watchers**, taken from a 1987 ad campaign with the jingle, "I'm a Wheel Watcher," a parody of the '60s pop song, "I'm a Girl Watcher."

• Sixteen million people bought Alanis Morissette's *Jagged Little Pill*. Only the truly devoted, about three million, bought the follow-up, *Supposed Former Infatuation Junkie*. Those fans call themselves **Junkies**.

• Viewers of HBO's epic series *Game of Thrones* split themselves into two camps. **The Unsullied** are those who have not read the George R.R. Martin novels upon which the show is based, and **The Bookwalkers** are the ones who have.

• Onstage, rapper Nicki Minaj likes to dress like a bizarre version of Barbie, with bright yellow wigs and pink clothes. Minaj calls her female fans **Barbies** and her male fans **Kens**.

• People who love the rock band No Doubt are known as **No Doubters**.

• Benedict Cumberbatch is a British actor who shot to fame starring in the BBC's production of *Sherlock*, which aired on PBS in the U.S. At first, his female admirers called themselves **Cumberbitches**, but have since shown preference for two slightly gentler names: **The Ben-Addicted** or **Cucumbers**.

* * *

I'M FIRED!

"Faced with severe budget problems, Dan O'Leary, the city manager of Keller, Texas (pop. 27,000), was unable to avoid the sad job of handing out pink slips. He had determined that one of Keller's three city managers had to go—so he laid himself off. According to a March 2012 Fort Worth *Star-Telegram* report, O'Leary neither intended to retire nor had other offers pending, and he had aroused no negative suspicions as to motive. He simply realized the city could be managed more cost-effectively by the two lower-paid officials."

—News of the Weird

MEET THE MUCKRAKERS, PART I

The late 1800s through the early 1900s was the "muckraker" era. The term described the investigation and reporting of scandalous activity ("muck") by political and business leaders, usually with a "David and Goliath" or a common-man versus the rich-and-powerful flavor. It was the birth of modern investigative journalism. Here are a few stories from that time.

SUBJECT: Bloomingdale Asylum, an institution for the mentally ill, located in New York City

MUCKRAKER: In 1872 Julius Chambers, 22, was declared insane and committed to Bloomingdale. Ten days later, his lawyer got him released. In the weeks that followed, a series of articles appeared in the *New York Tribune*...written by Julius Chambers.

EXPOSED! The 22-year-old was actually a reporter, and with the help of his editor and a lawyer—and after "practicing" acting insane—he'd gotten himself committed to Bloomingdale. His articles in the *Tribune* detailed the abuse of patients that went on behind the asylum's doors.

RAMIFICATIONS: Chambers's groundbreaking undercover journalism led to firings of Bloomingdale staff and improvements in conditions, and even got 12 inmates freed—after they were found to be perfectly sane. In 1876 he wrote a novel on the investigation titled *A Mad World and Its Inhabitants*. Historians consider Chambers the first modern investigative journalist.

SUBJECT: Blackwell Island Insane Asylum, New York

MUCKRAKER: In 1887 Nellie Bly, a 23-year-old reporter for Joseph Pulitzer's *New York World* newspaper, duplicated Julius Chambers's investigation—but with far greater impact. Bly secured lodging in a home for working women in Manhattan, pretended she didn't know who she was, and, in a frighteningly simple process, got herself committed to Blackwell Island Asylum, on what is now Roosevelt Island in New York's East River.

..."Elvis Presley TCB Tribute Revolver." (Price: $2,195.)

EXPOSED! After ten days, Bly's editor got her released, and over the next several weeks, *New York World* readers learned how she was committed and of the horrific conditions inside Blackwell—which included forced freezing baths, rancid food, severe beatings, and the cruel torment of patients.

RAMIFICATIONS: A grand jury was launched to investigate the asylum, which eventually led to major changes in conditions there. Changes were also made to the committal process, and funding for care of the insane in New York City was increased by more than $850,000 the following year. (Note: Bly's real name was Elizabeth Jane Cochran. It was the custom at the time for female writers to use pseudonyms.)

SUBJECT: The Ku Klux Klan

MUCKRAKER: In 1920 Herbert Bayard Swope, one of the nation's most respected journalists, became editor of the *New York World* (the same paper Nellie Bly wrote for). In 1917 he'd won the very first Pulitzer Prize for Reporting for a series of stories on the German Empire during World War I. Now in charge of one of America's most powerful newspapers, he decided to focus on what he saw as a new but powerful menace: the Ku Klux Klan. After being decimated in the late 1870s (it was founded in 1865), the white-supremacist organization had been restarted in Georgia in 1916 and was suddenly back in force. By 1920 the KKK had hundreds of thousands of members, and the number of cross-burnings, church bombings, and lynchings was growing. Swope launched an in-depth investigation into the Klan's doings.

EXPOSED! Over 21 days in October 1921, the *World* published "The Secrets of the Ku Klux Klan Exposed." Readers learned of secret handshakes, bank accounts, terror tactics, and the identities of politicians and other prominent citizens with ties to the organization.

RAMIFICATIONS: The story—which was syndicated and therefore read by millions all across the country—is credited with helping to turn public sentiment against the Klan and contributing to its eventual demise. The story won the *World* the 1922 Pulitzer Prize for Public Service.

Worldwide, more molten steel is poured in 1 hour than all the gold found in recorded history.

FIRST DATE? *LAST* DATE!

Just about everyone has a story about a first date that went really badly…but probably not nearly as badly as these folks'.

First Date: In September 2011, Dean Piraneo, 48, of Waxhaw, North Carolina, took a female acquaintance out for dinner to a steakhouse in Charlotte.

…Last Date: The trouble started when the pair got into Piraneo's SUV to drive home. That's when Piraneo, perhaps trying to impress his date with the gun he keeps in the vehicle for his own protection, accidentally shot himself. According to the police report, Piraneo "was reaching for his gun, which was chained up in a bicycle lock underneath the car seat. The gun went off as he was pulling on it, which shot him in the left leg."

Shooting Blanks: Piraneo was taken to the hospital with a non-life-threatening leg injury, but his budding romance was not expected to survive. No charges were filed.

First Date: In August 2009, a 27-year-old woman from Ferndale, Michigan, met a 23-year-old man named "Chris" at a Detroit casino. The two hit it off and exchanged phone numbers; Chris sent a picture of himself to her phone. A week later, he asked her out to dinner.

…Last Date: The pair went to the Buffalo Wild Wings restaurant in Ferndale. Because Chris didn't own a car, the woman picked him up in hers. When it was time to leave, Chris told the woman he'd left his wallet in her car and asked for the keys so that he could retrieve it and pay the bill. According to the police report, "From where she was sitting she saw him get in her car and he drove off at a high rate of speed," sticking his date with the check *and* stealing her car.

Photo Finish: "Chris" probably wishes he'd never used his phone to send a picture of himself to the woman's phone. That was how police tracked him down and identified him by his real name, Terrance McCoy. Police recovered the car (minus the stereo) two weeks later. At last report, McCoy was in jail awaiting trial. If convicted, he could get five years.

DNA paternity tests are now commonly performed on show dogs and racehorses.

First Date: Not long after Leah Gibbs, 23, of Tylorstown, Wales (U.K.), split up with the father of her two kids, an old friend of hers named Adam Minton, 21, contacted her through Facebook. After chatting a few times online, he asked her out; she agreed to meet him for drinks the next day.

...Last Date: When Gibbs arrived at Minton's house, he asked her to give him a ride "to his friend's house to pick something up." She dropped him off in front of Ladbrokes, the local betting parlor, then waited in the car for him to return. A few minutes later, she saw Minton come running out of Ladbrokes with a knife in one hand and a bag of money in the other. "He dived, rather than climbed, into the passenger seat, then screamed, 'Go! Go! Go!'" Gibbs told *The Mirror* newspaper. Police caught up with the pair a short time later and arrested them both: Minton for robbing the bookie—and Gibbs for *driving the getaway car*. "I began sobbing hysterically and said there had been a terrible mistake, but Adam just sat next to me completely silent," Gibbs told the reporter.

True Confessions: Gibbs spent a night in jail before Minton 'fessed up and told authorities that she'd had nothing to do with the heist. All charges against Gibbs were dropped; today she's back at home with her kids. Minton, who unbeknownst to Gibbs had a drug problem and a criminal record, got 4½ years.

First Date: In June 2008, a divorced 53-year-old former jockey named Angel Valdez invited Patricia Curtice, 55, who tends bar in Florida, to go horseback riding near his home in Spring Hill, about 40 miles north of Tampa. Curtice rode a Quarter Horse named Duke; Valdez rode a mare named Emma.

...Last Date: Valdez was a perfect gentleman, and his horses were well behaved. So what went wrong? As they were riding through a wooded area, two donkeys appeared out of the tall grass and charged the horses. Valdez jumped off his horse, but before Curtice could get off hers, the donkeys bit the horse in his hindquarters. Duke reared up and tossed Patricia to the ground, where she was stomped by all three animals until Duke galloped off, with the donkeys in hot pursuit.

Who knew donkeys could be trained as guard animals? Turns out they lived on a nearby cattle ranch owned by a multimillionaire auto dealer named Frank Morsani, where they were used to

Eau d'armpit: Sweat was once used as an ingredient in perfume and love potions.

protect the herd from coyotes and other varmints. The donkeys may have been stressed that day because a number of cattle had escaped through a hole in the fence. Sensing a threat when Curtice and Valdez rode by, they attacked.

Horse Sense: Curtice suffered seven broken ribs and bruises to her lungs and spine, injuries that left her unable to tend bar. She also racked up more than $80,000 in hospital bills. At last report, she was suing Morsani for negligence for letting his animals get out. The good news? Curtice and Valdez are engaged. "I told him, 'We're together. Because I'm not going on a second date!'"

* * *

NAME THAT PRODUCT

"Kleenex" is probably the most famous example of a "genericized trademark"—a product so popular that people use the brand-name to identify it. You've probably heard someone ask for a "Kleenex" more often than they ask for a "tissue." Here are some other name brands that have gone generic…and what, technically speaking, you should be calling them.

- **Bubble Wrap:** *Inflated cushioning*
- **Dumpster:** *Front-loader waste container*
- **Chapstick:** *Lip balm*
- **Lava Lamp:** *Liquid motion lamp*
- **Frisbee:** *Flying disc*
- **Hacky Sack:** *Footbag*
- **Jet Ski:** *Personal watercraft*
- **Jacuzzi:** *Whirlpool bath*
- **AstroTurf:** *Artificial turf*
- **JumboTron:** *Large-screen television*
- **Onesie:** *Infant bodysuit*
- **Superglue:** *Cyanoacrylate adhesive*
- **Rollerblades:** *Inline skates*
- **Tivo:** *Digital video recorder*
- **Speedos:** *Swim briefs*
- **Styrofoam:** *Extruded polystyrene foam*

JOKE ORIGINS

Classic jokes are essentially oral traditions that get passed from person to person for decades until someone decides to write them down. We asked our resident jokestorian, Bozo Newman, to find the origins of a few classics. Honk honk!

KNOCK-KNOCK!

During Prohibition in the 1930s, if you wanted to get into a speakeasy, you would knock on the door, someone would ask, "Who's there?" and you'd have to say a password. According to joke historian Charlie Orr, drunken patrons often had fun with the password custom as the night wore on, and that's how the knock-knock joke was born. Orr claimed that the very first knock-knock joke was told in the restroom of a Philadelphia hotel. The first guy said, "Knock-knock." His friend replied, "Who's there?" "Ranger." "Ranger who?" "Ranger clothes before you leave here!"

TOM SWIFTIES

Uncle John's favorite type of pun consists of a made-up quotation followed by a clever attribute that reinforces what was said:

- "I feel like raising the dead," said Tom, cryptically.
- "That's the last time I stick my arm in a lion's mouth," said Tom off-handedly.

These puns parody the writing style in the Tom Swift book series. Created in 1910 by Edward Stratemeyer (who also created the Hardy Boys and Nancy Drew), Tom Swift is a teenaged hero who uses his wits to thwart bad guys. Stratemeyer used clever wordplay, such as, "'We must hurry,' said Tom swiftly." The pun style was originally called Tom Swiftly, later shortened to Tom Swifty.

POLISH JOKES

Blame Adolf Hitler for these. In his quest to conquer Poland in the 1930s, Hitler pushed the racist "dumb Polack" stereotype so the rest of Europe wouldn't sympathize with the country's fate. The Nazi propaganda machine claimed, among other things, that Polish soldiers on horseback had once attacked German tanks with swords. That stereotype spread to the U.S. after the war, and by the 1960s, Poles had become a punchline. The TV show *Laugh-in* (1967–73) featured a regular segment dedicated to Polish jokes. Books of Polish jokes followed over the next decade. The perception began to change in 1978 when Cardinal Karol Wojtyla became the first Polish pope (John Paul II). The fad tapered off after the fall of the Soviet Union in 1991.

YO' MAMA

These jokes became popular in the 1960s in inner cities as part of a trash-talking game called the Dozens. Two African Americans would trade insults until one of them couldn't think of a comeback. The Dozens, which is considered a progenitor of free-style rap music, goes back centuries. According to Mona Lisa Saloy's book, *Still Laughing to Keep from Crying*, "The Dozens has its origins in the slave trade of New Orleans, where deformed slaves—punished with dismemberment for disobedience—were grouped in lots of a 'cheap dozen.' To be sold as part of the 'dozens' was the lowest blow possible." And in the insult game that came out of it, there is no lower blow than one directed at your opponent's mama:

- Yo' mama so hairy, Bigfoot was taking *her* picture!
- Yo' mama so stupid, she cooks with Old Spice!
- Yo' Mama so fat, she went to the movies and sat next to everyone!

MORE CLASSIC JOKES

• **The Chicken Joke:** First appeared in print in 1847 in a New York magazine called *The Knickerbocker*, on a page titled "Gossip with Readers and Correspondents." A reader wrote in:

> There are "quips and quillets" which seem actual conundrums, but yet are none. Of such is this: "Why does a chicken cross the street?" Are you "out of town?" Do you "give it up?" Well, then: "Because it wants to get on the other side!"

• **The Newspaper Joke:** What's black and white and red all over? A newspaper, of course. The joke first appeared in an American humor anthology in 1917.

• **Elephant Jokes:** How do you get six elephants in a Volkswagen? Three in the front and three in the back. This fad began in 1960, when Wisconsin toymaker L.M. Becker Co. released a set of 50 elephant-joke trading cards. (That one is card #12.)

...countries: The French say "*toc-toc*"; the Japanese say "*kon-kon*."

WIKIALITY CHECK

We live in an age when you can alter "reality" with the click of a button.

ELEPHANTS

On a 2006 episode of his Comedy Central show *The Colbert Report*, Stephen Colbert made fun of mainstream news outlets for using the online website Wikipedia as a research source. Colbert's issue: The website allows anyone—expert or not—to edit any of its 22 million articles. "If everyone agrees that what's in Wikipedia is true," he said, "then anyone can change reality simply by editing Wikipedia."

He called this new reality "wikiality" and suggested his viewers edit the Wikipedia article on elephants to read: "Elephant population in Africa has tripled over the past six months." A fan complied. A Wikipedia staffer removed the line; another fan put it back. After this happened a few more times, Wikipedia "locked" the elephants article so no more edits could be made. Here are a few other instances of people creating their own wikialities.

SARAH PALIN

In 2012 the former VP candidate was touring historic sites in Boston when she mentioned that on Paul Revere's famous ride in 1775, he was "ringin' those bells." Palin's history was off: Revere didn't ring any bells. The press mocked her, but she stood by her version of the events. Meanwhile, one of her supporters edited the Wikipedia entry on Paul Revere to reflect Palin's version. Wikipedia fixed the article and locked out any further changes. (Colbert later tried to "help" Palin by asking his viewers to change the entry on bells to include Palin's account of Revere's ride.)

JUSTIN BIEBER

In 2011, after jazz singer and bassist Esperanza Spalding won the Best New Artist Grammy over Bieber, his fans were upset. In the hours that followed, Spalding's Wikipedia entry was edited more than 90 times with such new "facts" as: "JUSTIN BIEBER DESERVED IT GO DIE IN A HOLE!" Another disgruntled fan changed Spalding's middle name to Quesadilla.

In *Sesame Street's* first season, Oscar the Grouch was orange.

HALLE BERRY

An anonymous Wikipedia user named "Ciii" added this quotation to Berry's biography in 2006: "I've always loved to sing and this album will show people that I can do more than act." Based on that, several news outlets, including the *Washington Post*, *Rock & Roll Daily*, and *Rolling Stone* magazine, reported that the Oscar winner was about to record a pop album. That prompted an official denial from Berry, who has no plans to become a singer.

BATMAN

In 2007 some joker deleted all of the text from the article on the Caped Crusader and replaced it with this:

> ## Batman
> From Wikipedia, the free encyclopedia
>
> DUH NUH NUH NUH NUH NUH DUH NUH NUH NUH NUH NUH BATMAN! DUH NUH NUH NUH NUH NUH DUH NUH NUH NUH NUH NUH BATMAN! DUH NUH NUH NUH NUH NUH DUH NUH NUH NUH NUH NUH BATMAN! BATMAN! BATMAN! DUH NUH NUH NUH NUH NUH DUH NUH NUH NUH NUH NUH BATMAN! DUH NUH NUH NUH NUH NUH DUH NUH NUH NUH NUH NUH **BATMAN**!!!!!!!!!!!!!!!!!!!!!

(If you're not familiar, those are the "lyrics" to the theme song of the campy 1960s *Batman* TV show.)

TITIAN

In the British House of Commons in 2009, Labour Party head Gordon Brown said during a speech that 16th-century Italian painter Titian died when he was 90. Conservative leader David Cameron later claimed that Titian died when he was 86…and then mocked Brown for his "lack of education." Later that day, one of Cameron's staffers called the BBC News and told them to go to Titian's Wikipedia page…which proved that Cameron—not Brown—was correct. Suspicious, a BBC reporter discovered that Titian's Wikipedia entry had recently been changed to reflect Cameron's version of the truth. When pressed, Cameron admitted that one of his staffers was responsible. (Titian's actual birth date is unknown.)

So that's why the freeways are crowded: One out of every eight Americans lives in California.

THE HALLS OF CONGRESS

• **Rep. Joe Donnelly (D-IA)** deleted the fact that he broke with Democratic leadership on several budget issues to maintain his reputation as a more conservative "Blue Dog" Democrat.

• **Vice President Joe Biden**'s staffers removed references to alleged plagiarism in his speeches.

• **Rep. John Mica (R-FL)** quashed reports that he wore a toupee—rumors started by Stephen Colbert.

THE SEIGENTHALER INCIDENT

In 2005 an anonymous Wikipedia user created a fake page about NBC News journalist John Seigenthaler, claiming that he was a suspect in the assassinations of both John F. and Robert Kennedy and that he had lived in the Soviet Union from 1971 to 1984. None of it is remotely true, but somehow the hoax went unnoticed for more than four months. Wikipedia eventually tracked down the saboteur: Brian Chase, 38, a delivery service manager in Nashville. "It was just a joke," Chase claimed, adding that he thought the site was "some sort of gag encyclopedia." He was forced to resign from his job. Chase later called Seigenthaler to apologize, saying he didn't think anyone would take it seriously.

The incident prompted Wikipedia to add more editorial oversight to its articles, which is why suspect entries have disclaimers at the top. The rules were changed so that a person must register on the site before they can make any changes (but they don't have to use their real name). In 2012 the company added new software that alerts a core group of trusted editors of article changes so that, if necessary, they can be fixed immediately. However, errant "facts" can still slip through the cracks. Seigenthaler summed up his experience in an editorial in *USA Today*: "We live in a universe of new media with phenomenal opportunities for worldwide communications and research—but populated by volunteer vandals with poison-pen intellects."

* * *

"It takes courage to grow up and turn out to be who you really are." —**e.e. cummings**

SCI-FI VIDEO TREASURES

For all the sci-fi fans out there, searching the aisles of the video store or clicking around Netflix looking for an obscure science fiction gem, here are a few you might have missed.

MOON (2009) *Psychological Drama*
Review: "This mesmerizing mind-bender sneaks up and hits you hard. Sam Rockwell is an astronaut finishing up a three-year stint on the moon, mining energy from lunar rock. He wants to be back on Earth with his wife and daughter. His only contact is GERTY, a robot with the sweet-sinister voice of Kevin Spacey. There's an accident. A new astronaut appears, looking just like the old one. I'll say no more." (*Rolling Stone*)

BROTHER FROM ANOTHER PLANET (1984) *Comedy*
Review: "John Sayles' first bona fide box-office success, *Brother* centers on a black escaped slave from a faraway planet who finds himself on the mean streets of Harlem. Though the locals are put off by the slave's inability to speak, they are won over by his technical wizardry. He is adopted as a 'brother' by his new friends, who protect him from pursuing white aliens played by director Sayles and David Strathairn." (*Rottentomatoes.com*)

THE MAN WHO FELL TO EARTH (1976) *Drama*
Review: "David Bowie is haunting, androgynous, and ethereal as a spaceman hoping to return to his dying world with fresh water. Instead he succumbs to human vices while shocking our economy with disruptive new technologies. A main-street American girl falls in love with this strange, vulnerable visitor and witnesses his descent into isolation and paranoia. A more poignant portrait of extraterrestrial homesickness than *E.T.*" (*Minneapolis Star Tribune*)

FANTASTIC PLANET (1973) *Animation*
Review: "It's not every midnight movie that can stand a second viewing in the sober light of day. Based on a novel by Czech fantasist Stefan Wul, *Planet* opens on an ominous note: A ragged woman clutching a baby runs through a thorny wilderness, sharp Yellow Submarineish squiggles and spikes raining onto her path.

Country with the highest marriage rate: the U.S. Highest divorce rate: the U.S.

The cause of her trouble is soon revealed when a giant blue hand appears, casually flicking her about until her small body lies in a broken heap. The hand belongs to a child of the Draag race, hundred-foot-tall, azure-skinned beings who brought the little Oms to their home planet centuries ago, alternately keeping them as pets and decrying them as fast-breeding vermin." (*Village Voice*)

GATTACA (1997) *Thriller*

Review: "In a near-future in which DNA is destiny and custom genetic makeups are for sale, Vincent Freeman (Ethan Hawke) is a nearsighted 'love child' with a burning desire to join the Gattaca Aerospace Corporation's flight program. Through a complicated process that involves tiny baggies full of dead skin, plastic sacks of urine, and peel-off fingertips, Vincent assumes another identity and rises through the Gattaca ranks. This stunningly beautiful picture evokes a future in which present-day prejudices and neuroses have been taken to insidious heights." (*TV Guide's Movie Guide*)

MAD MAX BEYOND THUNDERDOME (1985) *Action*

Review: "From its opening shot of a bizarre vehicle being pulled by camels through the desert, this film places us firmly within its apocalyptic postnuclear world. Mad Max (Mel Gibson), former cop, now freelance nomad, makes his way to Bartertown, a quasi-Casablanca hammered together out of spare parts, where you go to buy, trade, or sell anything—or anybody. It is ruled by an imperious queen named Aunty Entity (Tina Turner) and powered by an energy source that is a compelling argument against nuclear war: piggy-do. This is a movie that strains at the leash of the possible, a movie of great visionary wonder." (*Roger Ebert's Four-Star Reviews*)

IDIOCRACY (2006) *Comedy*

Review: "Director Mike Judge (*Office Space*) indicts American culture with scathing humor, as he projects what the country will look like 500 years from now. His dystopian vision includes avalanches of trash, a U.S. government that has been purchased for corporate sponsorship by a sports drink, and a citizenry that has become congenitally fat, lazy, and stupid. A trashed-out landscape that's part zombie film and part broken-down *Blade Runner*, the America of *Idiocracy* has become one vast junk food-entertainment complex. It is essential viewing." (*Washington Post*)

Coldest place in the solar system: Triton, a moon of Neptune (-240°C).

A FISHY BUSINESS

If you've never had a pedicure, or it's been a while since you have, say hello to Garra rufa.

JAWS

Any nail salon can trim your toenails, apply nail polish, and maybe scrub away the dead skin with a pumice stone. All in all, a pedicure is a pretty routine experience…unless your salon uses "doctor" fish—*Garra rufa*, a tiny species of carp about the size of your toe. They're also known as "nibble fish" because they will eat dead skin cells. Hundreds of nail salons in North America, Asia, and Europe have incorporated the fish into the pedicure routine. Instead of a beauty technician scrubbing feet with a stone or other tools for half an hour, dozens of garra rufa feast on the customer's feet. What's it feel like? Some have compared it to ants running across their skin, or the feeling of a limb being "asleep."

As bizarre as it sounds, using such fish dates back to Turkey in the early 1800s. According to local legend, a shepherd hurt his foot one day, so he stuck it in a hot spring to ease the pain. There, a bunch of tiny fish chewed on his feet until his wound was healed. Whether or not that's actually how the fish were first discovered, in the years that followed, fish clinics for skin ailments became commonplace throughout Turkey and eastern Asia.

CUTS LIKE A FISH

Garra rufa—the preferred fish for these treatments—are typically found in warm-water ponds that don't support much other aquatic life. As such, they've evolved into scavengers. They eat whatever they can find, even dead skin. They're also born without teeth. Instead, they have rough scalelike mesh, a trait that makes them perfect for sloughing off dead, flaking skin but incapable of biting off "live" skin (which they won't eat, anyway).

While they've been used as beauty treatments in Turkey for almost 200 years, doctor fish were unheard of in the United States until 2008. John Ho and his wife, Yvonne Le, the owners of two salons in Virginia, had been searching for an alternative to pedi-

First video game to feature a playable black character: the Atari 800's 1979 game *Basketball*.

cure razors, which tend to cut live tissue as well a dead skin. When a customer told them about the popularity of skin-eating fish in Asia, they booked a trip to China. After a treatment at a spa in Chengdu, Ho immediately contacted a dealer and paid $40,000 to have 10,000 fish shipped to back to Virgina.

POOL SHARKS

Right from the start, Ho and Le faced resistance from health inspectors, who classified the communal tub (with doctor fish in it) a "swimming pool," and closed it over sanitary concerns and the fear that the fish could spread blood-borne illnesses, such as hepatitis or HIV. The couple quickly created a workaround: a separate Plexiglas fish tank for each customer. The popularity of their aquatic foot-munchers took off. In July 2008, Ho appeared on *Good Morning America* and convinced host Diane Sawyer to stick her feet in one of his tanks. She compared it to "tiny, little delicate kisses."

Ho and Le opened more salons, and started encouraging other salon owners to do the same. The fad has spread to England, too. The first UK-based fish pedicurist opened in 2008; by 2011 there were 279 British salons using doctor fish.

SMELLS FISHY

But almost as soon as the fish started biting, regulators bit back. As of 2012, fourteen states have banned doctor fish for cosmetic use. The problem: Many states have laws requiring cosmetology tools to be sanitized or discarded after each use. Properly "sterilizing" doctor fish would require them to be heated for at least 30 minutes at 350 degrees…which would kill them. The other option, to throw away the fish after a single use, would be cost-prohibitive (not to mention cruel).

Salon owners who have invested thousands of dollars in fish and equipment are pretty unhappy about the situation. Many turned to the fish to help their businesses survive tough economic times. In 2009, one salon owner in Arizona filed a lawsuit against the state's Board of Cosmetology after they closed down her *Garra rufa* tanks. That case is currently on appeal, but despite the ongoing controversy about them, fish pedicures continue to be a worldwide phenomenon…however fishy the whole thing seems.

Dolphins don't drink water.

YOU CAN FIND THEM IN THE DICTIONARY

Here's a list of words added to English dictionaries since 2000. It's a mini time capsule of turn-of-the 21st-century culture...and you don't have to wait 100 years to look inside. Some words are so familar that it's easy to forget they weren't around just a few years ago. And others, well, the definitions are included.

- **ADULT CHILD (2011):** Someone who is 25 or older and still shows no interest in joining the real world.
- **ALPHA GEEK (2012):** A person who has great expertise, especially in computing and related technology.
- **AEROMEDICINE (2008):** A branch of medicine relating to physical and psychological stresses specific to flight.
- **ASPERGER'S SYNDROME (2002)**
- **BLOGOSPHERE (2009):** Personal websites and blogs collectively.
- **BAILOUT (2009)**
- **CLICK-THROUGH (2009):** The action of following a hypertext link to a particular website, especially a commercial one.
- **CRYOPRESERVE (2004):** To preserve by cooling them to below the freezing point of water.
- **DEADHEAD (2005)**
- **EARWORM (2011):** A catchy song or tune that runs continually through someone's mind.
- **ECO-WARRIOR (2001)**
- **ETHNIC CLEANSING (2001)**
- **INFOMANIA (2012):** The compulsive desire to check or accumulate news and information, typically via cell phone or computer.
- **ISLAMISCISM (2012):** Islamic militancy or fundamentalism.
- **SUPERBUG (2010):** A bacterium that is resistant to antibiotics.

• **LATTE (2004)**

• **TIME SUCK (2008):** Something so engrossing that it keeps you from doing more important things; a time waster.

• **POST-GUTENBERG (2006):** The shift from delivering knowledge through print to delivering it through digital media, over the Internet.

• **REVERSE ENGINEERING (2010):** The reproduction of another manufacturer's product following detailed examination of its construction.

• **SEXTING (2011):** Sending sexually explicit photographs or messages via mobile phone.

• **OUT-OF-BODY EXPERIENCE (2004)**

• **SUPER PAC (2012):** An independent political action committee that may raise unlimited sums of money.

• **PAPARAZZI (2005)**

• **TIGER MOM (2011):** (Coined by author Amy Chua) A strict or demanding mother who pushes her children to high levels of achievement using methods regarded as typical of child rearing in East Asia.

• **PODCAST (2008)**

• **UPSELLING (2007):** Talking a customer into buying something more expensive.

* * *

JUMBO SHRIMP

In 2005 University of Melbourne biology student Anna McCallum discovered a new species of shrimp off the southwest coast of Australia. That gave her the right to name the species herself, but she decided to auction off that right on eBay to raise funds for the Australian Marine Conservation Society. Winning bidder: Luc Longley, the 7'2" Australian-born forward for the Chicago Bulls. (He won three straight NBA championships along with teammate Michael Jordan.) Longley, an avid environmentalist, paid $2,900 for the naming rights, and dubbed the new species *Lebbeus clarehanna*—after his 15-year-old daughter, Clare Hanna Longley. "You get to name a species and you get to donate to charity at the same time," Longley told reporters. "It's a fabulous concept."

Speed dating was invented by Yaacov Deyo, a Los Angeles rabbi, in 1998.

MAN MEETS CARTOON

Since the dawn of cinema, filmmakers have tried to combine cartoon characters with the real-life world. Here's the history of animation in live action films.

GERTIE THE DINOSAUR

In the early-1910s, American cartoonist Winsor McCay wanted to break into the nascent motion picture business. At the time, he was best known for *Little Nemo in Slumberland*, a comic strip that followed the adventures of a young boy in a magical dreamworld. After two unsuccessful attempts at animation, McCay created a 12-minute silent film called *Gertie the Dinosaur* that debuted on February 8, 1914, at Chicago's Palace Theater.

Audiences were astounded. *Gertie* was as much "performance art" as it was a film. The initial screenings featured McCay dressed in a tuxedo and carrying a whip, standing in front of a movie screen, pretending to interact with a cartoon brontosaurus named Gertie. Much like a lion tamer at a circus, the cartoonist instructed the dinosaur to perform various tricks such as "catching" treats and dancing on her hind legs. And for the big finale, the real McCay ducked out of sight, allowing a previously filmed, on-screen version of himself to be picked up and carried away by Gertie.

McCay's animation was rudimentary by today's standards. Without techniques like cel animation, which allows parts of each frame—characters and backgrounds—to be reused, the production was incredibly labor-intensive. The artist himself painted thousands of frames on rice paper. But McCay invented time-saving tricks, such as registration marks and cycling (the reuse of animation in later scenes), that are still being used today. Following the success of the first shows, a revamped version of *Gertie* with a live-action prologue toured the country, and McCay returned to his day job.

THE ALICE COMEDIES

Gertie heavily inspired a young animator named Walt Disney. After his Kansas City–based Laugh-O-Gram studio went bust in 1923, Walt and his brother Roy pooled their resources to open a

In the Hawaiian language, the apostrophe symbol in words like *Hawai'i* is called the *'okina.*

new operation in Hollywood. Once there, they shopped around *Alice's Wonderland*, a 10-minute short loosely based on the character created by Lewis Carroll. In the film, which was as reality-blurring as *Gertie*, Alice encounters a group of cartoon animals while touring an animation studio. Although it was never released theatrically, it impressed investors—so much so that the Disneys were able to raise the funds to produce their next film project (unrelated to Carroll's characters), the Alice Comedies.

Starring child actress Virginia Davis as Alice, a typical installment followed her adventures with a cartoon cat named Julius as they roamed various animated backdrops that included a Wild West town and the ocean floor. In order to create the illusion that she was interacting with an animated environment, Roy filmed Virginia's performances in front of a white backdrop (often in a single take because they didn't have enough film for reshoots). Then Walt took the footage and combined it with sparse cartoon backgrounds and characters drawn on white paper.

Compared to Disney's later films, the Alice Comedies are stark and unpolished, and some have racist elements. In *Alice Cans the Cannibals*, for example, Alice thwarts a village of African cannibals in grass skirts (who look like they stepped out of a minstrel show), and in *Alice and the Dog Catcher*, Alice is the leader of the Klix Klax Klub, a group of kids who wear paper bags over their heads, à la the Ku Klux Klan. But the films were acceptable—and successful—in their day. Disney released 57 Alice Comedies before turning his attention to a cheaper animated series starring Oswald the Lucky Rabbit, precursor to a certain animated rodent.

THE ROTOSCOPE

During this same period, animator Max Fleischer, best known for bringing Popeye and Betty Boop to the big screen, also experimented with live action–animation combinations. In 1915 he invented *rotoscoping*, a technique in which animators painstakingly trace over filmed images, frame by frame, thereby combining the two forms. He filmed his brother Dave in a clown suit and then rotoscoped the image, transforming it into Koko the Clown for his "Out of the Inkwell" series, which ran from 1918 to 1926. In 1923 he produced two 20-minute educational films that used the rotoscope technique—*Theory of Relativity* and *Theory of Evolution*—explaining the works of Albert Einstein and Charles

Warner Music earns $5,000 a day in royalties for the song "Happy Birthday to You."

Darwin. (In one scene involving an X-ray machine, an actor's hand morphs into an illustration of the bones underneath his skin.) As the sound era emerged, Fleischer used rotoscoping to incorporate performances of jazz musicians Cab Calloway and Louis Armstrong into cartoons. He used it in animated *Superman* shorts and feature films, and Disney used it in *Snow White*.

TOON TOWN

In the years that followed, studios continued to experiment with the live-animated format. Notable moments:

• **1940.** Warner Bros.' *You Ought to Be in Pictures*, a short starring Porky Pig and Daffy Duck. At the beginning of the nine-minute film, Daffy convinces Porky to jump off a drawing board into the real world in order to look for a better-paying job at another studio. Unlike the Alice Comedies, the short featured animated characters running around a live environment, rather than vice versa. Few advanced special effects were used to combine Porky and Daffy with the live footage—for many scenes, animators simply enlarged still photographs and added animation cels over them.

• **1945.** In the feature-length comedy *Anchors Away*, Gene Kelly performed a four-minute tap-dance routine with Jerry Mouse, of Tom and Jerry. (Producers wanted him to dance with Mickey Mouse, but Roy Disney reportedly said no.)

• **1964.** In a scene in Disney's *Mary Poppins*, Julie Andrews and Dick Van Dyke jump into an animated chalk drawing, ride animated merry-go-round horses into an animated countryside, and dance with animated penguins.

THE COMPUTER AGE

In 1976 *Futureworld*, a sequel to the hit *Westworld*, became the first major theatrical release to utilize computer animation to create a special hand-and-face effect, for actor Edward Catmull. After that, computer-generated imagery (CGI) became the standard for creating special film effects that combine live action with animation, from the computerized worlds of *Tron* (1982) and the realistic dinosaurs of *Jurassic Park* (1993), to the alien world of Pandora in *Avatar* (2009).

ONE-LINERS

Classic schtick from 20th-century comics.

"My wife has a slight impediment in her speech. Every now and then she stops to breathe."

—Jimmy Durante

"I just bought a new house. It has no plumbing. It's un-can-ny."

—Morey Amsterdam

"I'm 83, and I feel like a 20-year-old, but unfortunately there's never one around."

—Milton Berle

"I was so ugly my mother used to feed me with a slingshot."

—Rodney Dangerfield

"A man says, 'Doc, I gotta strawberry growing out of my head!' The doc says, 'Here's some cream to put on it.'"

—Tommy Cooper

"My hotel room is so small, when I put the key in, I broke the window."

—Henny Youngman

"Want to wake up with a smile on your face? Go to sleep with a clothes hanger in your mouth."

—Totie Fields

"My wife said to me, 'If you won the lottery, would you still love me?' I said, 'Of course I would. I'd miss you, but I'd still love you.'"

—Frank Carson

"My cooking is so bad my kids thought Thanksgiving was to commemorate Pearl Harbor."

—Phyllis Diller

"An undertaker calls a man, 'About your mother-in-law, should we embalm her, cremate her, or bury her?' He says, 'Do all three. Don't take chances.'"

—Myron Cohen

"Drinking removes warts and pimples. Not from me—from the people I look at."

—Jackie Gleason

"I used the be quite the athlete—big chest, hard stomach. But that's all behind me now."

—Bob Hope

"Lawyers practice law because it gives them a grand and glorious feeling. You give them a grand and they feel glorious."

—Milton Berle

When her husband was president, Julia Tyler used the title "Mrs. Presidentress."

BATHROOM NEWS: AIRPLANE EDITION

Here are a few fascinating bits of bathroom news that we've flushed out from airplane bathrooms around the world.

ON A ROLL

In September 2011, an All Nippon Airways flight from the island of Okinawa to Tokyo was cruising uneventfully at 41,000 feet when the captain got up to take a bathroom break. The *break* was uneventful, but when the captain returned to the cockpit and the copilot tried to let him in, instead of pushing the button that unlocks the cockpit door, he accidentally hit the rudder trim knob. That sent the jet into a steep dive and caused it to roll almost completely upside down. In the 30 seconds that it took the copilot to wrestle the plane back under control, it fell 6,234 feet. Two flight attendants were injured and six passengers became airsick as a result of the incident. The good news: Because the plane was flying over water at night, it was so dark outside that many passengers, securely belted in their seats, had no idea the plane was nearly upside down. "We are deeply sorry for causing anxiety to our passengers," an ANA spokesperson said afterward.

KNOCK, KNOCK! WHO'S THERE?

Two months later, in November 2011, the captain of a Delta flight from North Carolina to New York took a bathroom break after an air traffic controller advised him that the plane was likely to be put in a holding pattern when it arrived at LaGuardia Airport, 30 minutes away. Unlike his counterpart on the All Nippon Airways flight, this captain never made it out of the restroom: When he tried to unlock the door, the latch broke, trapping him inside.

FAA regulations require that at least two people be in the cockpit at all times. So when the captain left for his break, the lone flight attendant on the small commuter jet joined the copilot in the (locked) cockpit. That meant that the only people left in the passenger section to hear the captain pounding on the bathroom door for assistance were the passengers. When a passenger in the first row offered to assist, the captain gave him the secret password to let him into the cockpit, so that he could tell the copilot and flight attendant what had happened. Only problem: The passenger had what the copilot later described as a "Middle-Eastern" accent. When the well-meaning man knocked on the door to the cockpit, the copilot feared that the captain might have been overpowered by hijackers. "The captain has disappeared in the back. What I'm being told is he's stuck in the john. Someone with a thick foreign accent is giving me a password to access the cockpit, and I'm not about to let him in," the rattled copilot radioed to air traffic controllers.

Fighter planes were alerted and the copilot was preparing to make an emergency landing when the captain finally forced his way out of the bathroom, returned to the cockpit, and assured the co-pilot and air traffic control that everything was fine. "No one was ever in danger and everyone, including the good Samaritan who tried to help the captain, and the crew, are to be commended for their actions," the airline said in a statement.

LOCATION, LOCATION, LOCATION

In February 2012, Artie Hughes and his wife were enjoying a barbecue at their New York home—which happens to be in the flight path of JFK Airport—when a jumbo jet passed overhead and spattered them with an oily black liquid. Fearing the material was engine oil, hydraulic fluid, or some other critical substance, they quickly called the airport police so that the aircraft could be identified and warned that it might have mechanical problems. The responding police officer had other ideas. "Looks like something nastier than that," he said. He was right: The substance turned out to be chemically treated sewage from a leaky holding tank. At last report, the couple were asking for an investigation…and nothing more. "I think they should find out what happened," said Hughes. "Was a button pushed? Was the lavatory filled to capacity before it left the ground?"

WINDOW SEAT

When the long-awaited Boeing 787 Dreamliner entered service in October 2011, the planes were brimming with state-of-the-art features, like TVs on every seat back, an LED lighting system that reduces jet lag, higher cabin humidity for greater passenger comfort, and the largest cabin windows of any commercial aircraft in history, complete with auto-dimming "smart glass" that can be darkened with the push of a button instead of pulling down a shade. But the most interesting new feature (at least as far as Uncle John is concerned): Even the *bathrooms* have windows, so you can enjoy the view while answering nature's call at 43,000 feet. "We're making flying fun again," said Boeing spokesperson Mary Hanson.

Not everyone was impressed with the bathroom windows when they were first introduced to the public. One woman who toured an early Dreamliner mock-up in Seattle complained that the prodigious portholes were an invasion of privacy. Duly noted, and ignored. "I told the lady that if someone was close enough to look in the window, she had a much bigger problem than being seen on the toilet," said Boeing senior engineer Ken Price.

* * *

A GOOD DAY TO DIE

On the morning of December 17, 2003, the website of the National Weather Service posted an especially stressful advisory for Missouri residents:

> URGENT-WEATHER MESSAGE: UNUSUALLY HOT WEATHER HAS ENTERED THE REGION FOR DECEMBER ... AS THE EARTH HAS LEFT ITS ORBIT AND IS HURTLING TOWARD THE SUN... EXCESSIVE HEAT WATCH IN EFFECT FROM THIS AFTERNOON TO LATE TONIGHT ...
>
> UNUSUALLY HOT WEATHER WILL OCCUR FOR AT LEAST THE NEXT SEVERAL DAYS AS THE EARTH DRAWS EVER NEARER TO THE SUN. THEREFORE...AN EXCESSIVE HEAT WATCH HAS BEEN POSTED.

The alert turned out to be a test message accidentally posted during a training session; it was removed later in the day and replaced by a correction...and an apology.

WEIRD BEQUESTS

You can't take it with you...so you might as well have a little fun when you leave it behind.

SKULLDUGGERY

In 1955 an Argentine man named Juan Potomachi bequeathed 200,000 pesos (about $43,000) to the Teatro Dramatico theater in Buenos Aires. The catch: His skull got to "play" Yorick, the skull Hamlet holds up for his soliloquy in Act V. A year later, Potomachi's skull "co-starred" in a production of *Hamlet*.

STAKEOUT

Harold West of London, England, died in 1972, terrified of vampires to the end. In his will, he instructed his doctor "to drive a steel stake through my heart to make sure that I am properly dead." (No word on whether his wish was carried out.)

SWAN SONG

McNair Ilgenfritz of Sedalia, Missouri, died in 1953. Part of a family that owned a large hardware business, Ilgenfritz died unfulfilled: He'd wanted to be a composer, but never had any luck getting his works produced. So in his will, he left the majority of his $150,000 estate to New York's Metropolitan Opera...on one condition: that the world-famous opera company stage one of his works, either *La Passant* or *Phedre*. The Met initially accepted the offer, but after a few years, changed their mind and returned the money to Ilgenfritz's family.

HEAD OF THE CLASS

In 1826 Jeremy Bentham, one of the most important philosophers in England's history, helped found the University of London. He so loved the school that he bequeathed his body to them, to be dissected by an anatomy class. He also requested that afterward, his skeleton be put on display in a glass cabinet at the college, clothed and topped with a wax replica of his head. Upon his death in 1836, Bentham was indeed dissected and preserved. His remains now reside in a glass case at the university.

Apple's initial public offering in 1980 was the largest since the Ford Motor Company's...

BY THE BOOK

Mark Gruenwald was an editor for Marvel Comics for decades, spending most of his career working on Captain America. He died in 1996, and in his will, asked that he be cremated so that his ashes could be mixed into comic book ink. Marvel obliged, and a little bit of Gruenwald was placed in every issue of the 4,000-copy paperback bind-up of one of his final projects, *Squadron Supreme*.

HUM DRUM

A man known only as S. Sanborn was a hatmaker who died in Massachusetts in 1871. He left his body to science, specifically asking that famous scientist and Harvard anatomy professor Oliver Wendell Holmes be given access to it. Then, Sanborn instructed, Holmes was to turn Sanborn's skin into two drums, which he was to give to a friend. The friend was to go to Boston at dawn every June 17, the anniversary of the Battle of Bunker Hill in the Revolutionary War, and play "Yankee Doodle." Sanborn requested that the rest of his body be "composted for a fertilizer to contribute to the growth of an American elm." His wishes were carried out.

LAST LAUGH

In 1994, a Portuguese aristocrat named Luis Carlos de Nornha Cabral da Camara went to a registry office in Lisbon with two witnesses to lay out the terms of his will (wills are not customary in Portugal). In front of the witnesses and a government official, da Camara picked 70 names randomly out of the Lisbon phone book and made them the beneficiaries of his estate. In 2007, da Camara died, and 70 Portuguese people got very surprising phone calls, informing them they'd inherited items from a man they'd never met—like a 12-room apartment, a country house, a car, and 25,000 euros. "He was a good man," said one of da Camara's neighbors, "although he drank a lot." "I'm sure he just wanted to create confusion," said another. "That amused him."

* * *

"When I was a little kid, I wished the first word I said was 'quote,' so that, when I died, I could say 'unquote.'"

—Steven Wright

LOVE THY NEIGHBOR

When people live close to each other, tensions can flare.

OFFENSE: A 24-year-old man named Zbigniew Filo liked to drive his souped-up Ford Escort at high speeds through his neighborhood in Lubczyna, Poland.

RETALIATION: He went out to his car one morning in May 2012 to discover that it had been hoisted 20 feet up a tree. None of Filo's neighbors admitted to having done it, although one did say that his crane had been "borrowed."

OFFENSE: A Polk County, Florida, man wouldn't water his lawn, despite numerous requests to do so from his neighbor, Joe Florence.

RETALIATION: Florence finally just pulled his own hose over to the yard and started watering. The neighbor called the police. When they arrived a few minutes later, they ordered Florence to put down the hose. He refused. A struggle ensued, and Florence ended up with two black eyes and numerous charges against him, including resisting arrest and trespassing.

OFFENSE: At 8:30 one morning in 2011, a 10-year-old Lakeland, Florida, boy was shooting baskets in his driveway. Next door, 48-year-old Ellenbeth Wachs was trying to sleep. She yelled out her window for the boy to be quiet, but he kept playing.

RETALIATION: Wachs began making loud, moaning sounds of a sexual nature. According to the boy's father, "She screamed, 'Oh, John! Oh, John!' over and over again and kept increasing the volume until it was a loud scream." Wachs—not the boy—was cited for disturbing the peace.

OFFENSE: Bob Furnad of Covington, Georgia, accused his neighbor of spreading "vicious lies" about him.

RETALIATION: One day in 2012, the neighbor found a bag of dog doo inside his mailbox. Surveillance video showed Furnad placing it in there. He was fined, and the story made headlines because Furnad is the former president of CNN Headline News.

In 1904 the first performance of Puccini's opera *Madame Butterfly* was booed.

REAL-LIFE SUPERHEROES

Here's a look at a once-obscure phenomenon that has blossomed into a full-blown fad with the help of social networking sites Myspace and Facebook: grown-ups dressing up as superheroes to battle evildoers.

KID STUFF

Just about every kid who grew up reading comic books and watching superheroes in the movies and on TV has wondered what it would be like to really put on a superhero costume and fight bad guys. Until recently, few people (few adults, anyway) ever got up the nerve to do it. Superhero costumes were like teddy bears and tree forts: When you reached a certain age, you gave them up. If you didn't (and if your childhood was anything like Uncle John's), your friends teased you mercilessly until you did. Peer pressure has killed more superheroes than kryptonite ever did.

VIRTUAL BATCAVES

Then in the 1990s, the Internet began to make it possible for aspiring costumed crusaders to live out their fantasies online. Even if they were too intimidated to wear their costumes around town, they could post pictures and videos of themselves on the Web. Social media sites like Myspace and Facebook, and video-sharing sites like YouTube, made it that much easier for real-life superheroes or "reals," as many prefer to call themselves, to find each other, and to realize that they aren't alone. As the online community developed, more superheroes were willing to venture out of their homes in full costume. Many cite the 9/11 attacks as intensifying their desire to confront evil in the world.

Their numbers have grown over the years. By 2011, there were some 300 real-life (mostly male) superheroes active in the United States, and another 75 to 100 around the world. In many places where more than one real-life superhero is active, they have organized into groups like the Great Lakes Heroes Guild (Min-

Wizardly word origin: *Dumbledore* is an Old English word meaning "bumblebee."

neapolis), Superheroes Anonymous (New York), and the Black Monday Society (Salt Lake City).

THANKS...BUT

As many costumed crime fighters have discovered, battling the bad guys in real life doesn't always play out the way it does in the comic books. Crime has been trending downward since the 1980s; neither the police nor the general public feel there's a need for assistance from unpredictable and (some would say) unbalanced superheroes with no law-enforcement training whatsoever.

When police respond to a call, the last thing they want to see is someone wearing a mask. Most people who wear masks, after all, are bank robbers and other criminals. One night when a group of Seattle superheroes called Rain City Superhero Movement pulled up in front of a Shell station to begin a patrol, a bystander called police. He thought they were there to rob the gas station. The Seattle Police Department had to issue a departmental memo warning its officers not to assume that masked adults are criminals.

Who are those masked men (and women)? Here's a look at some real-life superheroes.

CAPTAIN STICKY (San Diego)

Secret Identity: Richard Pesta, a consumer advocate. (Why "Captain Sticky"? Peanut butter was his favorite food.)

Costume: Blue tights and a gold lamé cape

Details: Standing over 6' tall, weighing more than 400 pounds, and driving a custom bubble-topped Lincoln Continental "Stickymobile," this self-proclaimed Mighty Man of Carbohydrates was one of the earliest caped crusaders and predates the Internet generation of superheroes by 20 years. In the early 1970s, Pesta began holding press conferences dressed in his superhero costume, shining the light on crooked auto mechanics, health insurance fraudsters, and other villains who preyed on the public. And he got results: His campaign against nursing home abuses was so effective that the California state legislature set up a task force to investigate the issue and invited him to serve on it.

PHOENIX JONES (Seattle)

Secret Identity: Ben Fodor, a social worker and amateur mixed-

On August 28, 1991, the crew of the space shuttle *Atlantis* sent the first e-mail from space.

martial-arts fighter in his mid-20s. He picked the name "Phoenix" because it's the name of a mythological bird that rises out of the ashes, and "Jones" because it's one of the most common surnames in the English language—he sees himself as a common man rising from the ashes.

Costume: A full-body black-and-gold superhero suit that includes a bulletproof vest, "stab plates," a "ballistic cup," and a utility belt containing handcuffs, pepper spray, a Taser, and a first aid kit.

Details: The most famous real-life superhero in recent years, Fodor made news in October 2011 when he broke up a "fight" outside a Seattle nightclub and pepper-sprayed four people. Only afterward did he learn that the people weren't fighting, just frolicking noisily on their way out of the club. After being chased off by a woman he pepper-sprayed while "saving" her, Fodor was arrested, and his costume and pepper spray were confiscated by police as evidence. "Recently there have been increased reports of citizens being pepper-sprayed by [Fodor] and his group," the police report notes. "Although he has been advised to observe and report incidents to 911, he continues to try to resolve things on his own."

Though no charges were filed against Fodor, the publicity—and the exposure of his true identity, which until his arrest had remained a secret—caused him to be suspended from his job working with autistic children and barred from working with kids and vulnerable adults while the case was under investigation. Not that it stopped Fodor. After his court appearance, he suited back up as Phoenix Jones and returned to patrolling the streets.

PHANTOM ZERO (Central New Jersey)

Secret Identity: A call-center worker in his 30s, real name unknown

Costume: Phantom Zero dresses in black from head to toe and wears a black cloak with a hood. His face is made up to look like a skull. He carries a walking stick. His only splash of color: a red-and-white cravat that he tucks into his shirt.

Details: Phantom Zero started out as a crime fighter like Phoenix Jones, then switched to costumed activism à la Captain Sticky. Why? When he started patrolling Lindenhurst, New York, in 2007, the only villains he found were drunks urinating in public.

Brazil's largest private employer: McDonald's.

When he moved to New Jersey, his new community was even quieter, so he dropped crime fighting in favor of supporting local charities and people in need.

MR. INVISIBLE (Los Angeles)

Secret Identity: A 29-year-old insurance salesman who took up superheroing in 2008, real name unknown

Costume: A gray one-piece "invisibility suit" that was difficult to see in the dark, enabling Mr. Invisible to hide in the shadows.

Details: The suit was a little too invisible. One night while Mr. Invisible was hiding in an alley, someone walked up and boldly went where no man had gone before, peeing on the superhero without even realizing he was there. The only other crime Mr. Invisible encountered in his short career was an argument between a small woman and her very large boyfriend. When he inserted himself into the middle of their argument to calm the boyfriend down, the woman punched him in the face. At 0-and-2 after just a week on the job, Mr. Invisible hung up his superhero suit and "refocused" his energies on his insurance career. "It's dangerous out there," he said.

ANGLE GRINDER MAN (London, England)

Secret Identity: An unemployed odd-jobber, real name unknown

Costume: Sky-blue leotard worn with gold lamé briefs, boots, gloves, kneepads, cape, and mask

Details: Most superheroes are sworn to uphold the law, but for Angle Grinder Man, unfair parking laws are the villain. In central London, the authorities attach steel clamps to the wheels of illegally parked cars to immobilize them until the owner pays a steep fine. Angle Grinder Man thinks that's unfair, so he uses his angle grinder to cut the clamps off, freeing drivers to go on their merry way without paying the fines. He got the idea when his own car was clamped and the cost to remove it was £95 (about $150). When he realized that angle grinders rent for just £30 an hour, a superhero was born. "My obsession with wheel-clamping is actually a rebellion against a much deeper malaise, namely, the arrogant contempt that politicians hold for the people who put them into power, and whom they claim to represent," he says.

DC'S GUARDIAN (Washington, D.C.)

Secret Identity: A man in his 40s with a military or national-defense background, real name unknown

Costume: A red, white, and blue leather tunic over blue spandex leggings, red leather boots, and a blue spandex mask with red "Mercury" ears. The mask, which covers his entire head, like Spider-Man's, is worn over red goggles or sunglasses. DC's Guardian wears a costume that is deliberately designed to conceal every inch of his body, "to allow black, white, Asian, or Hispanic people to see themselves behind the mask," he says.

Details: When DC's Guardian isn't patrolling a dangerous neighborhood behind the Capitol building, he's out on the National Mall passing out pocket-size copies of the Declaration of Independence, the U.S. Constitution, and the Bill of Rights to tourists and other passersby. "America has a lot to offer—if people stand up for the foundation it was built upon," he says.

For more real-life superheroes, turn to page 401

* * *

COMEDIAN RANTS

"Eggs! They're not a food, they belong in no group! They're just farts clothed in substance!"

—Dylan Moran

"Swimming is not a sport! Swimming is a way to keep from drowning. That's just common sense!"

—George Carlin

"When people blow their noses, they always look into their hankies to see what came out. Why? What exactly do you expect to find?"

—Billy Connolly

"I am sick of reading on message boards that I am one of these 'foul-mouthed modern comedians.' I am absolutely not! Honestly, who are these [censored]?"

—Stewart Lee

POLICE BLOTTER: CHEESEBURGER EDITION

On February 21, 2012, a man attempted to trick the employees of a Denny's restaurant in Madison, Wisconsin, into believing that he was their new general manager. This is the actual police report describing the incident, written by the Madison Police Department's information officer, Joel DeSpain, who, we're pretty sure, secretly dreams of writing crime novels.

INCIDENT: Disturbance
DATE: 02/21/2012 - 4:32 p.m.
ADDRESS: 1798 Thierer Road (Denny's)

ARRESTED: James B. Summers, age 52, Madison. Mr. Summers was arrested for Fraud, Disorderly Conduct, Possession of Drug Paraphernalia, and Possession of an Electric Weapon.

VICTIM: Female, age 38, Madison

DETAILS: He never announced he was one of the pros from Dover, but the briefcase-toting gentleman wearing a maroon tie and long black trench coat was quite clear: He had been sent by Corporate. He claimed he was the new general manager, that he had worked for the restaurant chain for 30 years and that he was starting his new job—right now.

The gray-haired stranger with the goatee had just arrived yesterday afternoon, unannounced, at the private office door of the restaurant manager. She was in the process of counting the day's receipts at the Denny's on Thierer Road. Surprised, and a bit shocked, the 38-year-old thought, "Surely this must be a mistake." She had heard nothing from Corporate about a new general manager, and politely told the man so. "Perhaps," she said to him, "you have arrived at the wrong restaurant."

This conversation developed into a tête-à-tête or a "nose-to-nose," to quote the manager, as the man asserted his new role and she told him she thought not. This went on until he said it was final, he was going to commence his duties. It was at this point that the manager began making calls up the chain. She was able to reach the man in charge of all hiring at her location. By this time the new "GM" had left the office, but not the restaurant, and she had shut the office door in order to carry out this important, private conversation.

While on the phone, she waved off kitchen staff as they rapped on her door, trying to get her attention. She was not to be interrupted while talking with Corporate. What the staff wanted her to know was that the new "GM" was cooking a cheeseburger and fries for himself and had gotten himself a soda. He was in the midst of dining when she let him know that the gig was up: She had talked with Corporate, and he was no new hire. Unfazed, he continued to brush off her remarks, saying she just had not yet gotten the memo. It was about this time the manager called 911. When the responding officer arrived, he saw the suspect walking away from the restaurant. Upon contact, he told the officer there was a misunderstanding, that he was the new GM, but there must have been a paperwork goof-up. He agreed to return to the restaurant so both sides could present their case.

The manager prevailed and the man was arrested. The officer found, beneath the man's trench coat and suit jacket, that he was packing a stun gun on his belt. The officer asked if the suspect had a concealed carry permit. The man replied, "It's in the pipeline." He was cooperative with the officer, but as he was being led from the restaurant, he yelled out to those eating: "This is why you don't dine and dash, kiddies."

* * *

KNOW YOUR -OLOGIES

- **Momilogy** is the study of mummies.
- **Astacology** is the study of crayfish.
- **Deltiology** is the study of postcards.
- **Fromology** is the study of cheese.
- **Tsiganology** is the study of gypsies.
- **Parthenology** is the study of virgins.
- **Splanchnology** is the study of entrails
- **Gelotology** is the study of the laughter.

Neon, the 4th most abundant element in the universe, makes up .0018% of our atmosphere.

THE MAGIC NUMBER

In honor of the Bathroom Reader's *25th anniversary...*

25 is the 26th number in the Arabic numeral system. (The first number is 0.)

25 is a *square number*—the product of a number multiplied by itself, in this case 5 x 5.

25 is the smallest square number that is also a sum of two squares ($3^2 + 4^2$).

25 is the smallest Friedman Number—a number is one that can be expressed as an equation (using addition, subtraction, multiplication, or division) in which the number's own digits are used. In this case 5^2, which uses the digits 2 and 5, equals 25.

25 is the number of chipmunk species in North America.

25 is the atomic number of the element *manganese*, commonly found in nature in manganese dioxide. This soft, dark-colored solid was used to make cave paintings, such as those in Lascaux, France, 25,000 years ago.

25 is the number of players on a Major League Baseball roster (until August 31, after which teams may expand rosters to 40 players).

25 is the minimum legal age of candidates for election to the U.S. House of Representatives.

25 is a jersey number often reserved for a Major League Baseball team's slugger. Examples: Mark McGwire, Barry Bonds, Jim Thome, and Carlos Delgado.

25 is the sum of the first five odd numbers: 1 + 3 + 5 + 7 + 9 = 25.

25 is the number of the U.S. Interstate highway that runs from I-90 in Wyoming south to I-10 in New Mexico. Along the way it runs through Cheyenne, Denver, Santa Fe, and Albuquerque.

25 was the age of death of poet John Keats (1821), R&B crooner Johnny Ace (1954), rapper Tupac Shakur (1996), and actor Brad Renfro (2008).

EXTREME SPORT: BASE JUMPING

"Extreme" equals "dangerous." You might want to think twice before taking up this pastime.

WAY OFF BASE

In 1783 Louis-Sébastien Lenormand climbed to the top of a tower in Montpellier, France...and jumped. The people down below probably thought he was nuts, but thanks to the contraption on his back, he landed without a scratch—it was the first parachute (it looked like a large umbrella), and Lenormand's jump was a precursor to a modern extreme sport: BASE jumping.

If Lenormand's jump had been filmed, he might be called the father of modern BASE jumping. Instead, the title goes to filmmaker Carl Boenish. On August 18, 1978, Boenish and three other expert skydivers put on their parachutes and went "hucking," an extreme sports term meaning recklessly throwing oneself into the air from a launching pad. For their launching pad, Boenish and his buddies used the 3,198-foot granite monolith El Capitan, in California's Yosemite National Park. They filmed their jumps and transformed a crazy stunt into a crazy sport that has, to date, claimed at least 186 lives.

BASE-ICALLY INSANE

BASE stands for **B**uilding, **A**ntenna, **S**pan (like bridges), and **E**arth (like cliffs)—the launching pads from which the jumpers jump. To receive an "official" BASE number, a jumper has to complete a jump from all four categories. Dangerous? Some cynics say the acronym should stand for "**B**ones **A**nd **S**@*! **E**verywhere." During a BASE jump, anything can go wrong and probably will. The jumpers smash into cliffs, collide with guy wires, go down in deep water, or hit the ground headfirst. And even though many fall victim to parachute malfunctions, BASE jumpers don't use reserve chutes. Why not? Because the relatively low heights from which they plummet give them about six seconds to reach the

First non-documentary ever to film in Mecca: Spike Lee's *Malcolm X* (1992).

ground: If a chute doesn't work, there's no time to deploy a backup. It should come as no surprise, then, that Boenish died in 1984 while BASE jumping from Trollveggen, Europe's highest vertical rock face at 3,600 feet. What went wrong? His chute didn't open.

FATAL ATTRACTION

Because BASE jumping is so dangerous, it's illegal in almost every American city and national park. West Virginia allows it, but only on a single day each year—New River Gorge Bridge Day. Before you go, consider a few facts from the Bridge Day FAQ page:

- Some of the smartest BASE jumpers in the world have been injured or killed BASE jumping.
- It's not "if" but "when" you get busted up in this sport, so get good medical insurance.
- It's a good idea to let your family know what you're doing so they won't be surprised if something happens.

One BASE jump instructor puts it like this, "If you are not ready to *die* BASE jumping, you are not ready to *go* BASE jumping." Since 1979 four people have died doing a Bridge Day jump.

HIGH JUMPER

While the number-one requirement for BASE jumping is obvious—guts—the number-two requirement might not be: superb free-fall skills. Knowing how to free-fall helps insure that the first jump isn't the last. In 1996, when Felix Baumgartner made his first jump, he was prepared. He'd learned about targeted skydiving as a special-forces parachutist with the Austrian military. (That was before he was labeled a troublemaker and kicked out.) For his first jump, Baumgartner headed to the New River Gorge Bridge—and survived.

As for illegal jumps, Baumgartner thrives on them, and he doesn't mind a bit of troublemaking if it will help him accomplish his goals. In 1999 he spent two months scoping out one of the world's tallest buildings—Kuala Lumpur's 1,483-foot Petronas Twin Towers. For days he watched security guards patrolling the towers and paid close attention to the businessmen who frequented the building. Then he walked into the building disguised in an expensive suit with a briefcase and phony I.D. card. He took an elevator to the 88th floor, where he opened his briefcase and

Post it, but don't copy it: The shade of yellow on Post-it Notes is trademarked by 3M.

pulled out a parachute and camcorder. After readying his gear, he climbed up a window-washing crane…and jumped—for eight seconds of free fall. The leap earned Baumgartner the record for world's highest building jump.

JESUS SAVES

Baumgartner also holds the record for the world's shortest BASE jump. His target: the famous Christ the Redeemer statue in Rio de Janeiro. In 2009 Baumgartner and his team managed to hide out in the security area at the base of the statue. At 4:00 a.m., they crept outside so the daredevil could shoot an arrow carrying a steel cable over the outstretched arm of the giant Jesus. He attached ropes to the cable and climbed to his perch—the right hand of Christ—and then vaulted 95 feet to the ground. The amount of time Baumgartner had to get his parachute open (and say his prayers): 1.5 seconds. "Every one of us has to die at some point," Baumgartner says, "so there's no point living in fear of it. Unfortunately, it's easier said than done when you're waiting for the ideal conditions to make the jump—and thinking about the twelve colleagues who died last year."

Not had your fill of deadly thrills? There's more. Check out our story of the second most dangerous sport: free-solo climbing. ***It falls on page 366.***

*   *   *

SUPERHEROES' RELIGIOUS AFFILIATIONS

Based on actual references in comic books.

- Superman—Methodist
- Batman—Episcopalian
- The Hulk—Catholic
- Wonder Twins—Mormon
- The Thing (Fantastic Four)—Jewish
- Wolverine (X–Men)—Buddhist
- Ghost Rider—Baptist
- The Human Torch (Fantastic Four)—Episcopalian
- Thor—Norse pantheon (of which he is a member)

The human population of the world inhales more than 6 billion tons of oxygen annually.

MUCH ADO ABOUT JUGS AND SCREWS

Freedom of speech does have limits. You can't yell "Fire!" in a crowded theater, for example. Many governments place greater restrictions on free speech than the U.S. does...or at least they try to.

NAUGHTY OR NICE

In 2011 the Pakistan Telecommunication Authority (PTA), which regulates that country's mobile phone industry, announced a plan to prevent Pakistanis from sending text messages it deemed offensive, sexually explicit, or counter to "the glory of Islam" (97% of Pakistanis are Muslim). PTA bureaucrats drew up a list of 1,500 naughty English and Urdu words and gave it to cell-phone service providers, ordering them to block any text messages that included those words. It gave cell-phone companies just a week to put the program in place.

The list of banned words soon found its way onto the Internet, where it was protested by free-speech activists...and mocked by ordinary Pakistanis, who were baffled by some of the words on the list. A few were genuinely obscene; others were simply medical terms. But most of the banned words were completely innocuous, perhaps with suggestive connotations, but only if used in a slangy context. Why they ended up on the list remains a mystery.

EXPLETIVES DELETED

Here are some of the words and phrases on the PTA's English list:

Athlete's Foot
Back Door
Barf
Bite Me
Budweiser
Cocktail
Condom
Creamy
Crotch Rot
Cumquat
Deeper
Deposit
Dipstick
Dome
Dope
Drunk
Fairy
Fart
Finger Food
Flasher
Fondle
Four Twenty
Genital
Glazed Donut
Harder
Harem
Headlights
Henhouse
Herpes
Hobo

Hole
Honkey
Hoser
Hostage
Hussy
Hustler
Idiot
In the Buff
Interracial
Jack the Ripper
Jug
Kmart
Knocker
Lactate
Lavender

Lolita
Lotion
Lowlife
Lube Job
Mango
Mary Jane
Murder
Oui
Period
Poor White Trash
Premature
Prime Time
Pussycat
Quickie
Rear End

Sucker
Red Light
Ribbed
Roach
Robber
Satan
Screw
Shag
Showtime
Six Six Six
Slant
Sleazeball
Slime
Snatch
Sniper
Spit

Stagg
Stroke
Stupid
Sucker
Suicide
Syphilis
Tampon
Testicle
The Trots
Tongue
Trailer Trash
Tramp
Trojan
Tunnel of Love
XXX

POTTY MOUTHS

The ban backfired badly. The number of obscene texts originating in Pakistan soared after the list was published, as millions of Pakistanis tested the system to see which dirty words got through and which ones didn't. Instead of protecting children—one of the ban's stated goals—it gave them a state-sponsored education in obscenity. "Well done!" one Pakistani posted to his Twitter account. "The banned list has made it all over Pakistan, and kids are swearing more elaborately and frequently than ever." Less than a week after the list was made public, the PTA scrapped it and announced it was beginning "consultations" to pare the list down to as few as a dozen words.

End Note: The original list included 26 expressions *containing* the word "butt," but not the word "butt" itself. Why? Butt is a common last name in Pakistan, a relic of the British colonial period when officials spelled the Kashmiri surname *Bhat* as you-know-what.

CITY NICKNAMES

Where would you rather live: Naptown or the Big Tomato?

TERRE HAUTE, INDIANA: "Pittsburgh of the West"
A curious nickname, because Indiana isn't really in the west, and Terra Haute is only 400 miles from Pittsburgh. The nickname stems from Terra Haute's status as, like Pittsburgh, a center of steel production during the Industrial Revolution.

BRAHAM, MINNESOTA: "Pie Capital of Minnesota"
Braham is between the major cities of Duluth and Minneapolis. In the 1930s and '40s, travelers made a popular destination out of the city's Park Café, which offered many homemade pies. In 1990 the town made the first Friday in August "Pie Day," when residents gather to consume pie and ice cream and raise money for charities. On the first Pie Day, Minnesota governor Rudy Perpich declared Braham the Homemade Pie Capital of Minnesota.

INDIANAPOLIS: "Naptown"
Because city ordinances made businesses close early, Indianapolis became something of a social ghost town, or sleepy, leading traveling jazz musicians to nickname it "Naptown." It's also a play on words, because "nap" is in the middle of "Indianapolis."

ANTHONY, TEXAS: "Leap Year Capital of the World"
Anthony resident Mary Ann Brown was born on February 29—Leap Day. In 1988 she proposed that the Chamber of Commerce host a festival on that day every four years. Anthony is the first city in the world to host such an event. It's also the home of the Worldwide Leap Year Birthday Club, an organization of people with a birthday on February 29.

NASHVILLE, TENNESSEE: "The Protestant Vatican"
Besides being the home of the country-music industry, Nashville is also a center of Christian thought, educational institutions, and religious industries. Bible publisher Thomas Nelson is headquartered there, as is the Southern Baptist Convention and the United

Methodist Church. Nashville is also the location of half a dozen major Christian colleges and more than 700 churches.

WACO, TEXAS: "Buckle of the Bible Belt"
If you picture the Bible Belt as a long swath that stretches across the South and west to Arizona, then Waco would be roughly where the buckle on that belt would sit. (Large decorative belt buckles are also very popular in the Bible Belt.)

YAKIMA, WASHINGTON: "Palm Springs of Washington"
Most of Washington has a rainy climate. Not so in south-central Washington, which is dry and arid, much like Palm Springs, California.

SACRAMENTO: "The Big Tomato"
A play on New York City's nickname, "The Big Apple," this nickname dating to the 1970s refers to Sacramento valley's many tomato farms and canneries.

RUMNEY, NEW HAMPSHIRE: "Crutch Capital of the World"
At one point, during and immediately after World War I, when demand was especially high, Rumney really was the world's top producer of crutches. The Loveland Company made more than 3,000 pairs a week.

QUINTER, KANSAS: "Half-Mile City"
Denver is the "Mile-High City" because its average official elevation is 5,280 feet—exactly one mile. Quinter (population: 981) has an average elevation of 2,681 feet, over half a mile.

ALGONA, IOWA: "Home of the World's Largest Cheeto"
In 2003 Algona resident Mike Evans opened a bag of Cheetos and found one that was a round blob (rather than a long, thin curlicue) about the size of strawberry. That may not seem huge, but it is the biggest Cheeto on record, and the town is very proud of it—so proud that they celebrate the cheesy snack each year on March 13, "Giant Cheeto Day."

MARRIAGE FIRSTS

For better or for worse, we present for your reading pleasure this bevy of betrothals that, in one way or another, were the very first of their kind.

FIRST (ENGLISH) MARRIAGE IN THE NEW WORLD

John Laydon, 28, a carpenter, married Anne Burras, 14, a maid, in Jamestown, Virginia, in December 1608. Their oldest daughter was the first European child born in North America.

FIRST (ENGLISH) DIVORCE IN THE NEW WORLD

When James Luxford was revealed as a bigamist in 1639, the court in Plymouth Colony dissolved his second marriage, sentenced him to an hour in the stocks, and ordered him "sent away to England at the earliest opportunity." His ex-wife got all his stuff. (Really.)

FIRST WEDDING BY TELEGRAPH

When a wealthy Boston merchant discovered that his daughter wanted to marry one of his clerks, he sent the young man away on business. He'd forgotten one thing: the telegraph. His daughter, on the other hand, had not. She headed to a Boston telegraph office and the man of her dreams hurried to a New York office with a magistrate in tow. In an "electric flash," they were wed.

FIRST ELOPEMENT BY AIRPLANE

Barnstorming pilot Art "The Smash-Up Kid" Smith, 19, wanted to marry 18-year-old Aimee Cour, but Indiana law required parental consent, and Aimee's parents wouldn't give it. Michigan laws were looser, so on October 26, 1912, they flew the coop. (Art crashed the plane.) Art loved flying more than he loved Aimee, and they divorced in 1917. He died in a final plane crash in 1926.

FIRST WEDDING BY TELEPHONE

Bertil Clason of Flint, Michigan, planned to marry his sweetheart, Sigrid Carlson, in the United States, but strict immigration laws kept her in Sweden. So on December 2, 1933, Bertil and a pastor picked up telephones in Detroit and called Sigrid in Stockholm, 4,100 miles away. The wedding service took only seven minutes. (In those days, overseas calls cost $12 per minute—$200 today.)

First wedding aloft in a balloon: two performers in PT Barnum's circus (Ohio, Oct. 1874).

TOWNS FOR SALE

What's the easiest way to become mayor if you don't want to run for office? Buy the town, of course! Here's a look at a few burgs that have gone on the block in recent years.

HENRY RIVER MILL VILLAGE, NC (Population: 0)

Includes: Twenty-two abandoned buildings, including homes and commercial buildings, on 72 acres

Asking Price: $1.2 million

Details: If you've seen the hit film *The Hunger Games*, you've seen this town. In 1977 the Henry River textile mill burned down, and the town, built in the 1920s to house the mill workers, was abandoned. Three decades later it was so run down that when Hollywood scouts came to North Carolina looking for a location dilapidated enough to serve as the movie's "District 12" (where the main characters live), the village was perfect for their needs. Soon after *The Hunger Games* hit theaters, fans began pouring into the village. That was more than 83-year-old Wade Shepherd, the owner of Henry River Mill Village, could handle. "I'm getting too many visitors. Day and night, they're driving through, taking pictures, getting out and walking. I'm just bombarded with people," he told the *Associated Press* in April 2012.

Sold! Fearful of being sued if a fan was injured on his property—which, after all, consists of *abandoned buildings*—Shepherd sold the village to an auction house called Profiles in History, which planned to auction it off in August 2012.

ALBERT, TEXAS (Population: 25)

Includes: A tavern, dance hall, tractor shed, a three-bedroom house, and 13 acres of land

Asking Price: $2.5 million

Details: In 2003 an insurance broker named Bobby Cave bought this town in the Texas Hill Country for $216,000. He planned to develop it as a tourist attraction, complete with a restaurant and cabins, but he only managed to finish the tavern. In 2007 he put the town up for sale on eBay, with a reserve price of $2.5 million. Winning bid: $3.8 million, by an Italian bidder...who never paid.

Q: What celebrity last name means "son of a stonemason" in Armenian? A: Kardashian

Cave relisted the property with an asking price of $883,000, and in 2009 he finally sold the town to a family from Austin, Texas, who now operate the tavern, a dance hall, and an outdoor pavilion.

Final price: Despite the public's curiosity, neither the buyers nor the seller would disclose how much the town was sold for.

SECRET TOWN WITH NO NAME, LATVIA

(Population: 0)

Includes: Seventy buildings, including 10 apartment buildings, two nightclubs, a school, hotel, shopping center, hospital, army barracks, and sauna complex, on 111 acres

Opening Bid: 150,000 *lats* ($285,000), about the price of a four-room apartment in Riga, the nation's capital city

Details: Latvia, a country on the Baltic Sea in northeastern Europe, was seized by the Soviet Union in 1940. In the 1960s the Soviets built this town to house two secret radar installations designed to detect a possible U.S. nuclear attack. At its peak, the town was home to 5,000 people, but it was so secret that it did not appear on maps and was never officially named. In documents it was identified only as Skrunda-1, because of its location near the town of Skrunda. When the USSR collapsed in the early 1990s and Latvia reclaimed its independence, the Russians dismantled their radar systems and went home.

Sold! The town sat abandoned until February 2010, when the Latvian government put it up for public auction. Winning bid: 5.9 million *lats* ($3.1 million), by a Russian company that planned to turn the entire town into a pig farm. That deal fell through, so four months later a Latvian company bought the town for the greatly reduced price of $323,000. At last report the company was still trying to figure out what to do with it.

* * *

PITTER PAT

In 2011 a couple hunting on a remote mountain in Sweden's northern province of Jaemtland were surprised to find 70 pairs of shoes spread out in the snow. The 140 shoes—ranging from high heels and tap shoes to kids' and men's sneakers—were each filled with about a pound of butter. Officials have no suspects.

THE PETE BEST AWARDS

Who's Pete Best? He was the Beatles' first drummer, replaced by Ringo Starr just before the band made it big. Sadly, Best never got to share his bandmates' success...and neither did any of these folks.

MUSICIAN: Laura Lynch, of the Dixie Chicks

STORY: Along with sisters Emily and Martie Erwin, Lynch founded the Dixie Chicks in 1989. After several years of playing clubs and music festivals, the group's modern bluegrass/country sound attracted the attention of Sony Records. It was right around that time that Lynch decided to quit the Dixie Chicks. Why? She was older than her bandmates (Lynch was 37; the Erwins were 23 and 26) and felt she was neglecting her 14-year-old daughter. Just before they made their first album for Sony, Lynch was replaced by Natalie Maines. The Dixie Chicks went on to become one of the most successful country groups of the 1990s and 2000s, selling 26 million albums.

FINAL NOTE: Lynch later told an interviewer that she "cried for months" after leaving the group, if only because she missed playing music. The money didn't matter—in 1999 Lynch's husband won $29 million in the Texas Lottery.

MUSICIAN: Doug Hopkins, of the Gin Blossoms

STORY: The Gin Blossoms' biggest hits—1993's "Hey Jealousy" and 1994's "Found Out About You"—were both written by Hopkins, the band's founder, songwriter, and guitarist. But by the time those songs were hits, Hopkins was long gone. Why? Drugs and alcohol. The other Gin Blossoms had to decide whether they would support their bandmate, or risk taking so long to record the album that A&M Records might drop them. Decision: They kicked Hopkins out of the band. And they wouldn't give him his share of the advance ($15,000) unless he agreed to give up his share of the group's publishing royalties. Hopkins was broke, so he took the deal. *New Miserable Experience* sold three million copies.

FINAL NOTE: As the Gin Blossoms became more successful, Hopkins got more depressed, drank more, and ultimately took his own life in December 1993.

Rats do not have gallbladders or tonsils. (But they do have belly buttons.)

MUSICIAN: Chad Channing, of Nirvana

STORY: Channing wasn't Nirvana's first drummer, but he was the first one to record with Kurt Cobain and Krist Novoselic—he played on the group's (first independently released) album, *Bleach*, in 1989. Channing was still in the band when, on the strength of *Bleach*, Nirvana was signed to Geffen Records and was starting to record *Nevermind*. By that point, Cobain had grown dissatisfied with Channing's drumming, and Channing was frustrated by not being allowed to contribute to the songwriting. Channing left the band amicably...and watched from the sidelines as Nirvana hit superstardom with new drummer Dave Grohl.

MUSICIAN: Jason Cropper, of Weezer

STORY: Cropper was the pop-rock band's original guitarist. He was present at their first rehearsal in February 1992 and played on the demos that got the band signed with Geffen Records. Less than two years later, however, Cropper was out and new guitarist Brian Bell was in. In May 1994, Weezer's self-titled album was released. It sold three million copies and launched the career of one of the most high-profile rock bands of the last two decades. Curiously, Cropper signed a non-disclosure agreement as to the reason for his departure. The gag order remains in effect to this day.

FINAL NOTE: Cropper and his wife, Amy Wellner Cropper, formed a new band called Chopper One. The band made a few independent albums; the Croppers divorced in 2004.

MUSICIAN: Dave Sabo, of Bon Jovi

STORY: Bon Jovi isn't run like other bands, where each member usually has an equal say. Lead singer Jon Bon Jovi actually owns the band and everything associated with it; all the musicians are his employees. (They are very well-paid and have stayed together for more than 25 years.) Bon Jovi formed the band around himself in 1984 to promote his first commercially released single, "Runaway." One of the musicians he hired was a guitarist named Dave Sabo. After "Runaway" garnered Bon Jovi national attention, Sabo was fired and replaced by Richie Sambora, who's still in the group.

FINAL NOTE: Sabo started the 1980s heavy metal band Skid Row. They had two top-10 hits and sold 20 million albums.

It takes your brain about 0.0004 seconds to retrieve a memory. (Or was it 0.0005? Whatever.)

NUDES AND PRUDES

Sometimes it seems like the world can be divided into two kinds of people—those who are offended by public nudity...and those who are offended by those who are offended by public nudity.

NUDE: Pasco County, on the west coast of Florida, has been home to nudist colonies since the 1940s, but the county reached a new milestone in 2011 when officials decided to use taxpayer money to market Pasco's naked charms to the outside world. In December the county awarded $3,818 to the Pasco Area Naturist Development Association (PANDAbare) to promote Pasco as a nude hub for foreign naturists visiting Disney World, the Space Coast, and Florida's other clothing-mandatory tourist spots. In Europe "there are over 19 million practicing nudists, so heck, if we just garner a hundredth of one percent, that's a lot of tourism coming in," said a PANDAbare spokesperson.

PRUDE: Just because Pasco County subsidizes nudity with taxpayer dollars, that doesn't mean it doesn't have limits: In 2008 the nudist Caliente Resort asked for a clothing-optional polling place for that November's presidential election. Request denied. To cite just one logistical problem, where would nude poll workers pin their badges? "Even if I was behind what they were asking for, which I'm not, it's just too much to ask right now," Brian Corley, county supervisor of elections, told *The St. Petersburg Times*.

NUDE: In January 2012, Brian Coldin, a Canadian crusader for the rights of nudists, lost his court fight challenging the constitutionality of Canada's anti-nudity laws. The case dealt with two incidents in which Coldin pulled up to fast food drive-up windows in the buff. In years past he has also been cited for being naked on the side of a highway and in a public park. In his defense, Coldin argued that 1) the citations violated his constitutional right to self-expression, and 2) since a 1978 Supreme Court ruling defined "nude" as "*completely* bare," his state of undress did not meet the legal definition of nudity, since he was wearing sandals and the necklace that he clips his cell phone to. No dice: The judge found Coldin guilty on four counts of public nudity. He was sentenced to

According to a study, the most hated word in the English language is "hate." #2: "moist."

two years probation and fined $3,000.

PRUDE: In March 2011, the Dean of St. Peter's College, Oxford, part of England's famed Oxford University, barred a circus dwarf named "Demon Dan" Blackner from performing at an end-of-year ball. Demon Dan eats glass, opens beer bottles using his eye socket, and "dangles a bowling ball from a 'lower appendage' not normally accustomed to carrying such a heavy load." His most famous trick—and the one that got him barred from Oxford—is the one in which he drags a vacuum cleaner across the stage using the aforementioned lower appendage. "I think it's ridiculous for the Dean to try and decide what people should or should not see," responded Doctor Haze, creator of the Circus of Horrors, where Demon Dan is a headliner.

NUDE: In April 2010, two dozen young women marched topless through Farmington, Maine, to protest the double standard that allows men to remove their shirts on hot days but expects women to keep their tops on. Is it *illegal* for women to go topless in Maine? No...so why have the march? To make it more *socially* acceptable. One protester vowed to "keep making a big deal about it until it's not a big deal."

PRUDE: In June 2011, just months after Demon Dan was barred from performing at a year-end party (see above), Oxford University struck another blow against exhibitionism when the Worcester College library put an end to the Half-Naked Half-Hour—a tradition where, every Wednesday afternoon, a group of male and female students removed their tops and studied in a state of semi-undress for 30 minutes. Were Oxford just another university, the practice might have been permitted to continue, but it is a world-class institution that receives international visitors, many of whom tour the library. "While it may have seemed like a piece of harmless fun," the librarian warned the student body via e-mail, "we ask you please to stop this kind of behaviour in the library. If the inappropriate behaviour continues, library staff will refer the matter to the Dean."

Z - PEOPLE

You know where the Zulu live—or do you? Here's a little information about them and other cultural groups whose names begin with the letter Z.

Zaghawa: A tribe of semi-nomadic farmers living mostly on the border of Chad and Sudan in north-central Africa. **Total population:** about 170,000

Zambo: The Spanish name for a people of mixed African and native descent in Latin America, primarily in Columbia, Peru, Ecuador, and Venezuela. **Total population:** about 5.5 million

Zapotec: Descendants of the builders of the 2,500-year-old ruins of Monte Alban in southern Mexico, they are Mexico's largest indigenous group. Many still speak the ancient Zapotec language. **Total population:** about 900,000

Zarma: They live primarily as subsistence farmers in villages in Niger, with smaller numbers in neighboring West African countries. **Total population:** about 3.5 million

Zaza: An ethnic group related to Iranians, living in nearby eastern Turkey (many have migrated to European countries). Their language: Zazaki. **Total population:** about 1.1 million

Zhuang: China's largest minority group. (The Han make up China's majority.) Most Zhuang live in Guangxi Province in south-central China. **Total population:** about 18 million

Zou: An indigenous group living in the hilly border regions of India and Burma. Their language, like the Burmese language, is related to Tibetan. **Total population:** about 80,000

Zulu: South Africa's largest ethnic group. Most Zulu live in KwaZulu-Natal Province on the country's east coast. **Total population:** about 11 million

Zuni: A federally recognized Native American tribe. Most live on the Zuni Indian Reservation in western New Mexico. Archeological records show they've lived and farmed in the region for 3,000 years. **Total population:** about 10,000

Loners: More Americans live by themselves than people in any other country.

GROANERS

Because every pun is its own reword.

THE STUDENTS who toured the SevenUp factory should have known there'd be a pop quiz.

EINSTEIN DEVELOPED a theory about space, and it was about time, too.

WOULD YOU like this dead battery? It's free of charge.

THE SOLDIER who survived attacks of mustard gas and pepper spray is now a seasoned veteran.

I WAS UP all night looking for the sun. Then it dawned on me.

I WONDERED why the rock was getting larger. Then it hit me.

I CHANGED the name of my MP3 player to *Titanic* because it's always syncing.

DESPITE ALL OUR hard work, we couldn't get the tent up. Too many missed stakes.

HOW DOES MOSES make his tea? Hebrews it.

KIM SAID she knew me from the vegetarian restaurant, but I'd never met herbivore.

DID YOU HEAR about the indecisive plastic surgeon? He couldn't pick his own nose.

JON'S ADDICTED to brake fluid. He says he can stop any time.

HAUNTED FRENCH pancakes give me the crepes.

VELCRO IS such a rip-off!

I USED TO BE a banker, but then I lost interest.

STUDYING FUNGUS is a cultured way to mold young minds.

THE KITCHEN remodelers were very counterproductive.

THE CROSS-EYED teacher got fired because she couldn't control her pupils.

GERMAN SAUSAGE is the wurst.

DON'T YOU limp in here late with a lame excuse!

"The goodness of the true pun is in the direct ratio of its intolerability." —Edgar Allan Poe

WHERE DID THE MOON COME FROM?

We know it's not made of cheese. What else do we know about it?

LUNA 101

What we know for sure about Earth's only natural satellite is that it's a 2,159-mile-wide collection of minerals that orbits our planet about a quarter-million miles away. NASA visited the moon six times between 1969 and 1972, and astronauts brought back hundreds of pounds of rocks, from which geologists determined that the moon is about 10 percent iron, 50 percent oxygen isotopes, 20 percent magnesium, 20 percent silicon, and the rest trace elements like calcium, aluminum, and niobium.

But how did it get there? Through history, there have been four predominant theories.

1. COLLISION-CONDENSATION THEORY

Details: The early universe was a gaseous cloud of material, organized by gravity into vast collections of matter from which galaxies were created, as were flat spinning discs that later became solar systems. Almost all (99.9 percent) of the material in one such disc gravitated toward itself and became the Sun. The remaining 0.1 percent stayed in orbit around the Sun and separated into smaller spirals. Eight of the spirals were big enough to become planets (nine, if you count Pluto) and exert their own gravitational pull. Whatever material was still floating around the planets condensed into orbiting clumps of rock. There are 166 of these "clumps" in our solar system—our moon is one of them.

Supporting Evidence: Everything that formed from that first spiral of material is still spinning in the same direction it always has. Looking down from the North Pole, the Earth spins in a counterclockwise direction, and so does almost everything else in the solar system, including planets, moons, comets, and the asteroid belt.

Detracting Evidence: If the moon and Earth condensed from the same cloud at the same time, the moon should have an iron core similar to Earth's. But Earth is 30 percent iron while the moon is only 10 percent, which suggests that perhaps they did not form at the same time and place.

2. FISSION THEORY

Details: The moon is made of material that was once part of Earth. The hypothesis is that a young, malleable Earth was spinning so fast that part of it detached and flew off into space, where some of it eventually came together as the moon.

Supporting Evidence: A third of Earth is iron, but most of that is in the core, where heavier elements coalesced inside the young planet. The iron content near the Earth's surface is closer to what you would find on the moon. Possible site of the detachment: the Pacific Ocean.

Detracting Evidence: While this may sound like a good theory, there isn't much real evidence to back it up.

3. CAPTURE THEORY

Details: The moon wasn't made from, near, or with Earth, but was a wayward traveler spinning through space until it happened to get close enough for the planet's gravitational field to grab it.

Supporting Evidence: Every meteor crater in the solar system is proof that rogue asteroids and planetoids were everywhere in the early solar system. Billions of years of gravitational attraction (that is, meteors smashing into things) has "cleaned up" most of the debris, but the asteroid belt between Mars and Jupiter remains as a reminder.

Detracting Evidence: Unusual things do happen in the universe, so it's hard to say this is impossible. But the specific weights, speeds, distances, and gravitational effects needed for this theory to work make it statistically unlikely.

4. GIANT IMPACTOR THEORY

Details: The world's leading moon scientists held a conference in Hawaii in 1984, during which they devised this fourth theory. It goes like this: 4.5 billion years ago, a planetoid called Theia, about the size of Mars, crashed into a still-forming Earth. The impact was 100 million times more powerful than the asteroid believed to have killed the dinosaurs. It was probably only a glancing blow rather than a full-on collision, so it didn't reach the iron in Earth's core. Still, it sent enormous amounts of "earth" into space. As the ejected material orbited around Earth over the next few billion years, some of it rained back down onto the planet, some spun away into the solar system, and the rest settled into a single body: the moon.

Detracting Evidence: About 40 percent of the moon would be made of the remnants of Theia; the other 60 percent would have been Earth. But evidence published in 2012 shows that certain titanium isotopes are just as abundant in Earth rocks as in moon rocks, suggesting that they both formed from the same debris field.

GOING, GOING GONE

While the question of the moon's origin is debated, one thing is certain. The satellite is moving away from Earth at about four centimeters per year, and in time will drift so far that Earth's gravity won't be able to hold it. The moon will shrink in the sky until it disappears into the heavens. Don't worry, though! You'll be able to enjoy moonlit nights for at least a few billion years longer.

*   *   *

NICE TRY

In July 2012, San Francisco Giants outfielder Melkey Cabrera was the MVP of the All-Star Game, and leading the league in hits. A month later, Cabrera received a 50-game suspension when he tested positive for a synthetic testosterone, a performance-enhancing substance banned by Major League Baseball. The MLB will reverse suspensions if a player can prove he took banned substances through no fault of his own. That's exactly what happened, Cabrera argued. He claimed he had purchased and used a topical cream that, unbeknownst to him, contained synthetic testosterone. Naturally, investigators had some questions, such as "What kind of product?" and "Who runs the company?" It was quickly discovered that an associate of Cabrera's had paid $10,000 to set up a fake website for the company that supposedly had sold Cabrera's muscle cream, and put an ad for the muscle cream on the site. The suspension stood.

Five of the ten most costly hurricanes in the U.S. have occurred since 1990.

SNAP, CRACKLE...FLOP

Wheaties and Rice Krispies have taken up permanent residency in America's breakfast bowls—these forgotten cereals, not so much.

Fruit Brute: General Mills debuted a line of five monster cereals in the 1970s: Franken Berry, Yummy Mummy, Count Chocula, Boo Berry, and Fruit Brute. The biggest flop of the bunch: Fruit Brute. But it has a cool factor—filmmaker Quentin Tarantino collects old cereals, and his personal box of Fruit Brute has appeared in his movies *Reservoir Dogs* and *Pulp Fiction*.

Graham Crackos: Kellogg's released this graham-cracker-flavored cereal in the late-1970s, a few years before the crack-cocaine epidemic that hit American cities. In light of this, old commercials for Crackos become unsettling. In one, a character named George arrives at a suburban house to deliver a box of Crackos to a family. In the background, a cheery balladeer sings, "Something new is comin' to town, George the Milkman is bringin' it 'round." After the mother takes a bite, she asks George if the cereal will help slow her kids down. "Long enough for them to eat," he replies.

Mr. T Cereal: Based on the fool-pitying strongman's animated self in *Mister T*, his early-1980s cartoon show, it was made up of crispy corn chunks shaped like the letter T. Essentially, Mr. T Cereal was a clone of Alpha-Bits, but with just one letter.

Ice Cream Cones: Available in two flavors, chocolate-chip or vanilla, this cereal consisted of crunchy puffs and sugary cones. The brand—which featured a smiling cartoon character named Ice Cream Jones who delivered the cereal to kids on a bicycle—disappeared within a year of its 1987 debut, possibly because parents didn't fall for the claim that the ice cream-flavored cereal contained "four wholesome grains and eight essential vitamins!"

Prince of Thieves: This cash-in on the 1991 film *Robin Hood: Prince of Thieves* had a couple of problems: 1) Manufacturer Ralston-Purina couldn't get the rights to *Thieves* star Kevin Costner's likeness, so they had to put a generic Robin Hood image on the box, and 2) the cereal was supposed to look like little arrows, but came out resembling a certain part of the male anatomy.

The beat goes on: Capuchin monkeys use large branches to club snakes.

PORTMANTEAU WORDS

These words combine parts or all of two different words, taking on aspects of both meanings. The term was coined in 1871 by author Lewis Carroll. Here are a few modern examples:

ADVERTORIAL

From: *Advertisement* and *editorial*

Meaning: An ad designed to look like a news story

Origin: The word first appeared in the mid-1940s and was widely used by the late 1950s. But while the term is fairly recent, the practice of making newspaper and magazine ads look like editorials or news stories, and even placing them in sections normally reserved for editorials and news, has been going on for centuries. Today it's illegal to use them without proper notification, which is why you often see—in teensy-weensy letters—the words "Paid Advertisement" hidden somewhere on an advertorial.

BEEFALO

From: *Beef* and *buffalo*

Meaning: Cattle that are the result of crossbreeding common cows with American bison ("buffalo"). And it's not just any old mix: Official beefalo must be 3⁄8 bison and 5⁄8 cattle breed such as Angus or Hereford. If they're more than 3⁄8 bison, they're known as "bison hybrids."

Origin: It was coined by beefalo breeders as a name they thought would help sell meat from these animals to the public. The first known use was in 1973, and credit is usually given to one breeder in particular, a California rancher named Bud Basolo.

Bonus: One of the first people to try crossbreeding cattle and bison was legendary Texas Panhandle rancher Charles Goodnight, who bred female bison with bull cattle in 1870. He hoped the result would be cattle with thick fur, which would help them withstand the region's harsh winters, but was ultimately unsuccessful—the resulting calves were often either sterile or very aggressive. Goodnight didn't call them "beefalo"—he called them "cattalo."

Egyptian Pharaoh Pepi II had his slaves smeared with honey to attract flies away from him.

MALWARE

From: *Malicious* and *software*

Meaning: Any software, files, code, or programs designed to harm or interfere with the operation of a computer

Origin: In the 1970s and 1980s, computer scientists began using the terms *worm*, *virus*, and *Trojan horse* to describe programs that attack computers. They all do damage differently: A *worm* installs itself on a computer, then replicates and spreads to other computers, consuming bandwidth and crippling networks; a *virus* infects and corrupts data on files and programs; and a *Trojan horse* is a program designed to look like a harmless file that, once installed, can destroy files or allow hackers access to a computer. Computer geeks argued about the use of these terms for years, so in 1990, someone—some say it was an Israeli security expert named Yisrael Radai—came up with the all-encompassing term *malware*.

STAYCATION

From: *Stay* and *vacation*

Meaning: To spend vacation time at home rather than travel

Origin: Canadian comedian Brent Butt is credited with inventing this word in the October 24, 2005, episode of his hit sitcom, *Corner Gas*. The word became popular in the English-speaking world after the financial crisis struck in 2008 and millions of people were forced to take "staycations" due to financial circumstances. It was made an official word when *Merriam-Webster* added it in 2009.

NETIQUETTE

From: *Net* and *etiquette*

Meaning: Conventions of polite behavior on the Internet

Origin: The word was coined in 1982—three years before the word "Internet" was invented and a full ten years before the Internet became widely popular. Scientists and university students involved with the development of the Internet, however, had been communicating on early prototypes, such as USENET and ARPANET, since the 1970s, and someone came up with the very polite term "netiquette" for them.

DUSTBIN OF HISTORY: BARBARA HUTTON

On page 73 we told you the story of tycoon Frank W. Woolworth's untimely demise. Here's the story of his granddaughter—and heir—Barbara Hutton, aka "the poor little rich girl."

WILL POWER

Frank Woolworth, founder of the F.W. Woolworth chain of five-and-ten-cent stores, was updating his will when he fell ill and died suddenly in April 1919. The new will would have dispersed his fortune among many heirs, including his wife, daughters, grandchildren, close friends, business associates, and charities. But he died before he'd signed it—which meant that an earlier will, drafted in 1899 when his estate was significantly smaller, was the one that counted.

That will left his entire fortune to his ailing widow, Jennie. When she passed away a few years later, the estate was divided equally among just three heirs: two surviving daughters and a granddaughter, 12-year-old Barbara Hutton. Barbara was the only child of Woolworth's third daughter, Edna Woolworth Hutton, who had committed suicide in 1917.

THANKS, DAD

Barbara's one-third share of the Woolworth fortune came to about $28 million (roughly $377 million in today's dollars). It was held in trust until she reached her 21st birthday, and was managed by her father, a wealthy stockbroker named Franklyn Hutton. (The last name might sound familiar: Hutton and his brother, Edward Francis Hutton, founded the E. F. Hutton brokerage firm in 1904.)

Franklyn Hutton was a shrewd investor even by Wall Street standards: By the time Barbara turned 21, he'd nearly doubled her fortune to $50 million (about $870 million today). Then he locked in her gains by getting out of the stock market just months before the October 1929 crash. The rest of the country slid into the Great Depression, but thanks to her father, 21-year-old Barbara Hutton was one of the wealthiest women in the world.

Take that, Italy! Galileo's middle finger is on display at Italy's Museum of Science.

THE MARRY-GO-ROUND

Franklyn Hutton may have been good with money, but he was a terrible family man. He was a blatant womanizer and a heavy drinker, and his behavior helped to drive his wife, Edna, over the edge. After she killed herself, Franklyn sent Barbara, then only four, to live with relatives until she was old enough to be packed off to boarding school.

Barbara Hutton's painful childhood left her needy and insecure. Perhaps because of it, at the age of 20, she began a nearly life-long pattern of marrying the fortune seekers who were drawn to her like mosquitos. Hutton would wed seven times: to a self-styled "prince" from Soviet Georgia (1933–35), a Danish count (1935–41), actor Cary Grant (1942–45), a Lithuanian prince (1947–51), a Dominican playboy and diplomat (1953; the marriage lasted only 53 days), a German baron and former tennis pro (1955–59), and a Vietnamese chemist who became a Laotian prince *after* Hutton paid $50,000 for his title (1964–66). With the exception of Cary Grant, who had his own money and neither asked for nor received alimony, each of Hutton's husbands walked away with millions.

BANK-ACCOUNT BARBIE

The money that Hutton's husbands couldn't get their hands on she spent herself, on exquisite jewels, fine art, yachts, palatial homes in the United States, Great Britain, Morocco, and elsewhere, an army of servants, and anything else she wanted. She gave away money compulsively, not just to friends, servants, and toadies, but also to hard-luck cases she'd read about in the newspaper and strangers she met on the street. She was also public spirited: During World War II she donated her yacht to Britain's Royal Navy; after the war she gave Winfield House, her London mansion, to the U.S. State Department to be used as the ambassador's residence, a purpose it still serves today.

Hutton's fabulous wealth, her numerous marriages and affairs, and her connection to the dime-store chain where so many Americans shopped, made her irresistible fodder for the newspapers, which called her "the poor little rich girl." (After she married Cary Grant, the pair ended up with a new nickname: "Cash and Cary.") Although much of the coverage was negative, it made her one of the most famous women of her time.

FOR SALE—CHEAP

If you inherited the equivalent of $870 million, do you think you could make it last? In the late 1960s, when Hutton was in her late 50s and estranged from her seventh and final husband, she started running out of ready cash. Her financial advisers began selling off the homes, jewels, and other items she'd accumulated over the years to raise the money she needed to live in the high style to which she was accustomed. There was plenty of stuff to sell, but thanks to a lot of self-dealing and sweetheart deals, many of Hutton's assets, including valuable real estate, sold for a fraction of what they were worth, causing her fortune to dissipate even faster.

Money wasn't Hutton's only problem: A lifetime lived in the headlines as she careened from one bad relationship to another had taken its toll. By her early 60s, she'd become a chain-smoking alcoholic, addicted to prescription drugs. When her only son, fathered by the Danish count, died in a plane crash in 1972, she sank into a depression that would last the rest of her life.

By the late 1970s, Hutton was a virtual recluse, living in a $10,000-a-month suite in the Beverly Wilshire hotel in Los Angeles. There she existed on Coca-Cola, vodka, cigarettes, prescription drugs and not much else, as her advisors scrambled to sell ever more of her assets to raise the $25,000 a month needed to cover her living expenses.

INTO THE DUSTBIN

The advisers managed to stretch Hutton's fortune to the end of her days, but only barely. Though she still owned a lot of jewelry, when she died from a heart attack in her hotel suite in May 1979, most of her other possessions had been sold. She had just $3,500 left in her bank account.

The Woolworth dime-store chain that had provided Hutton with her wealth didn't outlast her by much. Unable to compete against Walmart and other competitors, in the 1980s the company shifted its focus to its more successful specialty chains and let the original Woolworth stores wither away. The last Woolworth's in the United States closed in 1997. Four years later, the parent company renamed itself after its most successful specialty chain: Foot Locker.

...*Neighborhood?* A: Hischer Booptrunk. (It was Fred Rogers' childhood toy.)

HOUSEHOLD HINTS

Sent in by our readers.

Having trouble getting a key on a tight metal key ring? Use a staple remover to pry it apart and hold it open.

Rub a walnut (the nut, not the shell) on small dings and dents in wooden furniture to make them disappear.

To prevent your kid from falling out of bed, put a foam pool-noodle under the fitted sheet to make a bed bumper.

Place cleaning products in a hanging plastic shoe rack, and hang the rack on the back of a door. That keeps them away from your kids, and easily accessible for you.

To cut open plastic "blister" packages, try using a can opener.

To vacuum tricky corners or under furniture, stick an empty paper-towel or gift-wrap roll into the end of the hose.

Sprinkle cayenne pepper on plants to keep squirrels from nibbling them. It won't affect the plants.

Lost an earring? Put pantyhose over a vacuum hose and vacuum the area—the machine will suck up the earring, but the pantyhose will prevent it from going inside.

Put a dryer sheet in your pocket to help keep mosquitos away. (They hate the smell.)

To remove soap and mildew buildup from a shower head, tie a vinegar-filled baggie around it and leave overnight. (But don't forget to remove it before you shower.)

Want a less toxic alternative to bug spray? Try cornmeal. Put small piles of it where you see ants. They'll take it back to the colony to share, but none of them can digest it.

If you break a glass and you're not sure you swept up all the tiny shards, dab at the area with a wet cotton ball or Q-tip, or a wad of damp paper towel.

The fastest way to de-fog a windshield: a chalkboard eraser. The fastest way to clean foggy headlights: toothpaste.

***Star Wars* quiz: Who was Ralph McQuarrie? The artist who designed Darth Vader's helmet.**

AMERICA IS...

...the greatest nation? Not according to these folks.

"We Americans are the best informed people on earth as to the events of the last twenty-four hours; we are not the best informed as to the events of the last sixty centuries."

—Will Durant

"Americans will put up with anything, provided it doesn't block traffic."

—Dan Rather

"In our brief national history we have shot four of our presidents, worried five of them to death, impeached one, and hounded another out of office. And when all else fails, we hold an election and assassinate their character."

—P. J. O'Rourke

"America is a country that doesn't know where it's going, but is determined to set a speed record getting there."

—Laurence J. Peter

"In America any boy may become president, and I suppose it's just one of the risks he takes."

—Adlai Stevenson

"Very little is known about the War of 1812 because the Americans lost it."

—Eric Nicol

"The Americans are a funny lot; they drink whiskey to keep them warm; then they put some ice in it to keep it cool; they put some sugar in it to make it sweet; and then they put a slice of lemon in it to make it sour. Then they say 'here's to you' and drink it themselves."

—B. N. Chakravaty

"America is a land where a citizen will cross the ocean to fight for democracy and won't cross the street to vote in a national election."

—Bill Vaughan

"Illegal aliens have always been a problem in the United States. Ask any Indian."

—Robert Orben

"Thanks to the Interstate Highway System, it is now possible to travel from coast to coast without seeing anything."

—Charles Kuralt

First American to win the Nobel Peace Prize: Theodore Roosevelt (1906).

THE FIRE ANT DANCE

If you're wondering how to get lounge lizards onto the dance floor, here's the answer. Bring on the fire ants!

ANT INVASION

In the 1930s, a few red fire ant colonies were accidentally loaded onto ships bound from South America (their home) to Mobile, Alabama. The stowaways were offloaded at the port and quickly made themselves at home in Alabama's warm, fertile soil. Because they had left behind all the viruses, fungi, roundworms, flies, and parasites that kept them in check in South America, they quickly spread across the Southern United States.

Red fire ants (*Solenopsis invicta*) are extremely aggressive: They not only bite, they sting, injecting their prey with venom that paralyzes it, giving them time to eat their lunch...to the bone. What has happened since the South American fire ant invasion suggests that it doesn't take millenia for a species to evolve. Sometimes it only takes a tiny insect.

GET OFF THE FENCE

Eastern fence lizards (*Sceloporus undulatus*) were easy prey for the invasive fire ants. These 4- to 7-inch reptiles are known for lounging on sunny fence rails, and not getting worked up about anything as inconsequential as a few bugs crawling on them. In fact, fence lizards are accustomed to staying very still when an insect climbs aboard. They don't want to scare away an easy, self-delivered meal.

This strategy worked fine with harmless native bugs. But fire ants are *not* harmless. They will bite anything that looks like food. If there are enough of them, they can strip a newborn calf down to the bones. Fence lizards? A dozen fire ants can kill a lizard in a minute or less.

In the early years of the fire ant invasion, adult fence lizards seemed unaware of the danger—they continued to lounge around as fire ants swarmed over them, lifted up their scales, injected them with paralyzing poison, and then chowed down. Good for the fire ants; bad for the fence lizards.

It was once illegal to sell *E.T. The Extra-terrestrial* dolls in France.

Fortunately for the species, young fence lizards displayed a different reaction to the fire ants—they "dance." Because their scales are softer than an adult's, they're more vulnerable. (They're also only about the size of a house key.) So they react the way most people do when a bug crawls on them: They jump up, shake the insect off, and run away.

LET'S DANCE

Like every species, fence lizards have variations in behavior between individuals. Just as some humans stop acting like babies at age four but others still exhibit infantile behaviors into their 40s, some fence lizards stop doing their defensive ant dance earlier than others. Predictably, precocious fence lizards—those that give up dancing sooner—are at a disadvantage when it comes to fire ants. They get eaten. Lizards that carry the dancing behavior into their adult years tend to live longer (because they're not being eaten alive). Result: Fence lizards that keep dancing have a better chance of passing the dancing gene to their offspring.

YOU SAY YOU WANT AN EVOLUTION

Apparently some situations press the fast forward button on natural selection. Invasions are one of them. Penn State biologist Tracy Langkilde did a study in which she compared adult fence lizards from fire ant-infested areas with those from areas without fire ants. She discovered something that Charles Darwin might have predicted: In areas not infested by fire ants, only 40 to 50 percent of the adults danced when exposed to crawling insects. In contrast, in areas infested for at least 70 years, *80 percent* of adults danced. Fence lizards exposed to the ant invasion had evolved.

"They do this big body shimmy, or a body twitch," Langkilde told *LiveScience*. "They shake their body to fling the ants off them, and then they run away from the ant mound."

Langkilde found one other difference: Fence lizards in fire ant-infested areas had hind legs that were five percent longer than those in uninfested areas. Fire ant exposure, it turned out, had caused the lizards to evolve longer back legs. That extra length adds more velocity to the lizards' dancin' and shakin', which sends the ants flying faster and farther, *and* it adds greater speed for quicker get-aways from the vicious ants.

In physics, there are 6 types, or "flavors," of quarks: up, down, strange, charm, top & bottom.

IT'S LIKE A SIMILE

As you may remember from English class, a simile is a figure of speech that compares two things using the words like *or* as. *These literary examples come from Terence Hodgson's collection* Eyes Like Butterflies.

"The acne on your face is like an ancient map of Ireland after a smattering of napalm."

—Desmond Hogan, *Martyrs*

"She had skin like vacuum-cleaner bags hanging from between her elbows and armpits."

—Clyde Edgerton, *In Memory of Junior*

"The elderly American ladies leaning on their canes listed toward me like towers of Pisa."

—Vladimir Nabokov, *Lolita*

"I felt like a small valise that had been used for baggage-handler soccer all the way from Reykjavik to Delhi, including connecting flights."

—Toby Litt, *Finding Myself*

"Her breasts were like people, two slouching fat white people in caps having a conversation across the four-lane highway of her rib cage."

—T. C. Boyle, *Drop City*

"He felt like a potato in the soil dreaming of the vodka that was to be made of it."

—Penelope Gilliatt, *Known for Her Frankness*

"A thought passes through my mind like a cat walking on my shoulders behind my neck."

—Harold Brodkey, *A Guest in the Universe*

"His tongue rolled in his mouth like a frightened frankfurter."

—Angela Carter, *Shadow Dance*

"The air felt clotted, sluggish, hot, partisan, and impassioned, like the breathing of a vindictive judge."

—Cynthia Ozick, *The Doctor's Wife*

"The hours creep like slugs in a headwind."

—Richard Powers, *Plowing the Dark*

"The dusk raked like a black searchlight across the hills."

—Martin Amis, *Dead Babies*

Hedgehogs were a delicacy in ancient Egypt. (They're supposedly very fatty.)

UNDERWEAR IN THE NEWS

Except for those who go commando, underwear is such a common part of our lives that it's bound to make headlines once in a while.

HOW'S TRICKS?

Russell Fitzgerald, chairman of the Abington, Massachusetts, school committee, tried to make meetings a little more fun by opening with a magic trick. Once he made a glass of water disappear; another time he did a rope trick. In September 2011, he tied the corners of two handkerchiefs together and asked a committee member named Ellen Killian to hold the knot against her chest. Fitzgerald and a high school teacher he recruited as an unwitting assistant each held the other corners of the hankies, and at the count of three, gave them a pull. Where the knot had been, out popped a bra, creating the impression that Fitzgerald had yanked Ellen Killian's bra from beneath her blouse.

A simple illusion, and under other circumstances (a college party, perhaps), fairly innocent and even funny. But the meeting was being broadcast live over the community access cable channel, so "funny" wasn't how it went over. The trick was met with dead silence. Killian, red faced, returned to her seat, and Fitzgerald apologized, but it wasn't enough to save him: A few days later, he resigned his chairmanship after 11 years of volunteer service.

SHOPGIRLS BY DECREE

In January 2012, Saudi Arabia's King Abdullah issued a decree ordering that the all-male workforce in the ultraconservative kingdom's 7,300 lingerie shops be fired and replaced by women. This was expected to create jobs for as many as 40,000 Saudi women. Saudi women are traditionally barred from working in retail sales—even in stores that sell women's underwear—because the job might require interacting with men. (Women buying underwear from male salesclerks was considered permissible because Saudi women are always accompanied by a male relative when

In Zimbabwe the importation and sale of second-hand underwear was banned in 2011.

they shop.) Since women are prohibited from driving cars, the new salesclerks will still need to be driven to their jobs by a male family member. The decree may spur an increase in domestic sales of ladies underwear—in the past women who could afford to buy their unmentionables abroad often did so to avoid the embarrassment of giving their underwear size to the male salesclerks in Saudi stores.

SOLD!

One of the ways that the victims of Ponzi schemer Bernie Madoff received partial restitution for their $64 billion in losses was through the auctioning off of Madoff's personal effects, from his mansions, yachts, and cars to his golf clubs, sweaters, pants, shoes...and underwear. One bidder snapped up 14 pairs of underpants for $200; another paid $1,700 for 11 pairs of monogrammed boxer shorts grouped with 138 pairs of "ultra-luxurious Charvet socks" (which retail for $60). The winning bidder, who asked not to be identified, said he was interested only in the socks. "They're brand new, so I don't have to buy socks for the next two or three years," he explained to the *New York Post* in November 2010. So what was his plan for Madoff's monogrammed boxer shorts? "They're a great Christmas gift because it's not something people would buy for themselves."

* * *

SILLY (REAL) MOVIE MERCHANDISE

- *The Hunger Games* cookbook
- *Transformers* shaving kit
- *The Avengers* hamburger patties
- *Sex and the City* thongs
- *Star Wars* toaster (puts an imprint of Darth Vader on toast)
- *Letters to E.T.* (a book of letters from kids to the title character)
- *Harry Potter* slacks.
- *The Incredible Hulk*'s Hulkie Pokey Hulk. A stuffed animal for kids.
- *Twilight* condoms
- *The Passion of the Christ* crucifixion nail pendants.
- *Footloose* nail polish
- *Planet of the Apes* boomerang. Or as it was labeled, a "boom-a-rang-utang."(Get it?)

"DO YOUR BEST!"

...and other suggestions from the kamikaze training manual.

BACKGROUND

During World War II, Japan had a terrifying secret weapon: A group of pilots who were specially trained to crash their planes into enemy warships, killing sailors and, hopefully, sinking the ships. Over the course of the war, thousands of suicide missions managed to damage or sink hundreds of Allied battleships, killing 3,000 British and American sailors. The pilots' code name was the "To-Go Fliers," but outside the military they were known as *kamikaze* ("Divine Wind").

How did the Japanese air force convince these young pilots to give up their lives on suicide missions? With advice like this, taken from their manual, *Basic Instructions for To-Go Fliers*, which was translated into English for the first time in 2002.

- "When you eliminate thoughts about life and death, it will enable you to concentrate your attention on eradicating the enemy and reinforcing your excellence in flight skills."
- "Breathe deeply three times. Proceed straight ahead on the airstrip."
- "When you take this walk, be aware of your surroundings. What are the obstacles: an electric pole, a tree, a hill?"
- "Many have crashed into the target with wide-open eyes. They will tell you what fun they had."
- "You must prepare well your inner self. Some people say that spirit comes before skill, but they are wrong. Spirit and skill are one. The two elements must be mastered together."
- "The spirits of your dead comrades are watching you intently. It is essential that you do not shut your eyes so as not to miss the target."
- "Keep your health in the very best condition. You cannot deftly manipulate the control stick if you are suffering diarrhea."
- "Be always cheerful."

Earliest-known picture of a volcano: an 8,000-year-old wall painting in Turkey.

• "Where should you aim? When diving onto a ship, aim for a point between the bridge tower and smokestacks. Entering the stack is also effective."

• "You view all that you experienced in your 20-odd years of life in rapid succession. You may wonder what happened. You may even hear a final sound like the breaking of crystal. Then you are no more. At that moment, all the cherry blossoms at Yasukuni Shrine in Tokyo will smile brightly at you."

• "You have lived for 20 years or more. You must exert your full might for the last time in your life. Exert supernatural strength."

• "Remember when diving into the enemy ship to shout at the top of your lungs: *Hissatsu*! (Sink without fail!)"

• "You will sense that your speed has suddenly increased. It is like a long shot in a movie suddenly turning into a close-up and the scene expands in your face."

• "If you are not in top physical condition, you will not be able to achieve an ideal hit by body-crashing."

• "In the event of poor weather conditions when you cannot locate the target, don't be discouraged. Do not waste your life lightly. You should return to the base jovially and without remorse."

• "You are two or three meters from the target. At that moment, you see your mother's face. She is not smiling or crying. It is her usual face."

• "At the very moment of impact: Do your best."

* * *

YOU LIGHT UP MY LIFE

In October 2008, an early morning fire ripped through the Resort Hotel in Yamanashi Prefecture, Japan. No one was killed or injured, but enough damage was sustained that Tatushiko Kawata cancelled his wedding, scheduled to be held at the hotel that weekend. A few hours later, police arrested a man who they believed purposely set fire to the hotel: Tatushiko Kawata. He admitted the arson, telling police, "If I set a fire I thought I wouldn't have to go through with the wedding."

Americans throw away enough paper annually to build a wall 12' high from L.A. to NY.

THE WORST BUSINESS DECISION EVER?

In Uncle John's Unstoppable Bathroom Reader, *we told you the story of Charles Bennett, who passed on a chance to buy as much as half of the Ford Motor Company for as little as $75,000. Was it the worst business decision ever? Before you answer, consider the case of Ron Wayne.*

APPLE SEEDS

In February 1974, a 20-year-old college dropout named Steve Jobs answered a newspaper classified ad and landed a $5-per-hour job as a technician at a new company in Los Gatos, California, called Atari. If you're old enough to remember the 1970s, you probably remember the name: Atari is the company that essentially invented the video game industry when they introduced the game *Pong* in 1972.

At Atari, Jobs soon earned a reputation for being, well, a bit of a jerk. He was brilliant, and he knew it. He was also quick to let his coworkers know when he thought he was smarter than they were. He called them names to their faces. As if that wasn't bad enough, Jobs, who was a vegetarian, had somehow gotten the idea that his meatless diet eliminated his body odor. That, he felt, made it unnecessary for him to bathe regularly, so he didn't. (But he did soak his dirty bare feet in workplace toilets.)

BEEN THERE, DONE THAT

As anyone who worked around Jobs during his Atari days would assure you, conceit does not win you friends, and vegetarian diets do not eliminate body odor. The stinky, stuck-up prodigy was soon banished to the night shift, where his brains could be put to work for the company without his offensive personality and pungent aroma driving coworkers out into the street.

One man at Atari that Jobs *did* get along with was the chief draftsman, Ron Wayne. Jobs was intrigued with the idea of one day starting his own business, and Wayne, who was in his early 40s, had done this before. Jobs looked up to him as a mentor, and his advice would come in handy when Jobs and a high-school friend named Steve Wozniak considered launching their own company together in 1976.

LIGHT SHOW

Jobs's and Wozniak's decision to start a business together grew out of their participation in the Homebrew Computer Club, a group of hobbyists who built computers from mail-order kits or by scrounging parts from surplus military equipment and old office machines. The computers they were building were primitive: If you saw one today, you'd have trouble recognizing it as a computer.

Consider the Altair 8800, the machine that inspired the founding of the Homebrew club: Sold in kit form through *Popular Electronics* magazine, it was little more than a metal box with rows of lights and toggle switches on the front. It had no keyboard and no monitor. You "programmed" the Altair by flipping the toggle switches on and off to enter binary computer code. Once entered, the code made the lights blink in a specific sequence.

That was it—making lights flash on command was the only thing that the Altair 8800 could do. And yet it was so dazzling and so powerful a machine for its time that it not only inspired the founding of the Homebrew Computer Club, it also inspired a Harvard student named Bill Gates to drop out of college and form a business with his friend Paul Allen—a company they named Micro-Soft—to create a programming language for the machine.

THINKING SMALL

Wozniak, an engineer at Hewlett-Packard's calculator division, wanted to design a home computer that could do more than the Altair 8800. There were computers at the time that were capable of performing much more powerful operations, but they were enormous machines that took up entire rooms and cost so much money that only universities, large corporations, and government agencies could afford them. Some of these big computers could be accessed remotely over telephone lines, using a *video terminal*—a video monitor and keyboard that connected to the computer using a dial-up modem.

Wozniak thought that the newest microprocessor chips were powerful enough to enable video terminals to have small computer brains of their own, so that they wouldn't need to connect to

Meditate on this: For his hobby, the Dalai Lama likes to repair watches.

big computers far away. He decided to try to build one: Working in his Hewlett-Packard cubicle at night and on weekends, Wozniak designed and built a computer that had a keyboard, an ordinary TV for a video display (he thought computer monitors were too expensive), and a whopping 8 kb of memory. He also wrote the software that made the computer work.

On Sunday, June 29, 1975, Wozniak finished the computer and started it up. He typed a character, and it appeared on the screen! That's something we take for granted today, but Wozniak's machine was the very first "personal computer"—as they would soon be known—capable of such a feat. Wozniak didn't know it at the time, but with that single keystroke, he had brought the era of toggle switches and flashing lights to a close. The personal computer revolution had begun.

A COMPANY IS BORN

Wozniak had designed his computer simply for the fun of the challenge. He planned to print up the plans and give them away at meetings of the Homebrew Computer Club, so that the members could build their own computers. It did not occur to him that money could be made from his invention—that was where Steve Jobs came in.

Jobs thought they could make circuit boards pre-printed with Wozniak's design, almost like a paint-by-numbers kit, so that hobbyists would know where to install each component. He figured he could sell the circuit boards to members of the Homebrew Club for $50 apiece. So when Wozniak and Jobs decided to form a company in 1976, that was all they set out to make: pre-printed circuit boards.

NOT FAR FROM THE TREE

To raise the money, they needed to launch their company and print the first batch of circuit boards. Jobs sold his Volkswagen van for $1,500 and Wozniak sold his programmable calculator for $250. Next they needed a name for their company, and tried out techie-sounding ones like "Executek" and "Matrix Electronics." Jobs was on an all-fruit diet at the time (which proved no better that his old vegetarian diet at controlling body odor), and had recently returned from an Oregon commune, where he'd pruned some Gravenstein apple trees. He suggested "Apple Computer." That sounded better than anything else they could think of, *and* it came before Atari in the phone book, so Apple it was.

APPLES AND ORANGES

It was probably inevitable that Wozniak, who created things for fun and liked to give them away, would clash with Jobs, who wanted to build a business by selling things for profit. The two had their first big disagreement when Wozniak balked at giving Apple Computer the exclusive rights to his invention; he wanted to give his plans away free to Homebrew members who didn't buy the circuit boards. And since he'd built the computer at his Hewlett-Packard workbench after hours, he felt that HP also had a claim to the technology.

Jobs, on the other hand, was convinced that Wozniak's computer was the heart of Apple's business, and without the exclusive use of that technology the company would have no value. He shared his concerns with Ron Wayne, his friend at Atari, and Wayne agreed.

MR. 10 PERCENT

Wayne offered to have the pair over to his apartment, where he would try to convince Wozniak that Apple needed the exclusive rights to his design. It took about two hours to do it, but by the time Wayne was finished, Wozniak was a believer. His invention would be Apple's and Apple's alone.

Wayne was 20 years older than Jobs and Wozniak, and more mature than either of them. They were impressed by his business sense, and decided to make him a partner in the company. Instead of splitting ownership of Apple Computer 50/50 as they had planned, Wozniak and Jobs each took a 45 percent stake in the company, and gave Wayne the remaining 10 percent. That way, whenever they couldn't agree on something, Wayne would serve as a tiebreaker, giving the winner the 55 percent majority needed to prevail.

Ten percent of Apple Computer for two hours' work—what could possibly go wrong? ***To find out, turn to page 384.***

LAUGH LINES

People who are paid to be funny earn their money.

"The hardest part about going to Hypochondriacs Anonymous is admitting that you don't have a problem."

—Gene Hunt

"I stop my microwave at 0:01 to feel like I'm a bomb defuser."

—Jerry Seinfeld

"You offer a sincere compliment on a great mustache and suddenly she's not your friend."

—Marty Feldman

"I bet a cannibal's fridge would look a lot like an office fridge: full of containers labeled with people's names."

—Julius Sharpe

"Dad always thought laughter was the best medicine, which I guess is why several of us died of tuberculosis."

—Jack Handey

"There are no B batteries. If there were, you wouldn't know if someone was stuttering. 'Hello I'd like some B-batteries.' 'What kind?' 'B-batteries.' 'What kind?!'"

—Demetri Martin

"George Washington's brother, Lawrence, was the Uncle of Our Country."

—George Carlin

"I was on a plane recently reading an article about environmentalism in the in-flight magazine. That's right—I was reading about the environment while sitting on a pollution machine that can fly."

—Hari Kondabolu

"I hope cell phones aren't bad for us, but I would like the excuse: 'I can't talk right now. You're giving me cancer.'"

—Whitney Cummings

"So all my friends have kids now…which I think is rude."

—David Cross

"If you were to send a werewolf to the moon, would he be a werewolf permanently?"

—Kristen Schaal

"I was out with a guy who told me I didn't need to drink to make myself more fun to be around. I said, 'I'm drinking so *you're* more fun to be around.'"

—Chelsea Handler

People in big cities produce more earwax than people in rural areas.

A BAD CASE OF THE FLUE

You've heard the expression "caught between a rock and a hard place"? These folks got caught between some bricks...and some other bricks.

Flue Sufferer: Alejandro Valencio, a spurned suitor living in Evansville, Indiana

Down: In September 2007, Valencio and his girlfriend of several months split up. A few weeks later, an intoxicated Valencio showed up at her house at 3:30 in the morning. She refused to let him in, so he climbed onto the roof, lowered himself down the chimney, and got stuck.

...and Out: When firefighters arrived to extricate Valencio from the chimney, his ex-girlfriend wouldn't let them work. "Leave him in the chimney and let him die," she said. The firefighters called the police, the police arrested the ex-girlfriend, and then the firefighters broke Valencio out of the chimney. So did loverboy learn his lesson? Nope. Only hours later he was back...with a TV news crew in tow. By then his ex was back too, and she was not happy to see him. She attacked Valencio with a garbage can and threw bottles at him until he finally left. "I've dated a lot of psychos in my life, but nobody like that," the woman told reporters," Valencio commented. "Everyone do stupid things sometimes when they're drunk."

Flue Sufferer: Michael Urbano, 23, of Hayward, California

Down: One night in 2006, Urbano returned home from a night of bar hopping and realized he was locked out of his stepmom's house. She wasn't home, so he did what anyone else would do: He climbed onto the roof, disconnected the TV cable, and tried to use it to rappel down the inside of the chimney like a mountain climber. But first he stripped naked, figuring that his skin would have less "friction" against the inside of the chimney. He only made it partway before the cable snapped and he fell, getting stuck (naked) three quarters of the way down.

...and Out: No one heard Urbano's chimney-muffled cries until neighbors on a 6:30 a.m. stroll called police. The cops couldn't determine where the screams were coming from until they noticed

In Japan, work-related suicide is considered an occupational hazard.

the spark arrester from the chimney sitting on the roof. Firefighters were then dispatched to get Urbano out. Showing an amazing dedication to duty, one of them climbed into the fireplace and shoved his feet up to the naked Urbano, freeing him enough that the firefighters on the roof were able to pull him to safety. Police arrested Urbano on suspicion of being under the influence of drugs. (No word on whether he still lives with his stepmom.)

Flue Sufferers: Bonnie Earle, 10, and Nicole Jones, 6, of San Mateo, California

Down: When the two girls accidently got locked out of Nicole's grandparents' house in July 1991, they decided to try and get in through the chimney. Bonnie lowered Nicole down feet first, but Bonnie's hands slipped and Nicole dropped all the way down the chimney, where her foot got stuck in the damper. Bonnie tried to climb down the chimney to rescue her friend and got stuck too.

...and Out: Luckily for the girls, a third kid saw what happened and told an adult, who called 911. The girls spent an hour in the chimney before firefighters pulled them to safety, unharmed. "They just needed a bath," said a fire department spokesperson.

Flue Sufferer: Glenn Clark, 25, of Trenton, New Jersey

Down: On April 13, 1981, Clark and an accomplice were burglarizing Reiss Men's and Boys' Shop in Trenton when they set off an alarm. Police responded and caught the accomplice, but not Clark, who ran past them and disappeared. When police couldn't find him, they assumed he'd somehow escaped, but he hadn't—he was hiding inside the building's chimney, hanging by his fingertips. Before Clark could climb out, his fingers slipped and he fell 16 feet into the chimney.

...and Out: Clark spent six days in complete darkness. He might still be in the chimney today, were it not for the fact that Easter fell on April 19 that year. On ordinary days, the street noise was so loud that no one could hear Clark screaming for help. But when the Easter holiday arrived, things quieted down just enough for a woman walking her dog past the store to hear his cries. Firefighters smashed their way into the brick chimney with hammers and chisels and pulled Clark to safety. After a checkup (he had scrapes and bruises, but was OK), he was arrested for burglary.

We're on a collision course with the Andromeda galaxy. Crash date: 3 billion years from now.

Flue Sufferer: Joseph Schexnider, 22, who lived in Abbeville, Louisiana, 150 miles west of New Orleans

Down: In 1984 Schexnider disappeared from Abbeville shortly before he was scheduled to appear in court on charges of possessing a stolen vehicle. He was a vagabond and had traveled with circuses and carnivals in the past, so when he got into trouble with the law no one was surprised that he seemed to skip town. His family never reported him missing, even though he stayed away for nearly 30 years.

...and Out: In May 2011, a contractor renovating the second floor of the Abbeville Bank noticed a piece of fabric hanging inside an old chimney. He gave it a tug…and skeletal human remains fell into the fireplace. The skeleton was wearing a shirt, jeans, sneakers, and a pair of underwear. Schexnider's name was written on the waistband of the underwear, and his birth certificate and social security card were found in a wallet in the back pocket of the jeans. DNA tests confirmed that it was Schexnider, but due to the advanced state of decomposition, coroners were unable to determine a specific cause of death. No one knows why Schexnider was on the roof of the bank or why he tried to climb down the chimney. He wasn't carrying burglary tools or anything that could have been used to carry money, so he probably wasn't there to rob the bank. It's possible that he was simply fooling around. The rooftops of the buildings in that part of town are easily accessible, and playing on the roofs is a popular pastime for local kids. "He was the kind of guy," a family friend told reporters, "who would do things without really thinking them through."

* * *

SEVEN THINGS YOU CAN DO WITH MAYONNAISE...AT YOUR OWN RISK

1. Remove gum from hair.
2. Clean piano keys.
3. Condition your hair.
4. Polish plant leaves.
5. Kill head lice.
6. Get tree sap off of cars.
7. Cool a sunburn.

WORLD'S HIGHEST...

Scared of heights? Stay away from these places!

SWIMMING POOL

The pool at the Hong Kong Ritz-Carlton Hotel is on the 116th floor of the city's tallest building: the 1,600-foot International Commerce Centre. Hotel guests can float around at an elevation nearly 100 feet higher than the top of the highest building in the United States, Chicago's Willis Tower (formerly the Sears Tower).

GLASS OBSERVATION DECK

The floor of the 200-foot-long glass-bottomed Skywalk juts out from the side of a 4,691-foot cliff on Tianmen Mountain in Hunan Province, China. The walkway is three feet wide, but visitors tend to cling to the cliff face. Opened in late 2011, it is nearly 700 feet higher than the Skywalk on the West Rim of the Grand Canyon.

FLAGPOLE

In 2010 the government of Azerbaijan celebrated the nation's independence by building a 531-foot freestanding flagpole at the National Flag Square in the capitol city of Baku. It was the highest in the world...for six months, until Trident Support, the California company that built the huge pole, beat its own record by 10 feet at the Palace of the Nation in Dushanbe, Tajikistan.

CHIMNEY

In 1899 a Kazakhstani mineral explorer named Kosym Pshembayev founded a city in Russia on two giant mounds of salt. He called the city *Ekibastuz*, which means "two lumps of salt." In 1987 the coal-fired Gres-2 Power Station in Ekibastuz, which provides power to 40 percent of the country, built another landmark—the world's highest chimney. (Tall chimneys allow pollutants to spread out over a larger area before they return to the ground.) The 1,377-foot steel-reinforced concrete smokestack is taller than the roof of the Empire State Building.

What's *nomophobia*? The fear of being out of cell phone contact. (It's short for "no mobile.")

BRIDGE

Traffic got so bad on the N9 highway near Millau, France, that in 2005 engineers from the French company Eiffage were hired to build a bypass. Called the Millau Viaduct, it's an 8,000-foot suspension bridge that carries cars 885 feet above Millau and the nearby Tarn River Valley. The spires of the bridge top out at 1,125 feet, making it about 150 feet higher than another structure that Eiffage built—the Eiffel Tower.

AQUEDUCT

Two thousand years ago, a friend of Augustus Caesar named Marcus Agrippa brought fresh water to the people of Nemausus, which today is the city of Nimes, France. The closest freshwater spring was more than 12 miles away, and a straight path to Nemausus would have required a five-mile tunnel, an impossible feat for ancient Roman technology. Instead, Agrippa stacked six-ton blocks of stone into a triple-bridge system that carried water 160-feet high across the countryside. Sections of the aqueduct, which Agrippa built without mortar, are still standing.

HOTEL ROOM

Most of the world's tallest buildings are office buildings or tourist attrations—you can't actually stay the night in many of them. But you can at the fourth largest building in the world. The top 17 stories—floors 102 through 118—of the International Commerce Center in Hong Kong are occupied by a branch of the Ritz Carlton hotel chain. A room on the 118th floor places a visitor 1,587 feet in the air. It's the highest penthouse in the world.

TOILET

We're sure that more than one man has written his name in the snow at the summit of Mt. Everest. But the world's highest *constructed* toilet is an odorless, eco-friendly "Saniverte" outhouse 14,300 feet up on Europe's highest mountain, Mont Blanc in France. A French "dry-toilet" company called Ecosphere built the self-composting commode after locals complained of yellow and brown spots dotting the mountain.

THE CURIOUS CASE OF THE AMERICAN ACCENT, PART I

Hey, youz! Whah do 'mericuns have all differnt aks-ay-ents? It's, like, totally confusing and somewhat bizzahh, dontcha know.

TALK THIS WAY

An *accent* is "a manner of pronunciation peculiar to a particular individual, location, or nation." That's not to be confused with a *dialect*, which is a specific form of a language that has its own unique lexicon (words), grammatical structures, and *phonology* (a fancy word for accent). So an accent can be a part of a dialect, but not vice versa. Because dialects can be traced to geographic regions, they give linguists important clues to the origins of accents. And discovering where accents came from can explain why an American says "ta-may-toe" and a Brit says "ta-mah-toe," or why a Bostonian says "pahk the cah" and a Nebraskan says "park the car."

BRITISH INVASIONS

The United States began as colonies of Great Britain, but the settlers didn't trickle across the Atlantic at random. According to Brandeis University Professor David Hackett Fischer in his book *Albion's Seed*, there are four primary American accents, which derive from the major migrations from England to the New World in the 17th and 18th centuries.

1. East Anglia to Massachusetts (1620–40). Puritans who fled to the New World to escape religious persecution were, by and large, from the eastern counties of England. To this day, in remote parts of East Anglia, there are rural folk who speak in what is sometimes referred to as the "Norfolk whine." When they came to New England, that accent came along with them. You may recall the TV commercials where an old fellow says, "Pepperidge Fahm remembahs..." That's the Norfolk whine.

There is no U.S. federal law against owning a flamethrower (but it is a misdemeanor in Calif).

2. South and West of England to Virginia (1642–75). Immigrants who settled in the colony of Virginia tended to be wealthy Cavaliers (that is, loyal to the King) who came to the New World to become planters. Many elements of their accent can still be heard in rural Virginia, such as their penchant for elongated vowels—stretching *you* into "yeew," and shortened consonants—"ax" for *ask*, and "dis" and "dat" for *this* and *that*.

3. North Midlands to Pennsylvania and Delaware (1675–1725). In another flight to escape religious persecution, Quakers, largely from the northern and middle parts of England, also settled in the New World. Their speech patterns, characterized by shorter vowel sounds—a short "a" for *dance*, not the Yankee and East Anglian "dahnce," or the South England and Virginia "day-ence"—formed the basis for the flat Midwestern American accent we hear today, which has since been adopted as the standard American "non-regional" accent spoken by most newscasters.

4. Borderlands to the Backcountry (1715–75). The so-called "Scotch-Irish" fled their poverty-stricken homeland of northern England and southern Scotland, first to northern Ireland and then to America's mid-Atlantic coast. These new arrivals were considered uncultured and unruly and didn't mix well with the established settlers, so most kept going to settle in the backcountry of the Appalachian Mountains. Their distinctive accent can still be heard in many southern regions: "far" for *fire*, and "winder" for *window*. The Borderlands accent gave rise to the twangy "country" accent heard in poorer parts of the South—as opposed to the south-of-England "Southern gentleman" drawl heard in more affluent regions. Think Yosemite Sam for the former and Foghorn Leghorn for the latter.

THE HUDDLED MASSES

After achieving independence, the United States expanded westward and fresh waves of immigrants arrived in New York, New Orleans, and other port cities. The Northeast kept closer ties with Britain, which explains why Bostonians caught onto the English trend of broadening the "a" in bath, while the flatter pronunciation was used in most of the rest of the country.

For the impact the rest of the world has had on the American accent, go to page 437.

Thirty American towns have the word "liberty" in them. Largest: Liberty, MO, pop. 29,000.

SILVER MEDAL SHOCKER

After 25 years of publishing Bathroom Readers, *we at the BRI are proud to claim our silver medals! But this story isn't about us—it's about the Olympics, where silver means second-best, not 25 years. Here's the story of how the 1972 U.S. men's Olympic basketball team and how they refused to accept second place.*

THREE SECONDS TO GOLD!

Before 1972 no U.S. men's basketball team had ever lost in Olympic play. Starting in 1936 (the year basketball became an Olympic sport), U.S. men's teams won 63 consecutive games—and seven straight gold medals. But just after midnight on September 10, 1972, in Munich, Germany, that golden winning streak came to a screeching end, courtesy of the Soviet Union. The final three seconds of that game may be the most controversial Olympic finish of all time, because officials allowed those three historic seconds to be played not once, not twice, but *three* times.

TEAM OF DESTINY

Although the U.S. was favored to win, the Soviet team was not only good, it was seasoned, having played hundreds of games together. The American team, on the other hand, was basically a college all-star team; most of its members had played together only a few times before the Olympics. According to U.S. assistant coach John Bach, the team's experience amounted to 12 exhibition games plus the Olympic trials. To top it off, the 1972 squad was the youngest ever to represent the United States in Olympic competition. They had two things going for them—they were tall (average height: 6'7") and they were talented (an amazing 10 members of the team went on to become first-round NBA draft choices.) "These were the two strongest countries in the world fighting for supremacy, and basketball was *ours*," said U.S. guard Doug Collins, now head coach of the Philadelphia 76ers.

Surprisingly—at least to those who believed the U.S. couldn't lose at men's basketball—the Soviets built a 10-point lead in the second half. They kept that lead for several minutes before U.S.

More than 1,000 bags of Cracker Jack are sold at every Boston Red Sox game.

guard Kevin Joyce led a furious comeback. Pressing and hustling, the Americans whittled the lead down to a single point at 49–48 with 38 seconds left. But the Soviets had the ball. Intent on running out the clock, they passed back and forth, keeping the ball away from the Americans.

With just 10 seconds left, Joyce deflected a pass from Aleksandr Belov, and teammate Doug Collins scooped it up. Collins drove toward the basket to make the winning shot. "As I picked up my dribble," Collins recalled 40 years later, "I saw the guy from Russia. He was not going to be able to get an offensive foul—he couldn't get there. So basically he was just going to cut my legs out from underneath me." Soviet player Zurab Sakandelidze fouled Collins so hard that he fell against the basket stanchion, which he said "knocked him woozy." An intentional foul was called against Sakandelidze. With three seconds on the clock, Collins gathered his wits and sank two free throws, giving the U.S. a one-point lead. The score: 50–49. It looked like another Olympic championship would be theirs.

LET THE DO-OVERS BEGIN

After the free throws, only one second remained on the clock. A single second wouldn't give the Soviets enough time to in-bound the ball and drive to the hoop. Game over? No. A referee blew his whistle and stopped the game. He'd noticed a Soviet assistant coach gesturing frantically that they had signaled for a time-out *between* Collins's two free throws and been ignored.

Lead referee Renato Righetto allowed the time-out. When play resumed, according to Righetto, the clock should have been reset to show one second remaining. It wasn't. William Jones, secretary general of the International Basketball Federation (FIBA), came out of the stands and ordered the time keepers to turn the clock back *three* seconds—the time from the whistle of the foul against the Soviet Union to when the U.S. team scored two free throws would be played again. "Jones overruled the referee and the official scorer," said U.S. team captain Kenny Davis. "He had no power at all to do that."

Did he? To find out, dribble over to page 303 for Part II of the story.

First president to be photographed at his inauguration: Abraham...

THE NEANDERTHALS

Were they too dumb to compete with Homo sapiens*—or were they the original modern stone-age family?*

WHAT MAKES A MAN?

Neanderthals were an ancient race of homonids that developed alongside early humans. They shared almost all the same genetic classifications—kingdom (animal), phylum (chordata), class (mammal), order (primate), family (hominid), and genus (*homo*)—but differed in the final category, species (*neanderthalensis*).

Neanderthals first appeared in Africa about 600,000 years ago and slowly migrated into Europe and the Middle East. Between 100,000 and 35,000 years ago (scientists aren't exactly sure), *Homo sapiens*, migrated from Africa to the same areas. Up until that time, Neanderthals were the most successful hominids in the region, but by that time their population had dwindled, possibly because of freezing temperatures during the last Ice Age. After about 40,000 years of sharing territory, the remaining Neanderthals died out while *Homo sapiens* kept evolving. So why didn't the Neanderthals survive?

• **Theory #1: They weren't smart enough.** It was long conventional wisdom among anthropologists that Neanderthals were not very smart, and were outpaced and outsmarted by their clever human cousins, fading away because they lacked survival skills. Now scientists aren't so sure. Findings suggest Neanderthals had bigger heads and brains than humans, and probably weren't so dumb after all.

• **Theory #2: They weren't good hunters.** It was once thought that Neanderthals might have been poorer hunters than *Homo sapiens*, and so when species of large game dwindled, they couldn't survive. But it turns out that Neanderthal tools were actually more efficient than those crafted by early humans. Neanderthals are also believed by some experts to have had control over fire before *Homo sapiens* did and to have cooked, rather than gathered, much of their food. Aside from game, there is evidence that they dined

...Lincoln. Standing near him in the photo: John Wilkes Booth.

on birds and fish, and beach-combed for mollusks. And contrary to popular belief, their diet was not dependent on meat. Researchers have recently found bits of seeds, dates, beans, peas, and cooked grains stuck in Neanderthal teeth.

• **Theory #3: They lacked mobility.** There is evidence that Neanderthals took to the sea long before *Homo sapiens*. Neanderthal relics dating back more than 100,000 years have been found on Mediterranean islands that were unreachable other than by watercraft (evidence of which has not yet been found). Modern humans are thought to have built their first ocean-going vehicles only about 50,000 years ago, or about 50,000 years *after* Neanderthals would have been making theirs.

• **Theory #4: They couldn't communicate well.** More recent studies of Neanderthal voice boxes have led some scientists to conclude that Neanderthal voices were not incoherent grunts, as once believed, but high-pitched and melodic, and that their means of communicating may have been a combination of language, pitch, and song.

A CLOSER LOOK

Far from being the brutish creatures of cliché, Neanderthals were probably the first hominids to bury their dead, often leaving flowers on the gravesites. They also made and wore jewelry, and Neanderthal cave paintings from 42,000 years ago have been found in southern Spain. It is true that Neanderthals and humans looked different: Neanderthals were shorter and broader, with a heavier brow. But it seems there were similarities. About the same percentage of Neanderthal and human DNA includes the genetic mutation that inhibits brown pigmentation, so Neanderthals were about as likely as humans to be pale-skinned, blond, or redheaded.

Native Africans, whose ancestors never lived alongside Neanderthals in Europe, have no Neanderthal DNA in their genomes—but pretty much all other people do. According to most studies, about 2.5 percent of most modern human DNA was contributed by Neanderthals, proving that they interbred with Homo sapiens. So when the last of them disappeared about 25,000 years ago, it's possible they had already assimilated into the larger human population. Where did the Neanderthals go? Look in the mirror.

If all the neurons in your brain were lined up, they'd stretch 600 miles.

POETIC JUSTICE

"You have an obligation as a judge to be right, but you have no obligation to be dull."
—Judge J. Michael Eakin

BARD OF THE BENCH

In 2001 J. Michael Eakin was elected to the Pennsylvania Supreme Court after 11 years as the Cumberland County District Attorney. Like all judges, Eakin writes important legal decisions every day. Unlike other judges, he makes his into poetry. Eakin won a second 10-year term in 2011 with 74 percent of the vote. Apparently the public doesn't mind Eakin's poetic judgments, but not everybody thinks it's appropriate—his fellow justices, for instance. "It reflects poorly on the Supreme Court of Pennsylvania," said Chief Justice Stephen Zappala. In his defense, Eakin doesn't always give a rhyming opinion, only when he feels the case is light-hearted or needs an injection of levity. Here's a sampling of Eakin's creativity.

Riding Under the Influence. In 2004 it was up to Eakin and six other Justices to either reverse or uphold a lower court's decision that a person cannot be arrested for DUI if they're on a horse. Eakin disagreed with the lower court, and set his dissent to the theme song from the TV show *Mister Ed.*

> A horse is a horse, of course, of course / but the Vehicle Code does not divorce / its application from, perforce / a steed, as my colleagues said. / "It's not vague," I'll say until I'm hoarse / and whether a car, a truck or horse / this law applies with equal force / and I'd reverse instead.

Pro-Poodle Poetry. In 1999 Julia Zangrando sued Jan Sipula over veterinarian bills for her poodle, Angel. An Allegheny County Court ruled Sipula had negligently struck the dog with his car, and Sipula was asking for a re-trial. Eakin's ruling was a 59-verse sonnet. (We're only printing a fraction.)

> To appellee this was nothing short of an unmitigated disaster / the wingless Angel'd taken flight and ascended quickly past her / The bill for Angel's treatment, though, was

anything but small, / and appellee felt that in the end, appellant should pay it all / 15 miles an hour he claims as his maximum rate of speed / quite a cautious, prudent rate, not very fast indeed / It's also hard to quarrel here with what the trial court said / That speed's not fast enough to launch a poodle overhead / We must conclude the issues raised do not warrant a new trial / and all that we may offer now is this respectful rhymed denial.

A Verse on Divorce. Louis Porreco's divorce got ugly in 2000, when his wife Susan—they married when she was 19 and he was in his 40s—found out that her $21,000 diamond engagement ring was a fake. In addition to alimony, Susan sued Louis for fraud. The Supreme Court sided with Mr. Porreco; Eakin dissented:

A groom must expect matrimonial pandemonium / When his spouse finds he's given her cubic zirconium / Given their history and Pygmalion relation / I find her reliance was with justification.

Flightless and Fruitless. Delores Liddle wanted to breed emus, and in 2001 paid Denise Scholze $48,000 for a pair named Nicholas and Savannah. The emus failed to conceive, so Scholze offered Liddle 12 emu chicks to replace the two adults. Liddle declined, and when she later found out Nicholas was, in fact, a female emu, she sued. Eakin ruled that since Scholze had tried to remedy the situation, she was not liable for the fruitless fowl.

The fault's the emus', not that of Liddle / or Scholze, or the court placed in the middle / Fruitless in Pennsylvania and Louisiana / the blame's on Nicholas and Savannah.

Ode to an Overhaul. In 2000 a Pennsylvania court ruled that an auto-body shop called Limerick Collision had to change its name rather than infringe on the business of nearby Limerick Auto Body. Both shops are named after the Philadelphia suburb where they do business, but Limerick Auto Body was there first. Justice Eakin upheld the earlier court's decision, but he couldn't resist writing—of course—a limerick about the Limerick case.

"Limerick Auto" and "Limerick Collision" / Are so close one may clearly envision / That the two were the same / so a limerick I frame / And join in my colleagues' decision.

Male western gray kangaroos smell like curry. It's so powerful they're called "stinkers."

FOOD FIRSTS

The first thing Uncle John consumes in the morning: a handful of wasabi peas, washed down with black coffee. Here are some other landmark moments in the history of food.

First Indian restaurant in the West: In 1810 Sake Dean Mahomed, a captain in the British East India Company, opened a restaurant in London that served authentic food from his native India. He called it the Hindoostanee Coffee House. The restaurant closed within the year...but by the mid-20th century, "curry houses" were the most popular form of ethnic food *and* fast food in England.

First food eaten in space: On his orbit around the Earth in 1962, astronaut John Glenn ate applesauce.

First food magazine in the U.S.: *Gourmet*, which began publishing in 1941 and closed down in 2009. The first issue contained a recipe for wild bear.

First American culinary school: When American restaurants faced a labor shortage during and after World War II, the New Haven Restaurant Institute was founded in Connecticut to train new chefs. It's now the Culinary Institute of America.

First genetically engineered food: The Flavr Savr, a breed of tomato bioengineered by food scientists, who altered and combined the genes of several different tomato varieties to make one that was more resistant to spoilage. It was approved for sale by the FDA in 1994.

First branded food: Quaker Oats became the first trademarked breakfast cereal in 1877 and uses essentially the same label today.

First commercially available microwave oven: The Radarange, produced by Amana, went on sale in 1947. Cost: $3,000 (about $29,000 today).

First "Weird Al" Yankovic song about food: The comedy singer is best known for food-related parodies such as "Eat It" and "Fat." His first food song was the second song he ever released: "My

Bologna," a 1980 parody of the Knack's "My Sharona." The original version featured Weird Al—solo—on vocal and accordion. He recorded it in his bathroom.

First diet soda: Kirsch Bottling, a Brooklyn company that catered primarily to hospitals, launched a locally distributed sugar-free ginger ale in 1952. Called No-Cal, it was marketed to diabetics and dieters. The first nationally available diet soda: Royal Crown's Diet Rite Cola (1958).

First bananas in the United States: The 1876 Philadelphia Centennial Exposition featured a tropical plant exhibit, where vendors sold bananas for 10 cents each (about $2 today).

First weight-loss program: Jean Nidetch had a private weight-loss club for fellow New York City housewives. It did so well when she started it in 1963 that she formed Weight Watchers later that year.

First foods introduced to the New World: Christopher Columbus introduced Native Americans to the onions, garlic, wheat, barley, olives, and lettuce he brought from Spain. In return, he took back to Europe tomatos, potatoes, corn, beans, squash, and avocados.

First pizza delivery: In 1889 Naples, Italy, pizzeria owner Raffaele Esposito hand delivered a pie to a private home where the king and queen of Italy were staying on a visit to the city.

First commercially available canned food: Condensed milk. Gail Borden started condensing and canning milk in 1856. The business took off when he got a government contract to supply canned milk to the Union Army during the Civil War.

First Chinese restaurant in the United States: An influx of workers from China poured into northern California immediately after the Gold Rush of 1848. Chinese immigrant Norman Asing opened a restaurant serving Chinese food in San Francisco a year later—Macao and Woosung, an all-you-can-eat buffet. Cost: $1.

* * *

"To avoid trouble and insure safety, breathe through your nose. It keeps the mouth shut." **—Uncle John**

Syrupy sentiment: The maple leaf is a symbol of love in China and Japan.

ANTIPODES 101

Every point on Earth has its antipode *(Greek for "opposed foot"), the place where you'd end up if you tunneled straight through the center of the Earth and out the other side.*

ON THE OTHER FOOT

• Antipodes are true opposites. If you're in the Western Hemisphere, your antipode is in the Eastern Hemisphere. If you're in the Northern, it's in the Southern. It is literally the farthest place on Earth from wherever you are right now. The North Pole, in the Arctic, is the antipode of the South Pole, in the *Ant*arctic (literally, "opposite of arctic").

• That's not all. If it's noon where you are, it's midnight in your antipode. If you are in summer, your antipode is in winter (unless you're near the equator, where there are no seasons). Half of each day, your antipode's calendar isn't even on the same date as yours.

• There are plenty of apps and websites that can tell you exactly where your antipode is. But don't bother getting out your digging shovel. Odds are good that your antipode is under an ocean.

• In fact, only about four percent of Earth's land mass has a dry antipode. That's partly because so much of the planet is covered by water—about 70 percent, but also because so much of the dry land is in the Northern Hemisphere and so little is in the Southern.

• If you live in the Southern Hemisphere, your odds of having a dry antipode are vastly improved. Kids in Chile and Argentina really could end up in China if they dug straight down.

• Very little of North America has land in its antipodal region. Most of it is in the Indian Ocean between Africa and Australia. However, the extreme northern part of Canada and Alaska is the antipode to the far edge of Antarctica.

• For American kids who have their hearts set on digging through the center of the Earth, we suggest you start digging from Hawaii. It's the only U.S. state where you're safe from being flooded by seawater on the other side, because your hole will emerge in the landlocked country of Botswana in southern Africa.

WHEN TOILETS EXPLODE

The bathroom is supposed to be a place of peace and calm, a refuge in our modern world of toil and strife. But as the unfortunate folks below discovered, it doesn't always work out that way.

Victims: Workers at the General Services Administration in Washington, D.C.

Boom! In September 2011, the water pressure system in the GSA headquarters failed, allowing air into the water lines and causing pressure to climb far beyond what the system was designed to handle. By 11:30 a.m. the pressure was so great that when a federal worker tried to flush one of the toilets, it shattered, spraying her with toilet water and shards of porcelain. She wasn't seriously hurt, but when a second employee was cut on the leg by an exploding toilet minutes later, every bathroom in the building was closed until the problem was identified and repaired. CNN and other news outlets covered the story, and the response from the public was predictable: "A new way to get government employees off their butts," one reader commented to *The Huffington Post*. "Now we need to install the same equipment in Congress."

Victim: Carolyn Novak, a woman living in Troy, New York

Boom! Novak had just finished her shower one morning in January 1999 when water suddenly blasted out of her toilet "like a geyser," she told the Albany *Times Union*. When she heard a second explosion down the street a few seconds later, she assumed the neighborhood was under attack. Not quite: The blasts were caused when a neighbor, Thomas Brooks, tried to replace the gas tank in his Cadillac Coupe de Ville. He got rid of the gas in the old tank by pouring it down the drain and into the sewer, where it ignited. The resulting explosion blew out two manhole covers plus the contents of Novak's toilet and those of several of her neighbors, filling their homes with dangerous fumes. But the worst victim: Novak's minivan—it was parked over one of the manhole covers, and sustained more than $1,000 in damages. While his neighbors aired out their homes, Brooks was arrested and charged with criminal mischief and reckless endangerment of property.

Said Assistant Fire Chief Craig LeRoy, "He was trying to get rid of what he called 'a little gasoline,' and he made a very poor choice."

Victims: Workers in an office building in Tauranga, New Zealand

Boom! New Zealand isn't the kind of place usually associated with domestic terrorism, so it came as a surprise in September 2010 when police attributed an explosion in the restroom of a two-story commercial building in Tauranga to a homemade "basic incendiary device" powerful enough to smash the restroom door and hurl chunks of it 30 feet into an adjacent parking lot. "I heard an almighty bang," travel agent Jolene Purdy told *The New Zealand Herald*. "Everyone started shouting, 'We have to go. We have to go.' I couldn't talk, it was such a loud blast." After a more thorough investigation, police concluded the explosion had actually been caused by someone smoking in the restroom, which was also used to store flammable cleaning supplies. When the fumes came in contact with the lit cigarette—BOOM! (Luckily no one was injured in the explosion, not even the smoker.)

Victim: Benjamin Barad, 84, a retired teacher from Palm Beach, Florida

Boom! In 1990 Barad and his wife were traveling by train from Lorton, Virginia, to Sanford, Florida, when Barad had to use the washroom. When he tried to flush the pressurized toilet, it backfired, covering him with the contents of the septic tank. Because there was no running water on the train (that was broken, too), Barad had no way to clean himself off. He had clean clothes in his car, which was also aboard the train, but Amtrak would have had to stop the train for him to get to his car...and Amtrak refused to stop the train. So the retired hygiene teacher (yes, a *hygiene* teacher) had to sit in sewage-soaked clothes for the next 12 hours until the train reached its destination and he and his wife could clean up in a hotel room. At last report Barad was suing Amtrak for $10,000. "Trains only stop if there's a medical emergency. Other than that, we can't comment on a case in litigation," an Amtrak spokesperson said.

* * *

"Drink to the point of hilarity." —**St. Thomas Aquinas**

LAND OF THE RISING FUN

Japanese popular culture has made two major contributions to the rest of the world: video games and really weird stuff. Here's where the two meet—weird video games from Japan.

I'M *SORRY* (1985)

Former Japanese Prime Minister Kakuei Tanaka serves as the main character in this bizarre game, which satirizes the politician and his involvement in various bribery scandals in the early 1980s. Players control Tanaka as he makes his way through a series of maze-like levels while gobbling up gold bars, kind of like in *Pac-Man*. But unlike Pac-Man, whose enemies are a group of multicolored ghosts, *I'm Sorry*'s protagonist faces an onslaught from a group of celebrity enemies, including Michael Jackson, Carl Lewis, Madonna, and Japanese sumo wrestler Shohei Baba. If one of Tanaka's pursuers manages to capture him, they strip him down to a diaper and whip him as he begs for mercy.

Bonus: The title, *I'm Sorry*, is a play on the Japanese word *sori*, which means "prime minister."

SUB MARINE CATCHER (1994)

For decades, American arcades and pizza parlors have had "claw games," where the player controls a claw in order to grab and win a stuffed animal or a toy. Japanese arcades have a variant called *Sub Marine Catcher*. Instead of snatching a Hello Kitty doll or a miniature teddy bear, players can fish a live lobster out of a tank. Should they manage to snag one of the crustaceans, lucky winners are presented with a bag of water by an arcade clerk so they can take their prize catch home.

BOONG-GA, BOONG-GA (2001)

In the U.S., bullies employ the "wedgie" to terrorize their victims. In Japan, they have *kancho*, a less cruel, slightly less intrusive bit of mischief in which the prankster pokes someone in the butt (crack) with two fingers. *Boong-Ga, Boong-Ga* is a video-game version of *kancho*. Players select from a list of eight characters to "punish." Among them: "Ex-girlfriend," "Ex-boyfriend," "Mother-in-Law," "Gold Digger," and "Gangster."

Bonus: Game play is interactive—players poke a denim-covered fake butt, which is attached to the front of the game's cabinet.

THE TABLECLOTH HOUR (2010)

This game gives players the opportunity to do what usually only magicians can pull off—yanking a tablecloth out from underneath an elaborate place setting, leaving the dishes and silverware intact and in place. The screen shows a red sheet loaded with cute, anthropomorphized dishes and silverware. The player must then press a button at just the right moment to pull the tablecloth in order for the dishes to remain perfectly still (You win!) or fly off the table (Game Over). Believe it or not, *The Tablecloth Hour* is actually the second in a series of games about table settings. *Ultra Low Dining Table* has a completely opposite objective: The more objects that fall off the table, the more points the player scores.

TOYLETS (2010)

This one consists of an LCD screen placed above a urinal that contains pressure sensors capable of turning the player's "stream" into a game controler. The four *Toylets* games, from simple to bizarre:

- **"Mannekin Pis"** measures how hard the player can pee.
- **"Graffiti Eraser"** washes graffiti off walls.
- **"The Northern Wind, The Sun and Me":** The player must provide enough "force" to make a video gust of wind blow up a woman's skirt. (The harder you pee, the harder the wind blows.)
- **"Battle! Milk From Nose":** A test of "strength" against the previous player, in which the player's stream is translated into milk spraying out of his nose. If your stream is stronger, your milk stream knocks your opponent out of the ring.

* * *

Helpful Household Tip: If you're trying to fill a bucket with water, and it's too big to fit in your sink, put a dustpan in the sink, and angle it under the faucet so the water runs down the curved handle into the bucket on the floor.

WHO MADE JACK "THE RIPPER"?

Most serial killers get their nicknames from the press; some come from the cops. The creepiest names are the ones serial killers give themselves. Here are some grisly examples of all three.

JACK THE RIPPER (1888). He was the first serial killer around which a media frenzy was born, and that frenzy was related to his famous nickname. Between August and November 1888, five women were brutally murdered in the Whitechapel section of London. While the murders were still occurring, London's Central News Agency published a letter they said they'd received from someone claiming to be the killer. Known as the "Dear Boss" letter (that's how the letter began), it was signed "Jack the Ripper." News of the letter made headlines worldwide—something unheard of at the time—and the name "Jack the Ripper" stuck. But was the letter really from the murderer? Police believed it was actually written by a reporter from the Central News Agency who created the "Ripper" sign-off to drum up newspaper sales. The truth will never be known.

THE CHESSBOARD KILLER (2006). Russian Alexander Pichushkin killed 49 people in Moscow between 1992 and his arrest in 2006. After he was arrested, he told interrogators his goal was to kill exactly 64 people—enough to fill all the spots on a chessboard. That information was leaked, Russian newspapers ran with it, and he's been "The Chessboard Killer" ever since. (Pichushkin later claimed he was lying, and that he would have gone on killing indefinitely if he hadn't been caught.)

THE ZODIAC KILLER (1969). This still-unknown killer murdered eight people, possibly more, in Northern California in 1968 and 1969. During the murders, and for some years afterward, he sent taunting letters to San Francisco area media organizations. One to the *San Francisco Examiner* began, "Dear Editor, this is the Zodiac speaking." The killer would identify himself by this name in several more letters. Some of them included elaborate puzzles, including four cryptograms—pages of coded text—only one of which has been solved to date. The significance of the name was never explained, but is believed to simply be another of the killer's puzzles.

THE GRIM SLEEPER (2007). Between 1985 and 1988, someone killed eight women, all African Americans, in Los Angeles. Fourteen years passed. Then, between 2002 and 2007, three more African-American women were murdered. In 2007 using ballistics and DNA evidence, police learned that the same man had committed all eleven murders. Christine Pelisek, a reporter for the *LA Weekly*, dubbed the killer "The Grim Sleeper"—because of the 14-year lapse between his killing sprees. In 2010 police arrested 57-year-old Lonnie David Franklin Jr., alleging that his DNA matched evidence left at several of the murders. He is still awaiting trial.

THE CASANOVA KILLER (1974). Paul John Knowles, a "ruggedly handsome redhead," as newspapers described him, killed at least 18 people (he claimed he killed 35) during a vicious seven-month cross-country killing spree in 1974. Near the end of that run, Knowles met 40-year-old British journalist Sandra Fawkes in a Holiday Inn bar in Atlanta, Georgia. Fawkes became the killer's lover and spent three days with him—and somehow came out of it alive. She later described him as "a cross between Robert Redford and Ryan O'Neal." Just 13 days later, Knowles was arrested, and the media, noting his good looks and Fawkes's story, dubbed him "The Casanova Killer." (Knowles was shot dead by a police officer while attempting to take another officer's sidearm just a few weeks later.)

THE UNABOMBER (1979). Ted Kaczynski killed three people and injured 23 others in his notorious bombing campaign spanning nearly two decades, from 1978 until his arrest in 1995. Because the usual targets of his attacks were universities and airlines, the FBI labeled the secret taskforce investigating the crimes "UNABOM" —for **UN**iversity and **A**irline **BOM**bing. Agents referred to the unknown assailant as the "Unabomber" and that was picked up by the press.

THE GORILLA KILLER (1926). Between February 1926 and June 1927, Earle Leonard Nelson murdered 22 women, all boarding-house landladies, in various locations across the United States and Canada. He was convicted of two of the murders and executed by hanging in Winnipeg, Manitoba, in 1928. The exact story of how he got his nickname appears to have been lost, and several versions are passed around today. One suggests that he got the name because of the strength he exhibited in carrying out his crimes: Nelson strangled all his victims with his bare hands. (Gorillas are not known to practice strangulation.) Another story says that he had a severely receding forehead, large protruding lips, and very large hands, the combination of which made him look like a gorilla. And the oddest version: Investigators interviewed Nelson's aunt during his killing spree, and she told them that as a young boy, Nelson had been struck by a trolley and sent into a coma for several days. After he woke up, he suffered periods of mania, during which he would curl up his legs and walk around on his hands, making him look, she said, like a gorilla.

SON OF SAM (1977). David Berkowitz murdered six people, wounded several others, and committed arson around New York City in 1976 and 1977. He was first known in the press as the ".44 Caliber Killer," after the weapon he used in most of his attacks. In April 1977, Berkowitz left a letter at the scene of a double murder in the Bronx. A month later, he sent another to *New York Daily News* columnist Jimmy Breslin. In both letters he referred to himself as "Son of Sam," explaining that "Sam" was some kind of evil spirit that compelled him to kill: "Sam loves to drink blood," one read. "'Go out and kill' commands father Sam." (Berkowitz later said "Sam" was a demon that possessed his neighbor's dog.) Police eventually released that information to the press—and the rest is serial-killer history. Berkowitz was captured in August 1977 (his first words to police: "You got me. What took you so long?"), and is now serving 25 years to life for each murder.

Update: Berkowitz became a born-again Christian in prison in 1987. On his personal website—yep, he has one, reportedly administered with the help of friends outside of prison—he says he no longer wants to be known as "Son of Sam," but now goes by the name "Son of Hope."

VOMIT COMETS

Theme-park rides keep getting bigger and faster. Here are a few from around the world guaranteed to make you lose your lunch.

KINGDA KA

Location: Six Flags Great Adventure (Jackson, New Jersey)

Details: It's one of the tallest and fastest roller coasters on the planet. A ride on Kingda Ka lasts only 28 seconds, but it's a thrill ride. You're catapulted by cable-launch, going from 0 to 128 mph in a mere 3.5 seconds, soaring up a 456-foot incline, through a 270-degree spiral, and finally plummeting 418 feet straight down. Those brave enough to get aboard are said to experience near-weightlessness during the ride. Further adding to Ka's reputation: a real live Bengal tiger paces back and forth in a pen next to the coaster.

FORMULA ROSSA

Location: Ferrari World (Abu Dhabi)

Details: Formula Rossa stole the "World's Fastest" title from Kingda Ka when it opened in November 2010. The coaster begins on a platform inside the theme park before slinging riders along a track that runs out into a barren stretch of desert and back in again. Rossa reaches its top speed of 150 mph in 4.9 seconds, and utilizes a cable-launch system modeled after the mechanized catapults that send jets off the decks of aircraft carriers. Bonus: Riders sit in cars designed to look like Formula One Ferraris. (There are 20 Ferrari-themed attractions in Ferrari World, including a carousel with Ferrari prototypes instead of horses, and a flume ride "through the heart of a Ferrari 599 engine.")

MISSION: SPACE

Location: Epcot (Orlando, Florida)

Details: Disney theme parks are known for their family-friendly attractions, but this ride is about as far removed from "It's a Small World" as it gets. Since this motion simulator (in which riders experience G-forces similar to those endured by astronauts during a rocket launch) first opened in 2003, dozens of riders have been rushed to the hospital complaining of nausea and chest pains. Result: Disney engineers had to add airsickness bags, a first in theme-park history. In 2006 after numerous incidents—including two fatalites—and complaints from guests (and from the park employees who had to clean up after them), Epcot introduced a toned-down, non-spinning version of the ride.

X-SCREAM

Location: The Stratosphere (Las Vegas, Nevada)

Details: This ride might not be so intimidating if it wasn't on top of the tallest structure in Las Vegas. X-Scream features an open-top car attached to a pivoting 69-foot track. The track seesaws, sending the car directly over the edge of the Stratosphere hotel, giving riders the sensation of plummeting toward the pavement 866 feet below. X-Scream's software is programmed to further strike terror into riders' hearts: At one point, the car lurches forward a second time, briefly convincing those onboard that something's wrong with the brakes.

NOTHIN' BUT NET

Location: Zero Gravity Thrill Park (Dallas, Texas)

Details: It's an incredibly simple (but incredibly scary) concept: Adrenaline junkies climb to the top of the 16-story structure and then free fall—backwards—into a specially-designed net 130 feet below. The ride simulates the feeling of falling backward off the top of a cliff, which, according to participants, is terrifying. Dr. David Eagleman, a professor at Baylor College of Medicine in Houston, used the attraction in a study on how the brain perceives time during moments of panic and terror.

* * *

DUMB BUNNY JOKES

Q: How do you catch a unique rabbit?

A: Unique up on it.

Q: How do you catch a tame rabbit?

A: Tame way, unique up on it.

LAST TWEETS

What makes uninteresting tweets interesting? When the Twitter.com users are famous, and they don't know they will die soon after sending it.

"Somebody convince me to stay with AT&T. What do they offer that's better than even Metro PCS?"

—Comedian Patrice O'Neal

"Sunday evening. Been an awful week, but my friends have been great. But now I have to somehow pull myself together and finish with the HELLS ANGELS & PROLIFIC DEMONS!"

—Fashion designer Alexander McQueen

"'To Paris with Love' is #4 on the Billboard Dance Club Play Charts! xo"

—Donna Summer

"New you, New York, big city of dreams, but everything in New York ain't always what it seems."

—Musician DJ AM

"I called you a putz, cause I thought you were being intentionally disingenuous. If not, I apologize."

—Political writer Andrew Breitbart, to a reader

"Time to get back into the run of things. I'm filled up on eggnog, figgy pudding, and all that other Christmas stuff. Time for the gym, baby!"

—Wrestler Randy "Macho Man" Savage

"Oinka oinka oinka, why you awake?"

—Amy Winehouse

"My interview in *Bazaar* with Kim Kardashian came out!!!"

—Elizabeth Taylor

"In Japan there's a 20 foot picture of me endorsing one of my favorite hotels. Seeing it is surreal. PS. Stay there. Put food on my table!"

—Dennis Hopper

"BE INSPIRED!"

—Rapper Heavy D

"My new album, *The Titanic Requiem*, is in stores in UK today and rest of Europe later this week. Hope you enjoy it!"

—Robin Gibb (of the Bee Gees)

Canada's official motto, A *Mari Usque ad Mare*, means "From sea to sea."

IT'S A GUN AND A...

People seem to love objects that are designed to serve multiple purposes. Thomas Jefferson designed a table that converts to a chair. (Genius!) Collectors prize Amphicars—cars that can drive into water and become boats. Here are a few vintage guns that were designed to do double or even triple duty.

APACHE REVOLVER (1870)

Special Feature: A built-in knife and brass knuckles

Details: Manufactured from 1870 until 1900 by a Belgian company, L. Dolne a Liege, the Apache looked sort of like a standard revolver except that the handle was a set of brass knuckles, and the barrel was replaced with a knife blade. The gun folded up so that it could be hidden in a pocket or used as brass knuckles. Unfolded, it could be shot as a gun or used as a knife to stab someone. The lack of a barrel and the small size of the gun limited its firepower, though it could still be deadly at point-blank range...to the owner as well as to a victim: There was no trigger guard or safety lock to prevent the gun from firing accidentally while being carried.

KEY GUNS (1500s)

Special Feature: Ability to unlock doors

Details: These guns, made from the 16th to the 19th centuries, were designed with a particularly vulnerable person in mind: a jailer unlocking a cell door. To make it less tempting for an inmate to rush the jailer when his hands were occupied with opening or closing the cell door, the key itself became a weapon. If the keyhole passed all the way through the door, the jailer could shoot right through it at an attacking inmate.

COFFEE-MILL SHARPS CARBINE (1859)

Special Feature: Coffee grinder in the wooden shoulder stock

Details: Thousands of ordinary Sharps carbines were issued to Union soldiers during the Civil War. In those days it was still common for troops to live off the land, so the military outfitted some of the carbines with hand-cranked coffee grinders, enabling

Elvis Presley recorded more than 600 songs, but didn't write any of them.

soldiers to grind not just coffee—they could use it to grind grain into flour, as well. The idea was to issue one soldier in every unit a coffee-mill carbine, but the plan was never realized and relatively few of the guns were ever issued. (No water for the coffee? No problem. Colt, another gunmaker, made a pistol with a canteen in its stock.)

RS KNIFE GUN (1990s)

Special Feature: You guessed it—it's a knife *and* a gun

Details: Designed by a company called Global Research and Development, the knife had a five-shot revolver concealed inside the handle. When trouble struck, twisting a latch on the handle 180 degrees caused a spring-loaded trigger to pop into position, and the gun was now ready to fire its bullets through a hole in the front of the handle. G.R.A.D. made fewer than 500 knife guns before it went out of business.

PRATT HELMET (circa 1910)

Special Feature: A helmet complete with "head gun"

Details: Invented by a Vermont man named Albert Pratt, the steel helmet had a large spike on top, like the helmets Germans wore in World War I. It also had a gun barrel sticking out the front, and a gun sight that hung down into the wearer's line of sight. A pneumatic tube running from the rear of the helmet to the wearer's mouth served as the trigger. To fire, just blow. According to Pratt's patent application, the gun was aimed by the "marksman" turning his head in the direction of the target, "leaving his hands and feet free to further defend himself."

Extra-Special Feature: The top of the hat was removable and could be "inverted and used as a cooking utensil," with the gun barrel doing double duty as a pot handle, and the spike, stuck into the dirt, holding the pot steady over a fire.

* * *

"It's all about perspective. The sinking of the *Titanic* was a miracle to the lobsters in the ship's kitchen."

—Wynne McGlaughlin

$toned: Studies show coming into money can have the same effect on the brain as drug use.

SHRIMP

A few little shrimp facts.

Shrimp exist in a dazzling array of shapes, sizes, and colors. They comprise 2,000 species and are found in deep ocean waters, shallow tidal waters, and freshwater, in every region of every continent but Antarctica.

They are *arthropods*—the shelled, segmented phylum that includes all insects, arachnids, and crustaceans. More specifically, shrimp are part of the order *Decapoda*. All decapods have ten legs, a trait shrimps share with their cousins—crabs and lobsters.

Large shrimp are often called prawns, and vice versa. While they look very much alike, shrimp are more closely related to crabs and lobsters than they are to prawns. Prawns differ in that they have three pairs of pincers rather than a shrimp's two, they don't have a pronounced abdomen bend, and they don't "brood" their eggs—females release them right into the water.

Shrimp are primarily swimmers, not crawlers.

"Cleaner shrimp" survive by eating parasites and dead tissue off of other creatures. Many of these shrimp species live in coral reefs, where they hang out at what biologists call "cleaning stations"—places where fish, sea turtles, and eels go to be nibbled clean.

Shrimp can breed only after a female molts. A male deposits sperm on a female's underbelly. The female releases eggs (25,000 to a million at a time), which pass through the sperm and are fertilized. She carries the eggs on hair-like structures on her legs, where they're protected by the shell that soon regrows. Weeks later, the tiny hatchlings are dispersed into the water.

While most shrimp species live from 9 to 18 months, some, such as the North Atlantic shrimp, live to eight years.

The 2011 movie *The Muppets* is rated PG for "sex and nudity."

STEAMERS & WONGERS

Just because you came to Las Vegas in a $50,000 Mercedes and left in a $250,000 Greyhound bus, that doesn't mean you can't learn some casino slang and at least sound *like you know what you're doing.*

Action Jackson: A gambler who plays around the clock.

Arm: A craps player so skilled at throwing dice that with the flick of the wrist they can alter the odds of the game.

Bricks/Flats: Dice that have been shaved or otherwise altered for the purpose of cheating.

Bad Beat: When a good hand loses to an even better hand.

Toking: Tipping the dealer.

George: A good toker.

Tom: A bad toker.

Stiff: A player who never tokes, no matter how much they win.

Steamer: A player who bets wildly in an attempt to make up for past losses. Also called a *chaser* or *plunger*.

Playing the Rush: A player who plays more aggressively or loosely after winning several bets in close succession.

Firing: Repeatedly placing big bets.

Rail Bird: Someone who stands back from the table and watches other people gamble.

Silver Miner: Someone who wanders the casino floor looking for coins in unattended slot machines.

Calling Station: A poker player who frequently calls (matches the bets of other players), but rarely raises or folds.

Washing: The rubbing hand motion a croupier or dealer makes when leaving the table, to show they aren't stealing any chips.

Wonging: Counting cards at a blackjack table and joining the game only when the count indicates players have the advantage. (Named after a professional gambler named Stanford Wong.)

Flea: A small-stakes gambler who still expects to be "comped" by the casino with free meals, rooms, chips, etc.

What does the EPA use to decontaminate people exposed to anthrax? Household bleach.

ALL ABOUT CORDUROY

A few lines about fabric with lines.

Corduroy is a type of fabric characterized by its ribbed, or "corded," texture. It was first made in the textile manufacturing center of Manchester, England, in the late 1700s.

• **The word "corduroy" dates to the 1780s.** Its exact origin is unknown, but most etymologists believe it's a combination of the words *cord*, as in a ropelike cord, and *duroy*, an obsolete type of fabric once made in England. Some sources say the word derives from the French *corde du roi*, meaning "king's cord." This is false.

• **Corduroy is a type of woven textile known as a cut-pile fabric.** The weaving process results in one of the fabric's surfaces being loose loops of thread, or *pile*. After weaving, the fabric is passed through a machine that cuts the loops relatively close to the surface. The process also "brushes" the fabric, causing the threads to tuft. All of this results in the fuzzy texture that cut-pile fabrics are known for. Other cut-pile fabrics include velvet and velour. A pile fabric in which the loops of thread are *not* cut: terry cloth. In corduroy manufacture, the pile is cut into orderly vertical ribs and valleys—giving corduroy its "corded" texture.

• **The ribs (or cords) are known as "wales."** Corduroy comes in different types, based on the width of the wales:

Broadwale has wide wales—4 to 6 per inch of fabric

Midwale has medium-sized wales—8 to 10 per inch

Pinwale, also called pincord—12 to 16 wales per inch

Babycord has very narrow wales—18 to 30 per inch

• **Filmmaker Wes Anderson is a corduroy freak.** He had his personal tailor, Vahram Mateosian, design a corduroy wardrobe for the cast of his 2001 film *The Royal Tenenbaums*.

• **Eddie Vedder was inspired to write Pearl Jam's 1994 hit "Corduroy" when he saw an "Eddie Vedder" corduroy jacket being sold for $650.** It was modeled on one Vedder wore, which he said he bought in a thrift store for $12.

The Corduroy Appreciation Club (yes, there really is one) calls both Jan. 1 (1 | 1)...

A DARK AND STORMY WRITE

Alas, life just isn't fair. Consider the case of Edward Bulwer-Lytton, a successful 19th-century author who was forgotten by history, then rediscovered...but only so that readers could ridicule him for one really bad opening line.

BAD TO THE BONE

It's a rare author who can generate a single sentence that inspires ridicule from writers as divergent as Edgar Allen Poe and Charles Schulz. But that's what Edward Bulwer-Lytton succeeded in doing. The terrible line that sealed his reputation is the opening of his 1830 novel *Paul Clifford*:

> It was a dark and stormy night; the rain fell in torrents—except at occasional intervals, when it was checked by a violent gust of wind which swept up the streets (for it is in London that our scene lies), rattling along the housetops, and fiercely agitating the scanty flame of the lamps that struggled against the darkness.

Interestingly, when Charles Schulz used it in 1965 in the comic strip *Peanuts* (it was the opening line of Snoopy's forever unfinished novel), he probably improved the line greatly simply by stopping after the first seven words, because part of the awfulness of the line is the way it goes on and on (and on).

CONTEST NAMESAKE

Today the British author's name may be best known for being attached to a challenge dedicated to bad writing. The Bulwer-Lytton Fiction Contest, sponsored by San Jose State University in California, attracts tens of thousands of entries every year, each writer hoping to be recognized as the author of the worst opening line of a fictitious novel. The winner of the 2011 competition:

> Cheryl's mind turned like the vanes of a wind-powered turbine, chopping her sparrow-like thoughts into bloody pieces that fell onto a growing pile of forgotten memories.
>
> —Sue Fondrie, Oshkosh, Wisconsin

...and Nov. 11 (11|11) official "Corduroy Appreciation Day" (the dates look like corduroy).

But not all of Bulwer-Lytton's writing was bad. Some reviewers considered him equal to—or even better than—his contemporary Charles Dickens. In fact, Dickens consulted with Bulwer-Lytton about the manuscript of *Great Expectations* and took his advice in changing the unbearably sad ending (lovers forever part) to a happy one (lovers meet again and vow never to part).

Here are some more facts about the contest's namesake.

LIFE STORY

• Bulwer-Lytton published his first volume of poetry in 1818, at the age of 15, following with three plays and 29 novels ranging in subject from the historical (*The Last Days of Pompei*) to horror (*The Haunted and the Haunters, or The House and the Brain*) to romance, and a very early piece of science fiction about a race of beings living inside Earth (*Vril: The Power of the Coming Race*).

• Two of his novels became operas, including *Rienzi, the Last of the Roman Tribunes*, adapted by Richard Wagner, and *Leonora*, the first opera composed in the United States.

• Another book, *Ernest Maltravers* (1879), was the first Western novel ever translated into Japanese.

• Several phrases coined by Bulwer-Lytton have been quoted and requoted to the point of becoming cliches, including "pursuit of the almighty dollar," "the great unwashed," and "the pen is mightier than the sword."

LOVE STORY

• Bulwer-Lytton's personal life was a soap opera. Despite being high-born, he ended up having to work for a living because he married a woman of whom his mother did not approve, so she cut off his allowance. He split with great acrimony from the woman he married, Rosina Doyle Wheeler, after five years of marriage, two children, and a series of mistresses.

Wheeler got even by writing a wicked satire of her husband called *Cheveley, or the Man of Honor*. In return, he threatened her publisher with a libel lawsuit, had her committed to an insane asylum, took away her allowance, and denied her access to their children. His actions provoked so much bad publicity that he had her released from the asylum after only a few weeks. She promptly set

Average cost of a traditional Thanksgiving meal: $4.20 per person.

to work on her memoirs, in which she again savaged her husband, this time without hiding behind the veneer of fiction.

BIG HOUSE

• Bulwer-Lytton's forebears and descendants have lived in the stately Knebworth House since 1490. Its current occupant, also a descendant of Bulwer-Lytton, keeps the property intact through paid tours, and renting it out for events and films. The building has appeared as Bruce Wayne's manor in *Batman*, the Mallory Gallery in *The Great Muppet Caper*, Balmoral Castle in *The King's Speech*, and parts of Hogwarts School in the Harry Potter films.

• Bulwer-Lytton died a few days before his 70th birthday from an abscess that formed after a doctor operated on his ear. He let it be known beforehand that he wouldn't be caught dead being interred at Westminster Abbey, but since he was a baron, a former member of Parliament, and a famous author, that's exactly what happened.

• Ironically, Bulwer-Lytton wasn't the first to use the phrase "It was a dark and stormy night..." in a literary work. Twenty-one years earlier, Washington Irving had used the exact same phrase in his book *The History of New York*:

> It was a dark and stormy night when the good Antony arrived at the creek (sagely denominated Haerlem River) which separates the island of Manna-hata from the mainland. The wind was high, the elements were in an uproar....

The rambling, parenthetical sentence structure is so similar to what Bulwer-Lytton wrote in 1830 that scholars assume Bulwer-Lytton work was satirizing Irving's work.

• He wasn't the last to use it, either: Other works that have begun with the same seven words include *A Wrinkle in Time* by Madeleine L'Engle, *Let's All Kill Constance* by Ray Bradbury, chapter 65 of Alexandre Dumas' *The Three Musketeers*, and Joni Mitchell's song "The Crazy Cries of Love." Conversely, Terry Pratchett and Neil Gaiman began their book *Good Omens* with: "It wasn't a dark and stormy night."

* * *

"Truth is the safest lie." —**Jewish proverb**

MONEY IS NO OBJECT!

Are you a billionaire? Here's a shopping list of household items you might need.

Mattress. The Vividus (Latin for "full of life") from Swedish company Hästens is entirely handmade from a blend of natural fibers (including horsehair) and built to your individual specifications. You can only buy one in a Hästens store, and you can only see them by appointment. Cost: $69,500.

Toaster. Dualit is a 65-year-old British company that makes a variety of high-end handmade appliances, including the Combi toaster, which can toast four slices of bread in your home or toast 80 sandwiches an hour in your restaurant. Cost: $382.

Bicycle. The Aurumania Gold Bike Crystal edition is entirely 24-karat gold-plated, even the sprockets and spokes. The saddle and handlebar grips are made of handsewn leather, and there are more than 600 Swarovski crystals embedded in the bike's frame. The name "Aurumania" is written in Swarovski crystals on the cross-bar—in Braille. Cost: $114,464.

Blender. The Blendtec Smoother Q-Series comes with a heavy-duty 20 amp motor, which means this commercial blender can make endless rounds of margaritas or blended coffee drinks. And the see-through "copolyester sound enclosure" makes it very sleek and very quiet. Cost: $1,199.95

Trash Can. The "i" in German manufacturer Wesco's i.Master wastecan stands for "intelligent." It has a battery-powered infrared sensor that automatically opens the lid when your hand gets near. (It also has a foot pedal.) And it's fire-resistant. Cost: $430.

Pair of Jeans. Levi's "Spin Jeans," made in collaboration with artist Damien Hirst, are multicolored, splatter-patterned jeans, reminiscent of spin-art that you'd make at a carnival. Only eight pairs were made. (All were sold.) Cost: $27,000.

Bathtub. Kallista, the copper-smithing company that made the copper "fire" in the Statue of Liberty's torch, also makes tubs. Its Archeo model is solid copper. Five feet long, 21 inches deep, and with a 71-gallon capacity, it comfortably seats two. Cost: $67,557.

First pro wrestler to be inducted into the WWF Hall of Fame: Andre the Giant.

TOO CHEAP FOR GRACELAND

With tickets to the King's home running as high as $70 apiece, it's easy to understand why some fans might have to give his castle a pass. Luckily, there are plenty of other places to get an Elvis fix.

THE ELVIS MUSEUM, Pigeon Forge, Tennessee

Cost: $25 gets you admission to the museum *and* a live show by an Elvis impersonator ($17 for just the museum).

Background: Founder Mike L. Moon got his start collecting Elvis memorabilia in 1971 after he met the King in person and admired a belt he was wearing. Elvis removed the belt and gave it to Moon on the spot. "This generous act made a lasting impression, and Mr. Moon became an avid follower and fan, collecting authentic Elvis memorabilia as opportunities arose," says the museum's website.

Taking Care of Business: After Elvis died in 1977, Moon stepped up his collecting, purchasing items from the Presley family, the Memphis Mafia (Elvis's hangers-on), and others close to the King. He assembled what he calls The World's Largest Private Collection of Elvis Memorabilia. Included in the hoard are numerous pieces of jewelry, including one of Elvis's TCB ("Taking Care of Business") rings, clothing, jumpsuits, guitars, back and foot massagers, a telephone, and "Elvis's last limousine," which the King bought after admiring it in the movie *Shaft*.

Bonus: If you go, you'll want to know that Pigeon Forge is also home to Dollywood, Dolly Parton's theme park (which has a museum dedicated to her), and a *Titanic* museum housed in a building *shaped like the Titanic*.

SIERRA SID'S TRUCK STOP/CASINO, Sparks, Nevada

Cost: Free. The truck stop and the casino are open 24 hours.

Background: When Elvis's father, Vernon Presley, died in 1979, his fiancée, Sandy Miller, inherited a number of Elvis's personal effects. She sold them to truck-stop owner "Sierra" Sid Doan, who put them on display at the truck stop. They're still there.

Taking Care of Business: The main attractions are the three guns that belonged to Elvis—an engraved gold Smith & Wesson .38 Special, a .44 magnum Ruger Blackhawk he bought while serving in the Army in Germany, and an 1897 Colt .38 that he used in the 1964 film *Viva Las Vegas*. Note: These are *not* the guns that Elvis used to shoot his TV when singer Robert Goulet appeared on the tube. (But he did use the Colt .38 to shoot at light bulbs he tossed into Graceland's swimming pool.)

GRACELAND TOO, Holly Springs, Mississippi

Cost: $5 for the 1½ hour tour. (Three visits entitle you to free admission for the rest of your life.)

Background: Located just 30 miles south of Memphis, this two-story columned antebellum home bears some resemblance to Elvis's former home, except that it's smaller and usually painted in a garish color like hot pink or baby blue. Owner/hoarder Paul MacLeod has crammed it full of more than ten million items of Presleyana, including records, magazines, scrapbooks filled with newspaper clippings, old candy wrappers, bags stuffed with dead flowers from Elvis' funeral, and plastic storage tubs filled with carpet scraps tossed out by the *real* Graceland.

Taking Care of Business: The house opened to the public in 1990 and has been open 24 hours a day, 365 days a year ever since. MacLeod, who sleeps only four hours a night, snoozes on a couch near the front door so that he can hear the doorbell at any hour. As soon as it rings he springs into action, fueled by the 24 cans of Coca-Cola he drinks each day. He used to give tours with the help of his son, Elvis Aron Presley MacLeod, but his son moved to New York. Don't expect to see McLeod's former wife around the place, either. "My ex-wife told me, 'Make up your mind. Either me or the Elvis collection.' So that put an end to that," he explains.

FT. CHAFFEE BARBERSHOP MUSEUM, Arkansas

Cost: Free

Background: When Elvis entered the Army in 1958, he had to get a regulation buzz cut just like every other inductee. But because his was one of the most famous heads of hair in the world, *his* haircut made history. In 2008 Fort Chaffee's barbershop was lovingly restored to look just like it did on March 25, 1958, the

First film ever made in Hollywood: D. W. Griffith's 1910 *In Old California*.

day the King was cropped. The museum features pictures of Elvis getting his haircut and other period artifacts. (One thing you won't see: Elvis's hair clippings. The barber, James "Pete" Peterson, was ordered to mix the King's clippings with other hair while an Army major watched; then, when he took the hair out to the dumpster, he was escorted by military police to make sure fans didn't steal it.) In 2011 the barbershop and surrounding barracks were added to the National Register of Historic Places.

Taking Care of Business: Each March 25, the nearby town of Fort Smith celebrates Elvis Haircut Day, complete with—if you dare—free "authentic G.I. buzz cuts" given by Peterson's son, Jimmy Don.

Coming Soon: The adjacent Fort Chaffee *Barracks* Museum, "where Elvis Presley slept during his tenure (three days) at Fort Chaffee."

THE EVERYTHING ELVIS MUSEUM, Cornelia, Georgia

Cost: $5

Background: Art student Joni Mabe's obsession with the King began on the day he died, August 16, 1977. She was washing her car when the radio station announced his death and started playing Elvis songs. Mabe, who calls herself "The Queen of the King," was inspired to create Elvis-themed artwork and to start a collection of Elvis memorabilia that has grown to more than 30,000 objects.

Taking Care of Business: The two most impressive items in her collection are 1) The Elvis Wart, an actual wart removed from the back of Elvis's right hand in 1957 and purchased for "a substantial sum" from the doctor who removed it; and 2) The Maybe Elvis Toenail, which Mabe says she plucked from the green shag carpet in Graceland's Jungle Room while touring the holy of holies in 1983. (Get it? *Maybe* it's Elvis's toenail, and *maybe* it isn't.) Despite having one and possibly two sources of Elvis's DNA, Mabe has refused all requests to clone the King. "I would never want Elvis cloned. Ever," she told *Weird Georgia* author Jim Miles, "because then he wouldn't have a mama." Besides, Mabe asks, "How can anybody be sure that they won't actually create an Elvis monster?" (The museum's most popular souvenir: T-shirts that read, "The King is Gone...But the Wart Lives On.")

The world's 1st "scented billboard" was put up in Mooresville, NC, in 2010. The scent: steak.

THE ELVIS PRESLEY FIGHT SCENE, Madison, Wisconsin

Price: Free

Background: At 1:00 a.m. on the morning of June 24, 1977, two teenage punks were beating up a third kid in front of the Skyland gas station when two limousines rolled up and stopped at a red light. Elvis, in town for a concert, was riding in the second car.

Taking Care of Business: The King jumped out of the car and assumed a "classic karate stance," challenging the punks to a fight. That stopped them in their tracks. The kids shook hands with Elvis and each other. "Is everything settled now?" Elvis asked. When the boys promised not to fight anymore, Presley got back in his limousine and sped off. The incident would likely have been forgotten, had the King not died less than two months later. The fight remained fresh in local memory for 30 years, and in 2007, a granite marker was placed on the spot. The Skyland station is long gone; today it's a car dealership. But the marker is still there.

IT'S NOW OR NEVER

If you want to visit the museums listed above, don't put it off. Without Graceland's deep pockets, they can go under without warning. Here's one alternative Elvis venue that has already left the building.

• **The Elvis Is Alive Museum, Wright City, Missouri.** Opened in 1990 by Bill Beeny (a Baptist preacher, real estate salesman, conspiracy theorist, and occasional Elvis impersonator) the museum featured an Elvis funeral display with a dummy in an open coffin. ("It doesn't look like Elvis, but neither did the guy in the casket," Beeny said.) Other exhibits included documents from Elvis' FBI file, a recording of a message the King left on an answering machine six years after he "died," and results from a DNA test comparing Elvis' DNA to the body in the casket at Elvis's funeral. ("They did not match! Elvis was not in the casket!"). In 2007 Beany sold the collection on eBay for $8,000. The new owner reopened the museum in Mississippi, then closed it several months later and put the collection back up for sale on eBay—twice. (No takers.) The museum is currently in storage, but the website is still up. There, visitors can buy Beeny's book, *Elvis's DNA Proves He's Alive*, and post messages for the King to read. "Since Elvis did not die on August 16, 1977 and always enjoyed fan mail, we think he'd still enjoy hearing from you," says the site.

***Star Trek's* Lieutenant Uhura's name means "freedom" in Swahili.**

MYTH CONCEPTIONS

"Common knowledge" is frequently wrong. Here are some examples of things that many people believe but, according to our sources, just aren't true.

Myth: St. Patrick was Irish.

Truth: The patron saint of Ireland was actually born in Scotland in the late 4th century. When he was a teenager, Palladius (his real name) was kidnapped and sold into slavery in Ireland. Six years later, he escaped and went back to Scotland, where he joined a monastery. As an adult, Palladius returned to Ireland as a missionary, where he lived for 40 years, dying in A.D. 461 (And he didn't drive away any snakes—there weren't any.)

Myth: Jogging will wear out your knees.

Truth: Quite the opposite, actually. According to an 18-year study by Stanford University (from 1984 to 2002), running and jogging on a regular basis will make your knees stronger and your joints better lubricated. So if you go jogging and your knees hurt, most likely it's because you're out of shape or there's a preexisting problem that you're aggravating.

Myth: Greco-Roman architecture and statues were white.

Truth: They may look white now, but ancient traces of pigment have been detected on many of these structures, leading archeologists to believe that buildings like the famed Parthenon were probably *very* colorfully and elaborately painted.

Myth: Florida's Everglades is a giant swamp.

Truth: The Everglades is actually a very slow-moving river, 60 miles wide and 100 miles long. It flows from Lake Okeechobee and lets out in the Florida Bay.

Myth: The phrase "up to par" means a task has been performed satisfactorily, but not great—more like "average."

Fact: In golf, where this phrase comes from, *par* refers to the score an expert golfer should achieve on a hole. So if you perform a task "up to par," it technically means you've done it perfectly, without making a single error—which is a lot better than "average."

Myth: The popular Christmas carol contains the yuletide phrase "God rest you, merry gentleman."

Truth: The comma is in the wrong place. The original phrase, which dates to the 1400s, was "God rest you merry, gentlemen." The phrase "God rest you merry" uses *rest* not in the sense of "relaxing," but more like the phrase *rest assured*. So in essence, the song is saying, "May God keep you merry, gentlemen."

Myth: Searing meat seals in the juices.

Truth: If searing truly did create a seal, the fluid inside would boil and your steak would pop like a big piece of popcorn. Browning (or searing) the outside of your meat in a pan before baking it actually removes some of the moisture, which makes the meat a little bit drier…but also a lot tastier.

Myth: Buddha was fat.

Truth: He was thin. The man who we know today as Buddha, Siddhartha Gautama, lived 2,500 years ago in India. No pictures of him exist, but he was said to be "tall and slender." Other men after him have also been given the title *Buddha*, which means "one who has achieved a state of perfect enlightenment." The portlier version, known as the "laughing Buddha," was a 10th-century A.D. Chinese folk hero known as Budai.

Myth: In Shakespeare's *Romeo and Juliet*, when Juliet stands on the balcony and asks, "Wherefore art thou, Romeo?" she is looking for him.

Truth: In Elizabethan times, *wherefore* meant "why," so Juliet was asking, "Why are you Romeo?" She was lamenting the fact that he came from a rival family, forcing them to keep their love a secret.

Myth: You "sweat out toxins" when you exercise.

Truth: Sweat's one-and-only duty is to cool off the body. As such, it's made up of water and trace minerals. Toxins are processed through the liver and kidneys and then excreted during what you are most likely doing right now.

The first airplane to fly across the United States took 49 days to do it.

MUPPET FACTS

"It's time to put on makeup. It's time to light the lights. It's time to get things started with some Muppet facts tonight."

• Disney bought the Muppets in 2003, but only the "classic Muppets" (the ones from *The Muppet Show* and the Muppet movies). *Sesame Street* characters are owned by the Sesame Workshop, and the Fraggles are owned by the Jim Henson Company.

• In Portugal, Kermit the Frog is named "Cocas." In Spain, he's "Gustavo."

• The two hecklers in the balcony on *The Muppet Show* are named Statler and Waldorf. Statler is the one with the grey hair; Waldorf is the one with the mustache. (Waldorf's wife is named "Astoria.")

• Until 1983, HBO aired only movies and sports. Its first show was *Fraggle Rock.*

• Telly initially had dazed eyes and a TV antenna on his head. Ironically, during the first few seasons of *Sesame Street*, he was supposed to warn children that they shouldn't watch too much TV.

• An early draft of the screenplay for *The Muppet Movie* included a recurring role for Secretary of State Henry Kissinger. He was supposed to appear several times, disguised as a sheriff, a busboy, an extra, and as a head on Mount Rushmore.

• The Muppet characters' frames are made out of flexible polyfoam (foam rubber isn't used because it disintegrates). The "skin" is made out of a synthetic material called *antron fleece*, which is furry, dyeable (very important), and doesn't get fuzzballs.

• Miss Piggy's full, original name was Miss Piggy Lee.

• The protoype of Kermit was a lizard made from cardboard and covered in material cut from Henson's mother's fuzzy green coat. The eyes were two halves of Wacky Stacks, a 1970s line of toy plastic eggs. (When the manufacturer went out of business, Henson bought their entire stock so he'd have Muppet eyes forever.)

If a rattlesnake doesn't find shelter from the hot sun, it will die within 20 minutes.

• Two Muppet-sung songs made the pop chart: "Rubber Duckie," by *Sesame Street's* Ernie, hit #16 in 1970, and "Rainbow Connection," by Kermit the Frog, reached #25 in 1979.

• The first season of *Saturday Night Live* featured regular Muppet sequences. New characters from "The Land of Gorch" were created for the show, including "King Ploovis," "Queen Peuta" (she has three feet), and "The Mighty Favog." The adult-oriented sketches weren't very popular with audiences or the writers, and were discontinued in early 1976.

• *Meep! Meep!* In more than 30 years, Beaker from *The Muppet Show* has spoken only three lines: "Sadly, temporary," "Makeup ready," and "Bye-bye!"

• In 2005 Kermit the Frog was given the key to the city of Kermit, Texas.

• Oscar the Grouch around the world: In Pakistan, he's "Akhtar" and lives in an oil drum. In Turkey, he's called "Kirpik" and resides in a basket. There is no Oscar in the Israeli version of *Sesame Street*. Instead they have Oscar's cousin, "Moishe Oofnik," who lives in an abandoned car.

* * *

QUEEN ELIZABETH FACTS

• The United States has had 44 presidents in 225 years. Queen Elizabeth II (crowned in 1952) is just the 40th English monarch since 1066. She's outlasted 12 prime ministers of England.

• In her 60-year reign, she has conferred more than 400,000 awards and honors through 610 "investiture" ceremonies.

• More than 1.5 million people have attended garden parties at one of the Queen's royal palaces.

• She has received 3.5 million pieces of correspondence.

• The Queen is the legal owner of the swans who live in the Thames River, as well as the whales and dolphins in the waters surrounding the United Kingdom.

• The Queen doesn't need a driver's license or license plates when she drives.

• Her dogs don't need licenses either.

In 2011 the U.S. Treasury had an operating cash balance of $73.7 bil. Apple: $76.4 bil.

LIFE IMITATES ART

Countless movies and TV shows are inspired by real-life events. But when real-life events are inspired by fiction, Uncle John takes notice.

ON THE RADIO: In 1984 "Weird Al" Yankovic released "I Lost on *Jeopardy*," a parody of Greg Kihn's hit "Jeopardy." In the song and video, Yankovic loses spectacularly on the TV game show *Jeopardy!*

IN REAL LIFE: In 2000 Yankovic was a celebrity contestant on VH1's *Rock & Roll Jeopardy*!, which features questions and answers about rock music. He lost.

ON THE SCREEN: Actor Simon Pegg has appeared in dozens of films and TV shows, but his breakthrough was as writer and star of the British TV comedy *Spaced*, about a science-fiction-loving slacker. In one episode, he states, "As sure as the day is long, the night is dark, and every odd-numbered *Star Trek* movie is sh*t."

IN REAL LIFE: Pegg starred as Scotty in the 2009 reboot of the *Star Trek* movie franchise...the 11th movie in the series.

ON THE SCREEN: One of Fox's first shows was *Second Chance*, which aired in 1987. It was about a man named Charles who dies and gets another shot at life by going back in time to guide his teenage self through life. In the first episode, Charles dies and goes to heaven. Date: July 2011. Also shown awaiting judgment before St. Peter is Libyan dictator Muammar Gaddafi.

IN REAL LIFE: Gaddafi was toppled and killed in October 2011, just three months later than *Second Chance*'s prediction.

ON THE SCREEN: On its December 12, 1998, episode, *Saturday Night Live* cast member Jimmy Fallon appeared in a *Christmas Carol* parody. He played the "Ghost of Hosts Future," and predicted that he himself would host the December 12, 2011, episode.

IN REAL LIFE: By 2011 Fallon had become a huge star, hosting *Late Night with Jimmy Fallon* on NBC. On December 17, 2011, he did in fact host *Saturday Night Live*. (The prediction couldn't completely come true—December 12, 2011, was a Monday.)

NOT-SO-STUPID DISHWASHER TRICKS

A dishwasher takes up a lot of space in your kitchen. Ever feel that it's not pulling its fair share? Turns out there are many surprising ways you can increase your appliance's productivity.

NO-BRAINER ADAPTATIONS

Many people have found themselves one rack short of a full load, and grabbed something close at hand, such as greasy drip pans or scuzzy soap dishes, to fill up the dishwasher. Maybe you've put your refrigerator shelves in there, too. That's a good start, but it's not nearly the extent of a dishwasher's ability. Look around the house and you'll see a lot of things that could use a good dishwashin'. Here's a list of items that other kitchen adventurers have successfully cleaned in the DW:

- Small window screens
- The greasy fan vent screen above the stove
- Stove burner drip pans (Do it weekly to prevent carbon buildup. Don't wait until they're already caked with blackened crud.)
- Glass light globes (Glass only—no wires or electrical parts.)
- Ashtrays (Empty out the butts first, no matter how good your dishwasher claims to be.)
- Non-paper vacuum filters
- Household sponges

OUT OF THE KITCHEN

Even those who avoid the dishwasher for its normal purposes can get caught up in adapting it to new purposes.

- Non-power tools (Gets off the dirt and grime.)
- Hubcaps and wheel covers
- Heat registers
- Cabinet knobs and handles
- Inexpensive ceramic figurines
- Non-electronic toys, from plastic dinosaurs to Barbies to teething

An average potato will make about 36 potato chips.

rings to action figures to Legos (inside a nylon bag...unless you want to spend a lot of time fishing them out of the bottom)

- Dog toys
- Combs

STRETCHING IT

- Bowling balls (Believe it or not, dishwashing removes that oil they use on the bowling lanes, giving you more spin control and fewer oil stains on clothes and accessories.)
- Garden gnomes, frogs, plastic flamingos—any plastic items from your garden menagerie that will fit
- Baseball caps (They can lose their shape in a clothes washer, but DW advocates say that tucking them between dishes with the open side down does the trick. Still worried that they'll lose their shape? Buy a wire cap-supporting frame made for this purpose.)
- Rubber boots
- Knee, shin, and elbow pads
- Athletic shoes (The dishwasher gets the water hot enough to kill any fungi or microbes.)
- Brooms, brushes, dustpans, and plastic trash can lids
- Toilet seats (Don't do this one while you're washing the dishes.)

YOU'RE KIDDING ME, RIGHT?

This is the "Now you're on your own" section of this article. We can't vouch for the next few items, but they're so far out that we had to include them. Proceed at your own risk!

- Poaching fish (There are "cooks" who swear that if you wrap a fish in aluminum foil and seal it well, there will be no soap smell on the fish and no fish smell on the dishes.)
- Parboiling large quantities of corn on the cob prior to canning or freezing (Use the hottest rinse cycle only.)
- Cleaning potatoes (Why scrub your spuds with a brush? For best results, lay them between the bowls and glasses.)

NOTE: For just about everything listed here, it's best to use the top rack if possible and *not* to use the heated air-dry option. And remember this rule of thumb: "If it's something you'd cry over hurting, harming, or losing, DON'T put it in."

Money to burn: Collectively, Americans spend about $211 million on fireworks every year.

LOADED WORDS

Surprisingly, there are a lot of euphemisms to describe what we all do in the bathroom. Because they're so colorful, they are remarkably disgusting, yet eerily compelling. (Enjoy.)

Bake brownies

Clip a biscuit

Bust a grumpy

See a man about a dog

Release the hostages

Free the chickens from the coop

Let the firetrucks loose

Bust a dookie

Dispatch a Yankee

Squeeze a steamer

Ride the porcelain bus

Stock the lake with brown trout

Pinch a loaf

Lose a farting contest

Mold an action figure

Step into the office

Blow mud

Murder a mud bunny

Build a log cabin

Grease the punchbowl

Free the turtles

Lay hot snakes

Lay wolf bait

Give birth to a food baby

Expel the hamster

Take the Browns to the Super Bowl

Crank an 8-ball

Make a delivery

Hang a root

Empty the manure spreader

Go number 2

Park a custard

Log out

Burn a mule

Send some sailors out to sea

Sink submarines

Pop a squat

Drop a deuce

Sprout a tail

Drop the kids off at the pool

Give birth to sewer bass

Throw a chip

Unhitch a load

Trash the hash

Eat backwards

Visit the chamber of commerce

Duke it out

Lose 10 pounds in one minute

Talk to John

Misfart

CHAIN-STORE ORIGINS

From humble beginnings to the major stores we know today.

BEST BUY

Richard Shulze opened a small stereo store called Sound of Music in St. Paul, Minnesota, in 1966. Like most electronics stores of the time, it catered to stereo buffs, but as audio components and car stereos became more affordable in the 1970s, Sound of Music grew. By 1976 Shulze had opened eight more stores in the Twin Cities, then expanded into appliances and electronics, including the latest gadget, the VCR. The stores were always small, until a local disaster gave Shulze an idea. In 1981 a tornado destroyed the flagship store. Most of his inventory was undamaged, though, so Shulze held a "Tornado Sale" in the parking lot and heavily advertised it, adding products from the other stores (closed for the day to reroute sales traffic) to make the event appear even bigger. From the success of that sale, Shulze decided that big stores were the way to go. In 1983 he renamed the company Best Buy and opened a "superstore" in Burnsville, Minnesota. Today there are more than 1,000 locations worldwide.

TARGET

Dayton's was Minneapolis's top department store in the early 20th century. When founder George Dayton died in 1938, his sons, George and Douglas, took over and began to expand. In the 1950s, more Dayton's stores opened in Rochester, Minnesota, then in suburban Minneapolis's Southdale Mall, the first indoor shopping center in the U.S. (and the first of four Dayton-owned-and-anchored malls opened in the next decade). In 1962 the company made a risky move into "discount retailing"—a department store-size combination of drugstore and dime store. They turned out to be pioneers of the "big box" store. The publicity team debated over more than 200 names, ultimately deciding on Target, in order to be "on target" with customer service and value. The first one opened in Roseville, Minnesota. By the end of the year, there were five Targets statewide. Denver got one in 1966, followed by St. Louis, Dallas, and Houston. There were 74 Targets by 1980; today, there are more than 1,500.

By the 4th century B.C., the Chinese were drilling for natural gas and using it for heat.

And Dayton's? They're gone. They merged with Hudson's department store in 1969, then with Marshall Field's in 1990. The last Dayton's and Hudson's in Minnesota were converted into Marshall Field's in 2001. Today they're all Macy's stores.

J.C. PENNEY

In 1898, 23-year-old James Cash Penney took a job as a sales clerk at the Golden Rule dry goods store in Colorado. He was an enthusiastic employee and the top salesman. After four years on the job, the owners presented him with an opportunity. They were opening a branch in the small town of Kemmerer, Wyoming, and offered Penney a one-third share in that store if he would move there and run it. He accepted, and the store thrived under his management. In 1907 he bought out his partners and expanded to three stores. In 1909 he moved his offices from Kemmerer to Salt Lake City so he could be closer to banks and railroads, facilitating shipping to what had become a chain of six stores. By 1911 Penney had 22 stores, earning $1 million a year (around $23 million today). Two years later, he changed the name from Golden Rule to The J.C. Penney Company. In 1926, with a staggering 500 stores, the company became "the world's largest department store." Penney died in 1971. There are now more than 1,100 JCP stores.

HOME DEPOT

In 1978 Bernie Marcus and Arthur Blank were laid off from their executive jobs at Handy Dan Home Improvement, a chain of hardware and construction supply stores. Within a year, the duo had leased four former Treasure Island grocery stores in Atlanta and turned them into Home Depots. Their business model was different from most hardware stores: Home Depot bought directly from manufacturers, not from distributors, so its prices were lower. Marcus and Blank also set their store apart from their competitors' with size: Those initial stores were each more than 60,000 square feet and stocked with more than 25,000 products. Riding the wave of the growing "do-it-yourself" trend, within two years, they had 50 locations. When Marcus and Blank retired in 2000, there were more than 1,500 Home Depot stores, measuring on average about 100,000 square feet. (Handy Dan went out of business in 1989.)

The Butterfinger candy bar got its name in a contest in...

HOMONYM QUIZ

Homonyms are words that are spelled and pronounced alike but have different meanings. Examples: squash *(the plant) and* squash *(as in "crush"). In this quiz we give you one homonym and two meanings—and you have to guess which meaning entered the English language first.* *(Answers on page 601.)*

WHICH MEANING CAME FIRST?

1. **WORD:** Bank
MEANINGS:
a) a financial institution
b) a river's edge

2. **WORD:** Bat
MEANINGS:
a) a flying mammal
b) to flutter one's eyelashes

3. **WORD:** Cordial
MEANINGS:
a) sincere, friendly
b) a medicine or drink

4. **WORD:** Maroon
MEANINGS:
a) a dark reddish-brown
b) to strand, as on a desolate island

5. **WORD:** Moor
MEANINGS:
a) a person from North Africa of mixed Arab and Berber descent
b) marshy land

6. **WORD:** Fluke
MEANINGS:
a) a whale's tail
b) a stroke of good luck

7. **WORD:** Quarry
MEANINGS:
a) hunters' prey
b) a pit from which stone is excavated

8. **WORD:** Hail
MEANINGS:
a) freezing rain
b) to call from afar

9. **WORD:** Hawk
MEANINGS:
a) to sell or peddle
b) to clear one's throat

10. **WORD:** Trip
MEANINGS:
a) a hallucinatory drug experience
b) to release a switch or catch

...1923. Winner: a klutz named Nicola "Butterfingers" Jovanovic, who sent in his nickname.

11. WORD: Hip
MEANINGS:
a) informed ("I'm hip.")
b) a cheer ("Hip hooray!")

12. WORD: Magazine
MEANINGS:
a) a munitions storehouse
b) a periodic publication

13. WORD: Mummy
MEANINGS:
a) an embalmed body
b) a term for "mother"

14. WORD: Porter
MEANINGS:
a) a dark beer
b) a person hired to carry

15. WORD: Squash
MEANINGS:
a) a popular vegetable
b) to crush

16. WORD: Yank
MEANINGS:
a) an American
b) to tug or pull

* * *

RANDOM BOOK FACTS

• Before parchment, Europeans wrote on thin peels of bark. The word "book" is derived from *bog*, the Danish word for birch, the preferred writing bark in Denmark.

• Only writer to turn down the Pulitzer Prize for Fiction: Sinclair Lewis, for *Arrowsmith* in 1926. He thought that the prize should be given to books that celebrate American ideals and that *Arrowsmith* was critical of them.

• First e-book reader on the market: the Sony Bookman in 1992. (It flopped.)

• About 50 percent of adults read five or more books a year. About 25 percent don't read any.

• Most prolific author: Brazilian novelist José Carlos Ryoki d'Alpoim Inoiue. He published 1,058 novels between 1986 and 1996—about one every three days.

• St. Jerome is the patron saint of librarians; St. John is the patron saint of book sellers; St. Christopher is the patron saint of bookbinders.

• What *is* a book, exactly? In 1950 the United Nations defined one as "a non-periodical literary publication containing 49 or more pages, not counting the covers." (Oh.)

71% of Americans believe the government knows more than it is telling us about UFOs.

PUT A CORK IN IT!

New technology isn't always better.

CORK CONDITIONS

For centuries, wine bottles have been capped with cork stoppers made from the bark of *Quercus suber* (also known as the cork oak tree), which grows primarily near the Mediterranean Sea, in countries such as Portugal, Spain, Tunisia, Italy, Algeria, and Morocco. The hardy yet springy material is ideally suited for the job of preventing air and toxins from entering a bottle, without decomposing or interacting with the wine.

But cork is not perfect. Between 1 and 10 percent of all wines with cork stoppers fall prey to "cork taint," which occurs when a natural mold inside a cork causes a chemical reaction that results in trichloroanisole, or TCA for short. When this happens, wine develops a musty odor that experts compare to the scent of wet newspapers. It will also taste vinegary or bitter and, more often than not, become discolored. In short, it is undrinkable.

NEW STOPPERS

The obvious solution to cork taint: Use different materials. And winemakers have been experimenting with other ways to seal bottles for decades, for both quality control and cost savings.

• **Plastic corks.** First introduced in the mid-1950s for cheaper wines, they are now fairly common, but come with their own set of drawbacks. First off, they can start letting small but steady streams of air leak into bottles after only 18 months—which is fine if a wine is sold and consumed quickly, but for wines that are left to age and improve, that's disastrous. Second, they're more difficult to open than cork closures, and using them to reseal a bottle can be an exercise in frustration. Perhaps most damning: Because they're made with chemicals, synthetic corks can give wines a slight chemical flavor. Nevertheless, wines sealed with plastic corks have a failure rate of only 1 percent.

• **Aluminum screw caps.** What they lack in elegance, they more than make up for in practicality. For one thing, they're a cinch to open and they don't require a corkscrew. Plus, these closures (widely adopted by Australian winemakers in the 1970s) make preservation easier for both the public and producers. The caps do an excellent job of keeping out oxygen by forming a tighter seal than tops made from cork, thus improving a wine's aging potential. The failure rate is about 0.5 percent. And wine drinkers can simply screw the top back on after pouring a glass. Disregarding some slight change in taste that they give to wines made from sauvignon blanc grapes, switching to screw caps should be a no-brainer for winemakers, right? Wrong—and cork advocates are not about to go down without a fight.

CORK CONSTITUENCY

While many large-scale wine operations have given up on cork stoppers, plenty of their competitors are sticking with them. Advocates argue that the statistics on cork taint are overblown. Corks too often get the blame, they say, for wines that are stored improperly or were not very good to begin with.

Fans of cork also contend that harvesting the stuff is an environmentally friendly practice. The manufacturing process for cork tops yields low carbon emissions, especially compared to the industrial operations involved with the production of synthetic corks and screw tops. It's also cheaper to make corks than it is to manufacture and mold closures out of plastic or aluminum. Furthermore, purists claim, it's more environmentally sustainable. Cork oak trees are easy to grow and live a long time, and harvesting the cork bark is done with little or no environmental damage.

Need another reason to love corks? It's hard to overlook hundreds of years of tradition...and the satisfying "POP" a cork makes when it's pulled from a bottle of wine.

*   *   *

FEELING GROOVY

Skeletal remains show that ancient Viking warriors filed horizontal grooves into their front teeth to signify their rank. Evidence shows that some grooves may have been filled with dye. This may explain why a famous Danish king was called "Harald Bluetooth."

Valentine "conversation heart" candies have a shelf life of 5 years.

MUSICAL FLOPS

They can't all be "singular sensations." Here are a few musicals—each with impressive pedigrees—that went dark shortly after their debuts.

ANNIE 2: MISS HANNIGAN'S REVENGE

Annie, the Broadway musical based on the classic comic strip *Little Orphan Annie*, debuted in 1977 and ran for nearly six years at the Alvin Theatre. It inspired a successful film in 1982 and thousands of stage productions around the world. Despite the fact that there had never been a truly successful sequel to any stage musical, *Annie* was such a hit that the decision to make a sequel seemed like a no-brainer. So with a book, music, lyrics, and direction by the same team that had created *Annie*, *Annie 2: Miss Hannigan's Revenge* debuted at the Kennedy Center in Washington, D.C. in December 1989. "We're very well liked in Washington," the director told reporters. "I have a feeling we'll take Washington by storm." They didn't. Reviews for preview shows were terrible, one reviewer calling it "witless and belabored." But producers were determined to make it work. They cut an hour from the three-and-a-half hour show and had the composers rewrite the entire score in time for a March 1990 Broadway debut. It still didn't work. The show never opened on Broadway; it was shuttered after four weeks in Washington.

ANNIE WARBUCKS

Somehow, the failure of *Annie 2* didn't stop producers from making another attempt at an *Annie* sequel in 1993. *Annie Warbucks*, a heavily rewritten version of *Annie 2*, takes place immediately after *Annie*. The plot: When a Child Welfare commissioner orders Daddy Warbucks to either get married or lose custody of the cute orphan, the billionaire scrambles to find a bride. This version received solid reviews and did very well during an off-Broadway run. It was all set to debut on Broadway in January 1994...until the show was abruptly cancelled with only a single day's notice. Why? Investors learned the show couldn't be moved to Broadway in time to qualify for the Tony Awards, so they pulled its funding.

If you met one person per second, it would take over 200 years to meet everyone now living.

THE BEST LITTLE WHOREHOUSE GOES PUBLIC (1994)

The Best Little Whorehouse in Texas was a Broadway hit in the late 1970s and ran for 1,700 performances, which led to a film version starring Burt Reynolds and Dolly Parton in 1982—the top-grossing movie musical of the 1980s. Peter Masterson and Carol Hall, who wrote the music for the original, signed up to write the music and lyrics and score for the sequel. The premise: Miss Mona, the madam of the whorehouse, is lured out of retirement to save the Las Vegas brothel Stallion Fields after the IRS comes after them for millions in back taxes. Mona, the hookers, and the Feds come up with a way to raise the money—they decide to sell shares in the whorehouse on the Stock Exchange.

The show opened on May 10, 1994, at New York's Lunt-Fontanne Theatre. It flopped. The bizarre mixture of high finance lingo and low-brow sex talk was a hard sell, as was the decision to have one actor to simultaneously play two characters based on Siegfried and Roy (one side of his body was Siegfried, the other, Roy). "It's too dopey to be effective as political satire, too tame to qualify as raunch," said one critic. The musical closed after 16 performances.

LESTAT (2006)

This one seemed like a sure bet. The source material, the phenomenally successful Vampire Chronicles series by Anne Rice (which includes *Interview With the Vampire*) was rich with gothic characters and storylines reminiscent of the Broadway smash, *Phantom of the Opera*. Elton John and lyricist Bernie Taupin came on board to write the score, following their critically-acclaimed collaboration on *The Lion King* and *Billy Elliot*. After a hugely successful pre-Broadway run in San Francisco, the producers felt *Lestat* was almost ready to sink its teeth into the Great White Way. For Broadway, they decided to cut many of the San Francisco staging's elaborate special effects (such as ghostly film projections) along with several songs. The result was, as the *New York Times* put it, "a musical sleeping pill." *Lestat* was staked through the heart after only 39 performances.

Only puppet in history to testify before Congress: *Sesame Street's* Elmo.

"NO REGERTS"

Some people find fame by winning an Oscar, running the world's fastest mile, or getting elected president. Others get photos of their misspelled tattoos posted all over the internet. Here are some of our favorites.

"Get Rich Our Die Tryin"

"Happyness Comes No Matter Rain or Shine"

"Last of a Dieing Breed"

"My Mom Is My Angle"

"Poporn"

"Go Whereever The Wind Takes You"

"Imermanence is Forever"

"Music Are The Words I Cant Speek"

"Success is a Procss"

"Only God Will Juge Me"

"Oylmic Torch Bearer"

"It's Get Better"

"Dance Like Noone Is Watching"

"Black Sabbaht"

"Your The ~~Pettle~~ Petal* To My Rose"

"Tragdey/Comedy"

"Strenth & Courage"

"[Bleep] the Systsem"

"You Only Life Once"

"What Didn't Killed Me Made Me Stronger!"

"No Regerts"

"Belife Makes Things Real"

"Stanley Cup Champians"

"Tomarrow Never Knows"

"Ill Keep Apart of You With Me & Every Where I Am There You'll Be"

"Live is Hard/ Don't Give Up"

"...Are You Jalous¿"

"Everyone Elese Does"

"Sweet Pee"

"Ledgends Live On"

"My Love Runs Deeper Then My Wounds"

"See You At The Cossroads"

"Too Liggett To Quit"

"Your Next"

Eating .001% of your body weight in salt is enough to kill you.

TOILET PAPER IN THE NEWS

TP is such a "regular" part of our daily lives that it's bound to end up in the news once in a while.

FILM ROLL

Starring in eight different *Harry Potter* films over the years has made actor Daniel Radcliffe, who played Harry, a millionaire many times over. But not all of that money comes from the movies. Warner Bros. licenses Radcliffe's image for use on toys, children's clothing, and countless other products sold worldwide. Radcliffe gets a slice of the profits from the sale of this merchandise...including, apparently, a certain flushable bathroom product sold in Thailand. "I've heard my face is on toilet paper, but I haven't seen it and I don't know if it's much of a compliment," he told the *Sun* newspaper in 2011.

ROCK 'N' ROLL

In 1980 the British music company EMI auctioned off memorabilia it had accumulated during its many years in the recording business. Some items were from the company's Abbey Road studios, where the Beatles recorded their famous album of the same name. A Beatles fan named Barry Thomas went to the auction hoping to buy a souvenir from the Fab Four days. He found one: Thomas paid £85 (about $200) for a roll of studio toilet paper that the Beatles had refused to use during their *Abbey Road* recording sessions. Why? The paper was too "hard and shiny." Plus EMI's initials were stamped on every sheet (probably to deter theft). After the band complained, studio manager Ken Townsend provided them with toilet paper more to their liking...but kept the offending roll as a souvenir, until he let EMI auction it off. More than 30 years later, Thomas still owns the roll. He keeps it—and a letter of authenticity signed by Townsend—in a custom display case. In 2011 he tried to have it appraised on the *Antiques Roadshow*, but "they couldn't price such an odd object," he says. The only fair estimate of its value is the £1,000 ($1,500) a Japanese collector offered him for a single square. No dice. Thomas couldn't bring himself to tear a sheet from the roll. "It's such an original and unique thing," he told the *Daily Mail* newspaper. "People have the memories and the signed records and pictures and stuff, but no one else can say they have a toilet roll John Lennon rejected."

ROLLING ON THE RIVER

In July 2011, a truck driver hauling eight gigantic rolls of toilet paper to a processing plant that makes them into consumer-sized rolls lost control of his big rig on a curvy stretch of U.S. Highway 12 in Idaho. The truck hit the guardrail and overturned, dumping the toilet paper into the Lochsa River. The huge rolls, which weighed 8,000 pounds dry, swelled to 30,000 pounds each as they became saturated with river water. Even worse (at least as far as the cleanup was concerned), toilet paper is designed to disintegrate in water. The crew made such a mess hauling the two least-saturated rolls of toilet paper out of the river that the rest of the cleanup was postponed until the middle of August, when the river level had dropped enough for the other six rolls to dry out. Then the cleanup crews returned, wrapped the rolls in fine mesh to keep them from falling apart, and hauled them out of the river with a tow truck.

THE TAX ROLLS

In March 2011, Omaha, Nebraska, mayor Jim Suttle made headlines around the world when he proposed a national tax on toilet paper to pay for federally mandated improvements to state and local sewer systems. The 10 percent tax would have increased the price of every roll of toilet paper by about a dime, had it ever been implemented. It wasn't: Even as Suttle was proposing the idea (which he'd read about when it was turned down in Oregon), he reversed his position mid-sentence, perhaps when it dawned on him that he'd have to run for re-election as The Man Who Taxed Toilet Paper. "I heard about it and said, 'Well, this is simple. Let's put it on the table,'" he told the *Omaha World-Herald*. "That doesn't mean I endorse it."

THE ROLL OF GOVERNMENT

In March 2012, every agency of the city government of Trenton,

Of the 11 countries where the average woman has more than six children, 10 are in Africa.

New Jersey—including city hall, the police and fire departments, a water plant, and a number of senior-citizens centers—came within a day or two of running out of toilet paper, thanks to a budget fight between the mayor and the city council. The trouble began in September 2011, when the council rejected a request to spend $4,000 for a year's worth of hot-drink cups. That invalidated the contract for *all* of the city's paper purchases for the fiscal year…including toilet paper. Mayor Tony Mack removed the cups from the contract and resubmitted it, but legal technicalities and objections, including complaints that Mack wasn't doing enough to stop city employees from stealing the TP, killed the contract again and again. In mid-March, when the city government was down to its very last box, the council finally voted to buy more.

Crisis averted? Nope. The council approved an "emergency" purchase of paper products to last only through the end of the fiscal year, three and a half months away. After that, the battle over whether to supply city workers with toilet paper would begin anew. "We're the laughingstock not only of this nation, but the world," said council president Kathy McBride.

* * *

KEEPING UP WITH THE TERRORISTS

In 2012 a man named Jonathan Lee Riches filed a lawsuit against rapper Kanye West and his girlfriend, TV personality Kim Kardashian. The charges: West and Kardashian, along with the entire Kardashian family (including stepdad Bruce Jenner) are secret terrorists, aligned with Al-Qaeda, and that they're a danger to the American public. "On 6/17/2012, I was in West Virginia," reads the suit, "deep in the hills and I stumbled upon the defendants who were all at a Al-Qaeda secret training camp." Riches also claims to have seen Kardashian and West take an Al-Qaeda loyalty oath, burn the U.S. flag, stomp on a picture of President Obama, shoot AK-47s into the air, then perform a concert for other terrorist trainees. Riches, it's worth noting, is listed in the *Guinness World Records* as the "World's Most Litigious Man," having filed more than 5,000 lawsuits. At the time of his filing the suit against the Kardashians, he had just been released from prison, where he was serving time for fraud.

Thomas Edison was homeschooled by his mom.

DUMB CROOKS: BLABBER EDITION

These criminals probably could have gotten away with their crimes...if they hadn't bragged about them.

STATUS UPDATE: JESSE GETS 60 YEARS

Jesse Hippolite, 23, went on a bank-robbing spree in Brooklyn, New York, in 2011, handing tellers a note that read "GIVE ME ALL THE MONEY OR ELSE EVERYBODY DIES!!!" (He never actually brandished a weapon.) A partial license plate number from the getaway car led cops to Hippolite and they hit pay dirt on his Facebook page. Hippolite had posted a photo of himself wearing the same sweatshirt he'd worn in the robberies and holding a wad of cash. Two of his posts: "Crime pays my bills" and "What if we all got fed up with this recession and started running inside every f*cking bank to give us the money that belong to us???" Hippolite was arrested and now faces 60 years in prison.

AIRWAVE AIRHEAD

In June 2011, Susan Cole of Denver, Colorado, was called for jury duty. The 56-year-old beautician didn't want to serve, so she showed up at the courthouse wearing blotchy makeup, curlers, reindeer socks, and mismatched shoes. She then fabricated a sad story to District Judge Anne Mansfield: "I broke out of domestic violence in the military. And I have a lot of repercussions. One is post-traumatic stress disorder." Mansfield immediately dismissed her. A few months later, the topic on a Denver talk radio show was "How to Avoid Jury Duty." Cole was listening that day. She called in and described her ruse in detail. Guess who else tuned in that day: Judge Mansfield. Cole was charged with first-degree perjury.

TRÈS STUPIDE

A French computer hacker, known only as "Carl," specialized in stealing people's credit information. He'd done it hundreds of times but had never been detected. In 2011 the self-described "hacktivist" appeared on the French reality show *Further Investigation*, and not only did he demonstrate how he hacked—he bragged about *who* he hacked: the French military and the Thales Group, a company that provides "information systems and services for the aerospace, defense, and security markets." Thales Group officials alerted the police. They tracked "Carl" to his home, where they found victims' bank data on his hard drive. He was promptly arrested.

PHOTO OOPS

One day in 2011, Rodney Knight, Jr., 19, broke into the home of a Washington, D.C., family. King grabbed as much loot as he could and snuck out before anyone got home. The house belonged to *Washington Post* reporter Marc Fisher, who wrote that the burglar had left a parting shot:

> Compelled to showboat about his big achievement, he opened my son's computer, took a photo of himself sneering as he pointed to the cash lifted from my son's desk, and then went on my son's Facebook account and posted the picture for 400 teenagers to see. In the picture, the man is wearing my new winter coat.

The photo made it easy for police to track down Knight. Said one officer: "He's the most stupid criminal I've ever seen."

INK-COMPREHENSIBLE

In 2004 a Los Angeles gang member named Anthony Garcia gunned down a rival gangster in front of a liquor store. Homicide investigators were unable to link anyone to the murder, and the case was marked "unsolved." Afterward, Garcia had a detailed tattoo of the crime scene inked across his chest. A few years later, when he was arrested on an unrelated charge, police took a picture of his tattoo. Two years after that, L.A. County homicide investigator Kevin Lloyd was reviewing photos of gangster tattoos when Garcia's stopped him cold. Lloyd had worked on the liquor store case and was still bothered that the killer had never been caught. Could it be the same crime scene? He retrieved the case photos, and sure enough, there were details in the tattoo that only the killer could know, including "the direction the victim's body fell, the bowed streetlamp across the way, and the street sign." The investigation was reopened, and in 2011 Garcia was convicted of first-degree murder. He faces up to 65 years.

Tough guys: Ostrich leather is 7 times stronger than cowhide. Stingray skin: 25 times.

DON'T WORRY

Stop biting your fingernails long enough to read these quotes. (Now resume biting.)

"The game is supposed to be fun. If you have a bad day, don't worry about it. You can't expect to get a hit every game."

—Yogi Berra

"It ain't no use putting up your umbrella until it rains."

—Alice Hegan Rice

"For fast-acting relief, try slowing down."

—Lily Tomlin

"What we anticipate seldom occurs; what we least expected generally happens."

—Benjamin Disraeli

"Worry is rust upon the blade."

—Henry Ward Hughes

"We are more disturbed by a calamity which threatens us than by one which has befallen us."

—John Lancaster Spalding

"I read an article that said the symptoms of stress are eating too much, smoking too much, impulse buying, and driving too fast. Are they kidding? That's my idea of a great day!"

—Monica Piper

"Worry is interest paid on trouble before it falls due."

—Dean Inge

"Worry is like a rocking chair; it gives you something to do but it doesn't get you anywhere."

—Harold Stephens

"My advice to actresses is, don't worry about your looks. The one thing that makes you unhappy in your appearance could be the one thing to make you a star."

—Estelle Winwood

"If you're too busy worrying about the competition, you don't focus enough on what you're doing."

—Katie Couric

"A day of worry is more exhausting than a day of work."

—John Lubbock

"When I look back on all these worries, I remember the story of the old man who said on his deathbed that he had had a lot of trouble in his life, most of which had never happened."

—Winston Churchill

On average, daters will have their first kiss on the second date.

"DEATH IS COMING, WARNS WEATHERMAN"

A few more phony headlines from the satirical news agencies file.

E-TRADE BABY JAILED IN INSIDER-TRADING SCANDAL
(*Humor Gazette*, August 2011)

SELF-DESCRIBED "SUPER BUSY" WOMAN REALLY JUST BAD AT TIME MANAGEMENT
(*Red Schtick Magazine*, Jun. 2012)

FIRST "BIG-BONED" SKELETON DISCOVERED
(*Surreal Scoop*, Dec. 2011)

Baltimore Ravens Kicker Blames Missed Field Goal on 'Do-Nothing Congress'
(*The Daily Rash*, Jan. 2012)

SANTA PISSED OFF AFTER WIKILEAKS REVEALS XMAS LIST
(*The Daily Squib*, Nov. 2011)

Saudi Women's Beach Volleyball Team Set to Ruin It for Everyone
(*News Biscuit*, June 2012)

GOD NAMES NEXT "CHOSEN PEOPLE"; IT'S JEWS AGAIN
(*The Satire Wire*, Nov. 2010)

Atheist Sees Image of Big Bang in Piece of Toast
(*Satire and Comment*, Jun. 2011)

ISRAELI RESEARCHERS DEVELOP MARIJUANA WITHOUT THE ANNOYING HIGH
(*The Sarcasmist*, July 2012)

Release of Aung San Suu Kyi Another Example of Myanmar's Shameful Revolving-Door House Arrest System
(*The Daily Grind*, Nov. 2010)

DEATH IS COMING, WARNS WEATHERMAN
(*The Nev Filter*, August 2011)

AFTERBIRTHERS DEMAND TO SEE OBAMA'S PLACENTA
(*The Onion*, August 2009)

How to Sell Your Soul to the Devil
(*Weekly World News*, May 2009)

'HEINEKEN MAKES YOU BETTER AT DRIVING' AD BANNED
(*The Oxymoron*, Sept. 2009)

Are they nuts? The FDA allows frozen strawberries to have up to a 45% mold count.

BANNED!

It's human nature: If authorities outlaw something, suddenly more people than ever will want it...and someone will find a loophole and get around the ban.

BEER ON THE ROCKS

In 1908 the people of Iceland voted to ban alcoholic beverages. The law went into effect in 1915 but was relaxed in 1935, permitting the sale of spirits and "near" beer—beer with a low alcohol content of 2.25 percent or less. But thirsty Icelanders still figured out a way to get drunk on beer. How? Bartenders poured shots of hard alcohol into beers and served them that way. It was a more cost-effective way to get drunk than buying a few high-priced shots, or a lot of weak beer. (The ban was lifted in 1989.)

THE GOOSE IS COOKED

Foie gras is a French delicacy—the fatty liver of an overfed goose or duck. Animal rights activists believe the process of overfeeding immobile birds in tiny pens is cruel, and in 2012 convinced the California legislature to ban the sale of foie gras in that state. But *consuming* foie gras isn't illegal there. Chez TJ, a restaurant in Mountain View, California, stockpiled it in the months leading up to the ban and now serves the delicacy as a "free item" with the purchase of a $130 tasting menu. Chicago also briefly banned the food, from 2006 to 2008. That ban was a failure because of the widespread practice of upscale restaurants charging $30 for bottles of mineral water that came with "free" foie gras.

A COLORFUL STORY

In 2011 St. Joseph Catholic Secondary School in Mississauga, Ontario, banned any decorations with a rainbow. Reason: It's used as a symbol of the Gay Pride movement, and the school doesn't want to promote that. St. Joseph's did, however, allow a group of students to hold an anti-homophobia rally, as long as no rainbows appeared on signs, posters, or shirts. The students got around the ban by baking and distributing rainbow-colored cupcakes, which didn't qualify as "decorations."

What are Spirit Bombs, Gerbils, and Kurukuru Milks? Official yo-yo tricks.

LE SMOKE

France became one of the first countries in the world to ban smoking at indoor public places in 2007. Smoking is much more prevalent in Europe than in the United States, particularly in France. By 2012 dozens of cafés and restaurants in and around Paris had sidestepped the ban by allowing patrons to smoke on terraces, which are technically considered "outside." Smokers are protected from the rain and wind because the terraces are covered on all sides by transparent plastic tarps.

SMOKING POT(VIN)

The New York Rangers and New York Islanders are crosstown NHL rivals. In a February 1979 game, Islanders star Denis Potvin body checked the Rangers' Ulf Nilsson, causing Nilsson to break his ankle and miss the rest of the season. That intensified anti-Islander sentiment among Ranger fans. After that, whenever the organist played the popular rally song "Let's Go Blue" at Rangers home games, for the last three notes of the song, the crowd chanted "Pot-vin sucks!" Result: The arena banned its organists from playing "Let's Go Blue." But Ranger crowds got around the ban by whistling the tune in mass unison and chanting "Potvin sucks" at the end. Thirty years later, the ban is still in place and Ranger fans still whistle—and chant—the tune. (Potvin retired in 1988.)

SING, SING, SING!

The purpose of a labor strike is to force management into meeting workers' demands, because without workers, nothing can get done. Sometimes crafty bosses find ways around strikes. In January 1948 the American Federation of Musicians, the primary labor union of performing and recording musicians at the time, went on strike. AFM president James Petrillo barred all members from attending recording sessions as a way to force the music industry to pay royalties to the union. But before the strike was settled, some record companies replaced their musicians with a capella choirs and other vocal groups who sang the instrumental parts, ushering in the pop vocal era that replaced the big band era.

KHAN THE MAN

Genghis Khan (1162–1227), creator of the Mongol Empire: ruthless conqueror or peaceful nation-builder?

• Genghis Khan conquered more of the world than any person before or since.

• His empire was twice the size of Rome's, stretching from the Pacific Ocean in the east to the Caspian Sea in the west. His successors extended the borders into modern-day Poland, Korea, and southern China. The boundaries of India, China, and Iran are direct results of his conquests.

• He was born Temujin. *Genghis Khan*, which means "universal leader," is a title that was bestowed on him by the Mongol tribes when he was 50 years old.

• Despite the power he attained, he never once slept indoors. He preferred the *ger*, a circular tent made of wood poles and covered with felt. Today it's called a *yurt* and it's still the most common type of Mongolian dwelling. More than half the population of the capital city of Ulaanbaatar live in a yurts.

• When Temujin was eight years old, his half-brother Begter stole a fish from him. Angered that Begter was keeping food from the family, Temujin killed him with a bow and arrow. For this crime he was held in slavery for five years.

• He was said to be terrified of just two things: barking dogs and his mother.

• After they became his subjects, former enemies received the same rights as his most loyal citizens and were able to rise to the highest offices.

• Any tribe that would not swear allegiance to Genghis Khan left itself open to be conquered, and he went after them mercilessly. However, he knew that kidnapping women and stealing livestock led to war with neighboring tribes, so he made those crimes punishable by death.

• Other crimes punishable by death in the Mongol Empire: lying, adultery, sorcery, and urinating into water.

• After conquering the Bokhara people in modern Kazakhstan, he suspected them of hiding their treasure deep in a palace. "If you ask me what proof I have," he said, "it is because I am the punishment of God." He found the treasure and divided it among his warriors.

• Conquered armies served in battle...but only on the front lines. If they survived, they could be granted citizenship. Genghis Khan's own elite Mongolian warriors stayed farther back.

• Genghis Khan was known to give his soldiers uniforms that had armor only on the front, so that if they retreated, they'd be vulnerable. Result: an army that never retreated.

• Genghis Khan invented the concept of "diplomatic immunity." "Kings do not kill envoys," he said. But he didn't mind when his generals held a victory banquet on a wooden platform...slowly crushing to death the six enemy princes they had put underneath.

• He created a code of laws, a post office, and a network of toll roads throughout his empire. The highways were guarded by a police force, and messengers could cover 250 miles in a day.

• In the Mongol Empire, doctors, lawyers, and priests were exempt from paying taxes. Also tax-exempt: people who washed dead bodies.

• He was "green," declaring that hunting season be in the winter only so that elk herds would have time to replenish.

* * *

CANNED

"Irish airline Ryanair has sacked two of its workers who sat in an overcrowded plane's toilets for a flight from Spain because there were no other seats. The captain of the packed flight from Girona, near Barcelona, to Dublin resigned after he gave the two cabin crew permission. 'This is the first such incident of staff travelling on an already full aircraft in the 20-year history of Ryanair,' the company said in a statement."

—***Reuters***, 2004

CANADA'S MÉTIS PEOPLE

Canadians—you most likely already know this story. Americans—here's some fascinating information about your neighbors to the north.

BACKGROUND

The Canadian government officially recognizes three distinct groups of aboriginal peoples: the Inuit of the Arctic north; the First Nations peoples (comprising the Cree, Ojibwe, Blackfoot, Tlingit, and more than 600 other nations); and the Métis—unique as an officially recognized aboriginal group in that it is mixed-race.

The story of the Métis—pronounced "MAY tee"—begins in the 1600s, with the establishment of the European fur trade in the central Canadian interior. As the number of fur trading posts grew and spread deeper into the land of native peoples, more and more French and British traders married and had families with native women. The practice was actually encouraged by the French, less so by the British. Good relations with native peoples aided the smooth operation of the extremely lucrative fur trade. One consequence of those "good relations": an increasing number of children, and, as the decades passed, adults who were both European and native, yet belonged to neither group.

HALF-BREED (THAT'S ALL I EVER HEARD)

That growing subset came to be known by a number of different names—none flattering—by both Europeans and natives: "Halfbreed," "Country-born," "Black Scots," and "Bois Brûlé." The last term meant "burnt-wood," a French appropriation of the Ojibwa name for mixed-blood people, *wissakodewinmi*, meaning "half-burnt woodsmen"—a reference to the fact that they had lighter skin than full-blood Indians. They were also known as "Métis," French for "mixed." Over time, this is the name they took for themselves.

By the mid-1700s, after several generations of intermarriage and forming their own communities, a unique Métis culture began to emerge: religion, music, dance, food, and language became a mix of French, English, and native cultures. And the fact that the

Métis could speak French, English, and native languages made them successful in the fur trade, which, while run by the Europeans, had always relied on native help. By the mid-1800s, Métis communities flourished wherever that trade could be found. The area with the highest population: the Red River Valley, in the region around what is today the city of Winnipeg, Manitoba, where thousands of Métis lived in independent and self-sufficient communities. But trouble was on its way.

THE CANADIANS ARE COMING...

The British North America Act of 1867 established the modern nation of Canada—although it contained only the provinces of New Brunswick, Nova Scotia, and parts of modern Quebec and Ontario at that time. Two years later, the Canadian government purchased almost all of the land owned by the Hudson's Bay Company—a gargantuan stretch that included most of Saskatchewan, parts of both Alberta and Nunavut, and all of Manitoba. Not consulted in the negotiations: the roughly 9,000 Métis who lived in the Red River Valley.

When the government attempted to take control of the region, the Métis wouldn't let them. What followed was years of resistance, the two key events being the Red River Rebellion of 1869 and the North-West Rebellion (in Saskatchewan) in 1885, both led by Métis leader Louis Riel. There were some successes—Riel and the Métis were able to negotiate the formation of the province of Manitoba with the Canadian government, including some recognition of Métis landholdings. But the rebellion ultimately ended in 1885 with Riel's trial and execution on charges of treason.

MODERN MÉTIS

In the 20th century, the Métis, like all native North American groups, went through decades of political struggle, with varying degrees of mostly non-success. But in 1982, those efforts were rewarded when the Métis (along with the First Nations and Inuit) were designated one of Canada's three official aboriginal groups—making them the only mixed-blood people in the world fully recognized as an aboriginal nation.

Today, there are about 400,000 Métis in Canada, the majority in Manitoba, Saskatchewan, Alberta, and the Northwest

Sudan is the only country in which the official method of execution is crucifixion.

Territories. They are organized nationally—with their own prime minister—and provincially. Official Métis languages spoken today include English, French, *Michif*—a blend of French, English, Cree, Ojibwe, and Assiniboine—and *Bungi Creole*, a mix of Scottish English, Cree, Ojibwe, and Gaelic.

RANDOM FACTS

• For much of Métis history, there were two distinct Métis groups: Franco-Métis—descendants of French and native marriages, who spoke primarily French and native languages; and Anglo-Métis—descendants of British, especially Scottish, and native marriages, who spoke primarily English and native languages, and were the smaller group. The two groups were distinct for decades, but eventually merged into the one Métis people they are today.

• There are Métis communities in the United States—in Montana, North Dakota, and Minnesota—but they are not recognized as a distinct aboriginal group.

• "Métis fiddle" is a music genre featuring a very percussive (and uniquely tuned) fiddle, a percussion instrument (often spoons), and somtimes foot stamping and spoken lyrics. It's a Métis mix of European (especially Celtic) and First Nations music, dance, and storytelling traditions.

• Métis celebrities: actress Tantoo Cardinal, who played Black Shawl, wife of Kicking Bird (Graham Greene) in *Dances with Wolves*; former Canadian Prime Minister Paul Martin (2003–2006); and NHL Hall of Famer Bryan Trottier.

• In 1992 the Canadian parliament passed a resolution recognizing Louis Riel as one of the founders of the province of Manitoba. A statue of Riel stands in front of the Manitoba Legislature Building in downtown Winnipeg.

* * *

"Knowing who your are is confidence. Cockiness is knowing who you are and pushing it down everyone's throat."

—Mila Kunis

ODD BODY TIPS & TRICKS

Some strange tips sent in by readers who swear they work.

• **About to sneeze?** Push the tip of your tongue upward against the roof of your mouth where the hard palate ends and the soft palate begins (between your back teeth).

• **Chopping an onion?** Avoid the tears by lighting a candle. The heat will attract (and burn) the sulfide fumes.

• **Keep an injection from hurting** by pressing on the spot where you're about to get the needle. By overloading the nerve endings in that area, you deaden the pain.

• **Stop the gag reflex** by clenching your thumb in your fist.

• **Lost your car?** If you have a remote control to unlock the doors, hold it under your chin and press the button that beeps the horn. The shape of your skull intensifies the radio signal. Open your mouth, and the signal will go even farther.

• **Have a small burn?** Press on the spot with your finger. The best way to avoid blisters is to return the burned spot to its normal temperature quickly. (But it won't stop the pain.)

• **Leg fall asleep?** Change the position of your hip to adjust the blood flow to your lower body. End pins and needles in your hands by shaking your head. It loosens the pressure on nerves in your neck.

• **Getting a shot?** Coughing during the injection will ease the pain by putting pressure on the spinal canal, making it harder for the pain message to reach your brain.

• **For a toothache,** rub some ice on the back of your hand between the thumb and index finger. There's a nerve cluster there that affects pain sensations in the face and hands.

• **"Brain freeze"** occurs when the nerves in the back of your mouth suddenly get very cold, giving you a brief (but strong) headache. A quick way to stop it is to warm the nerve endings by drinking a glass of water (no ice).

More modern than you think: The ancient Greeks played with hula hoops.

LEGAL BRIEFS

If "going commando" has one advantage over wearing underwear, it's that you're less likely to end up in court on an underwear-related charge. (Less likely, but not impossible…)

CASE: Seth Brigham v. City of Boulder, Colorado

DETAILS: In February 2010, Brigham attended a Boulder City Council meeting with the intent of speaking during the televised public-comment period, as he'd done dozens of times in the past. There's nothing wrong with that…except that Brigham, who wanted to criticize a proposed city ordinance making it illegal to be naked in public, stripped down to his underpants to make his point. He opened his remarks by criticizing two council members by name, which prompted the mayor to tell him not to make personal attacks. When Brigham complained about being interrupted, a police officer asked him to leave the podium. Brigham refused and was arrested. He was charged with trespassing and obstructing the police.

OUTCOME: Ten days later, the city dropped the charges after the city attorney concluded the arrest was unjustified. When Brigham said he was considering suing the city for violating his civil rights, the city paid him $10,000 to settle the claim. Brigham said he planned to buy a scooter and possibly some underwear. "Maybe I'll buy myself some nice pairs of boxers—one for every City Council meeting," he told the local paper.

CASE: Albert Freed v. Hanes Underwear

DETAILS: In 2007 Freed won a trip to Hawaii for himself and his wife for selling more than $20,000 worth of diet products. To celebrate, his wife bought him eight new pairs of Hanes men's briefs for the trip. At the beach in Hawaii, Freed got sand in his swim trunks, which irritated his private parts. The new underwear made the injury much, much worse, he alleged, because it had a defective fly that "gaped open and acted like sandpaper on my privates." This, Freed claimed, caused excruciating pain that ruined the only vacation he'd taken in 40 years. Freed, who acted as his own attorney, sued Hanes in small claims court for $5,000.

OUTCOME: Freed lost. The court found that Freed failed to prove either that his underwear was defective or that it was responsible for making his injury worse. Freed himself was more likely to blame, the court found, because he ignored his original injury and also because he has an unusual way of putting on his underwear: "Plaintiff testified that he dresses by placing his underwear inside the pants he plans to wear that day and then pulls both on together. He testified that he never puts his underwear on and adjusts himself to get comfortable—that is 'just not how he does things,'" the judge wrote in her decision.

CASE: Charles "Beau" Wiseman v. Washoe County, Nevada

DETAILS: Wiseman, a county employee, claimed in 1998 that his boss, County Manager John MacIntyre, forced him to attend a "quasi-religious and cult-like" personal-growth seminar as a condition for keeping his job. At the seminar, Wiseman and other employees had to watch MacIntyre do a striptease in his underpants. "Mr. MacIntyre stripped down to his underwear and moved his pelvis and gyrated sexually until the group clapped and applauded," the lawsuit alleged. The strain of this and other "sexually seductive and gender-inappropriate" exercises, plus having to relive painful Vietnam War memories in a "group encounter," caused Wiseman to relapse into alcoholism after 13 years of sobriety. He took medical leave and sued the county for $50,000 in damages, alleging emotional and mental distress, negligence, false imprisonment, discrimination, civil rights violations, plus religious and sexual harassment. (MacIntyre claimed he only "suggested" that Wiseman attend the seminar.)

OUTCOME: Case dismissed. The county did, however, fire MacIntyre. Two county commissioners later told reporters that his firing was due in part to the seminars.

*   *   *

"Some people drink from the fountain of knowledge, others just gargle."

—Robert Anthony

IT'S A WEIRD, WEIRD WORLD

Here's proof that truth is stranger than fiction.

A CRYIN' SHAME

The 2011 Bar-B-Que cookoff in Houston came to an abrupt halt after one of the grillers, 51-year-old Mike Hamby, threw a canister of tear gas into a rival team's tent. The noxious fumes quickly spread to other tents. Dozens of people were sickened, and the contest was postponed. It's unclear why Hamby threw the canister, but apparently there was a "disagreement." After the smoke cleared, he was taken into custody…and later fired from his job as an officer with the Houston Police Department.

CHECKING YOU OUT

For one day in November 2010, the Toronto Public Library allowed patrons to check out an actual human being. Officials explained that the project was a way for people to spend half an hour of one-on-one time with someone they'd never normally get to interact with—including a stand-up comedian, a homeless person, a Buddhist monk, and a former prostitute.

EXTREME NAPPING

In 2012 Yan Yan Ch'eng, a 28-year-old Chinese student, was sunbathing when she fell asleep on a narrow concrete ledge five stories above the ground. Then she rolled over. Luckily, she woke and was able to grab hold of the ledge and hang on. Too scared to climb back up, she screamed for help as a crowd of people watched from below. Firefighters eventually pulled her to safety.

DYING TO BE ON TV

Law Lok-lam died five times in one day in April 2011. The popular Chinese actor appeared on five different shows as five different characters—each of whom met his end. Two of the deaths occurred off-screen. One—a Ming emperor—died of an illness.

The other two characters met their ends in martial arts dramas with Law coughing and spitting up blood as he perished. According to his fans, five TV deaths in a single day is a world record.

WITCH WAY DID SHE GO?

Eilish De'Avalon, a 40-year-old Australian woman, was pulled over in 2010 for talking on her cell phone while driving. When officer Andrew Logan gave her a citation, De'Avalon told him that she was exempt from traffic rules because she's a witch. "Your laws and penalties do not apply to me. I'm sorry, I must go. Thank you." As she started to drive away, Logan tried to take her keys, but his arm got caught in the window, and he was dragged 300 feet before he could pull the keys out of the ignition. De'Avalon was sentenced to two months in jail for severely injuring Logan's shoulder. She apologized and offered him "spiritual healing and a massage." He declined.

GENDER BENDER

Jenny Johnsson, a preschool teacher in Stockholm, Sweden, has banned the use of the words "him" and "her" in her classroom. Instead, the children must refer to each other as "friend." "That way," said Johnsson, "they can be whoever they want to be!" Some of the parents have criticized the taxpayer-funded school for "brainwashing" their boys and girls, but Johnsson claims she is simply following the state-approved national curriculum in Sweden, which aims to eliminate "oppressive" gender stereotypes.

CHICKEN LITTLE WAS RIGHT!

Radivoje Lajic's house in Bosnia has been struck by six meteorites: the first in 2007, another a few months later, and four more over the next three years. Scientists from Belgrade University confirmed that the six objects are indeed space rocks. What makes the strikes more curious? They only occur when it's raining heavily. "I don't know what I have done to annoy the aliens, but there is no other explanation that makes sense," said Lajic, 50. "The odds of being hit by a meteorite are so small that getting hit six times has to be deliberate. They are playing games with me." Lajic sold one of the meteorites to a school in the Netherlands and used the money to install steel reinforcements in his roof for protection.

Coincidence? In Japanese, the word rambo means "rowdy" or "violent."

Q&A: ASK THE EXPERTS

More questions and answers from some of the world's top trivia experts.

TO THE LETTER

Q: *Why are there A, C, and D batteries, but no B batteries?*

A: "Battery letter designations are based on the size of the battery: For common sizes, A is the smallest and D is the largest. By the same logic, AA batteries are larger than AAA. You never see B batteries because they aren't very useful. The size never caught on in products made for consumers, so stores didn't carry them. They are sold, but only in Europe, where they're used primarily to power bicycle lamps." (From *Mental Floss: The Book*)

LIME TIME

Q: *Why is "limey" a derogatory name for British people?*

A: "It's short for 'lime-juicer.' British sailors of the 1800s got lemon juice with their food in order to prevent scurvy, a condition characterized by weak knees and fatigue. In the 1750s, Scottish naval surgeon James Lind found that the juice alone from lemons and limes and oranges could prevent scurvy. The navy eventually took Lind's advice and put lemon juice aboard British ships. By the mid-1800s, limes were cheaper than lemons, so lime juice was used instead. The British sailors became 'lime-juicers,' then 'limeys.'" (From *Why Socks Disappear in the Wash*, by Don Glass)

HEADS DOWN

Q: *How can a chicken run around with its head cut off?*

A: "It's true that freshly decapitated chickens will run around for a few seconds, flapping their wings wildly. How does this happen? The chicken isn't really running, but it looks like it is. The adrenaline in the muscle tissue gives the bird convulsions, making it look like it is still alive. Chickens flap and flop around for about 30 seconds before they are totally dead." (From *Funny You Should Ask*, by Marg Meikle)

Colombians like their hot dogs with hard-boiled quail eggs on top.

MUSIC ON TV

If you're a child of the 1960s, you'll remember some of these shows. If not, you won't believe how silly their names were. *(For Part 1, turn to page 125.)*

***HOOTENANNY* (April 6, 1963).** Aimed to document the folk-music revival that was happening around America, *Hootenanny* was filmed at a different college campus each week. The first show took place at the University of Michigan in Ann Arbor. The Limeliters were the headliners and played three songs, the first of which was "If I Had a Mule." After two seasons, *Hootenanny* was cancelled. Reason: By 1964 the Beatles and the British Invasion had replaced folk music as the latest music craze. *Hootenanny*'s replacement was *Shindig!*

***TOP OF THE POPS* (January 1, 1964).** This BBC series counted down the Top 10 songs of the week, with some of the songs' artists lip-synching to their hits in the studio while teenagers danced around them. The first act was the Rolling Stones, who sang their #10 song "I Wanna Be Your Man." More than 2,200 episodes later, the show was cancelled in June 2006.

***SHINDIG!* (September 16, 1964).** This weekly pop-music series featured the top rock acts of the day, but always opened with a medley of songs performed by the show's in-house singers, Jackie & Gayle, the Wellingtons, and the Blossoms. The first medley consisted of "There's Music in the Air" from Jackie & Gayle, "Yes, Indeed" by the Wellingtons (the group that sang the *Gilligan's Island* theme song) and the Blossoms, "Gonna Build a Mountain" by Jackie & Gayle, then a reprise of "There's Music in the Air" by everybody, along with guests the Righteous Brothers and the Everly Brothers. *Shindig!* was an instant hit but was gone after only two seasons.

***HULLABALOO* (January 12, 1965).** NBC responded to the success of ABC's *Shindig!* with its own pop-music show with a silly name. Like *Shindig!*, *Hullabaloo* featured performances by popular hitmakers, but the producers didn't quite understand the rock-lov-

Kids, don't try this at home: If you fill a swimming pool with mercury, bricks will float in it.

ing kids they were trying to court—the first show's guest host was old-time crooner Jack Jones, who sang "Hello Young Lovers." After one season, *Hullaballoo* was replaced by *The Monkees*.

WHERE THE ACTION IS! (June 28, 1965). By 1965 ABC had moved *American Bandstand* to weekends, leaving no show with teenage appeal in the daily afternoon schedule of any TV network. So Dick Clark produced this show, a daily 30-minute series showcasing the pop and rock songs of the day. Like *Bandstand*, top performers (such as Johnny Rivers, Dusty Springfield, and the Animals) would come on and lip-synch to their songs. Like *The Lawrence Welk Show*, *Where the Action Is!* had a resident cast of performers, including fading early '60s pop star Linda Scott, minor teen idol Steve Alaimo, and house band Paul Revere and the Raiders. The show was an immediate hit—it was a summer show, so it had a captive audience of kids home from school. Freddy "Boom Boom" Cannon made the show's theme song, "Action," a Top 20 hit. *Where the Action Is!* was cancelled in early 1967, unable to recover from the 1966 departure of rising stars Paul Revere and the Raiders. The first act to perform on the debut episode was surf duo Jan and Dean, with their hit "Surf City."

SOUL TRAIN (August 17, 1970). If *American Bandstand* exposed millions of teenagers to the sounds and styles of rock 'n' roll, then *Soul Train* did the same thing with R&B music. Creator Don Cornelius was a veteran of Chicago radio and local TV. While a sportscaster on WCIU's *A Black's View of the News*, he pitched an idea for a dance show featuring soul music targeted at African-American audiences. WCIU said they'd give him airtime and studio space if he'd pay for the show himself. Cornelius agreed (good move—it gave him ownership of the show). After seeing dancers at a local talent show dance in a line that reminded him of a train, Cornelius came up with the name *Soul Train*. The show launched in Chicago in August 1970. An immediate hit, it expanded to seven cities by 1971, 25 by 1972, and to most of the country after that. The first national episode, on October 2, 1971, featured Gladys Knight and the Pips performing "The Friendship Train."

With an atmosphere meant to evoke a nightclub, *Soul Train* was the first African-American variety show on American television. Memorable elements: the Soul Train dance line, the Soul

Train Dancers (who introduced new dance moves), the Soul Train Scramble Board (a puzzle game), and performances by the nation's top soul performers. Cornelius retired from hosting in 1993, but continued to produce until 2006, when "the hippest trip in America" wished viewers "love, peace, and soul" for the last time. *Soul Train*'s 35-year run makes it the longest syndicated TV series ever.

***THE MIDNIGHT SPECIAL* (August 19, 1972).** The NBC concert series was first hosted by John Denver, who performed the first song: "Take Me Home, Country Roads." This show is notable because it brought live pop and rock performances—from acts as varied as Blondie, Barry Manilow, and Bo Diddley—to TV. (*American Bandstand* featured rock music, but its performers always lip-synched to pre-recorded tracks.) In 1978, however, rock music was eclipsed by disco, so the show's set was updated to look like a nightclub, and disco acts came on to perform, usually lip-synching. Viewers who remember this show probably think that gravelly voiced radio veteran Wolfman Jack was the host. He wasn't—he was the announcer. The show used guest hosts, such as Ray Charles, Paul Anka, and Richard Pryor. *The Midnight Special* was cancelled in 1981, ultimately replaced in its post–*Tonight Show* time slot by *Late Night With David Letterman*.

The music doesn't stop. For the '80s, '90s, and new millennium, go to page 467.

*   *   *

BIG FRACKING MISTAKE

State Rep. Becky Carney, a five-term Democrat from North Carolina, was strongly against a bill that would allow a fracking operation in her state. It would take 72 votes to kill the bill, and the Democrats had 71. After an hours-long debate, Carney had the deciding vote. She pressed the button, looked down, and said, "Oh my gosh. I pushed the wrong one!" In tears, she begged for a do-over, but the Republicans said no, and the fracking bill passed.

NFL DRAFT FLOPS

Great athletic ability and a good college record will generally push players to the top of the NFL draft...but it's no guarantee they're going to be any good when they turn pro. Or if they'll even get to play.

JAMARCUS RUSSELL (2007)

Vital Stats: Louisiana State University had a great season in 2006, finishing ranked #4 and winning the Sugar Bowl. A major part of that success: quarterback JaMarcus Russell, who threw for 3,129 yards with 28 touchdowns.

Drafted! As a junior, he decided to skip his senior year to go directly into the NFL, and the Oakland Raiders took him at #1 in the 2007 draft. But he refused to play until he got the contract he wanted. He held out through training camp, the preseason, and into the regular season, when he agreed to $32 million.

Fumble! Top NFL quarterbacks routinely pass for 4,000 yards per season. Russell threw for 4,083 yards in his entire career, which lasted only three years. And when he did throw the ball to somebody who caught it, it was often to the wrong team—he had 31 turnovers and 23 interceptions in just 31 games. In early 2010, the Raiders released him. Later that year, he was arrested for illegal possession of codeine cough syrup, and Russell admitted he was addicted to it. He hasn't played professional football since.

RYAN LEAF (1998)

Vital Stats: Leaf brought glory to Washington State University. He threw for nearly 4,000 yards and a Pac-10 conference-record 33 touchdowns. Under Leaf, WSU won its first-ever conference title and, its first Rose Bowl since 1931, and achieved a #9 ranking. Leaf finished third in Heisman Trophy voting and looked to have a stellar NFL career for whoever was lucky enough to draft him.

Drafted! The Indianapolis Colts had the #1 pick in the 1998 draft and invited prospects for interviews. Leaf skipped his. The Colts dropped him from consideration and drafted future superstar Peyton Manning. Leaf went #2, to the San Diego Chargers.

Fumble! In three years, he played in just 25 games, threw for

...the first $1 bill in 1862, he put his own face on it.

3,666 yards total (less than in his last year at WSU), and was intercepted 36 times. He was traded and played on practice squads for the Tampa Bay Buccaneers and Seattle Seahawks, but was finished by 2002. His last job in football was as an unpaid quarterbacks coach at tiny West Texas A&M from 2006 to 2008.

TONY MANDARICH (1989)

Vital Stats: Just prior to the draft, *Sports Illustrated* gushed over the Michigan State offensive tackle, putting the 6'6", 315-pound offensive tackle on the cover, and calling him "The Incredible Bulk: the best offensive line prospect ever."

Drafted! He was the #2 pick, and went to the Green Bay Packers.

Fumble! That year's top five included four future Hall of Famers: Troy Aikman, Barry Sanders, Derrick Thomas, and Deion Sanders. But not Mandarich, who played in six seasons out of the next 10 years and was sidelined from 1992 to '94 with substance-abuse problems. *Sports Illustrated* atoned for its bad prediction with another cover story that called Mandarich "The Incredible Bust."

ART SCHLICHTER (1982)

Vital Stats: Quarterback Schlichter was a Heisman Trophy finalist in three of his four years at Ohio State. He had a whopping 7,547 passing yards and threw 50 touchdowns, along with rushing for 1,303 yards and 35 rushing touchdowns.

Drafted! The Indianapolis Colts took him at #4 in the 1982 draft.

Fumble! At the end of training camp, Schlichter unexpectedly lost the starting job to fellow rookie Mike Pagel, leaving him as the backup QB with plenty of time to kill on the sidelines. Turns out Schlichter had a gambling problem. Rather than chart plays, as backup QBs are supposed to do, Schlichter called in bets on college and NFL games. When a players' strike shortened the season, Schlichter had more time to gamble. (He estimates he lost $700,000 during the work stoppage.) When bookies threatened to expose him, he went to the FBI and the NFL, which suspended him for the entire 1983 season, fearing he might throw games he was playing in. The Colts released him five games into the 1985 season. After he was arrested for his involvement in an illegal gambling operation in 1987, NFL commissioner Pete Rozelle banned him from the league.

Chicago's Sears Tower contains enough concrete to build an 8-lane highway 5 miles long.

LOONY LAWS

Believe it or not, these are real laws.

• In Spokane, Washington, it's against the law to interrupt a religious service with a horse race.

• It's illegal to go to church in disguise in Texas.

• Pictures of dead ex-presidents may not be used to sell alcohol in Michigan.

• Women serving on a jury in Mexico, Missouri, may not knit while doing so.

• Burning leather for fuel is prohibited in Fort Wayne, Indiana.

• It's against the law to store snowballs in a refrigerator in Scottsbluff, Nebraska.

• An old law in Linden, Alabama, states that women of "uncertain chastity" must be home by 9:00 p.m.

• In San Francisco, it's illegal to enter a bar on horseback.

• It's against the law in Pennsylvania to sleep on top of a refrigerator outdoors.

• It's illegal in Canada to enter a plane mid-flight.

• If you get run over by a train and killed in Kansas, good news: The law requires the train company to give your corpse a free ticket.

• In Florida, unmarried women may not parachute on Sundays.

• Vermont law states that restaurants may use margarine instead of butter, provided they note it on the menu in two-inch letters and serve it in triangle-shaped portions.

• In Idaho, it's illegal to sell chickens after dark (unless you have a permit).

• You may not loiter in the Detroit city morgue.

• Running for office in Simsbury, Connecticut? It's illegal to campaign at the dump.

• Anyone who detonates a nuclear bomb within the city limits of Chico, California, is subject to a $500 fine.

• If there's a donkey sleeping in your bathtub after 7:00 p.m. in Oklahoma, you're breaking the law.

Every member of Teddy Roosevelt's family owned a pair of stilts, including the First Lady.

WELCOME TO YEAR ZERO

One of the privileges of inventing a new calendar is choosing where it starts. If you created a new calendar, where would you put year zero?

IN THE BEGINNING

Even if you don't know much about our calendar—the Gregorian calendar—you can probably guess that it has religious origins. The years are numbered in relation to the approximate birth date of Jesus Christ, who was thought to have been born in year 1. Years preceding that date have the designation B.C. ("Before Christ"); year 1 and all the years afterward are designated A.D. (*Anno Domini*, Latin for "the year of our lord"). Today the more religiously neutral abbreviations B.C.E. ("Before the Common Era") and C.E. ("Common Era") are often used instead of B.C. and A.D.

The person who picked 1 A.D. as the year that Jesus was born was a 6th-century monk named Dionysius Exiguus (Dennis the Short). That's an ironic name, considering that modern scholars estimate that Jesus was more likely born between 7 B.C. and 2 B.C., meaning Dennis was at least three years off. By the time anyone realized that Dennis the Short had come up short, it was too late to change the calendar. Two other religion-based calendars:

- **The Hebrew calendar.** Uses the Gregorian equivalent of 3761 B.C. as its "year zero." A 4th-century A.D. religious leader named Hillel II fixed that date as the year that God created the world.

- **The Islamic calendar.** Uses the Gregorian equivalent of 622 A.D. as its "year zero." That's the year of the Hegira, when the prophet Muhammad learned of a plot to assassinate him and secretly escaped Mecca for the city of Medina, 200 miles away.

Creating a new calendar with a new starting date is one thing; getting people to actually use it is another. Here's a look at some calendars that have had a little more trouble catching on.

THE HUMAN ERA CALENDAR (1993)

Year Zero: 10,000 B.C.

Details: First proposed by an Italian-American geologist named

Cesare Emiliani in 1993, the Human Era calendar uses the dawn of human civilization, when the first hunter-gatherers abandoned their nomadic way of life in favor of agriculture and permanent settlements, as its starting point. The year 10,000 B.C. also happens to be a nice round number, which makes converting Gregorian dates to their Human Era (HE) equivalents a snap: Just add 10,000. The year 2013 A.D., for example, converts to 12013 HE. To convert B.C. dates, subtract them from 10,001. (The extra year compensates for the fact that the Gregorian calendar has no year zero.) The year 1323 B.C., when King Tut died, for example, translates to 8678 HE.

What Happened: Old habits die hard. For all the Human Era calendar's simplicity and ability to put the march of human progress into chronological perspective, it has not yet caught on.

THE JUCHE CALENDAR (1997)

Day One, Year Zero: April 15, 1912

Details: North Korea uses the Gregorian calendar when dealing with the outside world, but internally it uses the Juche calendar. What's so special about the Juche calendar? Its starting date is the birth date of the country's founder and "Eternal President," Kim Il-sung. He created the communist nation's philosophy of *Juche* (loosely translated as "spirit of self-reliance"), for which the calendar was named. Unlike the Gregorian calendar, the Juche calendar has no designations for dates before year zero; all dates before the birth of Kim Il-sung are expressed using the Gregorian calendar.

What Happened: North Korea isn't called "the Hermit Kingdom" for nothing. The communist state is almost completely cut off from the rest of the world, and though the Juche calendar is still in use there, it hasn't caught on anywhere else.

THE TRANQUILITY CALENDAR (1989)

Day One, Year Zero: July 20, 1969

Details: This calendar uses as its starting point "Moon Landing Day," or more precisely, the moment (20 hours, 18 minutes, 1.2 seconds) when *Apollo 11* set down on the moon and Neil Armstrong said over the radio to NASA's Mission Control, "Houston, Tranquility Base Here. The *Eagle* has landed." Dates before and after Moon Landing Day are designated as BT ("Before Tranquility") and AT ("After Tranquility").

Like the Positivist and International Fixed calendars on page 412, the Tranquility calendar is a perpetual calendar with 13 months of 28 days each. That adds up to 364 days. The anniversary of Moon Landing Day, called "Armstrong Day," serves as the 365th day. It is a "blank day" that is not part of any week or month. On leap years, a second blank day, called "Aldrin Day" after Neal Armstrong's crewmate Buzz Aldrin, is also added.

What Happened: The Tranquility calendar was first proposed by its creator, Jeff Siggins, in the July 1989 issue of *Omni* magazine. Like other 13-month calendars, it was just too unusual for it to catch on. It still has a few fans on the Internet, but that's about it.

THE MARTIAN BUSINESS CALENDAR (1985)

Day One, Year Zero: March 11, 1609 A.D.

Details: The Martian Business Calendar is one of more than a dozen mathematically similar calendars that have been designed for use on Mars, either by astronauts or by mission specialists on Earth who need to be on Martian time. This one was devised by an Australian astronomer named Bruce Mills.

Mars is about 1½ times farther from the sun than we are on planet Earth, and because of this, Mars takes longer to orbit the Sun. There are just over 668 Martian days in a Martian year, making it nearly twice as long as an Earth year. (The Martian day is, on average, 24 hours and 39 minutes long.) Mills's calendar has 23 months of 28 days each, and a 24th month that is 21 days long. Every other year is a leap year, with an extra "leap week" added to the 24th month to make it 28 days long. Mills doesn't name the months—he just numbers them from 1 to 24. He sets the starting date as the equinox of the year that corresponds to 1609 and 1610 A.D. Galileo Galilei began observing Mars through a telescope in 1610, and picking this as the starting date ensures that all of the major Mars observations and discoveries are given a positive date.

What Happened: NASA and other space agencies have sent unmanned missions to Mars, but none of them have seen fit to put this or any other Martian calendar to use. They just count forward from the day the mission arrives on Mars (Day 1, Day 2, and so on). But if there ever is a human settlement on the Red Planet, it's a pretty good bet that the calendar they use will be similar to this one.

PLAIN DRESSING

The Amish and similar groups call themselves "plain people." Here's the plain truth about the "plain" way they dress.

HUMBLE BEGINNINGS

In the 16th century, a radical group of Protestant Christians from Switzerland and Germany formed their own sect based on the belief that only adults could make the conscious choice to accept God. So even though they had been baptized as infants, this new group had themselves re-baptized, earning them the name Anabaptists (ana is Greek for "repeat" or "again"). Humility was the cornerstone of Anabaptist belief. They rejected pride, shunned non-believers, and refused to take part in any military action. They took no oaths, not even wedding vows, and firmly believed in the separation of church and state.

The Anabaptists were fiercely persecuted in Europe, which led to mass migrations in the early 19th century to the more tolerant United States. By this time the Anabaptists had split into a number of separate sects, most of them named after their spiritual leaders: the Amish, led by Jakob Amman; Mennonites, founded by Menno Simons; the Hutterites by Jacob Hutter; and the Brethren in Christ. Each branch established its own rules for living and for what devotees could and could not wear. They lived simply and dressed simply, which earned them the nickname "plain people." Their style of dress became known as "plain dress."

OLD-FASHIONED

Plain people believe that beauty comes from within. Any sort of fancy dress or ornamentation that calls attention to the physical body is against their *ordnung*, or church rules. Their dress is an expression of humility, and non-conformity with the outside world. Many people assume that plain dress is a 16th-century style, but it's really a mishmash of styles from different time periods. Today plain women wear 17th-century long-sleeved dresses with 18th-century bonnets and 19th-century shawls. Many plain men wear a style of frock coat that Ben Franklin might have worn in the 1700s, but instead of Ben's knee breeches, they wear long broadfall pants held up by suspenders, both of which date from the 1800s. Instead of a button fly, broadfall pants are faced with a wide swath of material that buttons at each hip, similar to sailor pants. Their black felt, broad-brimmed hats date from the 16th century and are similar to those worn by Hasidic Jews. No two communities are exactly alike in their fashion choices and plain dress can vary by the width of a hat brim or the choice of a button over a hook and eye on a coat. Having hooks and eyes on men's black coats and vests is important to the Amish but not necessary for Mennonites.

FABRIC OF SOCIETY

Even color can make a statement. When black became fashionable in the 19th century, plain men changed to grays, browns and navy blues. Many have since returned to basic black.

The Amish wear solid, bright colors like blue, burgundy, and the recognizable purple of the oldest-existing settlement in Lancaster, Pennsylvania. Mennonites, Hutterites and Brethren tend to mix it up with patterned fabrics because those don't show dirt as easily. The patterns are, of course, small and unobtrusive. Hutterite women are especially fond of polka dot headscarves. Black stockings of varying thickness are worn by women in most sects, as are linen caps, which come with or without ties and pleats. In some sects, unmarried women wear black linen caps to church. Women's hemlines vary but always hover somewhere between well below the knee and just above the ankle.

No jewelry is allowed, not even wedding rings. Watches can be worn, but only if the wristband looks like a band, not like a piece of jewelry. Eyeglasses must be non-decorative, which is why one Mennonite sect requests eyeglass makers remove any gold that glimmers on any part of a frame. Women never cut their hair and wear it parted in the middle and pulled into a bun. Men cut their hair, but avoid anything that looks like a hairstyle with blunt bangs and a chopped look for the rest. In some sects, the men wear chinstrap beards; in others they are clean-shaven.

COVERING UP

Men's clothing isn't designed to hide anything, but concealment is a large part of the women's design. In nearly every sect, women

The sound created by crashing waves comes mostly from popping air bubbles.

wear a "cape" called a *hals duch* (neck cloth). It's really just a folded triangle of cloth that drapes across her shoulders. The center point, which can be a matching or contrasting color, drapes down her back. The other points cross in the front and are pinned at the waist. If they don't cross, they are pinned straight down in front to the waistband. Designed for modesty, a hals duch conceals a woman's neckline and bust. Add an apron to cover the stomach and it's difficult to determine any real shape under all the fabric. The idea of maternity clothes has been a subject of debate in many sects and rejected. Why? Because it announces the wearer's condition, which is just another way of saying, "Look at me!" and vanity of any kind is frowned upon.

KID STUFF

Children have a little more fashion freedom than adults, only because they don't become members of the church until they are baptized—generally between age 16 and 25. During the rite of passage known as *rumspringa* (German for "running around"), Amish teens get the opportunity to wear what other teens are wearing: short skirts, sport shorts, tank tops, high-heels, and sneakers. *Rumspringa* is the plain people's way of allowing kids to experience the outside world before making a fully-informed commitment to the Amish way of life. Once they make that commitment and are baptized, they go "full-plain."

PLAIN FACTS

- The largest populations of plain people are in Pennsylvania, Indiana, and Ohio.
- There are more than 250,000 Amish in the United States. Of these, 150,000 can trace their roots to 200 Swiss-German founding members. The number of Amish in the U.S. continues to grow because the average number of kids in a family is seven.
- Old Order Amish will not use technology that is connected to electrical or telephone lines because those lines connect the community to the outside world. (Some wireless technology is ok.)
- Automobiles may not be owned because of the prideful "Look at me, I own a car" factor. However, the Amish may *ride* in cars—they simply hire drivers.

How about you? Less than 1% of the world's population is truly ambidextrous.

SILVER LININGS

A lustrous look at all things silver.

There is no word in the English language that rhymes with the word "silver." Except *chilver*—a female lamb—although many sources list this as obsolete.

The word silver comes from the Old English word for the metal, *seolfor*. It shares a root with the words for silver in several other languages: German is *silber*; Dutch is *zilver*; Swedish is *silver*; Danish is *sølv*; Basque is *zilar*.

The Latin word for silver is *argentum*. This is why the chemical symbol for silver is Ag, and it's also the source of the word for silver in languages such as French—*argent*; Romanian—*argint*; and Irish Gaelic—*airgead*.

The Spanish word for silver, *plata*, derives from the Latin *plata*, meaning "flat piece of metal," which comes from the ancient Greek *platys*, "flat, broad." The English word *plate*, as in "dinner plate" and "silver-plated," comes from the same root.

The British pound is also known as the "pound sterling," which basically means "a pound of silver." This goes back to the year A.D. 775, when the Anglo-Saxon currency was silver pennies. That's where the monetary unit came from: 240 pennies weighed exactly one pound.

In the 13th century, those silver pennies became known as "sterlings." Exactly why is unknown. The *Oxford English Dictionary* says it was most likely a derivation of the Old English *steorling*, meaning "little star." Not because these silver coins shined like stars, but because many early versions of them had depictions of stars on them—so the coins became known as "little stars."

Quicksilver is a common name for the element mercury. The name comes from the Old English *cwicseseolfor*, which meant "living silver"—an allusion to mercury's silvery look and its natural liquid state.

The term "silver screen" comes from a type of movie screen used in the early days of motion pictures that was embossed with actual silver, which made it highly reflective. As projector and screen technology improved over the years, the use of silver in screenmaking became unnecessary, but "silver screen" remained as a nickname in the Hollywood film industry.

"Sterling silver" eventually became the name of an alloy of silver mixed with small amounts of other metals. Pure silver is too soft to be useful in common applications, such as in coin- and jewelry-making, and mixing it with other metals made it much harder. This was first achieved at least 1,000 years ago. Sterling silver today is 92.5 percent silver and 7.5 percent other metals, usually copper.

Nickel silver is an alloy first produced in China centuries ago. It was introduced to European metal manufacturers in the 18th century, and is still used today—most commonly in industrial machine parts, and for musical instruments such as flutes and saxophones. Interestingly, nickel silver looks a lot like silver, but it contains no silver at all. It's made of copper, nickel, and zinc. It's also known as German silver, new silver, and alpaca or alpacca silver—the last one apparently because it is commonly used in faux silver jewelry from South America.

* * *

ROBOT FIRSTS

• **First robot to perform surgery:** In 1995, the FDA approved Robodoc to perform hip replacements. It can cut bone with 40 times more precision than a human surgeon.

• **First robot duck:** French scientist Jacques de Vaucanson invented one in 1737. Made of wood and the size of a real duck, it could be wound up to fly, swim, and mock-defecate.

• **First robot to knight a king:** In the 14th century, King Alfonso XI of Castile wanted to be knighted (even though he was already a king), and custom said he couldn't knight himself, and neither could a person of lower rank. Since no one outranked him, he had an automaton of St. James built, and then it knighted him.

Children's dreams are shorter than adults' dreams.

FOR YOUR READING PLEASURE

Over the years we've stumbled on a lot of weird-but-true book titles. Hard to believe, but these titles were chosen and published in all seriousness. How would you like to spend an evening reading...

If God Loves Me, Why Can't I Get My Locker Open?, by Lorraine Peterson (2006)

Johnny's Such a Bright Boy, What a Shame He's Retarded, by Kate Long (1977)

Pooh Gets Stuck, by Isabel Gaines (1998)

Inflammatory Bowel Diseases: A Personal View, by Henry D. Janowitz (1985)

Build Your Own Hindenburg, by Alan Rose (1983)

The Inheritance of Hairy Ear Rims, by Reginald Gates (1961)

The Foul and the Fragrant: Odor and the French Social Imagination, by Alain Corbin (1986)

Whose Bottom Is This? A Lift-the-Flap Book, by Wayne Lynch (2000)

Who's Who in Barbed Wire, Rabbit Ear Publishing (1970)

My Invisible Friend Explains the Bible, by J. G. Bogusz (1971)

Your Three Year Old: Friend or Enemy, by Louise Ames (1980)

Beyond Leaf Raking, by Peter L. Benson (1993)

The Best Dad is a Good Lover, by Charlie Shedd (1977)

The Baby Jesus Touch-and-Feel Book, by Linda and Alan Parry (1995)

Welcome to Your Face Lift, by Helen Bransford (1997)

Home and Recreational Use of High Explosives, by Ragnar Benson (1988)

The Lull Before Dorking, (Chiswick Press, 1871)

All About Scabs, (Genichiro Yagyu, 1998)

I Was a Kamikazi, (Ryuji Nagatsuka, 1973)

During the famous "chest bursting" scene in *Alien* (1979), director Ridley Scott...

UNDERWEAR IN THE AIR

Look—up in the sky: It's a bird, it's a plane, it's...underwear?

NO BUTTS ABOUT IT

In June 2011, a University of New Mexico football player was arrested and removed from a US Airways flight from Fort Lauderdale, Florida, to Phoenix, Arizona, after he refused a crew member's instruction to hike up his sagging pajama pants. The airline claimed that part of the man's rear end was showing; the player's lawyer said his client's butt was *not* visible, and that he was singled out because he is African American. The situation got worse when a US Airways passenger circulated a photo she'd taken of a *white* businessman in his mid-sixties who *was* allowed to board her flight, even though he was dressed only in ladies' underwear, a see-through top, thigh-high black stockings, and black high-heeled shoes. So does US Airways have a double standard? Not according to the airline: "We don't have a dress code policy," an airline spokesperson told the London *Daily Mail*. "But if they're not exposing their private parts, they're allowed to fly."

THE LONG AND THE SHORT OF IT

In July 2010, a New York financial consultant named Malinda Knowles boarded a JetBlue flight to Florida dressed in an oversized T-shirt and short shorts. The T-shirt completely obscured her shorts, prompting a JetBlue supervisor to wonder if the T-shirt was the only thing she was wearing. The supervisor tested his theory by putting the antenna of a walkie-talkie between her legs. "He said, 'I don't want to see your panties or anything, but do you have any on?'" Knowles said. "It was really crazy. I've never had a corporate employee ask me about my underwear."

Knowles was escorted off the plane and taken to a hangar, where she was told to lift up her T-shirt to prove she wasn't naked from the waist down. That satisfied the JetBlue dress code, but Knowles had been delayed so long that she couldn't get back on the flight. Instead, she had to catch a different flight four hours later. She sued the airline for assault and battery plus intentional infliction of emotional distress.

EARLY BIRD

During a company-wide drive to improve on-time arrivals in the late 1990s, a British Airways crew working a flight from London to Genoa, Italy, bet each other on whether the flight would arrive 20 minutes ahead of schedule. Flight attendant Andrea O'Neill bet that it wouldn't…and lost. Her punishment: run around outside the plane wearing only her underwear, the captain's hat, and a fluorescent orange safety vest. Afterward, one of O'Neill's co-workers complained to the airline, and she was placed under investigation for "inappropriate behavior." British Airways let her off with a reprimand. "She has apologized for the prank, and we are treating the incident with leniency," an airline spokesperson told reporters. "I guess we ought to take our hats off to her—but nothing else—for achieving such wonderful exposure of our brilliant timekeeping record."

BY THE SEAT OF THEIR (UNDER)PANTS

On a 13-hour flight from Buenos Aires to London in 1994, a fun-loving British Airways crew (pilot, co-pilot, and navigator) decided to make the entire flight wearing only their underwear and headsets. Unluckily for them, a British Airways executive was a passenger on the flight, and when he found out what was going on in the cockpit, he reported it to his superiors. The two senior-most crew members had their pay docked and the third was given a dressing down (so to speak). "This was obviously a practical joke," a British Airways official told reporters, "but not the sort of thing we expect from our flight crews."

* * *

MOVIE STARS WHO HATED THEIR MOVIES

"It's the worst film I have ever made. When my kids get out of line, they're sent to their room and forced to watch it 10 times."

—Arnold Schwarzenegger, *Red Sonja*

"The worst film I've ever made by far. Maybe one of the worst films in the entire solar system, including alien productions we've never seen."

—Sylvester Stallone, *Stop! Or My Mom Will Shoot!*

AHEAD OF THEIR TIME

Some things that seem like they belong to the modern world actually date back much further.

PARKING FINES

Assyria's King Sennacheribe (705–681 B.C.) had signs posted along the highway that read, "Royal Road—let no man decrease it," meaning don't park chariots on the shoulder. How high was the fine? Anyone illegally parked would be "put to death, with his head impaled on a pole in front of his house."

CLOTHES DRYERS

Invented by a Frenchman named M. Pochon in 1800, the "Ventilator" was a hand-cranked metal drum that the user placed over an open fire. Freshly washed and wrung clothes were put in the drum and the crank turned. If the fire was small enough and the crank turned quickly enough, the clothes came out only *smelling* like the fire, not burned by it. Whether they were still clean was another matter. Most people preferred the clothesline, for obvious reasons. The Ventilator never caught on.

PERSONAL ADS

The oldest one found to date was posted in *Collection for the Improvement of Husbandry and Trade*, an English publication, in 1695. It read, "A Gentleman about 30 Years of Age, that says He has a Very Good Estate, would willingly Match Himself to some Good Young Gentlewoman, that has a Fortune of £3,000 or thereabout, and he will make Settlement to Content." No word on whether there were any takers.

TISSUES

An English visitor to Japan in 1637 was stunned to see Japanese people "blow their noses with a certain soft paper which they carry about them in small pieces, which having been used, they fling away as a filthy thing." What the Japanese called *hanagami* ("sneezing paper") was ordinary rice paper crumpled repeatedly to make it soft.

SURVIVAL STORIES

Here are some amazing stories of people who survived near-death experiences—some by their own wits and some by dumb luck.

SPIN CYCLE

In May 2011, a tornado was roaring through Lenox, Iowa, when 11-year-old Austin Miller got a call from his mother, Jessica, who was at work: "Get in the laundry room NOW!" Jessica tried to drive home, but her way was blocked by a wall of debris, so she took shelter in her mother-in-law's cellar. After the tornado passed, she ran to her own house. The roof had collapsed, and there was no sign of Austin. Just then, the clothes-dryer door popped open and out he came. He had squeezed in just in time to ride out the storm.

CAN YOU HEAR ME NOW?

In May 2010, a Canadian man (unidentified in press reports) broke his leg and got lost in a remote forest near Wollaston Lake in Saskatchewan. After four days, no rescuers came, so the desperate man crawled through the forest with his ax until he found a power-line pole and chopped it down. A helicopter was dispatched by SaskPower to investigate the incident and found the man "in a very distressed state." He later made a full recovery.

GREAT WHITE FLOSSER

Martin Kane, 62, was paddling his surf-ski (a type of sea kayak) off the coast of Perth, Western Australia, in June 2012, when he felt a big BUMP—which is not something you want to feel in the middle of the ocean. At first he thought he'd been rammed by a Jet Ski, but then he saw the fin. It belonged to a Great White shark, and it was coming back for more. Before Kane knew it, his surf-ski had been bitten in half and he was in the water fighting off the shark with his paddle. Suddenly the shark stopped attacking but continued to thrash around. Another paddler came over and scooped Kane from the water. As they made their way back to shore, Kane figured out why the shark had let up: "Its teeth were caught up in the stringers that run down the length of the ski. It was too bothered trying to get rid of the ski to chase me."

How the French say "lol" in text messages: *mdr,* short for *mort de rive*—"I died of laughter."

DRINK PLENTY OF FLUIDS

Hank Miller, 84, of Anthem, Arizona, got lost in 2011 after he took the wrong highway exit and ended up 20 miles down a dirt road with his SUV stuck, unable to get back on the road. Miller used the floor mats as a blanket to stay warm at night, but ran out of food and water quickly. Days passed. With no other sustenance, he opened the truck's hood and dipped a napkin into the windshield washer fluid basin to keep hydrated. After five days, a helicopter pilot found Miller; he was weak but in good spirits. His friends weren't the least bit surprised he survived the ordeal. Said one, "That's just Hank being Hank."

TORRENTIAL DRAINS

Eight-year-old Kenny Markiewicz was playing in a big puddle in Proctor, Minnesota, the day after major flooding occurred in 2012. All of a sudden, he was gone. His mom, Amber, felt around for him when a powerful suction nearly pulled her into a small culvert opening barely 2½-feet wide. Sometime later, more than half a mile a way, a searcher heard crying in the forest. It was Kenny—bleeding and dazed. He'd been sucked into the storm drain and carried six blocks before being dumped out in the woods. "I hate that ride!" he said.

A WOMB WITH A VIEW

In 1992 Jessica Evers took a gunshot to the arm—and she hadn't even been born. It was the second day of major rioting in Los Angeles. Jessica's mother, Elvira—seven-months pregnant at the time—was shot in the stomach while trying to get to her apartment. With no ambulances available, a friend drove her to the hospital, where she fell into a coma. When she awoke a week later, she cried, "Oh my God, my baby!" But the nurse calmed her down and explained that an emergency C-section had saved the little girl. (The bullet was removed post-delivery.) In a way, the baby saved her mother's life. "If Jessica hadn't caught that bullet in her arm," said Elvira, "we'd both be dead." In 2012 MSNBC interviewed 20-year-old Jessica, who said her prenatal brush with death had impacted her entire life. "As each day goes by, I try to find out what I'm here for. I'm innocent, but then again there are other innocent people that got hurt, too. One thing's for sure, I'm still here."

Rule of thumb: The longer the bone in the finger or toe, the faster the nail will grow.

UNCLE JOHN'S CREATIVE TEACHING AWARDS

If schools handed out degrees for dumb, these teachers would have earned a Ph.D.

Subject: Math

Winner: An unnamed third-grade teacher at Beaver Ridge Elementary School in suburban Atlanta, Georgia

Approach: His students were studying slavery and the life of the abolitionist leader Frederick Douglass, so the teacher decided to give their math lessons a historical spin, too—he assigned 20 slavery-themed math questions for homework. "Each tree has 56 oranges. If eight slaves pick them equally, how much would each slave pick?" one question asked. (Answer: seven oranges.) "If Frederick got two beatings per day, how many beatings did he get in a week?" asked another. (Answer: 14 beatings.) Four different teachers used the questions as homework for their classes.

What Happened: When parents complained, the teacher who created the assignment resigned. The school district won't say whether the other three teachers were disciplined. "Something like that shouldn't be embedded into a kid of the third, fourth, fifth, any grade," one parent told reporters. "I'm having to explain to my eight-year-old why slavery or beatings are in a math problem. That hurts."

Subject: Conflict Resolution

Winner: Patrick Kocsis, 39, a science teacher at the McMillan Magnet Center middle school in Omaha, Nebraska

Approach: When two of his eighth-grade students got into a shoving match in August 2011, Kocsis broke up the fight and then escorted the boys from the classroom. But instead of taking them to the principal's office, he brought them outside and told them to "slap it out" until they resolved their dispute. The boys were still going at it *20 minutes later* when the principal and a school security officer intervened and ended the fight.

What Happened: Both boys were suspended, but their suspensions were later removed from their records—the teacher *told* them to fight, after all. Kocsis was cited on two counts of misdemeanor child neglect (later dropped) and placed on leave. Two weeks later, the school board voted 11–1 to fire him. (No word on whether Kocsis plans to *fight* his dismissal.)

Subject: Religious Studies

Winner: Harlan Porter, 31, a teacher at the B.C. Haynie Elementary School in Morrow, Georgia

Approach: One afternoon in April 2011, not long after the school day ended (and he learned his contract wasn't being renewed), Porter attained what he called "a new level of enlightenment" and acknowledged it by stripping off his clothes and wandering the halls naked. He did it, he later explained, so that everyone would know "that his third eye was open."

What Happened: A teacher who saw Porter called police, who found him—still nude—hanging out in the teachers' lounge. "I explained the obvious problem with his third eye being open in public. He readily agreed that his decision to remove his clothing caused a problem," the officer noted in the police report. Porter was charged with misdemeanor public indecency. Had any children seen him naked, he would have been charged with child molestation, a felony. According to the report, Porter admitted that his days as an elementary-school teacher were over, but that he hoped to continue teaching "on a new level, with hands in the earth, gathering the essence and learning how to love one another and fully appreciate the spiritual realm."

Subject: Anatomy and cinematography

Winner: Benedict Garrett, 31, the head of "Personal, Social, and Health Education" (in other words, sex education) at Beal High School in southern England

Approach: You can't accuse Garrett of not knowing the material. In July 2010, administrators learned he was moonlighting as both a stripper and a nude butler, *and* starring in adult films under the alias "Johnny Anglais." He got caught when his pupils found the trailers for *European Honeyz 4* and other movies online.

Aramaic, the language Jesus spoke, is now spoken only in three remote villages in Syria.

What Happened: Garrett was suspended from teaching and later resigned. At his disciplinary hearing, he argued that 1) stripping and appearing in adult films was not incompatible with teaching high school, and 2) he was being discriminated against and punished unjustly. "While a teacher working in the sex industry must be banned, teachers who publicly indulge in activities that are linked to thousands of deaths each and every year—such as smoking, drinking, and overeating—are tolerated," he wrote. Believe it or not, Garrett's explanation worked…sort of. The investigating committee reprimanded him for "unacceptable professional conduct," but did not take away his teaching license. "The committee is content that you would not repeat this behavior should you resume teaching and considers it unlikely that you will seek to return to the teaching profession whilst working as a stripper or in pornographic films," it concluded in its report. If and when Garrett retires from his adult-themed work, he's free to return to teaching. "Whether any school will employ me, that is another question," he said.

* * *

REDUNDANT REDUNDANCIES

Why say in one word what you can say in two or more?

Proceed forward
Evolve over time
Mental telepathy
Cacophony of sound
Unexpected surprise
Visible to the eye
Splice together
Past memories
Kitty cat
Reply back
Basic fundamentals
Surrounded on all sides
Two equal halves
Complete stop
Same exact

Reason why
Kneel down
Live studio audience
Adequate enough
Eliminate altogether
Very unique
Over exaggerate
Major breakthrough
Filled to capacity
PIN number
ATM machine
Unintended mistake
Final outcome
Cease and desist
Raid Kills Bugs Dead

SILVER MEDAL SHOCKER, PART II

Here's the next part of the story about the U.S. Olympic team that wouldn't accept being #2. (Part I is on page 211.)

GROUNDHOG DAY

William Jones may not have had the authority to overrule the official scorer, but that's exactly what he did. The clock started ticking off those three seconds again. The Soviets inbounded the ball and went for a long pass. The pass failed, and the buzzer sounded to end the game. The Americans celebrated wildly.

Then, suddenly, officials stopped the celebration, cleared the floor, and ordered three seconds showing on the clock *again*. Apparently the time keepers had still been fiddling around with the clock trying to reset it when play resumed. U.S. players stood in shock. "We couldn't believe that they were giving them all these chances," said forward Mike Bantom. "It was like they were going to let them do it until they got it right."

REVERSAL OF FORTUNE

When play continued, Ivan Edeshko threw a full-court pass to Aleksandr Belov, the player who'd made the bad pass moments earlier. Belov caught it and laid the ball into the hoop just as the clock expired again. Final score at the horn: 51–50, in favor of the Soviet team. Belov raced back to his teammates with his arms held high, a newly minted hero, while the U.S. men's team lost an Olympic basketball game...for the first time ever.

"It was sort of like being on top of the Sears Tower in Chicago celebrating and then being thrown off and falling 100 floors to the ground," said Doug Collins.

AND THE WINNER IS...THE COLD WAR!

Referee Righetto would not sign the official scorebook until the word PROTEST had been stamped on it, and the U.S. team filed an immediate formal protest with the International Basketball Federation. The next day, a five-member FIBA Jury of Appeals met to decide the winner. On the panel: three jurors from Communist countries Cuba, Poland, and Hungary, one from Puerto Rico, and one from Italy.

According to *Sports Illustrated* writer Gary Smith, "Everything progressed according to strictly Cold War politics. There were three Communist Bloc judges. It was a three to two vote. America loses. The Soviet Union wins the gold medal, and at that point the American players are facing a stark reality. Do they accept the silver medal?"

The U.S. team voted to reject the silver. "We do not feel like accepting the silver medal because we feel we are worth the gold," said Bill Summers, chairman of the U.S. Olympic Basketball Committee and manager of the U.S. team.

BEAT...OR CHEAT

Forty years later, team members still won't accept second place. Their silver medals remain in a vault in Lausanne, Switzerland, and none of the players wants them. In fact, team captain Kenny Davis said, "I have placed it in my will that my wife and my children can never, ever receive that medal from the '72 Olympic Games. I don't want it. I don't deserve it. And I want nothing to do with it." U.S. forward Mike Bantom agreed: "If we had gotten beat, I would be proud to display my silver medal. But, we didn't get beat, we got cheated."

As for the Soviets, Edeshko—the player who threw the game-winning pass for his team—voiced the opposite viewpoint: "It was the Cold War. Americans, out of their own natural pride and love of country, didn't want to lose and admit loss. They didn't want to lose in anything, especially basketball."

The last word goes to lead referee Renato Righetto. In a signed affidavit to the International Olympic Committee, he wrote, "I consider what happened as completely illegal and an infraction to the rules of a Basketball game."

That's not quite the whole story. For some basic background and poignant postscripts, turn to page 421.

Karl Marx, the father of communism, never visited Russia.

IT'S WHAT'S INSIDE THAT COUNTS

Thrift shops and yard sales teem with dusty old stuff that doesn't look very valuable. Sometimes that stuff is more valuable than you'd think, and sometimes the real treasure is the stuff inside *the stuff.*

CASE STUDY

Find: A purple suitcase

Where It Was Found: In a Salvation Army store in St. John's, Newfoundland, Canada

Story: In 2009 Tonya Ritchie and her husband traveled to a wedding in Newfoundland. They wanted to bring some frozen fish back home to Shelburne, Ontario, and rather than risk ruining their luggage, Tonya bought an old suitcase at the Salvation Army thrift store in St. John's for $5. When they got home, Tonya put the suitcase away in the attic, where it remained until she took it down to use it again in early 2012. While packing, she found three reels of 8mm film—the kind used in home-movie cameras in the 1960s and '70s in one of the pockets.

The rolls were labeled "James Brander, Glen Williams, Ontario." Tonya knew someone from the town of Glen Williams—her friend Janet Piper, who lived three doors down. When Tonya's husband showed Janet's husband the films and asked if the couple knew anyone by that name, he gasped—James Brander, who'd died nine years earlier, was Janet's father. The reels were home movies of Janet's childhood. No one can explain how the films ended up in Newfoundland, a place that Brander had never visited. No one recognized the purple suitcase, either. "It's just bizarre, the chances of me picking it up is crazy," Tonya Ritchie said. "It's the best five bucks I've ever spent."

WORTH A THOUSAND WORDS

Find: An old Polaroid camera

Where It Was Found: At a garage sale in Wichita, Kansas

Story: One Thursday in May 2012, 13-year-old Addison Logan tagged along with his grandmother Lois as she made the rounds of Wichita garage sales. At their third stop, he bought an old Polaroid camera for $1, then when he got it home he looked it up online to see how it worked. He opened the camera, removed the film cartridge inside...and saw that it contained a photograph of a young man and woman sitting on a sofa. The picture looked like it had been taken 30 or 40 years earlier. Addison didn't recognize the people in the photograph, but when he showed it to his grandmother she was stunned. "That's your uncle," Lois Logan said. The man in the picture was her son Scott, who'd died in a car accident in 1989. The woman was his high school girlfriend, Susan Ely.

The Logans returned to the garage sale to find out more about the camera, but the seller, who buys things at other garage sales to sell at his, could not remember when or where he bought it. "I'm just shocked," Addison's dad (and Scott's brother) told *The Wichita Eagle*. "The more time that passes, the more in disbelief I am. So many things have to come together for that to happen. It just seems supernatural."

INNER CHILD

Find: An old painting

Where It Was Found: At a garage sale in Las Vegas

Story: English businessman Andy Fields, 48, was visiting Las Vegas in 2010 when he decided to check out some local garage sales. At one of them, he bought five framed sketches. Price: $5. The man selling them bragged that his aunt babysat for Andy Warhol when he was a child, but Fields didn't pay much attention until he decided to reframe one of the sketches in 2012...and found a second sketch hidden inside the frame. "I took the backing off and saw a picture looking back at me," he told the BBC. The sketch, signed by Warhol, is of the 1930s singer Rudy Vallee (with bright red lips), and is believed to date back to when Warhol was just 10 or 11 years old. Estimated value: between $1 and $2 million.

* * *

"Just remember, once you're over the hill you begin to pick up speed."

—**Charles Schulz**

ANY RELATION?

Genealogist Mark Humphrys traced his family tree back 1,000 years. Along the way he found these famous people who are all descended from royalty.

Monarch: Louis IV, King of the Franks (920–954)
Descendants: Authors Louisa May Alcott (*Little Women*) and L. Frank Baum (*The Wonderful Wizard of Oz*); actors Katharine Hepburn and Anthony Perkins (*Psycho*)

Monarch: Hugh Capet, the first person to be called "King of France" (938–996)
Descendants: U.S. presidents Rutherford B. Hayes, Franklin D. Roosevelt, George H. W. Bush, and George W. Bush

Monarch: Otto II, Holy Roman Emperor (955–983)
Descendants: Danish astronomer Tycho Brahe (1546–1601), novelist Leo Tolstoy (*War and Peace*)

Monarch: Vlad the Impaler, (1431–1376) the Transylvanian prince said to be the inspiration for Count Dracula
Descendant: Actor Robert Pattinson, who played the vampire Edward in the *Twilight* movies

Monarch: Henry I of England (1069–1135)
Descendants: Nancy Reagan, actress Sigourney Weaver, Bill Gates, politician Mike Huckabee, actor Clint Eastwood

Monarch: William the Conquerer, King of England (1027–1087)
Descendant: French impressionist painter Edouard Manet

Monarch: Alfonso VII of Castile and Léon (now Spain), (1105–1157)
Descendant: Argentinian revolutionary Che Guevara

Monarch: Philip II of France (1165–1223)
Descendants: Former Canadian prime minister Jean Chrétien, singer Celine Dion, and actress Angelina Jolie

Monarch: Charlemagne (747–814), the King of Franks and Holy Roman Emperor
Descendants: Every other person on this page

A dark-chocolate bar contains around 12 grams of sugar. A glass of orange juice: 22.

BIRD BRAINS

These quotes are for the birds. (Well, they're about them, at least.)

"There's an unseen force which lets birds know when you've just washed your car."

—Denis Norden

"Much talking is the cause of danger. Silence is the means of avoiding misfortune. The talkative parrot is shut up in a cage. Other birds, without speech, fly freely."

—Saskya Pandita

"There is nothing in which the birds differ more from man than the way they can build and yet leave a landscape as it was before."

—Robert Lynd

"I hope you love birds. It is economical. It saves going to heaven."

—Emily Dickinson

"A bird does not sing because it has an answer. It sings because it has a song."

—Chinese proverb

"Everyone wants to understand painting. Why is there no attempt to understand the song of the birds?"

—Pablo Picasso

"Birds scream at the top of their lungs in horrified hellish rage every morning at daybreak to warn us all of the truth. But sadly we don't speak bird."

—Kurt Cobain

"When birds burp, it must taste like bugs."

—Calvin, *Calvin and Hobbes*

"Birds know themselves not to be at the center of anything, but at the margins of everything."

—Gregory Maguire

"Always behave like a duck—keep calm and unruffled on the surface but paddle like the devil underneath."

—Jacob Braude

"I don't ask for the meaning of the song of a bird, or the rising of the sun on a misty morning. There they are, and they are beautiful."

—Pete Hamill

"Eagles may soar, but weasels don't get sucked into jet engines."

—John Benfield

The word "mouse" is from the ancient Sanskrit word *mus*, meaning "thief."

ME: THE MOVIE

Why hire actors to play famous people when they are more than willing to play themselves?

Movie: *Viva Knievel!* (1977)

Starring: Evel Knievel

Details: In the 1970s, daredevil Evel Knievel was a one-man thrill show and a marketing genius, announcing months ahead of time the next seemingly impossible jump he planned to make on his red-white-and-blue motorcycle—over a row of buses or across Snake River Canyon, for example. Knievel TV specials attracted millions, and kids couldn't wait to buy Evel Knievel action figures and toy motorcycles. Part of the cultural phenomenon was the 1977 movie *Viva Knievel!*, starring Evel Knievel as himself. The plot: Knievel is planning a tremendous jump in Mexico, but there's a nefarious plan to kill him, masterminded by a drug lord played by Leslie Nielsen. Knievel saves the day, and he even inspires a crippled orphan to walk. (Really.)

Movie: *Tears and Laughter* (1994)

Starring: Joan and Melissa Rivers

Details: Joan Rivers was one of the first women to make it in the male-dominated field of stand-up comedy. She and husband Edgar Rosenberg had a daughter, Melissa, who made a career in show business hosting TV specials and occasionally acting. In 1987 Rosenberg, suffering from depression, took his own life. Seven years later, this story was sold as a made-for-TV movie. Joan and Melissa, at that point best known for hawking jewelry on home shopping channels, starred as themselves, reliving the tragedy of Rosenberg's death.

Movie: *The Jackie Robinson Story* (1950)

Starring: Jackie Robinson

Details: An important figure in history, sports, and civil rights, Jackie Robinson broke Major League Baseball's color barrier in 1947, enduring the open racial hostility of players and the public. But in addition to great fortitude, Robinson had great skills. He

Westinghouse released the first color TV in 1953. Cost: $1,250 (about $10,000 today).

was an excellent ballplayer, winning a Rookie of the Year award, an MVP award, a World Series, and starting spots on six All-Star teams. It would make a good movie, wouldn't it? That's what Hollywood thought…except that there were no major African-American movie stars to play him. So Robinson played himself. *The Jackie Robinson Story* told his life story—discovering baseball as a child, being spurned as a young man despite his abilities, and finally, breaking into the majors. It ends with Robinson, as Robinson, giving a stirring speech to Congress.

Movie: *The Greatest* (1977)

Starring: Muhammad Ali

Details: Will Smith played him in 2001's *Ali*, but at his peak, Ali was so relentlessly self-promoting that no one could have played him except Ali himself. Based on his autobiography, *The Greatest* covers the 14 biggest years in Ali's life, from his gold-medal win in the 1960 Olympics to 1974's "Rumble in the Jungle," when he defeated George Foreman in Zaire. The film also has a few real actors—James Earl Jones as Malcolm X, Roger Mosley as Sonny Liston, Ernest Borgnine as Angelo Dundee—and features archival footage of his boxing matches. And it's the source of what would become Whitney Houston's signature song, "The Greatest Love of All," originally written and sung by George Benson for this movie.

Movie: *The Ann Jillian Story* (1988)

Starring: Ann Jillian

Details: Jillian was a mainstay of forgettable 1980s television, starring in the sitcoms *Jennifer Slept Here* (as a flirty ghost) and *It's a Living* (as a flirty waitress), on Bob Hope specials, and in more than a dozen made-for-TV movies. Jillian's career came to a sudden halt in 1986 when she was diagnosed with breast cancer. She underwent a double mastectomy, beat cancer, and returned to work in made-for-TV movies. Her first role: *The Ann Jillian Story*, which dramatizes how she struggled to win parts on TV and Broadway, how she rose to stardom, how she met her husband (a cop), and how she dealt with and beat cancer. She also sang the theme song. Happy ending: Jillian won a Golden Globe for her performance.

Official name of Mexico: *Estados Unidos Mexicanos* (United Mexican States).

THE SMARTPHONE AUTOCORRECT QUIZ

It can be annoying (and amusing) when a smartphone's autocorrect feature "corrects" misspelled words. We typed some famous names into an iPhone ...and got these. Can you tell who they are? (Answers on page 600.)

1) Bigfoot Mittens (actor)

2) Eerily Legalese (TV chef)

3) Bonus Wager (baseball legend)

4) Stockyard Canning (actress)

5) Ravens-Gnome (Disney star)

6) Skiing Leprous (actor)

7) Beyond Knowing (singer)

8) Matt Frowning (cartoonist)

9) Dark Nitwit (NBA star)

10) Marissa Jar Gutsy (actress)

11) Kiss Sheldon (creator of *Buffy the Vampire Slayer*)

12) Sweet Ill Zappity (musician and rock star progeny)

13) Even Knives (daredevil)

14) Tipsy Shamir (rapper)

15) Care Blanket (actress)

16) Favorite Siding (actress)

17) Gerald Departure (actor)

18) Latent Nester (star of *Gossip Girl*)

19) Sits Von Reese (burlesque performer)

20) Bounteous Bounteous Gal (diplomat)

21) Zachary Halifax (actor)

22) Bing Thames (actor)

23) Chance Billions (NBA star)

24) Mikey Chris (singer)

25) Humid Hemstitcher ('60s rock star)

26) Alligator Cookie (Former *Masterpiece Theater* host)

Only U.S. pres. to work in a national park: Gerald Ford, in Yellowstone. (Park ranger, '36).

HEY, JAY! PAY FAY WRAY. TODAY, OKAY?

Word origins in the key of "AY."

BAY: The Latin *baia* meant "open out," as a bay opens out to the sea. The word may have come from an ancient spa on the Bay of Naples called *Baiae*. It entered English in the late 1300s as *baye*.

BRAY: The donkey's call is from the Old Irish *braigid*, which means "break wind."

CLAY: This word predates Latin to an ancient language known as *Proto-Indo-European* (PIE), where it first showed up as the root *glei-*, meaning "stick together," like *glue*—a word that comes from the same root.

DAY: From the Old English *dæg*, which comes from the PIE *dhegh*, for "burn." *Day* only meant "daylight hours" until the 1750s, when *solar day* was coined.

(INTO THE) FRAY: This term for a fight or brawl comes from Middle English *affray* (14th century), which also gave us the word *afraid*.

GAY: Entered English in the 1300s from the Middle-French word *gai* ("joyful, laughing"). Linguists trace its homosexual meaning to the late-1800s slang term *gaycat*: "a young hobo who latches onto an older hobo to learn the ropes." In the late 1960s, gay rights activists claimed the term.

GRAY: It entered English in the 700s as *græg*. In Great Britain, South Africa, New Zealand, and Australia, it's spelled *grey*. However, starting in the 1820s, *gray* became the preferred American spelling (although "greyhound" always has an "e").

HEY: The "hello" meaning only dates to the 19th-century American South, but nearly every language has a similar interjection to express surprise. The Greeks cried *eia!*; the Romans, *eho!*

The average American goes to the movies about 5 times a year. The average Japanese: once.

JAY: Comes from the Latin *gaius*, meaning "full of joy." To the Romans, that's what the squawks of these blue-feathered members of the crow family sounded like.

PAY: The Latin *pax* ("peace") became *pacare*, which meant "to pacify a debtor to keep the peace." In the 1300s, it came to English as *payen*.

PLAY: Comes from the Dutch *pleien*, meaning "dance, leap for joy, and rejoice."

PRAY: From the PIE root *prek-*, the word showed up in ancient Rome as *precari*, meaning "to ask earnestly, to beg." (It's also the root of *precarious*, because when you beg, you're put in a precarious position.)

PREY: Both *prey* and *predator* come from the Latin verb *prædari*, which means "to rob, to plunder."

RAY: Derived from the Latin *radius*, meaning "rod, spoke" (like a sunray), it entered English in the 14th century from the Anglo-French *rai*.

SPRAY: From the Middle Dutch *sprayen*, "a jet of water."

STAY: From the PIE root *sta-*, which meant "stand." Until the 1400s, *stay* meant "stop," as in "come to a halt," before taking on the added meaning of "remain where you are."

STRAY: The Latin *estree* ("street") became the Old French verb *estraier* ("to wander about the street"), and strayed into English in the 1300s.

WAY: From yet another PIE word, *wegh*, which meant "road," or "path." It was in use in Old English as early as the 700s as *weg*. The phrase *a-weg* gave us the word *away*.

WEIGH: Also from the PIE word *wegh*, in this sense "to move." Old English added the meaning "to lift" and then to "measure how much is being lifted." *Weigh* took on the figurative meaning "to ponder" in the 14th century.

*　*　*

"Without question, the greatest invention in the history of mankind is beer. Oh, I grant you that the wheel was also a fine invention, but the wheel does not go nearly as well with pizza."

—**Dave Barry**

THE REAL SCROOGE

One of the hallmarks of the work of 19th-century author Charles Dickens is his oddball characters and their fanciful names: Uriah Heep, Martin Chuzzlewit, Lady Honorie Dedlock, Pip Pirrip, Abel Magwich, Miss LaCreevy, and Bardle the Beadle, to name a few. Perhaps Dickens's best-known character is Ebenezer Scrooge, from A Christmas Carol*—who, it turns out, was inspired by a real person.*

THE MISER

John Elwes (1714–1789) was born John Meggot. He was orphaned at an early age. His father, a wealthy London brewer named Robert Meggot, died when the boy was only four. His mother, Amy Elwes, followed not too long afterward. When she died, the family fortune, an estimated £100,000 (about $29 million today), passed to her son.

John was educated at the Westminster School, an exclusive boarding school at Westminster Abbey in London. He spent more than a decade there, then lived in Switzerland for a few years before returning to England. When he was in his twenties and thirties, Meggot gave little hint of the man he would become. He dressed well, spent money freely, and moved among London's most fashionable circles. He developed a taste for French wines and fine dining. He was a skilled horseman and fox hunter, and he had a passion for gambling—he bet, and often lost, thousands of pounds in card games.

THE FAMILY WAY

Unfortunately for Meggot, hoarding money seems to have run in the family, at least on his mother's side. If contemporary accounts are to be believed, Amy Elwes went to her early grave because she refused to dip into the family fortune to buy food, and literally starved herself to death. Her brother, Harvey, was a miser in his own right. He lived on a country estate inherited from his father's side of the family, and though he would grow his inheritance to more than £250,000 ($72 million), he allowed the estate itself to fall to ruin. The manor house's roof leaked, and rainwater stained the crumbling, mildewed walls. Broken windows were "repaired"

Parkfield, CA, the "earthquake capital of the world," has a bridge spanning 2 tectonic plates.

with paper, and the furniture was infested with worms.

Rather than buy his own clothes, Uncle Harvey wore the old clothes of the dead relative who left him his fortune. And like his sister, he hated buying food; he spent his days wandering the estate hunting partridges and small game that he could eat for free. On cold evenings he kept warm by pacing back and forth in the great hall of his drafty mansion, rather than waste wood in a fire. Too cheap to marry, he lived like a hermit for more than 50 years "to avoid the expense of company." Not surprisingly, he produced no heirs.

DINNERS WITH UNCLE HARVEY

Since Harvey had no children, John hoped to inherit his uncle's fortune. That's why, in 1751, he changed his last name from Meggot to Elwes—to assure his uncle that the family name would survive him. That's also why Elwes visited his uncle regularly and pretended to share his miserly ways. But before arriving at his uncle's estate—where the meals were certain to be meager—he'd drop in on friends and fill up on their food. Then he'd stop at a roadside inn to change out of his fashionable clothes and into the tattered garments he kept for that purpose, and continue on to his uncle's.

For dinner Elwes and Uncle Harvey ate whatever fish, partridges, or other small game Harvey had managed to kill that day. As they ate they talked about money and how others wasted it. "There they would sit—saving souls!—with a single stick upon the fire and with one glass of wine, occasionally, betwixt them, talking of the extravagance of the times," Elwes's friend and biographer Edward Topham wrote. "When evening shut, they would retire to rest—as 'going to bed saved candle light.' "

THE FAMILY FOOTSTEPS

John's years of toadying paid off: When Harvey died in September 1763, he left his nephew, now in his late forties, his entire fortune. John Elwes was now worth over £350,000, the equivalent of more than $100 million today. By then Elwes had assumed many of his uncle's habits, but not all of them. He still had expensive tastes, and as long as someone else paid the bill, he happily indulged them, gorging himself at other people's tables as he warmed himself for free by their fires. He still loved to gamble huge sums of money in card games, he gladly lent huge sums to friends and associates when asked, no matter how frivolous the purpose. If a borrower defaulted, Elwes never demanded repayment, explaining that "it was impossible to ask a gentleman for money."

DON'T MIND IF I DON'T

But where his own material comfort and well-being were concerned, Elwes would not part with a penny. Where once he had dressed in rags only to impress his uncle, he now wore them all the time, and never cleaned his shoes—that might wear them out faster. Friends said he looked "like a prisoner confined for debt."

Like his uncle, Elwes allowed his estates to fall into ruin. He refused to buy a carriage and wondered how anyone could think he could afford one. Riding a horse was cheaper, especially the way he did it: Before setting off on a journey, he filled his pockets with hardboiled eggs so he wouldn't have to pay for meals in taverns. He rode in the soft dirt by the side of the road rather than on the road itself, so that he wouldn't have to buy horseshoes for his horse. He traveled hours out of his way to avoid toll roads. If he needed to stop for the night, he'd find a spot by the side of the road that had lots of grass (so that his horse could eat for free) and sleep beneath a tree to save the price of a room at an inn.

Elwes's mania for frugality extended to his own family. He had two sons out of wedlock (because marriages cost *money*) and refused to pay for their education. "Putting things into people's heads," he explained, "was the sure way to take money out of their pockets."

MISER OF PARLIAMENT

In 1774 Elwes was offered a chance to succeed a retiring Member of Parliament in the British House of Commons, and accepted ...provided he wouldn't have to spend money on his campaign. He spent just 18 pence—on a meal for himself—and won the election. Politics didn't change him, though. During his 12 years in office, Elwes dressed as shabbily as he ever had. He walked everywhere, even in the rain, to save the cost of sharing a coach with other MPs. He looked so destitute tramping around London that people often stopped him in the street to force pennies into his hand. If he arrived home drenched from a downpour, like his Uncle Harvey he'd sit in his wet clothes rather than light a fire.

Yet even though Elwes lived so frugally, he continued to lend

Einstein's eyes are currently sitting in a safe deposit box in New York City.

generously to friends and to invest in their speculative ventures. In all, it's estimated that he lost some £150,000 in bad loans and investments. No matter: His fortune kept growing. By the mid-1780s, he was worth nearly £1,000,000 (about $290 million).

A MOVEABLE FEAST

In 1784 Elwes retired from Parliament rather than spend even a pittance on what would have been certain re-election. With the distraction of public office gone from his life, his penny-pinching intensified. His diet suffered most of all. On one occasion he ate a dead bird that a rat had dragged out of a river; on another he caught a fish with a partially eaten smaller fish in its stomach. "Aye! This was killing two birds with one stone!" he said, then ate them both.

On those rare occasions when Elwes bought lamb or other meat from the butcher, he bought the entire animal to get the best price, and then ate every bit of it. In an age before refrigeration, this meant that he often ate meat that had reached "the last stage of putrefaction," a friend wrote. "Meat that walked about on his plate, would he continue to eat, rather than have new things killed before the old provision was finished."

OPEN HOUSE

Elwes had inherited several properties in London, and he added to their number until he owned more than 100. Keeping them rented took work, and yet for all the time Elwes spent in London, he never set up a household for himself. He and the old woman who served as his cook and maid stayed in whichever of his properties was vacant, but only as long as it took to find a tenant. Their household possessions were limited to a bed for himself and one for the maid, a table, and a couple of chairs. When a tenant was found, sometimes after Elwes and his maid had spent just a night or two in the place, they packed their things and moved to another vacant property.

The constant moving almost cost Elwes his life. Once when he and his maid both fell deathly ill at the same time, nobody knew where they were. Luckily for Elwes, his nephew went looking for him and found a boy who'd seen "a poor old man" enter one of Elwes's properties on Great Marlborough Street. The nephew rushed there and found Elwes near death. He was too late to save

Oldest surviving stadium in the NFL: the Chicago Bears' Soldier Field, built in 1924.

the maid: Her body was found in another room; she'd been dead for two or three days.

CASH ON HAND

Elwes recovered physically from the ordeal, but his mental state, already declining due to his penurious lifestyle and advancing age, got worse. His obsession with money narrowed until he became fixated on the change he had in his pocket. He'd wrap each coin in a piece of paper and hide it somewhere in his rooms, then stay up half the night wandering the house in an agitated state, trying to remember where he'd hidden the coins. In time he came to believe the change was all the money he had in the world. Terrified of dying penniless, he often woke in the middle of the night screaming at imaginary thieves: "I will keep my money, I will! Nobody shall rob me of my property!"

In November 1789, Elwes fell ill and took to his bed. He died eight days later. "I hope I have left you what you wish," he told one of his sons before he died. He probably did: Each of them inherited nearly £500,000 ($145 million).

As far as anyone knows, neither of them ever became a miser.

A LITERARY INSPIRATION

Edward Topham was fascinated by his friend's odd lifestyle, and in 1790 he wrote *The Life of the Late John Elwes, Esquire*. The book was a bestseller, with 12 printings by 1805. Its success inspired other books and articles, and Elwes's name soon became a household word, one synonymous with penny-pinching.

Charles Dickens knew the story and mentioned Elwes both in letters and in his 1865 novel *Our Mutual Friend*. Though he apparently never said so explicitly, Dickens is widely believed to have modeled Ebenezer Scrooge, the miser in *A Christmas Carol*, on Elwes. The artwork in the first edition of the story, published in 1843, bears this out: Dickens worked closely with his illustrators to create images of his characters that were exactly as he envisioned them—and the illustrations of Ebenezer Scrooge bear a striking resemblance to John Elwes.

Don't be stingy—spend your time wisely and learn how Scrooge (maybe) got his name. That story is on page 529.

SHOE FADS

These once-popular shoes aren't what you'd call "sole survivors."

THE REEBOK PUMP (1989)

This innovative sneaker featured an inflation system with a basketball-shaped pump on the tongue of each shoe that created a tighter "custom fit" around the ankle and top of the foot. Despite a retail price upwards of $150, stores could hardly keep them in stock, probably because they were endorsed by NBA All-Star Dominique Wilkins and Slam Dunk champion Dee Brown. When they started to cut into Nike Air Jordan's market share, competitors introduced similar air-pump shoes, such as L.A. Gear's Regulars and Nike's Air Pressure. Neither could touch the Pump, but the fad was over by 1993—basketball players both pro and amateur went back to their Air Jordans.

LIGHT-UP SHOES (1992)

L.A. Lights, produced by L.A. Gear, were introduced at Foot Locker stores and sold for around $50. They featured red LED lights, embedded in the soles, that lit up every time the wearer took a step. The shoes became a hit with teens and adults, but despite selling 40 million pairs at Foot Locker in the 1990s, L.A. Gear filed for bankruptcy in 1998. Light-up shoes are still moderately popular…among children. A different company, Skechers, controls that market today.

HEELYS (2000)

Heelys, marketed to teens and pre-teens, were sneakers with retractable wheels in the soles. They allowed the wearer to roller-skate around one second and casually walk the next by simply shifting their weight onto a trigger located in the heels. Predictably, the "heeling" fad led to numerous of accidents and injuries and at least one death, according to the U.S. Product Safety Commission. Heelys eventually became considered dangerous (and annoying) enough to warrant them being banned in schools, stores, and amusement parks across North America and Europe.

The Arabs invented caramel and used it as a hair remover for harem women.

SINE OF THE TIMES

Do these math puns add up? We're divided.

"Help me, Doc," said the math book. "I've got problems."

A nice view out the window is a weapon of math disruption.

That mathematician ate the bunch of fruit so fast that it was gone in a bananasecond.

Trigonometry for farmers: swines and coswines.

Algebra is the loneliest of the maths because it always wants you to find its X.

"My life is pointless," said the retired geometry teacher. (At least he's not going in circles.)

Don't worry about running out of math teachers. They're always multiplying.

For a good prime, call 555.793.7319.

The math teacher's pet parrot refused to eat, so he called it Polynomial. Then it died, so he called it Polygon.

There are 10 kinds of people, those who understand binary, and those who don't.

I didn't say you were average, just mean.

"Three!" said one math prof. "No, five!" said the other. They were at odds.

I'll do trigonometry, I'll do algebra, I'll even do statistics, but graphing is where I draw the line!

I personally found Newton's *Principia Mathematica* to be quite derivative.

I didn't understand addition, so the teacher summed it up for me.

Who's the fattest knight at the Round Table? Sir Cumference. Why so big? Too much pi.

Pickup line: Don't think me obtuse, but you're acute girl.

The geometry student was denied a loan because he couldn't get a cosine.

I'm partial to fractions.

Atheists can't solve exponential equations because they don't believe in higher powers.

I failed math so many times I've lost count.

Uncle John's favorite three-digit number? Too farty.

POP MUSIC: 1987

Why 1987? That's when the Bathroom Reader *was born. Rad!*

***Billboard*'s top 5 singles of the year:**

1. "Walk like an Egyptian" (The Bangles)
2. "Alone" (Heart)
3. "Shake You Down" (Gregory Abbott)
4. "I Wanna Dance With Somebody" (Whitney Houston)
5. "Nothing's Gonna Stop Us Now" (Starship)

Notable one-hit wonders:

• Cars bassist Benjamin Orr, "Stay the Night"
• Bruce Willis, "Respect Yourself"
• The Grateful Dead, "Touch of Grey" (a #9 hit)

• On average, in most years, there are nine #1 hits. In 1987 there were 30—a *Billboard* record.

The 5 bestselling albums:

1. *Slippery When Wet* (Bon Jovi)
2. *Graceland* (Paul Simon)
3. *Licensed to Ill* (Beastie Boys)
4. *The Way It Is* (Bruce Hornsby)
5. *Control* (Janet Jackson)

Two covers of songs by the 1960s band Tommy James and the Shondells that went to #1 in 1987:

• Tiffany's "I Think We're Alone Now"
• Billy Idol's "Mony Mony"

Going solo for the first time:

• George Michael (Wham!)
• Belinda Carlisle (Go-Gos)
• Bobby Brown (without the rest of New Edition)

Grammy winners:

• Album of the Year: U2's *The Joshua Tree*, which won over Whitney Houston's *Whitney*, Prince's *Sign o' the Times*, and Michael Jackson's *Bad*.

• Record of the Year: Paul Simon's "Graceland."

Oscar winner for Best Song: "Take My Breath Away" from *Top Gun* by Giorgio Moroder and Tom Whitlock

MTV Video Music Award for Best New Artist: Crowded House. They hit #7 with "Something So Strong" in 1987...and never again had a hit in the United States.

People with myopia can see better underwater than people with normal vision.

ONE-MAN BANS

More stories of literary vigilantes who took book censorship into their own hands.

Book: *The Book of Bunny Suicides: Little Fluffy Rabbits Who Just Don't Want to Live Anymore*, by Andy Riley (2003)

Vigilante: Taffey Anderson, who was living with her 13-year-old son in Halsey, Oregon, in 2008

Story: In October 2008, Anderson's son checked Bunny Suicides out of the Central Linn High School library. The book features a series of cartoons in which one or more bunnies try to kill themselves using cigarettes, bowling balls, electric toasters, hand grenades, and other means. Anderson's son thought the book's dark humor was hilarious; so did his friends. But when his mom found the book in his backpack, she was mortified. She threatened to burn the book rather than return it to the library, where some other kid might read it. "I saw poor bunnies going through meat grinders—people, like, throwing them in there. And they're getting shot out," she told a reporter. "It's not a kid's book. I feel it's not even an adult book. It's not okay."

Outcome: The school board considered a ban...and then voted to keep the book. Anderson claimed she was "disappointed" with the decision. "It's not funny. Not at all," she said.

Books: Mystery novels based on the *Murder, She Wrote* TV series

Vigilante: Unknown

Story: In 2004, an unidentified patron of the Davis County Library in Layton, Utah, began crossing out words like "God," "hell," and "damn" (with a pen), and replacing them with milder versions like "gosh," "heck," and "darn." The damage was discovered by Charlene Heckert, a library patron and regular reader of the novels. "It bothers me because I'm trying to read a book," she told the *Deseret Morning News*. "It's distracting."

Outcome: The damaged books were tossed out; to this day no one knows whodunit to the whodunits. If the vandal is ever caught, he or she could be in big trouble: In Utah, defacing library books is punishable by up to six months in prison and a $1,000 fine.

Under the 1928 Kellogg-Briand Pact, most countries signed a treaty agreeing not...

Books: Dozens of titles in the Crandall Public Library

Vigilante: Raymond Barber, 79, a retired truck driver and decorated World War II veteran living in Glens Falls, New York, in 2004

Story: Over a three-year period, Barber used an ink pen to cross out the swear words in more than 300 library books, replacing them with religious phrases and often writing "God Is Enough" inside the front cover.

Outcome: When the library discovered the damage, they notified the police, who traced the trouble back to Barber. When confronted, He confessed, and was arrested and charged with second-degree criminal mischief, a *felony*. Estimated value of the books he damaged: $9,255. Barber's family was humiliated when his crimes made the front page of the local newspaper and the evening news. "Murderers and rapists get no TV coverage. He scribbled in some books, and he gets crucified on TV," his wife complained to a reporter (before slamming down the phone).

Book: Dozens of mystery novels in the library in Ledbury, England

Vigilante: Unknown

Story: Why stop with naughty words? In the late 1990s, someone began correcting misspellings, factual errors, and bad grammar with a pen, *and* using correction fluid to obliterate bad words, love scenes, and the names or descriptions of private anatomical parts.

Outcome: The mystery remains unsolved, but not for lack of trying. Ledbury is the kind of town where everybody knows everybody, and for months, the place was abuzz with speculation on who might be to blame. The community split on the issue of whether the culprit was a male or a female. Sharon Lippell, a woman in her late 40s who worked in a gift shop, thought the vandal had to be a man. "He's a middle-aged dapper chap, who's living a modest lifestyle but who's got a grudge," she told London's *Independent* newspaper. "Somebody foreign. I don't know why; I've just got a funny feeling."

* * *

"Some books are to be tasted, others to be swallowed, and some few to be chewed and digested."

—**Francis Bacon**

...to use war to resolve disputes or conflicts. (It didn't work, but the treaty is still in force.)

THE POLICE BLOTTER

Actual police reports from around the country.

• "A caller in Amherst said a prowler was ringing the doorbell and banging on the door. Police determined that it was the complainant's brother, who should have gone to school."

• "Cheektowaga homeowners reported suspicious people in their backyard, which turned out to be a deer."

• "Caller reports chicken in the back parking lot of Wilson's Department Store. Officers sent, but unable to locate. Chicken possibly crossed the road."

• "Police were called to Market Square for a report about a 'suspicious coin.' Investigating officer determined it was a quarter."

• "Custer, South Dakota—Suspicious people were reportedly doing something with flashlights by the side of 5th Street. A deputy checked and found the people were not suspicious; they were Canadian."

• "A Mountain View Drive man brought in a cucumber that someone had given to him the day before. He said he didn't trust the person, so he threw it into the woods. During the night he heard a coyote crying in the woods. In the morning, he found the cucumber half-eaten, but no sign of the coyote. He was concerned that the cucumber might have been poisoned."

• "A resident reported that four males unloaded goats from a van and took them into the basement of a Wanda Ave. residence. She said she believed the goats would be slaughtered, because she's seen goats brought into the residence before, and 'they never leave.'"

• "A Transit Road resident reported a break-in and told police the suspect was the complainant's 'crack-head grandson.'"

• "After giving himself an enema, a Fallston man reportedly became extremely confused and argumentative."

• "2:05 p.m., 7500 Block of State Highway 7. Someone entered a home and left presents inside."

Technically speaking, Henry VIII had only two wives. Four of his marriages were annulled.

MEET THE MUCKRAKERS, PART II

On page 131, we told you about the era of "muckraking" journalism at the turn of the 20th century. Here are a few more muckraking stories that shook the world.

SUBJECT: Child prostitution, London, England

MUCKRAKER: In the decades leading up to the 1880s, British feminist groups tried again and again to get Parliament to pass laws protecting women—and especially girls—from London's prostitution rings. Parliament kept stalling, and by 1885, W.T. Stead, managing editor of London's leading newspaper, the *Pall Mall Gazette*, had had enough.

In May 1885, with the help of a few friends, Stead actually arranged to "buy" a 13-year-old girl named Eliza Armstrong from her severely alcoholic mother, have her set up in a London brothel (where Stead posed as her only customer), and then had the girl spirited away, across the English Channel and into France.

EXPOSED! Over three days in July 1885, the *Gazette* ran a story titled "The Maiden Tribute of Modern Babylon," telling, in lurid detail, the true story a of young girl named "Lily," who was sold into prostitution by her mother.

RAMIFICATIONS: The story caused an enormous uproar. Huge crowds fought on London's streets over copies of the papers, and anti-prostitution groups quickly formed. Fearing riots would overrun the city, the British government pleaded with Stead to cease publication. Stead replied by saying he would stop when Parliament did its part to protect women and children. Result: Within a month, the British parliament had passed the Criminal Law Amendment Act, a law designed to protect women and girls caught in lives of prostitution.

UNEXPECTED RAMIFICATIONS: Despite his good intentions, Stead and two women who had helped with the ruse were convicted of crimes involving the buying of Eliza Armstrong. Stead spent three months in prison; the two women spent six months. Upon his release, Stead said, "Never had I a pleasanter holiday!" and continued editing the *Gazette* for several more years.

Final Note: President William Howard Taft invited Stead to attend a peace congress at New York's Carnegie Hall in 1912. Stead set off for the event…on the *Titanic*. He did not survive.

SUBJECT: Standard Oil Company

MUCKRAKER: In 1890 the U.S. Congress passed the Sherman Antitrust Act, meant to combat the corrupt practices used by huge corporations—such as John D. Rockefeller's Standard Oil, the largest corporation in the world at the time—to destroy their competition. In the years that followed the act's passage, Standard Oil remained as large and aggressive as ever—and in 1900 *McClure's Magazine* sent Ida Tarbell to discover why.

EXPOSED! Tarbell spent nearly two years studying Standard Oil, traveling the country, digging up mountains of documents, interviewing the company's current and former employees—all the way up to the executive level—and investigating the company's competitors. She produced a work of reporting so comprehensive that historians credit it with changing the craft of journalism forever. Her story was finally published—it ran in installments over 19 issues of *McClures* from 1902 until 1904.

RAMIFICATIONS: Tarbell's story documented, with plenty of backup and in terms easily understandable to readers, how Standard Oil regularly employed unethical and illegal methods to squash competition. (A favored method was to simply flood a competitor's region with cheap oil—even at a loss—which Standard could easily recoup after driving the other companies out of business.) The story fueled the public's hunger for the hides of the era's ruthless tycoons, and is credited with spurring the U.S. Justice Department to take legal action against Standard Oil, which it did in 1906, leading to the company's dissolution in 1911.

Final Note: Tarbell's story about Standard Oil was voted #5 on a 1999 *New York Times* list of "The Top 100 Works of Journalism in the United States in the 20th Century."

*　*　*

"Clean your finger before you point at my spots" **—Ben Franklin**

In 1642 Dutch explorer Abel Tasman sailed all the way around Australia and never saw it.

HIGH-TECH UNDERWEAR

Who says underwear should only be clean and comfortable? Here's a look at some skivvies with extra built-in features.

MIA BRA COLLECTION

What It Does: Uses NASA technology to regulate excess body heat

Details: "The movement of a fuller bust causes friction between the breast and the abdomen, and it is this friction that causes heat to build up," says bra manufacturer Amoena Mia. The company's bras, made with temperature-regulating fabric similar to the material used in NASA space suits, absorb this extra heat. "Intelligent micro-capsules" in the fabric trap the heat, then gently release it again when body temperature decreases.

INVISIBLE SHAPING BUM BOOSTERS

What They Do: Make your butt look more like Pippa Middleton's

Details: Kate wasn't the only Middleton who wowed the more than one billion television viewers who watched her wedding to England's Prince William in 2011. Her 27-year-old sister Pippa made quite an impression of her own in a curve-hugging white bridesmaid dress. Invisible Shaping Bum Boosters, invented soon afterward, were designed to address the "bum envy" that many woman felt after they got a look at Pippa's behind. The padded panties contain "discreet, cheek-enhancing structures built into the back of the lining to give extra bulk and curvature, turning a flat bottom into rear of the year." By November 2011, they were outselling ordinary panties in some British stores by 148 percent.

CALORIE SHAPER UNDERPANTS

What They Do: Help you lose weight

Details: An extension of Japan's MXP brand (which makes underwear designed to "absorb the body odor of middle-aged and elderly men"), Calorie Shapers take MXP into the weight-loss category:

What are *knismesis* and *gargalesis*? The scientific terms for soft and hard tickling.

The shorts incorporate a nonelastic honeycomb resin that stiffens the shorts, making them harder to move around in. That, in turn, increases the number of calories burned. The manufacturer claims that if a 140-pound man walks an average of 90 minutes a day wearing the underpants, in a week he'll burn as many extra calories as there are in a pint of beer.

GO FREE PANTS

What They Do: They make panties optional—because an underwear panel is built in

Details: Inventor Tina Ketchie Stearns didn't like unsightly panty lines, and hated "thong" underwear, which some women wear to avoid panty lines, even more. When she went "commando" in ordinary pants, the cross seam that runs from the front of the pants to the back was uncomfortable. Why not incorporate underwear *into* the pants? "That's when the patent-pending design for Go Free pants came to me," Stearns writes on her website. "I have replaced that uncomfortable cross seam with a smooth cotton panel sewn directly into the pants. That means undergarments are optional....no more panty or thong lines!"

THUNDERWEAR

What it Does: Allows you to carry a concealed gun in your underpants

Details: This holster, held in place with a strap worn around the waist, centers your handgun in front of your crotch and below the belt line, so that you can conceal your weapon beneath pants, shorts, or a bathing suit, even when you're not wearing a shirt. When you sit down, "the weapon fits down comfortably between your legs," says the manufacturer. When trouble strikes, just "take the thumb of your weak hand and pull away your belt, then with your strong hand reach in and draw your weapon."

Safety First: Because Thunderwear allows you to wear your handgun *in front of* your private parts, instead of being pointed *at them* (as it would if you stuck a gun in your waistband like the bad guys do in the movies), the most you risk is a gunshot to your leg or foot if the weapon misfires, not a life-altering "junk shot." Bonus: "Your weapon will act as a CUP to protect the sensitive area of your body if under physical attack!" says the manufacturer.

Pocket poopers: Marsupial babies go to the bathroom in their mother's pouches.

MILITARY FIRSTS

Some unusual military firsts.

FIRST U.S. MOTHER & SON TO ENLIST TOGETHER

When Ethel Fleming, 34, brought her 17-year-old son, Mike, to the Army recruiting office in Merced, California, in 1975, she was so impressed with the sales pitch that she signed up too.

FIRST "WORLD" WAR

Fought between the Netherlands and Portugal in 1645, the Sugar War was the first in which battles were fought in the Northern, Southern, Western, and Eastern Hemispheres. The Dutch captured the Spice Islands (part of modern-day Indonesia), but Portugal retained its colonies in Brazil, Angola, and Goa (in western India).

FIRST MILITARY UNIT ISSUED A FULL UNIFORM

England's Yeoman of the Guard, organized by King Henry VII in 1485 as his personal bodyguard, were issued special hats, tunics, and breeches to make them more presentable at court. The unit still exists, and still wears the same "beefeater" costumes.

FIRST AERIAL BOMBARDMENT OF A CITY

When Venice (then part of Austria) revolted in August 1849, Austria launched 200 unmanned bomb-carrying balloons against the city. The attack failed, but Austria won anyway. It didn't cede Venice to Italy until after it lost the Austro-Prussian War in 1866.

FIRST U.S. GENERALS WHO WERE BROTHER & SISTER

West Point graduate Perry Hoisington probably never imagined his sister, Elizabeth, would join him in the officer corps, but that's what she did. As he rose to the rank of major general in the U.S. Air Force after World War II, she made her mark in the Women's Army Corps (WACs). By 1966 she was its director, with the rank of colonel. In 1967 Congress authorized women to hold the rank of general, and on May 15, 1970, promoted two women—Anna Mae Hays and Elizabeth Hoisington—to the rank of brigadier general.

The *Brady Bunch* girls had a pet cat named Fluffy, but it only appeared in the pilot episode.

POLITICAL BRIEFS

Short tales from the wacky world of government.

RACE TO THE BOTTOM. In 2011 the Republican National Committee set up a Spanish-language web page designed to court the Latino vote. However, right after it was launched, several people informed the RNC that the "Latino" family in the stock photo at the top of the page was actually Asian.

LIVE FREE AND DIE. Giulio Cesare Fava, the mayor of Falciano del Massico, Italy, faced a crisis in 2012: The cemeteries in his small town were all full. Unable to raise the funds for a new graveyard, Fava issued this executive order: "It is forbidden for residents to go beyond the boundaries of earthly life, to go into to the afterlife." So far, two residents have disobeyed his order.

TELL IT LIKE IT IS. A 65-year-old civil servant in Menden, Germany, was informed in 2012 that his position had been eliminated. So on his last day of work, he sent an e-mail to co-workers admitting that in his last 14 years of employment, he'd hardly done any work at all. He blamed it on redundant positions and poor management, writing, "I had nothing to do."

THAT'S COLD. In the election for a seat on the Pentland Hills, Scotland, city council, the Liberal Democrat candidate, Stuart Bridges, received 370 votes, and the Green Party candidate, Phyl Stuart Meyer, received 322 votes. However, both got fewer than an independent candidate who called himself "Professor Pongoo" and campaigned wearing a penguin costume. He received 444 votes.

DINE-AND-DASH. In June 2012, President Barack Obama gave a speech on the economy in which he said, "The Republicans, they order a steak dinner and then, just as you're sitting down, they leave, and accuse you of running up the tab." The very next day, the president took two U.S. soldiers to Kenny's BBQ on Capitol Hill. After the meal, Obama and his entourage left without paying the bill.

Fore, eh! Canada has more recreational golfers per capita than any other country.

THE PRESIDENT'S MEDAL

The President of the United States can award the Presidential Medal of Freedom to anyone who has made a significant contribution to what Superman might call "the never-ending battle for truth, justice, and the American way." We thought you'd like to meet a few of the most notable—and controversial—recipients.

BACKGROUND

President Harry S. Truman started the tradition of giving medals to civilians for extraordinary service in 1945. The first recipients were four women, each of whom had risked her life during World War II to aid American and British troops. In 1963 President John F. Kennedy re-established the award as the Presidential Medal of Freedom. Since then the medal has been awarded more than 300 times, sometimes generating controversy in the process. Why? Because the president can give the medal to anyone he pleases. Those awarded to popular figures such as Walt Disney, Mother Teresa, Fred Rogers, or Helen Keller seldom draw fire, but other choices have caused sparks to fly.

Recipient: Magazine editor Whittaker Chambers (1984)
Awarded by: Ronald Reagan
Contribution: "Standing alone against the brooding terrors of our age"—in other words, being rabidly anti-Communist during America's post-WWII "Red Scare"
Controversy: The announcement that Chambers, a *Time* magazine editor during the 1940s and '50s, would be posthumously awarded the Medal of Freedom brought an outburst of protest from one of his former colleagues at *Time*. The problem: Chambers often rewrote reporters' field dispatches to alter the news so that it would support his personal anti-Communist crusade. When researchers in *Time*'s New York office protested, Chambers replied, "Truth doesn't matter."

By his own admission, before adopting his anti-Communist stance, Chambers had been a paid agent of the Soviet secret police assigned to cultivate Marxists in the U.S. government. In 1938, Chambers claimed, he rejected Communism and began his crusade against it. He wasn't alone in that crusade—1938 was also the year the House Un-American Activities Committee (HUAC) was created "to investigate disloyalty and subversive activities on the part of private citizens and organizations suspected of having Communist ties." HUAC could subpoena any American to testify, and in 1948, it called in Chambers. The former Soviet spy accused Alger Hiss, a former State Department official, of also being a Soviet spy, and he produced evidence: a hollowed-out pumpkin stuffed with 35-mm film wrapped in waxed paper. Chambers's claim that the film contained State Department documents delivered to him by Hiss helped to convict Hiss of perjury (though not of espionage) and launched HUAC on a Communist witch hunt that didn't truly end until the committee was disbanded by Congress in 1975.

What *was* on the film? In 1975, through the Freedom of Information Act, Hiss got a look at the contents of the pumpkin: one roll of blank film and two other rolls "so innocuous" they would have been "useless for espionage purposes." During the Hiss trial, Chambers repeatedly changed his testimony. "Lying comes easy to you," said Hiss's attorney. "I believe so," Chambers replied.

Recipient: San Francisco Supervisor Harvey Milk (awarded posthumously in 2009)

Awarded by: Barack Obama

Contribution: Being an advocate for gay civil rights as the first openly gay politician elected in a major American city. "Milk encouraged lesbian, gay, bisexual, and transgender citizens to live their lives openly and believed coming out was the only way they could achieve social equality," said the White House.

Controversy: The response was fast and furious, and it came largely from Randy Thomasson, president of conservative policy watchdog group Save California. He called Milk a "sexual predator" who was "undeserving of the medal." On the other end of the spectrum, entertainment publicist Jim Strzalkowski thought Milk deserved the honor, but said it was "too little, too late." Strzalkowski went on to point out that such honors might be more valuable to the living. (Milk was assassinated in November 1978.) "Harvey Milk is dead," said Strzalkowski. "And there are plenty of gays suffering around the country today who need to be honored."

Official color of the ribbon on the U.S. Presidential Medal of Freedom: "Freedom Blue."

Recipient: CIA Director George Tenet (2004)

Awarded by: George W. Bush

Contribution: Playing a pivotal role in events that "made our country more secure and advanced the cause of human liberty"

Controversy: Tenet was head of the Central Intelligence Agency during the September 11, 2001, attacks and was also key in providing the intelligence that led to the United States sending troops to Iraq in 2003. In his 2004 book *Plan of Attack*, Bob Woodward reported on a meeting in which Tenet advised President Bush about the case for Saddam Hussein having weapons of mass destruction. "George, how confident are you?" asked the president. Tenet replied, "Don't worry, it's a slam dunk."

After he received the Medal of Freedom, a group of former CIA officials wrote a letter to Tenet, saying, "The reality of Iraq has not made our nation more secure nor has the cause of human liberty been advanced. In fact, your tenure as head of the CIA has helped create a world that is more dangerous." They called on Tenet to give back his medal. His response? "Never."

Recipient: Polish resistance fighter Jan Karski (awarded posthumously in 2012)

Awarded by: Barack Obama

Contribution: Serving as a courier for the Polish resistance during World War II and delivering to President Roosevelt the news that Jews in Poland were being murdered by Nazis on a massive scale

Controversy: This time it wasn't the recipient who drew fire—it was the president. During his speech awarding the medal to Karski, President Obama used the words "Polish death camp." Polish Foreign Minister Radek Sikorski went ballistic. He called Obama's gaffe a matter of "ignorance and incompetence" and demanded an apology. The Polish government is so anxious to avoid the term "Polish death camps," it posts the "proper language" on its website, on a page called *Against Polish Death/Concentration Camps: A How-To Guide*. Obama's press secretary amended the president's official remarks to say that the language should have been, "Nazi death camps in German-occupied Poland. We regret the error."

MY MEDAL, MY CHOICE

Because presidents can award the Medal of Freedom to anyone they choose, some pundits claim that a list of recipients says more about the men who awarded the medals than about the honorees. Here are just a few of the hundreds of people favored by U.S. presidents.

• **Richard M. Nixon** honored *Apollo 11* astronauts Neil Armstrong and Edwin "Buzz" Aldrin, Jr., and the crew of *Apollo 13* (James A. Lovell, Jr.; John L. Swigert, Jr.; and Fred W. Haise, Jr.).

• **Lyndon Baines Johnson** gave medals to composer Aaron Copland, opera singer Leontyne Price, CBS newsman Edward R. Murrow, and poet Carl Sandburg.

• **Jimmy Carter** honored nature photographer Ansel Adams, environmental writer Rachel Carson, civil rights activist Martin Luther King, Jr., and naturalist and bird painter Roger Tory Peterson (of *Peterson's Guides* fame).

• **Gerald R. Ford** honored baseball legend Joe DiMaggio and track star Jesse Owens, as well as world historians Will and Ariel Durant, and Civil War historian Bruce Catton.

• **Ronald Reagan** awarded medals to Hollywood pals Jimmy Cagney, Frank Sinatra, and Jimmy Stewart, as well as to jazz pianist Count Basie and marine explorer Jacques Cousteau.

• **George H. W. Bush** gave medals to his Gulf War team, including Gen. "Stormin' Norman" Schwarzkopf, Gen. Colin Powell, Dick Cheney, and Brent Scowcroft.

• **Bill Clinton** honored Supreme Court Justice Thurgood Marshall and human rights activists Rosa Parks, Rev. Jesse Jackson, and Cesar Chavez.

• **George W. Bush** gave awards to British Prime Minister Tony Blair, Columbian President Alvaro Uribe Velez, South African President Nelson Mandela, and Australian Prime Minister John Howard.

• **Barack Obama** honored baseball's Stan "the Man" Musial, basketball's Bill Rusell, NCAA coach Pat Summit, as well as authors Maya Angelou and Toni Morrison, and cellist Yo-Yo Ma.

Divorce was illegal in Ireland until 1997.

MOVING DAY

Moving is a chore. Imagine if everyone had to do it at the same time.

PACK IT UP!

In 1626 Dutch explorer Peter Minuit set out from New Netherland (now Delaware) for the island of Manhattan, where he planned to start a colony. He arrived there on May 1. The following year the settlers of "New Amsterdam" (now New York City) celebrated the day with a parade. As the colony grew, May 1 grew in importance, ultimately being used as the end-date for housing leases. In time *every* residential lease in New York ended at the same time, 9:00 a.m. on May 1st. Any tenant who didn't renew had to move out. This meant that tens of thousands of families (and their possessions) converged onto the streets, rain or shine, every May Day.

The system worked fine when New Amsterdam had only a few thousand colonists, but by 1880 there were a million people living in New York City. By 1945 the population had grown to nearly eight million.

ESCAPE FROM NEW YORK

Every May 2 the city looked like a war zone. The streets were lined with discarded furniture, broken dishes, and forgotten possessions. Mirrors commonly didn't survive, and newspaper cartoons joked about families forgetting their babies. The city had laws to prohibit movers from price gouging, but cart men were such a commodity that they still charged whatever they wanted.

It seems unthinkable that New Yorkers would stick to an inefficient system that wreaked this kind of havoc, but even a strike by the movers themselves in the early part of the 20th century couldn't stop the tradition. It took World War II to finally end it. Most of the cartmen and movers were drafted into the military, and replacement movers were difficult to find. Thousands of returning GIs caused a housing shortage in New York. Result: When Moving Day 1945 rolled around, very few people moved. Today, landlords end leases on whatever date they choose.

Thanks, space aliens! The stealth aircraft used in the Bin Laden raid was developed in Area 51.

SIMPSONS MOVIES

Ever notice that when someone walks past a movie theater on The Simpsons, *hilarious fake movies like these are being advertised on the marquees?*

Transformers of the Caribbean

The Poke of Zorro

Eating Nemo

Das Booty Call

Canadian Graffiti

The Planet from Outer Space

Explosion 2

Face Puncher IV

Cars 3: New Merchandise

Space Mutants 4: The Trilogy Continues

Shakespeare in Heat

Honey, I Hit a School Bus

Too Many Premises!

Dude, Where's My Prostate?

Beach Blanket Beethoven

My Dinner with Jar Jar

Horrible Premise

Siskel and Ebert: The Movie

Diet Coke: The Movie

Wedgie: The Movie

Look Who's Oinking

Ernest Needs a Kidney

Ernest vs. the Pope

The Smell in Room 19

Happy Little Elves II: The Sequelf

Baby Cops 3: Tired and Cranky

Blacula Meets Black Dracula

The Re-Deadening

Jackass: The Funeral

Mars Needs Towels

Too Many Grandmas

Editor-in-Chimp

Colonel Dracula Joins the Navy

Clone Me an Angel

Kill Bill Maher

The Christmas That Almost Wasn't But Then Was

A Matrix Christmas

Final Chapter 4: A New Beginning

Hail to the Chimp

Freddy vs. Jason vs. Board of Education

Man of the cloth: Before he played baseball, Babe Ruth trained to be a tailor.

TOILET PAPER CAPERS

Toilet paper is such a "regular" part of our daily lives that it's probably inevitable that it will end up at the center of a crime every now and then.

ROLL PLAYING

In the summer of 2011, the Lawrence, Massachusetts, City Hall had a toilet paper problem: Rolls were inexplicably disappearing faster than usual. It appeared at first that city employees were stealing them...until police stopped a suspicious man as he was carrying a box of toilet paper out of the building. The man—who did *not* work at City Hall—identified himself as David Pinkham, and admitted he'd been stealing TP and other supplies from City Hall for some time. There were 20 rolls in the box when Pinkham was arrested, and when he was booked at the police station, officers found six more rolls, flattened and stuffed down his pants.

The police had their man, but it wasn't until the next day that they discovered who he really was. That was when the *real* David Pinkham opened the newspaper and saw his name in the paper, next to the booking photo of his brother, *Roger* Pinkham. Fingerprints soon confirmed that it was Roger, not David, who was sitting in jail. Roger pled guilty to one count of larceny under $250 and one count of furnishing a false name to a police officer. He was sentenced to 20 hours of community service and one year of probation, and ordered to keep away from city hall. (No word on whether he apologized to his brother.)

SHEET CHEATS

In February 2012, an Arizona woman named Cheryl Stephenson was convicted of two counts of wire fraud in connection with a scheme to dupe consumers into buying unnecessary septic-tank-treatment products. In the scheme, telemarketers at FBK Products told consumers that because of government-mandated changes in the composition of toilet paper, they needed a product called Septic Remedy (sold by FBK) to stop the new paper from clogging their septic systems. In addition to being tricked into buying huge quantities of Septic Remedy, "some elderly customers were defrauded into purchasing more than seventy years' worth of toilet paper," the U.S. Attorney's Office said in a press release. Customers gullible enough to fall for the swindle were put on FBK's "idiot list," which would have been used in future scams. Eight other FBK employees pled guilty or were awaiting trial in connection with the case. Estimated cost to the victims of the con: $1 million.

OH, WAD A NIGHT

In July 2010, a Reidsville, North Carolina, man was charged with assault with a deadly weapon after he stuffed a wad of toilet paper into a black-powder pistol and fired it at his wife. Lonnie Pinnix, 38, apparently got mad at his wife, Darlene, after she stayed out past midnight. He wanted her to leave the home; she refused and climbed into bed instead. That's when Lonnie shot her in the back with the wad of toilet paper. Darlene suffered powder burns and bruising but was otherwise uninjured. At last report Lonnie was still in the can, awaiting his day in court.

STOLEN ROLL

In October 2011, a 53-year-old South Carolina woman named Linda Kay Johnson was charged with assault and battery after she threw a glass ashtray at her nephew (she missed) and then punched him in the face. Why did she do it? The nephew, 27-year-old Johnathan West, had used some of her toilet paper. After the attack, West called 911. Police responding to the call arrived to find Johnson waiting on the front porch. "Just take me to jail. I'm ready," she told the cops. (They did.)

*   *   *

SIX DEGREES OF KYRA SEDGWICK

Actor Kevin Bacon is the subject of the party game "Six Degrees of Kevin Bacon," in which participants link Bacon to any other actor (alive or dead) within six degrees of separation. He's married to actress Kyra Sedgwick (one degree of separation) of the TNT drama *The Closer*. A geneaologist informed her that she is related to Richard Nixon, Jimmy Carter, Marilyn Monroe...and Kevin Bacon (they are 10th cousins, once removed).

The top 10 feet of the world's oceans holds as much heat as the entire atmosphere.

THEY WENT THATAWAY

More famous people who aren't remarkable just for how they lived, but also for how they died.

FRANK W. WOOLWORTH (1852–1919)

Claim to Fame: Retailing pioneer, founder of the F. W. Woolworth discount store chain, and builder of New York City's famous Woolworth building, then the tallest building in the world

How He Died: Killed by his pathological fear of dentists

Details: If you like shopping at dollar stores, you have Frank Woolworth (and his boss, William Moore) to thank for it. In 1878 when Woolworth was in his mid-20s and learning the retail business at the Moore & Smith dry goods store in Watertown, New York, Moore told him to stock a table with miscellaneous items and price them all for a nickel. The goods sold so quickly that Woolworth wondered if an entire store of merchandise priced at 5¢ or 10¢ would do well. In 1879 Moore staked him with $300 worth of merchandise to try it in a store of his own…and the Woolworth chain of "five-and-dime" discount stores was born. By 1912 it was one of the country's largest retail chains.

Woolworth never forgot what he learned at Moore's side, and when Moore died suddenly in 1915 after a visit to the dentist, Woolworth took one final "lesson" from his mentor: Going to the dentist can kill you. Four years later, he paid for that lesson with his life. He developed a painful toothache but was too afraid to go to a dentist. The infection worsened and five days before his 67th birthday it killed him. By then his chain had grown to more than 1,000 stores and was headquartered in the world's tallest building. Woolworth had commissioned the 792-foot building himself and paid for it with cash—every penny earned from nickels and dimes. (The story of his granddaughter and heiress, Barbara Hutton, is on page 187.)

BOBBY FULLER (1942–1966)

Claim to Fame: Lead singer and guitarist of the Bobby Fuller Four, known for their 1966 hit, "I Fought the Law (and the Law Won)"

As a young man, President Rutherford Hayes had *lyssophobia,* the fear of going insane.

How He Died: Mysterious inhalation of gasoline fumes

Details: On July 18, 1966, just four months after "I Fought the Law" reached #9 on the music charts, 23-year-old Fuller's body was found lying across the front seat of his family's Oldsmobile in the parking lot outside his Hollywood apartment. His body and clothes were soaked in gasoline, and a partially filled gas can was found inside the car. The coroner ruled the cause of death as "accidental," caused by inhalation of gasoline fumes inside the closed automobile. Fuller's fans, friends, and loved ones have wondered about his death ever since. His mother reportedly suspected that he was murdered by a member of the band who was jealous over the attention (and money) that Fuller received. Band members had been arguing in the weeks leading up to Fuller's death, and Fuller was apparently about to replace them with new backup musicians.

Another theory: Fuller was friendly with a woman whose ex-boyfriend had mob connections. The relationship was platonic, but the ex-boyfriend suspected otherwise and had Fuller roughed up and doused with gasoline as a warning to stay away from her. Fuller was then tossed into his mother's car, the theory goes, semi-conscious, where he later expired form from inhaling the gasoline fumes. Or perhaps he was murdered and his killers either fled or lost their nerve before igniting a fire to destroy the evidence. It's also possible that Fuller committed suicide. When his band hit the big time and signed with a record label, he lost control over the group's direction. His mother described him as being "despondent" in the weeks preceeding his death. "I don't know if it was suicide," his brother, Randy, told the *El Paso Times* in 1982. "Because he's my brother, I'd love to say that it wasn't. But I don't know." The police records remain sealed to this day.

HARRY F. YOUNG (18??–1923)

Claim to Fame: New York City's last (legal) "Human Fly"

How He Died: Not being able to fly

Details: On March 5, 1923, Young, whose age was not given in newspaper accounts, climbed the facade of New York City's Martinique Hotel. It was a paid gig: Young received $100 to promote a silent movie with the title *Safety Last* and was wearing a placard with the movie's title as he made his way up the building, climbing without ropes, harness, or safety net. "Frequently, in

Microsoft paid $9 million to use the Rolling Stones song "Start Me Up" in Windows 95 ads.

order to give the crowd an extra thrill, Young seemed purposely to let his foot slip," *The New York Times* reported. When Young reached the 11th story, his foot did slip—this time for real. The crowd gasped as he plunged to the street below, still wearing his *Safety Last* placard. He died the instant he hit the sidewalk. A month later the New York City Council banned "street exhibitions of a foolhardy character in climbing the outer walls of buildings by human beings." Scaling the city's buildings has been illegal ever since.

* * *

THE GOOD OLD DAYS?

• **Life expectancy:** In 1955 it was 68. In 2011 it was 78.

• **Car safety:** There were 63 million cars on American roads in 1963. Only 8 million of them had seatbelts, and none had additional safety features, such as antilock brakes or airbags. In 2011 there were 125 million cars on the road—virtually all have seatbelts and 80 percent are equipped with airbags.

• **Cold remedies:** The only real treatment options in the 1950s were Vicks VapoRub and inhaled steam. Fever-reducers like ibuprofen became available in the 1970s, followed soon after by Triaminic, Theraflu, Benadryl, Tylenol Cold, Zicam…

• **Measles:** Before a vaccination was introduced in 1963, 90 percent of American children contracted the illness. In 2012 most school districts won't admit a child unless they're vaccinated, a practice that has virtually eradicated the disease.

• **Graduation:** In 1965 half of high-school seniors graduated. In 2011 about 80 percent did.

• **Banking:** If you needed money over the weekend, you had to get it from a live bank teller (before Friday at 3:00 p.m. in most areas). Banks began issuing debit cards—and opening on Saturdays—in the early 1990s.

• **Asbestos:** It was known to be unsafe as an insulating and fireproofing material since the 1930s, but asbestos continued to be used in public buildings up to the 1970s. Breathing its fibers led to approximately 250,000 lung cancer deaths.

Mel Brooks's *Silent Movie* (1976) has only one spoken word: "Non," spoken by a mime.

IT'S ALL *BLAT* TO ME

You may have heard some of these terms from the old Soviet Union, because many of them are still used in English today. Now you'll know exactly what they mean, Comrade!

Agitprop: Derived from the words *agitatsii* and *propagandy*, meaning "agitation" and "propaganda," and created by the official Department of Agitation and Propaganda. It was the name given to all mass media—newspapers, radio, pamphlets, posters, etc.—used by the Soviet government to influence public opinion. *Agitprop* is sometimes used in the West today as a derogatory term for Left-leaning politically-based artwork, especially in the theater or in film, for example the work of documentary filmmaker Michael Moore.

Apparatchik: Referred to a loyal low-level member of the Communist *apparat* ("political apparatus"), especially an official in the Soviet government's gargantuan bureaucracy. It's still used in English as an insulting term for a blindly loyal member of a political party or other organization. (A CEO-friendly mid-level manager of a corporation might be described as an "apparatchik" for the CEO.)

Blat: Not really used in English, but interesting nonetheless, *blat* was a very common term in the Soviet Union. Its meaning was roughly "cronyism." Because virtually every aspect of Soviet society was strictly controlled by the government, a pervasive underground society developed, in which *blat*—connections to people with power within the Communist Party—was the most powerful currency. Using *blat*, people could be bribed or bartered with, to get food, accommodation, a television, a car, employment, etc.

Bolshevik: In 1898 several Russian revolutionary groups merged to form the Russian Social Democratic Labor Party. In 1903 that party broke into two factions, one led by Julius Martov, the other by Vladimir Lenin. Martov's group was smaller, and was therefore called the *Mensheviks*—derived from the Russian word for "minority." Lenin's larger group was called the *Bolsheviks*—from the Russian word for "majority." The Bolsheviks were the ones who overthrew the Tsar and founded the Soviet Union. The term is still used in the West as an insult for people with extreme Left-leaning political beliefs.

Glasnost: Literally meaning "openness," this was the policy initiated by Soviet leader Mikhail Gorbachev in the late 1980s, requiring the famously secretive Soviet government to become more transparent. The policy had enormous—and mostly unintended—consequences: It allowed Soviet citizens to learn things about their country they had never been privy to, including truths about the murderous policies of former leader Josef Stalin. By June 1988, so much had been revealed that final exams for the entire country's schoolchildren had to be cancelled, since by that time everyone knew that the official history books were almost complete fiction. *Glasnost* is credited as being one of the chief forces that resulted in the fall of the Soviet Union in 1991.

Gulag: An acronym for the agency that ran the notorious Soviet labor-camp system, the *Glavnoe upravlenie ispravitel'no-trudovykh lagerei*—or the "Main Directorate for Corrective Labor Camps"—which was made up of hundreds of camps (and larger "colonies") located all over the Soviet Union. *Gulag* camps were known for their extremely harsh conditions: meager food rations, virtually non-existent health care, forced labor, and extreme cold (many of the camps were located in Siberia). This prison system started in 1930 and lasted until 1961. More than 14 million people, many of them political prisoners, passed through the camps. The term "gulag" is commonly used today in English for an especially oppressive prison or other institution. (Note: The Soviets didn't invent the system: It was a revamping of the *katorga*, brutal labor camps used since the 1600s by the regime the Soviets overthrew—the Russian Tsars.)

Izvestia: Meaning "delivered messages," this was one of two major Soviet daily newspapers (along with *Pravda*). Both were 100 percent propaganda devices, but they were different: *Izvestia* was the voice of the Soviet government, while Pravda was the voice of the Communist Party. The leader of the Soviet Communist Party was often also the leader of the government, but not always, and when this was not the case, the party and the country's leader were often political rivals. This meant that the two publications were often at

The avg. African family uses about 5 gallons of water a day. The avg. American family: 250.

odds—which meant that the two papers were closely monitored by Western intelligence agencies for signs of strife within the Soviet government. *Izvestia* still exists.

KGB: The *Komitet gosudarstvennoi bezopasnosti* ("Committee for State Security") was the secret police and the national and international intelligence organization in the latter half of the Soviet Union's existence. It began as *Cheka* (another acronym), formed by Lenin himself as an "emergency" security organization after the 1917 revolution—and the "emergency" never seemed to go away. The organization went through several name changes over the decades, becoming the KGB in 1954. The agency's final act: The failed attempt to overthrow Mikhail Gorbachev's government, just before the dissolution of the Soviet Union in August 1991. The KGB was dissolved a few months later. Its modern successor: the FSB, or the Federal Security Service of the Russian Federation.

Kremlin: This was used as the name of the huge complex of buildings in Moscow that were the headquarters of the Soviet government, and was also used to refer to the Soviet government itself (much like "White House" is used for the American government). But *kremlin* is actually an old Russian word meaning "citadel" or "fortress." It refers to any such fortified structure, of which there are many in Russia. (The current headquarters of the Russian government isn't in the Moscow Kremlin—it's in another Soviet-built Moscow building known as the "Russian White House.")

Mir: This Russian word has several meanings, including "society," "world," and "peace," and was the name of the world's first long-term space station, launched by the Soviets in 1986 and maintained by the Russian government until it fell from orbit in 2001.

Perestroika: Meaning "restructuring," this was the name given to Gorbachev's democratization of the Soviet government beginning in 1986. Bolstered by *glasnost* (described earlier), *perestroika* led the way to the 1991 fall of the Soviet Union.

Pravda: Meaning "truth," *Pravda* (along with *Izvestia*) was one of two major Soviet daily newspapers. *Pravda* began publication in 1912, and is still in publication. The *Washington Post* is sometimes referred to by American conservatives as "*Pravda* on the Potomac" because of its perceived left-wing slant.

When the Karaya Indians of Brazil speak, they make some sounds through their nostrils.

Samizdat: Russian for "self-publication," this was the name given to the printing and distribution of illegal essays, stories, novels, poetry, etc., without the approval of official censors, primarily by dissidents in Eastern Bloc countries after the death of Stalin in 1953. Aleksandr Solzhenitsyn and Josef Brodsky—both Nobel Prize winners—took part in Samizdat activity starting in the 1950s.

SMERSH: This was a Soviet counter-intelligence agency formed in 1943 by Josef Stalin to infiltrate the Soviet military in search of spies. The name was invented by Stalin himself, derived from two Russian words that mean "death to spies." The unit was broken up after World War II ended. (SMERSH is also the name of the anti-intelligence unit in several of Ian Fleming's early James Bond novels. In the James Bond films, SMERSH became SPECTRE.)

Soviet: It literally means "council." The "Supreme Soviet of the Soviet Union," the Soviet equivalent of a parliament, and the highest legislative body in the nation, was, therefore, literally the "Supreme Council of the Union of Councils."

Zek: *Zek* was a slang term for a prisoner, derived from the Russian word for "incarcerated." It became known to the English-speaking world with the 1974 publication of Aleksandr Solzhenitsyn's *The Gulag Archipelago* (he likens the hundreds of labor camps that dotted the Soviet landscape to an archipelago—a string of islands), which follows the life of a *zek* through the Gulag system.

* * *

A GUIDE TO RUSSIAN PRISON TATTOOS

Barbed wire: Usually around the inmate's forehead, it means they're serving life without parole

Executioner: The inmate is a former hitman

Skulls: The inmate is a convicted murderer

Cathedrals: The number of spires indicate number of years served behind bars

Faces of Josef Stalin and Vladimir Lenin: During the Communist era, it was forbidden to deface an image of those leaders. So a prisoner would have the leaders' faces tattooed over his heart and lungs to prevent guards from hitting or shooting him there.

Worth it? The first pop-up toaster cost $150 in 1926, the equivalent of $1,900 today.

TAKE ONE!

Becoming a top film director takes time. Directors have to prove their abilities before studios will trust them to make big-budget movies. Until then, they hone their skills making edgy, weird, or just plain terrible movies.

KATHRYN BIGELOW

Then: Starting around 1990, Bigelow was a director-for-hire on TV dramas such as *Homicide* and *Wild Palms*, and flops like *Strange Days* and *K-19: The Widowmaker*. In 2005 her friend, journalist Mark Boal, brought her a screenplay he'd written called *The Something Jacket*, about his time as an embedded journalist in Iraq, and asked her to help him turn it into a movie. (They'd worked together on an episode of the 2002 summer TV series *The Inside*.)

Now: Retitled *The Hurt Locker*, the movie was an unlikely success. The gritty, unsettling, documentary-style take on what it was like to serve in the Iraq War surprisingly beat out *Avatar* to win the Oscars for Best Picture and Best Director. Bigelow became just the fourth woman nominated for the award, and the first to win.

PETER JACKSON

Then: Among underground film fans, Jackson was known as the creator of a comic/horror genre he called "splatstick." His early films include *Meet the Feebles*, an explicit comedy about the sex lives of Muppet-like puppets, and *Dead Alive*, in which zombies terrorize a town in 1950s New Zealand—notable for a five-minute scene in which the protagonist kills a horde of zombies with a lawnmower. His first "serious" film: 1994's *Heavenly Creatures*, the true-crime story of two teenagers who conspire to kill one of their mothers. It also depicted the girls' rich fantasy world, in which terra-cotta warriors came to life.

Now: *Heavenly Creatures*' detailed fantasy sequences caught the eye of executives at New Line Cinema, who were looking for the right someone to adapt J.R.R. Tolkien's *The Lord of the Rings* onto film. Jackson got the job. He directed, produced, and co-wrote all three films in the series, which were released between 2001 and 2003 and earned a combined $2.9 billion. The third film, *Return* *of the King*, won 11 Oscars, including Best Director, Best Adapted Screenplay, and Best Picture. Jackson has since gone on to make *King Kong*, *The Lovely Bones*, and three films based on Tolkien's *The Hobbit*.

PAUL HAGGIS

Then: Over the course of 25 years, Haggis worked his way slowly up the Hollywood ladder. His first job: staff writer for the Saturday morning cartoon *Richie Rich* in the 1980s. He moved on to sitcoms (*The Love Boat*, *One Day at a Time*, and *The Facts of Life*) and eventually segued into better television, Emmy winners *L.A. Law* and *thirtysomething*, while creating the Chuck Norris action show *Walker, Texas Ranger*.

Now: In 2004 Haggis sold a screenplay he'd written called *Crash*, a dramatic look at race relations in Los Angeles. The movie was released in 2005, made a respectable $65 million, and won Oscars for Best Picture and Best Original Screenplay (for Haggis). Now working exclusively in movies, Haggis wrote the acclaimed World War II drama *Flags of Our Fathers*, as well as *In the Valley of Elah* and the James Bond movies *Casino Royale* and *Quantum of Solace*.

FRANCIS FORD COPPOLA

Then: While still in film school in the early 1960s, Coppola made three films in rapid succession: *Tonight for Sure*, *The Bellboy and the Playgirls*, and *Dementia 13*. Never heard of them? That's because they were low-budget B-films, shown only in second-rate theaters and drive-ins. Coppola rose to the mainstream after writing and directing *You're a Big Boy Now* in 1966 (it was his master's thesis), which won him a chance to direct a movie version of the musical *Finian's Rainbow* in 1968, which won a Golden Globe nomination.

Now: Coppola is widely regarded as one of the finest film directors of all time. He's had a long career of commercially successful film classics, including *The Godfather*, *The Conversation*, and *Apocalypse Now*. A proponent of the *auteur* concept (that the director is *the* creative force behind a film), a theory that revolutionized movie making, he's also the head of a successful Hollywood family: His children are director Sofia Coppola (*Lost in Translation*) and writer Roman Coppola (*Moonrise Kingdom*), and his nephews are actors Nicolas Cage and Jason Schwartzman.

WHO ARE YOU?

Profound thoughts on identity.

"You aren't born as yourself. You're born facing a mass of possibilities, a mass of other people's ideas and preconceptions—and you have to mold a 'self' by working through those raw materials."

—V. S. Naipaul

"A human being is like a novel: until the last page you don't know how it will end. Or it wouldn't be worth reading."

—Yevgeny Zamyatin

"Do not free a camel of the burden of his hump; you may be freeing him from being a camel."

—G.K. Chesterton

"If you hate a person, you hate something in him that is part of yourself. What isn't part of ourselves doesn't disturb us."

—Herman Hesse

"My sense of my importance to myself is tremendous. I am all I have, to work with, to play with, to suffer and enjoy. It is not the eyes of others that I am wary of, but my own."

—Noel Coward

"I am a collection of water, calcium, and organic molecules called Carl Sagan."

—Carl Sagan

"I don't know who my grandfather was. I am much more concerned to know what his grandson will be."

—Abraham Lincoln

"Whenever two people meet, there are really six people present. There is each man as he sees himself, each as the other sees him, and each as he really is."

—William James

"Animals can learn, but it is not by learning that they become dogs, cats, or horses. Only man has to learn to become what he is supposed to be."

—Eric Hoffer

"If I try to be like him, who will be like me?"

—Yiddish proverb

"Know thyself? If I knew myself, I'd run away."

—Goethe

"IT WAS LIKE SADDLING A PORPOISE"

On page 194, we gave you some examples of literary similes. Here are some others—of a slightly grittier nature.

JUST THE FACTS

Before Jack Webb became famous for playing Sgt. Joe Friday on the 1950s and 1960s police drama *Dragnet*, he played the lead roles in two hard-boiled detective radio shows: *Jeff Regan, Investigator* and *Pat Novak...for Hire*. One thing both characters had in common: a penchant for over-the-top, corny similes. Here are some of our favorites.

"Things were starting to move like a hula dancer with the Hot Foot."

"He looked sad—like a water buffalo caught in a drought."

"That left me with as much chance as a blue peanut on a wedding cake."

"She had a voice that stole over you like a pint of Irish ale."

"He just kept looking at me and waiting, like a guy feeding arsenic to a rich aunt."

"She was wearing black lounging pajamas tied tight around her slim waist. She looked like a wasp with a nice sting."

"There was a pinball machine in one corner, a couple of last year's girls in this year's slacks, and a bleary-eyed little night clerk. He looked like a well-groomed laundry bag."

"It was hard to figure. It was like trying to throw a saddle on a porpoise."

"I felt like a man in quicksand complaining about his height."

"When she said, 'Hello,' it melted all over you, like honey on a hot biscuit."

"From up on the hill, the Chinatown tenements lined up below like sweaty little kids waiting for a shower."

A 60-year-old Hershey's bar retrieved from Adm. Byrd's 1939 South Pole trip was still edible.

"When I came out of it, I was all head—like tap beer in a cheap saloon."

"It was the kind of a neighborhood where a 'For Rent' sign reads like a ransom note."

"He was smiling like a vulture with the first option on a massacre."

"She looked real good sitting there in a white crepe dress. It was one of those tight-fitting babies that made a bathing suit look like a toga."

"When I got up, my face looked like a relief map of Death Valley."

"He looked unhappy, like someone had fed him a Vaseline sandwich."

"It was all crazy, like an Eskimo with a popsicle."

"Hellmann stood there a moment and smiled, like a guy who just killed a landlord."

"I didn't have any leads. There wasn't anything I could do but sit on my hands. It was like taking your niece to a nightclub."

"She opened the door with a nice easy motion, like a cat getting ready to eat its young."

"The rain hadn't helped the alley much. It's like washing your kid's face and finding out he was ugly to start with."

"He was shaking like a polar bear in a French bathing suit."

"I stood in the doorway and watched the dull neons through the rain. They looked splotched and dim like water colors rubbed with a damp rag."

"The place was about as cozy as an abandoned mine shaft."

"You start with trouble, and it never stops. It's like offering to buy aspirin for a two-headed boy."

"I tried to follow the conversation, but it was like trying to put a smoke ring in your pocket."

"My head must have looked like a jackpot—everyone in town was hitting it."

"He was draped over the curb like a tired carpet. And if his suit was a brighter yellow, he could have passed for a loading zone."

"She was kind of pretty, except you could see somebody had used her badly, like a dictionary in a stupid family."

OOPS!

After 25 years, we know a good blunder when we see one.

SELF-ENTRAPMENT

Fed up with drivers speeding down his road, Henrik Ismarker of Stockholm, Sweden, logged on to the police department's Twitter account in 2012 and asked them to start cracking down on speeders. An officer thanked Ismarker for his concern and agreed to set up a speed trap. The next day, Ismarker was driving home and realized just how easy it was to speed on his road—he was pulled over for going more than 10 mph over the limit. Facing a fine of 2,400 kronors ($358), Ismarker told the local news that it was "embarrassing, stupid, and a good lesson," but then added that he was "very satisfied with the police response."

SORRY, HARLEY

In northern California in 2012, a 19-year-old Toyota Prius driver found himself driving behind several Hells Angels riding Harley-Davidsons. The excited teen grabbed his video camera and started filming, but didn't realize how close he was—until he accidentally bumped one of the bikers, who then careened into another biker, sending both of them to the pavement. When paramedics arrived at the scene, they treated the two Hells Angels for minor injuries ...and the Prius driver for several punches to the face.

HOP TO IT!

Billing itself as the "world's leading security company," the firm G4S is hired by police departments to install electronic tags on criminals who are under house arrest. In 2012 two G4S techs showed up at the home of Christopher Lowcock, 29, of Rochdale, England, who was on a court-imposed curfew for drug and weapons charges. They installed a tag on Lowcock's leg and then left. Shortly afterward, Lowcock left, too. How? He simply removed his prosthetic leg—with the security tag still secured to it—and hobbled out of the house. He was later pulled over for a driving offense (with only one leg). G4S fired the two techs.

...to top the *New York Times* bestsellers list since *Charlotte's Web* in 1952.

YOU MUST REMEMBER THIS

Sometimes the easiest way to remember something is to come up with a memory trick (or mnemonic device*), just as school kids have been doing for ages.*

SCIENCE

Three segments of an insect's body: Picture a bug wearing a **hat—h**ead, **a**bdomen, **t**horax.

Biological groupings: **K**ind **p**igs **c**are **o**nly **f**or **g**ood **s**lop. (kingdom, phylum, class, order, family, genus, species)

Types of camels: **B**actrian (two humps), with a back that looks like a *B* turned on its side. The one-humped **d**romedary's back looks like a *D*.

8 Planets in Earth's Solar System (from the closest to the farthest from the Sun): **M**any **v**ery **e**vil **M**artians **j**ust **s**howed **u**p **n**aked. (Mercury, Venus, Earth, Mars, Jupiter, Saturn, Uranus, Neptune)

GEOGRAPHY

World's longest rivers: Just say **nay**! (**N**ile, **A**mazon, **Y**angtze)

The world's largest deserts: Deserts make me **sag** (**S**ahara, **A**rabian, **G**obi)

The 7 Continents: **E**at **a**n **a**spirin **a**fter **a** **n**asty **s**andwich. (Europe, Antarctica, Asia, Africa, Australia, North America, South America)

MATHEMATICS

Formula for calculating distance: DiRT
Distance=rate x time

First 15 digits of the mathematical constant *pi* (using the *number* of letters in each word)**:** "Now I need a drink, alcoholic of course, after the heavy lectures involving quantum mechanics." (3.14159265358979)

MISCELLANEOUS

Traditional diet for treating diarrhea: BRAT (bananas, rice, apples, toast)

The 7 Cardinal Virtues: **C**an **h**aving **p**et **c**amels **t**ame **d**aft **k**ids? (charity, humility, patience, chastity, temperance, diligence, kindness)

It would take four minutes of kissing to burn off the calories in a Hershey's Kiss.

The 7 Deadly Sins: Even good people sin when given lattes. (envy, greed, pride, sloth, wrath, gluttony, lust)

Army ranks: Privates can't salute without learning correct military command grades. (private, corporal, sergeant, warrant officer, lieutenant, captain, major, colonel, general)

Ranks of British Peerage, from highest to lowest: Do monkeys ever visit Britain? (duke, marquis, earl, viscount, baron)

Directions of the compass, clockwise: Never Eat Shredded Wheat (North, East, South, West)

Guitar strings, from thin to thick: Elephants and donkeys grow big ears. (E, A, D, G, B, E)

Four heads on Mt. Rushmore, in order: We Just Like Rushmore. (Washington, Jefferson, Lincoln, Roosevelt)

Colors of the rainbow: Roy G. Biv (red, orange, yellow, green, blue, indigo, violet)

NO-MONICS

(Things you'll probably never need to know)

North-to-south order of the streets in Seattle's downtown business district: Jesus Christ made Seattle under protest (Jefferson, James, Cherry, Columbia, Marion, Madison, Spring, Seneca, University, Union, Pike, Pine)

5 Known Dwarf Planets in Earth's Solar System: Pluto can't make me eat his cereal. (Pluto, Ceres, Makemake, Eris, Haumea)

Eight common law felonies: Mrs. Baker (murder, rape, sodomy, burglary, arson, kidnapping, escape, robbery)

Date and time Prohibition ended in Finland: 543210 (5th of April, 1932, 10 AM)

The Mohs scale of mineral hardness, from softest to hardest: Toronto girls can flirt and only quit to chase dwarves. (talc, gypsum, calcite, fluorite, apatite, orthoclase, quartz, topaz, corundum, diamond)

Orders of color on a TV test pattern: When You Catch German Measles Remain Between Blankets. (white, yellow, cyan, green, magenta, red, blue, black)

James Madison and Thomas Jefferson were once arrested for taking a carriage ride on a Sunday.

IRONIC, ISN'T IT?

There's nothing like a good dose of irony to put the problems of day-to-day life into proper perspective.

EAU DE IRONY

In 2011 the Susan G. Komen for the Cure foundation released a line of perfume with the proceeds going to fight breast cancer. Another foundation, the Breast Cancer Awareness Group, had the perfume tested and discovered—surprise!—that it contained ingredients shown to have a link to breast cancer. A Komen for the Cure representative insisted to reporters that their perfume had indeed been safety tested...but they would "reformulate" the next batch (just to be sure).

D.U.I-RONIC

Damien Bittar had been 21 years old for only 90 minutes when his drunken joyride in Eugene, Oregon, came to an abrupt end: He crashed into Serenity Lane, an alcohol rehabilitation center.

CLOGGED IRONIES

In 2011 a man suffered a massive heart attack after eating the Triple Bypass Burger at the Heart Attack Grill in Las Vegas. After the man was taken to the hospital (he survived), restaurant owner "Doctor" Jon Basso told the local news, "I actually felt horrible for the gentleman because the tourists were taking photos of him as if it were some type of stunt. Even with our own morbid sense of humor, we would never pull a stunt like that."

NAME THAT IRONY

- The legendary racehorse Man o' War won every race he ever ran—except one. A rival horse beat the champion thoroughbred on August 13, 1919. The winning horse's name: Upset.
- For a home game in April 2012, an Orlando, Florida, arena-football team held a promotion in support of National Child Abuse Prevention Month. The name of the team: the Predators.
- What's so ironic about Patrick J. Sullivan spending a night in jail? It was the Patrick J. Sullivan Detention Center—named in

his honor 10 years earlier, in 2002. Sullivan, a retired police officer who was once Colorado's "Sheriff of the Year," got an inside look at his namesake after he was arrested for possession of methamphetamine and solicitation of a prostitute.

A TASTE OF THEIR OWN IRONY

- In 2010 a debt collector from Reliant Financial Associates phoned Diana Mey of Wheeling, West Virginia, to tell her she'd lose her home if she didn't pay off an old loan. Mey didn't have any outstanding debt, but Reliant kept harassing her, so she sued them…and won $10 million. So far, though, Mey has been unable to collect. The matter's been handed over to a collection agency.
- The Pirate Bay, a Swedish website that distributes illegal copies of music, books, and movies, warned its users not to be fooled by a copycat company—also called The Pirate Bay—that does the same thing.

ALL THE IRONY THAT'S FIT TO PRINT

In June 2012, Mitt Romney held a fund-raiser at the Washington, D.C., Newseum, a museum that celebrates "freedom of the press." After a short speech, the Republican presidential candidate sat down for a roundtable discussion with prominent business leaders, prior to which all reporters were escorted out of the building.

SELF-INFLICTED IRONY

While hitchhiking in Montana, a writer named Ray Dolin told police he'd been shot in the arm by a man in a red pickup truck. When that lead didn't pan out, the cops got suspicious and questioned Dolin, who finally confessed that he'd shot *himself*. Why? To "drum up some publicity" for his new book, *Kindness in America*.

* * *

SIGN IN AN OLD RESTAURANT

We go to work
To earn the dough
To buy the bread
To gain the strength
To go to work.

The temperature of the lit end of a cigarette when the smoker is inhaling: 1,292°F.

SEND IN FOR IT!

When you were a kid, did you ever send in for one of these cheap toys, tricks, or joke items from the back of a comic book? (Uncle John did.)

BACKGROUND

In the late 19th and early 20th centuries, millions of Americans did a lot of their shopping through catalogs. One of the most famous was the 600-page Johnson Smith Catalog, established in 1914, which sold novelties, toys, and gag gifts. Among the offerings: rubber chickens, joy buzzers, and ventriloquist dummies. Johnson Smith made millions (and still does), remarkable in that most of its items cost less than a dollar and are marketed to children.

In the late 1930s, Johnson Smith began advertising in the back of comic books, where ad space was cheap. Since then, kids have sent away to them and to dozens of similar companies for such novelty items like glasses that let the wearer see through walls, and powder that could make an entire room full of people break into fits of uncontrollable sneezing. The possibility of pulling off pranks has enchanted generations of children, who crave a bit of control, even if the items sounded a little too good to be true. Here's a look at some of the merchandise sold by Johnson Smith, the S.S. Adams Company, and other companies that kids could own in exchange for a few coins and a reply coupon.

VENTRILO VOICE THROWER (25¢)

Pitch: "Throw your voice into trunks, behind doors, everywhere. Fool teacher, friends and family."

Reality: This low-rent ventriloquism aid from the 1950s was two half-inch pieces of metal held together with a ribbon. You were supposed to hold it in your mouth and breathe, making the metal chunks vibrate, which was supposed to mimic the sound of someone trapped inside an enclosed space. But unfortunately it didn't sound like the voice was coming from anywhere but your own mouth, and the device inhibited you from speaking actual words.

Over 1,000 elephants helped haul building materials to the Taj Mahal (in India, not Vegas).

HYPNO-COIN ($1)

Pitch: "With the magic power of hypnosis you can hypnotize at a glance, make people obey your commands, strengthen your memory, develop a strong personality, overcome bad habits."

Reality: The "coin" was a plastic disc with a 3D-effect, black-and-white pinwheel design on it. When the coin was wobbled, the pattern swirled, which was supposed to mesmerize the subject. Though sold in the 1960s, it came with a 1935 pamphlet called "25 Lessons in Hypnotism" that offered tips on stage hypnotism.

X-RAY SPEX ($1.25)

Pitch: "See through fingers, see yolk of egg, see lead in pencil."

Reality: Plastic eyeglass frames lined with two layers of cardboard. In between the layers were bird feathers, which diffracted light and created the illusion of two separate images of the same thing. Where the images overlapped was a dark area, which was supposed to be the "X-ray" of bones, egg yolk, pencil lead, etc. X-Ray Spex first appeared in comic books in the mid-1960s. Variations: Aqua-Spex (same as X-Ray Spex, but with adjustable tinting, based on available underwater light), and Hypno-Spex (with the same swirly surface as the Hypno-Coin). The whole line of spex was invented by mail-order kingpin Harold von Braunhut, who also devised Sea Monkeys.

U-CONTROL LIFE-SIZE GHOST (95¢)

Pitch: "Soars 30 to 40 feet or more in air. You control in secret. Conceal in pocket, ready to operate. Rises, falls, floats, dances. Spooky effects."

Reality: Kids in the early 1950s who ordered it got a thin white balloon for the head, a billowy white garbage bag for the body, and a spool of transparent fishing line, to "control" it. Contrary to the ghost's spooky face in the ad, the balloon came decorated with the face of Casper the Friendly Ghost…not exactly terrifying (and not exactly a legal use of the image).

GENUINE SOIL FROM DRACULA'S CASTLE ($19.95)

Pitch: "From the gold-plated chain is suspended a transparent miniature coffin containing one gram of genuine earth from the exact place were Vlad (Dracula) once made macabre history. No mystic powers are claimed for this amulet."

Reality: You've got to hand it to the marketers. There aren't too many ways you can make a tiny plastic coffin filled with dirt—and that's exactly what this was—exciting. And it came with a "Certificate of Authenticity" guaranteeing that the dirt really was from Transylvania. Offered in the late 1970s, the thimble-sized dirt holders were sold by Warren Publishing, the same company that owned the magazines *Creepy*, *Eerie*, and *Famous Monsters of Filmland.*

THE MONEY MAKER ($1.25)

Pitch: "Put in a blank piece of paper, turn the knob...out comes a REAL dollar bill! You can spend it!"

Reality: A lot of mid-1960s kids probably thought this was their ticket to neverending wealth...until they realized that they had to secretly stock a compartment in the Money Maker with their own real currency, which is what the blank paper "transformed" into.

SECRET AGENT SPY CAMERA ($1)

Pitch: "Easily concealed in the palm of your hand. Takes secret or surprise pictures as well as regular candid shots."

Reality: It was, in fact, a tiny working camera...except that these were notorious for leaking light and ruining pictures. And it took special film, which was next to impossible to purchase other than from the back of a comic book (cost for six 10-exposure rolls: $1), let alone find a late-1950s photo lab that would develop it.

SNEEZING POWDER (25¢)

Pitch: "Place a little of this powder on your hand, blow into the air, step back, and watch the fun begin. Everyone in the room will begin to sneeze without knowing why."

Reality: When it was first marketed by novelty maker S.S. Adams at the turn of the 20th century, the active ingredient was dianisidine, used as a chemical weapon in World War I and banned by the FDA in 1939. At some point, it became cheaper—and safer—to use black pepper, which is what it was when it appeared in comic books in the 1950s. But it could make people sneeze, if you got close enough to blow it into their faces.

The beam from the Texas Petawatt laser is brighter than the surface of the sun.

OUR LADY OF THE LITTLE GREEN MEN

If mainstream religions leave you cold, why not spice things up by throwing a few UFOs into the mix? Here's a look at some "religions" that draw inspiration from extraterrestrials.

THE SEEKERS

Close Encounter: In the early 1950s, a suburban Chicago housewife named Dorothy Martin began receiving "mental messages" from what she said were extraterrestrial guardians from a planet called Clarion. She attracted a little band of followers and formed them into one of the earliest UFO cults, which she called "The Seekers." The aliens reportedly told her that they'd discovered unstable fault lines in the Earth's crust while observing the planet from their flying saucers. The faults were going to rupture before dawn on December 21, 1954, and cause floods that would destroy much of North America. The good news: Just before midnight, a UFO would take Martin and the Seekers to safety on planet Clarion.

What Happened: On Martin's orders, Seekers quit their jobs and gave away their money and belongings in anticipation of a new life on Clarion. Some even divorced their spouses. About 20 Seekers gathered at Martin's house on December 20 to await the UFO. Midnight came...and went...and no spaceship arrived. The terrified Seekers huddled together until 4:45 a.m., when Martin claimed to receive another message from the aliens. More good news! The "God of Earth" was so impressed by the Seekers' devotion that he'd decided to spare North America. The crisis averted, the alien rescue saucer had returned to Clarion without picking up the Seekers.

Aftermath: Martin fled Chicago to avoid being sent to a mental hospital. She lived in Peru from 1954 to 1961, then returned to the U.S. Now calling herself "Sister Thedra" and leading a group called the Association of Sananda and Samat Kumara, she continued to relay messages from space aliens until her death in 1992. The Association of Sananda and Samat Kumara, headquartered in Sedona, Arizona, is still active.

SUMMUM

Close Encounter: One afternoon in October 1975, a former aerobics instructor named Claude King was relaxing, eyes closed, on the couch in his Salt Lake City, Utah, apartment. He'd had some ringing in his ears lately, but this time it was much more intense: King claimed he was "engulfed" by the sound and teleported to an alien world. When he opened his eyes, he was standing next to a giant pyramid on a green lawn, under a blue sky filled with stars. It was the first of many visits to the world of "angelic Beings" known as Summa Individuals, who transmitted their Summum philosophy ("Nothingness and Possibility come in and out of bond infinite times in a finite moment") to King via mental telepathy.

What Happened: King had his name legally changed to Summum Bonum Amon Ra (though he still went by his nickname, Corky). He then founded the ancient-Egypt-themed Summum religion, which today is headquartered in a pyramid-shaped temple in Salt Lake City and promotes the "Seven Summum Principles: Psychokinesis, Correspondence, Vibration, Opposition, Rhythm, Cause and Effect, and Gender."

The movement has even developed a form of mummification that draws inspiration from the practices of the ancient Egyptians but incorporates modern materials like fiberglass and polyurethane. The service is available to the public: Human mummification costs $67,000, pets around $6,000. Practitioners of Summum also make sacramental wine called "nectar publications" and meditate over it to fill it with "spiritual concepts." The group says it has given away more than 250,000 bottles over the years, but only to Summum adherents. Drinking the spiritually spiked wine is said to enhance seven different types of meditation.

Aftermath: The first human to be mummified using the Summum technique: Corky Ra himself, who died in 2008. His mummy is stored inside the Summum pyramid, in an upright gold "mummiform" coffin just like King Tut's (except that Corky's face served as the model for the face on the coffin). The group says that more than 100 people have signed up to be mummified when they die.

THE AETHERIUS SOCIETY

Close Encounter: On May 8, 1954, a London taxi driver and yoga enthusiast named George King was alone in his apartment when

In 1953 driver Tim Flock won a NASCAR race with a rhesus monkey as his "co-driver."

he heard a voice command, "Prepare yourself! You are to become the voice of Interplanetary Parliament." The message was from an alien named The Master Aetherius. King, by virtue of his mastery of yoga, had been selected to be "the Primary Terrestrial Mental Channel for the Cosmic Masters of the Solar System." These Masters, hailing from Venus, Mars, Jupiter, and Saturn, would use King to transmit their messages to the world.

What Happened: The Masters told King that selfishness, violence, and other human ills had knocked the Earth's karma out of balance, as evidenced by pollution, warfare, and other global ills. The aliens, who regularly visited Earth in their flying saucers, wanted to help restore the karmic balance, using spiritual energy generated by prayer circles practicing a "powerful new form of Karma Yoga." On the Cosmic Masters' instructions, King formed the Aetherius Society to get the message out.

There's certainly nothing unusual about praying for the purpose of achieving positive ends, but what sets the Aetherius Society apart are devices they use called "radionic batteries." These sit in the middle of each prayer circle and soak up the spiritual energy. The batteries are "charged" with prayer week after week; then when a disaster strikes, such as a hurricane or the earthquake, tsunami, and subsequent nuclear meltdown in Japan in 2011, the Society releases the energy using a machine called a "spiritual energy radiator" and transmits it directly to the trouble spot.

Aftermath: Dr. King died in Santa Barbara, California, in 1997, but the Aetherius Society, now headquartered in Hollywood, is still praying away. It has about 650 members worldwide.

THE INTERNATIONAL RAËLIAN MOVEMENT

Close Encounter: If prayer circles don't float your boat, perhaps the Raëlians are more your speed. As we told you in our book *The World's Gone Crazy*, the Raëlian movement was founded in 1973 by an aging French pop star named Claude Vorilhon after he went hiking in a dormant volcano crater in central France. There he met an alien with skin that was "white with a slightly greenish tinge, a bit like someone with liver trouble," he writes in his book, *The Message Given to Me by Extra-Terrestrials*. The alien, a member of an advanced race called the Elohim, invited Vorilhon back to his UFO. During this and subsequent visits, Vorilhon was

First Facebook page to reach 10 million fans: Michael Jackson's (after his death).

taught the true origin of humanity—namely that humans were created by the aliens in test tubes in a laboratory 25,000 years ago, and prophets like Moses, Jesus, and Buddha were emissaries of the aliens, just like Vorilhon. The aliens told him that when humans perfect cloning and develop the ability to transfer memory and personality from aging bodies into healthy new ones, they will live forever. They also told him that having unlimited, uninhibited sex would enable them to achieve "perfect freedom."

What Happened: After his first alien encounter, Vorilhon changed his name to Claude Raël and founded the International Raëlian Movement. He dressed in flowing white garments and grew a topknot of hair that he said was an antenna for receiving further messages from outer space. The messages revealed the extraterrestrial "truth" of stories in the Bible: Jesus walked on water using "antigravitational beams," Jonah was swallowed by an alien submarine he thought was a whale, and the ancient Hebrews became the chosen people by winning a contest.

Aftermath: Thrown out—and laughed out—of France in the mid-1980s, Raël moved to Spain and eventually to Canada. He and his free-loving followers still live there, in a compound near Montreal. They run a museum called UFOland that presents Raëlianism to the general public, and they're raising money to build a $20-million extraterrestrial "embassy" that will also serve as an alien spaceport. As soon as it's finished, Raël says, Moses, Jesus, and all the other prophets (who have been kept alive through cloning) will return to Earth in their UFOs.

The aliens have told Raël that they would prefer the embassy to be built in "neutral" territory on land donated by the Israeli government. But the Raëlian movement's symbol, a swastika inside of a Star of David, has complicated negotiations with the Israelis. (The Raëlians say they're trying to "reclaim" the swastika from the Nazis.) In 1991 the symbol was changed to a less offensive pinwheel appearance, but that didn't seem to help much. If the embassy ever really does get built, it probably *won't* be built in Israel. The Raëlians claim to have 65,000 members in more than 80 countries. (No word on how many of them are just in it for the unlimited, uninhibited sex.)

Of the 20 highest mountain peaks in the U.S., 17 are in Alaska.

NUDES AND PRUDES

More stories of nudes and the prudes who find the nudes to be rude and or lewd.

NUDE: Camp Pendleton, a military base on the Southern California coast, is where the U.S. Marines practice their amphibious assault landings. In 2011 the base was faced with an invasion of a different kind: nudists from the neighboring beach, a state park. Nudity was banned in the park in 2009. Since then nudists had been crossing onto the base's beaches in increasing numbers, trying to get away from the park rangers, who they claim were singling them out for harassment. "You have rangers hiding between the bushes, within rocks, in trees, with cameras trying to take pictures. It's insane," a beachgoer named John Squicciarini told the *Orange County Register*. The rangers' response: They're just enforcing the law. "The naturists are mischaracterizing this as usual," said a spokesperson.

PRUDE: In November 2009, the Swiss Alpine village of Appenzell introduced a law making nude hiking punishable by a fine of 200 Swiss francs (about $225). It did so after a German "naturist" organization, citing the region's lax regulations regarding nudity, named Appenzell as an ideal spot for hiking in the buff. The area was soon flooded by German hikers wearing hats, hiking boots, and not much else. Nude hiking was illegal even before the new law was introduced, but the police could respond only to formal public complaints, and few locals were willing to go on the record. Now police can cite nudists on their own authority. "It's a sort of joke," Stephanie Sutter, a tourist official, told London's *Independent* newspaper. "But there are lots of kids hiking in this area and they shouldn't have to face these people."

NUDES VS. NUDES: France's Cap d'Agde, also known as "Naked City," is Europe's largest nudist colony. The community of 40,000 nudists was also one of the most sedate…until the early 2000s, when swingers, exhibitionists, and other "libertines" began flocking to the seaside town. The two camps have been at war ever since. The libertines complain that traditional nudists are too

Originally, the term "movies" did not mean films, but the people who made them.

uptight, and the traditionalists are furious because the libertines—when they aren't wife-swapping or engaging in public displays of lewdness—*wear clothes*. "There are often more people walking around dressed than undressed. If you are just an ordinary nudist, they stare at you as if you were something bizarre," a traditionalist complained to the *Independent* newspaper in 2010. (Three libertine orgy clubs were destroyed by arson fires in 2008. The culprits were never found, but police suspect the fires were set by traditionalists to drive the libertines out.) Traditionalists dream of returning to the good old days of sinless, nonviolent public nudity, but Mayor Gilles d'Ettore thinks that's unlikely. "I can't put a policeman behind all 40,000 nudists," he says.

NUDES VS. PRUDES: Four years after members of the New Beginnings Ministries church in Warsaw, Ohio, began a weekly protest in front of the Fox Hole strip club, the strippers decided to give the church a taste of its own medicine: In August 2010, they began protesting in front of the church during religious services each Sunday. Dressed for the occasion in shorts and bikini tops, the strippers kept at it for three months, hoping to pressure the church into leaving the Fox Hole alone. They failed: The strippers no longer demonstrate in front of the church, but at last report churchgoers were still protesting in front of the strip joint. "We cannot share territory with the Devil," Pastor Bill Dunfee told the Associated Press. "Light and darkness cannot exist together, so the Fox Hole has got to go."

PRUDE NUDES: In March 2009, police were called to escort John Harrison and his wife, Lyn, from Australia's White Cockatoo resort in north Queensland. Reason: March is the resort's "clothing optional" month, and the Harrisons, who were dining away from the resort that evening, opted (necessarily) to dress. It turns out clothing wasn't so optional after all. When Harrison finished dressing and stepped outside to wait for his wife, four nude women took offense at his state of un-undress and complained. "They felt uncomfortable with him eyeing them," resort owner Tony Fox explains. "I asked him to show respect and take his clothes off. He threatened to bash me, there was some argy-bargy [pushing and shoving] and police were called."

Dogs of War: The ancient Romans and the Gauls trained dogs to fight in battle.

WARNING LABELS

Some things in life should go without saying, but there's always the occasional genius who needs to be told not to shave during an earthquake.

On a salt packet: "Warning: Contains salt."

On a can of aerosol cheese: "For best results, remove cap."

On an information booklet: "Do not use if you cannot see clearly to read the information in the information booklet."

On air freshener: "For use by trained personnel only."

On dog medicine: "Alcohol may intensify the effects."

On rubbing alcohol: "Avoid contact with eyes, ears, brain, and surrounding membranes."

On a letter opener: "Safety goggles recommended."

On a travel pillow: "Do not use while sleeping."

On a dust mask: "Does not supply oxygen."

On a disposable razor: "Do not use during an earthquake."

On a box of dice: "Not for human consumption."

On a toy called Rubber Band Shooter: "Caution: Shoots rubber bands."

On a bicycle: "Removing the wheel can influence the performance of the bicycle."

On a disc-shaped chocolate: "Do not place chocolate into any electronic equipment."

On a cleaner for eyeglasses: "Not for or direct use in eyes."

On a birthday badge for two-year-olds (it says "I am 2" on one side): "Not to be used by children under 3 yrs. of age."

On a dishwasher: "Do not allow children to play in the dishwasher."

On a can of tuna: "Caution: Contains fish."

On toilet bowl cleaner: "Safe around pets and children, although it's not recommended that either be permitted to drink from the toilet."

Japan has "cat cafés"—for people who can't have pets, but want to play with a kitty.

EXTREME SPORT: FREE-SOLO CLIMBING

Here's the rundown on another death-defying sport. (BASE jumping is on page 165.)

DANGER ZONE

When it comes to the deadliest adventure sport, free-solo climbing is a close second to BASE jumping. How does a climber free-solo? By leaving behind ropes, harnesses, and other protective gear and relying on three things: physical strength, climbing skill, and psychological fortitude. Without all three, say experts, the consequences can be deadly.

In 2011 Sacramento free-solo climber Alex Honnold scaled the sheer rock face of Yosemite's Sentinel Rock with TV's *60 Minutes* crew filming every move. Clinging to a crack in the granite wall more than 2,600 feet above solid ground, the 26-year-old climber was so high above Yosemite Valley's floor that the trees below looked like toothpicks. Within minutes of starting the Sentinel ascent, Honnold reached "the point of no return," at which a climber must confront the danger and continue…or lose his nerve and go back. Honnold's point of no return: wet rock. He clung to the wall despite the water oozing onto it and reached for the chalk bag tied around his waist. He managed to get enough chalk to absorb the moisture on his hands and continued to the top.

The 2011 ascent made Honnold the first person to climb the Chouinard-Herbert route without a safety harness or rope.

STAYING ALIVE

"Nobody ever thought about doing it before," said adventurer and rock climber John Long, who watched the mind-blowing climb from below. Long is the elder statesman of free-soloing, credited for starting the extreme sport in the 1970s. Even he admits that in this area, Honnold is "unquestionably, the best guy alive today."

The "alive" part is, of course, critical. When asked what he considered Honnold's greatest achievement to date, Long says, "That he's still alive. If you look at the past, people who have made a real habit of soloing, at least half of them are dead."

WHISTLE WHILE YOU WORK

Honnold's key to surviving: keeping his cool. His nickname among other climbers is "Alex No Big Deal." That attitude has helped him prevent the adrenalin-spiked jitters that can kill a free-soloer. Honnold has a method: When caught in a seemingly impossible situation, he starts whistling a favorite tune. And if he does get an adrenaline rush? "It means that something has gone horribly wrong," Honnold says. "The whole thing should be pretty slow and controlled...mellow."

"The real challenge about climbing without rope," Long explains, "is that 'the feeling' can come up in a split second and you have to dial that back quickly...or else you're not gonna be able to breathe." He should know. Sylvester Stallone's movie *Cliffhanger* was based on Long's novella *Rogue's Babylon*, which he based on his own climbing experiences. If fear takes over while you climb, Long says, "You have no chance. You're gonna die."

SHE'S A LADY

Illinois native Steph Davis made her first climb in 1990. At the time, Davis was a freshman at the University of Maryland. Before long, she'd switched to Colorado State University—not for the academics, but because she'd fallen in love with climbing and Colorado had higher mountains. Davis earned a master's degree in literature, then after five days of law school, she dropped out to become what she calls a "dirtbag climber." With her grandmother's beat-up Cutlass Sierra and a faithful Blue Heeler mix named Fletch in tow, all Davis needed was a mountain. She built a bed in the backseat of the car and spent seven years living out of it and waiting tables for cash before landing sponsors to help support her expeditions.

She pushed herself hard and in 2005 became the first woman to free-solo El Capitan's huge Salathe wall. The brutal climb took nearly two weeks, with Davis sleeping on ledges the width of a diving board until she reached the top. Davis says she took up free-soloing as a way of facing her biggest fear: death. "When I was soloing, I didn't think about death, I felt alive," she says. "Doing physical acts that I find scary, and figuring out how to feel in control, is part of understanding how to be free from it."

DON'T FEAR THE REAPER

Davis went head-to-head with death in 2007 when she decided to climb Longs Peak in Colorado's Rocky Mountain National Park. Elevation: 14,255 feet. (The famed British climber Doug Scott once said, "The Himalayas are a great place to train for Longs Peak.") She set her sights on the Diamond, 900 feet of vertical and overhanging terrain—in particular, Pervertical Sanctuary, a steep crack that goes straight up the Diamond's face. On the Class 1 to Class 6 Yosemite Decimal System (YDS), Class 5 denotes vertical rock requiring skill and a rope; falls from Class 5 climbs typically result in severe injury or death. The Pervertical Sanctuary is rated 5.11a.

Davis started her climb at 5:30 a.m. "Over and over in my mind, I repeated 'be relaxed, have good feelings,'" Davis said. If she made it to the top, she'd be only the second person with a recorded free-solo of Pervertical Sanctuary. The first: prolific British free-soloist Derek Hersey (who plunged 200 feet to his death in 1993 while free-soloing Yosemite's Sentinel Rock). The sky was clear, the air freezing, and she found herself climbing with cold feet and hands. That made it harder to relax. "I was hoping to feel solid," Davis said later. But instead, she found herself wedged in the bulging section of Pervertical Sanctuary with one hand in a hand jam and her feet splayed out. She stretched high for a side pull with one hand and checked again to make sure the other hand was securely jammed. "I reminded myself that I am a crack climber," Davis said, and climbed past her fear and onto Table Ledge—the top of the climb—at 7:45 a.m.

The athletes featured here have survived their deadly pursuits...so far. But others have not been as lucky. *On page 495,* *meet some of the daring sportsmen (and women) who paid the ultimate price for the chance to fly like an eagle or climb like Spider-Man.*

* * *

"The end is nothing, the road is all." —**Willa Cather**

Tater tots were created to use up the potato shreds left over from French-fry production.

RANDOM FIRSTS

Here at the Bathroom Readers' Institute, we love amazing origin stories. For example, you are reading the first-ever Bathroom Reader *to have parachuting duckies on the cover. (Just wait—parachuting duckies will soon be all the rage.) Here are a few more fun firsts.*

THE FIRST PRANK PHONE CALL

For years, author and Portland State University English professor Paul Collins has been searching for the first documented prank phone call. In 2011 he stumbled across this item in the February 2, 1884, edition of *The Electrical World:*

> A GRAVE JOKE ON UNDERTAKERS—Some malicious wag at Providence R.I. has been playing a grave practical joke on the undertakers there, by summoning them over the telephone to bring freezers, candlesticks and coffins for persons alleged to be dead. In each case the denouement was highly farcical, and the reputed corpses are now hunting in a lively manner for that telephonist.

Finding no evidence of an earlier prank call, Collins has deemed this the very first one.

THE FIRST COFFEEHOUSE

Nearly 500 years before Starbucks, there was Hakam and Shams. The two Syrian traders—Hakam from Aleppo, and Shams from Damascus—introduced coffee to Turkey in the 16th century. It was so popular that in 1554 they opened a shop in Constantinople to sell the new drink. Except for the fact that women weren't allowed in, Hakam and Shams's place wasn't too different from today's coffeehouses: It featured poetry readings, music recitals, and impromptu political debates concerning the reach of the Ottoman Empire. Or patrons could just sit and talk, play chess or backgammon, and, of course, sip coffee.

THE FIRST INTERNET COUPLE

In 1982 a Chicago woman named Pam Jensen logged onto a CompuServe CB Simulator, a very early Internet chat room. Before long, Jensen found herself having an online conversation with Chris Dunn, a computer geek living in New York. Their first chat

At any given time, about 4% of American women are pregnant.

lasted for five hours. They kept up their correspondence, and a few months later Dunn flew to Chicago to meet Jensen in person. A year later they were married. "At that time," recalled Jensen on their 25th wedding anniversary in 2008, "computers weren't as pervasive in our daily life. To a lot of people, especially my parents and their friends, it seemed very suspicious to even be communicating like that."

THE FIRST FRISBEE DOG

On August 5, 1974, during the eighth inning of a nationally televised Los Angeles Dodgers home game, 19-year-old Ohio State student Alex Stein ran onto the field and threw a Frisbee toward the outfield fence. To the crowd's delight, Stein's dog, Ashley Whippet, sprinted through the grass, leaped high in the air, and caught the disc in his teeth. Stein threw another; Ashley caught that one, too. By this time, police were chasing both of them as the crowd cheered wildly. Stein was arrested, but his stunt caught the attention of Irv Lander, director of the International Frisbee Association, and within a year, Stein and Ashley were the ambassadors of a new sport (officially called "Disc Dog"—Frisbee is trademarked). Ashley went on to perform his feats at the White House and Super Bowl before going to doggie heaven in 1984.

THE FIRST FASHION MODEL

Marie Vernet was an attractive young French woman in the 1840s when she met up-and-coming British clothier Charles Frederick Worth, now considered the father of *haute couture* (the creation of exclusive custom-fitted clothing). The two married, and Vernet became Worth's "living mannequin." In the 1850s, she traveled to the homes of the Paris elite to model Worth's creations, but as his wares became more in demand, the couple started holding fashion shows at their shop, where Vernet and other models would parade on a runway showing off new Worth creations. (He was also the first designer to put his name in his garments.) And with that, the modern fashion industry was born.

THE FIRST VENDING MACHINE

The first coin-operated vending machine debuted in London in the early 1880s. (It sold postcards.) But that was the first *modern* vending machine. Its design was actually based on a contraption invented in the first century A.D. by Greek mathematician Heron of Alexandria. Heron was commissioned by the church to build a device that would stop parishioners from taking too much holy water. Author Daniel Smith describes it in his book *Forgotten Firsts*:

> A coin was deposited through a slot in the top of the box and fell into a pan that, when weighed down, operated a lever. When the lever rose, it opened a valve that allowed holy water to flow out into a receptacle. When the lever had tilted far enough that the coin fell out of the pan, a counterweight returned it to its original position, closing off the valve and ceasing the flow of water.

THE FIRST BABY BOOMER

The post–World War II "baby boom" officially ran from January 1, 1946, to December 31, 1964. Of the approximately 78 million Americans born during that time, Kathleen Casey-Kirschling was the first. Born early on New Year's Day in 1946, she grew up to become a school teacher and is now retired and living in Florida. In 2011, on her 65th birthday, a reporter asked Casey-Kirschling to sum up her generation: "We get a bad reputation for being materialistic, but I think by our sheer numbers and our education—we're the most educated generation that's ever been—we really built a lot of what the country is today. A lot of it is very good. And, of course, some of it was on the negative side."

THE FIRST SILICONE BREAST IMPLANT RECIPIENT

Timmie Jean Lindsey is an octogenarian great-grandma living in Texas. In 1962 she wanted to have a tattoo removed from her chest (roses...but that's another story), so she went to a Houston doctor named Frank Gerow, who told her that she was the perfect candidate for an experimental procedure he'd invented—silicone implants designed to increase breast size. "I'd never heard the term 'guinea pig' back then," said Lindsey, "I just thought it was privilege to have it done." (She went from a B cup to a C cup.) Lindsey is proud of her increasing role in medical history.

* * *

"He who has a why to live can bear almost any how."

—**Friedrich Nietzsche**

If the name fits: A man who rents mobile jets to executives in Texas is named Rich Mann.

BATHROOM JOKES FOR 10-YEAR-OLDS

If you're an adult, society at large expects you restrain yourself from laughing at these jokes—not even a snicker through your nose. You've been warned.

Q: Why did Tigger put his head in the toilet?
A: He was looking for Pooh.

Kid #1: I have to go to the doctor to get my butt fixed.
Kid #2: Why?
Kid #1: It's got a crack in it!

A man goes to the store to buy some toilet paper. The clerk asks him what color he'd like. "White," the guy says. "I'll color it myself!"

Two old women are sitting on a bench waiting for a bus. "You know," one of the women says to the other, "I've been sitting here so long, my butt fell asleep." The other woman turns to her and says, "I know! I heard it snoring!"

A cowboy goes into an outhouse, and hears a strange noise. He looks down the hole—and sees an Indian. "How long you been down in that hole?" he asks. The Indian replies, "Many moons."

Q: If H2O is on the inside of a fire hydrant, what's on the outside?
A: K9P.

Mother: Billy! Why are you sitting on the toilet and hitting yourelf on the head?!
Billy: Works for ketchup!

Q: How can you tell if a woman is wearing pantyhose?
A: If she farts, her ankles swell.

Q: Why did the little boy put candles on his toilet?
A: He was having a bithday potty.

Did you hear about the constipated accountant?
—He couldn't budget.

Q: Why did God make farts smelly?
A: So deaf people can enjoy them too!

Confucius say: Man who fart in church sit in his own pew.

AMERICA'S FORGOTTEN FIRE

You've probably heard of the Great Chicago Fire that started on October 8, 1871. But have you ever heard of the devastating fire in Peshtigo, Wisconsin, just 250 miles north of Chicago? It made the Chicago Fire look like a marshmallow roast...and it occurred on the exact same day.

PRELUDE TO PERIL

In 1871 Peshtigo, Wisconsin, was a thriving lumber town in an area of virgin forest a few miles from the shores of Green Bay. As the town grew, it spiderwebbed outward along both sides of the Peshtigo River. It had a sawmill that produced 150,000 board feet of lumber a day and a woodenware factory—at the time, the country's largest—that made all kinds of products, from pails and tubs to tool handles and shingles, located on the river's edge. Almost all of the 2,000 people who lived in Peshtigo made a living from the forests that surrounded the town.

During the winter of 1870–71, little snow fell on the region's pine, oak, and tamarack forests. Spring brought far less rain than usual. As summer started, the forest-savvy folks of Peshtigo had sense enough to know that if drought set in, the town could be at risk, but no one was really worried. Loggers kept felling trees and piling up slash (treetops and branches). Railroad workers cleared brush and left it along the wayside. People piled bark against their homes for insulation.

May and June were parched; July saw a single cloudburst. In August, when springs started drying up and drinking water became scarce, a firebreak was cut between the forest and the town—just as a precaution. Loggers kept cutting trees, but with the woods bone-dry, they didn't dare burn the debris. By September, the forest was ankle-deep in dry slash.

JUDGEMENT DAY

In and around Peshtigo, small fires started popping up in the slashings, in the brush piles along railroad lines, and in the nearby peat bogs that had dried out during the scorching summer. The autumn air became so smoky that harbormasters on Lake Michigan blew their foghorns constantly to keep ships from running aground. On Sunday, October 8, 1871, a pall of brown smoke hung over Peshtigo. During the evening service at one of the town's two churches, the preacher reportedly said, "I have prophesied that the day would come when God would punish man's wanton destruction of the forests. That day is coming near!" As churchgoers headed home, a deathlike stillness hung over the town, but a half hour later, the eerie quiet was broken by an ominous roar from the south. Fire, whipped by the wind, was heading toward town.

RAINING FIRE

Near dusk, James Langworth, a farmer living on the outskirts of Peshtigo, saw dozens of rabbits, squirrels, chipmunks, and raccoons fleeing from the pines into the open area around his house. The warning gave him barely enough time to toss some valuables into a blanket, throw it over his shoulder, and run for his life. Not everyone was that lucky. As fire consumed the forest, it swept toward the farms outside of town. A farm family was later found huddled in a clearing near their home, apparently sure the flames would never reach them. They were wrong: The entire family had been incinerated.

Inside the town, encircled by the firebreak cut earlier in the summer, fathers reassured their families that the flames couldn't jump the fire line. What they didn't know was that a massive low-pressure system over the Midwest was turning what had been many small scattered forest fires into a single massive, unstoppable firestorm. At 9:00 p.m., pillars of fire towered into the sky south of town and church bells began to toll ominously. And then, in one survivor's words, "The heavens opened up and it rained fire."

NOWHERE TO RUN

The firestorm brought with it a cyclonic wind that exploded houses, sent roofs spinning through the air, and pulled flaming trees up by their roots. One eyewitness saw "large wooden houses torn from their foundations and caught up like straws by two opposing currents of air which raised them till they came in contact with the stream of fire." People panicked, rushing from both sides of town to the river that bisected Peshtigo.

Australian McDonald's restaurants offer the McOz, a cheeseburger with beets.

The fire sucked oxygen from the air, which became so superheated that some people literally burst into flame before they could reach the water. Those who managed to make it to the river converged on the wooden bridge from both sides, but the bridge was already burning. It strained and swayed as 300 frantic people streamed toward the middle. One survivor, a French missionary, reported seeing "cattle, vehicles, women, children, and men," on the bridge, "all pushing and crushing against each other." Unable to bear the strain, the flaming bridge collapsed, sending a roiling mass of people and animals into the river below. Many drowned. But what about the people who *didn't* reach the river? Peter Leschak, a firefighter and the author of *Ghosts of the Fireground*, says, "The ambient air temperature was probably between 500 and 700 degrees," hot enough to melt some metals.

ASH MONDAY

For a short time, a few firefighters tried to get the town's single horse-drawn steam pumper to pull water from the river, but the pump was designed for fighting structure fires, not for taking on a hurricane of flame. When the telegraph operator rushed out of the railroad station yelling, "Chicago is burning!" the firefighters lost hope. "Maybe the preacher was right," one of them said. "This is Judgement Day."

On Monday, October 9, 1871, Big John Mulligan, foreman of the Peshtigo lumber gang, wandered into Marinette, a village seven miles north of Peshtigo. Bewildered, covered with soot, his clothes nearly scorched from his body, he spread the news. "Peshtigo is gone," he said. "Not a building is standing. People are dead in the streets."

On Tuesday, October 10, while reporters nationwide rushed to file stories about the Great Chicago Fire, one reporter—from the *Marinette and Peshtigo Eagle*—went to view the devastation of Peshtigo. What he found: "Frightfully mutilated corpses of men, women, children, horses, oxen, cows, dogs, swine, and fowls. Every house, shed, barn, outhouse, or structure of any kind swept from the earth. No pen dipped in liquid fire can paint the scene or give the faintest impression of its horrors."

Survivors told horrific tales:

• One young woman's long hair caught fire, and the blaze sucked the air from her lungs, suffocating her instantly.

• A man jumped into a watering trough to escape the flames and was boiled alive.

• A farmer, realizing that it was too late to outrun the holocaust racing toward his farm, shot his cows, his family, and then himself.

• A group of men, women, and children huddled inside one of the town's few brick buildings. They were baked alive.

• A father slit his children's throats to spare them the agony of burning to death.

FOR WHOM THE BELL TOLLED

Everyone remembers the Great Chicago Fire, but few people (not counting anyone who went to elementary school in Wisconsin) have heard of Peshtigo. Was property damage what made Chicago's fire stand out? No. Each fire caused about $200 million in property loss. Size? No. Chicago's fire covered a little more than three square miles, while the Peshtigo Fire swept across 2,400 square miles and devastated 1.5 million acres of land—that's as much land as the entire state of Delaware.

Because Chicago was a major city with a population of 324,000, some might think that the Chicago Fire caused a far greater loss of life. It did not. Chicago's death toll: 250. The Peshtigo Fire death toll was somewhere between 1,200 and 2,400—but the exact number will never be known. Why? An 1873 report to the Wisconsin State Legislature offers this chilling explanation: "The very sands in the street were vitrified [turned to glass]. Many perished...of whom not a vestige remains."

So why *didn't* this monster firestorm blast Chicago's off the front page? Word of the Chicago fire went out quickly, but Peshtigo's single telegraph line burned along with everything else in town. When word finally reached the Wisconsin governor's mansion, the governor and most state officials were away, in Chicago, helping the victims there. America's forgotten fire has become a historical footnote to the Great Chicago Fire, yet it was, and remains to this day, the deadliest forest fire in modern world history.

Think a cow is the craziest theory behind the Chicago Fire? Turn to page 481.

THE QUICK BROWN FOX...

Pangrams *are sentences that contain all the letters of the alphabet. For example: "The quick brown fox jumped over the lazy dog." Other languages have them too...but we don't understand those languages, so we opted for these English translations.*

- **Italian:** "But the fox with her leap has reached the quiet Fido."
- **Icelandic:** "A cow in heat with such a limp would admittedly keep silent about drugs in sheep on a farm."
- **Portuguese:** "A curious little tortoise saw ten happy storks."
- **Danish:** "The quiz contestants ate strawberry with cream while Walter the circus clown played the xylophone."
- **Latvian:** "Glass shack gnomes steal Bach piano covers while inebriated."
- **Korean:** "The essential condition for a kiss is that lips meet and there is no special technique required."
- **Croatian:** "The overweight little schoolboy with a bike is holding hops and fine cotton in the pocket of his attire."
- **French:** "Mister Jack, you type much better than your friend Wolf."
- **Swedish:** "God help Zorn's maiden get trousers quickly."
- **Hebrew:** "A curious fish sailed the sea disappointedly, and suddenly found company."
- **Turkish:** "The patient in pajamas quickly trusted the swarthy driver."
- **Slovak:** "A flock of woodpeckers teach a horse to feed on bark."
- **Russian:** "So eat more of these soft French loaves, and have some tea!"
- **Polish:** "Come on, drop your sadness into the depth of a bottle!"
- **Romanian:** "Drinking whisky, the drunken jazzman threw up right in the tequila."
- **Bulgarian:** "For a moment I was in someone else's plush squeaking armchair."
- **Klingon:** "Because of your apparent audacity the depressed conqueror is willing to fight you."

NO DRIVE, NO FIVE!

More bowling lingo to help distract you from all those pumpkins you've been throwing lately.

Scenic Route: The long curving path a "hook" ball takes to the pins.

Suitcase Grip: Holding the ball as if it were a suitcase, to reduce the curve or hook.

Pin Monkey: A bowling-alley employee who watches the automatic pinsetter and ensures that it does not jam.

Beer Frame: The bowler who knocks down the fewest pins of a designated frame has to buy beer for the team.

Bowling with a House Ball: A term for any bowler who's having a bad night—i.e., bowling with one of the cheap balls the bowling alley provides for people who don't own a bowling ball.

Parking Lot: A bad lane, or other conditions that make accurate bowling impossible.

Pumpkin/Marshmallow: A ball that strikes the pins with little force.

Logs: Pins that seem "heavy" or difficult to knock down.

Greek Church: A split with three pins on one side of the lane and two pins on the other. (The pins are said to resemble the spires of a Greek Orthodox church.) Also known as the "big five."

Tap: A "perfect" hit that *should* have been a strike but left a single pin standing.

Part of the Building: A pin that's still standing after a tap is said to be "part of the building."

Chicken Wing: A throw made with your elbow sticking out, not down by your side.

Buzzard: Three splits in a row.

Pin Deck: The place where the pins are set up at the beginning of each frame.

Ten in the Pit: A strike that knocks all the pins off of the pin deck and into the sunken "pit" behind it.

No Drive, No Five: If a ball hits the 1 pin without enough power to knock down the 5 pin, you won't get a strike.

Serene and mean: When threatened, swans have been known to capsize boats.

DUMB CROOKS

More proof that crime doesn't pay.

SIGN OF THE TIMES

Residents of a Portland, Oregon, neighborhood were concerned about an alleged "drug house." They had tried numerous times to get the police to investigate it, but to no avail. Then, in late 2011, someone in the area saw a flier related to the house, removed it from a pole, and brought it to the cops. That was all they needed to secure a warrant. When officers raided the house, they discovered marijuana, heroin, a sawed-off shotgun, thousands of dollars in cash, and the materials for a meth lab. What did the flier say? "Heroin for Sale." And then it listed the address.

A CINDERELLA STORY

A thief in Severina, Brazil, stole a woman's purse and ran away. During his sprint, he put the purse strap in his mouth and dialed his cell phone (to order a pizza?). But the purse fell to the ground, and when he scooped it up, he left behind something else: his dentures. A witness found them and turned them over to the police. A brief investigation led officers to the home of Milton Cesar de Jesus, 34, who tried to keep his mouth closed. He was ordered to try on the dentures. They fit perfectly, and de Jesus was arrested.

TWO WRONGS

A 30-year-old metal thief broke into an abandoned hospital one night in Devon, England. He heard police entering the building, so he hid in an air duct. Meanwhile, a 19-year-old metal thief broke into the same hospital. *He* heard police enter the building, so he hid on the roof. Turned out that the two burglars hadn't heard the police—they'd heard each other. Neighbors heard the commotion and called the *actual* police. Both men were arrested.

THE LONG ARM OF THE LAWLESS

A 17-year-old crook tried to break into a Belfast, Ireland, home by reaching through the mail slot and unlocking the door. But his

Big deal? In a poll, 40% of Americans said they believe in the possible existence of Bigfoot.

arm got stuck. The homeowners arrived and called the police. Firefighters had to remove the door and then remove the mail slot frame from the door, but they still couldn't free the boy's arm. So he was taken to the police station—still stuck in the slot—and booked. His arm was finally freed that night; he was not.

LACK OF (BRAIN) POWER

First he charged his cell phone; then he got charged and put in a cell. The burglary occurred in early 2011 when a snowstorm knocked out power to thousands of homes in Silver Spring, Maryland. Cody Wilkins, 25, broke into a house (that still had power) and stole some jewelry. He also plugged in his phone charger because his own place had no power. But someone came home unexpectedly, and Wilkins had to make a quick getaway. Later, the homeowner discovered the strange phone plugged into the wall. That led police straight to Wilkins...and pictures on the phone's hard drive linked him to several more burglaries.

JACK ATTACK

A 41-year-old Brazilian man, Ricardo Sergio Freire de Barros, made his living by using fake IDs to open bank accounts and then get credit cards. The banks and the police were onto him, but he always managed to stay one step ahead...until he tried to open an account one day in 2011. What gave him away? The picture on the fake ID. It was movie star Jack Nicholson, who bears little resemblance to de Barros. The police were quietly alerted, and the joker was arrested.

SHOW NO MERCI

In 2010, Calgary Mountie Charanjit Meharu was called to a home where the owners claimed they'd been burgled. "I've lost everything!" said the woman. While her boyfriend was listing all of the missing items to Meharu, the woman received a call from her father in Quebec. Speaking French, she bragged on the phone that they'd hidden all of their jewelry and electronics, then staged the robbery as an insurance scam. When Meharu finished writing down his notes, he said to the couple, "*Merci beaucoup*," which means "Thank you very much" in French...which the Mountie could speak fluently. He arrested the couple for fraud.

Patrick Henry, of "Give me liberty or give me death" fame, owned 65 slaves.

MORE TUBA!

Looking for some trivia to amaze people with at your next party? Here's a list of actors who have played the tuba in a TV show or film!

GARY COOPER. Cooper is Longfellow Deeds in Frank Capra's 1936 classic, *Mr. Deeds Goes to Town*. Deeds is a tuba player from Mandrake Falls, Vermont, who unexpectedly inherits $20 million from a rich uncle. Deeds doesn't want money—he just wants to play his tuba. But he moves to New York City, where seemingly everyone tries to take advantage of him and his "hick" ways. In the end, Deeds outwits the city-slickers—and gets to play his tuba once in a while, too. *Mr. Deeds Goes to Town*—very likely the first tuba-player-based film of the sound era—won Capra his second Academy Award for Best Director, and earned Cooper his first-ever Best Actor nomination.

Tuba Bonus: Gary Cooper couldn't actually play the tuba. His part was recorded by a Hollywood studio tubist (that's what they're called) named Winthrop "Windy" Warner.

ROBERT WAGNER. Wagner is Willie Little, who plays the tuba for the Marine Corps Band in the 1952 film *Stars and Stripes Forever*. Not only that, he tinkers with the shape of a tuba so it wraps around his body and rests on his shoulder, making it easier to carry while marching. He names his new tuba-like instrument the "sousaphone"—after his conductor, John Philip Sousa, played in the film by Clifton Webb.

Tuba Bonus: The sousaphone is a real instrument with a sound that is virtually identical to the tuba, and it is commonly used in marching bands because it is (relatively) easy to carry. But the film, a biopic on the life of John Philip Sousa, bends the truth a bit: The first sousaphone was made in the 1890s by Philadelphia instrument-maker J. W. Pepper—at Sousa's request. Pepper named it in Sousa's honor.

DIANA RIGG. In a scene in a 1965 episode of *The Avengers* TV show titled "The Murder Market"—the very first with Diana Rigg in the role of Emma Peel—Peel sits on a sofa in John Steed's (Patrick Macnee) apartment, her long, nylon-clad legs stretched out before her, and, for no apparent reason, plays a few notes on a tuba. According to *TheAvengers.tv* website, Macnee was originally supposed to play the tuba, but suggested that Rigg do it instead. "The director balked, but Macnee insisted, and the result proved his instinct was right—thereby helping to shape Emma's character." (A tuba can be seen in many *Avengers* episodes, standing in a corner of Steed's living room with a bunch of carnations in its bell.)

Tuba Bonus: In a 1966 episode, a child's ball bounces into Steed's apartment. He picks it up...and realizes it's a bomb. So he pulls the flowers out of the tuba, throws the bomb into it, points it out the window, and KABOOM! (If you watch closely, you can see the prop bomb fall from the tuba as Steed points it out the window.)

BILL MURRAY. In the 2000 film *Charlie's Angels*, the Angels need a retinal scan of one of the bad guys. So they go to his house dressed in skimpy German milkmaid outfits and sing for him in his driveway while Bill Murray, in the role of Bosley, plays an "oom-pah" tune on a sousaphone...which happens to be equipped with a retinal scanner! Because the bad guy is so entranced by the Angels—Bosley is able to get the scan! (How did this movie not win an Oscar?)

Tuba Bonus: Murray's tuba part was played by Tommy Johnson, the "most heard tubist on the planet," according to his 2006 obituary in the *Washington Post*. Over a 50-year career, he played tuba in thousands of commercials, TV shows, and films, including *The Godfather* and *Jaws*, in which he plays the famous "bum-bum-bum-bum" sound you hear when the shark is near.

EXTRA TV AND FILM TUBA MOMENTS

• Hong Kong film legend Sammo Hung is the star of a 1986 screwball comedy in which he plays a police officer who would rather play the tuba than do police work. Title: *Where's Officer Tuba?* (This film is available in Chinese only.)

• In the 1944 Sherlock Holmes film *The Spider Woman*, Dr. Watson (Nigel Bruce) is seen playing the tuba in Holmes's study. He plays exactly 13 notes, is interrupted by a man from the "Bureau of Entomology" named Adam Gilflower, and never plays the tuba in that film—or any other Sherlock Holmes movie—again.

BISCUIT = COOKIE

Some words in British-English are different from American-English. The British "biscuit" is our "cookie," for example. Here are a few you might not have heard.

Noughts and Crosses: Tic-Tac-Toe

Ground floor: First floor (their "first floor" is our "second floor")

Baps: Hamburger Buns

Silencer: Muffler (on a car)

Welsh dresser: China hutch

Trolley: Grocery cart

Fairy cake: Cupcake

Aubergine: Eggplant

Zebra: Pedestrian crosswalk

Aluminium (pronounced al-yoo-MIN-ee-um): Aluminum

Cooker: Stove

Fish fingers: Fish sticks

To let: For rent

Girl Guides: Girl Scouts

Mince: Ground beef

Beetroot: Beet

Draughts: Checkers (the game)

Earth, or earthed: Ground, or grounded (electrical)

Bank holiday: Legal holiday

Tin: Can (of food)

Flyover: Overpass

Bedsit: Efficiency apartment

Fir apple: Pinecone

Tailback: Traffic jam

Articulated lorry: Semi-truck

Footpath: Sidewalk

Gaol: Jail

Caravan: Trailer

Drawing pin: Thumbtack

Treacle: Molasses

Dummy: Pacifier (for a baby)

Valve: Vacuum tube

Swede: Rutabaga (from "Swedish turnip")

Caretaker: Janitor

Spanner: Wrench

Torch: Flashlight

Anti-clockwise: Counter-clockwise

Peckish: Hungry

Full stop: Period (at the end of a sentence)

Boiler suit: Overalls

Facia pocket: Glove compartment

Gammon: Ham

Toilet: Bathroom

THE WORST BUSINESS DECISION EVER? PART II

Here's the second part of our story of one of the unluckiest executives in the history of Silicon Valley. (Part I is on page 199.)

SIGNED, SEALED, AND DELIVERED

Ron Wayne wasn't a lawyer, but he had "some background at writing in legalese," as he puts it in his book, *Adventures of an Apple Founder*. So when Steve Jobs and Steve Wozniak were ready to launch Apple Computer, he drafted the company's founding partnership agreement himself. In addition to dividing ownership between the three partners 45%–45%–10% as agreed, the contract stipulated that any expenditure of more than $100 would need the consent of at least two of the partners. The three men signed the contract on April 1, 1976, and Wayne filed it with the county registrar the next day. Apple Computer was in business.

BOARD OF EDUCATION

Wozniak and Jobs printed up their first batch of Apple circuit boards and brought them to the Homebrew Computer Club. They sold quite a few. One of their most promising prospects should have been Paul Terrell, owner of a small chain of electronics hobby stores called the Byte Shop. But Terrell wasn't interested, giving Jobs his business card and telling him to "keep in touch."

The next day, Jobs walked (barefoot) into the Byte Shop. "I'm keeping in touch," he told Terrell, and tried again to sell him some circuit boards. Terrell still wasn't interested. What he wanted, he explained to Jobs, was fully-assembled computers. He wanted 50 of them, and he was willing to pay $500 apiece, in cash, as soon as they were delivered.

In the years to come, Steve Jobs would be hailed as a visionary, and he was, after all, the guy who thought that pre-printed circuit boards would sell. But in those early days, even he didn't realize that there was a market for assembled computers, at least not until Terrell placed his order.

In the last section of the Declaration of Independence, "British" is misspelled as "Brittish."

THE HARD PART(S)

Wozniak, who made $24,000 a year at Hewlett-Packard, didn't need a computer to tell him that 50 computers purchased for $500 each added up to $25,000—not a bad sale for a company launched with $1,750 raised from the sale of an old Volkswagen van and a calculator just a few weeks earlier.

But there was a catch: The computer chips and other parts that were needed to build those 50 computers were going to cost about $15,000. Where would they get the money? Jobs tried to borrow it from a bank, but, not surprisingly for a man who still wasn't bathing regularly, he couldn't get a loan. He finally found a school friend whose father was willing to lend him $5,000 for three months, and he also talked an electronics company into selling him parts on 30-day credit.

PAYBACK

The clock was ticking. Apple Computer, with three partners and no employees, had 30 days to assemble and deliver 50 computers, something it had never done before. Then it had to collect $25,000, and pay for the parts. The $5,000 loan would come due 60 days after that. If there were any snags and the creditors weren't paid on time, they were likely to sue Jobs, Wozniak, and Wayne to recover their money.

And that's when Wayne really began to think about what it meant to be a partner in Apple Computer. According to the contract that he himself had drawn up only days before, Apple was legally defined as a partnership, not a corporation—and there's a big difference. Corporations have limited liability. If you buy shares in a corporation and the corporation goes bankrupt, your shares are wiped out and the money you've invested is gone. But that's it—creditors who are owed money by the corporation cannot seize personal assets, such as your house and bank accounts, to settle the corporation's debts.

A partnership is different: Each partner is personally liable for debts incurred by the partnership. It doesn't necessarily matter if they're major partners or minor partners, either. Wayne may have only had a 10 percent stake in Apple Computer, but he was just as liable for the company's debts as either Jobs or Wozniak. If they didn't have assets that could be seized to pay Apple's debts, the

It took 38 years for radio to reach 50 million users, and just 5 years for the Internet to do it.

creditors would likely try to seize Wayne's assets instead. In fact, Jobs and Wozniak *didn't* have any assets. That meant that, in effect, Ron Wayne was assuming 100 percent of the risk in exchange for 10 percent of the profits...if any were ever to materialize.

NEVER MIND

The simplest explanation for why Apple Computer started out as a partnership and not as a corporation is that nobody thought the company would ever amount to much. Remember, when Wayne drafted the founding document, Apple was gearing up to sell circuit boards to hobbyists. A hot dog cart on a busy street corner would have had brighter prospects, so what difference did it make what kind of papers were drawn up? Partnerships are simpler than corporations, and their taxes are often lower. When a business is small and likely to stay that way, a partnership is a good way to go.

Besides, how much debt could a circuit-board company pile up? A lot more than Wayne had bargained for, now that Apple Computer was really going to sell computers. Wayne had been involved in business failures before: A few years earlier a slot machine company he owned had gone under, and it had taken him nearly two years to repay his investors. When Jobs racked up $20,000 in debts to finance a single sale, Wayne thought long and hard about whether or not he wanted to remain associated with Apple Computer...and decided the risk was too great.

SO LONG

On April 12, 1976, just eleven days after helping to found Apple, Wayne returned to the Santa Clara County courthouse and filed a "Statement of Withdrawal," which would alter the course of his life forever. "Wayne shall hereafter cease to function in the status of 'Partner,'" the document read, noting that Wayne had received $800 from Jobs and Wozniak for relinquishing his 10 percent stake. As far as anyone knows, he never owned a single share of Apple Computer again.

For more bad decisions, turn to Part III of the story on page 497.

FLUBBED HEADLINES

More actual newsaper headlines you might have to read twice.

Write-in voting gets woman shot at school board

"Girls Gone Wild" Sting Results in 16 Busts

Escaped wallaby caught using huge fishing net

Hamsters Can't Have Babies if Both Are the Same Sex

A's HOLE KEEPS GETTING DEEPER

Man Seeking Help for Dog Charged with DUI

Woman with Dog's Head Taken To Hospital

Actor Sent to Jail for Not Finishing Sentence

Homicide Victims Rarely Talk to Police

School Two Easy for Kids?

EDITOR'S WIFE RENTED TO 2 SUSPECTS, FBI SAYS

QUEEN VISITS IRISH NATIONAL STUD

Astronaut Welcomes Baby from Space

Virgin to offer service to South Florida

CASH IS THE KEY TO ENDING FINANCIAL WOES

ATLANTIC COAST TO REMAIN

London Olympics Will Take Place in London

GOP aims to use terrorism to keep control of Hill

SHERIFF WANTS DRUGS

Hooker named indoor athlete of the year

Navy SEALS Responsible for Getting Osama Bin Laden to Be Honored at Museum

Rancho Bernardo's only full-sized community newspaper! Disturbing to over 18,000 households per week!

2 LINE HEADLINE FOR DA PORN GUY GOES HERE

Nature's head game? Humans have more brain cells at the age of 2 than at any other time.

JACK TALES

You probably know him best for climbing a beanstalk and killing a giant, but were you aware that Jack—the hero of English folklore—also showed up in the the U.S. South?

DOWN HOME

Following in the footsteps of renowned English folklorist Cecil Sharp, who traveled the back roads of the Appalachian Mountains in 1916 in search of traditional British ballads, a young man named Richard Chase went to southern Virginia to hunt down some folk songs of his own. One day in 1935, after a folk music festival in Raleigh, North Carolina, Chase's quest took an unexpected turn when a local man named Marshall Ward told him that there were more than just songs being passed from generation to generation—there were tales, too. "Mostly," explained Ward, "about a boy named Jack."

Chase realized he'd struck gold—a living oral tradition of storytelling, much as Sharp had discovered the tradition of folk songs two decades earlier. He spent the next several years with Ward and his extended family, listening to Jack tales that they'd been telling for at least three generations, and writing down every word in his notebook as quickly and as faithfully as he could, dialect and all. He collected dozens of stories, including "Jack and the Giant's Newground," "Jack and the Robbers," "Hardy Hardhead," "Jack and King Marock," and "Soldier Jack." In 1943 Chase published them in a book called *The Jack Tales*.

JACK OF ALL TRADES

Before arriving in the New World, the legendary Jack was an English folk hero, usually depicted as a brave and honorable young squire. Variations of the character showed up in "Jack and the Beanstalk" and "Jack the Giant-Killer," as well as in fairy tales and nursery rhymes—"Jack and Jill," "Jack Be Nimble Jack Be Quick," "The House That Jack Built," "Little Jack Horner," "Jack Frost," "Jack Sprat," "Jack in the Box," and many more. One of the earliest is a 15th-century British tale called "Jack and His Stepdame," in which the hero is beaten by his stepmother, but shares his food with an old beggar who grants him three magic gifts that help him bring his stepmother her comeuppance.

Jesse James refused to rob a bank in McKinney, TX. (His favorite chili parlor was there.)

Fueled by cheaply printed chapbooks, stories of Jack abounded in England in the 1700s. So it's not surprising that British settlers brought Jack with them to America, mostly relegated to the pages of children's storybooks. In the isolated hills of Appalachia, Jack thrived as an oral tradition for nearly two centuries—until Chase shared the stories with the rest of the world.

YOU DON'T KNOW JACK

The same basic plots showed up in the Jack tales of Appalachia—the biggest difference was Jack himself. Unlike his "proper" British cousin, the American Jack is more like Mark Twain's Huckleberry Finn. He is an easygoing, overalls-wearing farm boy who aims to make his fortune by relying on wits and luck. Rather than a noble squire who rescues princesses, this Jack, as one tale goes, "tricks farmers out of their barefoot daughters." He's not above using unscrupulous means to get what he wants, but his manner is so breezy and likable, it's hard not to forgive him his escapades.

The American Jack tales are a fascinating blend of two very distinct cultures: Many of the plots, names, and settings are English, but the dialect and attitude are indisputably American. That blend can be heard in this excerpt from "Jack and the Bean Tree," when the giant totes a shotgun and roars:

> FEE! FAW! FUM!
>
> I smell the blood of an Englishmun.
>
> Bein' he dead or bein' he alive,
>
> I'll grind his bones
>
> To eat with my pones!

Want to read one of Jack's mischievous tales? Turn to page 489.

* * *

"One glance at a book and you hear the voice of another person, perhaps someone dead for 1,000 years. To read is to voyage through time."

—**Carl Sagan**

How about you? 33% of Americans wear pajamas to bed.

HOW TO MAKE A "SOLAR STILL"

Here's how to create an emergency supply of drinking water using just a few items from a hardware store.

WHAT YOU NEED

1. Piece of clear plastic tarp about 6 feet square
2. Piece of plastic tubing 1/4 inch in diameter and 4 to 6 feet in length
3. Cup or other small container
4. Shovel

WHAT TO DO

1. Find a sunny spot where the soil is moist and not too compact, so that it is easy to dig.
2. Dig a hole 3 feet across and 1-1/2 feet deep. In the center of the hole, dig another small hole just large enough to hold the cup, and put the cup in the smaller hole.
3. Run the tubing from the cup to outside the hole.
4. Cover the hole with the plastic tarp.
5. Find a small rock and place it in the center of the plastic tarp directly over the cup. The idea is for the rock to weigh down the plastic, forming a cone whose lowest point is directly over the cup.
6. Cover the edges of the tarp with dirt to secure it in place.

HOW IT WORKS

As sunlight warms the air inside the hole, the moisture in the soil evaporates and saturates the air in the hole with water vapor. Because the air outside the hole is cooler, the water vapor will condense on the inside of the plastic tarp and form droplets. Gravity will cause the droplets to run down the sides of the cone and drip into the cup. When it does, you can suck the water out through the tubing. Yield: up to one quart of distilled fresh water a day.

UNCLE JOHN'S STALL OF FAME

Four more honorees who've earned recognition for the unusual ways they put bathrooms and toilets to use.

Honoree: The Organizing Committee for the 2012 Summer Olympics, held in London

Notable Achievement: Quizzing 70,000 volunteers to make sure their bathroom manners were up to snuff

True Story: The Committee required Olympic volunteers to attend four-hour training sessions that included a "Diversity and Inclusion" multiple-choice quiz. Part of the quiz dealt with how to handle situations involving race, gender, religion, and sexuality that might arise when dealing with the public. For example, how should you give directions to the nearest restroom if the volunteer can't tell whether the questioner is male or female? Possible answers: a) "Panic…Explain politely that you do not know and sadly cannot be of assistance," b) "Ask them politely if they are male or female, so that you can direct them," or c) "Tell them where the male, female, and disabled toilets are, just in case." Correct answer: c. "I thought the training was unnecessary and they could have spent the money in other ways," one volunteer told *The Times*. "By the end of the process, people were choosing silly answers on purpose."

Honoree: Macquarie University in New South Wales, Australia

Notable Achievement: Teaching international students some important bathroom lessons

True Story: Anyone who's ever lived in a college dormitory knows that cleaning crews have their hands full keeping the restrooms clean in the best of times. In the fall of 2010, however, the contractor who cleans the restrooms at Macquarie University complained that the facilities had suddenly gotten much, *much* worse. Were vandals to blame? Possibly, but the cleaning contractor had another theory: Some international students at Macquarie hail from parts of the world where squat toilets are the norm, and may be unfamiliar with how to use a "sit-down" toilet. Too embarrassed to ask for help, the contractor speculated, the students may have climbed up onto the toilet seats and squatted there. If you've ever tried to answer nature's call in such a fashion, you know that getting your aim right is just about impossible ...hence the nature and the scale of the mess facing the cleaners at Macquarie.

As far-fetched as the theory may have seemed, the university decided to print up some posters explaining how to use a western toilet. On the poster, a figure shown squatting on a toilet seat is crossed out in red. Another figure, squatting on the floor *next* to a toilet, is also crossed out. Arrows point away from these figures toward a third figure seated correctly on a toilet. The university posted the diagrams inside toilet cubicles on the door...and the problem vanished overnight.

Honoree: Freeman Anthony, an engineer with the Bellingham, Washington, Public Works Department

Notable Achievement: Blazing new trails with old toilets

True Story: In 2011 Anthony got a call from a local nonprofit group called Sustainable Connections. They were helping to replace more than 400 old toilets in public housing units with modern low-flow models and wanted to keep the old toilets out of landfills. But how? Anthony thought it might be possible to smash the toilets and use the porcelain pieces as a substitute for the gravel in concrete. A local gravel company agreed to give it a try. They tossed the toilets into their concrete crusher, and created enough gravel-sized chunks to fill a dump truck. These were then mixed with sand and cement to make what Anthony calls "poticrete," which he used to pave part of a bike and walking trail that runs through the city. The trail was completed in September 2011 and dedicated with a ceremonial toilet seat set into the wet poticrete (like a star on the Hollywood Walk of Fame). The surface is being monitored to see if it holds up over time. If it does, toilet-infused sidewalks, foot and bike paths, and possibly even roadways may be coming to a neighborhood near you.

Honoree: Fans of the Winnipeg Jets hockey team

Notable Achievement: Circulating a pee-tition to improve the

The inside of your elbow is a *ginglymus*; the back of your knee is your *popliteal*.

public restrooms at home games

True Story: The Jets used to play in the Winnipeg Arena but now play at MTS Centre. The men's rooms at the Centre are a little more upscale than the ones at the Arena: Instead of the old "trough-style" urinals that accommodate a dozen or more people at a time, the new restrooms have standard urinals that only one person can use at a time. That's good news for people suffering from "stage fright" (difficulty peeing in the presence of others), but the problem is there aren't enough urinals to go around. A typical MTS Centre restroom has only four, and the lines to use them can get pretty long, especially in between game periods.

In December 2011, the fans started an online petition to bring back the troughs. "After finishing four-plus beers, the average Joe has to go do his business," the petition reads. "The new washroom service in MTS Centre cannot handle the capacity." And capacity isn't the only issue. Some people actually prefer the camaraderie of the trough to the loneliness and isolation of a one-man urinal. "My fondest memory of the trough would be watching the cigarette butt from the guy around the corner finally go floating by," one signer of the petition commented. "Oh, the good old days…"

Update: So did the petition do any good? Nope. "We're comfortable with the washroom facilities as we have them in the building. I don't think at any point we will be bringing the trough back," a Jets spokesperson told *The Winnipeg Sun.*

* * *

LEGAL EAGLES

"Law: The only game where the best players get to sit on the bench."

—American proverb

"Judge: a law student who marks his own papers."

—H.L. Mencken

"A real patriot is the fellow who gets a parking ticket and rejoices that the system works."

—Bill Vaughan

BUSTED ON FACEBOOK

At last count, Uncle John had more than 13,000 fans on Facebook. If you log on and discover that that number has shrunk, it'll probably be because Uncle John posted a really boneheaded status update or photo, just like these people.

UNFRIEND

Friend: Dylan Osborn, 37, of Buckinghamshire, England

Story: Shortly after Osborn joined Facebook in 2007, a window appeared on the screen asking if he wanted to send "friend requests" to everyone on his e-mail list. He clicked "Yes." Result: A friend request went to his estranged wife, Claire Tarbox...with whom he was under court order to not have any contact.

Busted! Tarbox called police, and Osborn was arrested for sending the friend request and then sentenced by a judge to 10 days in jail. Osborn claimed that he hadn't understood how Facebook works and had no idea the request would be sent to Tarbox. "I didn't even know she *had* a Facebook account," he told reporters after his release. "To be honest, I don't think the judge understood how it works, either."

LUNCH LIZARDS

Friend: Vanessa Starr Palm, 23, of Illinois, and Alexander Daniel Rust, 24, of Indiana

Story: While Palm and Rust were on vacation in the Bahamas in 2009, they saw a wild iguana. They killed it. And then they cooked and ate it. And they took photos of the whole process—and posted them on their Facebook profiles.

Busted! Iguanas are endangered species in the Bahamas. Someone contacted authorities about the photos, and Bahamian police tracked down and arrested the couple. They were released from jail on $500 bail and eventually paid fines for their illegal meal.

DEAD WRONG

Friend: Mark Musarella, 46, of Staten Island, New York

Story: Musarella was an emergency medical technician with the Richmond University Medical Center. When he was called to an

If a monkey steals your ball while you're golfing in the kingdom of Tonga, there's no penalty.

apartment where a 26-year-old woman had been murdered, he took a photo of the dead body with his cell phone...and (you know what's coming next) posted the photo to his Facebook page.

Busted! One of Musarella's friends saw the photo and called the hospital where he worked. He was immediately fired, then arrested on charges of official misconduct and disorderly conduct. He was sentenced to 200 hours of community service. Musarella—a former highly decorated NYPD detective—also lost his EMT license.

THE KING AND I

Friend: Fouad Mourtada, 26, of Casablanca, Morocco

Story: Mourtada joined Facebook sometime in 2007, under a fake name. Whose name? Moulay Rachid—brother of Morocco's King Mohammed VI, and second in line to the Moroccan throne.

Busted! In February 2008, Mourtada was arrested. He confessed to having made the fake Facebook profile, explaining that he'd done it "to get girlfriends." Mourtada was quickly tried, convicted of "modifying and falsifying information technology data and usurping an official's identity," and sentenced to three years in prison. A month later, after intense international pressure at what was viewed as an unfair trial, "Prince" Fouad Mourtada was released ...after receiving a royal pardon.

FACEBOOK CROOK

Friend: Paul Franco, 38, of Queens, New York

Story: In February 2010, Franco hacked the Facebook account of his ex-girlfriend, Jessica Zamora-Anderson...and changed her sexual preference to "gay." Then he changed her password—and proceeded to hold the account hostage, demanding hundreds of dollars from her if she wanted it back. Zamora-Anderson had met Franco 16 months earlier...on Facebook. He posed as a 29-year-old English teacher at Queen's College, where she was taking classes. They started dating, and she eventually found out that he wasn't a teacher, but continued dating him because he claimed he had a tape of them having sex and said he'd put it on the Internet if she left him.

Busted! Zamora-Anderson finally had enough and called the police. Franco was arrested, and Zamora-Anderson got her Facebook account back. (And it turns out Franco didn't have a sex tape.)

Cadbury sells 200 million Creme Eggs in the U.K. each year—more than 3 per citizen.

SMOKIN'

Friend: Rachel Stieringer, 19, of Keystone Heights, Florida

Story: In July 2010, she posted a photo of her 11-month-old son on her Facebook profile. In the picture, the diapered boy appears to be smoking a bong. The photo became an Internet sensation.

Busted! A concerned citizen called a Florida child abuse hotline. A police investigation was started, and in August, Stieringer turned herself in to police. She said the photo was just a joke…and that the bong was "only used for tobacco." Stieringer was arrested, and Florida children's services ordered that both Stieringer and her son be tested for drugs. The baby tested negative, fortunately, but Stieringer did not. She was arrested for possessing drug paraphernalia and was ordered to attend both drug and parenting classes.

POOR JUDGEMENT

Friend: Steven Mulhall, 21, of Coral Springs, Florida

Story: Mulhall was in a Broward County, Florida, court on February 23, 2012, on a theft charge. That same day, someone noticed that the nameplate from the door of Judge Michael Orlando disappeared. Who could have stolen it?

Busted! In March an anonymous tipster called Broward County Sheriff Al Lamberti. The tipster advised him to go to a certain Facebook page. Lamberti did, and saw a photo of Steven Mulhall…proudly displaying the nameplate of Judge Michael Orlando. Mulhall was arrested. "The nameplate is like only $40," Lamberti told reporters, "not that big of a crime—but what an idiot. He's got multiple convictions for petty theft, so now this is a felony."

*   *   *

WHO'S UNAVAILABLE

Organizers of the 2012 Olympic Games in London sent a request to the rock band the Who to perform at the closing ceremony. They specifically asked if "drummer Keith Moon would be available." The band's manager replied, "Keith now resides in Golders Green crematorium, having lived up to the Who's anthemic line, 'I hope I die before I get old.'" Moon died in 1978.

The refrigerators Americans buy in a week would make a tower more than 80 miles high.

THE MOTHER SAUCES

Before refrigeration, sauces originated as a way to hide the taste of food that was staring to spoil. Then people started tinkering with them, and things got a lot tastier. Here are the five sauces that food historians say are the source of all other sauces that followed.

FLAVOR SAVOR

A skilled *saucier* ("sauce cook") can create thousands of sauces, many with similar ingredients. In the 19th century, Marie-Antoine Carême (1784–1833), the French chef credited as the father of gourmet, or *haute cuisine*, classified all sauces under four categories that became known as the "Mother Sauces." (His other claim to fame: inventing the chef's hat.)

Carême's four sauces were updated a century later by another legendary French chef, Auguste Escoffier (1846–1935), who modernized French cuisine in the late 1800s. Escoffier reclassified one of Carême's sauces, and then added another to get the five Mother Sauces that chefs recognize today.

1) BÉCHAMEL (White Sauce)

Béchamel (BEH-shah-mehl) is the most common and easiest to prepare of the Mother Sauces. Named for the man who perfected it, King Louis XIV's steward Louis de Béchamel (1603–1703), this sauce is a *butter-roux* (flour and butter, combined to a paste over low heat) mixed with milk. It can be thickened by adding more butter and flour. Béchamel is the base of most cheese sauces, including the cheesy part of macaroni and cheese, as well as Alfredo, and the cheese sauce used in Welsh Rarebit.

2) VELOUTÉ ("Velvety")

To make a *velouté* (veh-loo-TAY), start with a white soup stock (vegetables and meat cooked in water, then strained out), thicken it by adding roux, then let it simmer. Chicken velouté is the most common, but veloutés are commonly made with veal or fish stock. If a chef adds egg yolks, the result is an *allemande*, one of Carême's four original sauces, which Escoffier reclassified. Chefs recommend pairing a velouté with a dish made from the same thing; chicken

The St. Louis Gateway Arch has 900 tons of stainless steel, the most of any structure ever.

velouté should be used on chicken, veal velouté on veal, and so on. The most common veloute: white wine sauce.

3) ESPAGNOLE (Brown Sauce)

Espagnole (es-pah-NYOHL) is prepared like velouté, but with carmelized meat and vegetables to give the sauce a brown color. Sometimes tomato paste or puree is used, but an espagnole is typically made without tomatoes. The sauce gets its thickness by *reduction*: boiling it quickly so the water evaporates but the flavor stays concentrated. Common espagnoles: Madeira sauce, Sauce Diane, and demi-glace, made by adding red wine to the recipe, then reducing the sauce until it is thick enough to coat a spoon.

4) HOLLANDAISE

A rich, creamy yellow sauce made of clarified butter, egg yolk, and lemon juice, hollandaise is the most difficult of the Mother Sauces to make because it's an *emulsion*, meaning the ingredients are naturally inclined to separate. The secret to making a good hollandaise is to pour the butter slowly into the egg yolks while quickly stirring the mixture with a whisk. Chefs use clarified butter because whole butter contains milk solids which tend to break the emulsion. Hollandaise is the key ingredient in Eggs Benedict, and it's also the sauce in Filet Oscar, which is a filet mignon topped with crab meat and asparagus. Other emulsions similar to Hollandaise include mayonnaise, tartar sauce, and Béarnaise.

5) TOMATE (Tomato)

Auguste Escoffier added *sauce tomate* as the fifth Mother Sauce. In addition to tomatoes, his recipe calls for salt pork, carrots, onions, butter, veal stock, garlic, roux, and a few seasonings, but a simple tomato sauce doesn't need much more than tomatoes and seasonings. As with other sauces, the roux in a tomato sauce is a thickener, but the flesh of a tomato is hearty enough that a thickener isn't always necessary. One of the easiest sauces to create, tomato sauce is extremely versatile and can be paired with almost any meat, fish, or pasta. It's also easy to freeze and store, making it one of the most-used sauces in the culinary world. Common tomato sauces: Creole and Provençale, as well as Italian Carbonara, Pomodoro, and Marinara sauces.

Bird brains? Californians eat 3 lb. more turkey per year than the average American does.

AFTER THE CIVIL WAR

Ever wonder what happened to the major players in America's worst internal conflict? We did, and thought you might like to know, too.

JEFFERSON DAVIS

Claim to Fame: President of the Confederate States of America

After the War: The former president refused to sign the oath of allegiance that would have returned his U.S. citizenship. He ended up selling life insurance for a living, but the company he founded failed. More than 100 years after the Civil War ended, another southern president, Jimmy Carter, posthumously gave Davis back his citizenship.

SGT. BOSTON CORBETT

Claim to Fame: Shot and killed John Wilkes Booth

After the War: Corbett was arrested for disobeying orders *not* to shoot Booth, but then was released by Secretary of War Edwin Stanton. Corbett went on to become something of a hero to northerners until 1887, when, as an assistant doorkeeper for the Kansas Legislature, he decided the other officers were snubbing him. Corbett drew his revolver and chased them from the building. He ended up in the Topeka Asylum for the Insane.

MAJ. GEN. PHILIP H. SHERIDAN

Claim to Fame: Crushed Confederate forces in Virginia and used "scorched earth" tactics to destroy the South's food supply

After the War: Sheridan boasted that he'd left the Shenandoah Valley so devastated that "even a crow would be compelled to carry his own food." He took that philosophy to the Great Plains, where he defeated the Sioux by driving the American bison—the natives' primary food supply—nearly to extinction. Ironically, years later, he argued for the expansion of Yellowstone Park to provide protection for the buffalo. When Congress stripped Yellowstone's funding in 1886, Sheridan led the 1st U.S. Cavalry into the park and turned it into a military protectorate. The cavalry stayed until 1916, when the National Park Service took over.

The ancient Etruscans (northern Italy) were the first to use gold in dentistry (circa 600 B.C.).

GEN. ROBERT E. LEE

Claim to Fame: Commander of the Army of Northern Virginia; considered to be the Confederacy's greatest military leader

After the War: Even though the war left him broke and homeless, Lee turned down a chance to head the notorious Ku Klux Klan. Instead, he accepted an offer to serve as president of Washington College (now Washington and Lee University) in Lexington, Virginia. The school was as strapped for funds as the former general, and the trustees hoped his fame would help them raise money. It did. Within five years, enrollment had grown from 50 to nearly 400. Today, with more than 1,700 undergrads, WLU is ranked in the top 20 of the nation's best liberal arts colleges.

GEN. JAMES LONGSTREET

Claim to Fame: General Lee's right-hand man and second in command of the Confederate forces at the Battle of Gettysburg

After the War: Before the war, Longstreet was close friends with Ulysses S. Grant. He introduced Grant to his cousin, Julia Dent. When they married in 1848, Longstreet was part of the wedding party. After the war, Longstreet renewed his friendship with Grant. In 1880 Grant talked President Hayes into appointing Longstreet Ambassador to the Ottoman Empire (now Turkey). Longstreet's next post: Postmaster of Gainesville, Georgia.

GEN. ALEXANDER SCHIMMELFENNIG

Claim to Fame: Accepted the surrender of Charleston, South Carolina, on behalf of Union forces. But that's only part of the story. Not only did Schimmelfennig have the longest last name of any brigadier general, he may have held the record for injuries and illnesses. Early in the war, the general injured his ankle in a fall from his horse and contracted smallpox while recovering from the injury. He went on to Gettysburg, where he was accidentally hit over the head with the butt of a musket, knocked unconscious, and woke up to find himself behind Confederate lines. He hid behind a woodpile for three days until the Rebels retreated, and then returned to his troops only to fall victim to dysentery and malaria.

After the War: The Confederates officially surrendered on April 18, 1865. That same month, Schimmelfennig contracted tuberculosis. He died five months later.

Pour me a tall one! Only U.S. president who was a licensed bartender: Abraham Lincoln.

MORE REAL-LIFE SUPERHEROES

These costumed crusaders (and villains) aren't afraid to risk danger and public ridicule in the pursuit of justice. *(The first installment is on page 157.)*

THE MASKED VIPER (Columbia, Tennessee)

Secret Identity: Christian Tyler Hardee, 20, a chemistry and art major at Union University in nearby Jackson

Costume: A green-and-black bodysuit and matching mask that covers his entire head, like Spider-Man's. The Masked Viper carries plastic fighting sticks, ninja throwing stars, and a cell phone (to call the actual police if he sees any crimes being committed).

Details: Hardee patrolled the streets of Columbia in full costume until July 2010, when police told him that a city ordinance forbids the wearing of face-obscuring masks in public. Since then, the Masked Viper has patrolled without his mask. "I'm just a guy trying to do what's right, in tights," he says.

SHADOW HARE (Cincinnati, Ohio)

Secret Identity: A male in his early 20s, real name unknown

Costume: A black bodysuit with a Shadow Hare logo on the chest, a black cape, and a black-and-silver mask that covers his head. Shadow Hare carries handcuffs, pepper spray, and a Taser, and has been seen patrolling the city on a Segway.

Details: "I've stopped many evildoers...such as drug dealers, muggers, rapists, and crazy hobos with pipes," he writes on his Myspace page. Shadow Hare has two archenemies: 1) The High Noon Tortoise, who has vowed (on YouTube) to loiter at high noon "at every convenience store in the greater Cincinnati area" until Shadow Hare reveals his secret identity, and 2) The Consortium of Evil, a shadowy group that posted an ad on Craigslist offering a $10 reward to anyone who reveals Shadow Hare's real name. (No takers so far.) "I've heard about the lame bounty on my identity," said Shadow Hare. "My opinion is this: Who cares?"

Most takes for a single scene in a movie: 2,900, in the Jackie Chan film *Dragon Lord* (1982).

THE STATESMAN (Birmingham, England)

Secret Identity: Scott Cooke, a banker in his mid-20s and former soldier in the U.K.'s Territorial Army

Costume: A long-sleeved Union Jack shirt, black army pants, black combat boots, a black eye mask, and a black utility belt containing a flashlight, first aid kit, notepad, and a cell phone. The Statesman hides his costume beneath a trench coat, which he throws off when he springs into action.

Details: Cooke lives in West Heath, but patrols nearby Birmingham. When he started, he didn't tell his mom or his girlfriend what he was up to in the middle of the night; they thought he was sneaking out to drink or play poker with friends. They didn't find out he was a superhero until London's *Daily Mail* newspaper profiled him in February 2011. The press Cooke has received since then has been unflattering: The *Sunday Mercury* reviewed local statistics and found that during the month of January 2011, when Cooke was on patrol over in Birmingham, 99 crimes were committed in his own community of West Heath, including 10 burglaries and four violent crimes. The *Sun* reported that his mother still did his laundry, and nicknamed him "The Phan-tum" because of his chubby build. "If he does want to clean up the streets of Birmingham I am behind him all the way," a neighbor told the *Mercury*. "Maybe he can start by cleaning his garden as he has let it get a bit shabby recently. There are potato chip packets everywhere."

DARK GUARDIAN (New York City)

Secret Identity: Chris Pollack, 27, a martial arts instructor

Costume: A red-and-black leather motorcycle suit worn over a bulletproof vest. He carries mace, a flashlight, and a first aid kit.

Details: Pollack has been a superhero since 2003 and specializes in keeping drug dealers out of Washington Square Park in New York's Greenwich Village neighborhood. His technique: He sneaks up on the drug dealers at night, either alone or with other superheroes, shines flashlights in their eyes, and shouts, "THIS IS A DRUG-FREE PARK!" In one raid in 2009, he and a dozen other costumed superheroes used bullhorns and floodlights to drive druggies out of the park. "Some may call me a hero, a vigilante, or a nut job," he said, "but I fight for all that's right. I will drive myself into the ground to make this world a better place."

Coca-Cola and Pepsi are sold in every country in the world except North Korea.

THE HUMAN SHRUB (Colchester, England)

Secret Identity: A local resident, 39, real name unknown

Costume: A military camouflage suit that looks like a giant bush, worn with gardening gloves. The Human Shrub's only weapons: garden tools. His enemies: tight-fisted local officials.

Details: When the Colchester town council proposed tearing out 20 percent of the town's rosebushes and shrubbery as a cost-saving measure, the Human Shrub protested the decision by parading in front of the town hall in full shrubbery regalia. The bad publicity he generated pressured the council into reversing its decision, but when it continued to neglect the town's planters, the Human Shrub replanted them with his own flowers and bushes in protest.

The Human Shrub also uses Facebook to rally "flash mobs" of his supporters to pull weeds and tend neglected patches of land that are supposed to be maintained by the council. At these events the similarly dressed "Mrs. Shrub" feeds the volunteers tarts. "I have no idea who he is," one council member told *The Daily Mail.* "I could go up and tear all his shrubbery off to find out, but I might be arrested for assaulting a bush."

TERRIFICA (Brooklyn, New York)

Secret Identity: Sarah, 23, an employee of a computer consulting company, full name unknown

Costume: Red tights, red knee-high leather boots, a red headband and red cape, topped off with a gold bra, gold eye mask, platinum-blonde wig, and a red utility belt containing a cell phone, camera, log book, pepper spray, condoms, Terrifica "fortune cards," and Smarties (for energy).

Details: Beginning in 1995 and continuing for a decade (she is now retired), Terrifica staked out Brooklyn-area bars and nightclubs to rescue tipsy women in danger of going home with men they'd just met. When she found one, she'd give the woman advice, a condom, and one of her fortune cards printed with tips on how to decline sexual advances and get out of relationships. "I protect the single girl living in the big city," she told ABC News in 2004. "I do this because women are weak. They are easily manipulated, and they need to be protected from themselves and most certainly from men and their ill intentions toward them.

People are happiest when they're alone and living their solitary lives."

Terrifica's archenemy (besides intoxicated, amorous couples and bartenders who thought she was bad for business) was "Fantastico," a ladies' man who frequented the same watering holes and had Terrifica pull more than one woman from his clutches. "She seems to have it in for men," Fantastico told ABC News. "I'm convinced she is loveless and would love to have the rest of the city as loveless and miserable as she is."

And a real-life supervillain…

THE GOLDEN DON (Big Sky, Montana)

Secret Identity: Unknown

Costume: A dark hooded cloak and a golden mask that covers his face

Details: What's a superhero without supervillains? In the comic-book world, superheroes like Batman often arise in response to evil that has gotten out of control. In the real world, real-life supervillains like the Golden Don arise in order to poke fun at make-believe superheros. The Golden Don, a member of a group known as The Roaming Eye of Doom, says he was "born of hatred for silly people who dress up and go out and 'fight crime.' We want to disrupt, trip-up, and generally distract the silly and implausible villain community at large. And make low-quality but funny videos." Another villain group to watch for: the Ruthless Organization Against Citizen Heroes (ROACH).

* * *

OOPS!

In July 2012 Canadian Dale Whitmell, 40, was camping near Anjigami Lake in Ontario, when he tried to kill a mouse—and shot himself in the forehead instead. Whitnell had attempted to kill the mouse by crushing it with the butt of his rifle, which caused the rifle to go off. He was treated at a nearby hospital, after which police charged him with careless use of a firearm.

NAME THAT PRESIDENT

U.S. presidents can award the Presidential Medal of Freedom—America's highest civilian honor—to anyone they choose. Take this quiz to find out if their choices are predictably partisan or not. (You may be surprised.)

THE PRESIDENTS

Which of these U.S. presidents hung the Presidential Medal of Freedom around the neck of which honoree?

- Richard Nixon
- Jimmy Carter
- Gerald Ford
- George H. W. Bush
- Bill Clinton
- George W. Bush
- Barack Obama

THE RECIPIENTS

1. BOB DYLAN

The President said: "No one ever picks up a guitar thinking, 'You know what, if I keep this up, I could get a medal in the White House.'"

2. MARGARET THATCHER

The President said: "Never, ever will it be said that Margaret Thatcher went wobbly."

3. GEORGE H.W. BUSH

The President said: "When democratic revolution swept across Eastern Europe, President Bush made possible an achievement once thought impossible, ending the Cold War without firing a shot."

4. BOB DOLE

The President said: "In this city often known for taking itself too seriously, we are all better for his fine sense of humor." Dole's reply? "I had a dream that I would be receiving something from the president. But I thought it would be the front door key."

5. GEN. TOMMY FRANKS

The President said: "At a recent high school reunion, Tommy's old principal told the general, 'You weren't the brightest bulb in the socket,' to which the general replied, 'Ain't this a great country?'"

6. DAVE THOMAS (Founder of Wendy's)

The President said: "Americans are not always in the mood for exquisite meals—sometimes all they want is a hamburger at the drive-up window."

7. GERALD FORD

The President said: "I invited all the presidents to spend the night in the White House. I thought that would be a neat thing. President and Mrs. Ford said that they were going to spend the night in the hotel room where they had spent their first night as a married couple nearly 50 years before. I love that."

8. DUKE ELLINGTON

The President said: "Would you all stand and sing 'Happy Birthday' to him? And, please, in the key of G."

9. JULIETTE GORDON LOW (Founder of the Girl Scouts)

The President said: "She flew airplanes. She went swimming. She experimented with electricity for fun."

10. LUCILLE BALL

The President said: "She was like everyone's next-door neighbor, only funnier."

11. HYMAN RICKOVER

The President said: "This is one of the few times when Admiral Rickover has walked toward me that I didn't tremble in my shoes."

12. JOHN WAYNE

The President said: "Through his countless film roles, 'The Duke' still leads millions on heroic adventures on behalf of fairness and justice."

13. RICHARD PETTY

The President said: "I'm going to keep this short today because afterwards Richard Petty and I are going to take a few laps around the Ellipse in number 43."

14. GEN. COLIN POWELL

The President said: "Powell has won the Presidential Medal of Freedom twice—once with distinction. I'm not sure what happened the other time."

Answers are on Page 602.

THE STRANGE FATE OF EBEN BYERS

Some people become famous for the way they lived their lives...and some become famous for the way they, well, shuffled off this mortal coil. Eben Byers is one such unfortunate soul. (His coil glowed.)

FALL GUY

In November 1927, a wealthy industrialist named Eben Byers was returning from the annual Harvard-Yale football game aboard a special chartered train. Yale won the game 14–0, and Byers was a Yale alumnus. It's not clear whether the celebratory atmosphere aboard the train (or Byers's reputation as a ladies' man) had anything to do with it, but sometime during the trip he fell out of his upper sleeping berth and injured his arm. The injury interfered with Byers's golf game and his love life. He visited one doctor after another, but no one could ease his pain. Then a physician in Pittsburgh suggested he try Radithor, a patent medicine (which consisted of little more than the element radium in a distilled water solution).

Radithor was a product of the Bailey Radium Laboratory of East Orange, New Jersey, founded by one "Dr." William Bailey, a Harvard dropout who falsely claimed to have a medical degree from the University of Vienna. In 1915 he had served time in jail for mail fraud. A few years later, after a stint peddling strychnine, the active ingredient in rat poison, as an aphrodisiac under the brand name Las-I-Go For Superb Manhood, he began selling Radithor as "Pure Sunshine in a Bottle." He claimed it would cure more than 150 different ailments.

HOT STUFF

Drinking radioactive water to improve health may sound crazy today, but in the 1920s, when much less was known about radiation, it seemed to make sense. People had long wondered what gave natural hot springs their supposed healing properties. When the waters were found to be mildly radioactive due to the presence of dissolved radon gas in the water (an hour's soak in a hot spring exposed the soaker to as much radiation as an hour in the sunshine), the radon appeared to be the explanation.

It wasn't just quacks like Bailey who thought radiation was good for you. In an article in the *American Journal of Clinical Medicine*, a Dr. C. G. Davis claimed that "radioactivity prevents insanity, rouses noble emotions, retards old age, and creates a splendid youthful joyous life." Other experts credited radiation with stimulating the body to throw off waste products.

DRINK TO YOUR HEALTH

Water from natural hot springs was bottled and sold as a health tonic, but devotees claimed that the bottled stuff lost most of its healing properties after just a few days. This, too, appeared to be explained by the radon, which has a radioactive half-life of just 3.8 days. That means that half of the radon will decay into other substances in that time. At that rate, less than 1 percent of the radon would remain in the water after just one month.

If the radioactivity in spring water was what made it so beneficial, the thinking went, then water that had gone "flat" could be recharged by reirradiating it. There were numerous products on the market in the 1920s that enabled you to do just that: You could buy a Zimmer Radium Emanator that, when dunked in a bucket of water, irradiated it. Or you could store your water in a Revigator water crock, made from radioactive ore.

ALL BETTER NOW

Why stop with water? Companies sold radioactive hair tonic, face cream, toothpaste (for a glowing smile), blankets, soap, candy, chocolate bars, earplugs, hearing aids, laxatives, contraceptives, and countless other products that were credited with curing everything from pimples to high blood pressure to arthritis, gout, constipation, and chronic diarrhea.

In addition to Radithor radium water, William Bailey also sold radioactive flu and cough medicines, and an athletic supporter called a "radioendocrinator" that he claimed would cure impotence. Wearers were instructed to position the radium "under the scrotum as it should be. Wear at night. Radiate as directed...." Eben Byers took his doctor's advice and began drinking Radithor. A lot of it. He found the water so "invigorating" that he contin-

In 1989 the space shuttle carried 32 fertilized chicken eggs (a student experiment) into orbit.

ued drinking it long after his arm stopped hurting. Byers's cure was more likely due to the simple passage of time than to any purported healing effects of radium, but he didn't know that. In addition to downing as many as three bottles of Radithor a day for nearly three years, he sent cases of the stuff to associates and lady friends and urged *them* to drink it. He even instructed his stable boys to feed Radithor to his racehorses.

TOO MUCH OF A "GOOD" THING

Byers kept right on drinking Radithor into the early 1930s, when he began losing weight and suffering aches and pains all over his body. These symptoms were soon followed by blinding headaches and terrible pain in his jaw, but it wasn't until his bones began breaking and his teeth started falling out that he realized he was suffering from something much more serious than "inflamed sinuses," as his doctors had diagnosed.

Precisely what was wrong with him didn't become clear until X-rays of his deteriorating jaw were sent to a radiologist in New York. The radiologist was familiar with the case of the "Radium Girls"—factory workers who had died after ingesting the radium in glow-in-the-dark paint while painting watch dials during World War I. The lesions on Byers's jawbone were similar to the ones the Radium Girls had suffered. When the radiologist learned that Byers had consumed as many as 1,500 bottles of Radithor since 1927, his diagnosis, like Byers's fate, was sealed.

RADIOACTIVE MAN

Had Radithor been made with radon gas dissolved in water, like the waters in natural hot springs, Byers probably would have escaped serious injury. But Radithor wasn't made with radon, it was made with *radium*, a different radioactive element altogether. Radium's half-life isn't 3.8 days like radon's—it's 1,600 *years*. Even worse, because radium is chemically similar to calcium, instead of passing through the body in a day or two, which would have limited the amount of harm it caused, it accumulates in the bones, where the radiation it gives off destroys the surrounding bone marrow, blood cells, and other tissue. This was why Byers's bones were breaking and his teeth were falling out—they'd been destroyed by radiation and were now disintegrating. By the time he began to experience the first signs of radium poisoning, he had already

About a third of all the carpeting made in the U.S. contains recycled plastic water bottles.

consumed more than three times the lethal dose. He was doomed.

A GOVERNMENT INVESTIGATION

Even if the Food and Drug Administration had understood just how deadly radium was, in those days its powers to act were very limited. Radium was neither a food nor a drug, after all—it was a naturally occurring element, placing it outside the agency's jurisdiction. The only government agency capable of acting was the Federal Trade Commission, which was empowered to protect consumers against misleading trade practices, including false advertising claims. Ironically, the FTC had used this power to take action against companies selling products that *claimed* to contain radioactive materials but *didn't.*

By the time Byers fell ill, evidence of the dangers of radioactive products had begun to mount. The FTC opened an investigation into Radithor, which had been advertised as being "harmless in every respect." Clearly it wasn't, and in 1931 a legal team was dispatched to Byers's estate to record his testimony. By then he was too sick to appear in court. "A more gruesome experience in a more gorgeous setting would be hard to imagine," attorney Robert H. Winn remembered:

> We went to Southampton where Byers had a magnificent home. There we discovered him in a condition which beggars description. Young in years and mentally alert, he could hardly speak. His head was swathed in bandages. He had undergone two successful jaw operations and his whole upper jaw, excepting two front teeth, and most of his lower jaw had been removed. All the remaining bone tissue of his body was slowly disintegrating, and holes were actually forming in his skull.

THE FALLOUT

Thanks in large part to Byers's testimony, Radithor was pulled from the market in December 1931. Byers died three months later, at age 51. Any doubts that the radium killed him were resolved at the autopsy, when some of his teeth and a portion of his jawbone were set on a plate of unexposed photographic film: The radiation in the bones exposed the film just as if it had been used in an X-ray machine. To prevent the radiation in Byers's body from leaking out, he was buried in a coffin lined with lead.

No one knows how many people died from drinking Radithor.

The E. coli bacteria in your stomach help your body manufacture vitamin K.

At least one female friend of Byers died from radium poisoning after he introduced her to the product. In all, dozens or possibly even hundreds of people may have been killed. Considering that William Bailey is estimated to have sold more than 400,000 bottles of Radithor over the years, it's a wonder that more didn't die. Many were probably saved by the price: Even when it was sold by the case, Radithor cost $1.25 a bottle (around $15 in today's money). Few people would have been able to afford to consume as much as Byers had.

LIGHTS OUT

Byers's death received a lot more press than those of the Radium Girls. ("The Radium Water Worked Fine Until His Jaw Came Off" read a *Wall Street Journal* headline.) Reason: Byers was a millionaire socialite; the Radium Girls were working-class nobodies employed by a paint factory. Very few people worked in such a place, so their story wasn't as scary to readers as Byers's, who'd died because he drank a *health tonic* sold to the public.

The scandal surrounding Byers's death prompted the government to grant the FDA much broader powers to regulate patent medicines and protect the public from other dangerous products. Another result: Today the sale of "radiopharmaceuticals"—radioactive materials used in medicine—is restricted to authorized members of the medical profession.

CAVEAT EMPTOR

If you collect antiques, you may know that some shops and dealers specialize in medical objects. From time to time an empty bottle of Radithor pops up, but think twice before you buy one—even though the bottles have likely been empty since their original purchasers consumed the product more than 70 years ago, the bottles themselves remain dangerously radioactive. Just like Eben Byers, still at rest in his lead-lined coffin in a cemetery in Pennsylvania, they will be radioactive for thousands of years to come.

*   *   *

Don't test the river's depth with both feet. —**African proverb**

First national TV broadcast in color: the January 1, 1954, Tournament of Roses Parade.

NEW AND IMPROVED CALENDARS

The calendar most people use today, the Gregorian (introduced in 1582 and named for Pope Gregory XIII)—is a significant improvement over the Julian calendar it replaced. (The Julian was off by 11 minutes per year, which caused it to gain three days every 400 years.) But it's not perfect. Here are some proposed"improvements" to the Gregorian calendar .

DAYS OF OUR LIVES

Can you remember, without looking at a calendar, how many days there are in September? How about March? In a perfect world, you wouldn't have to remember whether November has 30 days or 31—the months would all be the same length. But that's not possible with the calendar we use today: There are 365 days in the year, and 365 isn't evenly divisible by 12, which it would have to be to get the same number of days in each month. Divide 365 by 12 and you get 30 with a remainder of 5. Those five extra days have to go somewhere.

It would also be a good thing if each year started on the same day of the week. A Sunday, say. That would make it a perpetual calendar, never changing from one year to the next. You wouldn't have to throw out your old calendars each year, and more importantly, schools and other organizations wouldn't have to go to all that trouble planning schedules months or even years in advance: They could use the same schedule over and over, year after year. But that's not possible either, because 365 isn't evenly divisible by seven, the number of days in the week. Divide 365 by 7 and you get 52 with a remainder of 1, meaning that there are 52 weeks in a year…plus one extra day. If you're reading this in a year that began on a Monday, that extra day means next year will begin on a Tuesday (or if this is a leap year, on a Wednesday).

Our calendar is based on a solar year. It takes the Earth exactly 365 days, 5 hours, 48 minutes, and 46 seconds to orbit the sun, and any calendar that doesn't take this into account isn't much good to anyone. Plenty of calendars have been proposed as improvements on the Gregorian calendar. For example…

THE POSITIVIST CALENDAR (1849)

Improvement: A perpetual calendar with 28 days in each month

Background: The Positivist Calender, invented by a 19th-century French philosopher named Auguste Comte, had 13 months instead of 12, with four 7-day weeks in each month. That adds up to 364 days. To stay synchronized with the solar year, a 365th "blank" day was added at the end of the year. During leap years, two blank days were added. Keeping those days blank—not part of any week, and not part of any month—made it possible to start every week, month, and year on the same day of the week (Monday).

What Happened: As if a calendar with 13 months and one or two blank days a year wasn't strange enough, Comte renamed all the months after historical figures, starting with Moses and working chronologically forward to Marie François Bichat, a pioneering 18th-century French surgeon. The calendar never caught on.

THE INTERNATIONAL FIXED CALENDAR (1894)

Improvement: A perpetual calendar with 28 days in each month

Background: Created by an Englishman named Moses Cotsworth, this 13-month calendar was a little more palatable: Instead of renaming the original 12 months, as the Positivist Calendar had done, Cotsworth left them alone. He inserted a 13th month, called *Sol*, between June and July, added a blank 365th day at the end of the year, and during leap years added a second blank day between June and July. Cotworth's calendar generated a lot of interest at the League of Nations, which considered it the best of the 130 proposals submitted to a calendar reform committee in 1923. Its biggest fan in the United States: George Eastman, founder of the Eastman Kodak Company. He adopted it for Kodak's internal business and helped fund the International Fixed Calendar League, which lobbied for the calendar's adoption worldwide.

What Happened: Inserting Sol between June and July may have doomed the calendar's chances for success in the United States. Independence Day fell on Sol 17, which didn't have quite the same ring to it as July 4th. Another problem: Because each month began on a Sunday, the calendar had 13 Friday the 13ths—one every month. But for all its flaws, George Eastman never wavered.

..."White Self-Existing Wizard." The calendar's creator says he got the names from a UFO.

He used the International Fixed Calendar until his death in 1932, and Kodak continued to use it internally until 1989.

THE SOVIET CALENDAR (1929)

Improvement: Five days in a week

Background: In 1929 the USSR introduced a calendar with 72 five-day weeks, for a total of 360 days, plus five holidays on important Communist Party anniversaries, for 365 days in all. The calendar's purpose: to squeeze more work out of the Worker's Paradise. Instead of having two days off every seven days (28.6 percent of the time), workers got one day off every five days (20 percent). On calendars, the five days of the week were printed in different colors, and each worker was assigned one of the colors to indicate which day was the day of rest. The new calendar eliminated the idea of one common weekend for everyone, and made it easier for factories to remain in operation every day of the week. It also furthered the ideological goal of de-emphasizing the importance of Sunday as the biblically ordained day of rest.

What Happened: The new system didn't increase productivity as much as hoped. Machinery that runs every day (often 24 hours a day) never stops long enough to receive proper maintenance, so under the new calendar, breakdowns were more frequent. In 1931 the five-day week was scrapped in favor of a six-day week with a single, common rest day for everyone. That lasted only until 1940, when the Soviets went back to the seven-day week.

THE WORLD CALENDAR (1930)

Improvement: A 12-month perpetual calendar

Background: In 1929 a rubber-manufacturing heiress named Elisabeth Achelis attended a lecture given by Melvil Dewey, inventor of the Dewey decimal system. Dewey spoke in favor of the 13-month International Fixed Calendar, but Achelis thought it was impractical. Two weeks later, she read a letter in *The New York Times* that proposed a system for a 12-month perpetual calendar and was inspired to create the World Calendar. Achelis's calendar doesn't have months of equal length—it has *quarters* of equal length. Each quarter begins with a 31-day month and is followed by two months of 30 days each, giving each quarter 91 days, or 364 days for the year. A blank day called "Worldsday" (W for short) was added after December 30 to give the calendar 365 days. During leap years, a blank "Leapyear Day" (also W for short) was inserted between June and July.

What Happened: Achelis founded and bankrolled the World Calendar Association, which lobbied for the calendar's adoption worldwide. In 1931 she gave a presentation to the League of Nations that prompted the League to drop its support for the International Fixed Calendar in favor of the World Calendar. That was as far as it ever got. Religious groups objected on the grounds that weeks with W days were in effect *eight*-day weeks, which disrupted the biblical commandment to observe every seventh day as the Sabbath. The W days caused the obligatory day of rest to drift one day earlier in each regular year and two days per leap year; on most years the Sabbath wouldn't even fall on a weekend. The United Nations shelved the World Calendar in 1955, but the World Calendar Association continues to lobby for it to this day.

THE PAX CALENDAR (1930)

Improvement: A 13-month perpetual calendar that preserves the seven-day Sabbath cycle

Background: Invented in 1930 by James A. Colligan, a member of the Jesuit religious order, the Pax Calendar addressed religious concerns about the Sabbath by creating a calendar with 13 months of 28 days each, for a total of 364 days. (The new 13th month, called Columbus, is inserted between November and December.) Instead of inserting a 365th blank day, the calendar is allowed to drift until it is seven days out of synch with the solar year; then a special seven-day "month" called Pax is inserted between Columbus and December.

What Happened: The Pax Calendar didn't disrupt the Sabbath cycle, but it did interfere with the way the Roman Catholic Church sets the date for Easter, the holiest day on the Christian calendar, and that was enough to kill it.

*   *   *

"The past is a ghost, the future a dream and all we ever have is now." —**Bill Cosby**

The Great Sphinx's name in Arabic: *Abu al Hul*, "The Terrifying One."

PRINCE IS 2 WEIRD

Over a 30-year music career, Prince has had 19 top-20 hits and five #1s. He's sold 80 million albums, starred in three movies, and written dozens of songs for other artists. But he's also known for his eccentricity. For example…

KEEPING A MUSIC VAULT

The guitarist reportedly has a vault filled with dozens of unreleased albums, films, and music videos. Fans have long speculated about it, but Prince won't reveal the vault's contents. Over time, though, several items have been identified by his collaborators or in press releases for projects that were later nixed. Among them: *Dream Factory*, a double album recorded in 1986 with his backup band, the Revolution; a children's album called *Happy Tears* recorded in the mid-90s; and an album called *Camille* with all of Prince's vocals sped-up to make him sound like a woman.

BEING A BAD TENANT

In the mid-2000s, Prince leased the Hollywood home of NBA star Carlos Boozer for a staggering $70,000 a month. Despite the high rent, Boozer was enraged when he discovered that the pop star had redecorated the $11.9 million mansion. He'd had the "Prince symbol" and purple stripes painted on the exterior, added the symbol to the front gates, dyed the water in an outdoor pond purple, and installed a hair salon and a monogrammed carpet in the master bedroom. Boozer tried to sue, but when Prince handed over a check for $1 million to cover the cost of removing his alterations, the lawsuit was dismissed.

BRAWLING WITH SINEAD O'CONNOR

O'Connor had a smash hit in 1991 with "Nothing Compares 2 U," a song Prince wrote and produced in 1984 for the Family, a funk band he managed. When their record flopped, Prince planned to remake the song with a female singer…until O'Connor recorded it. Prince invited O'Connor to his Los Angeles home to discuss the controversy. Instead, O'Connor told an interviewer, he criticized her for using foul language in front of reporters. She fired

Life was the first magazine to make $100 million per year selling ad space in its pages.

back, and the argument led to blows. According to O'Connor, the pint-sized singer (he's 5'2") was no match for her, although she did admit that "he can pack a punch."

OPENING FOR THE ROLLING STONES

Prince's first big shot at stardom came when he opened for the Rolling Stones on their "American Tour 1981." Rather than tone down his racy live act, the relatively unknown musician did the exact opposite. He went out on stage each night wearing just a trench coat and a pair of bikini briefs. The Stones' fans didn't know what to make of it. At the Los Angeles Coliseum, Prince was pelted with garbage. At another gig, he was booed off stage after only two songs.

THE PRINCE VS. THE KING

The only male pop star bigger than Prince in the '80s was Michael Jackson. That could explain why Prince engaged in a bitter—and one-sided—rivalry with the King of Pop. In 1986 the stars met at a Los Angeles studio, where Prince was working on audio for his film *Under the Cherry Moon*, and Jackson was working on his Disneyland movie *Captain EO*. Jackson started flirting with Prince's girlfriend, Sherilyn Fenn, so Prince challenged him to a game of ping-pong in front of their respective entourages. Jackson lightly hit the ball, until Prince egged him on, taunting, "Come on Michael, get into it! You want me to slam it?" according to Prince's drummer Bobby Z's account. As Prince moved to hit the ball, Jackson raised his hands to cover his face…and Prince hit the ball as hard as he could, right into Jackson's crotch. Declaring himself the victor, Prince pranced around, shouting, "Did you see that? He played like Helen Keller!" Jackson apparently held no ill will: A year later, when Jackson was recording *Bad*, the follow-up to his monster hit *Thriller*, he asked Prince to sing a duet with him on the proposed first single, "I'm Bad." But when Quincy Jones played a demo for Prince, the singer balked at the first line, "Your butt is mine." Meant to sound threatening, Prince thought it sounded too much like a come-on. "Now who's gonna sing that to who?" he reportedly said to Jones. "'Cause you sure ain't singing it to me. And I sure ain't singing it to you." Jackson recorded the song alone, and it was a #1 hit.

JUST PLANE WEIRD

If you happen to be reading this on an airplane, you might want to save it for when you're back on the ground.

WHEEL MAN

In October 2011, the fun at a small-town carnival in Taree, Australia, came to a sudden halt when a man named Paul Cox accidentally flew his ultralight airplane straight into the Ferris wheel. Cox, 53, had just taken off from an adjacent airstrip. He said he didn't see the giant wheel and at first didn't know why "everything stopped" when he slammed into it. "I just went to take off, do a go-around...and next thing I know I was stuck inside the Ferris wheel," he told the *Courier Mail* newspaper.

Two children were on the Ferris wheel at the time. Neither was injured, but it took rescuers 90 minutes to get them down. Cox and his son-in-law, both also unharmed, were stuck in their airplane, still wedged in the Ferris wheel, for three hours. A subsequent investigation revealed that Cox had falsified his flight-training experience when applying for his pilot's license and did not have permission to use the airstrip. Investigators are looking into "why a Ferris wheel was installed alongside an airstrip."

GAS MONEY

Not long after a Comtel Air flight touched down in Birmingham, England, in November 2011, a woman locked herself in the airplane's restroom and called 999 (the U.K. equivalent of 911) for help. "A planeload of passengers has just arrived from Vienna," she told the emergency operator. "We were held there against our will and we've just had to hand over 24,000 euros [$31,600]!"

The plane was immediately surrounded by airport police, who soon learned that it was the *airline*, not hijackers, that held the passengers against their will and demanded money. According to Comtel, the trouble started when a British tour organizer sold tickets for airline flights but did not forward the money to the airline. When the jet landed in Vienna to refuel, it couldn't pay its fuel and airport fees, so the airline forced the passengers to come up with the money (about $175 each) instead. Anyone who refused was threatened with arrest.

The frightened passengers ponied up. Those who didn't have cash on hand were escorted under armed guard to an ATM—and when the ATM ran out of cash, to the airport's currency exchange desk. After the money was collected (and counted by the pilot in the cockpit), the flight continued on to Birmingham. At least three other Comtel flights were cancelled for the same reason. The airline is now defunct.

JUVENILE BEHAVIOR

Shortly after audio recordings of a child directing planes from the control tower of New York's JFK International Airport were posted on an aviation website in 2010, the Federal Aviation Administration launched an investigation to determine if they were authentic. They were. One evening in February 2010, a controller named Glenn Duffy brought his nine-year-old son into the control tower of America's sixth-busiest airport and let him give instructions to departing flights. "Here's what you get when the kids are out of school," the proud papa joked to pilots over the air.

A few days later, after Duffy and his supervisor were suspended and facing dismissal, recordings of a little *girl* directing flights from JFK appeared on the same website. It turns out that Duffy has twins: He brought his nine-year-old daughter to work the day after his son. Both the FAA and the air traffic controllers' union condemned Duffy's actions, but his family is sticking by him. "We all bring our kids to work. This just happens to be his profession," Duffy's sister-in-law told the *New York Daily News*.

ONE-WAY TRIP

In August 2008, four Air Canada flight attendants, including attendant-in-charge Hugh Bouchard, arrived at Toronto's Pearson International Airport to work their scheduled flight to Paris. But when they saw who the captain was, they refused to board the plane. Replacement attendants were found and the plane continued on to Paris without incident. A federal health and safety officer later investigated and concluded that because the flight attendants' grievance with the pilot was a "normal working condition of employment," they had insufficient grounds to walk off the job. So what was their grievance? As the flight attendants explained in a statement, they were afraid the pilot might commit suicide during the flight. "Bouchard advised us that he had an in-flight incident where the captain had threatened to ditch the plane in the Atlantic. Hugh said that the captain had said he had nothing to lose as he was being fired, anyway."

The flight attendants appealed the ruling and won. "The court recognized that threats of ditching a plane in the ocean are not a normal working experience," employment lawyer Stacey Ball told the *National Post*. Air Canada claims it investigated the earlier incident cited by Bouchard and does not believe the pilot really threatened to kill himself. The flight attendants were "reacting to comments that were never made, as far as we can tell," an spokesperson told the *Post*. The unnamed pilot was never reprimanded or fired, and at last report was still flying for Air Canada.

LOOK—UP IN THE SKY!

In October 2011, a Southern California skydiving instructor named Alex Torres was fired from the Skydive Taft company for mixing his skydiving work with his other profession: starring in adult films. Torres, who goes by the name "Voodoo" at his other job, filmed a scene with the Skydive receptionist, Hope Howell. They began in the back of one of the company's planes as it flew toward the jump site, then bailed out of the plane nude (except for their parachutes) and finished their scene in midair.

Company owner Dave Chrouch says he didn't learn of the stunt until the footage began circulating at a nearby high school and he was contacted by police. He fired Torres and Howell, but they don't have to worry about going to jail, because none of the authorities could think of any criminal charges that would stick. They were consenting adults, after all, and because no one on the ground reported seeing their amorous airborne antics, they could not be charged with public nudity, lewd behavior, or anything else. The FAA concluded that their activity was not distracting to the pilot. "He was in complete control of the plane at all times," Chrouch told the *International Business Times*. "I mean, he looked back a couple of times—the same thing he does if there are other skydivers in the plane. He is going to look back, he's going to look around to see what everyone is doing."

During the 1890s temperance movement, marijuana was a recommended substitute for alcohol.

SILVER MEDAL SHOCKER, PART III

We forget, when we're watching the Olympics in our living room with a bowl of cereal in our laps, that it's more than the thrill of victory and the agony of defeat. It's politics, too. Here's Part III of the story—some background and postscripts to the '72 Munich Olympics. *(Part II is on page 303.)*

MUNICH AND BEYOND

Every Olympics has its share of stories: goals reached, hopes dashed, medals won and lost. But the 1972 Munich games went far beyond athletics. What happened there became part of world history. Here are a few significant facts:

• The 1972 Summer Olympics took place under a terrible pall. On September 5, members of a Palestinian terrorist organization calling itself Black September scaled the walls of the Olympic Village, where the athletes were housed. They took 11 Israelis hostage—five athletes, four coaches, one judge, and one referee—and demanded the release of Palestinian prisoners in exchange. By the time the siege ended, all 11 Israelis and one German policeman had been killed. "Each time that I feel sorry for myself that we don't have that gold medal," said U.S. basketball team captain Kenny Davis, "I think about those Israeli kids that they took out of there in caskets."

• After the massacre, the Americans and most of the other athletes attended a memorial service for the Israelis. Russian athletes did not. "Russia didn't recognize Israel and did not attend the services," said U.S. basketball forward Mike Bantom. "They practiced. It did not affect their concentration."

• Every year since 1976, Ankie Spitzer, widow of slain Israeli fencing coach Andre Spitzer, has asked the International Olympic Committee for a moment of silence at the opening ceremonies to honor the murdered Israelis. Every year since 1976, the IOC has refused her request.

• The 2012 Summer Olympics in London seemed to many to be

the perfect time to remember the Israeli athletes who had fallen 40 years before. More than 150,000 people from over 100 countries signed a petition asking for a moment of silence at the opening ceremonies. U.S. President Barack Obama endorsed the petition, and Secretary of State Hillary Rodham Clinton urged the IOC to grant the petition. It was denied.

• Scoring in a number of events at the Munich Olympics seemed to show bias from Communist judges. Results in gymnastics, wrestling, boxing, shooting, and diving had already been disputed before the final men's basketball match.

• The Soviet sports program peaked with the Munich Olympics. The USSR won 50 gold medals, compared with 29 in Mexico City in 1968.

• The foreman of the jury that gave the basketball win to the Soviet team was Ferenc Hepp, a Hungarian who was said to have "loathed" the Soviet Union because of their 1956 invasion of his country. The great suffering of the Hungarian people and murder of family members made it unlikely that he showed favoritism to the Soviet team.

• Aleksandr Belov, the Soviet player who scored the winning basket, died from a rare disease—cardiac sarcoma—just six years after the 1972 games. The 26-year-old basketball hero was buried with his gold medal around his neck.

• The 12 players from the 1972 USA Men's Basketball Team Olympic squad had not been together as a group since the Munich games. In August 2012, the squad held a reunion at Kentucky's Georgetown College to mark their game's 40th anniversary.

* * *

BONK!

From the "News That Sounds Like Satire" Department: "Britain's first 'Safe Text' street has been created in London complete with padded lampposts to protect mobile phone users from getting hurt in street accidents while walking and texting."

—***Daily Mail,*** 2008

It is possible to sneeze hard enough to fracture a rib.

WORDS TO LIVE BY

Some quotations about living life so it matters.

"There is only one quality worse than hardness of heart, and that is softness of head."

—Theodore Roosevelt

"You can't get spoiled if you do your own ironing."

—Meryl Streep

"All glory comes from daring to begin."

—Eugene Ware

"The world is full of willing people; some willing to work, the rest willing to let them."

—Robert Frost

"Live so you wouldn't be ashamed to sell the family parrot to the town gossip."

—Will Rogers

"Humility does not mean you think less of yourself. It means you think of yourself less."

—Kenneth Blanchard

"Some people feel the rain. Others just get wet."

—Bob Marley

"The man who is brutally honest generally enjoys the brutality almost as much as the honesty."

—Richard J. Needham

"The true measure of a man is how he treats someone who can do him absolutely no good."

—Samuel Johnson

"You never really learn much from hearing yourself talk."

—George Clooney

"Never mistake motion for action."

—Ernest Hemingway

"Don't say that you want to give, but go ahead and give. You'll never catch up with a mere hope."

—Johann von Goethe

"Never let the fear of striking out get in your way."

—Babe Ruth

"It is better to wear out than to rust out."

—Richard Cumberland

"The truth is, you don't know what is going to happen tomorrow. Life is a crazy ride, and nothing is guaranteed."

—Eminem

"If your ship doesn't come in, swim out to it."

—Jonathan Winters

Something about the letter Z? Zookeepers are bitten more by zebras than by any other animal.

TOTALLY 21ST CENTURY

New words don't automatically make it into a dictionary. First a word has to catch on with the public, then experts have to agree that it has "lasting potential" and "cultural significance." Here are some words that have been added to dictionaries since the year 2000. Lasting potential? You decide.

Mankini: A brief one-piece bathing garment for men, with a T-back

Breatharian: A person who believes that it's possible, through meditation, to reach a level of consciousness where one can obtain all the nutrients one needs from the air

LARPing: Live-action role-playing games during which participants portray characters through physical action, often in costume and with props

Sheeple: People who, like sheep, are docile, foolish, or easily led

Middlebrow: Books, movies, music, and art that are good but don't require a lot of thinking to understand

Terminator gene: A gene in a genetically modified crop plant that stops the plant from setting fertile seed, thus preventing the farmer from saving seed for the next season

Slactivism: Using the Internet to support a political or social cause, which requires no time or involvement other than signing an online petition, joining a campaign group, or clicking "like" on Facebook

Upcycling: To reuse discarded objects or material in such a way as to create a product of higher quality or value than the original

Blamestorming: A method of collectively finding someone to blame for a mistake no one is willing to confess to. Often occurs in the form of a meeting of colleagues at work, gathered to decide who is to blame for a screw up.

Robin Hood tax: Any tax aimed toward redistribution of resources in order to achieve greater social equality, such as taxes on transactions made by financial institutions

Chillax: To calm down and relax

Then it's all downhill: Your brain stops growing at about age 18.

Bridezilla: A woman whose behavior in planning her wedding is regarded as obsessive or intolerably demanding

Gazillionaire: An extremely rich person

Precycling: The practice of seeking to reduce consumer waste by avoiding prepackaged goods, buying only reusable or recyclable products, using one's own shopping bags, etc.

Meatspace: The physical world (as opposed to cyberspace)

Twitterati: Avid or frequent users of the social networking site Twitter

Cyberslacking: Using your employer's Internet and email facilities for personal activities during working hours

Ego-surfing: Searching the Internet for mentions of your own name or links to your own website

Globesity: The worldwide epidemic of obesity, a term coined by the World Health Organization in 2001

Sandwich generation: A generation of people, typically in their 30s or 40s, responsible for both bringing up their own children and caring for their aging parents

Brain candy: Broadly appealing, undemanding entertainment which is not intellectually stimulating.

Crowdsourcing: To canvass suggestions from the general public before adopting a course of action

* * *

TOY STORY STORY

• The working title of the 1995 movie was *You Are a Toy*.

• The first draft of the script was about a tin toy named Tinny getting lost and trying to find his way home, eventually ending up at a preschool. (That became the plot of *Toy Story 3*.)

• Buzz Lightyear was initially going to be named Lunar Larry.

• A rough, early cut had to be entirely scrapped when studio executives thought Woody (voiced by Tom Hanks) was too mean and sarcastic. The script was completely rewritten.

• Jim Carrey was the first choice to voice Buzz Lightyear. Billy Crystal was the second choice. (Tim Allen got the job.)

Richard Strauss's 1905 opera *Salome* was banned by the Metropolitan Opera (too naughty).

WORLD'S GREAT MARKETS AND BAZAARS

You know what would be a great trip? A trip where you went to all these places. (With a boat full of money. So you could buy stuff—and have a place to put it all!)

DJEMA el-FNA (Marrakech)
Djema el-Fna is the name of the square at the center of the old, walled section of this ancient Moroccan desert city—and it's been the home of an outdoor market on and off for more than 1,000 years. Today it's actually a collection of several *souks*—Arabic for "market"—overlapping in the square and extending into the mazelike alleyways around it. Fresh-squeezed orange juice stands and food stands are everywhere, intermixed with jugglers, musicians, storytellers, and merchants selling rugs, spices, brass-work, and a lot more. (The origin of "Djema el-Fna" is unknown; it means, roughly, "The Mosque at the End of the World.")
Highlight: The snake charmers. Every morning there are dozens of snake charmers with live cobras at Djema el-Fna.

PLAKA MARKET (Athens)
Plaka is a neighborhood in Athens, Greece, located in the shadow of the city's famed Acropolis. In the 1970s the nightclubs the neighborhood was known for began to close, and merchants moved in. Today it is a jam-packed madness of thousands of shops, and streetside stalls selling way too much to list. (The market is especially known for its embroidered fabrics, amber jewelry, and musical instruments. There are also a lot of cafes, restaurants, and world class museums. Bonus: No cars allowed. It's all foot traffic.
Highlight: Every Sunday (for the last 110 years) the Monastariki Flea Market takes place just a few streets from Plaka. Great place to get Greek antiques, backgammon sets, religious icons, etc.

MARCHÉ BASTILLE (Paris)
If you want to go someplace to see if you can slowly eat yourself to death over the course of one gluttonous, joy-filled day—this is the

place for you. It's all food, it's almost all gourmet food, and it's all laid out in the most brightly colored, eye- nose- and mouth-watering way over two city blocks in Paris's historic 11th Arrondissement, all of it under the eye of the July Column in the Place de la Bastille. Fresh breads, pastries, pies, cakes, crepes, cheeses; fish mongers with tables full of iced whole fresh fish; rotisserie chickens; huge slabs of lamb and pork; sausages and pates; jams, pastes, fruits, and vegetables; whole ethnic sections with Mediterranean, African, and Arab dishes—and wine after wine after wine. (Okay, we have to go now. To Paris. To the Marché Bastille. Possibly to die.) The Marché Bastille is open every Thursday and Sunday—so you have a few days to recover in between bouts!

Highlights: You want highlights—after that?

IZMAILOVSKY SOUVENIR MARKET (Moscow)

Only going since the fall of the Soviet Union in 1994, this is an already world famous market located amid the ancient Russian architecture of Moscow's Izmailovsky district. Some standout items: handmade Persian rugs and chess sets; mammoth tusk carvings; handmade samovars; Soviet memorabilia—and stalls full of those famous Russian Matreshka dolls (where one fits into another into another and so on).

Highlight: The market is right next to the Izmailovo Kremlin, a fantastically gaudy and faux-ancient (construction began in 1998) structure full of shops and museums. Among them: The History of Vodka Museum. Samples available!

ZANZIBAR STONE TOWN MARKET (Zanzibar City)

Zanzibar City is located on the island of Unguja, just off the coast of the East-African nation of Tanzania. The city is divided into two main parts, the new section, and Stone Town (or *Mji Mkongwe*—Swahili for "old town"). A mix of Swahili, Arab, Portuguese, and Indian influences, step into Stone Town and you are immediately lost in a densely packed maze of streets (most too narrow for cars), full of bikes, scooters, donkeys, and people. This is the Zanzibar Stone Town Market. There are literally thousands of stalls lining these ancient streets, and it isn't just for tourists: locals come to the market to get household goods, used clothes, tools, and, especially, food, including fruits, grains, vegetables, spices—

Pres. James Monroe once chased his Secretary of State from the White House with fire tongs.

and lots and lots of fresh-caught Indian Ocean seafood.

Highlight: The Anglican Christ Church Cathedral. It's right in the middle of Stone town—and it's built at the site of the Zanzibar Slave Market, the largest in eastern Africa during the slaving era, and the last legal operating slave market in history. (Slaves were sold there legally until the 1890s.) The site includes the shallow, stone, windowlesss cellars where people were kept before being brought above ground to be sold.

CHATUCHAK WEEKEND MARKET (Bangkok)

This is one of the largest outdoor markets in the world: it covers more than thirty acres, has more than 5,000 stalls, and sees more than 200,000 visitors every Saturday and Sunday. Located in central Bangkok, Chatuchak (alternatively spelled "Jatujak") Market is immensely crowded, loud, fast-paced, chaotic, hot, and full of exotic and mysterious people, sights, scents, and sounds. New sneakers? They've got 'em. Electronics? They've got 'em. Baby squirrels? They've got them. (We don't know why—we don't *want* to know why—but they do.)

Highlight: Those in the know say to ask around for the restaurant run by an ex-stewardess for Thai Airways, known around the world for its yellow curries and sweet and sour soups, and dishes like "pork & egg in five spice and coconut juice."

Extra: The Or Tor Kor Market, Bangkoks largest farmers market, is right across the street. It has produce of every kind, as well as prepared Thai dishes of numerous types, and a reputation as a very clean and friendly place.

BRIMFIELD FLEA MARKET (Brimfield, Massachusetts)

An auctioneer named Gordon Reid decided he wanted to set up a place to sell antiques—so he invited dealers to set up tables in his back yard. That was in Brimfield in 1959. The Brimfield Flea Market is now made up of, according to their website, "22 individually-owned and operated flea markets ranging in size from 15 dealers to over 1000," all of them sprawling on either side of Brimfield's Main Street. It is one of the largest flea markets in the U.S, with more than a million people coming to rummage through the tables and tarps for treasure every year. (The market was featured on *Good Morning America* in June 2012.) What can you find?

Food for thought: 41% of Americans say farming as a career has "very great prestige."

Antiques—a really lot of antiques, including glassware, tools, and especially furniture—from one of the oldest, post-European-settlement regions of the U.S. (And John Reid's daughters Jill and Judy still run market their father started in 1959.)

Highlights: It's New England—meaning there's cheap lobster right on site. Yum.

TONALÁ MARKET (Guadalajara)

Actually about ten miles outside of the west-coast Mexican city of Guadalajara, this outdoor market takes place in the streets and alleys of the suburb of Tonalá. And it's not just kitsch: Tonalá is the home to the largest community of artisans in all of Mexico, and has been the center of pottery making since before Europeans arrived. You can also find textiles, metal works (iron, brass, tin, and copper, especially) marble-carvings, papier-mâché works, blown glass, as well as all kinds of foods, drinks, and entertainers.

Highlight: You can make your own artworks: many of the artisans have workshops where you can learn their particular craft.

TSUKIJI FISH MARKET (Tokyo)

Prepare yourself—this place has a distinct odor: it's the largest wholesale seafood market on the planet. You want to see a bunch of buyers yelling and arguing and bidding on a whole, several-hundred-pound tuna—that may end up selling for several hundred thousand dollars? This is the place for you. Located both indoors and out (Tsukiji Market naturally needs indoor cold rooms) the Tsukiji market sells an astonishing $15.5 million worth of seafood *every day*. But don't worry—it's not just for wholesalers. There's also an entire section just for us regular folks, with an enormous variety of fresh seafood, fruits and veggies, and even Japanese kitchenware. (The maximum number of visitors to the tuna auctions is 120 per day—so get to the Osakana Fukyu Center (the "Fish Information Center") at the Kachidoki Gate by 5 a.m.)

Highlight: Sushi breakfast. There are sushi restaurants both inside and outside at Tsukiji market, open from about 5 a.m. until noon. They have, according to those who know such things, arguably the best sushi you can get anywhere in the world.

Good for you? In the 1920s, Listerine produced its own brand of "medicated" cigarettes.

GO COWBOYS!

NFL games weren't always the mega-events they are today. What changed them? The Dallas Cowboys Cheerleaders.

CASHING IN

On November 5, 1967, the Dallas Cowboys were hosting the Atlanta Falcons at the Cotton Bowl. During a break in the action, one of the spectators, "Bubbles" Cash, a well-known Dallas burlesque performer, decided to put on an impromptu performance. Dressed in a fringe halter top, short-shorts, and cowboy boots, and carrying cotton candy in each hand (to resemble pompoms), Cash jumped onto the field and strutted right down the 50-yard line, turning the heads of fans, players, and coaches as she went.

As the story made headlines, Cowboys general manager Tex Schramm was intrigued. Pro football was at a moment of change—the first Super Bowl had been held earlier that year, and Schramm was looking for ways to raise his team's profile…and increase its revenue. The answer, he realized, was in turning the games from regionally popular athletic contests into national entertainment. Inspired by Cash's stunt, Schramm decided to inject some sex appeal into the Cowboys.

OUT WITH THE OLD

The Dallas Cowboys already had a cheerleading squad called the CowBelles & Beaux. Adhering to the traditional Ivy League cheerleader format, the squad was co-ed; they led cheers and boosted team morale with rally cries and acrobatic stunts. And the CowBelles & Beaux crew was composed entirely of local high-school students. But in 1969 Schramm began putting his burlesque-inspired changes into motion. He dropped the male cheerleaders and simplified the squad's name to the Dallas Cowboys Cheerleaders. By 1970 he'd hired a director and charged her with altering the routines to make them more dance-oriented and less acrobatic.

FRINGE BENEFITS

In 1972 Schramm hired Texie Waterman, a Dallas choreographer who had worked in television (as a dancer on Sid Caesar's *Your Show of Shows*), to select and train a completely different squad. Requirements: The girls all had to be over 18, they had to be attractive, and they had to have talent. Schramm also asked Waterman to provide her crew with provocative uniforms.

Waterman hired designer Jody Van Amburgh to come up with something distinctly different from the classic sweater-and-skirt combo. The result: a fringed blue-and-white halter top (Cowboys team colors), white short-shorts, a belt buckle, and tall white boots. (Sound familiar?) Seamstress Leveta Crager made all of the uniforms by hand—and did all of the tailoring work on every single outfit until 1996. With some minor changes (crystals added to fringe, belt buckle removed and then added back), today's Dallas Cowboys Cheerleaders uniforms are basically the same as the ones from 1972—the design is even a registered trademark.

STARS OF THE WEST

The Dallas Cowboys became one of the NFL's most successful teams. They went to four Super Bowls in the 1970s, earning the nickname "America's Team." Their cheerleaders, meanwhile, became a pop-culture phenomenon.

- The squad, with new members every season, went on USO tours and became a fixture on 1970s TV variety shows.
- A TV special, *The 36 Most Beautiful Girls in Texas*, aired in 1978 before a Cowboys game on ABC's *Monday Night Football*.
- The squad guest-starred on a two-part episode of *The Love Boat* in 1979, and appeared for "Celebrity Week" on *Family Feud*.
- A 1979 made-for-TV movie called *The Dallas Cowboys Cheerleaders* (co-starring Bert Convy and Jane Seymour) was a big hit, and a sequel followed a year later.
- Through the 1980s and '90s, calendars, posters, and other merchandise bearing the images of the scantily clad cheerleaders flew off store shelves, and the Cheerleaders continued to make TV appearances, from *Saturday Night Live* to *Hee Haw*.

IF IT AIN'T BROKE

Before long other NFL teams followed suit and started cheerleading squads using the Cowboys formula—young women in small costumes dancing around on the sidelines, posing for calendars, and making public appearances. Some of the squads that started in the '70s include the Chicago Honey Bears, the Cincinnati Ben-Gals, the Dolphin Starbrites, the New Orleans Saintsations, the Liberty Bells (for the Philadelphia Eagles), the SwashBucklers (for the Tampa Bay Buccaneers), and the Derrick Dolls (for the Houston Oilers).

But the Cowboys are still the most famous. Through merchandise sales and public events, the squad currently earns more than $1 million per year for the franchise, but their value in shining a spotlight on pro football, and on the Dallas Cowboys, is immeasurable. Or maybe not. As of 2010, the Cowboys are one of just five football teams worth an estimated $1 billion or more.

* * *

LAST LAUGH: EPITAPHS

In Massachusetts:
Francis Magranis
My shoes are made
My work is done;
Yes, dear friends, I'm going home.
And where I've gone
And how I fare
There's nobody to know
And nobody to care.

In Vermont:
Unknown man shot in the Jennison & Gallup Co.'s store while in the act of burglarizing the safe Oct. 13, 1905.
(Stone bought with money found on his person.)

Here lies Johnny Cole,
Who died, on my soul,
after eating a plentiful dinner.
While chewing his crust.
He was turned into dust,
with his crimes undigested—poor sinner.

In Rhode Island:
Sidney Snyder
The wedding day decided was,
The wedding wine provided;
But ere the day did come along
He'd drunk it up and died, did.

G. Winch, the brewer is buried here.
In life he was both hale and stout.
Death brought him to his bitter bier.
Now in heaven he hops about.

In Vermont:
She lived—what more can then be said:
She died—and all we know she's dead.

Jedediah Goodwin
Auctioneer
Born 1828
Going!
Going!!
Gone!!!
1876

LEGAL BRIEFS

Lots of moms have told their kids to be sure to wear clean underwear just in case they end up in the emergency room. But how many moms have warned their kids that underwear might land them in court?

CASE: The Navajo Nation v. Urban Outfitters
DETAILS: When Urban Outfitters, a national chain of retail clothing stores, began selling "Navajo Hipster" panties in the fall of 2011, the Navajo Nation sent the company a cease-and-desist letter, demanding that the "derogatory and scandalous" panties, plus more than 60 other Navajo-themed products, be pulled from the store's shelves. Urban Outfitters removed the panties and some other products from its stores and its website, but it continued to sell others. The Navajo Nation sued, claiming that the company misappropriated the tribe's name and trademarks and illegally suggested that the panties and other products were made by American Indians. In their suit, the Navajos demanded all the profits generated by the sale of the goods, plus $1,000 per product per day for every day that the offending panties and other items were offered for sale.
OUTCOME: As of June 2012, the case was still working its way through the courts. (But no Navajo-themed items are currently for sale on the Urban Outfitters website.)

CASE: Carol Ketover v. Bloomingdale's
DETAILS: In 2004, Ketover, a 60-year-old real estate agent, picked out a pair of $200 designer slacks and was directed by store staff to a dressing room to try them on. Inside the dressing room were two large Bloomingdale's shopping bags in front of a chair, but Ketover thought nothing of it as she disrobed down to her thong underwear. "As I bent down to put my foot in the slacks, I saw a flash of light behind me. I pushed the shopping bags away from the chair, and I saw a [video] screen. As I bent closer, I saw my butt with my thong underwear across the screen," she told the New York *Daily News*. She discovered a video camera that was taking the image next to the mirror. After hearing laughter outside the dressing room, Ketover quickly dressed and fled the store.

Had a pervert rigged the dressing room for a peep show? Not quite: NBC's *Today* show was filming the department store for Fashion Week, and someone had stashed the camera and a video monitor in the changing room when they weren't being used. Though the equipment was apparently on, NBC says it wasn't recording, and the only monitor connected to the camera was the one that Ketover saw, so no one else saw her in her thong underwear (the laughter she heard outside the dressing room was apparently unrelated). No matter—Ketover sued Bloomingdale's and its parent company, Macy's, Inc., for invasion of privacy and asked for unspecified actual and punitive damages. "We should have put a sign on the dressing room that it was closed. But the producer told me the camera would only be working if someone was operating it," Bloomingdale's spokeswoman Anne Keating told the New York *Daily News*.

OUTCOME: According to the company, "Macy's, Inc. does not comment on litigation. Regards, Corporate Communications."

CASE: Sang Eun Lee v. the Ontario, Canada, Police Department

DETAILS: In January 2010, Lee was arrested on suspicion of impaired driving and taken to jail. There she was patted down by a female police officer to see if she was concealing any weapons, drugs, or other contraband on her person. She wasn't—but the officer noticed she was wearing an underwire bra and ordered her to remove it, on the grounds that the wire in the bra could be used as a weapon. Lee was humiliated at having to remove her bra, and at her trial, she argued that the impaired driving charge should be tossed out because being forced to remove her bra was a violation of her constitutional protection against unreasonable search and seizure.

OUTCOME: Lee lost the argument, and when the case went to trial, she lost that, too. She was fined $1,000, and her driver's license was suspended for a year.

CASE: Unidentified male employee v. Sterile Reprocessing Services, Inc., a Texas medical-supply company

DETAILS: One afternoon in 1992, the 31-year-old employee, who was not named in press accounts, and three female co-workers were talking about underwear. The man said that some days he didn't wear underpants, whereupon he was accosted by the women, who were eager to see if this was such a day. (It was.) "At one point, all three women pulled the plaintiff's pants to his knees and caused him to fall. While the man was struggling to get away, they dragged him across the floor by his pants," the man's lawyer said in documents filed with the court. (In their defense, the co-workers said they took the man's comments about his lack of underwear "as an invitation for an 'inspection.'") The man probably wishes he'd worn his underpants that day, because afterward the women took to calling him "Shorty," "Pee Wee," and other names. The man waited two years to report the incident to his employers, and then did so only after he was disciplined for an unauthorized absence. Company executives promised his complaint would be kept quiet, but word leaked out, and that, apparently, is what prompted the man to sue the company in 1996.

OUTCOME: The case was settled out of court in 1997 without Sterile Reprocessing admitting wrongdoing; the terms of the settlement were not disclosed. The *Houston Chronicle*'s headline: "Firm Settles Suit with Man Whose Pants Were Pulled Down."

* * *

MISS AMERICA STATISTICS

• Women from 31 states have won.

• The winningest states are California, Ohio, and Oklahoma, which have each produced six Miss Americas. The city to produce the most winners: Los Angeles, with three.

• Three states have done it consecutively: Pennsylvania (1935–36), Mississippi (1959–60), and Oklahoma (2006–07).

• Ohio produced winners in 1922 and 1923, but both wins went to Mary Campbell, the only woman to win the contest twice. She placed second in 1924. (It's now against the rules to even compete twice.)

• In order to represent a state at Miss America, entrants must win their state pageant. Those who finish in second place or are "first runner up" are invited to the Miss National Sweetheart pageant. Grand prize: a $1,000 scholarship and a necklace with a pendant that looks like an ear of corn. It's produced by the Jaycees of Hoopeston, Illinois, as part of the city's Sweetcorn Festival.

TAKING IT TO THE GRAVE

Undertakers will honor most funeral requests (as long as they're legal). Check out what these people took with them to eternity.

RECLINER. Reuben John Smith (d. 1899) liked to relax in life, so he asked that his eternal resting place be a leather recliner and that a checkerboard be placed in his lap. (Smith also asked to be buried with a key to his tomb in case the undertakers made a mistake.)

WHISTLE. In *To Have and Have Not* (1944), Lauren Bacall delivers a famous line to real-life future husband Humphrey Bogart: "You know how to whistle, don't you, Steve? You just put your lips together…and blow." After Bogart was cremated, Bacall put a golden whistle in the urn with his ashes.

PIPE AND TOBACCO. Sixteenth-century explorer Sir Walter Raleigh is credited with popularizing tobacco smoking in England, a habit he picked up on his travels to the New World. His last request before being executed for treason in 1618: one final smoke. Raleigh's will provided for "ten pounds of tobacco, and two pipes" for any smoker who attended his funeral, and requested that he be buried with his favorite pipe and some tobacco, in a coffin lined with wood from his cigar boxes.

PETS. Ancient Egyptians are famous for it, and people today still like the idea of being buried with their animal companions. Cemeteries have started selling combined burial plots so that owners can lie beside their beloved pets for eternity. One 68-year-old woman from Surrey, England, asked that her cat be put down and buried with her. (The funeral home refused.)

STETSON. Actor Tony Curtis died of heart failure in 2010. He asked for his casket to be filled with items he may "want in the next life," including a Stetson hat, an Armani scarf, and *Anthony Adverse*, the novel that inspired his screen name. His family also put his iPhone in the casket…just in case.

Karl Marx was once a correspondent for the *New York Daily Tribune*.

THE CURIOUS CASE OF THE AMERICAN ACCENT, PART II

There are hundreds—perhaps thousands—of distinct accents in the U.S. This article only scratches the surface of a fascinating linguistic puzzle. (Part I is on page 209.)

WORLD TOUR

Just as it was with the English, immigrants from other countries tended to stick together when they got to America. Here's a look at where they came from, where they ended up, and how the way they spoke then still affects the way people in the United States speak today.

• **Germany.** After England, Germany produced the largest wave of U.S. immigrants between the 1680s and 1760s. Arriving first in Pennsylvania, the newcomers adopted the nasal tones of their Quaker neighbors who had come from England, then added their own clipped German speech patterns. The biggest German influence is the hard "r" sound at the end of words—"river" vs. "rivah"—and is the feature that most distinguishes American speech from British. This trend spread as settlers moved into the Midwest and beyond.

• **The Netherlands.** When settlers from New England moved south to New York, there was already a sizable Dutch population. The mixture of the two groups formed the famous Brooklyn accent (think of Bugs Bunny), in which *bird* is pronounced as "boid," *these* and *those*, "deez" and "doze," and *coffee*, "caw-fee." Unlike most other immigrant languages, which were abandoned for English within a generation or two, the Dutch language lingered in New York City for three centuries. (Theodore Roosevelt grew up hearing his grandparents speak it at the dinner table as late as the 1860s.) While other immigrant groups have influenced the classic New York accent, it comes primarily from original Dutch settlers.

First woman to climb Colorado's Pikes Peak: Amelia Earhart's mother, Amy, in 1890.

• **Russia and Poland.** Arriving in New York in the late 1800s and early 1900s, Yiddish-speaking Jews from eastern Europe added many new words and humorous turns of phrase to English, including, "I should live so long," "I need it like I need a hole in the head!" and "What's up?" Interestingly, although "New Yawk tawk" has become strongly associated with Jewish immigrants, Yiddish seems to have had little effect on the accent itself, which was adopted by the Irish, Italians, Chinese, and dozens of other ethnicities who live in New York. Actual spoken Yiddish—which is very clipped and Germanic—sounds very little like the New York accent.

• **Scandinavia.** Immigrants from northern Europe settled in the Upper Midwest, and many aspects of their Old World accents persist to this day. Referred to as both the Minnesota accent and the Great Lakes accent, it is most notable for the overpronunciation of vowels, especially the long "o" sound, as in "dontcha know." If you've seen the 1996 dark comedy *Fargo*, that's a good example of the Minnesota accent (although most native speakers claim that it's a bit exaggerated in the film).

• **France.** Much of the French influence on the American accent ended up in Louisiana. Cajuns were originally French settlers who had moved down from Acadia in the eastern part of Canada. In 1765 the British took over, and loyal Acadians fled and resettled in New Orleans, still French territory. Cajun French is very old, dating from the 1600s. It might be understood by someone in Paris today, but only with some effort. The Cajun accent (like the food) has a very distinctive flavor—"un-YON," "ve-HIC-le," and "gay-RON-tee," and "LOO-ziana."

• **Africa.** The speech of slaves brought over from West Africa had a strong effect on American English. However, its exact origin is hard to trace. There are a number of West African languages, and slaves were intentionally separated from members of their own groups to make it difficult for them to conspire. That led to what are called *pidgins*—simple languages with few rules that were cobbled together from two or more languages. According to some theories, this was the origin of what is now called African American Vernacular English (AAVE). It has been called *ebonics*, but use of that term is controversial. Many linguists now believe that West

Almost 80% of Europe's forests are located in Russia.

African languages had little if any influence on AAVE, and that its origin can be traced to early Southern dialects brought over from England. Nevertheless, some of the cadence and lilt of the Southern accent—spoken by both blacks and whites—probably comes from African slaves. Some linguists believe this could be because black women served as nannies to white children, and those relationships helped blend the two speaking styles.

BARN IN THE USA

Not all accents were brought over from other countries. A few are as American as apple pie.

• In a small section of southern Utah, there is an accent in which "ar" sounds are transposed with "or" sounds. It's uncertain how this way of speaking came about, but people who live in this region don't say "born in a barn," rather, "barn in a born."

• A relatively young accent, Valley Girl, or "Valspeak," began in the 1980s. The most defining characteristic: Raising the intonation at the end of a sentence as if it were a question. Originating in the San Fernando Valley of southern California, Valspeak may be one of the most uniquely American accents. Some linguists speculate its roots may be traced to refugees from the Ozarks who moved to California during the Dust Bowl era of the 1930s.

HOMOGENIZATION

U.S. regional accents are in danger of being lost. Because of TV, movies, video games, and YouTube, kids learn less about speaking from their parents and their grandparents than they do from the likes of the Disney Channel, Nickelodeon, and Pixar. These entities tend to make the main characters speak with standard Midwestern American accents. Result: A young boy in Boston might pretend to "park the car," and a teenage girl in Georgia might roll her eyes when her mother says "y'all." If this trend continues, then perhaps some day there will be just one American accent.

* * *

"Man does not live by words alone, despite the fact that he sometimes has to eat them."

—**Adlai Stevenson**

THE #2 REPORT

Warning: Toilet talk ahead!

• First major world city to ban doing your business in the streets: Athens, in 320 B.C.

• A few centuries earlier in Rome, Emperor Claudius legalized farting at official state banquets.

• The average person eliminates nearly a pound a day, or about 360 pounds a year.

• Vegans poop more—and more often—than meat-eaters.

• It is not uncommon for long-distance runners to experience a bout of *peristalsis* during a marathon—in other words, going in their pants. (Grete Waitz did it in her running shorts en route to winning both the London and New York City Marathons in the early 1980s.)

• Where does it go when you flush? Human sewage can be re-pooposed into fertilizer, bio-fuel, and bricks. (They don't smell.)

• Maternal instinct: Studies show that mothers find the smell of their own baby's dirty diaper relatively more pleasant than one from another baby.

• On average, human solid waste is made up of

2–3 percent proteins (both undigested and body-made)
10–20 percent inorganic matter
10–20 percent fats and cholesterols
30 percent undigested (or undigestible) food
30 percent dead bacteria that the body is getting rid of

• It takes time to get things going down there. Your next three movements are already inside you, waiting "on deck."

• The New World's oldest human stool sample—or *coprolite* (fossilized excrement)—was discovered in 2002 in Oregon's Paisley Caves. Date of the "deposit": around 12000 B.C.

A quarter for your thoughts? In 1912 a penny was worth what a quarter is worth now.

JUST PLANE WEIRD: "OPEN MIC" EDITION

Two stories of what can happen when the pilot or the air traffic controller forgets that they are wearing a microphone connected to a radio.

THE BACHELOR

Pilots operating in the airspace over Texas one day in June 2011 were treated to an obscenity-laden diatribe by Southwest Airlines pilot James Taylor, who didn't realize that his radio microphone was on. Taylor was upset that the flight attendants he worked with were either too gay, too old, or too fat for him to hit on. "Eleven [expletive deleted] [expletive deleted] homosexuals and a granny. Eleven! I mean, think of the odds of that. It was a continuous stream of gays and grannies and grandes," the pilot complained (unknowingly) to air traffic control and anyone else listening on the tower frequency. He was two minutes into his rant when an air traffic controller broke in and advised him that he had an "open" microphone. Taylor was suspended without pay and given diversity training, after which he was allowed to return to work. "From now on," he wrote in an apology e-mailed to Southwest workers, "I will show nothing but the utmost respect during my interactions with all employees."

AS SEEN ON TV

Captain Taylor wasn't the only person plagued by an open mic in 2011: That April, an unnamed controller working the night shift at the Cleveland Air Route Traffic Control Center got caught watching a DVD in the tower when he should have been watching the airplanes. Pilots tuned to the center's frequency heard more than three minutes of dialogue from *Cleaner*, a 2007 film about an ex-cop who works as a crime scene cleaner. They might have gotten to hear the entire movie, had an Air Force pilot not called in on a separate military frequency and told the controller that his microphone was open. (At last report, the controller and his supervisor were suspended pending a review.)

TOWNS FOR SALE

We recently read about an entire town that was up for sale on eBay. That started us wondering: How frequently does that happen? Turns out it's not as rare as you'd think.

BRIDGEVILLE, CALIFORNIA (Population: 25)

Includes: Eight houses, four cabins, a machine shop, a cemetery, 1½ miles of riverfront and a post office, all on 83 acres of land. Bridgeville has its own zip code: 95526.

Asking Price: In 2002 Bridgeville made headlines when its owners, the Lapple family, put it up for sale on eBay with a minimum starting bid of $750,000. It was the first town ever listed for sale on the online auction site.

Details: The town, formerly a stagecoach stop on the road to Eureka on the northern California coast, attracted a high bid of $1.77 million...but that bidder backed out. The Lapples put it up for sale again (not on eBay) and an Orange County banker named Bruce Krall bought it. Price: $700,000. Krall planned to fix up the town, but that proved to be much more costly than he'd planned. In 2006 he re-listed Bridgeville on eBay and sold it to Thomas La Paille, a Los Angeles entertainment manager, for $1.25 million. La Paille also planned to fix up the town, but three months after buying Bridgeville he committed suicide in Los Angeles for reasons that his family says are unrelated to the purchase of the town.

Update: Since La Paille's death, his family has repeatedly tried to sell Bridgeville but have been unable to find a buyer. The latest attempt that made headlines was a sale to a group that wanted to turn Bridgeville into a homeless rehabilitation center. That sale fell through in February 2010. At last report Bridgeville was back on the market, this time for $995,000.

BUFORD, WYOMING (Population: 1)

Includes: The Buford Trading Post (gas station and convenience store), a three-bedroom home, a schoolhouse, ten acres and its own zip code (82052), on I-80 between Laramie and Cheyenne

Asking Price: The town was put up for auction in April 2012

with an opening bid of $100,000

Details: Buford got its start in 1866 as a fort to protect workers building the Transcontinental Railroad. The population had dwindled from 2,000 residents down to only three when "Mayor" Don Sammons, his wife and their son moved there from Los Angeles in 1980. By 2007 Sammons' wife had passed on and his son had moved on, leaving him as the town's lone resident. After five years of that he decided to sell out and move closer to his son. The auction took place outside the Buford Trading Post.

Sold! Winning bid: $900,000 by Pham Dinh Nguyen of Vietnam. He learned about the sale on the internet and made his first visit to the United States just to bid on the town. When the check cleared he became the new honorary mayor of Buford...and the only mayor of an American town who is not a U.S. citizen.

GOLFVIEW, FLORIDA (Population: 175)

Includes: 63 houses, 64 acres of land and the town hall

Asking Price: $35 million

Details: Famous in Florida real estate circles as "the town that killed itself," Golfview was built next to a golf course and a small airport, Morrison Field, in 1937. During World War II the U.S. government seized the golf course and used the land to turn Morrison Field into the much larger Morrison Air Force Base...which grew further to become Palm Beach International Airport in 1948, and it's still growing. The golf—and Golfview's views—having been ruined by progress, in 1990 the citizens voted to combine their homes into one huge lot and sell it for development. "Rather than get angry, people here said, 'We'll just zone commercial and sell out,'" town manager Pinky Yount told the *Associated Press*.

Sold! The residents *wanted* $35 million, but they didn't get it. In fact, they didn't find a buyer until 1998, when the county bought up all but three of the homes for $15.9 million.

COURBEFY, FRANCE (Population: 0)

Includes: Nineteen houses, a village hall, stables, tennis court, swimming pool, and the ruins of a 13th-century castle

Asking Price: €330,000 (about $436,000)

Details: Like many rural French villages, this one in the Limousin region began to empty out in the 1970s. By 2008 it was completely abandoned save for "thieves, drunks and squatters." Three attempts to turn Courbefy into a resort failed. When the last owners of the town defaulted on their mortgage in early 2012 the lender, Crédit Aricole, put the town up for sale through ordinary real estate channels.

Sold! There were no takers...until the bank issued a press release. Then the story of the entire French village for sale made international headlines. Within days the village was swarming with investors from all over the world. Winning bidder: Ahae, a Korean-born American photographer, who bid €200,000 ($665,000) for Courbefy in May 2012.

ASKHAM RICHARD, ENGLAND (Population: 273)

Includes: Fourteen houses and three farms on 800 acres

Asking Price: £6.5 million ($10 million)

Details: This picturesque North Yorkshire village, part of an estate that was put up for sale in November 2011, was marketed with a glossy brochure explaining that the original manor house "was sold off some years ago by a previous owner." In a classic case of *caveat emptor*, or "let the buyer beware," the brochure neglected to inform readers that the manor house was still standing and is now Her Majesty's Prison Askham Grange, a women's correctional facility. One further surprise: Because it's an "open prison," the inmates, including some murderers, are let out during the day and are free to wander the community. "Prisoners are a frequent sight pushing prams through the village, feeding the ducks, waiting for a bus to take them to a nearby supermarket or to work," the *Scottish Express* reported. Not that it bothers the locals: "I've just been into the prison to get my hair done," one 86-year-old woman told the paper. "They let you do that if they know you. It's £1.75 for a wash, blow dry and a set. You can't beat that."

* * *

SPIDER GOAT

Spider silk is stronger than steel, but scientists can't recreate it in the lab, so they're attempting to add spider silk to goat's milk via DNA splicing. If successful, the extracted "goat silk" could be used to make bridges and body armor, and maybe even to replace damaged ligaments—which might just create an actual...spider man.

GOLD RUSH GIRLS

During the California Gold Rush of the mid-1800s, thousands of men headed west with gold dust in their eyes. But what about women? For many of them, the untamed West wasn't just about gold—it was about finding a place where they could loosen their corsets and call their own shots.

THE INSIDE TRADER

Mary Ellen "Mammy" Pleasant started life as a slave in Georgia, but her lively intelligence—not to mention her beauty—caught the plantation owner's attention. He sent her to Boston to be educated, and he was right, she *was* smart—smart enough not to return. Instead, she married a wealthy black businessman. When he died, Pleasant took her $50,000 inheritance—an unheard of sum at a time when few black women saw $15 in a month—and headed to San Francisco.

Pleasant shrewdly invested in "swank boarding houses for bachelors" and brought in women with looks and class to keep the men company. Her houses attracted the wealthy and powerful, including senators, judges, and—most importantly—financiers. While she poured brandies for guests, Pleasant listened for insider information on stock investments. Before long, she had accumulated a hefty portfolio and was sharing tips as often as she received them. "The best way to get rich in San Francisco," said one wealthy patron, "is to know Mammy."

THE STAGE MOTHER

Mary Ann Crabtree always wanted to be an actress, but like most women of her time, she abandoned her dreams in favor of marriage. In 1852 she followed her gold-hungry husband, John, to California. When their daughter Lotta was born, Mary Ann put her energies into turning the little girl into a star. She enrolled Lotta in dancing classes, first in San Francisco and then in Grass Valley, but her hopes didn't get traction until a seasoned (and world-famous) entertainer named Lola Montez moved in next door and taught little Lotta the Irish jig.

It was the right dance to learn. In the 1850s, half of California's foreign-born population was Irish. Lotta's first job: Dancing for Irish miners gathered at Flippin's Blacksmith Shop. She kicked up her heels, red curls bouncing, while hammers pounded on anvils in the background. The miners adored the little girl—she reminded many of them of daughters they'd left behind in their quest for gold. They showed their appreciation by throwing sacks of gold dust at her feet. After Lotta's successful premiere, Mary Ann dragged her daughter from one mining camp to another. Pretty soon little Lotta was bringing in $13 in gold every night—far more than her luckless father had ever found. By age 12, Lotta had become a famous actress and the sole support of her parents and two brothers, and by age 23 she was reportedly earning $80,000 per year.

Mom kept track of every cent Lotta earned or spent. She gave Lotta an allowance to live on, but invested the bulk her earnings in real estate. She was so obsessed with tracking her daughter's money that when her own husband "borrowed" a few coins, she had him arrested for theft. In the end, Mom's money minding paid off big. When Mary Ann died, Lotta discovered that her investments had made her a fortune. At age 45, with $2 million in assets, Lotta retired.

THE CARD SHARK

Historical records say that Eleanor Dumont was a gorgeous young woman when she left her New Orleans home for the California gold fields. She moved to San Francisco in the early 1850s chasing the love of her life. "Not a man," said Dumont, "but that glittery rock lying among the foothills of the Gold Country." But the backbreaking life of a miner wasn't in the cards for Dumont. What was? Cards! In 1854 she opened a gambling den in Nevada City, California, and created a scandal when she started dealing blackjack. The townswomen saw the lovely female dealer with the French accent as a threat to their marriages, while the men happily lost the gold they dug trying to win the dealer's heart. None of them succeeded. At the end of every winning game of *vingt-et-un* ("21"), Dumont sat the loser down and had the bartender pour him a glass of milk. "Any man silly enough to lose his last cent to a woman deserves a milk diet," she liked to say.

By age 30, Dumont's life as a gold-country gambler had made her a fortune. It had also scrubbed away her good looks. She had so much dark hair growing above her upper lip, disgruntled gamblers started calling her Madame Mustache. As the gold mines began to play out, the number of players dwindled. In 1877, Dumont played a hand of faro that lost her what little money she had left. She ended her career as a card shark and mixed herself one last cocktail—rumored to have been half champagne and half cyanide.

THE CRUSADER

In 1854 Sarah Pellet stepped atop a dry-goods box in Weaverville, California, to decry the terrors of demon alcohol. One resident who stopped to listen wrote to his sister about Pellet's lecture: "She is not bad looking, and has a fine voice and a great flow of language. Did I say flow? It is a perfect torrent. She talked for an hour and never stopped to draw breath." But Pellet's lectures were so dull that even her promise to bring 5,000 "worthy" young New England women to the town wasn't enough to make Weaverville's men pass an ordinance outlawing liquor. So she hopped on a mule and went to Downieville, a mining town in California's Sierra Nevada mountains.

According to Robert Welles Ritchie, author of *The Hell-roarin' Forty-niners*, Downieville miners "made the week between Christmas and New Year one continuous bender." The town's mayor called the place "a vast field of labor for the cause of temperance." But would a bunch of hardscrabble miners stop drinking and start listening to lectures? You bet! According to Ritchie, here's why:

> Any kind of a woman was a novelty sufficiently compelling to cause men to drop their gold pans and hike ten miles over a trail just for a look at a crinoline. A woman preaching against the Demon was novelty with comedy trimmings.

Pellet and her petticoats convinced thousands of Downieville men to sign a promise to stop drinking. Yet newspapers of the time hint at a more mercenary motive for Pellet's temperance crusade. After her lectures, she would pass a hat to collect money to aid in her work. One attendee watched in amazement as two-and-a-half-dollar gold pieces "rattled like hail" into the four hats being passed. A reporter for the *Nevada Journal* called Pellet "a humbug" and lambasted her:

...same time: one for a newborn, and one for an older joey.

> Rumor has it Miss Pellet provided her purse with the necessary against a rainy day to the tune of $25,000. This can hardly be true, yet such has been the scarcity of women in certain parts of the mining region that Miss Pellet could not fail to accumulate something of a pile by merely exhibiting herself in woman's array at two bits a sight.

As for Downieville's Sons of Temperance, when Pellet packed up her crusade and headed to Oregon in 1855, they went right back to drinking.

THE SHE-DEVIL

Anti-Chinese sentiment ran high in gold country, but Donaldina Cameron couldn't have cared less. What did she care about was that, as gold nuggets became harder to find, a new "yellow currency" had come into play: Chinese girls—some as young as 11 years old—were being kidnapped in Hong Kong or Canton and shipped to San Francisco. The lucky ones were forced to work in sweatshops; the unlucky ones became sex slaves, working in brothels to earn food and clothing plus $300 per month to pad the pockets of their owners.

In the 1890s, Cameron joined forces with the Presbyterian Women's Home Society and threw herself into rescuing these girls. Historians say she barged into the underworld of San Francisco's Chinatown with "nothing but an umbrella and a police whistle." She groped her way along dark passages, broke down doors, and even dropped through skylights to rescue girls. The Chinese slave owners called Cameron *Fahn Quai*—"She-Devil"—and marked her for death. But Cameron not only eluded her would-be assassins, she outlived them, dying in 1968 at age 98. Cameron rescued thousands of "sing-song" girls, educated them, and helped them find husbands. The grateful girls had their own name for Cameron: *Lo Mo*—"Good Mother."

* * *

From the Police Blotter: "Police responded to an alarm at a home on LeBrun Circle where the woman on location was unable to provide identification or the proper alarm code. She told the alarm company she was 'the newest new wife.'"

Bank book: A single page of a first-edition Gutenberg bible is worth over $25,000.

MORE PORTMANTEAUS

We gave you the stories behind some interesting portmanteau words on page 185. Here are a few more—of the extra-rich variety.

AFFLUENZA

Combination of: *Affluent* and *influenza*

Meaning: A derogatory "psychological condition" suffered by the very wealthy, with symptoms such as as obsessive materialism, compulsive shopping, snobbery, stress, and guilt

Origin: In 2001 reporters for the *Chicago Tribune* traced the word back to an early 1980s study about actual psychological problems suffered by people who inherit large amounts. The study was written by San Francisco psychologist John Levy, who said he'd love to take credit for inventing the term, but he'd gotten it from the man who commissioned the study, Fred Whitman, a member of a prominent San Francisco family. Whitman, 87 years old at the time, said he had indeed coined the term "affluenza" in 1954. "Anybody I'd use it with thought it was a giggle," Whitman said.

CELEBUTANTE

Combination of: *Celebrity* and *debutante*

Meaning: A debutante who has attracted so much media attention as to achieve celebrity status

Origin: This word was coined by influential radio and newspaper reporter Walter Winchell in his column *On Broadway* in early 1939. He used the word to describe Brenda Frazier, the daughter of a prosperous Boston family. Frazier made her debut into adult high society in December 1938 at the age of 17 and subsequently became internationally famous, being written about like a movie star in tabloids all over the world. She even appeared on the cover of a 1938 issue of *Life* magazine, basically for being young, attractive, and wealthy. Modern celebutantes: Paris Hilton, Nicole Richie, and Kim Kardashian.

GLITTERATI

Combination of: *Glitter* and *literati*

Meaning: People who are wealthy, powerful, glamorous, and associated with the arts in some way

Origin: It was coined in 1956 (some sources say it first appeared in *Time* magazine) to describe the very elite writers and artists who were also glamorous and influential celebrities, such as Pablo Picasso and playwright Arthur Miller (who wrote *Death of a Salesman* and was married to Marilyn Monroe). The meaning of the term has expanded over the years to include jet-setters in general. Members of the glitterati who are still young teenagers are sometimes referred to as "ziteratti." Well-known users of the microblogging service Twitter have been labeled "twitterati."

TRUSTAFARIAN

Combination of: *Trust fund* and *Rastafarian*

Meaning: Derogatory term for wealthy young people who, while living off their parents' money, adopt a bohemian lifestyle, with casual attitudes toward dress, work, and drugs

Origin: In the 1970s, Rastafarian performers like Bob Marley made reggae music a global phenomenon, nowhere more so than in the UK. London was home to a large Rastafarian community and a vibrant reggae scene. Over the years, thousands of rich white British kids were drawn to the "Rasta" way of life—or at least the dreadlocks and marijuana parts of it—and in the 1990s, someone came up with the sarcastic term "trustafarian" to describe them. The term has since traveled to other parts of the world where trustafarians can be found. (Hello, Ashland, Oregon!)

* * *

THE NEWS IN BRIEF(S)

"An Austrian count who complained that his prison-issue underpants breached his human rights has been awarded almost £400,000 ($655,000) after he was held in custody for six days. Alfons Mensdorff-Pouilly, a multi-millionaire, also complained that he was not given a comb when he was detained in London as part of a Serious Fraud Office investigation into a BAE Systems arms deal. The Ministry of Justice was unable to say what the payment was for."

—*The Daily Telegraph* (London), 2011

ODD GUNS

When Uncle John read about these unusual firearms, the first thought that came to mind was, "who would buy a gun like that?"...followed by, "Ooh! I wish I had a gun like that!"

THE DUCK FOOT PISTOL

Unusual Feature: Multiple barrels

Details: Also known as "mob pistols," these guns were designed to enable one person—such as a captain of a ship or a guard in a bank—to hold off an angry mob using a gun that could shoot several people with a single pull of a trigger. They're called "duck foot" guns because the barrels fan like the webbed foot of a duck. Made in the 18th and 19th centuries, they were superseded by shotguns, which were better at accomplishing the same purpose.

THE SEDGLEY OSS .38

Unusual Feature: Gives a punch some extra BANG!

Details: Developed for the U.S. military during World War II, the OSS .38 was nicknamed the "glove gun" because it was riveted to the outside of a leather work glove and worn on the back of the hand. A metal rod that extended forward about an inch past the knuckles served as the trigger; when the wearer punched the enemy, the rod depressed on contact and fired the weapon.

The glove gun was reportedly issued to covert agents as an assassination weapon, but there's no evidence that it was ever used to assassinate anyone. Where it did find use (and did kill at least one enemy soldier) was as a "weapon of last resort" worn by crews building airfields on islands in the Pacific that had been liberated from the Japanese. There, the threat of enemy holdouts hiding in the jungle was real. Riveting a gun to crew members' work gloves gave them a chance of defending themselves against any sudden attack. Only about 50 of the guns were ever made; today the collectibles sell for upwards of $7,000.

THE CORNER SHOT

Unusual Feature: Shoots around corners

Details: Invented by an Israeli colonel in the early 2000s, the Corner Shot looks like an assault rifle, except that it has a pistol, video camera, and flashlight mounted like bayonets on the front of the weapon. Just behind these items is a hinge that allows the Corner Shot to bend up to 60°, enabling the pistol, the camera and the flashlight to "peek" around corners. A video monitor on the rear of the gun and a second trigger connected to the handgun allow users to see what's around a corner—and shoot at it—without exposing themselves to return fire.

THE HECKLER & KOCH P11

Unusual Feature: Shoots underwater

Details: Specially trained soldiers on underwater missions need weapons to defend themselves against an enemy's underwater forces. Conventional firearms don't work well below the waves: Even if the ammo doesn't get wet, the bullets don't travel very straight or very far, and the shock wave from a gunshot can damage both the gun itself and the hearing of the person firing the weapon. Developed in the 1970s, the P11 is believed to use an electronically ignited explosive similar to solid rocket fuel to fire four-inch metal darts instead of bullets. (Details are classified.) Limits: The gun is lethal only to a distance of about 50 feet. And once you fire the darts from their individual barrels, the gun has to be returned to the factory to be reloaded.

THE FISHHOOK GUN

Unusual Feature: Shoots underwater—*at fish*

Details: Patented in 1941 by a Mr. H. Heineke (who, presumably, was not a very skilled or enthusiastic fisherman), the device was an actual fishhook with a miniature single-shot "gun" inside. "When a fish gives a sudden jerk on the hook," says Heineke's patent application, "the firing pin is released to strike the cartridge, and the latter will be discharged, thus killing or stunning the fish."

THE CIVIL WAR ORDNANCE PLOW

Unusual Feature: It's a plow with a cannon inside.

Details: Why bother beating your sword into a plowshare when you can have it both ways? Normally the part of the plow that's attached to the horse is a solid piece of metal, but on *this* plow it was hollowed out to serve as a cannon. As "a means of defense in

Tetris, invented by Russian Alexey Pajitnov, was originally called "The Soviet Mind Game."

repelling surprises and skirmishing attacks on those engaged in a peaceful avocation, it is unrivaled," New York inventors C.M. French and W.H. Fancher wrote in their 1862 patent application.

THE PALM PISTOL

Unusual Feature: It's "the world's first ergonomically designed firearm," for people who lack the ability to fire ordinary handguns.

Details: The Palm Pistol is shaped like an egg with a gun barrel sticking out one side. You make a fist around the egg and let the barrel poke out between your middle and ring fingers. A button on top of the egg serves as the trigger; you fire it with your thumb. The gun is "ideal for seniors, the disabled, or others who may have limited strength or manual dexterity. Point and shoot couldn't be easier," says the company.

Bonus: The gun has been certified as a "Class I Medical Device," which means if it's prescribed by your doctor, the purchase price can be reimbursed by Medicare or private insurance. At last report, the inventor was hoping to begin production in 2012.

* * *

CHIM-CHIM CHA-REE!

In the 1920s, American psychologist Robert Yerkes wanted to see if he could teach apes to speak. So he bought two chimpanzees from a zoo, Chim and Panzee, and brought them home, where he first successfully taught them to eat with a knife and fork, and tried to teach them to speak. Chim was the star pupil. Yerkes' method for teaching Chim to speak: He'd pass bananas through a hole in Chim's cage, and say "ba-ba," hoping Chim would eventually make an association between the sound and the food but he didn't. Apparently both Yerkes and Chim lost interest in the twice-daily training within a few weeks. Chim ended up being the focus of a book Yerkes wrote, *Almost Human*. As it turned out, Chim wasn't a chimp, but an ape—that distinction wasn't made in the 1920s; all primates were "chimps." Nevertheless, *Almost Human* and Chim ignited interest in primates and their near-human qualities.

BRI'S PACKING TIPS

Uncle John travels the world, bringing fun facts to the masses. Here's how he packs everything he needs into as few bags as possible.

Pack coordinates. One jacket, two shirts, and two pairs of pants or shirts can be combined to create eight different outfits—a real space saver. Pack similar colors and remember that black goes with everything.

Pillowcases takes up less room than laundry bags and stow easily in a zippered pocket.

Roll up small items like exercise shorts, tank tops, and socks and place inside shoes (such as running shoes), filling what would otherwise be empty space.

To fold two pairs of pants, lay half of one pair on top of the other pair. Fold the bottom pair over the top pair. Then fold the other over the top. It creates a cushion effect, which reduces wrinkling.

Going to a colder place? Take clothing you can layer for warmth, rather than taking up valuable suitcase space with lots of bulky sweaters.

Packing a shirt or dress that needs to look good when you get there? Try folding the item in tissue paper and putting it between thin sheets of cardboard. Pack it last, so it's on top of everything else.

T-shirts are pliable. Roll them up and stack them.

You probably know that it saves space to use trial-size bottles for toiletries and personal care items. Clean contact-lens containers are an efficient way to pack very small amounts of these liquids.

Travel and storage stores sell a helpful gadget called a "compression bag." Fill this tough plastic bag with clothes, then squeeze out the air through a one-way valve. Great for packing dirty laundry to bring home.

Leave room for small souvenirs. Buy things that are flat or very small, and unbreakable. Remember: They have to fit!

Meeting your quota? The average American drinks 54 gallons of soda per year.

DUMB BLONDES

According to scientists, there's absolutely no link between hair color and intelligence. (There have actually been studies.) So why then does this stereotype—and all those dumb-blonde jokes—persist?

HEATING UP THE ICE AGE

Blondes are a relatively recent addition to the gene pool. For nearly all of human history—200,000 years or so—humans had dark skin, dark hair, and dark eyes. The nomads who made their way into Europe about 40,000 years ago began to develop lighter skin (possibly as a result of vitamin-D deficiencies), but retained their dark hair and eyes. Then, a mere 11,000 years ago, a change occurred.

It was the last Ice Age and food was scarce. To survive, the men had to roam the European tundra hunting bison and woolly mammoths. Many of them perished, and before long the females outnumbered the males. Unlike in warmer climates, where women could farm or gather fruit, in frozen Europe if a woman wanted to eat, she needed a man. That predicament led to fierce competition among females—and it allowed two random genetic mutations to take hold: blonde hair and blue eyes. Neither trait had any physiological survival value, and neither may have caught on if the conditions weren't so harsh, but these were desperate times.

According to Canadian anthropologist Peter Frost, "When an individual is faced with potential mates of equal value, it will tend to select the one that 'stands out from the crowd.'" Result: When the big, strong hunters arrived with their mammoth meat, the blondes made it to the front of the line.

DIM BULBS

But somewhere along the way to modern times, the stereotype emerged that blondes are not that bright. Some theories as to where this perception came from:

• In the Middle Ages, wealthy people spent most of their time indoors and out of the sun, which kept their hair darker, while the "dumb" poor spent their time working outside, their hair getting bleached by the sun.

Only she knows for sure: 1 in 3 U.S. Caucasian women have blonde hair; 1 in 20 naturally so.

• Only about 25 percent of women who were born blonde retain that hair color into adulthood. The same factor that connotes youth—which is attractive to men—can also lead to perceptions of childlike immaturity and naivete.

• Brunettes help perpetuate the dumb-blonde stereotype because they're envious that all a blonde has to do is look coy and a man will give her free stuff. Who needs brains when you've got blonde?

HOW CURIOUS

Another theory: Some blondes deliberately perpetuate the dumb stereotype themselves. That's what many historians believe Rosalie Duthé was doing. Widely considered to be modern history's first "dumb blonde," Duthé was an 18th-century French dancer, nude model, and courtesan. In addition to her looks, the voluptuous blonde was famous for her habit of taking long pauses before she spoke. Did this make her stupid? No, but it didn't matter. Duthé had men hanging on her every word. This peculiar habit was satirized in the 1775 play *Les curiosites de la Foire*, in which Duthé's long pauses were stretched out even longer for comedic effect. The play was a huge hit in Paris, sending the message that it was okay to laugh at the intelligence—or apparent lack thereof—of blondes. (Duthé had the last laugh; she became very wealthy and lived to the ripe old age of 82.)

PUTTIN' ON THE DITZ

The dumb-blonde stereotype gained traction in early-20th-century America thanks to a popular vaudeville act called a "Dumb Dora." The premise: A ditzy woman (not necessarily blonde) would play dumb for laughs. Comedienne Gracie Allen perfected the persona in her stage acts with George Burns. Allen wasn't a blonde (although her hair was lightened when she appeared on TV), but her ditzy persona drew so many laughs that she was often imitated.

A comic strip based on this persona, called *Dumb Dora*, ran from 1924 to 1935. Its creator, Chic Young, introduced his most famous comic strip in 1930: *Blondie*. (She started out as a Dumb Dora type, but soon transformed into a smart housewife.)

BLONDES ON FILM

The mid-20th century was a golden age for blondes. There were

Foreign bodies: People from different regions have different mouth bacteria.

the "ice-cold blondes"—including Grace Kelly, Kim Novak, and Mae Murray—and the "blonde bombshells," like Brigitte Bardot, Lana Turner, and Jean Harlow. But the most famous one was, of course, Marilyn Monroe (a natural brunette).

Monroe was by no means "dumb," but she cashed in on the stereotype when she starred as Lorelei Lee in the 1953 comedy *Gentlemen Prefer Blondes*. The character, created by author Anita Loos in the 1920s, is actually more superficial than stupid. Take this exchange from the film between Lorelei (Monroe) and Dorothy, her "smart" brunette best friend, played by Jane Russell.

Lorelei: Excuse me, but what is the way to Europe, France?

Dorothy: Honey, France is in Europe.

Lorelei: Well, who said it wasn't?

Dorothy: Well, you wouldn't say you wanted to go to North America, Mexico.

Lorelei: If that's where I wanted to go, I would.

Like Gracie Allen, Monroe spawned many imitators, including Goldie Hawn's ditzy characters on the 1960s variety show *Laugh-In*, Chrissy (Suzanne Somers) on the 1970s sitcom *Three's Company*, and Phoebe (Lisa Kudrow) on the 1990s sitcom *Friends*. In the 2000s, celebrities such as Jessica Simpson and Paris Hilton have lived up to that stereotype to great success. "I play dumb like Jessica Simpson plays dumb," said Hilton. "But we know exactly what we're doing. We're smart blondes."

"THERE'S WHITE-OUT ON THE SCREEN."

That's the punchline to one of thousands of dumb-blonde jokes. (Setup: *How can you tell if a blonde has been using the computer?*) Another big reason the stereotype won't go away is the enduring popularity of these jokes. The fad, which began in the 1980s, is as strong as ever today. But are they "harmless," as some claim? According to a study conducted by Thomas E. Ford, a psychology professor at Western Carolina University, "Sexist humor is not simply benign amusement. It can allow men to feel comfortable with sexism without the fear of disapproval of their peers." That acceptance, concluded Ford, keeps the jokes—and the stereotype—alive.

Studies that recorded people's reactions to pictures of women all point to the same conclusion: Subconsciously, both men *and*

As uncomfortable as it sounded? The ancient Romans wore underwear called *subligaculum*.

women tend to judge intelligence, as well as likability, by hair color. In fact, one study conducted by the University of Paris found that blondes actually make *guys* dumber: Men who interacted with attractive blonde women performed worse on cognitive tests than men who interacted with attractive brunettes.

LIFE'S A BLEACH

Many blonde women complain that it's harder for them to be taken seriously in society because of the dumb stereotype. Reese Witherspoon, who starred in the 2001 comedy *Legally Blonde*, about a seemingly dumb blonde college student whose boyfriend leaves her for a smart brunette, says the prejudice her character experienced in the movie happens to her in real life: "Immediately, when people meet me, they think of me as not being smart."

An English journalist—and brunette—named Joanna Pittman decided to find out firsthand how blondes are really treated. She bleached her hair, walked outside, and immediately noticed a difference. "I got wolfish looks from men and complicit smiles from blonde women, who seemed to acknowledge my beaconlike hair as if I was now a member of an elite club."

Inspired, Pittman began researching the history of the hair color and society's reactions to it, culminating in her 2003 book *On Blondes*. Her conclusion: "Every age has restyled blond hair in its own image and invested it with its own preoccupations. Blondeness became a prejudice in the Dark Ages, an obsession in the Renaissance, a mystique in Elizabethan England, a mythical fear in the 19th century, an ideology in the 1930s, and a sexual invitation in the 1950s."

Today, it's a punchline.

*　　*　　*

AN ELEPHANT JOKE

Q: How do you shoot a blue elephant?

A: With a blue elephant gun.

Q: How do you shoot a pink elephant?

A: Hold its nose until it turns blue, and then shoot it with the blue elephant gun.

What do the words *alcohol*, *lute*, and *magazine* have in common? They come from Arabic.

LIGHTEN UP!

On page 455 we looked at humanity's strange obsession with blonde women. Now we look at the hair color itself.

HITTING THE BOTTLE

There are eight basic types of blonde hair. Here's a list of those colors, along with examples of famous blondes who wear them. (Disclaimer: Celebrity examples of hair colors can and do change with the fashions.)

• **Blonde/flaxen:** The most common type of blonde hair. It's light but not whitish, and has no traces of red, gold, or brown. *Flaxen celebrities: Paris Hilton, Naomi Watts.*

• **Yellow blonde:** Darker than flaxen but with no other colors mixed in. *Yellow-blonde celebrities: Madonna, Christina Aguilera.*

• **Platinum blonde:** Whitish blonde. (When children have this hair color naturally, they are called "towheaded.") *Platinum-blonde celebrities: Marilyn Monroe, Gwen Stefani.*

• **Sandy blonde:** Grayish-hazel or cream-colored blonde. *Sandy-blonde celebrities: Jennifer Aniston, Cameron Diaz.*

• **Golden blonde:** A rich, darker, golden-yellow blonde. *Golden-blonde celebrities: Goldie Hawn and her daughter, Kate Hudson.*

• **Strawberry/honey blonde:** A light or dark amberish golden blonde. *Strawberry-blonde celebrities: Amy Adams, Nicole Kidman.*

• **Dirty blonde, or dishwater blonde:** Dark-blonde with flecks of golden-blonde and brown. *Dirty-blonde celebrities: Scarlett Johansson, Emma Watson.*

• **Ash blonde:** A bit darker than dirty blonde. *Ash-blonde celebrities: Hayden Panettiere, Taylor Swift.*

Feeling adventurous? Try one of these real blonde hair-dye colors: "Electric Banana," "Virgin Snow," "Sassy Gold," "Misty Starlight," "Palest Moonglow," "Whisper Soft," and "Bright as #$(@%! Yellow."

Q: What do you call a fear of palindromes? A: *Aibohphobia.* (Read it backwards.)

DUMB CROOKS: STONER EDITION

Weed been thinking about doing an article like this one for a while.

DUDE, WRONG HOUSE!

Andrew Kramer, 22, of Grant County, Washington, who cops said "reeked of pot," was trying to sell baggies of marijuana to passersby. What's so dumb about that? He was doing it in front of the Grant County Courthouse. (He was quickly arrested.)

WRONG WAY TO GET LEGAL ADVICE, DUDE!

Robert Michelson, 21, of Farmington, Connecticut, called 911 to ask if he could get arrested for growing just one marijuana plant. The dispatcher said yes, he could. There was a pause. Michelson said, "Thank you," and abruptly hung up. A few minutes later, the police showed up and cited him for growing one pot plant.

SHOULDA LEFT IT AT HOME, DUDE!

A 22-year-old Stamford, Connecticut, man was walking to the courthouse to testify in a drug case when he took a quick detour to hide his bag of marijuana under a rock in front of a nearby building. Office workers, seeing the suspicious activity, alerted the police...whose headquarters were across the street from the hiding place. When the man returned, instead of his weed, he found a note that read, "You're under arrest. Look up at the police station." He looked up and saw officers waving at him from the window.

DUDES, WRONG PLANT!

• A teenager in Daytona Beach, Florida, was arrested for stealing a tomato plant from a neighbor's garden. After he was detained by the homeowner, the boy told the cops he thought it was marijuana...even though it had tomatoes on it.

• A 58-year-old Swedish man was busted by police after they witnessed him buying a bag of something from another man. (The other man ran away.) When the officer looked in the bag, he discovered that it wasn't "grass," it was grass—as in lawn clippings.

The buyer told the officer that he'd haggled the price down from $62 to $15, and it would have been a great deal had it been *actual* marijuana. Because it wasn't, the man was not charged.

DUDE, WRONG STASH CONTAINER!

A Vero Beach, Florida, man went to the dry cleaners to drop off a bag of what he thought was his dirty laundry. It wasn't. There were three pounds of marijuana inside the bag. Police searched the man's home and found $80,000 worth of illegal drugs.

DUDE, JUST LET IT GO, 'CAUSE IT'S LIKE...GONE!

Late one night in 2009, Calvin Hoover, 21, of Salem, Oregon, left the Free Loader Tavern and discovered that someone had broken into his truck and stolen his coat—along with the bag of pot in the pocket. Furious, Hoover called 911 to report that "They stole my weed!" According to the dispatcher, Hoover was difficult to understand "because he kept stopping his truck to vomit." The police found him later that night walking around looking for his weed, and arrested him.

WRONG QUESTION, DUDE!

In 2011 Devonte Davon Jeter, 19, was in court on drug possession charges. His public defender told the judge that the marijuana could have belonged to any of the four men who were pulled over that day in Midland, Pennsylvania. Jeter had denied the baggie was his, even though it was found near his feet after he exited the vehicle. Without the officer actually seeing the marijuana on Jeter's person, the judge couldn't convict. But Jeter's case fell apart when the arresting officer testified that after he was released from custody on bail, he asked, "Can I have my weed back?"

BAD DOG, DUDE!

San Diego resident Joel Dobrin, 32, was pulled over in 2012 while driving through Oregon. He quickly tried to stuff his stash of hash into a gym sock, but his pit bull had other ideas: He grabbed the sock and started playing tug-of-war. Just as Officer John Terrel approached the truck, the sock flew out of the window and landed at his feet. "I wish everyone traveled with their own personal drug dog," Terrel said. "It sure would make our job easier."

If they stood close together, everyone on Earth could fit in a space half the size of Belgium.

FAMILY FEUD: THE GUCCIS

One of the secrets of operating a successful family business is figuring out how to pass it along to your heirs without ending up in business-school textbooks as an example of how NOT to pass your business along to your heirs. It's not as easy as it sounds.

BAG MAN

In the late 1800s, a young Italian man named Guccio Gucci hopped a freighter for England after his parents' straw-hat business in Florence went bankrupt. In London, Gucci found a job at the Savoy, then (and now) one of the most exclusive hotels in the city. Accounts vary as to what he did there—he may have been a waiter, a dishwasher, or a bellhop—but whatever it was, Gucci was struck by all the fancy luggage that wealthy people brought with them when they checked into the hotel. The elegant leather steamer trunks, suitcases, and handbags were more than just functional items, he realized. They also served as status symbols that communicated their owners' social standing to the world.

Four years later, Gucci returned to Florence, where he found work in the leather goods industry, married, and started a family. He spent years learning the leather business and then, in 1921, opened his own store in one of the city's fanciest shopping districts. He stocked it with a wide assortment of goods, both made in Italy and imported from abroad.

INTELLIGENT DESIGN

Gucci's years observing the upper crust at the Savoy paid off: He developed a knack for sensing what wealthy tourists were likely to buy. When he couldn't find what he wanted from his suppliers, he designed his own products and hired local craftspeople to make them. His shop developed a reputation for excellent service and well-made, stylish goods sold at reasonable prices. As his business grew, Gucci began to stock only the goods designed and made by

Guinea pigs can walk as soon as they're born.

his firm—and the Gucci luxury brand was born.

Gucci ran the company that bore his name for more than 30 years. By the time he died in 1953, the business had grown into one of the most exclusive designer labels in Europe. Sophia Loren owned Gucci bags; so did Elizabeth Taylor, Katharine Hepburn, Princess Grace of Monaco, and Jacqueline Bouvier, soon to marry Senator John F. Kennedy.

Guccio had always resisted expanding outside of Italy, and it was only two weeks before he died that his son Aldo finally managed to open a store in New York City. He did it with a $6,000 bank loan—because his father refused to give him the money.

The reading of the old man's will sparked the first Gucci family feud. That was when Grimalda, Guccio's only daughter, learned she'd been disinherited from the family business merely because she was a woman. Grimalda fought her brothers Aldo, Vasco, and Rodolfo for a share of the company, but she lost.

CRACKS IN THE ARMOR

Aldo became the head of Gucci; his brothers Rodolfo and Vasco worked in production and design. Unlike the old man, Aldo had no qualms about expanding. Why should Gucci wait for its foreign customers to come to Italy, he reasoned, when the company could go to them? In the years that followed, Aldo opened Gucci stores in London, Paris, Tokyo, Hong Kong, and other cities around the world. He also added new product lines, including designer shoes, ready-to-wear clothing, watches, perfume, and a line of lower-cost canvas-and-leather goods that brought hundreds of millions of dollars into the company.

It grated on Aldo that he owned just a third of the company, and his brothers Vasco and Rodolfo got two thirds of the profits he was most responsible for generating. The situation "improved" for Aldo when Vasco died childless in 1974. Aldo and Rodolfo bought out Vasco's widow, split the shares, and became 50/50 owners. Rodolfo held on to his shares for the rest of his life, while Aldo gave each of his three sons 3.3 percent of the business, leaving him with a minority stake of 40 percent. But he still ran the company, and half of its profits went to his side of the family.

Historians believe Christopher Columbus may have brought syphilis to the Americas.

GENERATION GAP

Aldo and Rodolfo had their differences, but they managed to get along. It wasn't until their children came into the picture in the 1970s that the problems at Gucci really started. The biggest troublemaker: Aldo's son Paolo, one of the most creative members of the Gucci clan…and one of the most difficult to work with. Paolo clashed with both his father and his uncle: He wanted to start an entirely new designer label within the company, one with its own stores and targeted at a much younger demographic. Aldo and Rodolfo said no and relegated him to a frustratingly small role. It didn't work. In 1980 Paolo secretly launched his own designer label without telling Aldo or Rodolfo. When they found out, they fired him and then sued to block him from using the Gucci name in business.

Paolo didn't work at Gucci anymore, but he still owned a 3.3 percent stake in the company. That gave him the right to attend board meetings and to ask embarrassing questions about the way Aldo had managed Gucci's finances over the years (and helped himself to millions in company funds). More than one board meeting ended in a physical fight. Paolo even filed documents in U.S. court that laid bare how Aldo had cheated the U.S. government out of $7 million in taxes.

Aldo eventually served a year in federal prison for tax evasion, but that wasn't the only humiliation he suffered at the hands of his son. Though Aldo owned just a 40 percent stake in Gucci, he still ran the business, and as long as his brother Rodolfo was alive Aldo never had to worry about losing control of the company. That changed when Rodolfo died in 1983 at the age of 71, and his 50 percent stake passed to his only child and heir, Maurizio.

IT'S MY PLEATHER

Like his cousin Paolo, Maurizio wanted to make changes at Gucci. The company made big profits in the early 1980s, but it did so at the expense of its exclusive image. Long gone were the days that Gucci was associated with Jackie Kennedy and Princess Grace. Now, thanks to the huge success of Gucci's cheaper, mass-market line of leather-and-canvas bags, sold not just in Gucci's boutiques but in almost any retail store willing to stock them, the brand had become a tacky icon of conspicuous consumption. Gucci bags were now the kind of things that tourists, yuppies, and pimps bought at the mall, the airport, or even the drugstore.

Maurizio wanted to restore Gucci's faded luster, but after 30 years at the helm, his uncle Aldo wouldn't take advice from anyone, not even from the firm's largest shareholder—especially not while Gucci was earning more than $50 million a year in profits, much of it from products that Maurizio wanted to get rid of.

LET'S MAKE A DEAL

In the summer of 1984, Maurizio and Paolo came to an agreement: Paolo would vote his shares with Maurizio's, enabling him to take control of Gucci. In return, Maurizio promised he would buy out his cousin's 3.3 percent stake for $22 million, giving Paolo the money he needed to bankroll his own designer-goods company. The following September, the cousins put their plan into action, stripping Aldo of his power. They offered to let him stay on in a figurehead role, but when Aldo tried to fight back, he was thrown out of the company entirely.

Maurizio and Paolo's deal fell apart just two months later, before Maurizio could get his hands on Paolo's shares. Paolo turned Maurizio in to the Italian authorities for cheating on inheritance taxes, forcing Maurizio to flee to Switzerland to avoid arrest. Maurizio cleared up his tax problems without going to jail, but Aldo, Paolo, and Paolo's brothers continued to fight him for control of the company.

Maurizio became convinced that the only way he was ever going to have a free hand at Gucci was to buy out his relatives. He didn't have the money to do it himself, so he began looking for an outside investor. In 1987 he found one: Investcorp, a Bahraini investment bank, which agreed to buy the shares. Paolo sold out first, followed by his brothers, and then Aldo, who sold his shares in April 1989.

DUMB AND DUMBER

Maurizio was finally free to run Gucci as he saw fit, and Paolo now had the money he needed to get his own designer label off the ground. Neither cousin lasted very long. Paolo was the first to fail: Through a combination of high living and incompetent business decisions, he managed to burn through $40 million of his own money without ever opening for business. In 1993 he filed for bankruptcy, so broke that he couldn't even pay his phone bill, let alone the more than $350,000 in back alimony and child support he owed his ex-wife. When he died from liver failure in 1995 at the age of 64, the Gucci company bought the rights to his name from the bankruptcy court.

Maurizio didn't fare much better: His instincts about returning Gucci to its glory days were good, but he killed off many of the company's most profitable product lines before there was anything new to replace them with. Its boutique stores empty and its coffers hemorrhaging cash, by the end of 1991 Gucci had a negative net worth of $17.3 million and was losing $30 million a year.

DOWNWARD SPIRAL

It's possible that none of this would have threatened Maurizio's hold on Gucci had he not also racked up $40 million in personal debts at the same time that he was running the company into the ground. Maurizio had used his Gucci shares as collateral for personal loans, and now that the company was losing money, he had no income...and no way to pay his debts. Investcorp was the only thing keeping the company afloat, but it had long since lost faith in Maurizio's abilities. It refused to pump any more money into Gucci until he was gone.

Gucci was less than 48 days away from closing its doors and having its assets sold at auction when Maurizio, himself nearly bankrupt for nonpayment of personal debts, gave up the fight and sold his 50-percent stake to Investcorp. For the first time since 1921, there were no Guccis at Gucci, and there probably never will be again.

OUT OF THE ASHES

It's a testament to the strength of the Gucci brand that once Maurizio Gucci was replaced with competent management, it took the company just five years to repair its tarnished image and make record profits on more than $1 billion a year in sales. Maurizio was not so lucky: In 1995, the same year that Gucci went public, he was gunned down in Milan by a hit man hired by his ex-wife. She is serving a 29-year sentence for the murder.

Thomas Jefferson cut a piece of wood off a chair once owned by Shakespeare to take...

MUSIC ON TV

More tube tunes, from the '80s, '90s, and last week.
(Parts 1 and 2 are on page 125 and 280.)

***Yo! MTV Raps* (August 6, 1988).** In 1988, MTV started to branch out from showing a wall of music videos in random order all day. First, they launched the TV-trivia game show *Remote Control,* and then its first show dedicated to one specific kind of music: rap. Already a cultural presence in urban areas with large African-American populations, the presentation of rap videos five days a week on MTV turned rap into one of the two most dominant kinds of pop music in the United States, taking it from the cities to the suburbs. Hosted by DJs Doctor Dre and Ed Lover, the first video shown on *Yo! MTV Raps* was "Follow the Leader" by Eric B. & Rakim.

***MTV Unplugged* (November 26, 1989).** While the show later featured just one artist per episode, performing their songs without the aid of electric instruments, the first episode had three acts: Squeeze, Syd Straw, and Elliot Easton. The first act Squeeze with an acoustic rendition of "Pulling Mussels From the Shell."

By 1992 going on *Unplugged* was a major career milestone for a rock or pop act, demonstrating that beneath studio production, there was a legitimate musical talent. LL Cool J appeared in 1991 with a live, acoustic band for a unique rendition of "Mama Said Knock You Out," and the original members of KISS performed for the first time in nearly two decades on a 1995 episode, which led to a reunion tour. Mariah Carey's *Unplugged* cover of the Jackson 5's "I'll Be There" went to #1, and Nirvana's acoustic album sold more than six million copies. But the biggest success to come out of *Unplugged* was Eric Clapton, long on the sidelines of the music mainstream because of drug addiction and personal problems. His acoustic *Unplugged* disc sold more than 10 million copies and won the Grammy Award for Album of the Year in 1993.

***Total Request Live* (September 14, 1998).** Almost since its inception in 1981, MTV has had some kind of show where it

...home as a souvenir. It's on display at Monticello, Jefferson's home in Virginia.

counts down its most requested videos of the day. The 1998 incarnation, *Total Request Live*, became a cultural phenomenon. Broadcast live from MTV's studios overlooking Times Square, the show's audience was primarily teenagers, and the power of getting a top video on *TRL* propelled two music fads: teen pop and rap-metal. Exposure on *TRL* made superstars out of Britney Spears, Christina Aguilera, and *NSYNC in the pop category, and Kid Rock, Korn, and Limp Bizkit in the rock class. The very first video played on the show was the #10 video of the day: "Space Lord," by alternative rock band Monster Magnet.

***American Idol* (June 11, 2002).** Fox didn't have high hopes for a show that let young, amateur singers compete for a recording contract, so it scheduled it as a summer show, when viewing levels are less than half of what they are the rest of the year. *American Idol* was originally filler (in fact, ABC and NBC both turned down the chance to air it), but today it's the #1 show on TV, and has been for a record seven years straight. It's made indisputable stars out of winners Kelly Clarkson and Carrie Underwood, as well as runners-up, Chris Daughtry and Jennifer Hudson. Judge Simon Cowell became a household name, and host Ryan Seacrest an entertainment mogul with a production company that creates top-rated reality shows. Young people singing for a chance at stardom seems like an easy premise to copy, which is why the other networks tried—and mostly failed—to find their *American Idol* with shows like *Duets*, *The One*, *America's Got Talent*, *The X Factor*, *Country Star*, *America's Next Greatest Rock Band*, and more. As it still does, footage from auditions made up the first few episodes of the first season of *Idol*. The first person shown singing was an unidentified blonde woman who sang a portion of Bryan Adams' "Heaven."

***Glee* (May 19, 2009).** One of the most spectacular failures in TV history is the 1989 series *Cop Rock*, which combined searing police drama…with cops and robbers spontaneously bursting into Broadway-style musical numbers. ABC cancelled the show in the middle of its first season; that same year, CBS tried a musical/drama hybrid, too, with *Hull High*. It was a bomb, too. Maybe those shows were just ahead of their time, because when *Glee* debuted in 2009, it was an instant hit. Fox savvily promoted the show about an Ohio high school choir made up of misfits by selling recordings

Hanako, the oldest known koi fish, lived for 226 years. Most koi don't live past 45.

of the music performed on the show—primarily the cast singing popular songs by acts like Journey, Queen, Rihanna, and Lady Gaga. Twelve soundtrack albums have been released, and most have sold 500,000 copies or more. The *Glee* cast holds the record for most singles to hit the *Billboard* Hot 100 chart—205 through the 2011-12 season. (By comparison, the Beatles hit the charts a total of 70 times.) *Glee* is a top-20 TV show among viewers under age 40, and in 2011 Fox gave it the plum post-Super Bowl slot. The first song sung on the singin' teens show was the soul classic "Respect," by Mercedes Jones (actress Amber Riley) in her audition for the glee club.

***The Voice* (April 26, 2011).** The first song on this show was sung by the four celebrity judges—Christina Aguilera, Blake Shelton, Adam Levine, and Cee Lo Green—performing Gnarls Barkley's "Crazy." (Green is a member of Gnarls Barkley.) Then the show moved into its audition rounds, where amateur and unsigned singers, as well as singers dropped from their record labels, auditioned "blindly" for the judges—the judges sat in high-backed chairs, and if they liked what they heard, they spun their chair around, got a look at the singer, and added them to their "team." The first season winner was a guy named Javier Colon. Since *American Idol* debuted in 2002, every broadcast network has tried to find some sort of talent contest to compete with the ratings juggernaut. *The Voice* is the only one that's come close. It finished the 2010-11 TV season at #20 in the ratings; the next season, *The Voice* finished #3...just behind *Idol's* Wednesday episodes, and three spots above its Thursday edition.

* * *

MARX MADNESS

Groucho: "Do you think a mustache ever gets lonely?"

Chico: "Sure it gets-a lonely. Hey, when my grandfather's beard gets here, I'd like it to meet your mustache."

Groucho: "I'll talk it over with my mustache. Tell me, has your grandfather's beard got any money?"

Chico: "Money? Why, he fell hair to a fortune."

—***Monkey Business***

In Mayan civilization, cacao beans were currency. Painted-clay counterfeit beans were common.

IT'S THE END OF THE WORLD AS THEY KNOW IT

Even if you don't know anything else about the Mayan calendar, you may have heard that it supposedly predicted that the world would end on December 21, 2012. Here's a look at some other doomsdays that have come and gone.

Doomsday: February 20, 1524

Predicted by: Johannes Stöffler, a German mathematician, astronomer, astrologer, and professor at the University of Tübingen

End Times: In 1499 Stöffler calculated that 20 planetary "conjunctions," or appearances of two or more planets in the same part of the sky, would occur in 1524, and that 16 of these would occur under the astrological sign of Pisces (February 19–March 20). Pisces is the water sign, so Stöffler took this to mean that the world would be destroyed in a second Great Flood. His prediction was taken seriously. Thanks to the invention of Gutenberg's printing press a few decades earlier, pamphlets telling of his prediction were spread far and wide. As the date drew near, many people built boats and loaded them with provisions. One wealthy German nobleman, Count von Iggleheim, built a three-story ark.

Moment of Truth: The year 1524 began with much of central Europe in a drought, which soothed fears...until it began to drizzle on February 20, sparking a panic. A terrified mob descended on Count von Iggleheim's ark and tried to force their way onto it. In the riot that followed, von Iggleheim was stoned to death and hundreds of people were crushed or trampled. Then the skies cleared...and the mob realized it had all been for nothing.

Aftermath: Stöffler tried to save face by "recalculating" the date to 1528, but few people paid attention. He died in 1531.

Doomsday: May 19, 1780

Predicted by: Residents of New England and eastern Canada

(with a lot of help from mother nature)

End Times: Doomsday predictions typically begin with a forecast of when the world is supposed to end, followed by a wait to see if anything happens on that date. In the case of May 19, 1780, the process was reversed: Odd things began to happen, causing people to fear that the world was coming to an end.

Moment of Truth: For several days leading up to the 19th, the sky in much of the Eastern United States and Canada was a hazy yellow, and the sun and moon glowed red. Then on the morning of the 19th, the sky quickly darkened and by noon was as black as night. "If every luminous body in the universe had been shrouded in impenetrable shades, or struck out of existence, the darkness could not have been more complete," a Massachusetts man named Samuel Tenney wrote. "A sheet of white paper held within a few inches of the eyes was equally visible with the blackest velvet." Birds sang their evening songs in the darkness and then fell silent for the "night," and cows returned to their barns to sleep. When night fell many people went to bed despairing of ever seeing the sun again. "It was the general opinion that the day of judgement was at hand," Yale president Timothy Dwight wrote. It wasn't. The sun did come up on May 20, though the sky was still darker than usual, but that passed after a couple of days and life returned to normal.

Aftermath: So what caused New England's "Dark Day," as it came to be known? Smoke from a massive forest fire, hundreds of miles west in what is now Ontario's Algonquin Park. Wind carried the smoke all the way to the eastern seaboard, where it combined with fog and already overcast skies to turn the day as black as night. News traveled much more slowly in the 1780s, and nobody in New England knew about the fire. (That's *one* explanation, anyway: To this day some religious groups believe that the Dark Day was the fulfillment of Biblical end-times prophesy, and a sign that the second coming of Jesus Christ is just around the corner.)

Doomsday: May 18, 1910

Predicted by: Camille Flammarion, a French astronomer and founder of the French Astronomical Society

End Times: Halley's Comet was due to reappear in 1910, and this time the pass was going to be unusually close. For six hours on

May 18, the Earth was actually going to pass through the comet's tail. Flammarion hypothesized that when it did, there was a good chance that deadly cyanogen gas from the tail of the comet would penetrate the atmosphere and wipe out all life on the planet. A minority opinion to be sure and one loudly dismissed by other prominent scientists. But the newspapers knew a good story when they heard one. Eager to cash in on public interest in the comet, they happily published Flammarion's prediction.

Terrified people in North America and Europe stocked up on oxygen canisters, gas masks, special umbrellas, quack medicine "comet pills," and other doomsday supplies, then barricaded themselves in basements or rooms that had been carefully sealed off against outside air. One man in Atlanta had himself lowered to the bottom of a 40-foot well, where he remained until the crisis passed. All-night church services were held in the United States, Russia, and other places. For those who preferred comfort of a different kind, many saloons stayed open all night as well.

Moment of Truth: The earth passed through the comet's tail, and as just about every distinguished scientist *besides* Flammarion had predicted, nothing happened.

Aftermath: Somehow, Flammarion's reputation did not suffer much when the world failed to end as he'd predicted. He remained a respected figure in astronomy. Two craters, one on the moon, one on Mars, have been named in his honor, as has the comet 1021 Flammario.

* * *

UNCLAIMED ODDITIES

The Unclaimed Baggage Store in Scottsboro, Alabama, sells items that travelers left behind at airports. Some of their weirder ones:

- Moose antlers
- Vacuum-packed frogs
- 19th-century suit of armor
- 4,000-year-old mummified hawk
- Live rattlesnake
- Shrunken human head
- U.S. Air Force missile guidance system

In ancient Rome, parsnips were thought to have aphrodisiac properties.

THE POLITICALLY CORRECT QUIZ

How sensitive are you? Here are some real-life examples of "politically correct" and "politically incorrect" behavior. Guess which answer is the "correct" one. *(Answers are on page 602.)*

1. In 2011 the city council of York, England, banned children in its Sure Start toddler group from making a gesture while singing a nursery rhyme. What gesture, which nursery rhyme, and why?

a) Touching thumbs and forefingers together to make a diamond-shaped "star" while singing "Twinkle, Twinkle, Little Star." (The gesture might offend deaf people.)

b) Falling down while singing "Ring Around the Rosie." (It might offend epileptics and people with balance problems.)

c) Clasping their arms together to make a rocking cradle while singing "Rock-a-bye Baby." (Not all families can afford cradles.)

2. In May 2011, the newly founded *Journal of Animal Ethics* (University of Illinois Press) asked its readers to do what?

a) Support the creation of a labor union for racehorses, work dogs, and other service animals.

b) Stop feeding meat-based pet foods to their pets, on the grounds that it's cruel to animals. (Bone-shaped dog biscuits are "simulated" animal cruelty and just as bad.)

c) Stop referring to animals as "animals." (It's a "term of abuse.")

3. In the spring of 2011, a Seattle elementary school renamed which of the following?

a) Easter eggs: "Too religious." The school calls them "spring spheres."

b) Tic-Tac-Toe: "Demeaning to kids with missing or deformed toes." The school now calls the game "Bic-Bac-Boe."

c) Mohawk haircuts: "Racism." Children as young as eight are permitted to wear them, but now they're called "Punk-O's."

4. In May 2010, administrators at Ireland's University College Cork disciplined Dr. Dylan Evans, a behavioral scientist, after a colleague accused him of sexual harassment. What spurred the colleague, Dr. Rossana Salerno-Kennedy, to make the accusation?

a) Dr. Evans insisted on calling her the department chair*woman*, not the *chair*. "Hey, you're a *woman*, not a chair," he said.

b) He showed her a peer-reviewed article from a scientific journal. Topic: the mating habits of fruit bats.

c) Every time someone asked Evans a question he pointed to Salerno-Kennedy and said, "Ask the rear admiral."

5. In 2003 the Park Road Junior Infant and Nursery School in Batley, England, banned children under seven from reading the book *The Three Little Pigs*. Why?

a) The Royal Society for the Protection of the English Wolf (PEW) objected to the stereotyping of the Big Bad Wolf as "bad."

b) The U.K. chapter of People for the Ethical Treatment of Animals (PETA) objected to the Big Bad Wolf eating two of the pigs. They also objected to the third pig cooking the Big Bad Wolf in a pot after he came down the chimney of the pig's brick house.

c) Stories about pigs are offensive to Muslims, who don't eat pork.

* * *

TEN TV SHOW TITLES THAT WERE CHANGED FOR RERUNS

1. *Laverne and Shirley* became *Laverne and Shirley and Company*

2. *I Love Lucy* became *Lucy in Connecticut*

3. *The Lucy-Desi Comedy Hour* became *We Love Lucy*

4. *Emergency!* became *Emergency One*

5. *CHiPs* became *CHiPs Patrol*

6. *Marcus Welby, MD* became *Robert Young, Family Doctor*

7. *The Carol Burnett Show* became *Carol Burnett and Friends*

8. *The Ropers* became *Three's Company's Friends: The Ropers*

9. *CSI* became *CSI: Las Vegas*

10. *Wagon Train* became *Major Adams, Trailmaster*

Ancient Greeks and Romans were short: men averaged 5' 5½"; women: 5' 2".

THE UNITED STATES OF *BELGIUM*?

In the late 18th century, the United States pioneered a unique form of government—semi-autonomous states joined together under a central federal government. Plenty of other places around the world have since tried to emulate the idea, establishing their own "United States." But the name alone does not guarantee success.

THE UNITED STATES OF COLOMBIA

United: In the early 19th century, Simon Bolivar led several fights for independence across South America, expelling Spain as the dominant power by 1819. Portions of countries that are today Panama, Peru, Brazil, Ecuador, Venezuela, and Colombia united in various permutations as one nation from 1819 to 1866 under the names Gran Colombia, the Republic of New Granada, the Granadine Confederation, and finally in 1863 as the United States of Colombia.

Un-stated: By that point, the federation included only Colombia and Panama. In 1903 Panamanian rebel groups began agitating for independence from Colombia, urged on and financed by American interests who wanted to build a canal across the isthmus of Panama. Panama got its freedom, Colombia got a little smaller, and the U.S. got its canal.

THE UNITED STATES OF BELGIUM

United: Between about 1500 and the early 1800s, Belgium was variously under the control of Burgundy, the Habsburg monarchy, Spain, Italy, Austria, and France. In 1790 Belgians revolted against then-ruling Habsburg emperor Joseph II and established the republic of the United States of Belgium.

Un-stated: It was short-lived—the Habsburgs regained control by the end of the year and retitled it the United Kingdom of the Netherlands. (Modern-day, independent Belgium emerged in 1830 after splitting from the Netherlands.)

THE UNITED STATES OF BRAZIL

United: Brazil won its independence from Portugal in 1822. The name "Brazil" (after the brasil tree, harvested for its red dye) had long been used by Portuguese settlers. In 1889, when Brazil became a republic, it adopted as its official name the Republic of the United States of Brazil.

Un-stated: In 1964 Brazil's left-wing president Joao Goulart was overthrown in a military coup after he tried to introduce socialism to Brazil. Seeking to distance itself from the republican and socialist eras, in 1967 the military changed the name of the country to the Federative Republic of Brazil.

THE UNITED STATES OF INDONESIA

United: At the end of World War II, the native people of the Dutch East Indies declared independence from the Netherlands, but it took four years of bloody fighting before the Dutch conceded the inevitable and granted independence to the "Republic of the United States of Indonesia," which consisted of Indonesia and fifteen smaller states created by the Dutch since 1945.

Un-stated: In early 1950 the fifteen other states were dissolved and incorporated into Indonesia. With no other states left in the United States, in August 1950, the RUSI was officially dissolved and the Republic of Indonesia was proclaimed a unitary state.

THE UNITED STATES OF STELLALAND

United: The Republic of Stellaland was a *Boer* (Dutch-speaking settler) republic in southern Africa that broke away from British Bechuanaland in 1882. The following year it merged with another breakaway Boer republic, the State of Goshen, to form the United States of Stellaland in the hope of better resisting the British.

Un-stated: It didn't work: In December 1884, the British invaded Stellaland, abolished the republic, and reabsorbed the territory into British Bechuanaland.

* * *

"Like Superman, I too have a Fortress of Solitude. Only mine flushes."

—**Jerry Thomas**

Acrobat Joseph Spah survived the *Hindenburg* disaster by diving out the zeppelin's window.

DON'T BELIEVE EVERYTHING YOU HEAR

At the BRI, one of our goals is to make readers look at the world in a new way. After reading this article, you'll also be listening *in a new way. Listening to what? To sounds that seem real...but aren't.*

WHAT'S NEW IS OLD AGAIN

Have you ever heard of a *skeuomorph?* Pronounced SKEW-a-morf, it's a feature that's been added to a new version of a product that, while not functionally necessary, makes consumers more at ease with the new technology. For example, the "PLAY" button on your DVD player has a little arrow on it that points to the right. There's nothing inside a digital player that actually moves to the right, but there was on old VHS tape players. The arrow remains because consumers are used to it.

When it comes to sound, skeuomorphs are a big deal: If a product doesn't sound right, it can be a very tough sell to consumers. Companies employ sound designers—not unlike the sound engineers who work on Hollywood movies—to ensure that every noise a product makes will be pleasing to the ears. Sometimes it's for nostalgia's sake; sometimes for safety...and sometimes for more nefarious reasons.

• **Digital cameras:** For more than a century, film cameras had mechanical shutters that clicked when the shutter button was pressed. Digital SLR cameras have a similar electro-mechanical shutter that also clicks, although not as loudly. But what about cell phone cameras and small point-and-shoots? They, too, have shutters, but they're so small that the sound they make is barely audible. So manufactures have added fake shutter sounds to let the picture-taker know that a picture has been taken. Many people find this feature annoying, and some camera models allow you to change the sound to a beep. A few models even allow you to turn off the sound altogether.

However, there's a movement underway to mandate that these fake shutter sounds not only remain, but that they become *louder*. Reason: to prevent creepy voyeurs from secretly snapping photos in locker rooms and dressing rooms. In 2009 U.S. Rep. Peter King (R-NY) drafted a bill called the "Camera Phone Predator Alert Act" which would "require mobile phones containing digital cameras to make a sound when a photograph is taken." In Japan and South Korea, the governments have urged camera makers to keep the fake shutter noise to deter people from secretly taking pictures up women's skirts (apparently a problem in the Far East). So far, camera makers haven't complied, and King's bill went nowhere, but the shutter-noise issue remains controversial.

• **Car doors:** When you close a steel car door, it's loud. In recent years, safety and emissions standards have forced auto makers to use lighter materials, resulting in new doors that sound more like toys. Because most people equate a lower pitch with power, and a higher pitch with weakness, auto engineers have redesigned lighter car doors with dampeners and other materials in order to replace the tinny "tink" with a much more satisfying "thunk."

• **Turn signals:** The "tick-tock" you hear in newer cars doesn't correspond to the actual signal mechanism, which is a silent electrical relay switch. The sound is there mainly to alert the driver that the signal is on, but it's been carefully crafted to be noticeable without being too loud, and to have a pleasing tone. (In fact, nearly *every* noise you hear in a new car has been labored over by engineers—from the seatbelt click to the sound the seat makes when your butt hits it. If the sound doesn't sound good enough, it will be tweaked until it does.)

• **Electric car motors:** To ensure that pedestrians and cyclists hear them coming, silent electric cars come with speakers under the hood that play a recorded engine noise. But not just any random engine noise will do: The designers of the electric Nissan Leaf, for example, hired focus groups to listen to dozens of engine sounds and then vote on the one they found the most satisfying.

• **Harley-Davidsons:** These motorcycles make a very distinctive "potato-potato" sound, but that wasn't originally by design; it was the result of the cylinders of the V-twin engines firing at an

Breath test: The Pyruvate scale measures pungency in onions and garlic.

uneven rate (which was necessary to pack more punch into a smaller engine). Over time that noise became so associated with Harleys that other bike makers tried to copy it, leading the company to attempt to trademark the sound in the 1990s. The trademark bid was unsuccessful, but Harley-Davidson claimed they had won "in the court of public opinion."

Ironically, in recent decades Harley engineers have had to perform some trickery to retain that distinctive sound. Because of tighter engine regulations, the cylinders now fire at a more even rate, so the company has set up a "Noise, Vibration & Harshness Department" tasked with meeting regulations, but also meeting riders' expectations of what a Hog should sound like.

• **Segways:** If you've heard a Segway scooter rolling down the sidewalk, you know it makes a very distinctive whir that sounds a bit like the futuristic vehicles from *The Jetsons*. That's no accident. Segway designers tweaked the two-stage transmission until both stages hit notes that are exactly one octave apart. That gives the Segway a modern, musical sound—whereas two random notes could have made it sound clunky and out of tune.

• **Computer mouses:** The Apple Mighty Mouse makes a clicking sound when the user scrolls, yet there's no actual mechanism that clicks. Instead, a tiny speaker inside the mouse plays a simulated clicking sound. (To see if your mouse has a speaker inside, unplug it and roll the scroll ball. If it's silent, the click is fake.)

• **Ebooks:** There are some aspects of reading a real book that simply can't be captured by reading an ebook...but that hasn't stopped ebook makers from trying. Some ebook readers feature faux paper texture, page-turning animation, and the actual sound of a paper page turning.

• **Slot machines:** As tickets replace coins in slot machines, the familiar "ching-ching" sound is in danger of going away. No problem: Newer slot machines that award tickets play recorded coin sounds. To entice non-gamblers into the room, the same sound is heard whether the player wins 25 cents or 25 dollars. And not just any "ching-ching" will do. As one slot machine designer explained, "We mix several recordings of coins falling on a metal tray and then fatten up the sound." On digital slots that don't have a spinning wheel inside, a simulated spinning sound is played. Same thing if there's no lever. In fact, some slot machines employ up to 40 fake sounds just to keep people gambling.

• **Phones:** You can set your phone's ring tone to whatever you want, but when you *make* a call—be it on a mobile phone or on a landline—you always hear the familiar "ring-ring" sound. Callers haven't actually heard the sound made by an phone ringing on the other end since the 1950s. It's been simulated ever since.

• **Football games:** Sports fans have certain auditory expectations when they go to the stadium, so little is left to chance. Even the vendors who walk through the stands are trained to yell "Get yer hot dogs!" and "Cold beer here!" in a certain way. That adds to the nostalgia value of going to a game. But some things you hear at a sporting venue may be designed to give the home team an advantage. In 2007 the Indianapolis Colts were accused of piping in fake crowd noise during a home game against the New England Patriots—but only when the Patriots had the ball and the snapper needed to hear the quarterback's call. Colts officials denied it, claiming that what fans watching on TV said sounded like a "CD skipping" was actually feedback caused by the CBS Sports broadcast of the game. Nevertheless, the NFL enacted strict rules against this practice, with heavy fines for offenders. Since then, a few other teams have been accused of using fake crowd noise, but nothing's been proven.

• **The Olympics:** During the 2012 broadcast of the Summer Games in London, NBC admitted to some fakery with the rowing races. Because the motors on the chase boats and the TV helicopters were so loud, it would have been impossible to pick up audio from the actual rowers. So the Games' official sound engineer, Dan Baxter, didn't even try to use the live audio. Result: The viewers watching at home heard a playback of rowers on a calm, quiet river that Baxter had recorded himself. "Some people think it's cheating," he said. "I don't think I'm cheating anybody. The sound is there. It's just not necessarily real time. When you see a rower, your mind thinks you should hear the rower and that's what we deliver."

A METEORIC FOOTNOTE

On page 373 we told you the story of the devastating Chicago and Peshtigo fires of October 8, 1871. Were they caused by the wrath of God, as many believed at the time? Were they caused by a long drought and a gigantic low-pressure system? Or did something else spark the fires on that fateful day? After almost 150 years, the debate rages on.

A HOT THEORY

The chance of two historically significant fires starting on the same day only 250 miles apart still baffles experts. No definitive conclusion has yet been reached about what started either fire or why they spread so fast and furiously.

In 2003 former fire captain Mica Calfee read an article about the fires in *Firehouse Magazine*. Like most people, Calfee knew about the Great Chicago Fire of 1871, but when he read that an even *bigger* fire had occurred nearby on the same night, he was astounded. Then he read this statement: "Some astronomers point out that there was a meteor shower that night and suggest this as a possible cause." Calfee decided to investigate.

FIRE IN THE SKY

Survivors of the Peshtigo Fire had described a "horizontal tornado, with tremendous winds blowing fire everywhere." These stories convinced Peshtigo historian Robert Couvillion that the meteor theory was true. To Calfee, that *sounded* like a meteor blast, but as a master firefighter, he also knew that any large fire—especially one as big as the Peshtigo inferno—could create a horizontal draft.

Several other sources, including retired McDonnell Douglas physicist Robert Wood, claimed that a comet called Biela was to blame for the 1871 fires. The periodic comet was first spotted in 1772. In 1846 observers noted that the comet had split in two. Both parts were spotted in 1852 and were due back in 1872, but they were never seen again.

What happened? Wood theorized that the primary or secondary part of Biela could have sped up as it passed Jupiter so that it arrived a year early...in 1871. "The debris carried a mixture of rock and ice when the Earth plowed through the field in October

1871," said Wood. "The result was hundreds of hot rocks flying through the atmosphere and in many cases striking tinder-dry woods."

Just after 9:00 p.m. on the evening of October 8, 1871, fires erupted almost simultaneously not just in Chicago and Peshtigo, but across *three different states* in the Great Lakes region—Wisconsin, Illinois, and Michigan. Eyewitness reports seem to support the meteor theory: A number of survivors reported seeing "balls of fire" or "flaming balloons" falling from the sky.

ARE YOU GUYS NUTS?

After writing about the meteor theory for *Meteorite Magazine*, Calfee was contacted by George Zay, a former tracker for the International Meteor Organization (the guys NASA calls when they need an expert opinion about meteor activity). His reaction: "If any astronomer suggests a meteor caused a fire somewhere, he might as well be reading tea leaves."

Wait! Everyone knows meteorites are red-hot when they strike the ground, right? "Wrong," said Zay. "If it weren't for the *ablation* process," he wrote, "there could be room for the validity of a meteorite reaching the ground hot. But ablation is there with every meteorite." What's the ablation process? Calfee's research had actually taught him a lot about it. Here are a few of the facts he shared in his article:

> When a meteoroid enters the atmosphere it does two things. Its surface heats up due to friction with the air and it begins to quickly slow down. The heating causes the outermost millimeter of material to melt and slough off. As the meteoroid loses mass during its flight it disperses its heat, thus cooling the outer surface. A freshly fallen meteorite is often cool, if not cold, to the touch. There are reports of ice condensing upon the surface of meteorites as they lay on the ground in warm conditions.

Much as he enjoyed researching the meteor theory, in the end, Calfee drew this conclusion: "It is probably safe to assume that the only way an object falling from outer space could have caused the Great Chicago Fire was if it had frightened Mrs. O'Leary's cow into kicking over the fabled lantern." (Which isn't true either.)

STALL OF FAME: MR. FLOATIE

If you've ever been to Victoria, B.C., you know it's one of North America's prettiest cities. You may also know that its sewer system is, well...Victorian. Here's the story of one person who decided to do something about that.

TROUBLED WATERS

James Skwarok was a university student and environmental activist living in Victoria in 2004. The city is a popular tourist destination, but it has a dirty secret: It's one of the very few Canadian cities that does not treat its sewage. The city's wastewater is screened to remove objects larger than 6 mm in diameter (¼ inch), but that's it. The raw sewage is then piped out into the Strait of Juan de Fuca, which separates Vancouver Island from the state of Washington. There, about a mile from shore and in waters more than 200 feet deep, it's released into the swift-moving currents through outflow pipes on the seafloor. Thirty-four million gallons of sewage are disposed of in this manner each day. It's something that would be illegal in Europe and in the United States, just 20 miles to the south. But not in Canada, which has no national wastewater treatment standards.

Skwarok was disgusted by the thought of that much sewage flowing into the waters off Victoria every day. He wanted to call attention to the problem with something more than just a bumper sticker, a pamphlet, or a website...but how? An idea came to him one night while watching the animated TV series *South Park*. The episode featured the character Mr. Hankey the Christmas Poo, a talking piece of excrement who wears a Santa hat. That got Skwarok thinking: Why not dress up as a giant ocean poo?

ALL DRESSED UP

Skwarok's friends thought his idea was hilarious. They formed an organization called People Opposed to Outfall Pollution (POOP) and set to work building a costume. Starting with a backpack frame, they added some plastic garden mesh to give it shape, then added a one-inch layer of mattress foam and covered it with

The Super Soaker was invented by a NASA engineer. Original name: the Power Drencher.

brown velour fabric. They made two eyes out of clay and a smiling red mouth out of latex, added a jaunty yellow sailor cap, and named their seven-foot-tall creation "Mr. Floatie."

MAKING A SPLASH

Mr. Floatie began showing up at festivals, parades, yacht races, town hall meetings, and anyplace else Skwarok thought would call attention to his cause. He made appearances at all the top tourist spots, even greeting cruise ships as they pulled into port on their way to Alaska. For more than one foreign visitor to the Garden City, the first Canadian they ever met was a walking, talking turd at the bottom of their cruise ship gangplank, passing out "business cards"—hand-stamped squares of toilet paper—and eager to bring outsiders up to date on the city's sewage problem. "I'm Mr. Floatie, the ocean poo, if you live in Victoria, I come from you," he'd sing. A catchy jingle to be sure, but one that probably kept the city's tourism officials up at night.

In the summer of 2005, POOP organized Victoria's first-ever Mr. Floatie Toilet Bowl Regatta, a flotilla of inflatable boats (all outfitted with porcelain toilets) with names like *Montezuma's Revenge* and *Gas Bag*. That fall Mr. Floatie entered the race for mayor of Victoria, but was blocked from participating in all-candidate meetings, and then ejected from the race when city officials went to court and complained that the law did not allow for "costumed characters" to run for office, only real people. ("Of course I'm not a real person," Mr. Floatie replied. "I'm a big piece of poop!")

CHANGING COURSE

Skwarok kept at it for three years. His antics made news all over the world ("Mr. Floatie Causes a Stink in Canada," read one South African newspaper headline)...and generated a lot of unflattering publicity for British Columbia, just as the province was hoping to shine in the buildup to the 2010 Winter Olympics, held 60 miles away in Vancouver. The attention helped pressure the city into re-examining its waste treatment policies: In September 2005, the Capital Regional District, which oversees the city's sewage (non)treatment, ordered a scientific and environmental review of the city's practices, giving new life to the debate over wastewater treatment that had been going on for years.

Language with the fewest vowels: Ubyx (Turkey), with 2. The last native speaker died in 1992.

DOOS AND DON'TS

Advocates for a sewage treatment plant argued that in addition to the "ick" factor associated with pumping 31 million gallons of raw sewage into the sea every day, there was a significant environmental impact as well. The wastewater contained chemicals, heavy metals, and other contaminants that are harmful to aquatic life. Any toxic chemicals that entered the water were likely to find their way into the food chain and accumulate at the top—namely, in the killer whales that live in the waters around Vancouver Island.

Opponents of sewage treatment argued that the estimated $1 billion cost of building a sewage treatment plant outweighed the benefits, and they questioned whether there were really any benefits at all. In treatment plants, sewage is exposed to oxygen and bacteria, which quickly break it down into less harmful substances. The opponents argued that a sewage treatment plant would only do artificially—and at great expense to the taxpayer—what the oxygen- and bacteria-rich waters around Vancouver Island were supposedly doing naturally. "In the oceans, there is the possibility of allowing the natural effect of heavily oxygenated sea water to treat sewage," the *Victoria Times Colonist* argued in an editorial. "Nature has provided us with a natural toilet, whose flushing action disperses our screened sewage far and wide."

TOP O' THE PIPE

As for the hazardous materials in wastewater, for years Victoria had pursued a "top-of-the-pipe" waste management strategy, requiring chemical companies, dental offices, and other hazardous-waste-generating businesses to outfit their operations with special waste traps, collectors, and separators to prevent harmful materials from entering city sewers in the first place. Victoria spent more than $1 million a year on these source-control efforts and an additional $1 million monitoring the sewage discharge area for signs of environmental damage. Opponents of the sewage treatment plant argued that it would be much more cost-effective to expand and improve these efforts than it would be to spend a billion dollars (or more) on a sewage treatment plant.

The scientific review was completed in July 2006. While it found little evidence of health risks or environmental degradation to date, given that the population of the greater Victoria area was expected to double by 2035, it also concluded that continued dumping of raw sewage into the sea was unsustainable.

Acting on this information, the B.C. government ordered Victoria to come up with a sewage treatment program. In 2009, the Capital Regional District approved a plan to build treatment plants in four different locations in and around Victoria, for a total cost of $1.2 billion, with the provincial government and the federal government picking up two-thirds of the construction costs. The plants are scheduled to come online in 2016. Estimated cost to local residents: about $700 a year, or just under $60 a month.

GOTTA GO!

As of 2012, Victoria's sewage is still untreated while the city waits for the treatment plants to come online, but Mr. Floatie rarely makes appearances anymore. James Skwarok has moved on to other issues. Now a substitute teacher, he dresses up in a red-and-yellow superhero costume in his spare time and battles global warming as "CO_2 Man," part of a campaign to pressure the Canadian government into placing strict caps on the country's greenhouse gas emissions.

Skwarok hopes his new character will be as effective as the old one. "Mr. Floatie definitely helped," he told an interviewer in 2006. "I mean, you can't ignore a seven-foot-tall walking, talking, dancing piece of poo."

* * *

GOOD LUCK, BAD LUCK

In 2000 the International Olympic Committee enacted a rule change that allowed athletes from less developed, less equipped countries into the Olympics without meeting minimum qualifications. Swimmer Eric Moussambani from Equatorial Guinea made it to the Olympics that way. His first event was the 100-meter freestyle...in which all seven of his competitors were disqualified for false starts. Result: Moussambani swam unopposed in his heat and won with the slowest winning time in Olympic swimming history, 1:52.72. (The eventual gold medalist, Pieter van den Hoogenband of the Netherlands, did it in just over 47 seconds.)

Most popular restaurant choice for a first date: Italian.

TURKEYS & WHALES

More casino terms to make even the lowest grind joint pokie pigeon sound like a whale with coattails.

Camouflage: Things an expert gambler does to look like a novice to casino security (like appearing drunk, wearing disguises, playing badly, etc.).

Grind Joint: A casino that caters to low rollers. Example: the El Cortez, a low-budget hotel off Fremont Street in Las Vegas.

Carpet Joint: A casino that caters to high rollers. Examples: the Bellagio, the MGM Grand, Mandalay Bay, etc.

Whale: The highest of the high-stakes gamblers. Whales bet a minimum of $500,000 an hour, for hours on end, without flinching. (Estimated worldwide whale population: 200–250.)

Nit: A poker player who only raises on their best hands.

Card Mechanic: A dealer who cheats by using sleight of hand to manipulate the cards.

Coattailing: Placing the same bets as a nearby gambler who is winning.

Top-hatter: Someone who tries to place a roulette bet after the wheel has stopped spinning.

Bustout Dealer: A crooked dealer who specializes in breaking winning streaks, so that gamblers don't leave with too much of the casino's money.

Bustout Joint: A gambling establishment where all the dealers are cheats.

Tell Player: A gambler who specializes in observing subtle, involuntary "tell" signs that reveal whether another player has good or bad cards.

Color Up: To trade in a large number of low-value chips for a smaller number of high-value chips.

Turkey: A player who's rude to the dealer.

Apple: A sucker. Also called a *cucumber*, *egg*, *fish*, *pigeon*, *sheep*, or *donkey*.

Soft Player: A sucker who keeps playing until all of their money is gone.

First president of the Republic of Chile: Bernardo O'Higgins, a Chilean of Irish descent.

OLDSTERS

Old age ain't no place for sissies."—Bette Davis

"Like everyone else who makes the mistake of getting older, I begin each day with coffee and obituaries."

—Bill Cosby

"Old age is like a plane flying through a storm. Once aboard, there's nothing you can do."

—Golda Meir

"I guess I don't so much mind being old, as I mind being fat and old."

—Peter Gabriel

"Age isn't important unless you're a cheese."

—Helen Hayes

"I'll tell you how to stay young: Hang around with older people."

—Bob Hope

"At 50, everyone has the face he deserves."

—George Orwell

"It's true, some wines improve with age, but only if the grapes were good in the first place."

—Abigail Van Buren

"You don't stop laughing when you grow old, you grow old when you stop laughing."

—George Bernard Shaw

"My dad's pants kept creeping up on him. By 65 he was just a pair of pants and a head."

—Jeff Altman

"After a man passes 60, his mischief is mainly in his head."

—Edgar Watson Howe

"You know you're getting old when all the names in your black book have M.D. after them."

—Harrison Ford

"It's paradoxical that the idea of living a long life appeals to everyone, but getting old doesn't appeal to anyone."

—Andy Rooney

"I was born in 1962. True. And the room next to me was 1963."

—Joan Rivers

"Wisdom is the reward for surviving our own stupidity."

—Brian Rathbone

"Don't complain about getting old. Many people don't have that privilege."

—Earl Warren

"The older I get, the better I used to be."

—Lee Trevino

What do Hawaii and the Galapagos Islands have in common? Earth's only green sand beaches.

"JACK AND THE HEIFER HIDE"

On page 388, we told you about Jack tales an' how they traveled all the way from the Old World to the hills and hollers of Appalachia. Here's one of Jack's most rip-roarin' stories (which we should warn you contains some debauchery and killin'). As master storyteller Monroe Ward said a century ago, "It'll not do just to read 'em out of a book, you gotta tell 'em to make 'em go right." So gather your kinfolk 'round and have yourselves an old-timey story-tellin' session!

JACK used to have two brothers. Will and Tom were their names. One day their daddy gave the three of 'em a patch of land way up in the Smoky Mountains to start a farm. He gave Will and Tom a horse apiece, but Jack, bein' the youngest—he didn't get nothin' but a little ol' heifer. (That's a cow for you city folk.)

The three brothers fixed themselves up a pole shanty and set to work a-clearin' new ground. Well, Will and Tom did, anyway. All Jack did was loaf around the rest of the day. His brothers didn't like that much and felled a tree upon Jack's heifer to get back at him. Jack didn't mind that none. He just skinned it and lived off the beef. Got so big, he plumb busted out of his overalls!

Time came that the beef all ran out, and Will and Tom wouldn't share none of their rations with Jack. All he had to his name was that heifer hide, and he thought long and hard about what he could do with it.

JACK hatched a plan. He studied up on proper preservation techniques and then salted the heifer hide to dry it. Then he stuffed it full of corn shucks and set off for low ground, a-draggin' that stuffed heifer behind him by the tail. It was near about the funniest thing you ever saw—Jack draggin' that old thing down the road, it a-goin' *fump fump fump* every step he took!

It was gettin' dark now, and Jack was hoping for a meal, so he stopped at a farmhouse and knocked on the door. A woman ran up—*clomp clomp clomp*—and opened it like she was all excited.

But then she frowned when she saw Jack and his heifer hide. "What do you want?" she asked.

"Just a floor to sleep on, ma'am, and perhaps a nibble to eat, and then I'll be on my way. I'm takin' this here magic heifer to the city tomorrow to sell it!"

"No," said the woman. "Blame the man of the house. He ain't here, and he wouldn't like it. And I don't believe in no magic."

"Surely you wouldn't deny a poor farm boy a floor to sleep on," Jack begged. She looked past him and quickly pulled him inside.

"You go up in the loft and keep quiet. If you don't say a word, I'll fix you up with some cornbread later." So Jack went up the stairs, dragging his heifer hide behind him—*fump fump fump*.

JACK heard someone come in the front door. He peeped down through a knothole in the floor to get a look. Now, Jack wasn't that old, but he'd been around long enough to know that somethin' fishy was up. This dandy feller who came in all dressed up in a collar and necktie was by no means the man of the house. "Well, I'll be," said Jack to himself. "She's a-courtin' another."

The woman told the dandy feller that her husband wasn't going to be home until late. "So you just sit here, and I'll feed you like a king!" She went to the cupboard and retrieved a veritable feast: fried ham and chicken pie and whiskey. "Mmm-mmm," said Jack. He looked on as the woman and the dandy feller started chowin' down. And Jack's poor old stomach a-started grumblin'—*fump fump fump*.

JACK heard the clip-clop of a horse and figgered that must be the old man ridin' up to the house. The woman yelled out, "Law! It's my old man! You best git out of sight!" So she pushed that dandy feller—collar and necktie and all—into an old chest a-sittin' in the corner. Then she hid the vittles and whiskey in the cupboard.

The old man pushed open the door and sat at the supper table. "Git me some vittles, wife," he barked. "I'm plumb starved to death!" Jack's eye was pressed almost all the way through that knot in the floor as he watched the woman give her hungry husband a not-so-feastly helping of stale cornbread and cold potatoes.

The ancient Etruscans were the first to use gold in dentistry (about 600 BC).

Just then, Jack done hatched another plan.

JACK picked up his heifer hide and went *thump thump thump* on the floor. "Now what in tarnation is that racket up there?" said the man of the house.

"Oh," replied his wife. "Just some poor farm boy who begged me to let him spend the night. Pay him no mind at all."

The old man yelled to the ceiling, "You come on down here!" So Jack came down a-dragging his heifer hide—*fump fump fump*.

"What's your name, stranger?" asked the old man.

"They call me Jack."

"Well, come and set down, Jack. Eat with me. T'aint much, but you're welcome to it."

Jack bit off a corner of his cornbread and started gasping like it was a-chokin' him. "I'm sorry to insult, sir," he said as he spit it out. "But this here food ain't fit enough to feed a pig."

"I'm inclined to agree," admitted the man. "Blame the woman of the house," he said with a sideways glare toward his wife.

JACK turned and looked at the heifer hide. "What's that?" he said to the dead animal. "There's some better food in *where*? Oh, hush. You ought not carry on like that."

The old man got a confused look upon his face and asked Jack, "What did that heifer tell you? Better food where? Speak up!"

"I cain't tell you what the magic heifer hide done said, sir," said Jack. "Might make the woman of the house angry."

"Don't blame the woman. Tell me what it said, Jack."

"Well, if'n you must know, it told me there was some fried ham and chicken pie up there in yon cupboard."

The old man looked at his wife. "Is this true, woman?"

"That boy is a liar, and that heifer ain't magic, and there ain't no more food in the cupboard!"

"Open it," said the old man.

So she did. "Well, what do you know? I guess I forgot about it."

JACK and the old man commenced to eatin' till they were fit to burst. Then Jack made like the heifer was talkin' to him again. "There's some whiskey *where*?" Then Jack pointed to the cupboard. The wife shot a nasty look at him and put the whiskey on the table. Then Jack and the old man got good an' likkered up, all the while the man was a-lookin' at that heifer hide. "I just got to have it," he finally said. "I know my woman is keeping secrets from me, and that old heifer is sure to keep her honest."

"I wouldn't sell my heifer hide for nothing!" said Jack. But then he sat back and said, "But I would sell it for something."

"Name your price, son."

"I'd let it go for a hunnerd guineas…and that old chest over there in the corner." (Now, you do remember that dandy feller was still hiding in that there chest, right?)

"You cain't have that chest!" shouted the wife. "It belonged to my great-grandmother, who gave it to my auntie, who gave it to her second cousin's half-sister, who gave it me!"

"Blame you an' all your kinfolks!" said the old man. "If Jack wants that musty old chest, he can have it. Yer just scared of the hide 'cause you cain't hide nothin' from me when it's around."

JACK bid farewell to his heifer hide and the bickering couple, and walked out with a hunnerd guineas in his pocket while a-draggin' the old chest behind him—*fump fump fump*. Finally, he set it down and said aloud, "I sure am tired of dragging this big ol' box around. Think I'll just chuck it off this old cliff right here."

"Please don't do that!" said the dandy feller, who'd been quiet as a mouse up until then. "Let me out, and I'll reward your kindness with a hunnerd guineas."

"Honest?" asked Jack. "You don't seem all too trustworthy." The dandy feller poked the money through a crack in the chest, and Jack obliged to let him out. He laughed as the dandy feller ran off as fast just as he could.

JACK went home a lot richer and told his brothers, Will and Tom, he made two hunnerd guineas just by sellin' off his heifer hide. So the next day, Will and Tom shot their horses and stuffed 'em with corn shucks, but they didn't use Jack's fancy preservation techniques, and the hides started to rot. They went to house after house a-tryin' to sell them stinky horses, but no one wanted 'em.

Will and Tom chucked their horse hides into the brush and

Oldest Declaration of Independence signer: Ben Franklin. He was 70.

headed on back home, mad as hornets. They grabbed Jack and put him in a sack and then dragged him down to the river to drown him. But Will and Tom—as you may have guessed by now aren't the sharpest tools in the shed—well, they forgot to bring a rope to secure the sack and had to go home to get one. So they put a big log on the sack to keep their little brother from a-gettin' away.

JACK heard an old shepherd a-drivin' a herd of sheep toward him. He started a-wrigglin' and a-hoppin' all around—*fump fump fump*. "Who's in that there sack?" yelled the old shepherd.

"Go 'way," said Jack. "I'm a-fixin' to go on up into heaven. The angels'll be back for me any minute."

"Law," said the old shepherd. "I'm ninety-three. I might never get another chance to go on up to heaven. How about I trade you this hunnerd head of sheep to swap places with you?"

"All right," said Jack. "It's a deal." So the old shepherd let Jack out and climbed on into the sack. Jack warned, "Don't say nothin' to the angels, so they won't know they got the wrong man."

JACK returned to the farm and waited for Will and Tom. Were they ever surprised to come home and find their deceased brother an' a hunnerd head of sheep! "Where'd you get them?" they asked.

"Why, I found 'em down in the river you done tossed me into!"

Will and Tom begged Jack to tie them up in sacks and chuck them in the river, too. Jack was only too happy to oblige. First, he threw Will in, and Tom asked, "What's he thrashin' around for?"

"He's a-gatherin' sheep," answered Jack.

"Quick," said Tom. "Chuck me in, too, afore he gets 'em all!"

That's just what Jack did. Then he returned to his cleared fields with his two-hunnerd guineas an' a hunnerd head of sheep.

Last I heard, Jack was doing right well.

*   *   *

WARNING LABELS

On a pack of Breath Savers: "Not for weight control."
On bottled water: "Throw top away. Do not put in mouth."
On a tube of deodorant: "Do not use intimately."

THE NEW LATIN LEXICON

Leaders of the Catholic Church correspond mostly in Italian (Vatican City is inside Rome), but its official language has always been Latin. In 2003 the Church updated the ancient language with modern phrases in a dictionary called the Lexicon Recentis Latinitatis. *Here's a sampling.*

Amnesia
memóriae amíssio

Blue jeans
bracae línteae caerúleae

Pizza
placenta compressa

Cowboy
armentárius

Weekend
éxiens hebdómada

Miniature golf
pilamálleus minutus

Laser
instrumentum laséricum

Karate
oppugnatio inermis Iapónica

Graffiti
figura gráphio exarata

Christmas tree
arbor natalícia

Traveler's Check
mandatum nummárium periegéticum

Jazz
iazensis música

Overdose
immódica medicamenti stupefactivi iniéctio

Smog
fumus et nébula

Kamikaze
voluntárius sui interemptor

Hot pants
brevíssimae bracae femíneae

Jeep
autocinetum locis iniquis aptum

Basketball
follis canistríque ludus

Pornographic film
pellicula cinematographica

Spaceship
navis sideralis

Computer
instrumentum computatórium

Snack bar
thermopólium potórium et gustatórium

Punk
punkianae catervae ássecla

Rush hour
tempus máximae frequéntiae

Gangster
gregalis latro

Miniskirt
tunícula mínima

Dishwasher
escariorum lavator

Thermos
lagoena calefactória

Flirt
amor levis

Sports fans
admiratores studiosíssimi

Vodka
válida pótio Slávica

Megalomania
effrenuta glóriae appeténtia

World's fastest manned aircraft: the *X-15*, with a top speed of 4,519 mph (1967).

THEY DIED WITH THEIR CHUTES ON

There's a reason BASE jumping is considered one of the most dangerous sports—even for those with plenty of experience. These athletes were among the many who didn't survive their jumps. (An intro to the sport is on page 165.)

Athlete: William Heidebrecht, age 41

Details: "Wingsuit flying" is another kind of BASE jumping. According to the United States Parachute Association, to fly in a wingsuit—a special jumpsuit with expanded surface area for increased lift—a BASE jumper must be a licensed skydiver with at least 200 free-fall skydives. Canadian firefighter Heidebrecht had that much experience and more. On September 14, 2010, he was in Lauterbrunnen Valley, Switzerland, doing what he loved to do: wearing his Vampire 3 wingsuit as he BASE jumped off a cliff known as "High Nose."

What Went Wrong? Heidebrecht's V3 wingsuit got damaged, so he put on his Phantom 1 wingsuit. When it came time to pull the parachute rip cord, Heidebrecht reached for the leg pouch as he did when flying the V3...but the P1's deployment cord is on the jumper's back.

Athlete: Kylie Tanti, age 42

Details: Friends called the Australian skydiver fearless, with a "mad passion" for BASE jumping. Tanti was the first woman to skysurf—skydiving on a surfboard. On September 27, 2010, she was making her third BASE jump from the 541-foot Alor Setar telecom tower in Malaysia. She ran into trouble with her parachute and hit the pavement below.

What Went Wrong? According to fellow BASE jumper Gary Cunningham, Tanti's parachute got tangled up with the camera on her safety helmet.

Athlete: Jan Davis, age 60

Details: Davis had done more than 70 jumps over a period of 16 years. She'd even jumped from Venezuela's Angel Falls—the highest waterfall in the world. And as a stuntwoman, she did skydiving sequences for James Bond movies. On October 22, 1999, Davis took part in a protest jump off Yosemite National Park's 3,198-foot El Capitan. The jump was meant to show park rangers that BASE jumping can be done "safely" and deserves a place in national parks. Organizers staged the jump after an illegal BASE jumper drowned while fleeing from rangers. Davis hit the talus slope (a formation of rock fragments) after about 20 seconds of free fall, never having deployed her chute.

What Went Wrong? Because the jump was illegal, the protestors had agreed that they would land in a designated area, get arrested by park rangers, forfeit their equipment, and then take their fight to court. As he watched his wife plummet from the cliff, Davis's husband was heard repeating, "If only she had used her own gear." Davis had used less expensive gear so that her personal parachute wouldn't be confiscated. The borrowed one had its rip cord on the leg, while the cord on Davis's gear was on the back.

Result: BASE jumping in the parks is still banned.

* * *

WORLD'S 10 DEADLIEST BASE JUMP SITES

1. Lauterbrunnen, Switzerland (28 deaths)
2. Monte Brento, Italy (9 deaths)
3. Lysebotn, Norway (7 deaths)
4. Trollveggen, Andalsnes, Norway (7 deaths)
5. Yosemite National Park, California (7 deaths)
6. Perrine Bridge, Twin Falls, Idaho (5 deaths)
7. Kjerag, Forsand, Norway (5 deaths)
8. New River Gorge, Fayetteville, West Virginia (4 deaths)
9. Sam Ford Fjord, Baffin Island, Canada (2 deaths)
10. Engelberg, Switzerland (2 deaths)

In WWII the Nazis made a candy-bar bomb designed to blow up when a piece was broken off.

THE WORST BUSINESS DECISION EVER? PART III

When life gives you lemons, make lemonade. And when life gives you Apple, don't sell your shares! Here's Part III of our story. *(Part II is on page 384.)*

THINKING OUTSIDE THE BOX

Steve Jobs, Steve Wozniak, and a handful of friends and family members set to work filling the Byte Shop's order of 50 computers. Working in a bedroom in Jobs's parents' house, then moving to the garage when the bedroom got too crowded, they finished with one day to spare. The Byte Shop got its computers, Apple got its money, and the bills got paid on time.

But as Paul Terrell, the owner of the Byte Shop, learned to his dismay, the Apple I "computer" was a very barebones product indeed: It was just a circuit board with the computer chips and other components installed, nothing more. The keyboard wasn't included, neither was the monitor, and there wasn't even a case to enclose the circuit board. Wozniak and Jobs still saw their computer as a product for hobbyists. They thought buyers would want to customize their machines by providing these parts themselves.

Terrell didn't agree. He thought that computers, like toasters, should work right out of the box, so he added his own keyboards, monitors, and enclosures before putting his Apples on sale. It didn't take Jobs and Wozniak long to see that he was right. They decided that the Apple II, which Wozniak was already developing, would have a case and a built-in keyboard, with an optional monitor for people who didn't have a spare TV.

NEW PARTNERS NO MORE

Jobs and Wozniak estimated that gearing up to manufacture the Apple II was going to cost at least $200,000. Once again, they didn't have the money. After searching around for investors, they found a Silicon Valley millionaire named Mike Markkula who was willing to put up nearly $100,000 of his own funds, plus personally guarantee a $250,000 line of credit from Bank of America. In return, Markkula became an equal partner. But rather than invest

Only about 200 Apple I computers were ever made. In 2010 one was auctioned for $213,000.

in the old partnership, on January 3, 1977, Jobs, Wozniak, and Markkula formed a new corporation—Apple Computer Inc.—which promptly bought out the old partnership for $5,309. To ensure that their old partner Ron Wayne wouldn't cause problems later, Jobs and Wozniak sent him a check for one third of that amount, or about $1,770, along with a letter asking him to forfeit any future claims against Apple Computer Inc. Wayne was surprised to receive money and happily signed the letter. Total compensation for signing away his Apple stake: $2,570.

WHAT COULD HAVE BEEN

When they formed Apple Computer Inc., Jobs, Wozniak, and Markkula each got 26 percent of the new corporation's stock, setting aside the remaining 22 percent of shares to be sold to investors at some future time. That means that Jobs's and Wozniak's combined stake in the new corporation was 52 percent. Since Wayne was a 10 percent owner of the old partnership, it's reasonable to assume that had he remained with the company, he would have received 10 percent of Jobs's and Wozniak's stake in the new corporation, or 5.2 percent, of Apple Computer Inc.

However relieved Wayne may have been at having exited Apple without losing everything he owned, his pleasure must surely have turned to pain when the Apple II became one of the bestselling personal computers of all time, raising the current partners' fortunes (but not his) with it. On December 12, 1980, not quite five years after Wayne made his escape, Apple Computer Inc. went public. By the end of the month, the company was valued at $1.79 *billion*. Had Wayne held onto his 5.2 percent stake, it would have been worth just over $93 million.

IT GETS WORSE

If you're an Apple fan, you know that the company has had its share of troubles over the years. Steve Wozniak ended his day-to-day involvement in the company in February 1985, and seven months later Steve Jobs left the company after losing a power struggle. With neither of the founders around to guide it, Apple foundered in the 1990s in the face of strong competition from computers that used the Microsoft Windows operating system. By the time Steve Jobs retook the helm as interim CEO in 1997,

Apple was less than 90 days away from bankruptcy. Under his leadership, the company revamped its computer offerings and introduced the iPod (2001), iTunes (2003), the iPhone (2007), and the iPad (2010). On the strength of these new offerings, the company roared back to life in what *Time* magazine called "the greatest comeback in the history of business."

Sadly, Jobs died from pancreatic cancer in October 2011. By then the business, now known as Apple Inc., had passed Exxon Mobil to become the most valuable publicly traded company on Earth. Its stock price continued to climb after his death: By January 2012, Apple had a market value of more than $393 billion.

Estimates of the present value of Ron Wayne's original Apple stake vary depending on what assumptions are made, but all the estimates are in the billions. If he had owned 5.2 percent of Apple in early 2012, it would have been worth more than $20 billion, making him one of the 13 richest people in the United States, just behind the Wal-Mart heirs and just ahead of Amazon.com founder, Jeff Bezos, and Google co-founders, Sergey Brin and Larry Page. He'd also be well ahead of Steve Jobs and Steve Wozniak, who sold much of their stock in the 1980s.

LIFE'S A GAMBLE

Wayne had continued to consult with Apple after withdrawing from the partnership. He designed the first Apple logo (an image of Sir Isaac Newton sitting under an apple tree), wrote the Apple I user's manual, and helped organize an inventory system. After he left Apple, he worked a variety of jobs in government and industry. He didn't own a computer until 1996. When he finally did get one, he bought a Dell. He didn't own any Apple products until 2011, when an event organizer gave him an iPad 2 during a personal appearance in the United Kingdom.

By 2012, Wayne had retired and was living in the desert community of Pahrump, Nevada, 60 miles west of Las Vegas. He still makes occasional appearances at Apple events. When he's in Pahrump, he supplements his social security income by selling rare stamps and coins from his home. For entertainment, he plays the penny slot machines in a nearby casino.

In interviews, Wayne invariably puts a brave face on his famous missed opportunity, but occasionally a twinge of regret

Better to drink soda? 30% of bottled water is contaminated with chemicals or bacteria.

does slip out. "Unfortunately my whole life has been a day late and a dollar short," he told a reporter in 2010.

JOIN THE CLUB

Ron Wayne wasn't the only one to say no to a big slice of Apple. Here are a few others who made the same regrettable decision.

Hewlett-Packard. Because he built the Apple I at his cubicle in the HP's calculator division, Steve Wozniak felt obliged to offer it to the company. The calculator division didn't want it, so an HP attorney called the heads of all the other departments and asked, "You interested in an $800 machine that can run BASIC (an early computer language) and hook up to a TV?" No one was. The lawyer drafted a letter renouncing any claim to ownership by HP and gave it to Wozniak for nothing. Later, after Wozniak finished work on the Apple II, he offered to join an HP team designing a personal computer. HP turned him down.

Haltek Surplus Electronics. Jobs offered Haltek a stake in Apple in exchange for the $15,000 in parts he needed to build the first 50 computers. No deal: The owner thought the "scruffy-looking" Jobs and Wozniak would never succeed in business. Haltek closed its doors in 2000 after the landlord raised the rent.

Atari. When HP turned Wozniak down, Jobs offered the Apple I to Atari, but they were busy creating a home version of *Pong* and passed. Later, when Jobs was trying to raise the $200,000 needed to launch the Apple II, he made Atari's founder, Nolan Bushnell, another offer: 30 percent of Apple Computer for $50,000. Bushnell said no. The Atari brand is still around, but the company is long gone. After losing $500 million in 1983, its parent company, Warner Communications, split Atari into two separate companies and unloaded them both. Both are now defunct.

Commodore Computers. After Atari said no to a 30-percent stake, Jobs tried to sell the entire company to Commodore Business Machines. Price: $100,000 in cash, plus some Commodore stock and $36,000-a-year jobs for both Jobs and Wozniak. Commodore passed on the offer and introduced its own computer in 1977. After years of losing market share to Apple and IBM PCs, Commodore filed for bankruptcy in 1994.

In ancient Rome, a father had the right to sell any member of his family into slavery.

THE INNOCENCE PROJECT

Today everyone knows about DNA evidence because it's a part of every cop show on TV and in the movies. But have you ever wondered about the cases and the people that started it all? We did.

A NEW CASE

In 1986 Barry Scheck, professor at the Benjamin Cardozo School of Law at Yeshiva University in Manhattan, and Peter Neufeld, who ran a private law practice nearby, were sent a case file regarding a man in a New York prison. Scheck and Neufeld had both started law school in the late 1960s, and both were steeped in the social justice themes that defined the era. As young lawyers in the 1970s, they'd cut their teeth as public defenders in the South Bronx, where they had worked on the most desperate cases—cases very similar to the one they'd just been handed.

Marion Coakley, 30, had been convicted of a violent robbery, kidnapping, and rape that had taken place in a Bronx, New York, hotel in 1983. The victim had described her attacker as a dark-skinned black man with a Jamaican accent and a short Afro. She later picked Coakley—a light-skinned black man with no Jamaican accent and no Afro—out of a police lineup. Seventeen people, including a priest, said they were with Coakley at a church meeting miles from the scene of the crime at the time it occurred, but he was convicted anyway.

A NEW TECHNOLOGY

Scheck and Neufeld agreed to look into the file. A blood expert they sometimes worked with, Robert Shaler, told them the case might be a good one to test out an emerging technology called "DNA testing." Naturally, the two criminal defense lawyers were interested in promising forensic technologies, so they took their colleague's advice. That DNA could be used to identify individuals had only been discovered a few years earlier, and it had never been used in a criminal case in the United States. Such testing was, in fact, being used for the very first time in a case in England. (For more on the story of DNA testing in forensics go to page 585.)

THE VERDICT

Scheck and Neufeld tried to use DNA testing to get Coakley's conviction overturned. It didn't work: Not enough DNA could be extracted from the evidence to identify the attacker. Fortunately, they were still able to get Coakley's conviction overturned by proving his innocence via other evidence, including a bloody palm print on the rearview mirror of the victim's car, which the actual assailant had stolen as part of the attack. Coakley was released in September 1987, after serving two years. But even though the use of the technology hadn't been successful, the die was cast. Scheck and Neufeld had been introduced to DNA testing—and they knew that it was going to be a game changer.

For the next couple of years, people in both law enforcement and science worked to figure out how DNA testing was going to fit into the world of forensics. Think about it: Fingerprinting alone took decades to be fully integrated into forensic science. If DNA testing was going be accepted, it would have to be made understandable to investigators, prosecutors, defense attorneys, judges, and—especially—juries. Scheck and Neufeld became closely involved with this process, and they are credited today with getting DNA testing to become a standard part of forensics as quickly and thoroughly as it did.

THE COURTS SPEAK

Two significant events occurred to push DNA testing along:

• In 1987 the West Virginia Supreme Court ruled that DNA evidence could be used in a trial (it was a rape case), giving the use of DNA evidence in a courtroom its first major legal precedent.

• In 1989 Gary Dotson of Chicago, Illinois, became the first person in history to have a conviction overturned through the use of DNA testing. It was a heart-rending case. Dotson had been convicted in 1979 of the violent rape of a 16-year-old girl and sentenced to 25 to 50 years in prison. Six years into his sentence, the "victim" admitted she'd made up the whole thing. Earlier that day, she'd had sex with her boyfriend for the first time, and was afraid she'd become pregnant. Yet even with that recantation, it took Dotson another four years—and, finally, DNA evidence proving that semen taken from the girl's underwear was her boyfriend's, not Dotson's—for him to be exonerated.

Scheck and Neufeld followed Dotson's case closely, and when he was finally proclaimed innocent, they decided it was time to put on their superhero costumes.

PUSHING THE ENVELOPE

Because they had used DNA testing early on, Scheck and Neufeld got letters from prison inmates pleading for their help. By the early 1990s, they were inundated. Neufeld described this period in 2001, in an interview with the University of California, Berkeley's online show, "Conversations with History":

> The first thing that happened is that we began doing these cases on an ad hoc basis. Someone would write us a letter; we would try and respond to it and take on the case. And we realized that this was inadequate.

In 1991 Scheck dealt with that inadequacy by starting an experimental project for some of his students at the Cardozo Law School: The students would read the letters from inmates and their lawyers, and develop a set of criteria a case would have to meet in order to be accepted. The most important: There had to be sufficient reason to believe that the person may have been wrongfully convicted (as in Marion Coakley's case), and there had to be *biological evidence*—blood, other body fluids, or hair—still available, from which DNA could be extracted. Scheck and Neufeld decided to call it "The Innocence Project."

When a case was accepted, the students would search through old evidence, do their best to find witnesses, and go over testimony, while Scheck and Neufeld would help on the larger legal issues. When they had what they thought was enough, they'd present what they'd discovered to the prosecutor where the case was tried, and ask that the prosecutor's office order a DNA test. Prosecutors hate having cases overturned, so it was an uphill battle....but sometimes it worked.

THE NEXT CASE

One such case was that of Kirk Bloodsworth. In April 1985, Kirk Noble Bloodsworth, 23, went on trial for the 1984 sexual assault and murder of a 9-year-old girl in Maryland. Bloodsworth, a former Marine with no criminal record, pleaded innocent. No physical evidence linked him to the crime, and he had witnesses who

Legal briefs: In Thailand, it's illegal to leave your house if you're not wearing underwear.

put him somewhere else at the time of the crime. In addition, the eyewitnesses who testified that they'd seen him near the scene of the crime were shaky at best: Two of them were boys aged 7 and 10, who had been unable to pick Bloodsworth—a large man with bright red hair and prominent sideburns—out of a police lineup. Despite all this, Bloodsworth was convicted and sentenced to death.

TRIED AND TRIED AGAIN

The trial was such a mess that the original conviction was overturned on appeal—but the second trial saw Bloodsworth convicted again. This time he was sentenced to two consecutive life terms. Seven years passed. Then, in 1992, Bloodsworth read a book that had a reference to DNA testing in it. He told his lawyer, Robert Morin, about it. Morin enlisted the help of The Innocence Project.

The team reviewing the court record was able to determine that biological evidence had been taken in the case. They asked for it, but were told it had been destroyed. The team persisted. The evidence suddenly "turned up." In April 1992, the prosecutor agreed to have DNA testing done. Another year passed. (Testing took much longer back then than it does today.) But on May 17, 1993, the DNA test conclusively proved that Kirk Bloodsworth could not have been the person who committed the crime for which he'd been convicted (twice) and for which he had already served eight years—two of them on death row. He was freed from prison, given a full pardon by the governor of Maryland, and in 1994, he was awarded $300,000 compensation.

The real rapist and killer in the Kirk Bloodsworth case wasn't discovered for another ten years after Bloodsworth's 1993 exoneration. When Bloodsworth heard the man's name—Kimberly Shay Ruffner—he said, "My God. I know him." Ruffner had spent five years in the same prison as Bloodsworth. "I gave him library books," Bloodsworth said, "and he never said a word."

SUCCESSES

Bloodsworth was just one of five wrongfully convicted people exonerated by DNA testing in 1992, all of them with at least some help from The Innocence Project. After that, things really got rolling. In the years since Scheck and Neufeld began their quest, The Innocence Project has become an enormous phenomenon, with chapters in all 50 states, as well as in several other countries. All of the cases are done pro bono. A few of the more notable ones:

• **The Ford Heights Four.** In July 1996, DNA evidence proved that Dennis Williams, Willie Rainge, Kenneth Adams, and Verneal Jimerson were not guilty of the 1978 rape and murder of a young couple in the Ford Heights neighborhood of Chicago. Williams, Rainge, and Adams spent almost 18 years in prison for that crime, Jimerson almost 11. In 1999 they settled with Cook County, Illinois, in a $36 million wrongful conviction lawsuit—the largest civil rights settlement in history at the time. (During the investigation that freed them, it was revealed that a witness had told police that four *other* men were seen running from the crime scene—but police never investigated that. In 1998, DNA evidence proved those four other men had committed the crimes. One was in jail for having murdered another woman.)

• **Marvin Anderson.** In 2001 Anderson was exonerated in the violent 1982 rape of a young woman in Hanover, Virginia. He was just 18 when he was convicted, and he had no criminal record. The only reason he was suspected in the case: The victim, who was white, told police that her assailant, who was black, said he had a white girlfriend—and Anderson was the only black man in the area that they knew of who had a white girlfriend. (He was convicted by an all-white jury in about 45 minutes—and sentenced to 210 years in prison.) In 1988 John Otis Lincoln, also from Hanover, admitted in a courtroom that he'd committed the crime—but the judge said he was lying. Anderson was freed on parole in 1997, after serving more than 15 years. It took another five years to get a DNA test done, which proved his innocence. In 2002 he was granted a full pardon. He was the 99th person in the United States exonerated, post-conviction, through the use of DNA evidence. (Further testing showed that John Otis Lincoln *had* committed the crime. He was convicted of the 1982 rape in 2003.)

• **James Bain.** In December 2009, James Bain of Brooklyn, New York, was proven by DNA testing to be innocent of the kidnapping, burglary, and rape of a 9-year-old boy—for which he had spent 35 years in prison. It's the longest sentence served by any

...Johnson (Robert C. Weaver, Secretary of Housing and Urban Development, 1966–68).

person exonerated by DNA evidence. One of the reasons Bain had been convicted: The victim picked him out of a police lineup. The boy admitted years later than he'd been directed to pick Bain.

So far, 289 wrongfully convicted people in the United States have been exonerated through the use of DNA evidence, most of them with the help of The Innocence Project or related organizations. Average length of time served: 13.5 years. Of the 289 total, 17 were freed from death row.

In 1994 the FBI began operating CODIS ("Combined DNA Index System"), a massive database of DNA profiles for millions of people who have been convicted of violent and sexual crimes. Of the 289 exoneration cases, use of CODIS has led to the arrests of 139 *actual* perpetrators. The prosecutor in Bloodsworth's case, Ann Brobst, finally apologized to him in 2003.

*   *   *

A LUCKY FIND

Zach Bodish, 46, of Columbus, Ohio, restores vintage furniture that he finds in thrift stores. One day in March 2012, he was perusing a local Volunteers of America store when he found what he thought was a poster that featured a reproduction of a Picasso print made for a 1958 exhibit of his pottery in France. Bodish bought the poster for $14.14.

When he got the poster home he noticed some French words written in pencil at the bottom. They translated as "original print, signed proof," and the notation "6/100." He also found some faded red pencil markings on the lower-right corner. The "poster," it turns out, was actually a limited-edition print—only 100 had been made. The low number, 6th out of the 100 printed, meant that it was an "artist's proof" that Picasso personally reviewed and approved before the remaining prints were made by the printer. Those faint red marks? Picasso's signature!

While Picasso's *paintings* have sold for more than $100 million apiece, his signed prints are worth far less. Bodish's print was appraised at just $4,000, but he found a buyer willing to pay him $7,000. "I realized it wasn't going to make me rich, but how often do you find a Picasso?"

The first TV broadcast of an atomic bomb detonation took place on station KTLA in 1952.

HIYO, SILVER—AWAY!

What better way to celebrate the silver anniversary of Uncle John's Bathroom Reader *than to "return to those thrilling days of yesteryear," when a masked man rode the plains on a horse named Silver?*

THE LONE STATION

In the late 1920s movie theater owner from Detroit named George W. Trendle convinced his business partner that they should expand into the fledgling medium of broadcast radio. They bought the local CBS affiliate, and promptly renamed it WXYZ.

Trendle didn't like the restrictions that came with being a network station, so within a year he left CBS and became independent. That meant producing his own radio shows, but in those first few years WXYZ had trouble coming up with anything that could compete with popular shows on CBS and NBC.

Trendle never lost money showing cowboy movies in his theaters, so in December 1932 he fired off a letter to Fran Striker, a prolific scriptwriter:

> Will you please write up three or four Wild West thrillers, including all the hokum of masked rider, rustler, killer Pete, heroine on the train tracks, fight on top of the boxcars, Indian bad men, two-gun bank robbers, etc.

SEEING IS BELIEVING

That was a lot of detail to cram into a couple of scripts (especially when Trendle was only paying $4 per script) so Striker reworked some old episodes of a show called *Covered Wagon Days* to include a cowboy who wears a mask. Striker made him a Texas Ranger who traveled and worked alone—a *lone* ranger.

Striker gave his masked man ivory-handled revolvers, bullets made of silver, and a white stallion named Silver as well. Vivid details like these were known in the radio business as "shiny things for the mind," and were considered essential because they enabled listeners to form sharp mental images of characters they could not see.

Because *The Lone Ranger* was going to be a children's show, it was important that the character be a strong role model for kids. The Lone Ranger would treat others with respect. Violence would be kept to a minimum: He would use his guns only as a last resort and only to disarm his opponents, not to deliberately harm or kill them. He wouldn't drink or smoke, and he would have no romances. George Trendle was a stickler for proper language, and in all his years on the air the Lone Ranger never used slang or poor grammar. He didn't even have a Texas accent. He also never removed his mask, except to don another disguise. (The one exception: When meeting President Ulysses S. Grant, who refused to talk to a masked man.)

EASY RIDER

The country was mired in the Great Depression in the early 1930s and Trendle, a penny-pincher in the best of times, was determined to cut costs wherever he could. The show needed a theme song, but Trendle didn't want to pay royalties to a composer. So he chose a classical selection: the finale to the *William Tell Overture* by Gioachino Rossini, who was long dead. That piece of music has been synonymous with *The Lone Ranger* ever since. The show aired for the first time on Monday, January 30, 1933, at 8:00 p.m. and was broadcast three times a week for the next 22 years—2,956 original episodes in all.

Because of the limitations of radio, the Lone Ranger wouldn't remain alone for long. In radio the storyline advances largely through dialogue—or in the case of the first ten episodes of *The Lone Ranger*, through *mono*logues. When the Lone Ranger was with other characters, he could talk to them, but when he was riding Silver, he rode alone. To prevent listeners from getting bored with one scene after another of the Lone Ranger talking to himself, Striker created the a "faithful Indian companion, Tonto," and introduced him in episode 11.

ME TONTO

In recent decades the pidgin-talking Tonto has come to be seen as a demeaning, stereotypical depiction of Native Americans and their culture. The Lone Ranger told Tonto what to do, never vice versa. The Lone Ranger spoke perfect English, while Tonto sounded more like Tarzan. Considering all of the character's flaws, it's

500,000 Twitter followers equals one "Wheaton" (after *Star Trek's* Wil Wheaton).

easy to forget just how ahead of its time, Tonto was for the early 1930s. *The Lone Ranger's* audience soon grew to nearly 250 stations all over the United States, including in the Jim Crow South, where racial segregation was the law of the land. There, as everywhere, children were being entertained by a white man whose sole trusted companion and *kemosabe*—"faithful friend"—was an Indian that he respected as an equal. *The Lone Ranger* would, in effect, slip its subtle message of racial tolerance, right past segregationist parents and into the hearts and minds of their children.

MAIL CALL

It didn't take long for Trendle and Striker to sense that they had a hit show on their hands, but just how big was it? In those days measuring the size of a radio show's audience wasn't easy. One way to do it was to offer a free premium to listeners and invite them to write in to get it. If the station received a lot of letters, they would know the show had a large audience.

A few months after *The Lone Ranger* hit the airwaves, WXYZ offered kids a free *Lone Ranger* pop gun. The station received 25,000 letters in three days. That July, when the Lone Ranger made a public appearance at a local park, more than 70,000 people turned out to see him. The show was on its way to becoming one of the most popular in the history of radio, enjoyed by nearly as many adult listeners as children. Kids everywhere—girls included—dressed in Lone Ranger and Tonto outfits, joined *Lone Ranger* safety clubs, played with *Lone Ranger* cap guns, and sent away for one premium after another, including badges, silver bullets, and the *Lone Ranger* six-shooter ring, which shot real sparks when "fired" by spinning a flint wheel.

KEEPING UP APPEARANCES

The first person to play the Lone Ranger was George Seaton who left the show after three months. He was replaced by a radio actor named Earl Graser, who signed on in April 1933. Graser *sounded* like the Lone Ranger, but didn't look like him at all. He was short and fat, he couldn't ride a horse, and he didn't like guns, either—not exactly the kind of guy you'd want to send out on public appearances. So WXYZ gave *that* part of the job to the show's announcer, 6'3" Brace Beemer, a skilled rider who looked great on a horse and was good with guns. When Earl Graser died in a car accident in 1941—"LONE RANGER DEAD; AUTO HIT TRAILER," read the headline in *The New York Times*—Beemer took over the voice job as well. He played the Lone Ranger for the rest of the radio show's run.

AS SEEN ON TV

But the actor who would become most closely associated with the Lone Ranger in the pubic mind was former circus acrobat Clayton Moore. Moore played the Lone Ranger on TV from 1949 to 1952, and, after sitting out a season over a pay dispute, again from 1953 to the show's end in 1957. Playing Tonto on the TV show was a Canadian Mohawk actor named Jay Silverheels. (Real name: Harold J. Smith. He got the nickname "Silverheels" years earlier, from his teammates on Canada's national lacrosse team, who were impressed with his speed and shiny athletic shoes).

The Lone Ranger was the first Western produced for television and ABC TV's first big hit. But Moore isn't the best-remembered Lone Ranger just because he played the character on TV. After the show ended in 1957, he continued to make personal appearances as the Lone Ranger for the next 40 years. And in all that time he never made a public appearance without wearing a mask...at least not until 1979. That's when the producers of the upcoming film *The Legend of the Lone Ranger* went to court to force him to give up the mask, out of fear that he would confuse movie goers into thinking that he, not the much younger actor they'd hired, was starring in the upcoming film.

Big mistake: Moore gave up the mask, only to switch to oversized sunglasses that *looked* like a mask, and then gave one TV interview after another generating terrible publicity for the film. All those kids who grew up watching Clayton Moore as *their* Lone Ranger boycotted what might have been a sure moneymaker. Result: The film lost $11 million, and Actor Klinton Spilsbury, who played the Lone Ranger, never worked in Hollywood again.

MISSING PERSONS

So how is it that a show that was so beloved for so long has been absent save for occasional TV reruns ever since? The fact that *The Legend of the Lone Ranger* bombed at the box office in 1981 cer-

Check it yourself: The bottom row of a QWERTY keyboard has no vowels.

tainly didn't help, but much of the trouble rests with Tonto. The character has not aged well. Even Jay Silverheels, who was popular in the role during the TV show's original run, came to be derided in later years as an "Uncle Tomahawk" for perpetuating negative Indian stereotypes.

When the 2013 Disney film *The Lone Ranger* was in the early stages of production in 2002, there was talk of tackling the issue by casting a woman as Tonto. Later it was decided that Tonto would be the lead character in the film, and Johnny Depp was cast in the role, with an actor named Armie Hammer playing the Lone Ranger. If the big-screen reboots of Superman, Batman, and Spider-Man are any guide, this latest film won't be the last time that the story is freshened up and presented to a new generation of fans.

"The Lone Ranger will never die," Clayton Moore told an interviewer not long before his death in 1999. "It's Americana: the cowboy, the cattle drive, the sheriff, the fight for law, order and justice—it's part of our history, and what that stands for can never be extinguished."

* * *

SO THAT'S WHY HE WEARS IT

For the first five years that *The Lone Ranger* was on the radio, the series made no attempt to explain his true identity, or why he wore his mask. It wasn't until the first movie serial, produced by Republic Pictures in 1938, that fans finally learned who their hero was. According to the script, six Texas Rangers were ambushed by outlaws as they rode through a canyon. The only survivor, named John Reid, was found and nursed back to health by Tonto, an Indian whose life Reid had saved when they were younger. ("You only ranger left," Tonto tells Reid after the attack. "You Lone Ranger.") Reid's older brother Dan was one of the rangers killed in the ambush. Reid makes a mask out of fabric taken from his dead brother's vest and wears it to prevent the outlaws from realizing he is still alive. Then he and Tonto set out to bring the murderers to justice. The origin story was so popular that it was adopted by the radio show and subsequent films as well.

Highest recorded temperature in Alaska: 100°F. Highest in Hawaii: 100°F.

Q&A: ASK THE EXPERTS

More questions, with answers from the world's top trivia experts.

SEEMS FISHY

Q: *Who do pizzerias offer anchovies, if nobody orders them?*

A: "When the dish was first developed, in Naples during the late 18th century, anchovies made an ideal topping—they were cheap, plentiful, and could be preserved almost indefinitely in oil and salt. When the first wave of Italian immigrants came to the U.S. in the late 1800s, they brought pizza with them. In the 1910s, as Anglo-Americans began to sample the exotic food, pizzerias started catering to local tastes, offering toppings like vegetables and pork, which crowded out the anchovy. Today it seems that pizzerias persist in offering them more out of nostalgia." (From *The Explainer,* by the editors of *Slate*)

BUTTERFLIES FLUTTER BY

Q: *What's the difference between a moth and a butterfly?*

A: "Though many people distinguish them by color (butterflies are often the more brightly colored), other features are better for telling them apart. Butterflies have slim bodies and moths have stout ones. The antennae on a butterfly are long, slender, and tipped with knobs, while those of moths are hairlike or feathery. Most moths fly at night; butterflies are active during the day." (From *Reader's Digest's ABCs of Nature: A Family Answer Book*)

PRUNE POWER

Q: *Why are prunes such a powerful laxative?*

A: "Prunes (or dried plums) are primarily famous for being a laxative because they are rich in fiber. Also, a prune contains more than one gram of sorbitol (a carbohydrate our bodies do not absorb well). Large amounts of sorbitol can cause diarrhea. Prunes also contain the laxative diphenylisatin." (From DiscoveryHealth.com)

It took author J. R. R. Tolkien 12 years to write the *Lord of the Rings* trilogy.

WHEN TOILETS EXPLODE

More terrifying tales of good thrones gone bad.

Victims: Employees and visitors to the King County Courthouse in Seattle

Boom! One morning in February 1989, the courthouse's toilets and urinals began erupting violently when anyone tried to flush them. "They started blowing at about 11:30 a.m. We think we've lost about twenty to twenty-five toilets. The porcelain is actually cracked," said building manager Bill Kemp. The problem was traced to work on a $430 million bus-tunnel project nearby, where someone had mistakenly connected an air compressor to a water line, causing the line to fill with more pressure than it was designed to handle. No one was injured, but several people were soaked by water from the exploding toilets.

Victim: Edmond Okolie of Seattle

Boom! What is it with Seattle public works projects? In November 2006, Okolie was inspecting a leaky toilet in the basement of an adult-care facility when it erupted with so much force that the toilet was blown off the floor, striking Okolie and knocking him to the ground. Raw sewage continued to gush from the hole in the floor until the entire basement was flooded. Okolie, bruised and drenched in sewage but otherwise unharmed, scrambled upstairs to safety. Investigators traced the problem to a nearby light-rail construction project, where workers had accidentally cut into or blocked the sewer line, causing pressure to build up in the line until it exploded. At last report Okolie was suing the transit line for unspecified damages.

Victims: Undergraduate students living in the University of Chicago's Pierce Tower dormitory

Boom! During the fall and winter of 2011–12, the 50-year-old dormitory had severe problems with its antiquated plumbing: leaking urinals, broken drains, showers, and erupting toilets that sounded like shotgun blasts and sprayed their contents onto bathroom ceilings. "In one twenty-four-hour period," a student complained on a web log set up to document Pierce Hall's problems, "the plumbing exploded twice, and exploded with such force and severity that a toilet bowl shattered, throwing porcelain shards across the bathroom. There were, on the floor, just rivers of excrement, urine and pieces of porcelain. And there were no e-mails from the university about the issue." The toilet blasts were usually accompanied by water outages that lasted many hours. One female student who was drenched with the contents of a toilet had to clean up with Clorox wipes because the water was out. It took months for the university to tackle the problem, but luckily when they finally did, spring break was just around the corner. While the students were away, the university overhauled the 10-story building's plumbing, replacing the faulty equipment that caused the toilet explosions and installing video displays next to the elevators on each floor, to warn students quickly if the problems return. (So far, they haven't.)

Victim: Dennis Bueller, a 14-year-old boy in Recklinghausen, Germany

Boom! In November 2008, Bueller used the bathroom and then reached for a can of air freshener. "I sprayed because it smelled, then I began fiddling with a cigarette lighter," he told London's *Daily Mail*. Big mistake: The lighter ignited the air freshener, causing a blast powerful enough to send Bueller flying out an open window. "There was this big orange whoosh of flame. I woke up outside with my clothes burned off and me smelling like a barbecue," he said. Bueller was hospitalized with burns to his upper body, but was expected to recover. "I think he realizes he was a bit dim in playing with a lighter," his father told reporters.

*   *   *

SIGN LANGUAGE

Over a trash can in Beijing: "Please don't throw rubbish away"

In Budapest, Hungary: "Tourists! Don't follow your guides!"

On a beach in Mexico: "Dangerous not to swim."

On a road in Jeju Island, South Korea: "Wayout Parking."

On a cafe storefront in Seoul, South Korea: "Hussy Coffee"

Inside Afghanistan's Kabul Museum: "Please Do Not Use the Flashy Cameras During the Photography"

The phrase "Don't Mess with Texas" was coined in 1985 as an anti-litter slogan.

NOT-MURDER MYSTERIES

When murder most foul turns out to be...not murder at all.

Victim: Todd Sommer of San Diego, California

Details: In 2002 Sommer, a 23-year-old Marine, died suddenly while on leave at his San Diego home. An autopsy found the cause of death to be a heart attack.

Murder! In 2005 more than three years later, Sommer's wife, Cynthia, was arrested for his murder. Marine investigators had reviewed the case and found that the arsenic levels in Todd Sommer's liver were more than a thousand times higher than normal. This could only have occurred via poisoning, they said. At the trial, jurors were told that Cynthia received $250,000 in veteran's benefits after her husband's death, and that within just a few months, she had used some of that money on breast implants and had been "sexually promiscuous." Based on that circumstantial evidence, in 2007 Cynthia Sommer was found guilty of murder. She faced life in prison with no possibility of parole.

...or Not: Sommer appealed the case and won a retrial. But before the second trial even began, prosecutors dropped the case. They'd redone Todd Sommer's lab tests, and the new results showed no sign of arsenic whatsoever. (The first lab had somehow contaminated the samples, they said.) Because the rest of the case was little more than character assassination, Cynthia Sommer was released, with all charges dropped. By that time, she'd spent more than two years in prison. Sommer filed a $20 million wrongful conviction lawsuit against the San Diego prosecutor's office in 2009.

Victims: Seven people in The Hague, Netherlands

Details: In September 2001, a six-month-old infant died at the Juliana Children's Hospital in The Hague. The death was deemed suspicious, prompting an investigation. Result: High levels of digoxin were found in the baby's blood. Digoxin is a medication used to treat heart conditions (for which the child was being treated), but it can be deadly when used improperly.

Murder! A few months later, a 28-year-old nurse named Lucia de

Berk was arrested. Police said she had been on duty at the time of the death, and that she had acted suspiciously when questioned. After further investigation, several earlier deaths and near-deaths —all of which had been viewed as unremarkable when they occurred, and all of which occurred while de Berk was on duty— were suddenly suspect. At the ensuing trial, prosecutors told jurors they had proof that de Berk had murdered three of the victims, and that there was an overwhelming statistical probability that she had killed or had tried to kill the others. (The odds that one nurse would be on duty for so many "suspicious" events, said prosecutors, were 1 in 342 million.) That convinced the jury, and in 2003, Lucia de Berk was convicted of murdering seven people and attempting to murder three more, making her the worst serial killer in Netherlands history. She was sentenced to life in prison without possibility of parole.

...or Not: In 2008, after years of serious questions regarding aspects of de Berk's case, a Dutch court ordered it reviewed. In 2009, the review's findings were released: The three murder victims for which prosecutors had said they had "proof" of de Berk's guilt—hadn't been murdered at all. They'd died of natural causes (not uncommon for very ill people at hospitals). As for the other deaths, they'd never been physically determined to be murders in the first place. Overzealous investigators and prosecutors, the review found, had used "statistical probabilities" to create suspicion where none was warranted. Result: Lucia de Berk was exonerated of all charges, and received an official apology—and an undisclosed amount of money—from the Dutch government. By the time of her release in 2010, she'd spent six years in prison.

Victim: Bob Woolmer of Cape Town, South Africa

Details: On March 18, 2007, international cricket star Bob Woolmer was found unconscious in a Jamaica hotel room and died a few hours later. At the time, he was the coach of Pakistan's national team; a day earlier the team had been knocked out of World Cup contention in an upset loss to Ireland. Newspapers reported that Woolmer had suffered a heart attack.

Murder! Four days later, Jamaican police announced that Woolmer hadn't died from a heart attack—he'd been strangled. In April, the BBC reported that the police had further determined

Value of all of the gold mined in a year worldwide: more than $12 billion.

that Woolmer had been poisoned before being strangled. Allegations that Woolmer had been murdered by gangsters—because he was about to reveal details of match-fixing in his sport—made headlines around the world.

...or Not: Nearly two months later, Jamaican police made yet another announcement: The earlier reports that Woolmer had been poisoned and strangled were wrong. He hadn't even been murdered. His death was caused by chronic bad health, possibly diabetes. Case closed. Understandably, the conflicting reports caused international embarrassment for Jamaican law enforcement and raised serious questions regarding what had actually happened. (Had cricket gangsters gotten to the Jamaican police?) In November 2007, an inquest into Woolmer's death was ordered. After five weeks of testimony, the jury returned an open verdict, meaning Woolmer may have been...and may *not* have been...murdered. Case closed again.

Victim: Nicholas Loris

Details: In February 1987, the body of six-year-old Nicholas Loris was found in a wooded area about 150 yards from his home in Davidson County, North Carolina. He'd been last seen leaving his home to walk his family's dog less than an hour earlier. Police reported that the boy had been badly beaten.

Murder! The county coroner ruled that the cause of Nicholas's death was strangulation. Because he was found so close to home, and because his single mother, Elizabeth Watkins, was the only person in the area at the time, Watkins became the chief suspect in her son's murder. But since police never found any evidence to support their suspicions, she was never brought to trial. She simply remained a suspect—a fact the police made no attempt to conceal from the public—for more than two decades.

...or Not: In January 2012, almost 25 years after the event, the Davidson County Sheriff's office made an announcement: They had reinvestigated the death using new technology and determined that the boy had been killed by a group of dogs. One or more of the dogs pulled tightly enough on Nicholas's sweatshirt to strangle him. After two and a half decades, Elizabeth Watkins was finally—and publicly—cleared of all suspicion.

Armadillos can hold their breath for up to 6 minutes.

A HISTORY OF Y

Why Y? Because it's our 25th anniversary and Y is the 25th letter of the alphabet.

BACKGROUND

The letter Y has been in the English alphabet since the beginning, sometime around the 7th century A.D., about 1,300 years ago. But the story of the letter—and why it's located at the end of our alphabet—is even older.

Y's ancestor, according to alphabetologists, is the letter *waw*, the sixth letter in the world's oldest alphabetic system, the Phoenician alphabet. "Waw" meant "hook," so the letter was drawn to look like one. The sound it represented is unknown, but linguists believe it was a long "u" sound, as in the word "tube." The seafaring Phoenicians developed their 22-character alphabet more than 3,000 years ago and over the following centuries spread its use from their home (modern-day Lebanon) throughout the Mediterranean.

IT'S GREEK TO THEM

In the 9th century B.C., the ancient Greeks, still centuries away from becoming the civilization that shaped the modern world, adopted the Phoenician alphabet. But they changed the name of the letter *waw* to *upsilon*—from *u psilon*, meaning "plain u"—to distinguish its "u" sound from similar sounds in their own language. (Some languages today still use this name—in German, for example, Y is called *ypsilon*.)

In the 1st century B.C., the Romans conquered the Greeks and, being admirers of Greek culture, added many Greek words to Latin. One problem: The Romans had their own alphabet, and couldn't properly spell some of their new Greek words. Because the words had an unfamiliar sound—the "u" mentioned above—the Romans added the letter upsilon to their own alphabet. Not long after, they stole the Greek letter Z, too. (That's why Y and Z are at the end of the Latin alphabet.)

THE ROAMIN' Y

The Romans called their new letter Y *igraeca* (meaning "Greek I") because the "u" sound it represented was somewhat similar to the sound represented by their Roman letter I. (This explains the letter's name in many Romance languages today: In French, for example, it's *i grek*; in Spanish it's *i griega*.) The Romans famously spread their alphabet over their vast empire, and although the empire came to an end in the 5th century A.D., the alphabet lived on.

In the 7th century, the Anglo-Saxons, a scruffy conglomeration of battling kingdoms in what is now England, scrapped their primitive, rune-based alphabet and took up the Latin alphabet the Romans had left behind. The Anglo-Saxons were descendants of Germanic tribes that had invaded England a few centuries earlier, which explains why the pronunciation of the letter Y changed a bit at this time, becoming more like the German ü—somewhat similar to the "eu" sound in "feud." The Anglo-Saxons also gave Y its modern name—"wye." Why? Nobody knows.

After the Norman Conquest of England in 1066, French became a major influence on English, and Y changed again: For the first time it was used as a consonant, representing the "yuh" sound in words like "you" and "voyeur." Over the next several centuries, it lost its "ü" sound altogether, kept the "yuh" sound, and gradually added all the vowel sounds we associate it with today—in words such as *try*, *day*, *myth*, and *happy*.

FINAL NOTE

You've probably seen Y used in place of "th" in the word "the"—for example, in the names of businesses like "Ye Olde Cake Shoppe." Reason: In the 1400s, the English alphabet had a letter called "thorn." It looked like **þ** and represented the sound "th." So words like "the" were spelled "þe." When the first printing presses were brought to England in the 1470s, the type was from non-English-speaking countries that had no letter "thorn," so printers used Y in its place, and words like "the" ended up being spelled "ye." This went on until the 1600s, when the letters T and H finally took over from Y in words like "the," and the letter thorn was lost for good.

BURNED AT THE SKATE

Why would a 16th-century king of Spain go nuts over ice skates? Blame it on the Dutch, a group so stubborn that they fought the mighty Spanish Empire through the 80 Years' War ...and (eventually) skated to a win.

ICE FOLLY

It's not like Spain, with its mild Mediterranean climate, is well known for its frozen lakes and canals. So why would its king contact craftsmen and tell them to drop everything and make 7,000 pairs of skates? And this was back in 1572, long before there were indoor skating rinks, hockey, couples-ice-dancing, or Disney on Ice. It's unlikely that there were 7,000 Spaniards who had even heard of skates, let alone who would have been willing to put them on and stand on a slippery surface.

THE SPANISH ACQUISTION

Remember, there was a time when Spain controlled much of the world—not just in the New World or Africa, but in Europe as well. One of their holdings was the "Seventeen Provinces," consisting of present-day Netherlands, Belgium, Luxembourg, and parts of France and Germany. The territory was acquired when the Duchess of Burgundy married into the Spanish royal family in 1482.

The Dutch got the rawest part of the deal. Being the farthest north of Spain's European holdings meant that obtaining even a minor bureaucratic decision could require weeks or months of waiting while horsemen or ships traveled the 2,200-mile round trip from Amsterdam to Seville.

That was bad enough. Then came the Spanish Inquisition.

INQUIRING MINDS

During this time, the Spanish king was also Emperor of the Holy Roman Empire of the German Nation. That was one of the reasons Spain's kings and queens tended to go brutally overboard in enforcing faith in the Roman Catholic Church. They forced Jews and Muslims to convert or get out of the country in 1492. Then they created the infamous Inquisition to root out atheists, freethinkers, Christians of the wrong kind, and "former" Jews and Muslims who were only pretending to be converts to Catholicism. Torture, forced confessions, and burning at the stake were common tools of saving the souls of those deemed insufficiently Catholic.

THE OTHER MARTIN LUTHER

In 1566 the Spanish king Philip II got disturbing news about its most northernly provinces. There, people like Martin Luther and John Calvin had planted the seeds of Protestantism, and the noxious weed was growing deep roots. After trying out slightly gentler methods, Philip sent in Spanish troops with orders to scare the devil out of the Dutch, by any means necessary. But instead of thanking Philip II for his concern about their immortal souls, the Dutch people rose up in rebellion.

Philip redoubled his efforts. The effect, of course, was to turn many of the Dutch provinces—even Catholics and normally pro-Spanish noble classes—against Spanish rule. Not all of them, however. Some towns were filled with people who still considered themselves Catholics and loyal subjects (or didn't want trouble) and went out of their way to welcome and placate the troops.

In November 1572, for example, the citizens of Naarden tried to negotiate surrender to the Spanish by inviting the invading army to a feast. After food and toasts and expressions of friendship, the army gathered the 3,000 townspeople into the church and attacked them with swords, then burned the survivors alive. Other cities and towns were similarly sacked, with an estimated 18,000 men, women, and children put to death.

DUTCH THREAT

The news quickly spread through the rest of the Netherlands that if cooperation and surrender weren't an option, resistance was the only alternative. But that wasn't going to be easy.

By late August 1573, the Spaniards were marching toward Amsterdam, and the small cities along the way didn't have armies to resist them. Their leaders desperately considered the nearly non-existent options: Cold weather was just around the corner

You're my inspiration: In Disney's *Fantasia* ('40), the Devil's face was modeled on Bela Lugosi.

and not even evacuating citizens to hide in the woods would work.

The Netherlands don't have high places to use defensively. On the contrary, much of the Dutch countryside is flat (Netherlands means "low lands"), created by filling in swamps, lakes, and even the ocean floor. Twenty-five percent of the country's land is below sea level, and most of the rest is just barely above. How do you defend a land like that?

AMSTERDAM *UN*DAMMED

Perhaps inspired by the bible story of Israelites luring the Egyptian army into death in a boggy sea, the leaders of Alkmar decided on a plan so crazy that it probably shouldn't have worked: They would save their cities and towns by flooding them. Volunteers with shovels and pick axes went to work, breaking holes into the levees and dikes that kept the rivers at bay. When the Spaniards arrived, they discovered a huge, shallow lake where the maps showed farmland. In the center, barely raised above the water, the city sat on an island.

Townspeople had flooded the land with just enough water to make it too shallow for troop transit boats, but too deep to cross on foot without succumbing to the cold or the arrows of marksmen hiding behind trees and dike walls. Even in warm weather, the water would slow attackers and leave them with nowhere to hide. The Spaniards looked at the setup and decided to go way around instead of through, leaving the city unharmed...for now.

Other towns followed suit, using small, fast flat-bottomed boats to get around. Since a lot of the land became a temporary inland sea, the Spanish retreated back to their ships and decided to attack Amsterdam through its harbor. They were aware that winter was coming on, but that didn't seem to be a problem. In fact, it might be a solution, because all those impassable water defenses would freeze into ice highways leading straight to the so-far unpunished Dutch strongholds. The Spanish watched and waited.

HANS BRINKERMANSHIP

A few months later, the ragtag Dutch fleet got frozen into the Amsterdam harbor, giving the Spanish a chance to try out their strategy. Taking advantage of the helpless ships and undefended

A healthy horse can travel up to 100 miles in a day (more if it's riding in a trailer).

coastline, Spanish troops got their marching orders and set off on foot across the ice to attack the sitting-duck ships.

As they stepped cautiously across the ice, they were confronted with a horrifying apparition. Off in the distance they saw a dark, shape-shifting mass of humanity moving toward them at terrific speed, then splitting amoeba-like and taking up positions on all sides of them.

HERE COMES TROUBLE

Skates were not known in Spain at the time, and the sight of Dutch soldiers gliding or flying across the ice with incredible speed, flitting into range just long enough to fire a musket before before retreating again behind ice walls, was unlike anything the Spaniards had ever seen. The Spanish at first thought the Dutch were using some sort of Lutheran voodoo to grow new appendages that let them travel on ice as fast as the steeds of Satan. "It was a thing never heard of before," Spain's appointed governor, the Duke of Alva, recounted later with grudging admiration, "to see a body of musketeers fighting like that on a frozen sea."

Alva didn't gawk for long. He ordered a quick retreat, or at least as quick as the Spanish soldiers could go with slippery shoes and frostbitten toes. The Dutch masters followed behind, skating Alva and his men off the ice and picking off several hundred of them in the process. The Dutch had won, for now.

General Alva eventually commandeered a pair of the skates. He sent them back to a Spain with a message: If you don't want to lose these faraway provinces, we need as many of these as possible, as soon as possible. And that's why the king of Spain ordered 7,000 pairs of skates, and up on mountain lakes, the Spanish military started offering mandatory skating lessons for the next battle.

COLD COMFORT

• The Dutch, of course, having learned to skate skillfully from childhood, maintained a certain level of tactical advantage, but the Spanish did become reasonably competent at skating. As defenders, however, the Dutch held on to a significant advantage: They were able to get the Spaniards skating on thin ice, literally, by cutting the ice at tactical spots, creating deadly weak spots luring their enemies into a deep, often fatal plunge into freezing water.

The first North American magazine ad appeared in Ben Franklin's *General Magazine* (1742).

• The Dutch doubled their forces by training civilian women to fight and to repair the ice walls under fire (often raiding Catholic churches for statues of saints, using them as building materials and missiles to taunt, anger, and demoralize the Spaniards).

• The war lasted for eight decades, alternating between years of stalemate and years of horrifying brutality. Finally, in 1648 the provinces of the Netherlands and Belgium were able to drive out the Spanish, already deep in debt and spread thin by having to defend their empire all over the world.

• The Dutch would continue to use and refine strategic flooding as a defensive tactic, adding mini-forts to hold tactical roads and bridges, often planting trees along them that could be half-felled toward the invading forces to create nearly impassable barriers. The "Dutch Water Line" tactic remained effective for nearly four centuries, until World War II's bombers and paratrooopers made it obsolete.

* * *

RANDOM ORIGIN: TARMAC

In the early 1800s, Scottish engineer John L. McAdam developed a roadmaking process that used pieces of broken-up rock about ¾" in diameter for a road's surface. With use the gravel became compacted, and the surface smooth and durable. "Macadamization," as it became known, was a vast improvement over other roadbuilding techniques at the time, and "macadam roads" could soon be found worldwide. Decades later, when the automobile came along, dust became a problem. In 1901 English engineer Edgar Hooley stumbled on a solution to that problem, He happened upon a macadam road on which tar had spilled. Someone had covered the spill with crushed *slag*—a byproduct of metal smelting—which absorbed the tar, took away its stickiness, and stopped dust accumulation. Within a year Hooley had patented a tar and slag mix which could be easily sprayed on macadam roads. He founded Tarmac Limited. By 1920 the term "tarmac" was being used to refer to airport runways, and eventually included roads and similar surfaces. McAdam's macadamization process, along with Hooley's addition of tar and slag, is still the most widely used roadmaking process in the world.

World's largest casino: China's Venetian Macao. It has 4,000 slot machines and gaming tables.

SERIAL KILLERS: UNSOLVED CASES

We like to cover a wide variety of subjects in every edition of Uncle John's Bathroom Reader. *We have never shied away from gross topics, nor have we demurred from gruesome ones. Even so, we feel compelled to warn you that this one, while fascinating, might make you a little queasy. So if you're squeamish, you might want to skip this article. (Uh-oh. Now you're hooked.)*

BACKGROUND

The most generally accepted definition of "serial killer" is someone who has killed at least three people over a period of at least a month, with a "cooling off" period in between the murders. (This is to differentiate from cases of "mass murder," where someone might kill many people in a single event.) Many serial killers are never caught, which means that some are still at large today. Here are the stories of unsolved serial murders from around the world.

THE FAMILY (Australia)

Between 1979 and 1983, five young men between the ages of 14 and 25 were kidnapped, drugged, tortured, and murdered in and around the South Australian city of Adelaide. In 1984 Bevan Spencer von Einem, an Adelaide accountant, was convicted of committing one of the murders and is currently serving a life sentence. Although police believe von Einem took part in *all* of the murders, they lacked sufficient evidence to prove it. And anonymous witnesses—anonymous because they'd been threatened—informed police that while von Einem was guilty, he wasn't alone: He was only one member of a shadowy group of prominent Adelaide citizens, including lawyers and doctors, who preyed on young men. Other members of this group, called "the Family" in the press, are believed to have taken part in all five murders—and possibly others—with von Einem. A $1 million reward still stands for information leading to further convictions.

America's tallest sand dunes are located in Colorado. They're 750 feet high.

RAINBOW MANIAC (Brazil)

Thirteen men between the ages of 20 and 50 were murdered in Paturis Park in the Brazilian city of Carapicuíba (near Sao Paolo) between July 2007 and August 2008. Twelve were shot; one was beaten to death. The killer was dubbed the "Rainbow Maniac" in reference to the gay-pride rainbow symbol, because all the victims are believed to have been gay. Four months after the thirteenth murder, police announced they had arrested Jairo Francisco Franco, a retired Sao Paolo police officer, after a witness told them he'd seen Franco commit the crime on August 19, 2008. Another witness told police that Franco regularly visited the park seeking gay men. Shortly after Franco's arrest, police inspector Paulo Fortunato told reporters, "We are convinced he is the 'Rainbow Maniac' we have been looking for." But more than four years have passed, and Franco has yet to be charged with this or any crime. The case remains officially unsolved.

HIGHWAY OF TEARS (Canada)

From the 1970s to the present day, numerous women have been murdered or have simply gone missing on what has been dubbed the "Highway of Tears," a remote 450-mile-long stretch of Highway 16 between the towns of Prince George and Prince Rupert in British Columbia. Royal Canadian Mounted Police say the number of women killed or missing there is 18, but Native leaders in the region (several victims were First Nations people) say the number is much higher, possibly even in the forties. While no one believes all of the murders are linked, police have indicated they believe a single serial killer is responsible for at least some, and possibly several, of the attacks. And while there have been many suspects in the case, nobody has ever been arrested.

STONEMAN (India)

This case spans two periods and two locations: The first, from 1985 to 1988 in Bombay; the second from June to December 1989 in Calcutta. During this time, 25 people were killed—12 in the first three-year span, and 13 more over just three months in Calcutta. The method in which "Stoneman" took his victims' lives was especially macabre, and earned him (or her) that odd nickname. In all of the cases, someone crept up to a destitute person sleeping outside alone on a street or in an alley, and dropped a

First U.S. city to host the summer Olympics: St. Louis, Missouri (1904).

large stone—weighing around 50 pounds—on the victim's head, crushing the person's skull and killing the victim instantly. Indian police aren't convinced that the two series of murders were carried out by the same person, saying instead that the Calcutta murders were probably carried out by a copycat killer. There has never been a suspect in the Stoneman cases.

BIBLE JOHN (Scotland)

Between February 1968 and October 1969, three women, aged 25, 29, and 32, were murdered in Glasgow, Scotland. Each had been raped and strangled. The clue that tied them together: All three victims were menstruating at the time of their deaths. Sanitary napkins or tampons had been placed near their bodies, and their purses—but not the contents of the purses—were stolen by their killer. And, most bizarrely, they had all met their murderer at the very same venue—the Barrowland Ballroom. According to police reports, several people actually saw the killer on the night of the third murder. Hellen Puttock, 29, had gone to Barrowland with her sister Jean. They met a man there who introduced himself as "John." After spending more than an hour together at the club, the three left in a taxi. The taxi first dropped off Jean at her home and then dropped off Helen and the man at Helen's home. Helen was found dead in her backyard the next day. Jean told police that the man had quoted the Old Testament during the taxi ride, leading the media to give him the name "Bible John." Although several people saw the killer that night, no arrests were ever made.

Update: In 2007 a Scottish man named Peter Tobin was convicted of the murders of three young women in Scotland and England between 1991 and 2007. Many people believe that Tobin—who lived in Glasgow until 1969 (he turned 23 that year)—is Bible John. This has not, however, been confirmed.

NEW BEDFORD HIGHWAY KILLER (United States)

For eleven harrowing months between July 1988 and June 1989, people in and around the town of New Bedford, Massachusetts, grew increasingly terrified as they heard over and over about the murder of yet another young woman. Before the killing spree ended, the bodies of nine women between the ages of 24 and 36 had been discovered along highways in the region. Two other women went missing in the same time period, and have never

Archaeologists have found ancient mummies with metal braces on their teeth.

been seen since. All of the victims are believed to have been in rough circumstances: All were either prostitutes or drug addicts. There have been a handful of suspects in the case over the years, and one man, Kenneth Ponte, an attorney who had represented several of the women before their deaths, was charged with one of the murders. But, due to lack of evidence, Ponte was never brought to trial, and he died in 2009. The murders remain unsolved today.

* * *

CONSUMER ELECTRONICS OF 1987

Video Games: The video game market crashed in 1983 after games for the Atari console saturated the market. It came back in a big way in late 1986 when Nintendo launched the Nintendo Entertainment System. The first system available was the Deluxe Set, which came with a game console, two "control pads" (joysticks), a "light gun" for shooting games, the shooting game *Duck Hunt,* the puzzle game *Gyromite*, and ROB, a small robot that helped the player with *Gyromite*. Total cost: $249 ($500 today).

Compact Discs: By 1987 compact discs were beginning to replace records and tapes as the dominant music format, with manufacturers shipping 100 million CDs. (Beatles albums were available on CD for the first time that February.) They still cost more than records or tapes, though—$10 on average, vs. $8 for a record or cassette. It would also cost you more to play them. One of the most popular CD players on the market in 1987 was the Magnavox CDB650, which cost $429, the equivalent of $900 today.

Laptops: The first portable or "laptop" computer from IBM had just come on the market in 1987—the IBM PC Convertible. Running on an electrical cord or battery, it was the first IBM computer with the 3.5-inch disk drive that would soon become industry standard. It weighed 13 pounds, the screen was two-tone green, and it ran on 256 kilobytes of RAM. A typical computer in 2012 has 4 gigabytes of RAM—meaning it's about 16,000 times more powerful than this laptop. Cost: $2,000, or $4,000 in today's money.

SCROGGIED

On page 314 we told you the story of how Charles Dickens got his inspiration for the character Ebenezer Scrooge from a real-life miser named John Elwes. But where did the name *Ebenezer Scrooge come from? Here's the tale of Ebenezer Lennox Scroggie, the man who is said to have inspired Dickens's most memorable moniker.*

GRAVE INDICTMENT

According to a story that surfaced in 1997, Dickens stumbled across an intriguing name in 1841 while visiting Edinburgh, Scotland, on a lecture tour. One evening when he had some time between public readings of his work, Dickens wandered through the Canongate Kirkyard (churchyard) along the city's Royal Mile. There he found the grave of one Ebenezer Lennox Scroggie, who was described on his own tombstone as a "mean man," in other words, a cheapskate.

Dickens is said to have been stunned by the inscription. The man's next of kin had gone to the trouble and expense of having his worst quality carved into his tombstone, making it an eternal reminder of what a flawed man he'd been. "I thought it was a grievous message for eternity," he is said to have written. "'Mean man' was an advertisement of a shriveled soul.... This was the emblem of a life surely wasted."

Scroggie's tombstone, the story goes, inspired Dickens to write *A Christmas Carol*, the story of man living just such a wasted life, who is given a chance to redeem himself. He already had John Elwes's life story to draw from. By jiggling the spelling of *Scroggie* to get the more distinctive *Scrooge*, he christened the character that would become the most famous miser in all of English literature.

MYTH-UNDERSTOOD

The second part of the Ebenezer Lennox Scroggie tale is every bit as interesting as the first. It suggests that Dickens evidently did little or no research into the "mean man's" life to find out what he was really like. He apparently didn't get a really good look at the tombstone, either. Because if he had, he would have noticed that the tombstone didn't say "*mean* man" at all. It said "meal man."

Ebenezer Scroggie (1772–1836) wasn't a miser. He was a dealer in *cornmeal*.

MR. FEZZIWIG

In addition to dealing corn, he sold wine and spirits, and is credited with having talked the Royal Navy into buying stores of Scotch whisky in addition to their traditional drink, rum.

Any similarities with the character Ebenezer Scrooge end there. Scroggie is said to have been a public-minded man. He served two terms as a town councilor in the city of Edinburgh. His contemporaries remembered him as a caring, generous, and fun-loving man, more like Scrooge's fun-loving former employer, Mr. Fezziwig, than Scrooge himself. Scroggie loved to spend money and threw wild parties. He was also a notorious womanizer. He is said to have pinched the Countess of Mansfield on the bottom during a church meeting, and was twice reprimanded for lewd behavior with women in the Canongate Kirkyard, once with a widow named Anabella Cameron, another time with a servant girl named Maggie Synge.

The second episode may have produced a child: Though Scroggie never admitted paternity, he did invite Maggie and her child to live with him. Scroggie never married Maggie Synge, but he did eventually wed one Griselda MacGregor, a widow. In 1826 he and Griselda are said to have written *Love in Caledonia: A Guide to Marriage*, "the nearest we have to a sex manual of the time."

GONE WITHOUT A TRACE

Scroggie died in 1836 and was buried in the same churchyard that he'd earlier put to other use. His grave was a sturdy one, complete with iron bars to keep out "resurrectionists" (grave robbers who sold corpses to surgeons for dissection). But if you dream of retracing Dickens's 1841 walk through the Canongate Kirkyard to Scroggie's tombstone, you're out of luck: His tombstone was removed in the 1930s during renovations and never replaced.

When Uncle John first learned of the tale of Ebenezer Lennox Scroggie, he couldn't help but wonder would have happened if Dickens had never stumbled across the tombstone. And what if he had read the tombstone correctly in the first place, or researched

At the game's peak, Farmville "farmers" outnumbered real farmers in the U.S. by 60 to 1.

the life of Scroggie and realized he wasn't a miser after all? Would Dickens ever have written *A Christmas Carol*? It's difficult to imagine Christmas without it. But what Uncle John wondered most of all was how such a fascinating story could have been forgotten for more than 150 years, only to reappear in 1997, seemingly out of the blue. That seemed a little odd, so Uncle John e-mailed the Edinburgh Civic Trust, the city's historical society, to learn more about it.

END OF THE LINE

And that's when the story of the happy-go-lusty cornmeal dealer began to fall apart. "Interesting tale but not necessarily based in fact," Euan Leitch, the Trust's assistant director, wrote:

> There's a notion that the story was created quite recently by someone to see how far you can spread an urban myth as there is no evidence of an Ebenezer Scroggie as a merchant in the post office directories for the period, the grave conveniently no longer exists and there is no parish burial record. I've also yet to see where the direct quote from Dickens comes from.

Uncle John then did a little more digging and traced the story to its origin—an article by journalist Peter Clarke. In 1997 Clarke was writing for an adult magazine called *The Erotic Review*. The *Review*'s editor was a woman named Rowan Pelling, and as she related in a column in *The Telegraph* newspaper in 2012, when Clarke came to her with the story in 1997, even she wondered if it was too good to be true. Had Clarke made the whole thing up?

Pelling concluded that he most likely had—that Ebenezer Lennox Scroggie was a figment of Clarke's imagination, nothing more. "I find myself complicit in a probable Dickens hoax," she admitted in 2012. "I published this literary 'exclusive' in 1997, in *The Erotic Review*. As we went to press, the facts were queried and it hit me that its author, Peter Clarke, was probably pulling my leg. No one could find any corroborating evidence, but it seemed a shame to let the facts obstruct a good yarn."

* * *

"Money—in its absence we are coarse; in its presence we are vulgar."

—Mignon McLaughlin

WEIRD NEWS

Ninety-nine bottles of beer edition.

REALITY BITES

One night in July 2010, Australian Michel Newman, 36, on vacation in the remote town of Broome, Western Australia, was thrown out of a pub for being too intoxicated. Unwilling to let that ruin his evening, Newman wandered over to the Broome Crocodile Park, where he climbed a fence and proceeded to sit on the back of "Fatso"—a 16-foot, 1,700-pound saltwater crocodile. Fatso immediately snapped around, latched his enormous jaws onto one of Newman's legs, and...let him go. Bleeding profusely, Newman scrambled over the fence and headed back to the pub. He was taken to the hospital, where he made a full recovery. Park owner Malcolm Douglas was surprised that Newman had survived. "Saltwater crocodiles, once they get hold of you," he said, "are not renowned for letting you go." He said that the fact that it had been an unusually cool night may have made Fatso sluggish—and that was probably the only reason Newman was still alive.

I (DON'T) HEAR THAT TRAIN A-COMIN'

In 2012 a man camping in southeast British Columbia downed several beers, then took a stroll, came upon a railroad track, lay down between the rails, and fell asleep. Minutes later, a 26-car train roared down the track. The conductor spotted the man and blasted the train's horn. He didn't move. The driver slammed on the brakes, generating a long, deafening metal-on-metal screech. He still didn't move. All 26 cars of the train rolled over him. The conductor and other train workers ran back to the spot, expecting to find a dead person (or pieces of one)—and were stunned to find the man, intact and alive, still between the rails. They nudged him. "He got up," RCMP Sgt. Dave Dubnyk told reporters, "grabbed his beer and walked away." Police found the man at the nearby campground. "I can't imagine being so passed out that you wouldn't hear a train," Sgt. Dubnyk said, "but if he had, and the train had startled him into sitting up, it would have been tragic." The still-intoxicated man was taken to jail for the night...for his own safety.

Vatican City is the only nation in the world that can lock its gates at night.

PRESIDENT CONAN O'BRIEN

...president of Harvard Lampoon *magazine, that is. Here are a few more who went on to bigger things.*

BACKGROUND

The *Harvard Lampoon*, founded more than 130 years ago in 1876, is the longest-running continuously published humor magazine in the world. A list of its writers through the years reads like a who's who of accomplished people, including William Randolph Hearst (newspaper publisher), George Santayana (philosopher), Patricia Marx (*New Yorker* and *Saturday Night Live* writer—and first woman elected to the *Lampoon* staff, in 1971), P. J. O'Rourke (political satirist), Al Franken (U.S. Senator), and Etan Cohen (*Beavis and Butthead* writer). The *Harvard Lampoon* is a magazine, but it's also a fraternal organization of sorts, so presidents are elected by a vote of the staff. Many presidents went on to live some pretty remarkable lives.

PRESIDENT JOHN REED (1910)

Reed was born to an upper-class Portland, Oregon, family and entered Harvard in 1906 (fellow students included two-time Pulitzer Prize–winning author and journalist Walter Lippmann, and poet T. S. Eliot). He joined the debating club, dramatic club, cheerleading squad, banjo club, mandolin club, glee club, and water polo team, and in the meantime studied to be a writer. In his junior year he became an editor of the *Lampoon*, and in his senior year its president. "Under Reed's term as president," according to the magazine's website, "the *Lampoon* evolved from salacious puns and localized 'Harvard humor' to highly literate, scathing social commentary."

After leaving Harvard, Reed established himself as one of the country's most popular freelance journalists (and poets). He also became a Communist. In 1917 Reed traveled to Russia to report on the Communist revolution, returned in 1918, was charged with sedition in 1919, fled the United States, and in 1920 died in

The red carpet at the Oscars is about 500 feet long and 33 feet wide.

Moscow. He then became one of the very few Americans ever to be buried at the Kremlin Wall Necropolis, the honored burial ground for heroes of the Communist revolution.

PRESIDENT GEORGE PLIMPTON (1949)

Plimpton grew up on Manhattan's Fifth Avenue and attended a series of elite schools, where he excelled at sports—but not in the classroom—and entered Harvard in 1944. ("It was a little easier to get into Harvard in those days," he remarked years later.) He joined the elite Porcellian Club—the Harvard equivalent of Yale's Skull and Bones—where he met writers and became interested in writing himself. Before long he was contributing to the *Lampoon*, and in his senior year was elected its president.

Plimpton graduated in 1950, and in 1952 he moved to Paris, where he co-founded the *Paris Review*, one of the world's most highly regarded literary magazines. Around this time he began specializing in a unique genre of non-fiction writing. He would become or play the part of something that most people never get a chance to do—usually involving sports—and then write about the experience. Examples: He fought bulls in Spain, pitched in a Major League Baseball All-Star Game, boxed against world light-heavyweight champion Archie Moore, participated in a flying trapeze act, and, in his most famous role, played quarterback for the NFL's Detroit Lions, which he wrote about in the book *Paper Lion*. (Alan Alda played Plimpton in the 1968 film version.) He also acted, appearing in *Lawrence of Arabia* (1962), *L.A. Story* (1991), and *Good Will Hunting* (1997). Plimpton continued to work, including editing the *Paris Review*, until his death in 2003 at age 76.

PRESIDENT FRED GWYNNE (1950)

The son of a Wall Street broker, Frederick Hubbard Gwynne entered Harvard in 1947. He was a gifted illustrator and worked as a cartoonist for the *Lampoon* before moving on to writing, and then became president. He was also a gifted singer (and part of the Harvard Krokodiloes *a capella* group) and actor (in the school's esteemed Hasty Pudding theatrical society).

After graduating, Gwynne moved to New York, found work on Broadway, and got his first movie part as an uncredited gang mem-

According to the U.S. census, one in three Americans adults are unmarried.

ber in 1954's *On the Waterfront* with Marlon Brando. In 1961 he got his first big television role, co-starring in the sitcom *Car 54, Where Are You?*, and in 1964 the 6'5" Gwynne landed his best-known role—the Frankenstein-ish Herman Munster on *The Munsters*. (He hated it because of the three-hour makeup sessions and 40 pounds of padding he had to wear.) Gwynne continued to act, write, and draw—he wrote and illustrated several acclaimed children's books—until his death at age 66 in 1993. His last role: a critically acclaimed performance as Judge Chamberlain Haller in 1992's *My Cousin Vinnie*.

PRESIDENT LISA HENSON (1981)

Henson, the daughter of Muppets creator Jim Henson, grew up in Westchester County, outside New York City. She entered Harvard in 1979 as a math major. A natural storyteller, she soon changed her major to mythology and folklore. During her freshman year she attended a recital by *Lampoon* president Andy Borowitz, who read a limerick "that involved Muppets performing sexual acts," Henson told *The Harvard Crimson*, the school's newspaper, in 2007. That got her interested in the *Lampoon*. She started working for it doing art and design work—which she had learned from her father—and by her senior year was such an integral part of the organization that she was elected its first female president.

After graduation she was hired by Warner Bros., where she worked on such films as the *Lethal Weapon* series, *Batman* in 1989, and *Free Willy* in 1993—by which time she was vice president. She then went to Columbia Pictures, where she became president. Today she's CEO of the Jim Henson Company, where she has led production of several hit TV shows, including *Dinosaur Train* and *Sid the Science Kid*.

PRESIDENT CONAN O'BRIEN (1983–84)

O'Brien was born in Brookline, Massachusetts, in 1963, graduated from Brookline High School—as class valedictorian—in 1981, and entered Harvard in 1982. He quickly became one of the *Lampoon*'s major writers, and was elected its president in his sophomore and junior years, making him only the second person in the magazine's history to serve as its president twice. (The other was humorist Robert Benchley, class of 1912.) If you're a fan, you probably already know about his career after Harvard: writing for *Not Necessarily the News*, *Saturday Night Live*, and *The Simpsons*; hosting *Late Night With Conan O'Brien* on NBC for 16 years; infamously replacing Jay Leno on *The Tonight Show* for just seven months before being re-replaced...by Jay Leno; and hosting a cable TV show, *Conan*. Something you may not know is that while O'Brien was president of the *Lampoon*, he and his fellow "pooners," as they are called, played a number of pranks on their longtime rivals—the staff of *The Harvard Crimson*. These included an early morning theft of the entire print run of the *Crimson* (during which O'Brien was arrested) and a *Lampoon* edition that included a fake phone-sex ad with the dorm room phone number of the *Crimson*'s president, Jeff Zucker. Who's he? The guy who became president of NBC in 2007—and oversaw the Conan O'Brien/*Tonight Show* debacle. (He's also the guy who called the police on O'Brien for taking all the *Crimson* newspapers.) So was the *Tonight Show* mess payback for President Conan O'Brien's prankster days at the *Lampoon*? We'll probably never know.

*   *   *

HE'S A REAL HOTHEAD

"A Georgia man was taken to a hospital in critical condition in 2012 after he allegedly encouraged his friends to set his head on fire at a bar by dousing him with 100-proof booze, police said. The 36-year-old man had originally phoned police to report several attackers had lit his head on fire, but police later learned otherwise by watching surveillance video captured at Allie Katz Bar in Augusta. Footage showed it took the man's friends two attempts to ignite the Bacardi 151 on his head before he rushed around the bar with his entire head ablaze. 'The man who was set on fire bet his friends that he was drinking with that he could set his face on fire. Obviously no one believed him and he proved them wrong,' Lt. Blaise Dresser told WJBF-TV. The man was released from hospital and police said he won't be charged because he's suffered enough."

—ABC News

"THIS PLACE IS A TOILET"

Normally when someone refers to a house, restaurant, or some other place as a "toilet," it's an insult. Sometimes it's just the truth.

OUT OF ORDER

You might not believe it when you can't find a restroom after a night of pub crawling in London or some other British city, but during the Victorian era, Great Britain was known for the quantity and quality of its public toilets. Great numbers of them were built in the late 1800s and early 1900s. Some were free-standing buildings of brick or stone while others were just below ground level, accessible via stairs. Many were quite ornate by modern standards.

Quite a few of these structures still stand, although they have fallen on hard times, victims of vandalism, shrinking government budgets, and plumbing that's now more than a century old. Some municipalities have stopped providing access to public restrooms altogether; others have found that it's cheaper to build new facilities than to modernize the old ones and make them accessible to disabled people. So what do you do with all those antique restrooms? Many have been converted to new—and fascinating—uses.

EASTVILLE PHARMACY

Location: Bristol

Story: For many years, Bristol's Eastville neighborhood didn't have a drugstore, which meant that residents, many of whom did not own cars, had to go miles out of their way to get prescriptions filled. In 2011 a businessman named Naveed Sahoor opened a pharmacy in a long-abandoned public toilet, one whose doors and windows had been bricked up for years. Sahoor spent £100,000 ($155,000) ripping out toilets and urinals and converting the building to its new purpose. He kept the TOILET signs "as a reminder of the building's history." Bonus: Because the neighborhood is home to a large South Asian population, customers can have their prescriptions filled by staffers speaking Urdu, Punjabi, or Hindi as well as English. "I am pleased with how the building

In 1999 the Grateful Dead's caterer, Charlie Ayers, became Google's first company chef.

looks and the quality of the premises," Sahoor said when his toilet pharmacy opened in July 2011.

THE BAY CAFÉ

Location: Canvey Island, Essex

Story: Barbara Power and Alan Stanard have been significant others for more than 30 years. But in 2009 Stanard, 59, became too sick to walk, so Power decided to convert a public restroom on the Canvey seafront into a health-food café. The couple borrowed £50,000 (about $78,500) to remake the toilet into a café with seating for 32 and an open kitchen that allows customers to watch their food being prepared. (The local council approved the change, provided that Power make the café's restroom available to the public.)

TEMPLE OF CONVENIENCE

Location: Manchester

Story: This small subterranean men's room beneath Manchester's Great Bridgewater Street has been reborn as a tiny—but popular—music bar. No band? No problem: The jukebox has one of the best selections of music in the city, and there's a great selection of beers as well. Get there early if you want a seat; they go fast. "This is the best bar in a toilet that I have ever been to," one customer wrote in an online review. "If you are one of the lucky smug few to get a seat then you can while away a cozy and intimate evening laughing at those fools who came to the toilet too late."

CORE BAR AND GRILL

Location: Southport, Merseyside

Story: Who says underground toilets have to be small? (Or toilets?) In 2002 the drainage problems in a large subterranean restroom in Southport got so bad that the local government solicited bids to fill the entire space with concrete. One of the bidders, Mark Ashton, thought it made more sense to fill the bathroom with paying customers, so he proposed converting it into a tapas bar. The council liked the idea so much that it awarded Ashton and his partner, Paul Townsend, a 125-year lease. The duo fixed the drainage problem, spent £300,000 (about $450,000) ripping out the plumbing and then remodeled the interior into a restaurant large enough to seat 100. When Core opened in 2005,

Older than you think: The phrase "kiss my ——" dates back to at least 1705.

Townsend predicted that the bar's unconventional history would be good for business: "It was always going to be in people's minds that they were toilets. Some customers do come in and say, 'That's where I used to pee.'" He was right: The bar is still in business.

THEATRE OF SMALL CONVENIENCE

Location: Malverne

Story: Opened by a puppeteer and part-time social worker named Dennis Neale in 1999, the theater was built in a wedge-shaped men's room that's 6 feet wide at one end, 10 feet wide at the other, and 16 feet long on the sides. Neale spent two years constructing the small but ornate venue, fitting it with intricate woodwork, murals on the ceiling and walls, seating for 12, and a five-foot stage at the narrow end. Over the years, the theater has been used for plays, poetry readings, musical performances, and Neale's eight-minute puppet shows, which he performs upon request every Saturday. In 2002 Guinness World Records recognized the playhouse as the smallest commercial theater in the world.

PUBLIC LIFE

Location: London

Story: Opened in 2000, Public Life is a bar, Internet cafe, and art space in a former men's room beneath Commercial Street, which separates the East End from the financial district. In the early 1990s, artist/activist Siraj Izhar used the abandoned restroom, then a popular haunt for junkies and prostitutes, as a free space for performance art. Why the toilet? He didn't have the money to do anything else. In 1995 he paired up with a financier named Neil Bell, who, with the help of public grants and donations from supporters, raised $290,000 to bring Public Life to life. The tile walls and checkerboard marble floor are original; the bar, LED lighting, and everything else is new. "Internet connectivity, plus a lively mix of neighborhood types, including bankers and prostitutes, are a part of the space's urban design," says the *New York Times*.

THE LOOKOUT

Location: Scarborough, Yorkshire

Story: Tracy Woodhouse and Graham Peck had long admired the boarded-up public toilet built into a cliff overlooking

First cat in outer space: Félicette, launched by the French in 1963. (She survived.)

Scarborough's North Bay. Whenever the couple walked past the dilapidated building with its beautiful stonework, Peck would talk about fixing it up. They got their chance in 2005, when the local government council offered the building for lease. Woodhouse and Peck put £15,000 down (about $27,000) for a seven-year lease and negotiated an additional 21-year lease for £1,800 ($3,200) a year. They spent an additional £35,000 ($64,000) converting the toilet into a one-bedroom home. Working on the project in their spare time, they finished in 2010 and named their new home the Lookout. (Get it? The *Loo*–kout.)

What once was the ladies' room now serves as Woodhouse and Peck's bedroom and bathroom. The men's room is now the living room, with a TV set where the urinals used to be. "Some people joke about it," Woodhouse told the *Daily Mail* in 2010. "At work they'll say things like, 'Oh yes, you're the couple who live in a lavatory.' But we now have a lovely little house with a sea view that used to be a loo." The Lookout has become a Scarborough tourist site, especially among visitors old enough to remember when the bathrooms were still in operation...and now assume they've re-opened. "We can be watching TV or washing the dishes and suddenly a face will peer through the window. I don't know who's more surprised, them or us," Peck says.

*   *   *

A VERY LONG SENTENCE

In 1976 Dudley Wayne Kyzer, 40, of Tuscaloosa, Alabama, was sentenced to death after being convicted of three murders. But four years later his conviction was overturned, he was retried, convicted again, and this time sentenced to two life sentences plus 10,000 years—the longest sentence ever imposed in the United States, according to *Guinness World Records*. Because of quirks in Alabama's sentencing laws, Kyzer became eligible for parole after ten years, and has been eligible every five years since then (they last turned him down in 2010), so his 10,000-year sentence still stands, which means, as of 2012 he still has 9,969 years left to go. He'll be out in the year 11981.

22% percent of all twins are left-handed. General population: 12%.

HUMAN GUINEA PIGS

Sometimes real-life scientists make the "mad" scientists from the movies look downright sane.

THE MONSTER STUDY

In 1939 Wendell Johnson, a speech pathologist at the University of Iowa, directed graduate student Mary Tudor in an experiment on six children, aged 5 to 15. For six months Tudor visited the kids (who lived in a nearby orphange) and conducted classes with them—and whenever they spoke she told them they had terrible speaking voices. She did this again and again. Why? To see if she could turn the kids—all of whom had perfectly normal speaking voices—into stutterers, thereby proving Johnson's hypothesis that stuttering is caused by conditioning rather than congenital defect. None of the kids became stutterers, but according to Tudor's own notes, all of them became afraid and ashamed to speak.

When the experiment was over, Tudor simply left. The children were never told anything. Johnson's peers were aghast when they heard what he'd done and dubbed his work "The Monster Study."

Update: The results were concealed for decades, but in 2001 they were discovered by a journalist. Later that year the University of Iowa issued a formal apology for the experiment. In 2007 three of the test subjects, along with the estates of the other three, were awarded $925,000 by the State of Iowa for what all described as the lifelong scars they suffered as a result of the "Monster Study."

SOVIET POISON TRIALS

Soviet biochemist Grigory Mairanovsky was the head of "Laboratory 1," a super-secret Moscow facility run by the KGB, from 1939 until 1946. His assignment: Develop a flavorless, odorless poison that is undetectable in an autopsy. To achieve this Mairanovsky personally directed experiments on humans—all of them political prisoners. They were given poisons with meals or in drinks, and tested for effects. (They were kept in bare cells and observed through small windows.) If the poison failed to kill them, the pris-

John Steinbeck's novel *Of Mice and Men* was almost called *Something That Happened.*

oner would be nursed back to health to await another round.

Records show that more than 100 people were tested in this way. Not one survived, and many died agonizing deaths. It's rumored that Mairanovsky did succeed in developing a poison (dubbed "K-2") during his time at Laboratory 1. It could reportedly kill within 15 minutes and was undetectable in an autopsy.

Update: The rumors have never been confirmed.

SOUTH AFRICAN ARMY SHOCK THERAPY

In the 1970s and '80s, South African army psychiatrists performed experiments on members of the nation's all-white military who were—or were suspected of being—gay or lesbian. The experiments involved encouraging subjects to fantasize about someone of the same sex and then delivering powerful electric shocks to them. If repeated treatments didn't "cure" them, other methods were tried, including hormone therapy and chemical castration. The exact number of men and women subjected to these experiments is unknown—some estimates put it as high as 900. News of the experiments wasn't made public until the end of South Africa's apartheid era in 1994.

Update: One psychiatrist believed to be involved in these experiments, Dr. Aubrey Levin—known as "Dr. Shock"—was allowed to emigrate to Canada in 1995, where he became a professor of psychiatry at the University of Calgary. Levin's psychiatry license was revoked in 2010, after he was charged with sexually assaulting male patients. He is still awaiting trial.

JAPANESE "UNIT 731" EXPERIMENTS

In 1937, during the Second Sino-Japanese War, the Japanese government built an enormous military complex in the puppet state of Manchukuo, in what is now northeast China. Called Unit 731, the facility was headed by General Shiro Ishii, the Japanese army's chief medical officer. Over the course of the following eight years, Ishii directed hundreds of doctors in an unimagineable nightmare of experiments on humans, mostly Chinese and Korean prisoners. This included exposure to biological and chemical warfare agents (such as plague, cholera, and mustard gas), unnecessary amputations, and surgery without painkillers.

The experiments were done in the name of medical research,

Moo-la: The first coins, from around 2000 B.C., were bronze pieces shaped like cattle.

but many had no discernible medical purpose whatsoever. With military defeat in sight, in 1945 General Ishii ordered the executions of all remaining prisoners and fled back to Japan. During his time as the head of Unit 731 more than 10,000 people were experimented upon; roughly 3,000 of them died in the process. Ishii was arrested by U.S. Occupation Authorities in 1945. He was granted immunity in exchange for information about Unit 731 and received no punishment for his crimes.

Update: Ishii died at home in 1959 at the age of 67.

GERMAN SULFONAMIDE TESTS

In 1942 doctors at the Ravensbrück concentration camp in northeastern Germany were ordered to test the effectiveness of a new kind of drug—an antibacterial called a sulfonamide. The Nazi government's goal was to reduce troop losses due to infection after injury, especially from gunshot wounds. To make conditions as true to life as possible, doctors at Ravensbrück were supplied with prisoner test subjects, most of them Polish women. Doctors cut long incisions into the women's calves, dabbed the wounds with virulent strains of bacteria, tied off the blood vessels at either end of the wounds—in order to simulate gunshot wounds—and then stitched up the incisions. Some of the women were given sulfonamide, some weren't; some were given small doses, some large. Their wounds were observed over the following weeks. Before the experiments ended in September 1943, 74 women had been subjected to the experiments. Eleven died. The rest suffered injuries to their legs that affected them for the rest of their lives.

CANADIAN "PSYCHIC DRIVING" PROCEDURE

In the early 1950s Scottish-born psychiatrist Dr. Ewen Cameron developed what he believed was a cure for schizophrenia, and in 1953 began testing it on patients at the Allan Memorial Clinic in Montreal. He called it "psychic driving." The treatment: Patients were drugged into unconsciousness with powerful sedatives, had earphones placed on their heads, and were subjected to repeated messages, such as "People like you" or "You have confidence in yourself," over and over...and over...for days, weeks, and, in some cases, months. Over a decade, Cameron subjected hundreds of people to "psychic driving." Not a single person is believed to have been cured or even helped by the treatment—and many were quite likely made worse off.

At the same time Cameron was performing these experiments, he was taking part in the CIA's notorious MK-ULTRA "mind-control" program, involving, among other things, dosing unwitting subjects with LSD. That's why Cameron's clinic was in Canada—it would have been illegal to do such things in the U.S.

THE "LITTLE ALBERT" EXPERIMENT

In 1920 American psychologist Dr. John B. Watson, a professor at Johns Hopkins University in Baltimore, performed an experiment on an nine-month-old boy Watson dubbed "Little Albert" (not his real name). Over the course of several days, Little Albert was introduced to a white rabbit, a white mouse, white pieces of cotton, and other white fuzzy things. He showed no fear of any of these things. Then he was reintroduced to them, but this time when he saw them Watson struck a piece of iron with a hammer behind Little Albert's head. The sudden loud noise would startle the boy, and he'd begin to cry. Watson did this again and again. After several days, whenever the rabbit, mouse, or other white things were shown to Little Albert, he would burst into tears. After 31 days Little Albert's mother took the boy home—and that was that. Watson had demonstrated that an infant could be conditioned to fear something through the use of loud noises. He published his findings, which became a standard part of psychology textbooks for decades.

Update: In 2009 a team of psychologists at Appalachian State University in North Carolina published a paper in which they claimed to have discovered the identity of Little Albert. His name was Douglas Merritte, the son of Arvilla Merritte, an unmarried nurse in training at Johns Hopkins. Douglas died of *hydrocephalus* (water on the brain) at the age of six. Modern psychologists say the most unfortunate aspect of Watson's experiment is that no effort was made to desensitize the boy once it was finished, and that he may have suffered long-term effects from it.

RAT-HEAD FACIAL EXPRESSION EXPERIMENT

In 1924 Carney Landis, a graduate psychology student at the University of Minnesota, designed an experiment to determine whether there is a basic underlying human facial expression for any given emotion. In the school's lab, Landis drew black lines on the faces of several volunteers (fellow grad students) to more easily track the movements of their facial muscles. He then photographed their faces as he exposed them to stimuli meant to evoke specific emotional responses, including exposing them to the smell of ammonia, having them stick their hands into a bucket of live frogs, and having them watch pornographic films. Then came the final experiment: Landis gave each of the students (one at a time, with no one else present) a live rat and a large sharp knife—and instructed each student to decapitate the rat. Two-thirds agreed to do it, and actually cut off the rats' heads. The other third refused, so Landis decapitated the rats for them, while taking photographs of their (disgusted) faces. Conclusion: Landis discovered no universal facial expressions, but did find that most test subjects will do whatever they're told to do. (Our conclusion: Landis liked to kill rats.)

*   *   *

NAUGHTY PENGUINS

In June 2012, a researcher at the London Natural History Museum discovered lost accounts of "depraved" penguin sexual activity that dated back 100 years. They were written by Dr. George Murray Levick, who accompanied explorer Robert Falcon Scott on his 1911 attempt to reach the South Pole. Levick studied Adélie penguins on that journey, and was so shocked by what he saw that he wrote his notes in Greek, so only "educated gentlemen" like himself would be able to read them. What penguin depravities did Levick observe? Penguins forcing other penguins to καλύψτε τα μάτια σας; penguins απόκρυψη των frozen penguins; and penguins κακός penguins κακός κακός penguins. (Sorry—this book is family-oriented.) Levick attempted to publish an academic paper on the penguins' "astonishing" behavior when he returned to London in 1913, but it was deemed so vulgar that no one would publish it. The report, titled *Sexual Habits of the Adélie Penguin*, was forgotten until a curator at the museum came across it in Levick's papers, which led to the report finally being published 99 years later.

BIG NOISE, LITTLE BUG

Cicadas are the vuvuzelas of the insect world. (What are vuvuzelas? Those loud horns that nearly caused soccer fans' brains to explode during the 2010 World Cup.) Vuvuzelas reach a decibel level of 60, but cicadas? These little bugs can reach a decibel level twice that loud. That's as loud as a rock concert or a jet engine.

BROODY BUGS

Cicadas are bizarre, especially the "periodical cicadas" that live only in eastern North America. What's odd about them is that they're on either a 13- or a 17-year cycle. They emerge in "broods" of so many bugs it's like some shock-and-awe insect invasion, make a lot of deafening noise, mate, lay eggs, and, within just a few weeks, die. Then they disappear again for an another exact number—13 or 17—of years. Entomologists are still trying to figure out what makes periodical cicadas tick. The main problem: those long cycles. It's difficult for scientists to study an insect that shows up only once or twice in their careers.

The name *cicada* is Latin for "tree cricket," which is actually incorrect: cicadas are not crickets. And though one species is commonly called the "17-year locust," they're not locusts, either. Locusts are "eating machines" that can devour entire crops. Cicadas don't eat leaves; they're sapsuckers, like their closest relatives leafhoppers and spittlebugs. Cicadas have also been called "jar flies," "harvest flies," and "dust flies," but their Australian nickname, "galang-galang," which echoes the racket they make, may be the most fitting.

THE DROP ZONE

Periodical cicadas wait a long time for their 15 minutes of fame, spending the bulk of their lives hidden underground. Each cicada begins as one of about 600 eggs embedded into V-shaped slits that a female cicada makes into new growth at the tips of tree twigs. The female makes the grooves using the sharp *proboscis* (feeding tube) under her chin. (It's the same tool cicadas stick into plant stems to suck out the sap, their main food.) The egg-laying process can cause the twig tips to turn brown but doesn't harm adult trees.

Saplings are a different story—too many cicada eggs can kill young trees.

When cicada eggs hatch it's kind of like a family riding the Drop Zone at an amusement park. After 6-10 weeks, baby cicadas emerge as "nymphs." They look like the adults they're going to become, except they're smaller (about the size of an ant) and they can't fly. That's why a nymph's intro to the cold cruel world is a sudden plummet from the tree to the ground below.

HIT THE GROUND RUNNING

After crash landing, cicada nymphs burrow into the ground, digging down 1 to 9 feet where they settle in next to a juicy root. They leach off the root for their entire 13 (or 17) years underground. During that time, periodical cicadas don't cocoon, they molt. Over and over. They eat, their bodies grow, and when they grow too big for their skin: *pop*! Their exoskeletons burst open, and a slightly bigger and more mature cicada emerges. This happens seven times before they become adults.

In the spring of their 13th (or 17th) years, the cicada's biological alarm clock sounds. As for the time of year, many experts think soil temperature triggers cicada nymphs to emerge. When it reaches a constant minimum of 64° F or 18° C, cicadas burrow to the surface for the first time since they dropped from the tree at hatching. If the ground is wet, "mud chimneys" appear on the ground as the nymphs tunnel upward. If the ground is dry, the emerging cicadas leave it pockmarked with round holes.

As soon as they reach the surface, cicadas scurry off to attach themselves to a plant (trees are particular favorites) for one final molt—this one will make them full-fledged adults. The skin down the middle of their backs splits open and the adult cicadas climb out, stretch their wings and wait for them to dry, and then fly off, leaving their empty skins hanging on the tree. (These look so much like live cicadas that they act as decoys for predators.) After about six days of hiding in leaves while their new outer shells harden, it's time to start singing.

THAT "COME HITHER" FLICK

Cicadas have a pair of stiff hollow membranes called *tymbals* located on the sides of their abdomens just behind their wings. When they flex the large muscles attached to the tymbals, the tymbals buckle inward. This buckling makes a vibrating click that's amplified by an air chamber in the insect's abdomen. As the muscle relaxes, the tymbal sounds again. Repeating this action quickly and repeatedly can sound like anything from a motorbike to the vuvuzela-infested soccer stadium. The specific sound depends on the species of cicada.

"Choruses" of male cicadas congregate in high tree branches, hoping to get lucky with a receptive female. The louder a cicada sings, the better its chance of attracting a mate. There are a lot of competitors: As many as 1.5 million cicadas can emerge in a single acre, but many of those are females whose biological clocks are ticking away the last few weeks of their lives. Females don't call. When they hear the singer of their dreams, they signal their interest with an alluring flick of their wings.

CAN YOU HEAR ME NOW?

Every species has its own song. Differences in tymbal size between species create different tones, which combine with the speed of clicking and the length of the call to make up each species' distinctive call. And like moms and elementary school teachers, cicadas have "selective hearing." Each cicada species clearly hears its call while remaining virtually deaf to the calls of other species. Result: A dozen cicada species could be buzzing their tymbals off in a single forest, and each cicada would be able to pick out the call of its own species above the din. But cicadas are often fooled by machines: Because they can only hear one narrow range of frequency, odds are good that some undertone or overtone of machine noise will match it. The sounds of lawnmowers, weed whackers, and other chugging two-cylinder machinery can sound quite attractive to a female cicada. ("He's playing our song.")

NOT QUIET ON THE SOUTHERN FRONT

Although cicadas are Johnny One-Note when it comes to pitch, they can modulate it a bit. Once a male attracts a female with its "calling song," it switches to a softer, more romantic "courtship song." Cicadas also have a "distress call" that they use when caught by a predator: They click erratically like a tiny engine revving and stopping as it runs out of gas.

The trash dumped into Earth's oceans each year weighs 3 times as much as the fish caught.

How loud a chorus gets depends on the concentration of cicadas in a given area. The noise *can* be as loud as 88–120 decibels (from a blender to a jet engine). Brood XIX, a 13-year brood also known as the Great Southern Brood, was scheduled to emerge in May 2011. Spurred on by horror movielike headlines, people from Virginia to Oklahoma started to worry about whether the "deafening" insects that were about to cover their trees could actually make them deaf. Biology professor Johannes Schul offered reassurance: "It won't damage anyone's hearing, and won't have any adverse health effects aside from stressing a few people out."

Don Griffith, a 70-year-old retired Georgia school superintendent experienced that stress first-hand during Brood XIX: "It sounds like a million little wooden boxes rattling with a million marbles. They'll land on your collar. They'll land on your head. It causes you to think maybe you're at war with them." Despite Griffith's periodical cicada paranoia, those masses of insects really are fighting for something: survival.

SURVIVAL OF THE LUCKY

Many animal species hang out in herds, schools, or flocks. Why? Because there's safety in numbers. Cicadas take this to an absurd length, coming out en masse, but not every year. Scientists theorize that if broods emerged every year, predator populations would be so well fed they'd increase. Every year, more and more predators would be standing around with their tongues hanging out, waiting for the cicadas to show up. Cicadas survive by going into hiding for so long that few individual predators live long enough to see the tasty bugs more than once in their lives.

Brood X, also known as the Great Eastern Brood, is on a 17-year cycle and last showed up in 2004. This brood's turf stretches from the Chesapeake Bay to the edge of the Great Plains. Scientists say the 2004 emergence was probably "the largest insect outbreak on Earth." How large? It produced an estimated one *trillion* cicadas. Scientists call this natural strategy "predator satiation." Predators that happen to be around gorged themselves until they can't eat another insect. After a few days, predators get sick of eating cicadas and leave them alone. "If you walked outside and found the world swarming with Hershey Kisses, eventually you'd get so sick of Hershey Kisses that you'd never ever want to eat

Who's John Tyndall? The Irish scientist who answered the question "Why is the sky blue?"

them again," said biologist and editor-in-chief of *American Entomologist*, Gene Kritsky. Most cicadas survive and go on to sing, mate, and lay eggs (if they're female) for about two weeks.

ON THE MENU

What eats cicadas? Just about any animal that isn't a vegetarian: birds, foxes, wolves, dogs, cats, opossums, pigs, squirrels, frogs, lizards, fish, other insects…and people. Since pre-history humans have been eating cicadas either fresh off the tree, stir fried, deep-fried, or roasted over fires. "They're high in protein, low in fat, no carbs," Kritsky told *National Geographic News* during the 2004 outbreak. "They're actually quite nutritious." (Female cicadas, by the way, have a reputation for being meatier and more succulent.)

If being eaten after 13 or 17 years stuck underground seems unfair, it may be preferable to two other fates. First, the cicada's most virulent enemy, *Massospora cicadina*. It's a fungal disease to which these insects are particularly susceptible. Spores can infect cicadas when they're still underground, resulting in malformed bodies and wings. Cicadas can also be infected as they emerge. If that happens, the infected individual's abdomen swells up and breaks off, exposing a white, chalky mass of spores. This sterilizes the cicada but does not kill it; infected cicadas pass the fungus on to others as they try to mate, infecting them, too.

KILLER QUEENS

Frankly, if we were cicadas, our least preferred predator would be the second one: the giant (2" long) cicada killer wasp (*Sphecius speciosis*). Instead of administering a quick death, the cicada killer queen swoops down and lands on an unsuspecting cicada. She administers a paralyzing sting, straddles the cicada, grasps it with her legs, and flies it to her underground nest, where she rolls the unlucky cicada into a cell, and lays an egg on it (if the egg is female, the wasp may provide two or three cicadas). Finally, she seals the cell to create a sort of climate-controlled incubator. Two to three days later, the egg hatches and the larva emerges to discover a juicy birthday breakfast. What makes this such a horrible death is that the cicada killer's paralyzing sting keeps the cicada *alive* so that the larvae can dine on living flesh for 10-14 days, until only the cicada's outer shell remains.

UNTIL WE MEET AGAIN

So, how does our cicada story end? With the entire brood dying off in a peaceful mass death like some insect Jonestown, leaving no survivors. (And predators wondering if that all-you-can-eat buffet was just some crazy dream.) From start to finish—from the time the first cicada nymph digs tunnels up until the final die-off—a brood's above-ground life lasts about 4–6 weeks. "They come and go so quickly," said University of Georgia entomologist Dr. Nancy C. Hinkle. But, at least we know one thing. "They'll be back..."

A FEW FACTS

• There are at least 2,500 species of cicadas. Africa has about 450, Australia 200, North America at least 105, and the British Isles 1.

• Some tropical species grow to as long as 6 inches. Some desert species can sweat to cool themselves. (Very rare among insects.) Some cold-weather cicadas can raise their body temperatures at will by more than 70°. (Very rare among not just insects, but most living things.)

• With two large red compound eyes on the sides of the head and three small *ocelli* (simple eyes) in a triangle on the front of the head, periodical cicadas have excellent vision.

• In India, one cicada species is called the "World Cup Cicada." It emerges in synch with the FIFA soccer tournament, held every four years from mid-June to mid-July. (Who needs vuvuzelas?)

• In China, cicada "flowers" (shells left behind after molting) are collected and used in traditional medicine. They're a common ingredient in formulas used to cure fevers, sore throats, blurry vision, spasms, and skin irritations.

• Because of its extended life cycle, the 17-year cicada is the world's longest-living insect.

• Most periodical cicadas have red eyes, but a small percentage have blue or white eyes. During the 2011 emergence of Brood XIX, which covers 15 states, word spread that researchers were paying $3,000 for specimens of blue-eyed cicadas, but according to Vanderbilt University biology professor Patrick Abbot, that was "a recurrent myth."

...George Washington. First: Washington, KY (1780).

• Scientists say its tough to understand the purpose of an insect as bizarre as the periodical cicada, but they do play positive roles: They are a food source for a wide variety of species. Their tunnels aerate the soil and aid tree growth. The twig damage caused by female egg-laying "prunes" trees and stimulates future growth.

• Periodical cicada nymphs that burrowed underground during the Clinton Administration will still be emerging until the year 2017.

• Because of the clearing of hardwood forests, several broods of periodical cicadas are now extinct.

• In 2004 University of Maryland grad-student Jenna Jadin put together a brochure called "Cicada-Licious: Cooking and Enjoying Periodical Cicada." Recipes include *El Chirper* Tacos, Cicada Dumplings, Cica-Delicious Pizza, Banana Cicada Bread, and Cicada-Rhubarb Pie. (The brochure can be found online.)

* * *

MUSTACHE QUOTES

"A man without a mustache is like a cup of tea without sugar."

—English Proverb

"My mustache gets so many questions he has his own agent now."

—Tom Selleck

"Hitler ruined that mustache. It's an interesting mustache, but now, no one can wear it!"

—Larry David

"Guys are lucky because they get to grow mustaches. I wish I could. It's like having a little pet for your face."

—Anita Wise

"You offer a sincere compliment on a great mustache and suddenly she's not your friend."

—Marty Feldman

BANNED BOOKS

Each September the American Library Association sponsors "Banned Books Week" to call attention to books that have been targeted for removal from schools, libraries, and even bookstores. Here are some of the more unusual cases.

CLIFFORD THE BIG RED DOG (1963)

Book Notes: This children's favorite, written by Norman Bridwell, is about a tiny red puppy that grows until he's 25 feet tall. There are more than 40 titles in the *Clifford* series to date, with more than 126 million books in print in 13 languages.

Banned! In 2006 the *Clifford* books were included on a list of 23 books that California's Wilsona School District voted to ban from the Vista San Gabriel Elementary School library. Other titles on the list: *Disney's Christmas Storybook*, *Harry Potter and the Half-Blood Prince*, the Artemis Fowl series (about "a boy-genius anti-hero and criminal mastermind"), and "all the princess books," one parent complained. Some books were banned because district trustees felt they were "inappropriate for children," others because they dealt in fantasy. "We want books to be things that children would be able to relate to in real life," Trustee Marlene Olivarez told the *Los Angeles Daily News*.

What Happened: The trustees later admitted that they hadn't actually read all the books they banned, and conceded that some were probably on the list "by mistake." At a subsequent meeting, the Clifford books, *Disney's Christmas Storybook*, and a number of other titles were *un*-banned. (Harry Potter and Artemis Fowl fans are still out of luck: Trustee Maurice Kunkel said the board wanted to support books that "are anti-witchcraft and anti-criminality.")

SYLVESTER AND THE MAGIC PEBBLE (1969)

Book Notes: This book, written by William Steig, won the Caldecott Medal, one of the most prestigious awards in children's literature. It tells the story of a donkey named Sylvester who finds a magic pebble that grants wishes.

Banned! At one point in the story, Sylvester fails to return home, and his parents go to the police...who are depicted as pigs. The book is full of animal characters, including pigs who aren't police officers, but law-enforcement organizations still took offense. Soon there were police-directed efforts to ban the book in 11 states. "Please check your grade school libraries and public library to see if the book is there," the Illinois Police Association wrote to member agencies. "If it is, please ask the library to remove it, and if they do not, please go to your local press."

Steig vehemently denied that the pigs were intended as a slur against the police. "All the characters in *Sylvester,* except for the villain lion, are domestic animals and very likable ones, and it should be obvious that no insult to anyone could possibly have been intended," he explained to the *New York Times*. "The story was written in 1968 when, as far as I know, the word 'pig' had not yet been used as a designation for police."

What Happened: The controversy helped sales of the book and probably spurred Steig's career: He wrote more than 30 children's books in all, including *Shrek!* (1990), which was made into the 2001 Oscar-winning film.

THE MERRIAM-WEBSTER COLLEGIATE DICTIONARY

Book Notes: The Oak Meadows Elementary School in Menifee, California, has a few college dictionaries on hand so that fourth and fifth graders can study word roots or prepare for spelling bees.

Banned! ...or at least they *did* until January 2010, when a parent volunteering in a classroom looked up some sexual acts in the dictionary and decided the definitions were too graphic for 9- and 10-year-olds. (No word on why the parent was looking up sex acts in the dictionary during school hours.) The tawdry tome was pulled from the shelf, and the difficult work of scouring other lexicons for lewdness began. "It's hard to sit and read the dictionary, but we'll be looking to find other things of a graphic nature," said a spokesperson.

What Happened: A few days later, the controversial dictionaries were back, but now only kids with signed permission slips are allowed to use them. Children without permission slips are directed to less offensive dictionaries (or, more likely, got their friends to look up the dirty words for them). Not all parents were impressed by the way the school handled the situation: Parent Jason Rogers asked, "What are they going to do next, pull encyclopedias because they list parts of the human anatomy?"

Who? First person on the cover of *Time* (1923): Speaker of the House Joseph G. Cannon.

BROWN BEAR, BROWN BEAR, WHAT DO YOU SEE?

Book Notes: Written in 1967 by Bill Martin, Jr., with illustrations by Eric Carle, this classic concept book teaches pre-readers about animals and colors using simple rhyming text.

Banned! In 2010 the Texas State Board of Education removed *Brown Bear* from the state's curriculum. But not because of anything objectionable in the book. Board member Pat Hardy requested that it be eliminated on the grounds that Bill Martin had written "very strong critiques of capitalism and the American system" in his books for adults, such as the 2008 work *Ethical Marxism: The Categorical Imperative of Liberation.*

What Happened: Hardy didn't do his homework. It turns out that Bill Martin, Jr., the author of *Brown Bear*, died in 2004, four years before *another* Bill Martin, this one a college professor, wrote *Ethical Marxism* in 2008. *Brown Bear* is back in the curriculum.

OTHER BOOKS TARGETED BY BANS

- ***The Higher Power of Lucky*** (2006). "The word 'scrotum' appears on the first page."
- ***Calvin and Hobbes*** (1987). "Allusions to murder and sex."
- ***Walter the Farting Dog*** (2001). "Focus on flatulence"; "offending words used twenty-four times in the book."
- ***The Adventures of Super Diaper Baby*** (2002). "Scatological humor and bad spelling make it inappropriate for kids."
- ***Bromley Climbs Uluru*** (1993). The story of a teddy bear that climbs the Australian landmark formerly known as Ayers Rock. "Offensive to Aboriginal peoples."
- ***On the Bright Side, I'm Now the Girlfriend of a Sex God*** (2000). "Parents objected to the 'sex god' title, not the book's content."
- ***World's Most Famous Ghosts*** (1989). "Pollutes the minds of teenagers."
- ***Freaky Friday*** (1972). "Words or deeds not permitted in school should not appear in the pages of school library books."

A salmon's sense of smell is thousands of times more acute than a dog's.

AUTHOR VS. AUTHOR

The pen truly is mightier than the sword.

Mary McCarthy on Lillian Hellman: "Every word she writes is a lie, including 'and' and 'the.'"

Robert Louis Stevenson on Walt Whitman: "A large, shaggy dog just unchained scouring the beaches of the world and baying at the moon."

Stephen King on Stephanie Meyer: "They both write for young people, but the real difference is that Jo Rowling is a terrific writer and Meyer can't write worth a darn."

Harold Bloom on J.K. Rowling: "If you cannot be persuaded to read anything better, Rowling will have to do."

D. H. Lawrence on Herman Melville: "Nobody is more clownish, more clumsy and sententiously in bad taste."

Truman Capote on Jack Kerouac: "That's not writing, that's typing."

Dorothy Parker on Ayn Rand: "*Atlas Shrugged* is not a novel to be tossed aside lightly. It should be thrown with great force."

Virginia Woolf on James Joyce: "*Ulysses* is the work of a queasy undergraduate scratching his pimples."

Salman Rushdie on Dan Brown: "Do not start me on *The Da Vinci Code*, a novel so bad that it gives bad novels a bad name."

Ralph Waldo Emerson on Jane Austen: "Vulgar in tone, sterile in artistic invention, imprisoned in the wretched conventions of English society, without genius, wit, or knowledge of the world. Never was life so pinched and narrow."

Mark Twain on Jane Austen: "Every time I read *Pride and Prejudice*, I want to dig her up and hit her over the skull with her own shin-bone."

William Faulkner on Mark Twain: "A hack writer who would not have been considered fourth rate in Europe, who tricked out a few of the old proven sure-fire literary skeletons with sufficient local color to intrigue the superficial and the lazy."

First college to offer a degree in surfing: England's University of Plymouth.

FROM GOLD MEDAL TO SILVER SCREEN

After the Olympics, there aren't a lot of options for athletes who want to stay in the public eye—it's not like they can go join a pro gymnastics team or National Weightlifting League. The destination: Hollywood.

Olympian: Jim Thorpe

Sport: Pentathlon and decathlon

Details: Thorpe was widely known as "the world's greatest athlete." That's because in addition to winning gold medals at the 1912 Stockholm Olympics in the pentathlon and decathlon, he'd also played pro football and semi-pro baseball. That led to his medals being taken away, because he wasn't really an "amateur," as the Olympics then required. Thorpe's popularity wasn't affected, and he was offered several movie roles. But because he was half Native American, they were mostly cameos as either an "Injun" or as himself. However, he starred as a football coach in the 1932 film *Always Kickin'* and as a baseball player in 1935's *One Run Elmer*. One movie Thorpe didn't appear in: *Jim Thorpe, All American*. (He was played by Burt Lancaster.)

Olympian: Mitch Gaylord

Sport: Gymnastics

Details: Gaylord won a gold medal at the Los Angeles Olympics in 1984. While female gymnasts are small and light, male gymnasts have huge upper bodies, making them naturals as action stars. Or so Gaylord thought. In 1986 he starred in the sports drama *American Anthem*. It should have been easy—he plays a guy who becomes an Olympic gymnast. But the film bombed, and Gaylord got a Razzie Award nomination for Worst New Star.

Olympian: Bruce Jenner

Sport: Decathlon

Details: Jenner became an American hero at the 1976 Summer Games thanks to three world-record-setting performances, which "took back" the decathlon gold medal from the Soviet Union.

Only country to not win a gold medal while hosting the Summer Olympics: Canada (1976).

After the Games, Jenner hung up his track shoes and went to Hollywood, hoping to cash in on his sex-symbol status. He auditioned for the lead role in the upcoming *Superman* movie, but lost the part to Christopher Reeve. Jenner did land a supporting role in 1980's *Can't Stop the Music*, a disco-themed musical starring the Village People. The film flopped; it received the Razzie Award for Worst Movie of the Year. Jenner went on to a modest TV career—including *CHiPs*, game shows, sportscasting, and *Keeping Up With the Kardashians*—but didn't make it back to the big screen for 30 years, when he appeared in Adam Sandler's 2011 comedy *Jack and Jill*...which also won the Razzie for Worst Movie.

Olympian: Kurt Thomas

Sport: Gymnastics

Details: One of many athletes whose Olympic dreams were shattered by the U.S. boycott of the 1980 Moscow Games, Thomas was predicted to take the gold in several events. By 1984 he was too old to compete at a world-class level, so he turned to Hollywood, where he was cast in the cult-classic B-movie *Gymkata*. Thomas plays Jonathan Cabot, an American spy who must infiltrate Communist territory in order to secure a mineral contract. Fortunately, every time the bad guys attack him in the woods, there's a tree or rock that looks and functions just like a pommel horse or high bar.

Olympian: Tonya Harding

Sport: Figure skating

Details: Tonya Harding is one of the most famous figure skaters ever, but not for skating—rather for conspiring to injure her rival, Nancy Kerrigan, in order to clear a path to victory in the 1994 Winter Olympics. Despite getting whacked on the knee with a police baton by Harding's hired hitman, Kerrigan still won silver; Harding finished eighth. Kerrigan hosted an episode of *Saturday Night Live* and bowed out of the limelight gracefully. Harding, meanwhile, became a tabloid fixture, mired in domestic disputes, leaked sex tapes, and a TV special called *Celebrity Boxing*, in which she fought fellow tabloid fixture Paula Jones. In 1996 she starred in her only dramatic role, a direct-to-video crime drama called *Breakaway*, about a drug mule who wants to retire after one last job. Harding plays "Gina," one of the mule's accomplices.

1.6 million people live in Manhattan...and 6.7 million people commute to work there daily.

WHAT'S ANOTHER WORD FOR "THESAURUS"?

Once there was a man, a biographer noted, "more interested in words than people." That turned out to be a great thing for BRI writers and other wordsmiths. It gave us a book that is of great use, utility, value, help, worth, *and* functionality.

THE LIST MAKER

Peter Mark Roget (1779–1869) was an unusual kid. In our time he would probably be diagnosed with obsessive-compulsive disorder or classified as having high-functioning Asperger's syndrome, and if he'd been born in the twenty-first century, an early intervention would have been put in place. But in the late eighteenth century, the London-born son of a clergyman had to find his own way to cope: He obsessively counted things and made lists. He recorded, for example, the total number of stair steps he climbed up each day, and kept a separate count of the steps he went down. Before age 8, he had already filled notebooks with lists of words grouped by categories: for example, all the animals he could think of, all the parts of the body, and even "Things Found in the Garden."

TAKE MY FAMILY, PLEASE

The young Roget was phobic about dirt and easily upset by a world he saw as random, messy, unpredictable, and disorderly. Worse, some of his loved ones were far more dysfunctional, filling his life with instability, insanity, and tragedy. His grandmother was a lifelong depressive and possibly a schizophrenic. His mother became psychotic after his father died. His sister suffered from depression and nervous breakdowns. But perhaps the worst experience of Roget's young life was having a grieving uncle slash his own throat and bleed to death right in the middle of a conversation they were having.

In the midst of such horror, Roget's ritualistic sorting practices must have calmed him and given him a sense of order, helping him to stay functional while those around him were not. In fact, young Roget managed to keep his idiosyncracies so well in check that he was invited to study medicine and the classics at Edin-

High society: Each member of a Swiss household may legally grow 4 cannabis plants.

burgh University when he was 14 years old.

NO LAUGHING MATTER

Roget earned his MD from Edinburgh in 1798. He was nineteen at the time, and perhaps it was this youthfulness that caused him to drift a bit. He hung out with scientific luminaries including Charles Darwin's grandfather, Erasmus (the young Roget found the elder Darwin to be fat and sloppy). He worked for awhile with Jeremy Bentham, inventor of the "frigidarium" (a device for keeping food cool and fresh), but was reportedly appalled by the "filthiness of his equipment." He moved on to participate as a subject in experiments with nitrous oxide but, Roget being Roget, he took the whole thing too seriously: After his first laughing gas exposure, he wrote that while others were laughing and acting giddy, "I experienced no pleasurable sensations of any kind."

After six weeks working on ways to repurpose London's sewage (we have no idea what he had in mind), Roget spent two years as a tutor and guide for two wealthy young gentlemen doing their "Grand Tour" of Europe (Paris: dirty. Napoleon's soldiers: pleasingly precise). At the ripe old age of 25, Roget was made a physician at the Manchester Royal Infirmary. He settled into a career and went to work introducing much-needed public-health reforms.

When Roget arrived in Manchester in 1804, the city's streets literally swam with garbage. "The town is horrible," he wrote, "dirty and black...the air always heavy by the smoke of the factories." Roget found the city so filthy and disorderly that he refused to go out for trivial reasons and spent most evenings and off-days indoors, tinkering and...making lists.

MOVING PICTURES & SLIDING RULES

While peering through the window blinds one day, Roget noticed something odd: The spokes of a cart's spinning wheels looked curved as they passed by. Roget ran outside and asked the cart driver to go back and forth in front of his home so he could study the effect. He decided that this optical allusion was due to what he called "the persistence of vision." In simpler words, the eye's retina sees movement not as a continuous flow but as a series of split-second still images that it projects to the brain, which interprets them as movement. This discovery led, in time, to the magic of movies. (More than a century later, movie executive Will H. Hays would credit Roget as being one of the fathers of the motion picture.)

Roget's biggest breakthrough, however, was inventing the "log-log scale" for slide rules. Adding a sliding piece of wood with precise numbers along its edges to the basic ruler allowed engineers, architects, and mathematicians to do complicated computations without spending hours working them out on paper.

Dr. Roget was something of a joiner: He was a Fellow of the Royal Society (made up of the world's most distinguished scientists), and a member of the Zoological Society of London, the Geological Society, and the Medical and Chirurgical (surgical) Society, among others. Despite his comfort with groups, he was less comfortable working one-on-one. His bedside manner was awkward at best, so he spent much of his career as a researcher and lecturer (and kept making list after list of words).

In 1840 Roget retired from medicine. He was 61 years old and could have justly rested on his laurels and gone down in history as a scientific footnote for his contributions to the slide rule and motion pictures. But a book by another compulsive list maker sent him back to his lists with a vengeance.

NOT A LISTLESS RETIREMENT

Enter the competition: Hester Lynch Piozzi. Piozzi had been interested in words and their usage all her life. In 1794 she wrote a guidebook of synonyms, titled (in the long-winded style of the time) *British Synonymy; or, An Attempt at Regulating the Choice of Words in Familiar Conversation*. Twenty-four years after her death, a publisher reprinted the volume and Roget got his hands on a copy.

He was appalled. To Roget, Piozzi's lists were not only haphazard, they were based on a faulty premise: that words could actually *be* synonymous. He believed that no two words were ever truly synonyms—each word had subtle differences in meaning and connotation. He also believed that the best word guide would provide a system of "verbal classification."

He dug up the lists of words organized by categories he'd started as a young doctor and set to work with new vigor, refining his categories and subcategories, carefully fitting each word into its proper place. For example, in the very long category of "Individual

Thanks to thinner air, airports at higher altitudes need longer runways than those at sea level.

Volition," he included a subcategory called "Cleanness" that starts with words related to perfection ("pure, spotless"), works its way through medium clean words ("untainted, like a cat in pattens"), and then tackles words related to extreme uncleanness ("rotten as cheese, crapulous"). Roget's way of classifying words would allow a wordsmith to pick just the right word to use when comparing, say, a well-maintained restaurant kitchen ("hygienic") with a teenager's bedroom ("foul").

ONE CLASSY BOOK

At age 73, Roget brought to his publisher a book that separated words into 1,000 categories and sorted them by class, division, and section (similar to the way natural historians sort animal species by phylum, class, and order). He saw it as a kind of "reverse dictionary" that would enable someone to find the word by which "an idea may be most fitly and aptly expressed."

It was an invaluable resource with one big problem: While Roget's method of organizing was brilliant (and fun to browse) it was extremely difficult to use as a reference tool. Luckily, his publisher convinced him to add an index, changing the book from an exhaustively fascinating oddity to a genuinely useful reference tool. It became a true *thesaurus*, which Roget would have been quick to point out means "treasury" and not, as most people believe, "a list of synonyms."

Published in 1852, Roget's book had a wordily worthy title: *Thesaurus of English Words and Phrases, Classified and Arranged So As To Facilitate the Expression of Ideas and Assist in Literary Composition*. It was a huge hit with the British public, and was an immediate success. A "bowdlerized" American edition (they took out the vulgar bits) came out two years later. Roget continued correcting and adding to subsequent editions until his death at age 90, and his heirs continued the task for another century by which time the name Roget's became so generic it was (sorry Mr. R.) synonymous with the word *thesaurus*.

* * *

"A synonym is a word you use when you can't spell the word you first thought of."

—**Burt Bacharach**

GANGRENE EXPLAINED

The BRI staff was sitting around talking about old Western movies, when Thom pointed out that it seemed like there was always someone in danger of getting "gangrene." There was a long pause, and then someone said, "What the heck is gangrene anyway?" And so an article was born. (Warning: Uncle John found this article especially creepy, but let us include it because, he said, "Science is fascinating...even when it makes you retch.")

WHAT IT IS: Gangrene is a medical condition in which body tissue dies due to loss of blood supply or bacterial infection. Many things can cause a loss of blood supply, including trauma and complications due to disease.

HISTORY: Before the modern era of medicine, gangrene was a common cause of death for people who had suffered some kind of injury, especially those resulting in an open wound. This was especially true of soldiers wounded in combat. During World War I, for example, it is believed that at least 100,000 wounded soldiers—and probably many more—died not directly due to their wounds, but due to the gangrene that set in afterwards. Since the development of antibiotics, which attack infection, wartime gangrene deaths have been almost nil.

WHERE IT STRIKES: Gangrene can occur anywhere on the body, even in internal organs, but it usually occurs at the extremities—hands, fingers, feet, toes—where conditions leading to compromised blood supply are much more common. There are two major types:

• **Wet gangrene** occurs when an area of the body already suffering from depleted blood supply—due to an artery being severed, for example—becomes infected which leads to: 1) swelling, which can further impede blood supply, 2) the production of foul-smelling pus, 3) change in skin color in the affected region from red, to brown, to black, 4) the loss of the dead tissue. Wet gangrene is by far the more dangerous type, as it can quickly lead to *sepsis* (a body-wide infection), which can lead to death in hours. The most common condition that causes wet gangrene is serious trauma, such as that suffered via gunshot, car accident, or fire.

An especially deadly form of wet gangrene is gas gangrene. It's caused when a strain of bacteria known as *Clostridium perfringens* enters the body, most commonly through an open wound. As the bacteria multiply, they produce toxins, which cause further tissue damage, plus gas, which causes intense swelling. Both speed the spread of infection, and, if untreated, will quickly lead to death. Textbook symptoms of gas gangrene are massive swelling, dark purplish skin, and large, tight bubble-blisters on the skin. (That's from the gas.)

• **Dry gangrene** develops much more slowly—it can actually take years to develop. It is the result of a gradual reduction of blood flow to an area. Affected tissue becomes cold, skin slowly becomes purplish, then black, and, if untreated, there can be loss of tissue. The most common cause of dry gangrene is vascular disease (such as *arteriosclerosis*, or hardening of the arteries) due to high cholesterol levels, diabetes, or cigarette smoking.

TREATMENT: Gangrene is always treated with antibiotics to fight infection, and with removal of dead tissue, as it is a breeding ground for bacteria. You may have heard of the use of maggots—fly larvae—to treat wounds. That's all about gangrene: Maggots eat dead tissue—and actually kill bacteria—and in so doing prevent the infection that can lead to gas gangrene. "Maggot therapy," as it's called, has been around since ancient times and was approved by the FDA in 2004. Treatment also may also include operations to return blood supply to affected areas, or in extreme cases, amputation.

PREVENTION: People with diabetes and people with chronic vascular problems should regularly check extremities for cuts, sores, swelling, or discoloration, and if any are found, should see a doctor.

FAMOUS VICTIMS:

• **King Herod of Judea.** He is believed to have died from a rare form of gangrene that affects the private parts.

• **President William McKinley.** He was shot twice in the abdomen on September 6, 1901, by Leon Czolgosz. McKinley survived the attack, and over the first few days doctors thought he was on the mend. But then he took a turn for the worse and died on September 14. Until an autopsy was performed, doctors were unaware that gangrene had set in all along the tracks of the bullets, from the entry wounds, through internal tissue, and turning the walls of the stomach, pancreas, and one kidney gangrenous.

• **Sarah Bernhardt.** The international stage star injured her right knee during a play in Rio de Janeiro, Brazil, in 1905. The knee never healed. Bernhardt was plagued by pain, and, more significantly, circulation problems, and over the years dry gangrene developed in her leg. In 1916, fully eleven years after the accident, Bernhardt, by this time 71 years old, ordered doctors to amputate the leg above the knee. She continued acting, mostly in a wheelchair (she never liked her wooden leg) until her death in 1923 at the age of 78.

FINAL NOTE: In the year 944, an estimated 20,000 people (some historians put it as high as 40,000) died in an epidemic that struck southern France. Experts who have studied the numerous writings about the outbreak say that although the people didn't know it at the time, their grain supply—especially rye—had become infected with a fungus known as *Claviceps purpurea.* This fungus contains toxins which build up in the bodies of those who consume it, eventually leading to a medical condition known as *ergotism*, which causes vomiting, seizures, hallucinations, discoloration of the skin, loss of fingers, toes, and even limbs, and, in almost all cases before the days of modern medicine, death. How? Chemicals in the toxins restrict blood vessels, which leads to loss of blood supply. That means that many of the 20,000 (or 40,000) people who died in southern France in 944—and the hundreds of thousands more in the many other ergotism outbreaks throughout history—actually died of dry gangrene.

* * *

6 REAL WRESTLER NAMES FROM THE WWF

1. Akeem the African Dream
2. Isaac Yankem, D.D.S.
3. Doinks the Clown
4. Johnny Attitude
5. Disco Inferno
6. Xanta Claus

Canada has the world's longest coastline, but only a 9,000-person navy. The US: 300,000.

LIFE BEFORE SPELL-CHECK

How did people remember how to spell tricky words before computers? With the aid of mnemonic (memory) devices. Once you learn them, you'll never again forget how to spell these words.

Word: Opposite
Memory Trick: "Often *p*rosperous *p*eople *o*pen *s*tores *i*n *t*he *e*ast."

Word: Illegible. (Does it have one *l* or two? Does it end in –gible or –gable?)
Memory Trick: "*Ill* on *gin*? Your writing will be illegible."

Word: Pneumonia
Memory Trick: "*P*eople *n*ever *e*xpected *us* to get pneumonia."

Word: Exaggerate. (Is it spelled with one *g* or two?)
Memory Trick: "If you're bragging, you're exaggerating."

Word: Champagne
Memory Trick: "A*gn*es loves to drink champagne."

Word: Lightning. (Is it spelled with or without an *e*?)
Memory Trick: "Leaving off the e lightens lightning's load."

Word: Grammar. (Is it spelled with one *m* or two?)
Memory Trick: "To*m m*arred his paper with bad grammar."

Word: Wednesday
Memory Trick: "*We d*o *n*ot *e*at *s*oup on Wednesdays."

Word: Embarrass. (One *r* or two? One *s* or two?)
Memory Trick: "People get *r*eally *r*ed and *s*mile *s*hyly when they're embarrassed."

Word: Marshmallow. (Is it spelled –mello or –mallo?)
Memory Trick: "They sell marshmallows at the *mall*."

Word: Indispensable. (Is it spelled –ible or –able?)
Memory Trick: "Only the most *able* are indispensable."

Word: Colonel
Memory Trick: "The colonel was *lone*ly."

Word: Overrated. (One *r* or two?)
Memory Trick: "Che*rr*ies are overrated."

Word: Lovely. (Spelled with an *e*? If so, where does it go?)
Memory Trick: "I *love* to get lovely gifts."

Heavyweight boxing champ Gene Tunney once lectured at Yale. Subject: Shakespeare.

SINGING ATHLETES

These days, it seems as if every basketball star or boxer is making a music video. Shaquille O'Neal, Kobe Bryant, Allen Iverson, and Chris Webber are on the long list of NBA stars who've cut rap songs, while Oscar De La Hoya, Roy Jones Jr., and Manny Pacquiao have all stepped out of the boxing ring to show their tender sides through song. Here's a look at a few of the best—and worst—musical athletes.

CARL LEWIS

Athletic Career: Lewis was a world-champion track-and-field star. He won nine Olympic gold medals—four in the 1984 games, two in '88, two in '92, and one in '96, all as a sprinter and long jumper.

Music Career: Shortly after the '84 Olympics, he recorded one of the most cringe-inducing videos of all time—"Break It Up," which intersperses footage of Lewis sprinting and jumping at the Olympics with close-ups of him singing while working out in a gym. In the video, he's wearing a skimpy one-piece black leotard (with a white belt). The song has a catchy techno/reggae beat and Lewis has a pleasant voice, but the images of him in the weight room are difficult to watch. (You've been warned!)

MIKE REID

Athletic Career: Reid was a first-round pick in the 1970 NFL draft. He went on to become a Pro Bowl offensive lineman in the Cincinnati Bengals and a standout for four pro seasons.

Music Career: After a knee injury led to his early retirement in 1974, Reid became a songwriter. Since then he's written at least a dozen songs that have hit #1 on the Billboard country charts, including "In This Life" by Collin Raye, "Forever's as Far as I'll Go" by Alabama, "Everywhere" by Tim McGraw, Reid's own "Walk in Faith," and "Stranger in My House" by Ronnie Milsap, which won the 1985 Grammy for Best Country Song. He also wrote Bonnie Raitt's "I Can't Make You Love Me." In 2005 Reid was inducted into the Nashville Songwriters Hall of Fame.

GUY LAFLEUR

Athletic Career: Known as "The Golden Demon" during his 14 seasons with the NHL's Montreal Canadiens, the two-time league MVP was inducted into the Hockey Hall of Fame in 1988.

Music Career: In 1979—right in the middle of his playing career—Lafleur made a detour into music. He was no singer, but he knew hockey and he knew pop culture. So he combined the two, making a series of (we kid you not) instructional hockey records set to disco music. Lafleur told listeners how to shoot, skate, face-off, check, and run a power play while disco music played in the background. And because he was so popular in Canada, he cut versions in both English and French.

BABE DIDRIKSON

Athletic Career: Didrikson has been called the greatest female athlete of all time. She won two gold medals in track-and-field events during the 1932 Olympic Games, after which she was determined to be a professional athlete in an era when there were absolutely no women making a living at it. She played baseball with the all-male House of David team. She was the only player without a beard, but that didn't stop her from striking out Joe DiMaggio during an exhibition game. She also toured with her own basketball team, Babe Didrikson's All-Americans.

Music Career: In the early 1930s, Didrikson ran out of money and teamed up with piano player and comedian George Libbey to perform on the Chicago vaudeville circuit. Libbey would start the show with comedy, then Didrikson would join him onstage. Here's how Russell Friedman described her performance in his biography, *Babe Didrikson Zaharias: Making of a Champion*:

> Babe pranced down the center aisle wearing a Panama hat, a green swagger coat, and high-heeled platform shoes, looking as though she had just returned from a winter vacation in Florida. After swapping a few vaudeville gags with Libbey, Babe burst into song, belting out the lyrics to "I'm Fit as a Fiddle and Ready for Love." Then she kicked off her high heels, put on a pair of rubber-soled track shoes, and swept off her coat to reveal a red, white, and blue jacket and satin shorts.

She then jumped onto a treadmill and started running, and finished with harmonica renditions of "When Irish Eyes Are Smiling" and "Jackass Blues." She was a huge hit and sometimes did five shows daily.

Reprise: Didrikson became an even bigger star later, when she took up golf. She won 82 tournaments between 1933 and 1953, including 17 successive tournament wins in the 1946–47 season, and she helped found the LPGA.

JOHN DALY

Athletic Career: Daly is probably better known for getting into trouble than for winning golf tournaments, but he has won a few big ones, including the 1991 PGA Championship and the 1995 British Open. Along the way, he's also been a heavy drinker and a gambling addict (he says he's lost millions on bets) and has been disqualified from tournaments for boorish behavior, including hitting a tee shot off the top of a beer can.

Music Career: Despite all that, Daly's demeanor is endearing to many, and he's tried to capitalize on it by recording a couple of country-inspired albums...but in this area of life, he knows his limits. "You can't do music half-a**ed the way I do and get any good," he admits. "I love it, but I'm not trying to fool myself that I'll ever be able to do anything more than fool around on the guitar." Daly's first album, *My Life*, included guest vocals by Willie Nelson and Johnny Lee. The song titles sound a lot like Daly's life: "I'm Drunk, Damn Broke," "Long Ball Rebel," and "All My Ex's Wear Rolexes."

NOLAN SHAHEED

Athletic Career: Shaheed may not be a household name, but in 2012 he ran a mile on the track in 4 minutes, 53 seconds. Since the four-minute-mile barrier was broken by Roger Bannister in 1954, what was so great about Shaheed's time? He was 62 years old. Shaheed holds several world track records in his age group, in distances ranging from 800 meters to 5,000 meters.

Music Career: He's a legitimate musician. Over his 40-year musical career, he's played lead trumpet in bands led by Marvin Gaye, Natalie Cole, Stevie Wonder, Diana Ross, Phil Collins, Count Basie, and Anita Baker. What do running and playing the trumpet have in common? Wind. In high school, Shaheed discovered that running was great for building lung capacity, a big plus for his

World's most expensive divorce: Rupert and Anna Murdoch ($1.7 billion in 1999).

trumpet playing. "My teacher pointed out that my chops were best when I was on the track team, so I joined the cross-country team, and sure enough, my trumpet playing got better," Shaheed said. "The harder I trained, the better I was on the trumpet, so I started training very hard and before I knew it I was running very fast as well." Shaheed finally had to cut down on touring, but age had nothing to do with it. The reason: The smoke-filled arenas and nightclubs he performed in were bad for his running.

THE CHICAGO BEARS

Athletic Career: The 1985–86 Bears racked up a 15–1 record in the regular season, then crushed the New York Giants in the divisional playoffs, beat the LA Rams in the NFC playoffs, and trounced the New England Patriots (46–10) in the 1986 Super Bowl.

Music Career: A few months before the big game, several members of the team made a music video: "The Super Bowl Shuffle." When it was released, the press called the video arrogant because the team had never made it to the Super Bowl before. But the single sold more than half a million copies and was nominated for a Grammy for best rhythm-and-blues performance by a group. Half of the proceeds went to a Chicago charity. (The producer got most of the rest.)

* * *

USELESS WEBSITES

You Sneezed! (*yousneezed.com*) It simply says "Bless you!

Am I Awesome? (*amiawesome.com*) It displays the word "very."

What I Would Name My Pet Unicorn If I Had One (*mypetunicorn.blogspot.com*) A listing of ideas for names that the site's owner would name his pet unicorn, should he ever get one

Is it Tuesday? (*isittuesday.com*) If it's Tuesday, it says "Yes" in big block letters. Otherwise, it says "No."

Sometimes Red, Sometimes Blue (*sometimesredsometimesblue.com*) Sometimes the page is red, sometimes blue.

Instant Rimshot (*instantrimshot.com*) Tell a joke, press the big red button, and the sound of a drum "rimshot" plays.

Antarctica's Horlick Mountains are named for William Horlick, the inventor of malted milk.

PRIVATE WOJTEK, THE SOLDIER BEAR

There are many stories of animals playing a part in World War II, from dogs to carrier pigeons, but did you know that a bear *also served in the war? Here's the story of the "Smiling Warrior."*

DOUBLE CROSS

For most Americans old enough to remember World War II, *their* war began on December 7, 1941, the day the Japanese bombed Pearl Harbor. But the war in Europe had been raging for more than two years, beginning when Nazi Germany invaded Poland on September 1, 1939. The Germans invaded from the west. Sixteen days later, the Soviet Union invaded from the east, part of a secret agreement between Adolf Hitler and Joseph Stalin to carve up the country for themselves.

Poland fell on October 6, and thousands of Polish soldiers captured in Soviet-occupied territory were shipped off to *gulag* labor camps in Siberia. But when Hitler betrayed Stalin and invaded the Soviet Union on June 22, 1941, Stalin released the Polish soldiers so that they could fight the Nazis. Some of them served in the Soviet Army; others made their way from the Soviet Union into neighboring Iran and from there to the British forces fighting in North Africa, where they were organized into Polish army units serving under British command.

NO PIG IN A POKE

It was while these soldiers were passing through Iran that a group of them came across a small boy carrying something inside a burlap bag. The soldiers gave the boy some food to eat, and then asked what was in the bag. He opened it to reveal a baby bear cub, not much larger than a teddy bear, that had been orphaned when its mother was killed by hunters. The soldiers bought the bear from the boy, trading a pocketknife, a chocolate bar, a can of corned beef, and some money for it. They named the bear *Wojtek* (pronounced "Voy-check"), which means "smiling warrior" in Polish.

BEARING RESPONSIBILITY

One of the soldiers, 46-year-old Peter Prendys, took responsibility for caring for Wojtek. The bear was tiny enough to sleep in a washbowl, but it preferred to snuggle with Prendys and the other soldiers in their beds, much as it would have slept with its mother in the wild. This, combined with being bottle fed until he was old enough to eat solid food, caused Wojtek to bond with the soldiers as if they were his mother. He became as tame around humans as a wild animal can be.

The soldiers were assigned to the 22nd Artillery Supply Company, a part of the Polish II Corps. They spent more than two years in North Africa, and in that time Wojtek grew rapidly on a diet of fruits, honey, meat, bread, biscuits, marmalade, and whatever else the soldiers fed him. By 1944 he weighed more than 500 pounds and stood over six feet tall.

MONKEY SEE, MONKEY DO

Bears are intelligent, social animals that learn by imitating the behavior they see around them. In the wild, they watch other bears; in the army, Wojtek watched the soldiers. He learned to stand on his hind legs and walk upright, and he often marched with the men. When someone saluted him, he saluted back. He loved to wrestle with the soldiers—one-on-one when he was smaller, then in groups as he grew larger. When the soldiers traveled around North Africa and the Middle East transporting materiel from one base to another, Wojtek went along with them, riding with Prendys in the passenger seat of his truck.

When Wojtek was naughty and Prendys had to scold him, the bear would cover his eyes with his paws and whimper for a time, then peek through his paws to see if Prendys was still mad. If he was, Wojtek kept whimpering until Prendys forgave him. Then he'd lie flat on his back in submission—his way, perhaps, of promising never to do it again.

SMOKE-Y BEAR

Like a lot of humans who serve in the armed forces, Wojtek picked up a few vices during his stint in the service. He developed a taste for beer and received a ration of two bottles a day, more on holidays and special occasions. He was fascinated by the sight of

The first text message was sent Dec. 3, 1992. The message: "Merry Christmas."

soldiers smoking cigarettes, so it was probably inevitable that sooner or later someone would give him one. He never did quite learn how to smoke them, but not for lack of trying: When he saw a soldier pull out a pack of cigarettes, he'd hold out his palm (which was about the size of a salad plate) and bum a smoke. Someone had to light the cigarette for him, and then he'd swallow it whole, letting out a contented puff of smoke as he did. The cigarette had to be lit—if it wasn't, Wojtek just threw it away.

BEARS WILL BE BEARS

When Prendys or another soldier was around to keep an eye on Wojtek, he was free to roam the camp at will. When they were busy or away, he was chained up for his own safety. He didn't like being chained, and he expressed his displeasure by pulling on the chain to trip soldiers up as they walked by. That wasn't his only mischievous habit: He liked to raid the cookhouse when nobody was looking, and he became so proficient at working the showers in the bath hut that it had to be locked to keep him from using up all the water.

Wojtek's shower habit may have saved lives: Once when the company was camped near Kirkuk, in Iraq, an Iraqi snuck into the camp in advance of a raid. He hid in the bath hut, where Wojtek found him while sneaking in to take a shower. He cornered the screaming man until help arrived. Terrified of being eaten by a bear, the man confessed and the raid was foiled.

BEARING A BURDEN

In February 1943, the 22nd Artillery Supply Company was ordered to move from North Africa to Italy to support the front-line troops battling their way north, toward Rome. Wojtek went along. It was the first time he'd ever gotten close to the fighting, but he quickly got used to the sounds of the exploding artillery shells and instead of hiding from the noise, he climbed to the tops of trees to get a better look at the action.

Yet no one ever expected Wojtek to participate in the war effort. It was assumed that he would just remain off to the side while the soldiers did their work. That changed during the Battle of Monte Cassino, one of the biggest battles of the war. One day while watching soldiers unloading 100-pound boxes of artillery shells from a

Highest-grossing movie never to be #1 at the box office: *My Big Fat Greek Wedding* (2002).

truck and carrying them over to the big guns, Wojtek ambled over to the truck, stood up on his hind legs, and gestured with his arms to the soldier on the truck, signaling him to hand him one of the boxes. The soldier did. Wojtek carried the box to where they were being stacked, handed it off to another soldier, and went back for another box. He kept at it until the trucks were unloaded.

PRIVATE WOJTEK

In all, it's estimated that the 22nd Company delivered more than 17,000 tons of ammunition to the front lines during the Battle of Monte Cassino, plus additional tons of fuel, food, and other supplies. It's not known how many boxes Wojtek carried, but he carried a lot of them and he never dropped a single one. His efforts did not go unnoticed. The 22nd Company soon adopted a new insignia: a bear walking upright and carrying an artillery shell. The insignia was stamped into badges that men of the 22nd wore on their uniforms, and the logo was painted on the company's trucks. (If you look on the Internet, you can find pictures of Wojtek sitting in a truck painted with his own insignia.)

Monte Cassino fell to the Allies on May 18, 1944, opening the way to Rome, which was captured on June 4, two days before the D-Day landings on the Normandy coast of France. The 22nd Company remained in Italy for the rest of the war, following the front-line troops northward as they advanced. Wojtek continued to help with the loading and unloading (at times he had to be bribed with food, cigarettes, or beer). And as of February 14, 1945, he did it as *Private* Wojtek—that was the day that he was officially enlisted as a soldier in the Polish Army in recognition of his contribution to the war effort.

VICTORY...OF SORTS

The 22nd Company fought its last battle on April 21, 1945, when it helped liberate the city of Bologna. German troops fighting in Italy surrendered on April 29; Hitler committed suicide the next day, and Germany itself surrendered to the Allies on May 7.

For most of the Allies, the end of the war in Europe was a time of celebration. But for the 22nd Company and other units made up of soldiers from eastern Poland, it was a time of bitter disappointment. After the war, Poland's borders shifted 150 miles to the west, as Stalin held on to the territory he seized in 1939. Poland was compensated with new territory in the west, taken from Germany. For Prendys and other Polish soldiers who'd survived the horrors of Soviet *gulag* prison camps, this meant that their homes were now part of the Soviet Union. (The rest of Poland didn't fare any better: After the war, its democratic institutions were crushed and replaced with a communist dictatorship controlled by Moscow.)

STARTING OVER

Few Polish soldiers had any intention of returning home now that home was a Soviet police state, and the handful that did were quickly arrested and imprisoned, or shot. Perhaps out of guilt for allowing Stalin a free hand in Poland, the British government created the Polish Resettlement Corps to help the Polish soldiers start new lives in the United Kingdom. When the soldiers of the 22nd Company were demobilized in 1946, they entered the Polish Resettlement Corps and went to live in the Winfield Camp for Displaced Persons, located in the Scottish countryside near the border with England.

Wojtek enjoyed a remarkable degree of freedom at Winfield. He was confined to his own sleeping quarters at night, but during the day he was free to roam the camp (with supervision), just as he'd done during the war. The Scottish public knew of his exploits and were eager to see the furry soldier bear up close. Kids who visited gave him candy and were allowed to climb on his back; the adults spoiled him with food and beer. And of course, if Wojtek saw someone smoking, out went his paw as he tried to bum a cigarette.

BEAR ABOUT TOWN

On weekends the Polish soldiers brought Wojtek into town with them. The bear was welcome at dances that the locals organized for the troops. If there was a live band, Wojtek sat upright on his hindquarters and stared with fascination at the musicians, sometimes even appearing to bob his head in time with the music.

Fast food: A star-nosed mole can find, identify, and eat a worm in 140 milliseconds.

Baked goodies were a staple at these gatherings, and though Wojtek was remarkably well mannered for a bear, he wasn't above trying to mooch a pie to go with the pints of beer the locals invariably bought him. When there weren't any dances to go to, Wojtek and the soldiers made the rounds of the pubs. They even visited one called the Brown Bear.

MOVING ON

Had Wojtek gotten his way, he might have stayed with the soldiers at the Winfield Displaced Persons Camp forever. But the soldiers—Peter Prendys included—were eager to begin their new lives. Now in his early 50s, Prendys had a wife and three children in Poland that he wanted to bring to the west. He had to learn English, he had to find a job, and he had to find a home for Wojtek. He eventually found it at the Edinburgh Zoo, which agreed to care for the bear for the rest of its life.

After living at Winfield for about a year, on November 15, 1947, Wojtek climbed into the bed of a pickup truck and was driven to his new home at the zoo. He and Prendys walked into the bear enclosure together; Prendys stayed for a few minutes with his friend, then said good-bye and left.

AT THE ZOO

Prendys appears to have held out hope of one day reuniting with Wojtek. "In Edinburgh Zoo I know he is safe," he told an acquaintance. "Now I have to look after me. Then we will see." He moved to London, found a job as a construction worker, and eventually reunited with his wife and children. But he could never bring himself to return to Edinburgh to visit his old friend. Having lived through so much trauma in his own life, and having cared for Wojtek since he was a cub, parting with the bear nearly broke him. The thought of going back was too painful. He may have also feared that a visit would be hard for Wojtek, so he never went back.

It took time for Wojtek to adjust to his new life at the zoo. He was fortunate that so many of his soldier friends had resettled in the U.K. They were a few hours away by train at most, and he received frequent visits in the years that followed. The zookeepers were sympathetic to the soldier bear's plight, too: They turned a blind eye when Wojtek's war buddies climbed into his enclosure to

Can you name the only two TV sitcoms that were #1 in the ratings...

wrestle with him and share a beer and a smoke. The bear was overjoyed when his friends came to see him, but for the first six months of his stay, when the visits were over he'd slip into a funk that lasted for days. Wojtek did not understand why his friends were leaving him and why he couldn't go with them.

In time, however, the zookeepers noticed that Wojtek remained happy long after his friends departed. The bear bonded with his new keepers, and he enjoyed the attention he received from the public. He especially perked up whenever he heard Polish being spoken, often by the young children born to the soldiers he'd known during the war. When they called out "hello," told him to wave, or whistled the Polish national anthem, he waved. He remained a popular attraction at the zoo for the rest of his life, and lived to the ripe old (bear) age of 22 before passing away in December 1963.

A TALE THAT BEARS REPEATING

Wojtek remained dear to the memories of the soldiers who knew him during the war, and to the people who saw him at the Edinburgh Zoo. But for the rest of the world, as the years passed, his story faded away. Even the plaque honoring him at the Edinburgh Zoo was taken down after he died. In recent years, however, there has been renewed interest in the story of the bear that fought in World War II. Wojtek has been the subject of several books, a documentary film, and exhibits at the Sikorski Institute and the Imperial War Museum, both in London, and the Canadian War Museum in Ottawa. In 2009 the Scottish Parliament hosted a reception in his honor. Plans are afoot to erect a statue, featuring Wojtek and Peter Prendys—who died in 1968—standing side by side.

* * *

THE OLD BALL AND CHAIN

In September 2006, Kandi Blakney went to the Wichita courthouse to get married. She arrived in a white wedding dress and reported to the clerk's office to get her marriage license. When the clerk pulled it up on her computer, she found two outstanding arrest warrants for violating probation on a drug charge. Instead of getting married, Blakney went to jail (in the white dress).

AT 25...

As Uncle John's Bathroom Reader *reaches the quarter-century mark, we thought it might be fun to check out what some other famous icons were up to during their 25th year of life.*

ALBERT EINSTEIN (1879–1955)

Claim to Fame: German-born scientist, considered the father of modern physics

At 25... Einstein was working at the Swiss Patent Office and was the father of a newborn son. While pushing Albert Jr.'s stroller through Bern, Switzerland, Einstein would often stop to scribble down mathematical notes. Those notes would form the basis for his theory of relativity.

GEORGE W. BUSH (1946–)

Claim to Fame: 43rd president of the United States

At 25... In what the press later dubbed his "missing year," 1st Lieutenant Bush was serving in the Texas Air National Guard, training to become a combat fighter pilot. As his 26th birthday approached in July 1972, Bush failed to show up for several weekend drill assignments, then skipped his annual physical. Result: His flight status was revoked and he never flew for the military again.

OPRAH WINFREY (1954–)

Claim to Fame: "She's Oprah Winfrey"

At 25... Winfrey had recently been fired from her first big TV gig, co-anchor of the 6:00 News at WJZ-TV in Baltimore. The other anchor, Jerry Turner, didn't like sharing the spotlight and often belittled Winfrey. To placate him, station managers "demoted" Winfrey to an early-morning talk show called *People Are Talking*. Her co-host there, Richard Sher, was much more amicable, and Winfrey soon realized that delivering the news wasn't for her: "I liked talking *to* people, not *about* them." In 1979 *People Are Talking* became a hit and 25-year-old Winfrey began forming her TV persona. She stayed for seven years before moving to Chicago, where she launched her own talk show in 1986.

According to studies, work-related stress can be as bad for your health as smoking.

WILLIAM SHAKESPEARE (1564–1616)

Claim to Fame: Most celebrated writer of the English language

At 25... Shakespeare became a playwright. Though little is known about his younger days, it's generally agreed that he penned his first play, *Henry VI, Part 1* around 1590. That's also about the time that the ambitious writer left his home in Stratford-upon-Avon to seek his fortune in London.

QUEEN ELIZABETH II (1926–)

Claim to Fame: Constitutional monarch of the United Kingdom, Canada, Australia, New Zealand, and several other countries for more than six decades

At 25... Elizabeth became Queen of England. On February 6, 1952, her father, King George VI, died, and the popular English princess ascended to the throne. She heard the news while she was in Kenya with her husband, Philip, as they were preparing to embark on a goodwill tour of Australia. Elizabeth rushed back to England, where she was instructed to choose a *regnal*, or ruling name. The new queen replied, "Why, Elizabeth, of course."

HARRISON FORD (1942–)

Claim to Fame: Hollywood's most bankable leading man in the late 1970s, 1980s, and 1990s, starring in such roles as Han Solo, Indiana Jones, Rick Deckard (*Blade Runner*), John Book (*Witness*), and Dr. Richard Kimble (*The Fugitive*)

At 25... Ford was a struggling young actor in Los Angeles, living on a $150-per-week contract with Columbia Pictures. He wasn't offered any good parts because powerful producer Jerry Tokofsky didn't like him; he called Ford "stiff and unappealing." Ford's one "big" speaking role in his 25th year was in the comedy *Luv*: After a Volkswagen Beetle backs into his convertible, an angry Ford jumps out, stomps up to the VW, says "Hi" to the lady driving, then punches Jack Lemmon in the nose. Bit parts like that didn't pay the bills, so Ford quit acting for a while and took up carpentry.

HILLARY CLINTON (1947–)

Claim to Fame: First Lady, Senator, and U.S. Secretary of State

At 25... Hillary Rodham graduated with honors from Yale Law

School. She stayed on at Yale as a research assistant, contributing to the seminal child psychology work *Beyond the Best Interests of the Child.* She also volunteered for the Children's Defense Fund, offering free legal services to child abuse victims. Also that year: Rodham turned down a marriage proposal from her boyfriend and future husband Bill Clinton.

WARREN BUFFETT (1930–)

Claim to Fame: American business mogul

At 25... Buffett made his "$50-billion decision." The young investor was so adept at the intricacies of finance that he was offered a prestigious job in New York by his mentor, Benjamin Graham. But Buffett politely declined, opting instead to return home to Omaha, Nebraska, and support his young family as an unemployed investor. "Although I had no idea, age 25 was a turning point," he later told *Forbes* magazine. "I was changing my life, setting up something that would turn into a fairly good-size partnership called Berkshire Hathaway. I wasn't scared. I was doing something I liked, and I'm still doing it."

CONDOLEEZZA RICE (1954–)

Claim to Fame: U.S. Secretary of State from 2005 to 2009

At 25... Rice had already been in college for a decade, having enrolled at 15. (She was so smart she skipped the first and seventh grades.) In 1980, 25-year-old Rice was working on her Ph.D. in political science at the University of Denver. She'd recently broken up with her fiancé, Denver Broncos star receiver Rick Upchurch, to focus on her studies. But Rice, a registered Democrat, was having a political identity crisis and found herself disagreeing with many of President Carter's foreign policy decisions. Two years later, she switched parties and rose to the top of the GOP (but never did get married).

DONALD TRUMP (1946–)

Claim to Fame: Business mogul and reality TV star

At 25... After deciding not to attend film school because he felt he could earn more money in real estate, Trump moved to Manhattan "practically broke" as he described it (despite his father's real estate fortune). But Trump had bigger dreams and saw Manhattan as a huge business opportunity. The young man (who even then had puffy hair) talked his way into elite social clubs and made friends with some of New York's most influential people. With financial backers, 25-year-old Trump convinced the cash-strapped City of New York to grant him a 40-year tax abatement to turn around the struggling Commodore Hotel. He later fixed it up, renamed it the Grand Hyatt, and was well on his way to becoming New York's most famous real estate tycoon.

JACKIE ROBINSON (1919–72)

Claim to Fame: Hall-of-Fame baseball player who became the first African American of the modern era to play in the Major Leagues

At 25... Robinson was already well-known for his stellar athletic career at UCLA, but he'd been drafted to fight in World War II. Rising to become one of the few African-American officers in the U.S. Army, Robinson was a 2nd lieutenant of the 761st Tank Battalion (the "Black Panthers") stationed at Camp Hood, near Waco, Texas. Shortly before his unit was to depart for Europe, Robinson boarded a bus going from the base hospital back to his barracks. The white bus driver, Milton Reneger, ordered Robinson to sit in the back of the bus. Robinson refused. After arriving at the base, Reneger called over two MPs and had them detain Robinson. During the interrogation, a white officer used a racial slur, and Robinson threatened to "break in two" anyone else who dared call him that. Not long after, he was charged with disorderly conduct and public drunkenness (even though he didn't drink). So instead of leaving for Europe, Robinson was court-martialed. After a contentious trial that drew lots of press, an all-white panel of officers voted unanimously to drop the charges. Robinson never did see combat and was honorably discharged in November 1944. A few months later, Brooklyn Dodgers general manager Branch Rickey hand-picked him to become the first African American to integrate the big leagues.

TINA FEY (1970–)

Claim to Fame: Emmy-winning TV writer and actress

At 25... Fey was waiting for her big break. Her dream was to get hired by *Saturday Night Live*, and she knew the best way to do that was to join the Second City improvisational comedy troupe in

Chicago. So during the days, she was a receptionist at the YMCA, and at night she performed with Second City. In 1995 the *SNL* scouts came to Second City. "We were like puppies," she recalled. "Pick me! Pick me!" But Fey didn't get picked. Her friend Adam McKay did, and became head writer. Two years later, producer Lorne Michaels was looking for new writers; McKay told him to check out Fey. In 2000 she became the first female head writer in *SNL's* history.

GROUCHO MARX (1890–1977)

Claim to Fame: American humorist, game-show host, and movie star

At 25... Julius Marx (his real name) and his brothers were just coming into their own as a comedy team on the vaudeville circuit. They'd started out as a musical troupe but found that crowds were more entertained when the brothers cracked jokes and insulted each other. This was a couple of years before Groucho donned his fake mustache and eyebrows. But he did have one thing: a catchy name. A year earlier, the Marx Brothers were playing in a poker game with comedian Art Fisher. In those days, many vaudevillians took on stage names that ended with "o," so as Fisher dealt each of the brothers a card, he gave them their new names: Leonard, the oldest, became Chico (he was a "chicken chaser," slang for a womanizer); Adolph became Harpo because he played the harp; Milton became Gummo because he liked to wear gumsoled shoes; and Julius became Groucho because he was "stern and serious."

J. K. ROWLING (1965–)

Claim to Fame: Creator of the Harry Potter books, which sold 400 million copies and were adapted into the highest-grossing film series of all time, making her the only author to ever become a billionaire

At 25... Joanna Rowling was a research assistant for Amnesty International. During a four-hour delay on a crowded train from Manchester to London, a story popped into her head "fully formed" about a boy wizard and his adventures at a wizard school. Rowling scribbled down a few notes and then started writing in earnest when she arrived back at her flat in London. Later that same year, Rowling's mother died. To deal with the loss, she decided that in her book, Harry would also lose his mother. "I thought I'd written something that a handful of people might quite like," she recalled.

BARACK OBAMA (1961–)

Claim to Fame: 44th president of the United States

At 25... In 1986 he was working as a community organizer in Chicago's poverty-stricken South Side. The recent Columbia University graduate had arrived there a year earlier after becoming bored with his job at a New York financial firm. He had two main goals in Chicago: 1) to try his hand at public service, and 2) to immerse himself in an African-American community. He'd been raised by his white mother in a white neighborhood, and wanted to connect with his roots. Serving as director of the Developing Communities Project, Obama tried to help low-income people find jobs, affordable housing, and get into college, and urged them to put pressure on City Hall to hire more police, fill in potholes, and remove asbestos from public housing projects. But it was an uphill battle, and, as he later recalled, "Victories were few." He soon realized, "I just can't get things done here without a law degree." So in 1988 Obama enrolled at Harvard Law School

FRANK SINATRA (1915–98)

Claim to Fame: American crooner

At 25... Sinatra became a household name and changed the music industry forever. After signing on as a singer in Tommy Dorsey's big band in 1940, Sinatra became the biggest draw. He toured the nation and appeared in his first full-length feature film, *Las Vegas Nights*. By May, Sinatra was the #1 singer in both *Billboard* and *Down Beat* magazines. "You could almost feel the excitement coming up out of the crowds when he stood up to sing," recalled Dorsey. "Just a skinny kid with big ears. I used to stand there so amazed that I'd almost forget to take my own solos." Sinatra's success proved to record-label executives that teenagers—especially girls—would buy records, which had, up to then, been marketed exclusively to their parents. A few weeks before Sinatra's 26th birthday, in December 1941, the United States entered World War II. He was drafted, but a congenital ear-drum injury kept him out of the military.

Chuck Norris invented his own martial arts style: Chun Kuk Do—"The Universal Way."

NAPOLEON BONAPARTE (1769–1821)

Claim to Fame: French military and political leader who ruled France and conquered much of Europe in the early 19th century

At 25... Napoleon was already a general known for his uncanny mastery of battlefield strategies. But he wasn't as deft in the battlefield of love. Engaged to Désirée Clary—the daughter of a wealthy silk merchant in Marseille, France—Napoleon was ready to tie the knot for the first time. That's when the 25-year-old general met a beautiful woman six years his senior named Josephine de Beauharnais. Napoleon was smitten, and left his bride-to-be for Josephine. (Désirée moved on and later became the Queen of Sweden.)

*   *   *

WEDDING BELL BLUES

• **Murphy's Law.** In 1995, Bebe Emerman and Steve Wolfe. organized a huge outdoor wedding at Yosemite National Park. A storm swept in, forcing the event to be held in a tent. Unfortunately the storm also flooded several roads into the park, which rerouted guests to additional roads that added 140 miles to their trip. The wedding ceremony itself went fine, But during the reception, a squirrel got into the tent and walked all over the wedding cake. Then the wedding photographer had to leave early because he was doubled over in pain with a kidney stone. And Emerman accidentally dropped the back of her dress into a toilet.

• **Crabby Day.** The night before Mary McPhail got married, she held her rehearsal dinner at the restaurant where she and her fiancé Geord Douglas had had their first date. Touched by the romantic gesture, the restaurant gave the party a surprise gift: a large tray of expensive stone crabs. The next day, McPhail felt ill, but attributed it to wedding day jitters. It wasn't. She made it down the aisle, and as she and Douglas were reciting their vows, she clenched her hand over her mouth to prevent herself from puking. Aware of the situation, the priest quickly wrapped up the ceremony and pronounced the couple married to get McPhail out the door. As soon as she left the church, she let loose, all over her gown. "I was mortified, but it was the highlight of everyone's day," said McPhail.

THE ORIGIN OF DNA TESTING

On page 501 we told you the story of the Innocence Project—the organization that uses DNA testing to help get people wrongfully convicted of crimes freed from prison. Here's how that technology was discovered in the first place.

EUREKA MOMENT

On September 10, 1984, geneticist Alec Jeffreys, 34, was working in his lab at the University of Leicester, in central England. More precisely, he was in the lab's darkroom, studying an X-ray that had been soaking in a developing tank over the weekend. The X-ray was the result of a process through which recently discovered DNA sequence anomalies appeared on a sheet of film as rows of black lines interspersed with blank spaces—almost like bar codes. The particular X-ray he was looking at showed DNA "bar codes" from three people: one of his technicians and her mother and father.

Jeffreys had no idea what to expect from the X-ray—he was just inventing this process, hoping to see evidence of change to specific regions of DNA between the parents and their daughter. But after looking at the blurry mess of dark and light spaces for a few moments, he suddenly realized that, completely by accident, he had discovered a way to tell if people were related. "It was an absolute Eureka moment," he told a reporter in a 2009 interview with *The Guardian* newspaper. "It was a blinding flash. In five golden minutes, my research career went whizzing off in a completely new direction."

AFTER THE EUREKA

What Jeffreys saw in that blurry X-ray: 1) each of the three family members had their own unique "bar code," 2) all three of the family members' bar codes related to one another (which makes perfect sense, as each of us gets our DNA as a combination of our parents' DNA), and 3) the relationships were plainly visible. Jeffreys quickly realized that his findings would have implications regarding paternity. With such technology you could prove with scientific certainty whether someone was—or wasn't—someone else's child. Or even whether they were closely related. The technology could be of use in criminal cases where the perpetrators left blood or other biological evidence behind.

Jeffreys had apparently discovered something extraordinary—but what to do with it? Surely it would take decades for it to have any applications in the real world, he thought. So he simply kept working on what he dubbed his "DNA fingerprint" process, trying to improve it. Meanwhile, he wrote a scientific paper titled "Individual-Specific Fingerprints of Human DNA," which was published in the scientific journal *Nature* in July 1985.

Two weeks later, he got a phone call.

TEST CASE: PATERNITY

The call came from a London lawyer who told Jeffreys she'd read a newspaper article about his "DNA fingerprinting" and wondered if it could be used in an immigration case she was handling. A British-Ghanaian woman's 13-year-old son had gone to stay with her estranged husband in Ghana for some time, and when he returned, British authorities didn't believe it was him. They thought the family was trying to sneak someone else—possibly a cousin—into the country on the son's passport, and they wanted to deport the boy. Could Jeffreys prove that the child was the woman's son?

Jeffreys agreed to give it a try. He took blood samples from the mother, three of her other children, and the boy in question, and made DNA bar codes for each of them. His conclusion: The boy was definitely the woman's son. The lawyer presented the evidence to the British Home Office, and even though DNA testing had never been used in a case before, they were convinced. The boy was legally accepted as the woman's son and allowed to stay in the country. Not only that, British immigration officials said they would allow DNA testing to decide any future cases that had paternity questions. The British Home Office had, perhaps without realizing it, made the brand-new, still not widely understood use of DNA testing a legally legitimate procedure.

Western diamondback rattlers bite more people in the U.S. than any other venomous snake.

TEST CASE: GUILT OR INNOCENCE

In November 1983, the body of 15-year-old Lynda Mann, of Narborough, Leicestershire (not far from where Jeffreys worked), was found. She had been raped and strangled. Three years later, in July 1986, the body of 15-year-old Dawn Ashworth, of the nearby town of Enderby, was found. She too had been raped and strangled. Evidence taken from both crimes showed only that the attacker in both cases had the same blood type.

Shortly after the second murder, Richard Buckland, a 17-year-old kitchen porter, was questioned by police. During interrogation he appeared to know facts about the crimes that only the killer could have known. He was arrested and subsequently confessed to the second murder. Police were convinced he had committed the first murder, too, but he insisted he had nothing to with it.

Having heard about the paternity case that Jeffreys had solved, police investigators asked the scientist to help them identify Buckland as the murderer of Lynda Mann. Jeffreys agreed to help. He extracted DNA from semen left at both crime scenes, and from a blood sample taken from Richard Buckland, then ran them through his process, made the bar codes, and established that one person had indeed carried out both attacks...except it *wasn't* Richard Buckland.

Nobody was more disappointed than Jeffreys. "As a man with a young family, living in the local area," Jeffreys told the BBC years later, "I was as keen as everyone else that our discovery should catch the killer. We couldn't believe what we were seeing. We'd tested and retested our findings."

BLOODHOUNDS

With Buckland off the hook, police were left with no suspects at all, so they decided to try something that had never been done before: In early 1987, they put out a call asking all male residents of the villages of Narborough and Endbury between the ages of 17 and 34 (about 5,000 men) to voluntarily submit to a DNA test. Some objected, seeing the request as an almost science-fiction-like infringement of their privacy rights. But most of the men, understandably distressed by the idea that a vicious killer might be in their midst, were behind it wholeheartedly.

Nearly all 5,000 men in the region voluntarily gave blood. And while Jeffreys's new forensic technology didn't solve the crimes directly, in the end it did help nab the killer. A man named Ian Kelly was overheard boasting in a pub that he'd been paid to give a blood sample in someone else's name. Police interrogated Kelly, then arrested a 27-year-old Leicester baker with the distinctive name of Colin Pitchfork. Pitchfork confessed immediately, and later pleaded guilty to the rapes and murders of both Lynda Mann and Dawn Ashworth. He was sentenced to life in prison with a minimum of 30 years served.

AFTERMATH

Christiana and Andrew Sarbah (the mother and son in the paternity case) were the first people in history to have a paternity case solved through DNA testing. Richard Buckland was the first person to be proven not guilty of a crime through the use of DNA, and Colin Pitchfork the first person convicted of a crime as a result of DNA testing. News of these events made global headlines. Within a year, DNA fingerprinting—now known as *DNA profiling*—was being used in the United States, and in just a few more years it was considered a standard part of forensics almost everywhere in the world. And not just to find out whodunnit—but also to determine who-didn't-dunnit.

Jeffreys is still a professor at the University of Leicester, although he is now known as *Sir* Alec Jeffreys. He was knighted by Queen Elizabeth II in 1994 for "Services to Science and Technology." He has received numerous other awards for what turned out to be one of the most momentous scientific discoveries of modern times. And it brought him some well-deserved fame: "Literally every two or three days I get an e-mail," he said in 2009, "mainly from the States, from school kids saying, 'I've got to do a project on a famous scientist, so I've chosen you,' and I love that. I always respond."

A FEW MORE FACTS

• It may seem elementary to *CSI* fans, but after his discovery on that fateful Monday morning in 1984, Jeffreys had no idea if the DNA in a bloodstain would be usable in his process. So he did the only thing a good scientist could:

> I spent the next two days cutting myself and leaving blood marks round the laboratory. Then we tested those bloodstains.

(It worked, of course.)

• Jeffreys's original X-rays—the ones mentioned at the start of the story, with the bar codes of the three family members—actually held 11 such codes. The other eight were made from the DNA of animals, including a mouse, a cow, and a baboon. And in case you were wondering, DNA testing works the same for animals as it does for humans.

* * *

UNCLE JOHN'S PUBLIC DOMAIN THEATRE

The opening lines of Hamlet, *by William Shakespeare*

ACT I, SCENE I

Elsinore. A platform before the castle.

FRANCISCO at his post. Enter to him BERNARDO

BERNARDO: Who's there?

FRANCISCO: Nay, answer me: stand, and unfold yourself.

BERNARDO: Long live the king!

FRANCISCO: Bernardo?

BERNARDO: He.

FRANCISCO: You come most carefully upon your hour.

BERNARDO: 'Tis now struck twelve; get thee to bed, Francisco.

FRANCISCO: For this relief much thanks: 'tis bitter cold, And I am sick at heart.

BERNARDO: Have you had quiet guard?

FRANCISCO: Not a mouse stirring.

BERNARDO: Well, good night.

THANKS FOR NOTHING

Aristotle didn't have it. Neither did Pythagoras or Euclid or other ancient mathematicians. We're talking about zero, which may sound like nothing, but, as it turns out, is a really big something. Here's the story.

COUNT LIKE A HINDU

Sometime in the early ninth century, a mathematician named Muhammad ibn Musa al-Khwarizmi (circa 780–850 A.D.) gained a key piece of knowledge that would eventually earn him the nickname "The Father of Algebra." What he discovered would also speed up mathematical calculation many times over and, eventually, make a host of amazing technological advances possible, up to and including cars, computers, space travel, and robots.

What was it? The Hindu number system (developed in India). The system intrigued al-Khwarizmi because it used nine different symbols to represent numbers, plus a small circle around empty space to represent *shunya*—"nothingness." To keep from having to use more and more symbols for larger numbers, the Hindu system was a *place system*. The value of a number could be determined by its place in a row of numbers: There was a row for 1s, a row for 10s, 100s, 1000s, and so on. If nine numerals and a circle to represent "nothing" sounds familiar, it should. Thanks to al-Khwarizmi, the Hindu number system (known in the West as "Arabic numerals") is the system used in most of the world today.

A ZERO IN THE HOUSE OF WISDOM

Al-Khwarizmi knew a good idea when he saw one. He was a scholar and worked in the House of Wisdom, a combination library, university, research lab, and translation service in Baghdad. At the time, the Abbassid caliphs—who claimed to be descendants of Abbas, the prophet Muhammad's youngest uncle—ruled the Persian Empire. They had turned their seat of power, Baghdad, into the "jewel of the world." Muhammad had exhorted his followers to "acquire knowledge" and to "seek learning though it be as far as China." So as Europe descended into the Dark Ages, the caliphs kept the light of knowledge burning bright. They collected as much of the world's written knowledge as they could get their hands on and had it translated into Arabic. At a time when the largest library in Europe contained far fewer than a thousand volumes, the Abbasids amassed a library believed to have held a million books.

While working for the Abbasids in The House of Wisdom, al-Khwarizmi specialized in astronomy and mathematics. He spent most of his time finding useful real-world applications for mathematical concepts and explaining them in ways that reasonably-intelligent non-mathematicians could understand. And those Hindu numbers opened up a whole new world of mathematical possibility. And he was especially intrigued by the symbol for "nothing."

HOLD THAT PLACE!

"The tenth figure in the shape of a circle," al-Khwarizmi wrote, would help prevent confusion when it came to balancing household accounts or parceling out a widow's dowry. The circle was the key: If no numeral fell into a particular column, the circle served as a placeholder, as al-Khwarizmi put it, "to keep the rows straight." A merchant (or mathematician) could run his finger down each column starting from the right and be confident that the ones, tens, hundreds, and so on, were in the correct place.

If this seems less than Earth-shaking, consider this: The Hindu system was based on the abacus, a counting device that some scholars say goes back 3000 B.C. The earliest versions used pebbles lined up in columns to represents 1s, 10s, 100s, 1000s, etc. Later versions used beads strung on wires inside a frame. With this type of abacus, when you counted past nine, you flipped one bead into the 10s column and pushed the beads in the 1s column back to nothing. British mathematician Lancelot Hogben succinctly explained what was so amazing about the Hindu circle:

> The invention of *sunya* (zero) liberated the human intellect from the prison bars of the counting frame. Once there was a sign for the empty column, 'carrying over' on a slate or paper was just as easy as carrying over on the abacus...and it could stretch as far as necessary in either direction.

That, in a nutshell, is the humble beginning of zero. But a circle used as a placeholder is only half of the story about nothing.

The U.S. Justice Dept. reported men are 4 times more likely than women to be murdered.

ZERO HOUR

For awhile, the Hindu circle remained a placeholder doing nothing more than showing that there was nothing in a particular column. But al-Khwarizmi wasn't content with that and went back to the books. He studied everything he could find about math from the ancient Greeks and others, and he began considering the existence of negative numbers, in particular what happens when you subtract a larger number from a smaller one. Something about the available literature bugged him. There was something missing.

Take a problem like 3 - 4 =___. Everybody had figured out that the answer was -1. But al-Khwarizmi knew that he couldn't arrive at that answer by starting at 3 and counting backward by 4 numbers. When he did that…2, 1, -1, -2…the fourth number was -2, and that's the wrong answer.

Al-Khwarizmi's "Ah-ha!" moment came when he realized that there was a missing number, one that signified "nothing." And—Eureka!—a symbol for nothing was already there in the Hindu system, stuck at the end of numerals like 10, 20, 30, 100, to indicate the numeral's place in a column of figures. That circle signifying "nothing" (*sunya* in Sanskrit, *sifr* in Arabic, and, in time, *cipher* in Latin) needed to be upgraded from a placeholder to a full-fledged numeral. Al-Khwarizmi gave zero its rightful place: right between +1 and -1. He began using the round placeholder (0) as the missing number in calculations, and suddenly math with negative numbers worked. (His zero also provoked heated philosophical discussions along the line of: "How can nothing be represented by something?" but that's a different topic.)

ALGEBRA 1

Around 825 A.D., al-Khwarizmi wrote a book to explain calculation using the Hindu number system. It was called, fittingly, *On the Calculation with Hindu Numerals*. But al-Khwarizmi didn't rest on his zeroes; he expanded his work, developing math that included rational and irrational numbers, negatives, equations, and all the other stuff you've forgotten from ninth grade.

Around 830 A.D., he wrote *al-Kitab al-mukhtasar fi hisab al-jabr wa'l-muqabala* (*The Compendious Book on Calculation by Completion and Balancing*). The title gave the world the term "algebra" (from *al-jabr*) and the content gave the world the advanced math that went with it. Al-Khwarizmi's intent wasn't to confuse future generations of middle school students with abstract equations. In his own words, it was to explain...

> ...what is easiest and most useful in arithmetic, such as men constantly require in cases of inheritance, legacies, partition, lawsuits, and trade, and in all their dealings with one another, or where the measuring of lands, the digging of canals, geometrical computation, and other objects of various sorts and kinds are concerned.

Al-Khwarizmi's books became popular throughout the Persian Empire, and not just with mathematicians. Storekeepers, bankers, builders, architects, and anyone else who needed math to do their jobs made use of Hindu numbers and al-Khwarizmi's algebra. But it would take a surprisingly long time before his concepts spread beyond the Muslim world and into Europe.

A POPE FAILS TO CONVERT

Despite the Biblical injunction to "go forth and multiply," convincing Christians to use this more advanced system of mathematics would take about 1,000 years. In al-Khwarizmi's time (late 8th- to mid-9th century), the Muslim world was in the middle of a golden age of learning. The Christian world: Not so golden. When the Roman Empire collapsed in 476 A.D., in the words of one modern historian, it was as if "Western Civilization went camping for five hundred years."

During the Middle Ages, much of the Christian world considered Muslims to be "heretics" who rejected the "true faith." What, then, could be learned from them? In the minds of most Europeans, the answer was an unequivocal "nothing." When it came to math, there was one notable exception: the 10th-century French monk, Gerbert of Aurillac. As a young monk, Gerbert had traveled to Muslim-controlled Spain to study advanced science, astronomy, and mathematics—disciplines that had been lost to the Western world. He discovered "Arabic numerals," learned how to use an abacus, and studied algebra. Gerbert couldn't wait to get back and share this knowledge. One man in particular was interested: Otto the Great, the Holy Roman Emperor. Otto took 20-year-old Gerbert into his court to tutor his 16-year-old heir, Otto II, in what was then called "mathesis." Otto II wasn't much of a scholar, but he knew a good teacher when he saw one. When his own heir, Otto III, needed a tutor, Gerbert was his man.

Over time Gerbert became an astronomer, an organ builder, a music theoretician, a mathematician, a philosopher, a teacher, and...the world's first French pope—Sylvester II. In 999, Otto III, in his new role as emperor of the Holy Roman Empire, used his influence to get his former teacher elected to the papacy. Gerbert saw his election as an opportunity to introduce Arabic numerals into the Church, replacing those unwieldy Roman numerals. Bad idea: Using Arabian "squiggles" to do math was, to many, a suspicious indication that Sylvester II had gone over to the dark side. Rumors spread that while in Spain the future pope had either learned the "magic" we call math from his teacher's secret book of magic...or studied with the Devil himself.

Whispers that Gerbert's math was a tool of Satan followed him into the papacy, and though he frequently displayed his abacus skills and wrote treatises on Arabic math, he died (in 1003) without convincing either the Church or the masses to adopt Arabic numerals. In 1096, just before the First Crusade to recapture Jerusalem from the Muslims began, the deceased pope was, according to *The Abacus and the Cross* by Nancy Marie Brown, "branded a sorcerer and devil-worshipper for having taught the mathematics and science that had come to Christian Europe from Islamic Spain."

ENTER FIBONACCI

Arabic numerals (and zero) made their next significant appearance in Western civilization nearly 200 years after Gerbert's death, courtesy of Leonardo Fibonacci. Born in Pisa to a wealthy Italian merchant around 1170, Leonardo is said to have been the best Western mathematician of the Middle Ages (not that he had a lot of competition). Leonardo was raised in northern Africa where his father oversaw Italy's coastal trading outposts and made sure his son was schooled in the math he would need to become an accountant. Leonardo's Arab teachers showed him al-Khwarizmi's Hindu-Arabic number system. "When I had been introduced to the art of the Indians' nine symbols, knowledge of the art very soon pleased me above all else," he later wrote.

As a young man, Fibonacci traveled enough to encounter other number systems being used in the West, including the awk-

In ancient times the symbol now known as the swastika was a symbol of good fortune.

ward Roman numeral system still reigning in Europe. (He also traveled enough to earn the nickname *Bigollo*, which means "vagabond" or "wanderer.") To Fibonacci, the Hindu-Arabic system he'd learned in the Arab world was far superior. He returned to Pisa as an adult and, in 1202, published *Liber Abaci* (*Book of Calculation*) to share the knowledge of how to use the Hindu-Arabic system in practical ways, including the conversion of measures and currency, allocation of profit, and the computation of interest. Italian merchants and bankers loved it. Soon most of them had switched over to the new system.

MUCH ADO ABOUT ZERO

That didn't end the push back against Arabic numerals. In 1259, a edict came from Florence forbidding bankers to use "the infidel symbols" and, in 1348, the University of Padua insisted that book prices be listed using "plain" letters (Roman numerals), not "ciphers" (al-Khwarizmi's *sifr*). Though Fibonacci's book is credited with bringing the zero (as well as its buddies, 1 to 9) to Europe, it took another 300 years for the system to spread beyond Italy. Why? For one thing, Fibonacci lived in the days before printing, so his books were hand written. If someone wanted a copy, it had to be copied by hand. In time, Fibonacci's book would be translated, plagiarized, and used as inspiration for books in many other languages. The first one in English was *The Crafte of Nombrynge*, published around 1350.

Zero finally came into its own in Europe during the Renaissance when it showed up in a variety of books, including Robert Recordes's popular math textbook *Ground of Artes* (1543). That book may have been read by one William Shakespeare, the first writer known to have used the Arabic zero in literature. In *King Lear*, the Fool tells Lear, "Thou are a 0 without a figure. I am better than thou art now, I am a Fool, thou art nothing."

MEANWHILE...

Lest we forget, advanced knowledge also developed in the New World, independently of Old World thought. The zero appears on a Mayan stela (a stone monument) carved sometime between 292 and 372 A.D. That's 400 to 500 years *before* al-Khwarizmi "discovered" it.

ANSWER PAGES

I'LL HAVE A FATSO BURGER

(Answers for page 108)

1. g) *Dogma.* All of director Kevin Smith's movies take place in the same "universe." Characters and institutions from one movie appear in others. In 1999's *Dogma*, two fallen angels (Matt Damon and Ben Affleck) break into the corporate boardroom of the Mooby's fast-food chain, call out the grave sins of each of the board members, then execute them all. In Smith's 2006 movie *Clerks II*, the main characters work at Mooby's.

2. c) *American Beauty.* When writer Lester Burnham (Kevin Spacey) has a midlife crisis, he tries to relive his teen years by buying a muscle car, smoking marijuana, and getting a job at a fast-food joint called Mr. Smiley's. But while he's working the drive-through line, he spots his wife (Annette Bening) as she drives through with her lover (Peter Gallagher). Unfazed, he offers her a "beef pot pie on a stick."

3. o) *The Simpsons.* The most popular hamburger joint in Springfield, it's owned by TV host Krusty the Klown. Once called "the unhealthiest restaurant in the world," it trotted out the vegetarian Mother Nature Burger…made with tainted barley. Other menu items include the Clogger, the Deep Fried Krusty Burger, and the Partially Gelatinated Nondairy Gum-Based Beverage (known in most restaurants as a "shake").

4. e) *Buffy the Vampire Slayer.* When Buffy (Sarah Michelle Gellar) wants to be a normal, non-vampire-fighting teen, she gets a job at Doublemeat Palace, which specializes in a sandwich made with one beef patty and one chicken patty. When body parts begin showing up in the kitchen, Buffy suspects human flesh is the secret ingredient, but the truth is far darker: The "meat" is made from vegetables and beef tallow.

5. d) *Roseanne.* In 1993 Roseanne and then-husband Tom Arnold bought a home in Iowa and opened up a "loosemeat" sandwich restaurant. Popular in the Midwest, they are sandwiches made of

In a photo of Lincoln's funeral procession, 6-year-old Teddy Roosevelt is looking out a window.

restaurant. Popular in the Midwest, they are sandwiches made of ground meat and sauce, sort of like sloppy joes. Roseanne's TV character opened one, too, in her fictional hometown of Lanford, Illinois.

6. m) *Breaking Bad.* Cancer patient and meth cooker Walter White (Bryan Cranston) gets into business with international drug kingpin Gus Fring (Giancarlo Esposito), who runs a chain of 13 fast-food chicken restaurants called Los Pollos Hermanos as a front for his drug business. They serve fried chicken, Mexican and South American dishes, and, if you know who to ask, methamphetamine.

7. n) *Coming to America.* A blatant parody of McDonald's, McDowell's shows up in the 1988 comedy starring Eddie Murphy as an African prince who gets a job there when he first arrives in New York. The chain's signature sandwich is the Big Mic, which consists of "two all-beef patties, special sauce, lettuce, cheese, pickles, and onions" on a bun. (No sesame seeds.)

8. p) *Doug.* On the 1990s Nickelodeon cartoon *Doug*, Honker Burger was the cool place where the cool kids went to hang out, with a 1950s diner look (rendered in pink and purple). You had to be in the know to know how to order at Honker Burger. Want a burger without pickles and onions? Then you say "a moo cow without cukes and sneakers." A fish sandwich? Order a "wet one."

9. i) *The Flintstones.* It has to be one of the first drive-in restaurants…because it existed in prehistoric times. Biggest thing on the menu: the car-size, car-toppling triceratops ribs.

10. f) *Saturday Night Live.* Taco Town appeared in a 2008 *SNL* commercial parody spoofing extreme fast food. Its signature item is the Pizza Crepe Taco Pancake Chili Bag. That's a crunchy taco wrapped in a flour tortilla, then wrapped in a corn tortilla, then wrapped in a crepe and deep-fried. Then it's rolled in a deep-dish pizza, rolled up in a blueberry pancake, and tossed in a tote bag, which is then filled with chili.

11. h) *SpongeBob SquarePants.* SpongeBob works as a short-order cook at the Krusty Krab restaurant flipping Krabby Patties. It's a popular place, much to the chagrin of its across-the-street rival, the disgusting Chum Bucket, run by the tiny Plankton, who is bent on

There are over 30,000 sushi restaurants in Japan. In the U.S.: about 10,000.

stealing the secret recipe for the Krusty Krab's Krabby Patties.

12. j) *Beavis and Butt-Head.* Another parody of McDonald's (its logo is upside-down golden arches, forming a W, for "World"), Burger World is where stupid, lazy teens Beavis and Butt-Head work...or are at least employed. They spend most of their time throwing random objects into the fryer or hanging out in the bathroom.

13. b) *Fast Times at Ridgemont High.* In the 1982 teen comedy, high-school senior Brad Hamilton (Judge Reinhold) is on the management track at Captain Hook's until he abruptly quits one day. Reason: He delivers an order and an attractive girl laughs at the silly pirate costume he has to wear.

14. l) *Futurama.* In the 2000 episode "The Problem With Popplers," the interstellar delivery crew finds a delicious, bite-size animal on a foreign planet and fills their earthbound spaceship with them. They sell millions to the Fishy Joe's fast-food chain, only to learn that they're actually the babies of a bloodthirsty race of aliens.

15. a) *Pulp Fiction*. Toward the beginning of the film, Vincent (John Travolta) and Jules (Samuel L. Jackson) go to collect a mysterious briefcase from the apartment of a trio of inept young criminals. Jules asks one of them for a bite of his hamburger, as he's heard that Big Kahuna makes "a tasty burger." Then Jules kills him.

16. k) *That '70s Show.* The fictional Wisconsin burger joint Fatso Burger figured prominently in the Fox TV series. Eric (Topher Grace) is forced by his father to get a job there. But he quits after a few days because his friends stole a statue of the restaurant's mascot, Fatso the clown.

17. q) *South Park.* City Wok is the only Asian food restaurant in the town of South Park. Proprietor Tuong Lu Kim has a thick accent, leading his pronunciation of the first word in the name of his restaurant to sound a lot like a swear word. But because he's technically saying "city," it got past TV censors (which is probably why show creators Trey Parker and Matt Stone named it "City Wok" in the first place).

First written mention of a kiss: in the Vedic Sanskrit texts (India, 1500 B.C.).

POLITICALLY CORRECT QUIZ

(Answers for page 473)

1. a) The diamond shape is *similar*, but not identical, to the British Sign Language symbol for "female genitalia." That symbol is formed by making the diamond shape over the crotch, with the forefingers pointing downward. The children make the "star" symbol over their heads with their forefingers pointing upward, but that was close enough for the city council. Banning the gesture was "a sensible decision taken to prevent deaf children or deaf parents being offended," a spokesperson told the *Daily Mail* newspaper. Not everyone agreed: "These are innocent children just making a sign to show a star," one parent told reporters. "No one would give it a second thought." (There were no deaf parents or deaf children enrolled in the toddler group at the time.)

2. c) "We do need to examine our language about animals because a lot of it is derogatory in the sense that it belittles them and our relations with them," said Dr. Andrew Linzey, the journal's co-editor. The journal suggests using either "differentiated beings" or "non-human animals" instead of "animals." (So why does the journal get to use "animal" in its title? "'Animal ethics' has become the established term within academia for the field of study," said Dr. Linzey.) The journal also requests that individual animals be referred to as "he" or "she," not "it," and that terms like "wild animal" and "wildlife" be avoided in favor of "free-living," "free-ranging," and "free-roaming." "For most, 'wildness' is synonymous with uncivilized, unrestrained, barbarous existence. There is an obvious prejudgement here that should be avoided," Dr. Linzey explained.

3. a) "We have a religion-accommodation policy, approved by the school board in 1983, stating that 'no religious belief or non-belief should be promoted by the school district or its employees, and none should be disparaged," the school board responded in a statement after the incident came to light. (Seattle's parks and recreation department has renamed its annual Easter egg hunt a "spring egg hunt.")

4. b) University investigators concluded that Evans intended no harm, but upheld the complaint anyway. The university's punishments—mandatory counseling and a two-year period of "monitor-

The smallest detectible computer mouse movement (less than 0.1 mm) is called a "mickey."

ing and appraisal"—were dismissed after a judge ruled they were "grossly disproportionate." In 2011 Evans left the school for a teaching job at the American University in Beirut. "If academics can't show a scientific paper to a colleague under these conditions for fear that the colleague might be offended, then I think academic freedom is truly dead at UCC," he says. (A few weeks after her complaint against Evans, Salerno-Kennedy accused a female colleague of "bullying" her. That claim was dismissed after investigators concluded it was baseless.)

5. c) "We try to be sensitive to the fact that for Muslims, talk of pigs is offensive," the school's head, Barbara Harris, told the *Yorkshire Evening Post*. The ban applied not just to *The Three Little Pigs*, but to any and all stories containing pigs, including *Charlotte's Web*, *Babe*, and any Winnie-the-Pooh story that mentions Piglet. The Muslim Council of Britain asked for the ban to be rescinded, calling it "well-intentioned but misguided." (Muslims are not allowed to *eat* pork, but are free to read and talk about pigs.) "The school has gone too far," said Barry Malik, a local magistrate and practicing Muslim. "What will they do next, ban the word 'cow' because the Hindus believe the cow is sacred?"

THE SMARTPHONE AUTOCORRECT QUIZ

(Answers for page 311)

1.Viggo Mortensen
2. Emeril Lagasse
3. Honus Wagner
4. Stockard Channing
5. Raven-Symoné
6. Shia LaBeouf
7. Beyoncé Knowles
8. Matt Groening
9. Dirk Nowitzki
10. Mariska Hargitay
11. Joss Whedon
12. Evel Knievel
13. Dweezil Zappa
14. Tupac Shakur
15. Cate Blanchett
16. Gabourey Sidibe
17. Gérard Depardieu
18. Leighton Meester
19. Dita Von Teese
20. Boutros Boutros-Ghali
21. Zach Galifianakis
22. Ving Rhames
23. Chauncey Billups
24. Miley Cyrus
25. Jimi Hendrix
26. Alistair Cooke

HOMONYM QUIZ

(Answers for page 253)

1. b) a river's edge. This meaning of *bank* is ancient, and has been in the English language since at least the year 1200. The financial *bank* didn't arrive until the late 1400s. Exact roots are unknown, but both words may have come from the same Old Germanic root, meaning "bench" or "shelf."

2. a) a flying mammal. *Bat* the winged mammal first showed up in the 1570s, from the Middle English *bakke*, which is believed to have been derived from an Old Scandinavian word meaning "flapper." To *bat* your eyelashes was first used in the 1840s, and came from a little-known word still used in falconry: A falcon *bates* when it flutters its wings strongly off its perch.

3. b) a medicine or drink. Both meanings for *cordial* have the same origin—the Latin *cordialis*, meaning "of the heart." *Cordial*, the drink or medicine meant to stimulate the heart, came into use in the late 1300s; *cordial*, meaning "sincere" or "from the heart," came about a century later.

4. b) to strand, as on a desolate island. In the 1720s, *maroon* was an English term for the black slaves who had escaped to live in the wild in the West Indies and Guiana (in northwestern South America). The name spread to other communities of fugitive slaves, as well as their descendants, who are still called Maroon people in some parts of the world today. (Harriet Beecher Stowe wrote about the Maroons who lived in a swampy region in Virginia and North Carolina in her 1856 novel *Dred: A Tale of the Great Dismal Swamp.*) That meaning for maroon is thought to have its origin in the Spanish word *cimarrón*, meaning "wild" or "untamed." The color *maroon*: That came into English in the 1790s, derived from the French *marron*, for "chestnut."

5. b) marshy land. The marshy *moor* came very early, before the year 1200, from the Old English word *mor*, meaning "morass" or "swamp." The *Moor* that refers to North Africans entered the English language in the late 1400s and comes from the Latin *Maurus*, for "inhabitant of Mauretania," an ancient African kingdom on the shores of the Mediterranean in what is now Morocco and part of western Algeria. (The modern nation of Mauritania, which lies to the southwest and on the Atlantic coast, was named after the ancient kingdom of the Moors.)

6. a) a whale's tail. In the 1720s, people started calling the whale's tail a *fluke*, which was derived from the term for the flared part of a ship's anchor—the part meant to dig into the sea floor—which has been called a *fluke* since the 1500s. (That word is believed to have its root in the German *flügel*, meaning "wing.") The lucky *fluke*: The earliest known reference to that meaning came in 1857, referring specifically to a lucky stroke in a game of billiards, although it can now apply to anything. Where that came from, no one knows.

7. a) hunters' prey. In the good old days, when a hunter bagged a buck or some other creature, he gutted it and placed some of its entrails on the animal's hide—for the dogs that had helped on the hunt. The name for the entrails: *qurrie*, which became *quarry* in the early 1300s. (*Quirre* comes from the Latin *cor*, meaning "heart.") The *quarry* where rocks are mined entered the language around 1400, from the Middle Latin *quarreria*, which meant "place where stones are squared," which goes back to the Latin *quadrare*, meaning "to square," referring to the process of chiseling rock into squarish shapes for building.

8. a) freezing rain. The frozen *hail* came to us in the 1100s, from the Old English word of the same meaning, *hægl*. That word is believed to have been derived from a very ancient Proto-Indo-European word *kaghlo*, meaning "pebble." The *hail* that means "to call from afar" arrived in the 1560s, its roots going back to the Old Norse *heill*, a greeting meaning "health," or "prosperity."

9. a) to sell or peddle. This meaning of *hawk* came to English in the late 1400s, as a back-formation of the older noun *hawker*, for a street vendor, which goes back to the Germanic *höken*, meaning "carry on the back." To *hawk* up loogies—that came in the 1580s. It was onomatopoeic: It sounds like "hawwwwk."

10. b) to release a switch or catch. *Trip* as in "trip a switch" was first used in the late 1890s, and was simply an imaginative use of the verb "to trip" as in catch your foot on something and stumble. *Trip* as in "Oh, wow, man..." entered the language in the late 1950s.

11. b) a cheer ("Hip hip hooray!"). The happy *hip* was coined in the 1820s, and is believed to come from the German *hepp*, a call made by hunters before attacking their quarry. The other meaning of *hip* came in the first decade of the 1900s, from an earlier word with the same meaning—*hep*. The origin of that word: unknown. Both were born as part of African-American slang; "hip" took over from "hep" completely by the 1950s.

12. a) a munitions storehouse. *Magazines* have been used for ammo since the 1580s, the root of this meaning going back to the old Arabic *makhazin*, meaning "storehouse." *Magazines* have been for reading (in the john!) since the very first one—*The Gentleman's Magazine*—was published in London in 1731. Publisher Edward Cave saw it as a "storehouse" for information.

13. a) an embalmed body. *Mummy* became an English word in the 1610s, from the Latin *mumia*, which came from the Arabic *mumiyah*, both meaning "embalmed body." (The word first entered English in the 1400s, but it meant "medicine made from an embalmed body." That's because back in those days mummies were ground into powder and sold as a medicine to be eaten. *Mummy* as a pet name for Mom didn't come along until the 1820s.

14. b) a person hired to carry. *Porter*, as in hotel porter, came from the Latin *portare*, meaning "to carry," in the 1200s. The dark beer became *porter*, after the hard-working porter 500 years later, in the 1720s.

15. b) to crush. You could first *squash* something (like a bug) in the 1560s, the root of the word being the Latin *quassare*, meaning "to shatter." The tasty *squash* was taken from the Narragansett people around Rhode Island in the 1640s. Their name for this food was *askutasquash*, a combination of their words *askut*, meaning "green or raw," and *asquash*, meaning "eaten."

16. a) an American. The earliest known shortening of "Yankee" to *Yank* was in 1778. The verb *yank*: 1822. And it appears to have been *yanked* out of nowhere: Its origin is unknown.

NAME THAT PRESIDENT

(Answers for page 405)

(Answers for page 405)

1. President Obama, 2011
2. President Obama, 2012
3. President Bush (Sr.), 1991
4. President Clinton, 1999
5. President Bush, 2004
6. President Bush, 2003
7. President Clinton, 1999
8. President Nixon, 1969
9. President Obama, 2012
10. President Carter, 1980
11. President Bush (Sr.), 1989
12. President Carter, 1980
13. President Bush (Sr.), 1992
14. Presidents George H.W. Bush (1991) and Bill Clinton (2002). Clinton upped the honor by awarding it "with distinction."

* * *

IMPOSSIBLE QUESTIONS
WEIRD TIME EDITION

1. What day is most likely to be the longest day of the year?

Answer: December 31. If you said June 20 or 21 (the Northern Hemisphere's Summer Solstice), you'd be right...if we were talking about the longest amount of *daylight* in the year. We're not: Despite the extra sunlight, those days are 24 hours long, just like every other day in a normal year. But not every year is normal. As astronomy and time measurement have become increasingly precise, official time gradually gets out of sync with the earth's rotation. Additions of "leap seconds" are required now and again to stay accurate. The International Earth Rotation and Reference Systems Service added 25 of them between 1972 and 2012. Fifteen "24:00:01 days" took place on December 31; ten, on June 30.

2. If you planned to drink a root beer for every hour it's your birthday somewhere on Earth, how many cans should you buy?

Answer: Forty-eight. If you started celebrating just west of the International Dateline, you could celebrate for 24 hours. Then at midnight you could step eastward over the Dateline, lose a day, and celebrate your birthday all over again for a total of 48 hours.

Charles Dickens made as much money from his lectures as he did from his 20 novels.

More UNCLE JOHN than you can shake a stick at!

Log onto our online store at *www.bathroomreader.com* for dozens more great titles in the Bathroom Reader line: You'll find puzzle books, regional-interest books, big books, little books, and introducing—e-books! Great reading no matter where you are!

UNCLE JOHN'S BATHROOM READER CLASSIC SERIES

Find these and other great titles from the *Uncle John's Bathroom Reader* Classic Series online at **www.bathroomreader.com**.

Bathroom Readers' Institute
P.O. Box 1117
Ashland, OR 97520

BATHROOM READER FOR KIDS ONLY!
Uncle John's BOOK of FUN
Uncle John's Facts to ANNOY Your Teacher
Uncle John's Top Secret! BATHROOM READER FOR KIDS ONLY!
Uncle John's KID TOPIA
Amazing Facts
Puzzles
Mazes
Brain Teasers
Jokes
Strange (but true) Tales
And Tons More
Uncle John's THE ENCHANTED TOILET
Magic, Mystery, Science, History and... Totally Twisted Tales
BATHROOM READER FOR KIDS ONLY!
By the Bathroom Readers' Institute

THE LAST PAGE

FELLOW BATHROOM READERS:

The fight for good bathroom reading should never be taken loosely—we must do our duty and sit firmly for what we believe in, even while the rest of the world is taking potshots at us.

We'll be brief. Now that we've proven we're not simply a flush-in-the-pan, we invite you to take the plunge: Sit Down and Be Counted! Log on to *www.bathroomreader.com* and earn a permanent spot on the BRI honor roll!

Well, we're out of space, and when you've gotta go, you've gotta go. Tanks for all your support. Hope to hear from you soon. Meanwhile, remember...

Keep on flushin'!